Colombia
a country study

Federal Research Division
Library of Congress
Edited by
Rex A. Hudson

On the cover: The Shamanic Flight, Iconic A, Tolima style, first mille-
nium AD, a gold pendant discovered in Quimbaya territory,
Quindío, The Gold Museum of the Central Bank, Bogotá
Courtesy Gerardo Reichel-Dolmatoff, *Orfebrería y chamanismo: Un
estudio iconográfico del Museo del Oro*, Medellín, 1988, 105

Fifth Edition, First Printing, 2010.

Library of Congress Cataloging-in-Publication Data

Colombia: a country study / Federal Research Division, Library of
Congress ; edited by Rex A. Hudson. -- 5th ed.
    p. cm. -- (Area handbook series, ISSN 1057-5294 ; 550-26)
ISBN 978-0-8444-9502-6
1. Colombia. I. Hudson, Rex A. II. Library of Congress. Federal Research
Division.
F2258.C64 2010-03-18
986.1--dc22
                                2010009203

For sale by the Superintendent of Documents, U.S. Government Printing Office
Internet: bookstore.gpo.gov Phone: toll free (866) 512–1800; DC area (202) 512–1800
Fax: (202) 512–2250 Mail: Stop SSOP, Washington, DC 20402–00001

ISBN 978–0–8444–9502–06

Foreword

This volume is one in a continuing series of books prepared by the Federal Research Divison of the Library of Congress under the Country Studies/Area Handbook Program, formerly sponsored by the Department of the Army and revived in FY 2004 with congressionally mandated funding under the sponsorship of the Joint Chiefs of Staff, Strategic Plans and Policy Directorate (J–5).

Most books in the series deal with a particular foreign country, describing and analyzing its political, economic, social, and national security systems and institutions, and examining the interrelationshps of those systems and the ways they are shaped by historical and cultural factors. Each study is written by a multidisciplinary team of social scientists. The authors seek to provide a basic understanding of the observed society, striving for a dynamic rather than a static portrayal. Particular attention is devoted to the people who make up the society, their origins, dominant beliefs and values, their common interests and the issues on which they are divided, the nature and extent of their involvement with national institutions, and their attitudes toward each other and toward their social system and political order.

The books represent the analysis of the authors and should not be construed as an expression of an official U.S. government position, policy, or decision. The authors have sought to adhere to accepted standards of scholarly objectivity. Corrections, additions, and suggestions for changes from readers will be welcomed for use in future editions.

David L. Osborne
Chief
Federal Research Division
Library of Congress
Washington, DC 20540–4840
E-mail: frds@loc.gov

Acknowledgments

The fifth edition of *Colombia: A Country Study* supersedes the 1990 edition edited by Dennis M. Hanratty and Sandra W. Meditz. The authors acknowledge general background information that the 1990 edition and earlier editions may have provided for the present volume, which is, however, a completely new edition. The book editor would like to thank the authorial team for their dedication in producing authoritative new material.

The authors are grateful to individuals in various agencies of the Colombian and U.S. governments and international organizations, including nongovernmental organizations, as well as scholars affiliated with universities or other institutions, who offered their time, expertise, or research facilities and materials to provide information and perspective. None of these individuals is, however, in any way responsible for the work or points of view of the authors.

The authors gratefully acknowledge any assistance, including chapter-review comments made by other chapter authors. The book editor is particularly indebted to Dr. David Bushnell. The book editor would also like to acknowledge the contributions to an early draft of chapter 2 made by Dr. Marta Juanita Villaveces Niño of the Economics Department of the University of El Rosario, Bogotá. The authors of chapter 3, Drs. Roberto Steiner and Hernán Vallejo, would like to thank two individuals in particular for helpful comments on their chapter: Professor Miguel Urrutia of Los Andes University (Uniandes), Bogotá; and Dr. Arturo Galindo, adviser, Ministry of Finance, Colombia. The author of chapter 5, Dr. Ann C. Mason, would like to thank the following experts for their invaluable research assistance: Catalina Arreaza of the Political Science Department at Uniandes; Sebastián Bitár, School of Government at Uniandes; and Mauricio Vargas of the Colombian government's National Planning Department (DNP). For their expert review of, and significant contributions to, various sections of the chapter, Dr. Mason is also grateful to Jaime Camacho of El Rosario University; María Victoria Llorente of the Center for Economic Development at Uniandes; Román Ortiz of the Political Science Department at Uniandes; security consultant David Spencer; and Professor Arlene Tickner, also of the Political Science Department faculty at Uniandes.

The book editor would also like to thank members of the Federal Research Division (FRD) of the Library of Congress who contributed directly to the preparation of the manuscript. These include Sandra W. Meditz, who reviewed all textual and graphic materials, served as liaison with the sponsoring agency, and managed editing and production, which included providing numerous substantive and technical contributions; Catherine Schwartzstein, who unflaggingly provided substantive and meticulous editing, helped with layout for images and figures, and prepared the index; Janie L. Gilchrist, who did the extensive word processing and prepared the camera-ready copy; and Katarina M. David, who provided technical help with processing the images, including scanning those used for the artwork. Christopher S. Robinson, an outside contractor, prepared the book's graphics based on FRD drafts, as well as the final digital manuscript for the U.S. Government Printing Office (GPO).

Finally, the book editor acknowledges the generosity of the individuals, diplomatic and international agencies and organizations, and the U.S. government for allowing their photographs to be used in this study. The illustrations for the cover and chapter title pages are based on published illustrations of indigenous artwork found in books in the Spanish-language collection of the Library of Congress.

Contents

List of Figures

Preface

Like its predecessor, this study is an attempt to treat in a concise and objective manner the dominant historical, social, political, economic, and national security aspects of contemporary Colombia. Sources of information included scholarly journals and monographs, official reports of governments and international organizations, foreign and domestic newspapers, and numerous periodicals and Internet sources, particularly official Colombian government Web sites. Chapter bibliographies appear at the end of the book; at the end of each chapter is a brief comment on some of the more valuable sources suggested as further reading. The Glossary provides supplementary explanations of words and terms used frequently or having particular importance. Measurements are given in the metric system; a conversion table is provided to assist those readers who are unfamiliar with metric measurements (see table 1, Appendix).

Although there are numerous variations, Spanish surnames generally consist of two parts: the patrilineal name followed by the matrilineal. In the instance of Álvaro Uribe Vélez, for example, Uribe is his father's name and Vélez is his mother's maiden name. In nonformal use, the matrilineal name is often dropped. Thus, after the first mention in each part of the book, Uribe is sufficient.

The use of foreign words and terms has been confined to those essential to understanding the text, with a brief definition upon first usage and additional treatment in the Glossary. A list of abbreviations and acronyms of Spanish names, with English translations, can be found in table A. The text uses the standard spelling of place-names sanctioned by the United States Board on Geographic Names.

The book's formal information cutoff date for the chapters is December 31, 2008. Certain parts of the text, however, contain later information, added as it became available since the completion of research. The Introduction provides a general update for 2009 and early 2010.

Table A. Selected Spanish Abbreviations and Acronyms

Abbreviation or Acronym	Organization
AD	Alternativa Democrática (Democratic Alternative)
AD M–19	Acción Democrática M–19 (Democratic Action M–19)
Afeur	Agrupación de Fuerzas Especiales Antiterroristas Urbanas (Urban Counterterrorist Special Forces Group)
AFP	Administradores de Fondos de Pensiones (Pension Funds Administrators)
AGC	Autodefensas Gaitanistas de Colombia (Gaitán Self-Defense Groups of Colombia)
Aico	Autoridades Indígenas de Colombia (Indigenous Authorities of Colombia)
ALADI	Asociación Latinoamericana de Integración (Latin American Integration Association)
ANDI	Asociación Nacional de Industriales (National Association of Industrialists)
Anapo	Alianza Nacional Popular (Popular National Alliance)
ANH	Agencia Nacional de Hidrocarburos (National Hydrocarbons Agency)
ANIF	Asociación Nacional de Instituciones Financieras (National Association of Financial Institutions)
ANUC	Asociación Nacional de Usuarios Campesinos (National Association of Peasant Land Users)
ARS	Administradoras del Régimen Subsidiado (Administrators of the Subsidized Regimen)
ASI	Alianza Social Indígena (Indigenous Social Alliance)
Asocaña	Asociación de Cultivadores de Caña de Azúcar de Colombia (Association of Colombian Sugarcane Growers)
Asocolflores	Asociación Colombiana de Exportadores de Flores (Colombian Association of Flower Exporters)
AUC	Autodefensas Unidas de Colombia (United Self-Defense Forces of Colombia)
Augura	Asociación de Bananeros de Colombia (Association of Colombian Banana Producers)
Bancoldex	Banco de Comercio Exterior (Foreign Trade Bank)
Banrep	Banco de la República (Bank of the Republic; Central Bank)
BBVA	Banco Bilbao Viscaya Argentaria
BCN	Bloque Cacique Nutibara (Cacique Nutibara Bloc)
Cacom	Comando Aéreo de Combate (Combat Air Command)
CAE	Comando Aéreo de Entrenamiento (Air Training Command)
CAEM	Curso de Altos Estudios Militares (Higher Military Studies Course)
CAIs	Centros de Atención Inmediata (Immediate Care Centers; police posts in large cities)
Cajanal	Caja Nacional de Previsión Social (National Social Pension Fund)
Caman	Comando Aéreo de Mantenimiento (Air Maintenance Command)
CAN	Centro de Administración Nacional (National Administration Center)
CAN	Comunidad Andina de Naciones (Andean Community of Nations)
Caracol	Caracol Televisión, S.A., previously Primera Cadena Radial Colombiana (Caracol Television, previously First Colombian Radio Channel)
Carbocol	Carbones de Colombia (Colombia Coal)
CARE	Comisión Asesora de Relaciones Exteriores (Advisory Commission on Foreign Relations)

Table A. Selected Spanish Abbreviations and Acronyms (Continued)

Abbreviation or Acronym	Organization
Catam	Comando Aéreo de Transporte Militar (Military Air Transport Command)
CAVs	Corporaciones de Ahorro y Vivienda (savings and loan corporations)
CCFs	Cajas de Compensación Familiar (Family Compensation Funds)
CCJ	Comisión Colombiana de Juristas (Colombian Commision of Jurists)
CCN	Comisión de Conciliación Nacional (National Reconciliation Commission)
CEC	Conferencia Episcopal de Colombia (Colombian Episcopal Conference)
CEDE	Centro de Estudios sobre Desarrollo Económico (Economic Development Studies Center)
Cedecol	Confederación Evangélica de Colombia (Evangelical Confederation of Colombia)
Celade	Centro Latinoamericano y Caribeño de Demografía (Latin American & Caribbean Demographic Centre)
Cenicaña	Centro de Investigación de la Caña de Azúcar de Colombia (Sugarcane Research Center of Colombia)
Cepal	Comisión Económica para América Latina y el Caribe (Economic Commission for Latin America and the Caribbean—ECLAC)
CGN	Consejo Gremial Nacional (National Business Council)
CGT	Confederación General del Trabajo (General Confederation of Labor)
CGTD	Confederación General del Trabajadores Democráticos (General Confederation of Democratic Workers)
CIAT	Centro Internacional de Agricultura Tropical (International Center for Tropical Agriculture)
CICAD	Comisión Interamericana para el Control del Abuso de Drogas (Inter-American Drug Abuse Control Commission)
Cidenal	Curso Integral de Defensa Nacional (Comprehensive Course of National Defense)
Cinep	Centro de Investigación y Educación Popular (Research and Public Education Center)
CNA	Coordinador Nacional Agrario (National Agrarian Coordinator)
CNC	Consejo Nacional Campesino (National Campesino Council)
CNE	Consejo Nacional Electoral (National Electoral Council)
CNRR	Comisión Nacional de Reparación y Reconciliación (National Commission for Reparation and Reconciliation)
CNU	Comando Nacional Unitario (National Unitary Command)
Codhes	Consultoría para los Derechos Humanos y el Desplazamiento (Consultancy for Human Rights and Displacement)
Conpes	Consejo Nacional de Política Económica y Social (National Council for Economic and Social Policy)
Cra	Comisión de Regulación de Agua Potable y Saneamiento Básico (Water and Basic Sanitation Regulatory Commission)
CREG	Comisión de Regulación de Energía y Gas (Energy and Gas Regulatory Commission)
CRIC	Consejo Regional Indígena del Cauca (Cauca Regional Indigenous Council)
CRT	Comisión de Regulación de Telecomunicaciones (Telecommunications Regulatory Commission)
CSSDN	Consejo Superior de Seguridad y Defensa Nacional (Superior Council on National Defense and Security, previously CSDN—Consejo Superior de la Defensa Nacional)

Table A. Selected Spanish Abbreviations and Acronyms (Continued)

Abbreviation or Acronym	Organization
CSJ	Consejo Superior de la Judicatura (Superior Judicial Council)
CTC	Confederación de Trabajadores de Colombia (Confederation of Colombian Workers)
CTI	Cuerpo Técnico de Investigación (Technical Investigation Corps)
CUT	Confederación Unitaria de Trabajadores (United Workers' Federation)
DAFP	Departamento Administrativo de la Función Pública (Administrative Department of the Public Function)
DANE	Departamento Administrativo Nacional de Estadística (National Administrative Department of Statistics)
Dansocial	Departamento Administrativo Nacional de la Economía Solidaria (National Administrative Department of Economic Solidarity)
DAPR	Departamento Administrativo de la Presidencia de la República (Administrative Department of the Presidency of the Republic)
DAS	Departamento Administrativo de Seguridad (Administrative Security Department)
DGPN	Dirección General de la Policía Nacional (General Directorate of the National Police)
DIC	Dirección de Investigación Criminal (Criminal Investigation Directorate)
Dijin	Dirección de Policía Judicial e Investigación (Judicial and Investigative Police Directorate)
DNP	Departamento Nacional de Planeación (National Planning Department)
EAE	Escuela de Aviación del Ejército (Army Aviation School)
Ecopetrol	Empresa Colombiana de Petróleos (Colombian Petroleum Enterprise)
EFIM	Escuela de Formación de Infantería de Marina (Marine Infantry Training School)
EFSP	Escuela de Formación de Soldados Profesionales (Training School for Professional Soldiers)
Ehfup	Escuela de Helicópteros de la Fuerza Pública (Helicopter School of the Public Force)
ELN	Ejército de Liberación Nacional (National Liberation Army)
Emavi	Escuela Militar de Aviación Marco Fidel Suárez (Military Aviation School)
Emcali	Empresas Públicas de Cali (Cali Public Companies)
Emcar	Esquadrón Móvil de Carabineros (Mobile Squadron of Mounted Police)
Enap	Escuela Naval de Cadetes Almirante Padilla (Naval Cadet School)
ENP	Escuela Nacional de Policía General Santander (Police Cadet School)
ENS	Escuela Nacional Sindical (National Union School)
ENSB	Escuela Naval de Suboficiales ARC Barranquilla (Naval School for Noncommissioned Officers)
EPL	Ejército de Liberación Popular (Popular Liberation Army)
EPM	Empresas Públicas de Medellín (Medellín Public Companies)
EPS	Entidades Promotoras de Salud (health insurance entities)
Esdegue	Escuela Superior de Guerra (Superior War College)
Esmic	Escuela Militar de Cadetes José María Córdova (Military Cadet School)
Esrem	Escuela de Relaciones Civiles y Militares (Civil–Military Relations School)
Esufa	Escuela de Suboficiales Capitán Andrés M. Diaz (Noncommissioned Officers School)

Table A. Selected Spanish Abbreviations and Acronyms (Continued)

Abbreviation or Acronym	Organization
ETB	Empresa de Teléfonos de Bogotá (Bogotá Telephone Company)
FAC	Fuerza Aérea Colombiana (Colombian Air Force)
Famig	Fundación de Atención al Migrante (Migrants' Care Foundation)
FARC	Fuerzas Armadas Revolucionarias de Colombia (Revolutionary Armed Forces of Colombia)
FEC	Fondo de Compensación Educativa (Education Compensation Fund)
Fecode	Federación Colombiana de Educadores (Colombian Federation of Educators)
Fedecafé	Federación Nacional de Cafeteros (National Federation of Coffee Growers)
Fedegan	Federación Colombiana de Ganaderos (Association of Colombian Stockbreeders)
Fedemunicipios	Federación Colombiana de Municipios (Colombian Federation of Municipalities)
Fenalco	Federación Nacional de Comerciantes (National Federation of Merchants)
Fedesarrollo	Fundación para la Educación Superior y el Desarrollo (Foundation for Higher Education and Development)
Finagro	Fondo para el Financiamento del Sector Agropecuario (Fund for the Finance of the Agricultural Sector)
FNG	Fondo Nacional del Ganado (National Livestock Fund)
FSP	Frente Social y Político (Social and Political Front)
Fudra	Fuerza de Despliegue Rápido (Rapid Deployment Force)
FUN	Federación Universitaria Nacional (National University Federation)
Gacar	Grupo Aéreo del Caribe (Caribbean Air Group)
Gaori	Grupo Aéreo del Oriente (Eastern Air Group)
Gaula	Grupos de Acción Unificada por la Libertad Personal (United Action Groups for Personal Freedom)
GEA	Grupo Empresarial Antioqueño (Antioquia Entrepreneurial Group)
ICBF	Instituto Colombiano de Bienestar Familiar (Colombian Family Welfare Institute)
IEPRI	Instituto de Estudios Políticos y Relaciones Internacionales (Institute for the Study of Politics and Foreign Relations)
IFI	Instituto de Fomento Industrial (Industrial Development Institute)
IMA	Instituto Militar Aeronáutico (Aeronautics Military Institute)
Incomex	Instituto del Comercio Exterior (Foreign Trade Institute)
Indumil	Industria Militar (Military Industry)
INEM	Institutos Nacionales de Enseñanza Media Diversificada (National Institutes of Diversified Intermediate Education)
Inpec	Instituto Nacional Penitenciario y Carcelario (National Jail and Penitentiary Institute)
INS	Instituto Nacional de Salud (National Health Institute)
IPS	Instituciones Prestadoras de Servicios de Salud (health care providers)
ISS	Instituto de Seguros Sociales (Social Security Institute)
Justapaz	Justicia, Paz y Acción No Violenta (Justice, Peace and Nonviolent Action)
M–19	Movimiento 19 de Abril (Nineteenth of April Movement)
MAQL	Movimiento Armado Quintín Lame (Quintín Lame Armed Movement)
MAS	Muerte a Secuestradores (Death to Kidnappers)
MCV	Movimiento Colombia Viva (Living Colombia Movement)

Table A. Selected Spanish Abbreviations and Acronyms (Continued)

Abbreviation or Acronym	Organization
Mercosur	Mercado Común del Sur (Common Market of the South)
MIC	Movimiento Indígena de Colombia (Colombian Indigenous Movement)
Minga	Asociación para la Promoción Social Alternativa (Alternative Social Development Association)
MIRA	Movimiento Independiente de Renovación Absoluta (Independent Movement of Absolute Renewal)
MSN	Movimiento de Salvación Nacional (National Salvation Movement)
MSR	Movimiento Socialista de Renovación (Renewed Socialist Movement)
MRTA	Movimiento Revolucionario Túpac Amaru (Túpac Amaru Revolutionary Movement)
OCNP	Oficina del Comisionado Nacional para la Policía (National Police Commissioner's Office)
OIE	Oficio de International des Epizooties (World Organization for Animal Health)
ONIC	Organización Nacional Indígena de Colombia (National Indigenous Organization of Colombia)
Opain	Operadora Aeroportuaria Internacional (International Airport Operator)
ORO	Organización Radial Olímpica (Olympic Radio Organization)
PAICMA	Programa Presidencial para la Acción Integral contra Minas (Presidential Program for Integral Action Against Antipersonnel Mines)
PC	Partido Conservador (Conservative Party)
PCC	Partido Comunista de Colombia (Communist Party of Colombia)
PCD	Partido Colombia Democrática (Democratic Colombia Party)
PCN	Proceso de las Comunidades Negras (Platform of the Black Communities)
PCR	Partido Cambio Radical (Radical Change Party)
PDA	Polo Democrático Alternativo (Alternative Democratic Pole)
PDI	Polo Democrático Independiente (Independent Democratic Pole)
PL	Partido Liberal (Liberal Party)
Procaña	Asociación Colombiana de Productores y Provedores de Caña de Azúcar (Colombian Association of Sugarcane Producers and Suppliers)
Proexpo	Fondo para la Promoción de Exportaciones (Export Promotion Fund)
PSUN	Partido Social de Unidad Nacional (also seen as Partido de La U; National Unity Social Party; Party of the U)
PUJ	Pontificia Universidad Javeriana (Javeriana University)
PVO	Partido Verde Oxígeno (Oxygen Green Party)
RAS	Red de Apoyo Social (Social Assistance Network)
RCN	Radio Cadena Nacional (National Radio Network; it has radio and television channels)
Redprodpaz	Red Nacional de Programas de Desarrollo y Paz (National Network of Development and Peace Programs)
RNC	Radiotelevisora Nacional de Colombia (National Radio and Television of Colombia)
RNEC	Registraduría Nacional del Estado Civil (National Registrar of Civil Status, or National Registrar's Office)
RSS	Red de Solidaridad Social (Social Solidarity Network)
RTVC	Radio y Televisión de Colombia (Radio and Television of Colombia)

Table A. Selected Spanish Abbreviations and Acronyms (Continued)

Abbreviation or Acronym	Organization
SAC	Sociedad de Agricultores de Colombia (Society of Colombian Farmers)
Sapol	Servicio Aéreo de Policía (Police Air Service)
SARC	Sistema de Administración de Riesgo de Crédito (Credit Risk Management System)
Sena	Servicio Nacional de Aprendizaje (National Apprenticeship Service)
SFC	Superintendencia Financiera de Colombia (also seen as Superfinanciera; Colombian Financial Superintendency)
SINA	Sistema Nacional Ambiental (National Environmental System)
SIC	Servicio de Inteligencia Colombiana (Colombian Intelligence Service)
SIC	Superintendencia de Industria y Comercio (Industry and Commerce Superintendency)
SIP	Sociedad Interamericana de Prensa (Interamerican Press Society)
Sisben	Sistema de Identificación de Potenciales Beneficiarios de los Programas Sociales (System for the Identification and Selection of Beneficiaries of Social Programs)
SNS	Superintendencia National de Salud (National Superintendency of Health)
SPEC	Secretariado Permanente de la Conferencia Episcopal (Permanent Secretariat of the Episcopal Conference)
SSPD	Superintendencia de Servicios Públicos Domiciliarios (Residential Public Services Superintendency)
Superfinanciera	See SFC
SVSP	Superintendencia de Vigilancia y Seguridad Privada (Superintendency of Guard Forces and Private Security Companies)
Telecom	Colombia Telecomunicaciones S.A. (Colombia Telecommunications)
TSM	Tribunal Superior Militar (Supreme Military Tribunal)
UAEAC	Unidad Administrativa Especial de Aeronáutica Civil (Special Administrative Unit of Civil Aeronautics)
UN, or Unal	Universidad Nacional (National University)
Unasur	Unión de Naciones Suramericanas (Union of South American Nations)
Uniandes	Universidad de los Andes (University of the Andes)
Uninorte	Universidad del Norte (University of the North)
UP	Unión Patriótica (Patriotic Union)
UPAC	Unidad de Poder Adquisitivo Constante (Unit of Constant Purchasing Power)
USO	Unión Social Obrera (Workers' Social Union)
UTC	Unión de Trabajadores de Colombia (Union of Colombian Workers)
UVR	Unidad de Valor Real (Real Value Unit)

Table B. Chronology of Important Events

EARLY HISTORY

20,000 BC	Approximate date of earliest evidence of human occupation in what is now Colombia.
9790 BC	Tibitó archaeological site near present-day Bogotá.
4000–2000 BC	Appearance of settled communities in Caribbean coastal plain.
AD 1000–1500	Flourishing of Tairona and Muisca cultures, respectively, in the Sierra Nevada de Santa Marta and eastern highlands.

COLONIAL ERA, 1499–1810

1499	First Spanish expedition, led by Alonso de Ojeda, accompanied by Amerigo Vespucci and Juan de la Cosa, reaches Colombian coast (in September).
1525	Rodrigo de Bastidas founds Santa Marta, first permanent Spanish settlement.
1536–38	Gonzalo Jiménez de Quesada leads expedition that conquers the Muiscas.
1538	Jiménez de Quesada founds Santafé, present-day Bogotá, known as Santa Fe during the colonial period (August 6).

New Kingdom of Granada, 1538–1717

1550	Royal high court, or *audiencia*, is established in Santa Fe. Jiménez de Quesada is appointed marshal of New Granada and councilor of Sante Fe.
1564	Arrival in Santa Fe of first captain general of New Granada, whose appointment represents consolidation of Spanish colonial government.
1566	Smallpox epidemic reduces population by 10 percent.
1580	Dominicans establish university-college of Santo Tomás, first institution of higher education in New Granada.
1615–50	Ministry of Jesuit Pedro Claver, later canonized, to African slaves arriving through port of Cartagena.
1629	Founding of Barranquilla, last established of today's principal Colombian cities.

Viceroyalty of the New Kingdom of Granada, 1717–23

1719	New Granada officially attains the temporary status of viceroyalty with Santa Fe as its capital; its territory includes present-day Colombia, Ecuador, Panama, and Venezuela.

Presidency of the New Kingdom of Granada, 1723–39

1738	First printing press begins operating in Santa Fe.

Viceroyalty of the New Kingdom of Granada, 1739–1810

1777	First public library opens in Santa Fe.
1781	Comunero Rebellion protests new tax policies.
1783	José Celestino Mutis leads expedition to search out and describe all botanical species in viceroyalty.
1794	Antonio Nariño is arrested and convicted of sedition for having printed a Spanish translation of the French "Declaration of the Rights of Man and Citizen."
1808	Abdication of Ferdinand VII, under pressure of Napoleonic France, creates vacancy on Spanish throne and opportunity for Spanish Americans to seek a form of self-government.

FOUNDING OF THE NATION, 1810–1903

1810	In Santa Fe and elsewhere, criollo revolutionists establish juntas to rule, ostensibly in the name of Ferdinand VII (interned in France).
1811	Act of Federation of the United Provinces is declared (November 27).

Table B. Chronology of Important Events (Continued)

United Provinces of New Granada, 1811–16

| 1816 | Royalist forces retake Santa Fe (in May) and restore the colonial regime in most of New Granada. |

| 1816–19 | Spanish Reconquest. |

Republic of Great Colombia, 1819–32

| 1819 | Simón Bolívar Palacios wins Battle of Boyacá (August 7), delivering all of central New Granada to the patriots; congress meeting in Angostura, Venezuela, creates Republic of Colombia, referred to retrospectively as Great Colombia (Gran Colombia), comprising all of former Viceroyalty of New Granada, with its capital in renamed Santa Fe de Bogotá. |

| 1821 | Congress of Cúcuta adopts new nation's first constitution, which is strictly centralist in organization but otherwise conventionally liberal. |

| 1823 | Royalist forces surrender at Puerto Cabello, following Battle of Maracaibo in Venezuela; independence struggle in new Republic of Colombia ends. |

| 1826 | Rebellion in Venezuela weakens Great Colombia union. |

| 1828 | Bolívar assumes dictatorial powers and later survives assassination attempt (on September 25). |

| 1830 | Assembly in Santa Fe de Bogotá issues new Colombian constitution; Ecuador and Venezuela secede; Bolívar resigns presidency and dies (on December 17) in Santa Marta. |

Republic of New Granada, 1832–58

| 1832 | Present-day Colombia plus Panama is reconstituted as the Republic of New Granada. Its constitution, adopted in 1832, closely resembles Colombian charter of 1821. Francisco de Paula Santander y Omaña, Colombian vice president whom Bolívar had sent into exile, becomes New Granada's first constitutional president. |

| 1837 | José Ignacio de Márquez Barreto defeats Santander's chosen successor in first fully contested presidential election. |

| 1840–42 | War of the Supreme Commanders is waged (and lost) by proto-Liberals against the proto-Conservatives who follow Santander in office, a watershed in development of two-party system. |

| 1843 | New constitution strengthens central executive. |

| 1847 | Regular steam navigation begins on the Magdalena. |

| 1848–49 | Liberal and Conservative parties evolve from main political factions in course of critical presidential election campaign. |

| 1849–52 | Election of the Liberal José Hilario López Valdéz is followed by a succession of reform measures: abolition of state tobacco monopoly (1850), abolition of clergy legal privileges (1850), and final elimination of slavery, effective January 1, 1852. |

| 1853 | New constitution grants suffrage to all adult males, enshrines full religious toleration, and makes concessions to provincial autonomy, although stopping short of outright federalism. |

| 1854 | Backed by disaffected military and artisans, General José María Dionisio Melo y Ortiz carries out a successful coup (on April 19) against Liberal president but is soon overthrown by Liberal–Conservative coalition (December). |

| 1855 | Constitution is amended to establish Panama as a federal state. |

| 1856 | Colombia's first railroad, across the Isthmus of Panama, is completed. |

Granadine Confederation, 1858–61

| 1858 | Still another new constitution establishes the Granadine Confederation and creates a federal organization for entire country. |

Table B. Chronology of Important Events (Continued)

1859–62	In response to election law dictated by Congress, former Conservative Tomás Cipriano de Mosquera y Arboleda leads Liberal revolution against the Conservatives who had regained control in Bogotá, the only full-fledged revolution (rather than civil or military coup) ever to overthrow a Colombian government.
1861	As provisional head of what is now called United States of New Granada, Mosquera expropriates most church property and punishes the church for its support of Conservatives.

United States of New Granada, 1861–63

1863	Liberals enact new constitution that carries both federal autonomy of states and individual liberties to new extremes, while allowing states to limit suffrage again.

United States of Colombia, 1863–86

1870	Presidential decree declares primary education free, obligatory, and religiously neutral throughout the nation.
1876	Abortive Conservative uprising becomes brief but bitter civil war sparked in large part by Roman Catholic indignation over education policy.
1878	Colombia grants concession to French interests for construction of canal across Panama.
1878–1900	Regeneration movement (most influential in this period).
1880–82	Independent Liberal President Rafael Wenceslao Núñez Moledo's program of Regeneration aims to promote order and progress through strengthened national government but is thwarted by opposition of mainstream Liberals.
1885	"Radical" Liberals launch a preemptive rebellion lest Núñez illegally change the constitution, providing him with pretext to declare the 1863 constitution null and void.
1886	Under Núñez's auspices, new constitution ends federalism in favor of highly centralized government and dilutes individual rights; United States of Colombia is renamed Republic of Colombia and is organized into departments rather than sovereign states.

Republic of Colombia, 1886–Present

1887	Concordat with Vatican restores special privileges to Roman Catholic Church and offers compensation for lost assets.
1889	Coffee comes to dominate Colombian exports.
1890	Establishment of protected indigenous reserves.
1895	Another unsuccessful Liberal uprising.
1899–1902	War of the Thousand Days, a final failed effort by Liberals to reverse Núñez's innovations, causes heavy loss of life and economic disruption.
1900	Conservatives take power by coup.
1902	Hay–Herrán Treaty is signed with U.S. government (in September), allowing United States to complete Panama Canal.
1903	United States approves Hay–Herrán Treaty. After the Colombian Senate refuses to ratify it (in August), a group of Panamanian politicians and foreign adventurers bring about Panama's secession from Colombia (on November 3).

RECONCILATION, 1904–30

1904–9	President Rafael Reyes Prieto, a pragmatic Conservative, introduces power sharing with opposition, restores government finances, and promotes public works.
1907	Coltejer, first major textile-manufacturing company, is founded in Medellín.
1909	Rail connection between Bogotá and the Magdalena is completed.
1914–18	Colombia remains neutral in World War I.

Table B. Chronology of Important Events (Continued)

1919	Colombian–German Air Transport Society, the airline that later becomes Avianca (one of first airlines in hemisphere), is founded.
1921	Ratification of Urrutia–Thomson Treaty restores normal U.S.–Colombian relations, damaged by U.S. role in support of Panamanian independence.
1922	United States pays Colombia US$25 million for loss of Panama.
1928	Violent repression of strike by United Fruit Company banana workers produces strong backlash against the company and the Conservative government.

REFORMISM, 1930–45

1930	Liberal Party wins peaceful elections; in some parts of the country, serious outbreaks of political violence follow; small Socialist Revolutionary Party formally becomes Communist Party of Colombia.
1932–34	Colombia and Peru engage in a conflict over Amazonian territory of Leticia; Peru recognizes Colombia's ownership of port.
1934–38	First presidency of Alfonso López Pumarejo, whose program, Revolution on the March, brings first agrarian reform law and government support of unions in labor disputes.
1936	Constitutional reform (Codification of 1936) sets limits on property rights, permanently restores universal male suffrage, and reopens church–state conflict.
1941–44	Colombia closely collaborates with United States in World War II, declaring war on the Axis in 1943.

LA VIOLENCIA, 1946–58

1946	Conservatives regain presidency as result of Liberal divisions; change is again accompanied by widespread political violence.
1948	Assassination of Liberal leader Jorge Eliécer Gaitán (on April 9) provokes wave of rioting (known as the Bogotazo but not limited to Bogotá).
1950	Conservative leader Laureano Gómez Castro is elected president, with Liberals boycotting polls as violence worsens in countryside.
1951	Gómez sends Colombian troops to fight alongside United Nations forces in Korean War; Tropical Oil Company concession reverts to government and forms basis for creation of Colombian Petroleum Enterprise (Ecopetrol).
1953	General Gustavo Rojas Pinilla stages coup to oust Gómez (on June 13) and rules as military dictator, although at first with widespread Liberal and other support.
1954	Introduction of television; suffrage for women is adopted but takes effect only when elections are held after the fall of Rojas.
1957	Liberal–Conservative alliance, strongly supported by business community, compels resignation of Rojas (on May 10); plebiscite approves establishment of National Front power-sharing arrangement between the two major parties.
1957–58	General Gabriel París Gordillo heads the military junta.

THE NATIONAL FRONT, 1958–78

1958	National Front is formed. Alberto Lleras Camargo takes office as its first president.
1961	Government sponsors new agrarian reform law.
1963–65	Military offensive, with some U.S. aid, overcomes most guerrillas and bandit groups but fails to capture Pedro Antonio Marín, alias Manuel Marulanda Vélez or Tiro Fijo, and his associates, nucleus of the Revolutionary Armed Forces of Colombia (FARC), formed in 1964.
1965–66	Radical priest Camilo Torres Restrepo joins the Cuban-inspired National Liberation Army (ELN), formed in 1964, and is killed in combat.
1967	Pro-Chinese Popular Liberation Army (EPL) begins operations.

Table B. Chronology of Important Events (Continued)

1970	Former dictator Rojas runs for president and narrowly loses attempt to regain power (on April 19).
1973	ELN is decimated by army campaign, Battle of Anorí (August 7–October 18), and internal feuds, but remnant survives to regain strength in next decade; Nineteenth of April Movement (M–19) forms in October.
1978	National Front power-sharing mandate ends.

TERRORISM AND COUNTERINSURGENCY, 1979–Present

1979	U.S.–Colombian extradition treaty for drug traffickers comes into operation.
1980	M–19 members seize diplomatic hostages at Dominican Republic Embassy and occupy it for 61 days.
1982	Novelist Gabriel García Márquez becomes first Colombian to win Nobel Prize.
1984	Assassination of Minister of Justice Rodrigo Lara Bonilla (on April 30), by narco-traffickers inspires first major, but unsuccessful, crackdown on illicit drug industry.
1985	In Bogotá M–19 members seize Palace of Justice (on November 6), which is destroyed during army counterassault, with more than 100 deaths, including half of Supreme Court; eruption of Nevado del Ruiz volcano destroys Armero, a town in Tolima Department, killing 25,000 people (on November 13).
1989–90	Luis Carlos Galán and two other presidential candidates are assassinated in the 1990 election campaign.
1989	Coffee loses first place among legal exports. M–19 disarms and creates a political party (October–November).
1991	New constitution goes far toward decentralizing power and enshrines long list of citizen guarantees.
1993	Medellín Cartel's Pablo Escobar Gaviria is killed (December).
1994	Ernesto Samper Pizano takes office as president amid accusations of accepting narco-traffickers' contributions to his campaign fund.
1997	Founding of United Self-Defense Forces of Colombia (AUC) unites paramilitary groups.
1998–2002	Presidency of Andrés Pastrana Arango, who cedes an extensive, although lightly populated, area (*despeje*) to FARC guerrillas to advance peace negotiations that eventually fail.
1999	FARC kidnaps and murders three U.S. citizens, who were activists for indigenous rights (in February).
2001	FARC kidnaps popular former Minister of Culture Consuelo Araújo Noguera and then murders her during army rescue attempt, provoking public outrage against the guerrillas and the peace process (in September).
2002	FARC's kidnapping of a senator prompts President Pastrana to end peace talks and to order army to retake FARC's demilitarized zone; FARC kidnaps presidential candidate Ingrid Betancourt Pulecio and her colleague, Clara Rojas (in February).
	Right-wing independent candidate Álvaro Uribe Vélez wins presidential elections with landslide in first round (in May).
	Attorney General's Office reactivates arrest orders for ELN commanders, including maximum chief Nicolás Rodríguez Bautista, alias El Gabino (in June).
	Uribe assumes presidency (on August 7).
2003	FARC takes hostage three U.S. drug-control contractors—Keith Stansell, Marc Goncalves, and Thomas Howes (in February).
	Government negotiators and AUC representatives sign accord at Santa Fe de Ralito marking the start of formal peace negotiations (in July).

Table B. Chronology of Important Events (Continued)

	President Uribe is defeated in a referendum, in which he sought sweeping powers to streamline the state, reform the bloated political apparatus, and attack corruption (in October).
2004	Dialogue between the government and the ELN begins after Mexico offers to mediate (in July).
	Congress passes Uribe's legislation allowing for presidents to serve two consecutive terms (in December).
2005	Constitutional Court ratifies legislation allowing presidents to serve a second consecutive term (in October).
	Controversial Justice and Peace Law, which grants AUC almost blanket amnesty, goes into effect, increasing AUC rate of demobilization (in December).
2006	Parapolitics scandal begins: 12 pro-Uribe legislators are arrested for alleged collusion with outlawed paramilitary groups (January–May).
	Parties associated with President Uribe win majority in both houses of Congress (in March).
	AUC demobilization is officially completed (April 18).
	Uribe easily wins presidential election in first round with 62 percent of the vote (in May).
	ELN and government tentatively agree to begin formal peace process (in October).
2007	FARC assassinates 11 regional legislators, kidnapped five years earlier in Cali, when a military group attempts to rescue them (in June).
	Samuel Moreno Rojas, candidate of left-wing Alternative Democratic Pole (PDA) and a political rival of President Uribe, is elected mayor of Bogotá (in October).
	International Court of Justice at The Hague recognizes validity of Treaty of Esguerra–Bárcenas, under which Nicaragua acknowledged Colombian sovereignty over the Archipiélago de San Andrés, Providencia y Santa Catalina. Colombia recognizes Nicaraguan sovereignty over the Costa de Mosquitos (in December).
2008	Nationwide demonstrations occur on February 4 to protest FARC kidnappings.
	With Venezuelan president Hugo Chávez Frías mediating, longtime FARC hostages Clara Rojas and Consuelo González de Perdomo are released, followed by four congressional hostages (in February).
	FARC Secretariat members Raúl Reyes and Iván Ríos are killed in cross-border strike into Ecuador, and Manuel Marulanda Vélez, FARC's founder and its supreme commander since 1964, dies (in March).
	Guillermo León Sáenz Vargas, alias Alfonso Cano, is named as Marulanda's replacement to lead FARC (in April).
	Supreme Court rules that a former legislator had received a bribe to ensure the passage of the constitutional amendment that allowed Uribe to run for a second term in 2006, prompting Uribe to call for a referendum on his rule (in June).
	FARC's four highest-profile hostages—former presidential candidate Ingrid Betancourt and three U.S. contractors—plus 11 military and police members are rescued (in July).
	Military "false positives" scandal emerges, revealing large-scale extrajudicial killings of impoverished young civilian men in order to raise guerrilla casualty counts (in September).
	Thousands of irate Colombians stage violent protests in 10 cities across the country after national Ponzi scheme victimizes hundreds of thousands (November 13).

Table B. Chronology of Important Events (Continued)

2009	FARC releases a Swede, Erik Roland Larsson, thought to be its last foreign hostage (March).
	Veteran Colombian journalist José Everardo Aguilar, 72, a noted critic of corruption, is assassinated (April 28).
	United Kingdom ends bilateral military aid to Colombia because of human rights concerns (April 29).
	Senate approves holding referendum on whether constitution should be changed to allow possibility of second Uribe reelection (May 19).
	President Uribe visits President Barack H. Obama at the White House (June 29).
	Supplemental Agreement for Cooperation and Technical Assistance in Defense and Security between the Governments of the United States of America and the Republic of Colombia, or Defense Cooperation Agreement, is signed in Bogotá (October 30).
	National Electoral Council (CNE) invalidates petition for referendum on a second presidential reelection bid by President Uribe (November 13).
	FARC kidnaps and murders governor of Caquetá Department (December 21).
2010	Inspector general of the nation endorses proposed referendum (January 13).
	FARC military chief Jorge Suárez Briceño, alias El Mono Jojoy, reaffirms FARC's armed struggle and rejects surrendering in letter to Military Forces general commander (February 13).
	Constitutional Court rules the proposed plebiscite unconstitutional (February 26).
	Legislative elections (March 14).
	Presidential election (May 30).

Country Profile

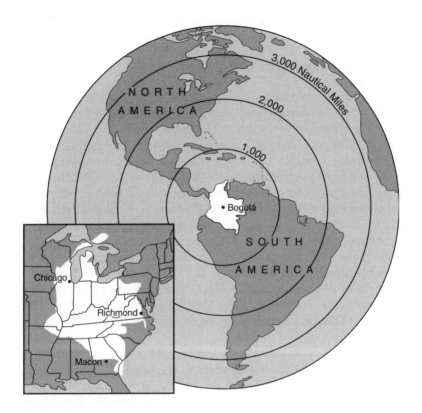

Country

Formal Name: Republic of Colombia (República de Colombia).

Short Form: Colombia.

Term for Citizen(s): Colombian(s).

Capital: Bogotá. Although officially called Distrito Capital de Santa Fe de Bogotá under the 1991 constitution, Santa Fe was formally dropped from the name of Bogotá in 2000.

Major Cities: In order of population, Bogotá, Medellín, Cali, Barranquilla, and Bucaramanga.

Independence: Colombia marks its independence from Spain on July 20, 1810, when criollo revolutionists established a ruling junta in the capital city of Santa Fe de Bogotá (present-day Bogotá).

Flag: Three horizontal bands of yellow (top, double-width), blue, and red.

Historical Background

By the time of the Spanish Conquest, the Chibcha, numbering 500,000 and split between two groups—Taironas and Muiscas—dominated the Central Highlands of what is now Colombia, where they had lived for at least 2,000 years and had become the most advanced of the indigenous peoples. Gonzalo Jiménez de Quesada led the first conquering expedition from Santa Marta to Sabana de Bogotá (1536–39). In 1538, when Jiménez de Quesada founded Santafé (Santa Fe during the colonial period) in the Bagatá zone of the country, Muiscas still lived in the hills overlooking the settlement, but their notable system of political centralization was crushed, and they became assimilated with the rest of the population. Conquistadors Nikolaus Federmann and Sebastián de Belalcázar led other expeditions in 1537–39 and 1538–39, respectively. In 1719 present-day Colombia, Venezuela, Ecuador, and Panama formed the Viceroyalty of the New Kingdom of Granada. In 1781 anger over Spanish taxation led to the Comunero Rebellion.

On July 20, 1810, revolutionary leaders took part in an uprising in Santa Fe, deposing the Spanish viceroy. On August 7, 1819, General Simón Bolívar Palacios defeated the Spanish at the Battle of Boyacá, allowing colonists to sever ties with Spain and form the Republic of Great Colombia, with its capital in renamed Santa Fe de Bogotá. Bolívar was the first president of Great Colombia, with fellow liberator General Francisco de Paula Santander as vice president. When Ecuador and Venezuela seceded in 1830, the remainder of Great Colombia soon became the Republic of New Granada, with Santander as its first president. From 1849 to 1886, Colombia oscillated between a liberal republic and a highly centralized, authoritarian government.

The 1886 constitution gave the country its present name, reversed the federalist trend, and inaugurated 45 years of Conservative rule. Factionalism within political parties and political and economic instability characterized the inaptly named Regeneration period (1878–1900). The War of a Thousand Days (1899–1902) between Liberals and Conservatives devastated the country. Panama declared its independence in 1903.

In 1948 the assassination of popular Liberal leader Jorge Eliécer Gaitán instigated major political rioting in Bogotá (the Bogotazo). Countrywide violence, known as La Violencia, which had begun in 1946, continued to rage until 1958, when the Conservatives and Liberals banded together in the National Front. The arrangement greatly reduced political violence in the early 1960s, but by excluding dissident political forces, it contributed to the emergence of guerrilla groups.

The National Front arrangement ended in 1978, but the tradition of presidents inviting opposition figures to hold cabinet positions continued. Following a constitutional reform convention, a new constitution was adopted in July 1991. The election of Álvaro Uribe Vélez (president, 2002–6, 2006–10), an independent, ended the Liberal–Conservative duopoly of political power. Immensely popular for his handling of the economy and his hard line against the insurgency, Uribe was reelected to a second term. In 2008 his popularity was strengthened by major setbacks to the insurgent Revolutionary Armed Forces of Colombia (FARC). In February 2010, a proposed referendum, which might have led to a second reelection, was declared unconstitutional.

Geography

Size and Location: Colombia measures 1,138,910 square kilometers, or slightly less than twice the size of Texas. The country lies in the northwestern part of South America, bordered by the Caribbean Sea to the north, the North Pacific Ocean and the Isthmus of Panama to the west, Ecuador and Peru to the south, and Brazil and Venezuela to the east.

Topography: Colombia has five major geographic regions: the Caribbean lowlands; the Pacific lowlands; the Andean region, including three rugged parallel, north–south mountain ranges; the vast eastern and northeastern grassy plains, known as llanos; and the Amazon region, which is tropical rainforest. Colombia's insular region includes four small islands. The most important rivers are the Magdalena, Cauca, and Putumayo.

Climate: Because of differences in elevation, Colombia has an extensive temperature range, with little seasonal variation. The hottest month is March (9° C–20° C); the coldest months are July and August (8° C–19° C). Precipitation is generally moderate to heavy with an annual average of 3,000 millimeters and considerable yearly and regional variations.

Natural Resources: Colombia is well endowed with energy resources and minerals, including coal, copper, emeralds, gold, hydropower, iron ore, natural gas, natural nickel, petroleum, platinum, and silver. Its coal reserves, totaling 7.4 billion metric tons, are foremost in Latin America and are concentrated in Península de La Guajira and the Andean foothills. Colombia's natural gas reserves, totaling 4 trillion cubic feet in 2007, and proven oil reserves, totaling 1.45 billion barrels in 2007, are located mostly in the eastern Andean foothills and Amazonian jungle. There are abundant renewable water resources. Only a small percentage (probably less than 3 percent) of Colombia's total land area, such as the fertile Andean mountainsides and valleys, is cultivated for crops.

Environmental Factors: Colombia's forests cover 578,000 square kilometers, and about 10 percent of the total land area is designated as a protected area in the national park system. The country's abundant rivers and streams have long been degraded by industrial and municipal pollution, as well as by guerrilla sabotage of oil pipelines and chemicals used in the coca-refining process. Other issues include deforestation in the jungles of the Amazon and in Chocó on the Pacific coast, air pollution (especially in Bogotá), and the use of herbicides. As a result of soil erosion, 65 percent of the country's municipalities face water shortages by 2015. Nearly 12 million Colombians have no access to clean water, and 4 million have only limited access.

Society

Population: Colombia is the third most populous country in Latin America, after Brazil and Mexico. The 2005 census put the national population residing in Colombia at 41,468,384; the average annual population growth rate during 2001–5 was 1.6 percent, falling to an estimated 1.4 percent in 2008. The estimated population in February 2010 was about 45.3 million. By 2005 the largely urban population had increased to 75 percent. The internal armed conflict as well as the violence generated by the illegal drug-trafficking industry caused massive displacement of the rural population, and many people fled to the cities. Population density per square kilometer averaged 44 in 2005, but with major regional variation. The 2005 census found that 3.3 million Colombians were living abroad because of insecurity and unemployment at home; external migration is primarily to Ecuador, the United States, and Venezuela. In 2008 some 29.4 percent of Colombians were aged 14 years or younger; 65.1 percent were in the 15–64 age-group; and only 5.5 percent were 65 or older. The estimated median age in 2008 was 26.8 years. The birthrate was 19.9 per 1,000 people; the estimated fertility rate was 2.5 children born per woman. The death rate was 5.5 deaths per 1,000 people. Overall life expectancy at birth was 72.5 years (males, 68.7 years; females, 76.5 years). The number of male homicide victims accounts for the significant gap between life expectancy for men and women.

Ethnic Groups and Languages: The official language is Spanish. The 2005 census reported that whites and mestizos (of mixed white and Amerindian ancestry) constituted 86 percent of the population. The Afro-Colombian population, including blacks, mulattoes (mixed black and white ancestry), and *zambos* (mixed Amerindian and black ancestry), accounted for 10.5 percent of the population; the indigenous population, for 3.4 percent; and the gypsy (Rom) population, for 0.01 percent. Colombia has about 78 living languages; there are about 500,000 speakers of Amerindian languages, but their numbers are diminishing rapidly.

Health: Health standards in Colombia have improved greatly since the 1980s. Employees must pay into health plans, to which employers also contribute. Although in 2005 the system covered 66 percent of the population, health disparities persist, with the poor suffering relatively high mortality rates. In 2005 Colombia had only 1.1 physicians per 1,000 people, compared to a Latin American average of 1.5. The health sector reportedly is plagued by rampant corruption, misallocation of funds, and evasion of health-fund contributions. Total expenditures on health constituted 5.6 percent of gross domestic product (GDP) in 2005. In 2002 Colombia had one of the world's highest homicide rates of more than 60 per 100,000 inhabitants, or 28,837. Some 17,206 violent deaths were recorded in 2006, the lowest figure since 1987, and the number was about the same in 2007, declining further to 16,359 in 2008. Other than homicide, heart disease is the main cause of premature death, followed by strokes, respiratory diseases, road accidents, and diabetes. Prevalent in lowland and coastal areas are waterborne diseases such as bacterial diarrhea, cerebral malaria, and leishmaniasis; water-contact diseases such as leptospirosis; and vectorborne diseases such as dengue fever, malaria, and yellow fever. In 2004 some 92 percent of infants under 12 months of age were immunized against measles. Acquired immune deficiency syndrome (AIDS) is also a major cause of death among those of working age, and the number of AIDS and hepatitis B cases has been rising.

Welfare: All Colombian workers are legally required to be affiliated with a basic pension and health provider. The Social Security Institute is one of Colombia's largest state companies and is the principal agency involved in the field of social security, with responsibility for pensions. Serious social problems include high rates of criminal violence; extensive societal discrimination against women, child abuse, and child prostitution; trafficking in women and girls for sexual exploitation; widespread child labor; extensive societal discrimination against indigenous people and minorities; drug addiction; poverty; and displacement of the rural population. Poverty remains widespread in Colombia, where income distribution has huge disparities. The proportion of the population living below the poverty line was estimated at between 50 and 60 percent in 2005, according to the Comptroller General's Office, with up to 40 percent of rural dwellers living in extreme poverty. The Economic Commission for Latin America and the Caribbean said that the overall poverty index had declined to 46.8 percent by 2005.

Religion: The constitution states somewhat ambiguously that there is no official church or religion, but the great majority of the population traditionally has been Roman Catholic. Statistics on religious affiliation in Colombia vary widely, however, and the National Administrative Department of Statistics (DANE) does not collect religious statistics. Between 80 and 90 percent of the population is Roman Catholic, at least nominally; approximately 10 percent of Colombians belong to other Christian denominations, particularly Protestant, or profess no belief. Very small percentages of Colombians adhere to Judaism, Islam, Hinduism, and Buddhism, as well as Afro-Colombian syncreticism. For political reasons, the illegal armed groups, both left-wing and paramilitary, have targeted religious leaders and practitioners.

Education and Literacy: Public spending on education was 4.7 percent of GDP in 2006, when the pupil/teacher ratio was 30:1. Many teachers are poorly qualified, particularly in rural areas, where only five years of primary school may be offered, although primary education for children between six and 12 years old and a total of nine years of education are free and compulsory. Secondary school begins at age 11 and lasts up to six years; graduates gain the *bachillerato* (high-school diploma). The 2005 census found that 50.3 percent of those aged between three and five were enrolled in school, as were 90.7 percent of those between six and 10 years old and 79.9 percent of those between 11 and 17. By 2008 literacy had risen to 93 percent of the general population; only 67 percent of rural dwellers were literate in 2004. The ratio of public to private primary and secondary schools was 3:1; at the tertiary level, the private sector dominated, with a ratio of 2.4:1. In 2004 Colombia had 279 institutions of higher learning, including professional technical schools, technological schools, colleges, and universities.

Economy

Overview: In 2007 Colombia had the fifth-largest economy in Latin America (after Brazil, Mexico, Argentina, and Venezuela), a status expected to continue through 2010; by regional standards, it is a diversified economy. Since 1991 a free-market economy has evolved through measures such as tariff reductions, financial deregulation, privatization of state-owned enterprises, and adoption of a more liberal foreign-exchange rate. In 2007 agriculture accounted for 13 percent of GDP, industry (including manufacturing and construction) for 29 percent, and services for the remaining 58 percent.

The economy became mired in a recession in 1998–99 as a result of external shocks and monetary tightening to curb inflation. It has rebounded since 2003 as a result of confidence in the political and economic policies of President Álvaro Uribe. The recovery of growth in the GDP in 2005 and an overall reduction in criminal and political violence contributed to favorable conditions that made 2007 one of the best economic years in recent history. The economy is expected to remain steady despite continuing weak domestic and foreign demand, slow GDP growth, austere government budgets, and serious internal armed conflict. Problems facing the government include reforming the pension system, reducing unemployment, and funding new exploration to offset declining oil production.

Gross Domestic Product (GDP): Overall GDP increased by 6.8 percent in 2006 and by 7.5 percent in 2007, when it totaled US$172 billion. Colombia is a lower middle-income country. Real GDP per capita contracted by 6 percent in 1998–2002 and only recovered its 1997 level in 2005, when it reached US$2,735 (or US$5,867 at purchasing power parity, or PPP, in current international dollars). The GDP per capita at PPP in 2008 was US$6,958. In 2005 the median household income was US$3,904.

Government Budget: Favorable international conditions such as higher oil prices and Colombia's economic expansion aided the efforts of the Uribe administration to bring Colombia's public finances under control. Public-sector debt has fallen as a share of GDP from 2002, when it was 63.5 percent of GDP, to 46.4 percent in 2009, but it was expected to rise to 48 percent in 2011. Under President Uribe's tax reforms, the income tax rate probably declined to 34 percent in 2008 and to about 33 percent in 2009, with lower corporate taxes and a simpler value-added tax. From a balance of 0.5 percent in 2008, the estimated deficit for 2009 was 2.8 percent of GDP, 3.1 percent for 2010, and 2.7 percent for 2011. Continuing foreign direct investment and other capital inflows to the oil sector were expected to allow the government's widening fiscal and current-account deficits to remain manageable.

Inflation: During 1990–2002, the inflation rate averaged 18.1 percent per year. Although it gradually fell to an estimated 4.5 percent in 2006, it rose to 5.7 percent in 2007 and registered 7.7 percent in 2008, well above the official year-end target of 3.5 to 4.5 percent.

Agriculture, Forestry, and Fishing: Diverse climate and topography allow cultivation of a wide variety of crops and other agricultural products, including bananas, beef, cassava, cocoa, coffee, corn, cotton, cut flowers, livestock, palm oil, potatoes, rice, soybeans, sugarcane, timber, and tobacco. Coffee remains Colombia's leading legal cash and export crop, still accounting for about one-third of employment in agriculture. Endemic guerrilla and paramilitary violence has plagued many campesinos and cattle-ranch owners and discouraged investment in the sector. Colombia has at least 53 million hectares of forest and woodland, but only 3 million hectares are commercially exploited. Roundwood removals in 2004 totaled 8.1 million cubic meters, and sawn-wood production totaled 622,000 cubic meters; much harvested wood is used as fuel. Coastlines on both the Caribbean Sea and Pacific Ocean provide Colombian fisheries with extensive and diverse resources. Nevertheless, low fish consumption and rudimentary fishing techniques apparently account for the relatively marginal performance of the fishing industry. The total catch in 2004 was 211,385 metric tons.

Mining, Minerals, and Energy: Colombia is a major producer of ferronickel and is famous for its gold, silver, platinum, and emeralds, accounting for 90 percent of the world's emerald production. Colombia was self-sufficient in energy in 2008, with substantial proven reserves of coal and natural gas and currently adequate petroleum, as well as vast hydroelectric potential.

Industry and Manufacturing: In 2007 this sector accounted for 29 percent of GDP and for 18.7 percent of employment. Major manufactured products include beverages, cardboard containers, cement, chemicals, electrical equipment, machinery, metal products, pharmaceuticals, plastic resins and manufactures, textiles and garments, transport equipment, and wood products. Construction, a growing subsector, contributed an estimated 6.7 percent of GDP in 2005.

Services: The services sector accounted for about 58 percent of GDP in 2007. The sector includes commerce; communications; electricity, gas, and water; financial services; tourism; and transportation. Representing nearly 18 percent of GDP, financial services are centered in Bogotá, Medellín, and, to a lesser extent, Cali.

Labor: During 2001–5 the generally well-educated and well-trained workforce grew by 1.4 percent. The unemployment rate was down to about 10–11 percent of a labor force of 18.8 million by 2007, but underemployment affected an estimated 35 percent of the working population.

Foreign Economic Relations: The United States is Colombia's most important trading partner; Andean countries are also major markets. Venezuela was an important trading partner until it began imposing restrictions on trade with Colombia in 2009. Others include Chile, Mexico, Caribbean Community and Common Market countries, and members of the European Union, especially Germany.

Imports: Imports of goods (free on board—f.o.b.) totaled US$37.5 billion in 2008. In 2006 some 26 percent of Colombia's total imports came from the United States, 9 percent each from China and Mexico, 7 percent from Brazil, 6 percent from Venezuela, 4 percent each from Germany and Japan, 3 percent from Ecuador, and 1 percent from Spain. Principal imports were machinery, industrial and oil and gas industry equipment, grains, chemicals, transportation equipment, mineral products, consumer products, metal and metal products, plastic and rubber, paper products, and aircraft supplies.

Exports: Exports of goods (f.o.b.) totaled US$38.5 billion in 2008. Exports were projected to have dropped significantly in 2009. Until 2008 the trend of increasing exports reflected higher commodity prices and growing foreign demand, as well as an export-oriented policy. The relative importance of coffee exports in the country's GDP plummeted from 51 percent in 1985 to less than 6 percent in 2006. Coal and oil are Colombia's two other primary export commodities, accounting for 38 percent of total exports in 2006. Traditional exports—oil, coal, coffee, and nickel—reached US$5 billion in 2005. In the 1980s and 1990s, manufacturing and new exports such as cut flowers began to earn more export revenue than the country's traditional products—coffee, bananas, and textiles. Colombia has become the world's second largest exporter of fresh-cut flowers. In addition to major oil and gas discoveries, mineral exports have strengthened the economy. Significant nontraditional exports include agricultural products (cut flowers and sugar), mining products (ferronickel, gold, cement, and emeralds), and industrial products (textiles and apparel, chemicals, pharmaceuticals, cardboard containers, printed material, plastic resins, and manufactures). The main destinations of 68 percent of total exports in 2006 were the United States, 40 percent; Venezuela, 11 percent; Ecuador, 5 percent; Mexico and Peru, 3 percent each; and Germany, Japan, and Belgium, 2 percent each.

Balance of Trade: Exports grew faster than imports during the 1999–2006 period, resulting in positive trade balances. In 2008 there was a positive balance of US$1 billion from total trade of US$76 billion.

Balance of Payments: Colombia has had a negative current account since 1993. The current-account deficit was 2.8 percent of GDP in 2007 and 2008, but continuing strong foreign investment was expected to fully finance the deficit. Nevertheless, the current-account deficit in 2009 was estimated at 2.4 percent of GDP. Foreign currency reserves totaled US$25.3 billion in 2009.

External Debt: The foreign debt level was high; external debt rose to US$44 billion in 2007.

Currency and Exchange Rate: Colombia uses the peso, formally abbreviated as COP and informally as COL$ or Ps. On February 16, 2010, COPs 1,900.8 equaled US$1.

Fiscal Year: Calendar year.

Transportation and Telecommunications

Overview: Almost 70 percent of cargo is transported by road, but Colombia has a very low ratio of paved roads per inhabitant; air and waterway routes are well developed. Waterways are the only means of transport in 40 percent of the country, but guerrilla groups imperil those in the south and southeast. By the 2000s, mass transportation systems existed in Bogotá, Medellín, and seven other cities. Traffic congestion in Bogotá was exacerbated by the lack of a rail system but eased by the TransMilenio Bus Rapid System and private cars being subjected to a daily rotating ban. Barranquilla has a similar bus rapid-transit system. Cali's transit system of articulated buses opened in late 2008. Medellín has a modern urban railroad connecting with the cities of Itagüí, Envigado, and Bello and an elevated cable-car system, added in 2004, linking some poorer mountainous neighborhoods with Metro de Medellín.

Civil Aviation and Airports: In 2009 Colombia had 992 airports (116 with paved runways), plus two heliports. Bogotá, Rionegro near Medellín, Cali, Barranquilla, Bucaramanga, Cartagena, Cúcuta, Leticia, Pereira, San Andrés, and Santa Marta have international airports. Bogotá's El Dorado International Airport handled 579,000 metric tons of cargo and 13.5 million passengers in 2008.

Inland Waterways: In 2008 some 18,300 kilometers were navigable by riverboats. Approximately 3.8 million metric tons of freight and more than 5.5 million passengers are transported annually, a majority on the Magdalena–Cauca, Atrato, Orinoco, and Amazon river systems.

Ports: Seaports handle around 80 percent of the country's international cargo. In 2005 a total of 105,251 metric tons of cargo was transported by water. Colombia's main ocean terminals are at Barranquilla, Cartagena, and Santa Marta on the Caribbean Coast and at Buenaventura and Tumaco on the Pacific Coast. Exports mostly pass through Cartagena and Santa Marta, while 65 percent of imports arrive at the port of Buenaventura.

Railroads: Colombia had 3,304 kilometers of rail lines in 2006. The rail network is underdeveloped, but much of the system was upgraded in 2004–6. Although the network links seven of 10 major cities, very little of it is used regularly because of security concerns, lack of maintenance, and the country's powerful road-transport union.

Roads: Of the 164,257 kilometers of roads, about 8 percent were paved in October 2008. Colombia has three main north–south highways, mostly in good condition. Despite major terrain obstacles, 70 percent of cross-border dry cargo is transported by road. Major road improvements are expected in the near future.

Telecommunications and Mass Media: Telecommunications constituted 3 percent of GDP in 2007, when Colombia had fewer than 8 million fixed telephone lines. According to the Industry and Commerce Superintendency (SIC), the Colombian cell-phone market reached 40.7 million subscriptions at the end of 2008, bringing the penetration rate to 91 percent. In 2008 Colombia had an estimated Internet penetration rate of 32.3 percent and broadband reception rate of 3.9 percent. In 2008 Colombia had five national channels, local and regional channels, 76 registered providers of cable television, one company broadcasting by satellite (DIRECTV), and about 12 million TV sets. In 2004 there were almost 1,300 radio stations. Ownership of news media is highly concentrated among wealthy families, national conglomerates, and major political parties. Journalists practice self-censorship for fear of corrupt officials, criminals, and members of illegal armed groups.

Government and Politics

Government Overview: The constitution of 1991 established a multiparty democracy in a unitary republic, a strong presidential regime, and separation of powers among the three branches of government. President Álvaro Uribe's broad congressional alliance and institutional stability have prevailed from 2002 to early 2010, despite endemic violence from guerrilla, paramilitary, and narcotics-trafficking activities, as well as high-level corruption associated with wealth created by the drug cartels that have undermined Colombia's political and social foundations.

Branches of Government: As chief of state and head of government, the president has executive power and strong policy-making authority and is elected for a four-year term. The president heads and is assisted by a cabinet. The bicameral Congress of the Republic consists of a 102-member Senate and 166-member House of Representatives, which includes 161 members elected to represent the 32 departments and one for the Distrito Capital de Bogotá, as well as an extra two members to represent Afro-Colombians, one for the indigenous population, one for the Colombians living abroad, and one for other political minorities. Members of both chambers are popularly elected with no reelection limit. The judicial branch is largely independent. It is composed, at the highest level, of a coequal Supreme Court of Justice, Council of State, Constitutional Court, and Superior Judicial Council. The system includes the Attorney General's Office, an autonomous judicial agency headed by an independent attorney general, elected for a four-year term by Congress and responsible for investigating criminal offenses and prosecutions. The military justice system, as part of the Ministry of National Defense, falls under the executive branch.

Administrative Divisions and Local Government: Colombia is divided into 32 administrative departments and the Distrito Capital de

Bogotá. In 2009 departments were subdivided into a total of 1,120 municipalities, each headed by a mayor. Citizens directly elect governors, deputies, mayors, municipal and district councils, and members of local administrative boards. Department governors are popularly elected for four-year terms. Each department has a popularly elected departmental assembly that oversees actions of the governors.

Politics: For 150 years after their official establishment in the mid-nineteenth century, the rival Liberal Party and Conservative Party dominated politics. In recent years, a multiparty system has developed, and in 2002 Álvaro Uribe became the first independent president in Colombian history. In the March 2006 congressional elections, winners were parties associated with President Uribe, including the Conservative Party in alliance with two main Uribista groupings. The center-left Liberal Party is still the largest party in Congress but is currently relatively powerless, as is the leftist Alternative Democratic Pole (PDA), but the Liberals have been moving to the center, while the PDA has been consolidating its ranks and expanding grassroots support. After the March 2006 elections, 16 recognized political parties had seats in Congress. Political parties generally operate freely and without government interference. Members of independent parties may be elected to regional or local office and may also win seats in Congress, as may dissidents from the two main parties. President Uribe has been very popular, owing to his success in improving domestic security and socioeconomic conditions, particularly containing the guerrillas, significantly reducing high rates of criminal and political violence, and reviving economic growth. The Uribe administration has stressed combating insurgency by providing internal security within the framework of democratic protections and guarantees. Other priorities are international trade, supporting alternative means of development, and reforming the judicial and tax systems.

Foreign Relations: Colombia has generally adopted a low profile, relying on international law and regional and international security organizations to pursue its interests. The country has good relations with the United States in its most important foreign relationship. U.S. aid, which totaled more than US$7 billion in 1999–2007, is designed to boost Colombian counternarcotics capabilities by providing helicopters and training, and to support human rights, humanitarian assistance, alternative development, and economic and judicial reforms. The main issues for the United States are Colombian drug trafficking and illegal Colombian immigrants to the United States. Regional relations remain good despite contentious issues with neighbors, especially the spillover from Colombia's civil conflict, including guerrillas moving across borders, the flow of refugees, and the spread of drug crops—activities of particular concern to the bordering countries of Brazil, Ecuador, Panama, Peru, and Venezuela. Brazil is the second-largest market in the world for Colombian cocaine after the United States and a source for weapons for Colombian guerrilla and paramilitary groups. Relations with Nicaragua and Venezuela have been strained over territorial disputes, Colombian complaints of Nicaraguan and Venezuelan support for the Revolutionary Armed Forces of Colombia (FARC), and from 2009, over Colombia's Defense Cooperation Agreement with the United States. Under the Uribe administration, relations with the European Union (EU) have been cool, with the EU critical of Colombia's counterinsurgency strategy and human rights abuses.

Major International Agreements and Treaties: Defense treaties to which Colombia is a party include the Inter-American Treaty of Reciprocal Assistance of 1947 (Rio Treaty). Regional treaties include the Andean Community of Nations (formerly the Andean Pact), which also includes Bolivia, Ecuador, Peru, and Venezuela and the bodies and institutions making up the Andean Integration System (AIS). Colombia has also signed, adhered to, and ratified 105 international treaties or agreements relating to the environment. Colombia is a signatory to the Treaty on the Non-Proliferation of Nuclear Weapons and is also a party to the Treaty for the Prohibition of Nuclear Weapons in Latin America (Treaty of Tlatelolco). By 1975 signatories to the 1974 Declaration of Ayacucho, including Colombia, had decided on limitations to nuclear, biological, and chemical weapons. Colombia is a party to the 1988 United Nations Drug Convention, and in 1994 it ratified the United Nations Convention Against Illicit Trafficking in Narcotics and Psychotropic Substances.

National Security

Armed Forces Overview: Under the constitution, the president is commander in chief, and, in practice, President Uribe exercises direct command over the military and security forces, leaving the minister of national defense with mostly administrative duties. The London-based International Institute for Strategic Studies (IISS) estimated 2008 active armed forces to total 267,231: army, 43,013 career active-duty plus 183,339 conscripts, for a total of 226,352; navy, 23,515 plus 7,214 conscripts, for a total of 30,729; and air force, 10,150. The IISS total does not include naval aviation, 146, and marines, 14,000. Reservists totaled an additional 61,900 (army 54,700; navy, 4,800; air force, 1,200; and joint, 1,200). In 2008 the army ranks included approximately 7,000 officers and 26,000 noncommissioned officers (NCOs).

Defense Budget: Colombia's defense budget and military expenditures have been rising in response to significant security challenges, including the continuing insurgency, massive narcotics trafficking, and an arms-buying spree by Venezuela. With U.S. aid under Plan Colombia, the defense budget's share of GDP has been expanding; in August 2008, it totaled US$12.25 billion, or 5.6 percent of GDP; and total defense spending per member of the armed forces totaled US$49,814, with budget increases funding additional professional soldiers and counterguerrilla battalions. In 2008 defense expenditures totaled US$8.27 billion, and the defense budget totaled US$5.55 billion. The army received US$2 billion in 2007, while US$1.8 billion went to the National Police, US$400 million to the navy, and US$392 million to the air force. On top of U.S. aid, much increased spending is funded by President Uribe's wealth tax levied on the country's richest individuals and enterprises; this tax is expected to raise up to US$3.7 billion in 2007–11.

Major Military Units: The army is organized into seven divisions subdivided into brigades and battalions; the navy is organized into three naval forces (Caribbean, Pacific, and Southern) and four commands (marine infantry, coast guard, naval aviation, and the Specific Command of San Andrés and Providencia); and the air force is organized into six combat air commands, three auxiliary commands, and two smaller air groups without operational aircraft. As of mid-2009, the military forces were undergoing radical change and were gradually introducing a new organization. The current structure will be replaced with five joint commands: Pacific (covering the western coastline and Ecuadorian border); Caribbean (created in 2005 and covering the north coast and Panamanian border); Eastern (the frontier with Venezuela); Central (the Andean heartland of Colombia); and the original pilot joint command called the Omega Force Command expanded to cover the southeast, including the borders with Peru and Brazil. The new organization is designed to encourage closer cooperation among different branches of the military and to ensure dedicated resources of troops and naval and air assets in all zones.

Major Military Equipment: In 2009 the army inventory included 176 light tanks and reconnaissance vehicles, 194 armored personnel carriers, 584 artillery pieces (including 101 towed and 483 mortars), 18 antitank guided weapons, 118 helicopters, and 27 aircraft. The navy had 4 submarines, 4 principal surface combatants (corvettes), 84 patrol and coastal combatants, 8 amphibious craft, and 6 logistical and support craft. In 2008 the navy received funds for programs including modernization of its FS–6 guided missile corvettes and new maritime patrol aircraft. Naval aviation had 11 aircraft and 10 helicopters. The air force inventory included 85 fighter jets and 114 helicopters of various kinds. In 2006 the air force signed a contract for 25 Brazilian Embraer EMB–314 Super Tucano light attack aircraft, the last of which was delivered in August 2008. The air force fleet of Israel Aerospace Industries Kfir TC–7 and C–7 aircraft and Dassault Aviation Mirage 5 COAMs and 5 CODMs, in service more than 30 years, is being upgraded to C–10s or replaced. In 2007 Colombia purchased 13 upgraded Israeli Kfir 2000 fighter jets fitted with electronic monitoring equipment, the first four of which were received in June 2009 (C–10 and C–12 versions). The National Police force had 65 aircraft and 60 utility helicopters.

Military Service: All nonstudent males reaching age 18 must present themselves for military service of 12–24 months; those who can afford to may buy their way out of serving, and those with high-school diplomas are exempt from combat, so it is mostly the poor with little education who actually serve. After military service, conscripts become part of the reserves. Females may volunteer for military service, which could be required in some circumstances.

Foreign Military Relations: Since the late 1980s, the United States has been the primary provider of military training and equipment to Colombia; other suppliers include Brazil, Spain, France, Germany, Italy, and Israel. Many Colombian military personnel have received training in the United States or U.S. instruction in Colombia. In 1999–2001 the U.S. government approved a US$1.3 billion aid package called Plan Colombia, mostly earmarked for military hardware for antidrug efforts, such as a fleet of 71 helicopters for spraying coca fields; subsequent aid also has been used for counterinsurgency. U.S. support for counternarcotics efforts included more than US$2.5 billion in aid between 2000 and 2004, making Colombia the third-largest recipient of U.S. aid, after Israel and Egypt. In fiscal year 2004, however, Colombia became the fifth-largest recipient of U.S. foreign aid, as a result of U.S. aid to Iraq and Afghanistan. Since 2004 U.S. military aid also has focused on increasing state presence by improving access to social services and supporting economic development through sustainable growth and trade. The United States has continued aid for counterinsurgency and counternarcotics efforts averaging

US$600 million per year through 2007; aid is devoted primarily to training units of the Urban Counterterrorist Special Forces Group (Afeur). Colombia has one infantry battalion in Egypt in support of the Multinational Force and Observers (MFO), an independent international peacekeeping organization established by Egypt and Israel to monitor the security arrangements of their 1979 Treaty of Peace. Some National Police personnel served with United Nations peace-keeping forces in Croatia and El Salvador. Between 120 and 150 Colombian soldiers were reportedly supporting the Spanish force in Afghanistan by the end of 2009.

Security Forces: In early 2008, armed security forces totaled at least 144,097 personnel, including 136,097 members of the National Police and 8,000 members of the rural militia. In addition to supporting the army in its internal security role, the police share some law-enforcement duties with elements of the Attorney General's Office. Highly trained United Action Groups for Personal Freedom have long enjoyed U.S. support and operate a fleet of Blackhawk helicopters and aircraft for the tasks of drug-crop eradication and antikidnapping and urban hostage-rescue operations. One of Colombia's most effective counternarcotics forces is a U.S.-trained and -funded force of 200 members of the Criminal Investigation Directorate.

Internal Threat

Insurgency, Counterinsurgency, and Narco-trafficking: The pro-Cuban National Liberation Army (ELN), Maoist People's Liberation Army (EPL), and pro-Soviet Revolutionary Armed Forces of Colombia (FARC) were founded in the mid-1960s; the FARC quickly became the largest guerrilla group. The ELN and FARC, as well as a dissident EPL element, have continued insurgent activities to the present day, although the ELN lost at least 30 percent of its members and the FARC, 60 percent during the 2002–8 period, from members deserting, being captured, or killed. In 2009 the ELN had an estimated 1,500 guerrillas and the FARC at least 11,000. By the mid-1980s, large narco-trafficking syndicates, particularly the Medellín and Cali cartels, gained wide power through terror and corruption. During the narco-terrorist era (1983–93), traffickers sponsored assassinations of numerous government officials, justices, and politicians, particularly those who favored an extradition treaty with the United States. Illegal armed groups increasingly depended on the drug trade to finance their insurgent operations. Despite the breakup of the big cartels, hundreds of smaller, lower-profile cartels have proliferated, often operating in association with the paramilitary and guerrilla groups.

Trafficking in processed cocaine and other illicit drugs accounts for more than US$5 billion a year and represents between 2.0 percent and 2.5 percent of GDP a year. Colombia is the world's leading coca cultivator and supplier of refined cocaine. More than 90 percent of the cocaine that enters the United States is produced, processed, or transshipped in Colombia. The country is also a growing source for heroin. Stepped-up government actions against insurgents since 2002, with significant U.S. military aid and growing professionalization of the armed forces and police, kept the guerrillas mostly withdrawn into the remote countryside. The FARC reaffirmed in mid-2008 that it has no intention of entering any peace negotiations and would continue the insurgency.

Paramilitary Partial Demobilization: Paramilitary groups that emerged in the early 1990s, particularly the United Self-Defense Forces of Colombia (AUC), the country's largest paramilitary organization, have fought guerrilla groups and terrorized campesinos and human rights workers suspected of supporting or sympathizing with them. Members of these paramilitary groups are sometimes in the pay of drug cartels or landowners or backed by elements in the army and police. After several years of negotiations and a demobilization process, on April 18, 2006, the government announced that the AUC had disbanded, with a formal demobilization of 30,150 paramilitaries, who surrendered about 17,000 weapons, 117 vehicles, 3 helicopters, 59 urban properties, and 24,000 hectares of land under the controversial Justice and Peace Law of July 22, 2005. Nevertheless, an estimated 2,000 paramilitaries belonging to other groups have remained outside the peace process altogether.

The Continuing Insurgency: At least 12,500 guerrillas were still active in late 2009. It is generally believed that the guerrillas have no realistic chance of taking power in Colombia, but the FARC and ELN remain well funded, well equipped, and capable of carrying out effective guerrilla attacks against military and security forces and occasional acts of urban terrorism in Bogotá. The FARC suffered major setbacks in 2008, including the rescue of its most important hostages and the capture or killing of several top leaders. The group became largely confined to remote jungle areas, but by 2010 it appeared to have regrouped and strengthened. The ELN has been involved in peace talks with the government since December 2006. Violent crime by common criminals is rampant in Colombia's major cities; homicide levels are among the highest in the world. Criminal bands specializing in kidnapping, extortion, and robbery target businesses and civilians.

After drug trafficking, the main illicit industries are contraband, forgery (principally of currency, clothing, books, CDs, and audio- and video-cassettes), and, more recently, the theft of gasoline.

Human Rights: The constitution provides for freedom of speech and the press, and the government generally respects these rights in practice. Individuals criticize the government both publicly and in private. The media express a wide spectrum of political viewpoints and often sharply criticize the government, all without fear of government reprisal. However, Colombia is one of the world's most dangerous countries in which to practice the profession of journalism; a few journalists are killed almost every year, and journalists continue to work in an atmosphere of threats and intimidation, in some instances from corrupt local officials in collaboration with paramilitary groups, but primarily from terrorist groups.

According to the U.S. Department of State's human rights report for 2008, the government's respect for human rights continued to improve, as seen particularly in the implementation of the Justice and Peace Law. Civilian authorities generally maintained effective control of the military and security forces, but there were instances in which elements of the security forces acted in violation of state policy. President Uribe generally has been quick to hold senior military officials accountable for criminal incidents within the ranks, causing considerable turnover in the military high command.

Police, prison guards, and military forces routinely mistreat detainees. Conditions in the severely overcrowded and underfunded prisons are harsh, especially for prisoners without significant outside support, and prisoners frequently rely on bribes for favorable treatment. The government claims not to hold any political prisoners. In 2008 there were 3,336 prisoners accused of rebellion or aiding and abetting insurgence, 2,263 of whom were accused of supporting the FARC.

Figure 1. Administrative Divisions of Colombia, 2009

Administrative Divisions of Colombia

Amazonas	32
Antioquia	10
Arauca	13
Archipiélago de San Andrés, Providencia y Santa Catalina	(see inset)
Atlántico	2
Bolívar	7
Boyacá	12
Caldas	16
Caquetá	27
Casanare	18
Cauca	25
César	4
Chocó	9
Córdoba	5
Cundinamarca	17
Distrito Capital de Bogotá*	22
Guainía	29
Guaviare	28
Huila	26
La Guajira	1
Magdalena	3
Meta	23
Nariño	24
Norte de Santander	8
Putumayo	31
Quindío	20
Risaralda	15
Santander	11
Sucre	6
Tolima	21
Valle del Cauca	14
Vaupés	30
Vichada	19

*Bogotá also serves as the capital of Cundinamarca Department.

Introduction

"PARADOXICAL" is how observers often describe the Republic of Colombia, and this contradictory characteristic is reflected in this fifth edition of *Colombia: A Country Study*. On the one hand, Colombia has a distinguished tradition of political stability as one of Latin America's longest-functioning democracies, with a lasting record of usually fair and regular elections and respect for political and civil rights. It is the only Latin American country with two rival traditional parties, the Conservative Party (Partido Conservador) and the Liberal Party (Partido Liberal), which have survived since their formation in the midnineteenth century.

Colombia is also one of South America's gems, not only for its spectacular geography but also for its cultural and intellectual life. Long a cultural leader in Latin America, it has produced internationally celebrated writers, such as Nobel Laureate Gabriel García Márquez, and artists, such as Fernando Botero and Alejandro Obregón. When German naturalist and statesman Alexander von Humboldt visited Santa Fe (present-day Bogotá) during 1800–1804, he named it the "Athens of America" in honor of its cultural and scientific institutions; the latter included South America's first astronomical observatory, founded by José Celestino Mutis. Bogotá enjoyed this appellation for most of the nineteenth century and part of the twentieth.

On the other hand, Colombia is a very fractured and polarized society where the tradition of electoral competition has existed alongside a history of various forms of political violence—insurgency, terrorism, narco-terrorism, and paramilitarism. After six interparty wars in the nineteenth century, the country enjoyed nearly a half-century of relative peace. However, the Bogotazo riots that followed the assassination of popular Liberal leader Jorge Eliécer Gaitán on April 9, 1948, destroyed downtown Bogotá, including the neoclassical Palace of Justice building, killed 2,000 people, and made the city more analogous to the Athens sacked by a Roman general in 86 B.C. The Bogotazo intensified a period of countrywide violence known as La Violencia (The Violence, 1946–58). Since the 1960s, the country has suffered a continuous insurgency.

The term *culture of violence* is often applied to Colombia. The late U.S. political scientist Robert H. Dix attributed the nation's violent legacy in part to the paradoxical and elitist nature of the political system; members of the traditional elite competed bitterly, and sometimes

li

violently, for control of the government through the Liberal and Conservative parties. What Dix termed the *inherited hatreds* of a person's identity, handed down from generation to generation, created an emotional bond to the chosen party, carrying members not only to the polls but periodically also into violent conflict with adherents of the opposing party. Constitutional order and institutional stability generally have prevailed, despite the continuing violence.

The interparty violence finally abated under a power-sharing arrangement during 1958–78 called the National Front (Frente Nacional). The pro–Conservative Party stance of the Roman Catholic Church and the anticlericalism of the Liberal Party had remained troublesome for both parties for about a hundred years, even though Colombia was the first country in Latin America to separate church and state in 1853. The longstanding argument between the Conservative Party's advocacy of centralized government and the profederalist Liberal Party's insistence on a decentralized form of state had been an equally contentious issue. By the 1980s, the two main areas that had so long antagonized the parties, church–state relations and centralism versus federalism, had been largely resolved. By then, however, Colombians were looking to third-party alternatives. The two traditional parties finally lost their duopoly of power in 2002 with the historic election of independent Álvaro Uribe Vélez (president 2002–6, 2006–10).

Colombia's autochthonous violence constitutes the central paradox that differentiates its political system from other Latin American countries. The negative international image created by the country's long-running insurgency, political violence, narco-terrorism, criminality, and political and military scandals has overshadowed many impressive features that distinguish Colombia as a major Latin American country. By discussing key aspects of the country's history, society and environment, economy, government and politics, and national security, the authors of this edition of the Country Study attempt to provide a multidimensional portrait of contemporary Colombia.

Even the etymology of Colombia's name is paradoxical, which may help to illustrate the country's almost schizophrenic character. Although Colombia's eponym honors Christopher Columbus (Cristóbal Colón), in homage to his early exploration of the New World, the Genoese-born navigator had a less well-known reputation as a failed administrator and a ruthless and greedy tyrant who enslaved the indigenous population of Hispaniola. Moreover, the closest that he ever got to present-day Colombia was the Golfo del Darién, during his fourth voyage to the New World in 1502–3. Nevertheless, Colombia's Great Liberator, Simón Bolívar Palacios, a Venezuelan, adopted the name Republic of

Great Colombia for a union of present-day Venezuela, Colombia, Ecuador, and Panama, which was established at the Congress of Angostura in Venezuela on December 17, 1819. Earlier, Venezuelan revolutionary Francisco José de Miranda had conceived the name Colombia as a suggested epithet for all of the New World, especially those territories and colonies under Spanish and Portuguese rule. A more historically based name would have been Nueva Granada (New Granada), considering that Spain's Granada was the toponym of what is now Colombia for most of the time before 1863. Nevertheless, the country adopted four additional names, including the United States of Colombia (1863–86). Finally, the 1886 constitution settled on the Republic of Colombia.

In his influence on Colombia's history, Bolívar towers over Columbus (as historian David Bushnell's numerous references to Bolívar, and none to Columbus, attest). Bolívar has not only Colombia's second-highest peak named after him, Pico Simón Bolívar (5,775 meters), located on Colombia's Caribbean coast near its twin, Pico Cristóbal Colón (5,776 meters), but also one of Colombia's 32 administrative departments, more than a dozen towns, and Bogotá's central plaza. Moreover, popular reservations about the country's namesake began surfacing in the 1920s, when Colombians and other Latin Americans adopted an alternative name for the holiday known in Hispanic America as Día de Colón (Columbus Day). The name Día de la Raza (Day of the Race) came to be preferred not only as an offshoot of growing resentment toward the United States, which was generally seen as interventionist, but also in acknowledgment of Columbus's legacy of slavery and brutal conquest of Amerindians (some use the term *genocide*).

Today, Amerindians constitute no more than 3.4 percent of the Colombian population, and demographers struggle to make racial and cultural distinctions between the mestizos, who account for about half of the population, and the whites, who make up at least a third. The Colombian population is ethnically homogeneous, compared to countries such as Brazil and the United States.

Because of its great geographical diversity, Colombia is one of Latin America's most regionalist nations, in which Colombians identify traditionally more closely with their regional origins than with the nation as a whole. The country's characteristic introversion prompted Alfonso López Michelsen (president, 1974–78) to refer to Colombia as "the Tibet of South America." Moreover, Colombians refer to the sharp contrast between the major cities, which are islands of relative safety and prosperity, and the rural areas by the anarchic expression *ausencia del estado* (absence of the state). Much of the countryside surrounding the major cities remains almost a battleground where the *ley del monte* (law of the jungle) applies. Because of Colombia's regionalism, national unity has eluded the country. Indeed, despite its democratic political system, common religion—like most Latin American countries, the vast majority of Colombia's population (between 80 and 90 percent) is, at least nominally, Roman Catholic—and common language (Spanish), Colombia is characterized more by social fragmentation than by national unity.

Regional disparities, especially between urban and rural areas, remain acute. Since 2000 Colombia's largest cities, particularly Bogotá (with more than 7 million inhabitants, or more than 8.2 million in the greater metropolitan area in 2007), and Medellín, have been undergoing a renaissance. They now have amenities that include modernized public transport, new libraries, outdoor cafés, art galleries, renovated parks, and bicycle paths. Yet, despite its progress, even Bogotá may not be a safe haven, if a global survey conducted by the Economist Intelligence Unit (EIU) on the "livability" of cities in 2009 is to be believed. It ranked Bogotá and Caracas at 127 and 118, respectively.

A highly stratified society, Colombia also remains characterized by considerable social exclusion and by sharp inequalities, not only in income but also between the standard of living in urban and rural areas and in the lack of opportunities for ethnic minorities, women, and the displaced population. Despite improvement in overall indicators in recent years, poverty affects at least half of the population, and Colombian income distribution remains the second most unequal in Latin America, after Brazil. The government figures for poverty and extreme poverty in Colombia in 2008 were: 46 percent, or 20.5 million Colombians; and 17.8 percent, or 7.9 million, respectively. Whereas the poverty rate fell 4.3 percent from 2005, abject poverty rose by 2.1 percent.

Making progress on an ambitious poverty-reduction strategy, unique in Latin America, was a major priority of the second administration of President Uribe. In 2007, however, Colombia was just starting the poverty-reduction process of the United Nations Millennium Development Goals project, adopted by 189 countries, to be accomplished by 2015. Colombia's slow progress in this regard has been blamed on the country's recession in 1999, the armed conflict, and population displacement. Five goals that Colombia is not expected to achieve by 2015 include: significant further reduction of poverty and of teenage pregnancies, greater vaccination coverage, improved housing in shantytowns, and expansion of preschool-education coverage. The decentralization process of the early 2000s, in which financial resources have devolved to the municipalities and private companies, ironically has worsened service quality, particularly in the public-health and education sectors. This deterioration in service is because municipal authorities and private companies often cannot be relied on to allocate the funds intended for national programs.

Despite the country's still-serious domestic security problems, Colombia's economy in recent years has been one of Latin America's most robust, and the country has been a model of economic stability. About US$40 billion in foreign investment flowed into the country during the first seven years of the twenty-first century. Reliable data exist only for the formal economy. In 2007 Colombia, with an impressive gross domestic product (GDP—see Glossary) growth rate of 7.5 percent (compared with –4.2 percent in 1999), had the fifth-largest economy in Latin America.

The combination of an economic revival in 2007, a hard-line strategy against the guerrillas, and improving domestic security and socioeconomic conditions enhanced President Uribe's image as a strong and capable leader and made him immensely popular with Colombians; his successes led to popularity ratings in the 70 to 80 percent range, according to Gallup polls. During his second term, Uribe focused on improving public finances, reducing inflation (at a record low of 2 percent at the end of 2009), and strengthening economic growth. Nevertheless, Uribe faced fiscal challenges during the remainder of his term, especially with an international financial crisis and a slowdown in the economies of its main trade partners, including the United States, which accounts for about one-third of Colombia's exports. In late 2008–early 2009, these conditions, which included the loss of 600,000 jobs in 2008, were seriously affecting the broader economy.

Colombia's GDP growth rate dropped 2.8 percent in 2008 and probably did no better than about zero in 2009. The construction and manufacturing sectors were down sharply in 2008, as were traditional exports such as coal and coffee. However, energy, mining, and financial services continued to grow in 2008, and oil production rose. The authors of the economy chapter point out that a key feature of Colombia's economy has been a growing dependence on remittances from abroad as a source of foreign exchange, but the Ministry of Finance and Public Credit has estimated that this income may have dropped by 20 percent in 2009, resulting in a US$1 billion reduction in remittances to US$4 billion.

The continuing juxtaposition of democracy, economic and political stability, and internal conflict—many years after other countries in Latin America managed to overcome their own insurgencies—makes Colombia an anomaly in the region. Colombia's insurgency is unique in the world because of its longevity, being a relic of the 1960s. The Colombian government has pacified a few of the illegal armed groups: the Nineteenth of April Movement (M–19) and the Maoist Popular Liberation Army (EPL) in the early 1990s, and the paramilitary United Self-Defense Forces of Colombia (AUC) in 2006. Nevertheless, the diehard leaders of the National Liberation Army (ELN) and the Revolutionary

Armed Forces of Colombia (FARC) have sustained the insurgency. Although the ELN has engaged in occasional peace talks since 2005, the FARC has yet to demonstrate that it is willing to undertake good-faith peace negotiations with the government, despite crippling setbacks that the organization suffered during 2008.

For many Colombians, the apparently never-ending conflict has scarred the face of the nation socially, psychologically, and ecologically, condemning them to live with it for their entire lives. The armed conflict is also somewhat anachronistic in that it has pitted the defunct political ideologies of the insurgents and their now-mostly demobilized paramilitary enemies against each other, in contrast to the religious fanaticism that characterizes many of the world's active extremist groups. Although the guerrilla forces still operating in the countryside generally wear uniforms, this does not mean that the rebels can be categorized ipso facto as legitimate insurgents under international law, which is how some Latin American governments—such as those of Ecuador, Nicaragua, and Venezuela—may see them. In urban areas, they operate in civilian guise. Canada, Colombia, the European Union (EU), and the United States have categorized the ELN and the FARC as terrorist organizations, but they are also drug-trafficking networks.

Narco-terrorism, and the military's often equally violent response to it, again turned the rebuilt Palace of Justice into a battleground on November 6–7, 1985. The Colombian government's Truth Commission determined in 2006 and reaffirmed in December 2009 that the Medellín Cartel funded the M–19's takeover of the Palace of Justice, in a failed effort to intimidate the government from extraditing cartel bosses to the United States. The free rein granted the military to deal with the Palace of Justice takeover, without regard for the lives of the justices and the employees, and subsequent military impunity for using violence against the civilian population in the countryside created the conditions for paramilitarism to thrive for the next two decades.

Since December 1997, when Colombia reauthorized the extradition of its nationals, at least 855 individuals have been extradited to the United States, including 789 since Uribe first assumed office, 208 of them in 2008 alone. In the narco-terrorism period of the 1980s and 1990s, the Extraditables' attitude toward extradition to the United States was summed up in their adage about preferring a grave in Colombia to a jail in the United States. Since 2007, however, in a paradoxical about-face, Colombian drug traffickers and paramilitary criminals facing prosecution for their crimes reportedly have been endeavoring to be extradited to the United States in order to be tried in U.S. courts. According to *Semana* magazine, they concluded that being tried in a Colombian court would likely result in an automatic 30-year sentence and lawsuits from their victims, as well as a high risk of being murdered in an overcrowded Colombian prison. They believed that a U.S. court would reduce their sentences by up to 70 percent in exchange for testifying against the big capos who were brought to trial, resulting in sentences of only two to four years. Moreover, they heard of fellow traffickers who, having settled their accounts with U.S. authorities, were able to start new lives in the United States.

The paramilitary warlords, guerrilla kidnappers, and drug kingpins who have been extradited to the United States and tried in U.S. courts have plenty of time to pine about a tomb in Colombia. For example, Diego Fernando Murillo Bejarano, alias Don Berna, a paramilitary chief extradited in May 2008, was sentenced to 31 years in prison and fined US$4 million for smuggling cocaine into the United States. Similarly, on May 1, 2009, a U.S. court sentenced Eugenio Montoya Sánchez, alias Héctor Fábio Carvajal, a leader of the Norte del Valle Cartel, to 30 years in prison. On December 12, 2008, Montoya's brother, Diego Montoya Sánchez, alias Don Diego, a former top-ten most-wanted fugitive of the U.S. Federal Bureau of Investigation and principal leader of the Norte del Valle Cartel, was extradited from Colombia to the United States to face federal charges.

Despite this extraordinary bilateral cooperation, there has been some nationalistic backlash to extradition in Colombia, in part because the victims of those who were extradited generally have been excluded from the judicial process in the United States and unable to seek reparations. Supreme Court of Justice decisions in February 2009 marked yet another major shift in extraditions from Colombia to the United States, raising perplexing questions about how to deal with future extradition requests. The Supreme Court blocked the extraditions of the FARC kidnappers of three former U.S. hostages—Marc Gonsalves, Thomas Howes, and Keith Stansell—ruling that the United States had no jurisdiction over Colombians in some crimes committed in Colombia, including taking hostages. In mid-2009, the U.S. government reaffirmed its commitment to ensuring that former paramilitary leaders imprisoned in the United States can continue testifying in judicial proceedings underway in Colombia, either by videoconferencing or in person.

The illegal armed groups in Colombia are criminal enterprises that are deeply involved in activities such as extortion and kidnapping for ransom, but primarily drug trafficking. Much of the violence in the Colombian countryside involves fighting among the FARC, paramilitaries, and narcotics cartels over coca-growing land, which is typically in remote and marginal areas. Moreover, endemic guerrilla and paramilitary violence has been a serious problem for many campesinos and cattle-ranchers, and it has discouraged investment in the agricultural sector. The FARC and the ELN control all aspects of the drug trade in their areas of influence; for example, they levy "taxes" at all levels of the narcotics production chain.

Over four decades of armed conflict, the countryside has been littered with land mines and other improvised explosive devices (IEDs). Between 2002 and 2007, these IEDs inflicted a minimum of 2,000 casualties and an additional 300 victims in the first nine months of 2008, according to the Presidential Program for Integral Action Against Antipersonnel Mines (PAICMA). According to the National Army, in 2008 troops destroyed 17,353 explosive devices, deactivated 405 land mines, and seized 118 tons of explosive material. The landmine problem worsened in 2008 after FARC commander Alfonso Cano ordered his guerrillas to sow more minefields. Moreover, the FARC mastered the manufacture of homemade land mines after receiving training from former members of the Irish Republican Army (IRA), according to Freddy Padilla de León, the general commander of the Military Forces. In August 2009, Vice President Francisco Santos Calderón denounced the FARC for using the planting of antipersonnel mines as a war strategy, and noted that mines had killed or injured an additional 370 victims during the year.

One reason why Colombia's internal armed conflict continues is the country's illegal drug industry, which, since the 1970s, has allowed the guerrillas and paramilitaries to fund their violent campaigns with a vast source of revenue. Today, the FARC continues to operate a guerrilla version of a drug cartel. According to the Colombian government, the FARC's annual revenues declined to about US$500 million in 2007. The group's cash reserves reportedly have been depleted as a result of a crackdown on exchange houses that the FARC used to launder money, while much of the reduction in revenues is because of competition from Mexican cartels. In August 2009, the U.S. Department of the Treasury identified an "important financial contact" of the FARC living in Costa Rica.

Despite counternarcotics efforts since the mid-1980s, the supply of drugs in 2006 remained steady, prices had fallen, and purity had increased. Colombia remained Latin America's largest exporter of illegal drugs. Increased aerial spraying under Plan Colombia, a U.S.-supported program for combating the insurgency and narcotics trade, temporarily reduced the coca-growing area under cultivation, primarily by displacing the local population. However, as much coca was cultivated in Colombia in 2006 as when aerial fumigation of the drug crop began in 2000. Instead, coca growing simply had been redistributed into smaller, harder-to-reach crops. Moreover, aerial spraying of coca crops along the border with Ecuador on December 11, 2006, caused a series of diplomatic incidents with that country and damaged bilateral relations. A U.S. Government Accountability Office (GAO) report released in November 2008 found that, although opium-poppy cultivation declined by about 50 percent from 2000 to 2006, coca-leaf production actually had increased by 15 percent over the same period. The report recommended cuts in U.S. funding of the program.

The Uribe government strongly disputed a report by the United Nations Office on Drugs and Crime (UNODC) that illicit crops increased by 27 percent in 2007. However, the government and the UNODC agreed that the area planted in coca in 2008 decreased from 99,000 to 81,000 hectares, as a result of record aerial spraying and manual-eradication efforts during the year. A collateral effect of the concentration of eradication and interdiction efforts in the agricultural zones of the interior was to displace coca-growing activity to the border regions and the Pacific coast.

Paradoxically, despite at least US$5 billion in U.S. counternarcotics aid under Plan Colombia, Colombia remains the world's leading coca cultivator and supplier of refined cocaine and a major source of heroin; in 2007 at least 70 percent of the cocaine entering the United States was produced, processed, or transshipped in Colombia. Trafficking in processed cocaine and other illicit drugs accounts for more than US$5 billion a year and represents between 2.0 percent and 2.5 percent of GDP a year. However, only an estimated one-half of these illicit revenues returns to Colombia.

The narco-terrorism that characterized the large drug cartels in the last decades of the twentieth century has abated, but the drug-smuggling industry is now dominated by hundreds of smaller, lower-profile syndicates, many of which are based in Venezuela and operate in association with the Colombian guerrilla and paramilitary groups. Moreover, the corruption that this illegal industry has spawned has remained widespread, as have criminal and political violence and abuse of human rights. The societal conditions that contributed to the country's internal violence have been aggravated by endemic poverty, inequality, social injustice, population displacement, and weak state institutions.

Colombia's long-running two-party rivalry was interrupted for the first time since the midnineteenth century in 2002, when Álvaro Uribe, an independent and Liberal Party dissident, won the presidency. Born on July 4, 1952, in Medellín, Uribe was a brilliant student, earning a doctorate in law and political science in Medellín. He also completed studies in administration and management at Harvard and conflict resolution at Oxford.

After the 2002 election, the two once-dominant traditional parties had to form alliances with some of the approximately 60 political parties then formally recognized, most of which were not represented in the Congress of the Republic (Congreso de la República) because they were too small. As if confirming the demise of the two-party system, Uribe easily won reelection on May 28, 2006, becoming the first Colombian president in 100 years to be reelected, thanks to a constitutional amendment authorizing reelection for a second consecutive term. Moreover, he won by a record majority (62 percent of the ballots) in the first round. With this strong electoral mandate and a working majority in Congress, Uribe began his second four-year term that August. His congressional alliance included independents, some former Liberal Party members, and the Conservative Party.

As a multiparty, constitutional democracy and a unitary republic with a strong presidential regime, Colombia is not unique in Latin America. Like numerous other countries from Mexico to Argentina, its national government has executive, legislative, and judicial branches that were established with separation of powers and with checks and balances. However, Colombia is unusual in the region in that its armed forces have seized power far less often than in many Latin American countries, on only three occasions—1830, 1854, and 1953. The informal ending in 1991 of the tradition of military defense ministers has ensured civilian oversight of the military. This trend was interrupted in May 2009, after Juan Manuel Santos Calderón resigned as minister of national defense in order to qualify as a potential presidential candidate, and President Uribe appointed General Padilla de León to act concurrently as the Military Forces general commander and his interim minister, pending consideration of other candidates for the post. Although Colombia subsequently has another civilian minister of national defense, as do the other South American nations, it stands out in the region as a militarized nation whose armed forces are second in size in Latin America only to those of Brazil.

This updated edition of *Colombia: A Country Study* reflects the reforms of the amended 1991 constitution, which was the first revised charter since 1886. These wide-ranging reforms of the country's institutions are aimed at establishing a new political and judicial model. They include the creation of institutions such as the Attorney General's Office (Fiscalía General de la Nación) to investigate criminal cases, the Human Rights Ombudsman's Office (Defensoría del Pueblo) to mediate between the state and its citizens, the Constitutional Court to provide constitutional oversight and to protect human rights, and the Superior Judicial Council (Consejo Superior de la Judicatura) to control and administer the judicial branch. In addition, they include tutelary mechanisms (*tutelas*), to protect basic human rights. With the main exception of these popular judicial improvements, however, Colombians reportedly have not been particularly impressed by the effect of the new constitution on their quality of life and have been especially frustrated by the lack of congressional reform, such as the system for electing senators, and the lack of accountability of public officials. In short, the new constitution has not proven to be the panacea for Colombia's problems that many had hoped it would be. Instead, it has strengthened presidentialism by allowing, as of 2005, for a president to be reelected to a second consecutive term and to invoke a referendum on possibly allowing yet a third successive term. In the view of some scholars, presidentialism is a prescription for authoritarianism, as in Venezuela, and the combination of presidentialism with a multiparty system is especially inimical to stable democracy.

Colombia's poor record on human rights makes it far from being a paragon as a constitutional democracy, despite a long history of party politics, usually fair and regular elections, and respect for political and civil rights. The systemic violence of the left-wing insurgents, right-wing paramilitaries, drug traffickers, and common criminals, as well as the often-indiscriminate counterinsurgency tactics of the Colombian military and security forces, have resulted in egregious human rights violations and massive population displacement.

Despite the persistence of serious problems, the government's respect for human rights has been improving, according to the U.S. Department of State's *Country Reports on Human Rights Practices for 2008*. A new Code of Criminal Procedure took effect at the start of 2008, raising hopes that it would reduce judicial impunity. According to Freedom House, in 2007 Colombia's freedom of the press status "improved from Not Free to Partly Free, owing to the increased willingness of journalists to report critically on political issues such as high-level corruption scandals, as well as a gradually improving security situation," although, the nongovernmental organization (NGO) added, "Colombia remains the most dangerous country for journalists in South America." Although no journalists were murdered for political reasons in 2008, three were killed in Colombia in the first half of 2009, as compared with four killed in Russia.

His electoral mandate to pursue further reforms in his second term notwithstanding, President Uribe's stellar image began to be sullied, at least internationally, in 2006, as reports of high-level governmental corruption surfaced. The harshest blow yet suffered by Uribe and his administration became known in 2006 as the *parapolítica* (parapolitics) scandal, which exposed the alliance between paramilitary groups and many politicians and other officials in the executive, legislative, and judicial branches, as well as the Military Forces and security personnel. The spreading parapolitics scandal and concerns over his administration's human rights record caused the U.S. Congress to reduce U.S. funding of Uribe's Plan Colombia. Although the scandal did not hurt Uribe personally or even lower his popularity ratings, it opened a fissure in his coalition. The Alternative Democratic Pole (PDA), a left-leaning party, underscored the Uribe government's weakened political influence by capturing the mayoralties of the three largest cities—Bogotá, Medellín, and Cali—in the regional elections for mayors and governors held on October 28, 2007.

The parapolitics scandal has debilitated not only the executive and legislative branches of government, but the judiciary as well. In 2008 relations between the executive and judiciary became increasingly tense as a result of the latter's investigations and prosecutions of legislators with suspected ties to paramilitary groups—some of the 95 lawmakers under arrest or investigation in 2008 were Uribistas. Another factor was President Uribe's frequent public verbal attacks on the judiciary, particularly on the criminal chamber of the Supreme Court for its role in the parapolitics investigations. On June 24, 2008, Yidis Medina, a former legislator, was convicted of accepting bribes in 2004 in exchange for supporting the legislation that approved the constitutional changes allowing Uribe to seek a second consecutive term. The conviction opened a debate within the judiciary over the legality of President Uribe's historic landslide election victory in May 2006. Claiming that Uribe was aware of the bribes, Medina told the court that she had supported the legislation after senior government officials offered political jobs to her supporters. The Constitutional Court subsequently reviewed the legislation that permitted Uribe to seek his second consecutive term in office. Uribe responded to the court's ruling by accusing its judges of political bias and asking Congress to authorize the holding of a national referendum, in which voters would be asked whether or not they wanted to hold new presidential elections. In August 2009, security measures in the Palace of Justice were intensified because of a growing campaign of threats against the justices.

The corruption and violence associated with the enormous wealth created by the drug cartels have undermined the country's political and social foundations. The illegal narcotics industry has corrupted every level of Colombian society, from the campesinos who grow and harvest the mostly illegal coca crops (as in Bolivia and Peru, however, a very small percentage of the coca crop is legal for domestic medicinal or traditional purposes) to some members of the government and military and security forces, who provide discreet services to the narcotics traffickers in exchange for a bribe.

International surveys that take such factors into account provide a comparative perspective of Colombia's global standing. Colombia ranked seventieth of 180 countries in Transparency International's Corruption Perceptions Index 2008, a significant decline from its better ranking in 2005 of fifty-fifth place. However, Colombia ranked thirteenth of 32 countries in the Americas, a relatively good rating, at least in comparison with its immediate neighbors, particularly Venezuela, which placed thirty-first. In a survey taken in Colombia in November 2008, Transparency International found that 41 percent of respondents considered political parties to be the most corrupt institutions in the country, while 26 percent said that Congress was.

Corruption is one of the political, economic, military, and social indicators of instability that contributed to Colombia's borderline ranking of 41 out of 60 countries surveyed in *Foreign Policy* magazine's pejoratively named Failed States Index 2009. The authors of this edition of the Country Study all agree that Colombia is far from being a "failed state," only a weak one. The Economist Intelligence Unit 2008 democracy index ranks Colombia 60 out of 167 countries, categorizing it as one of 52 "flawed democracies." Colombia has low scores in the EIU index for political culture and participation, mainly owing to low confidence in political parties, low levels of political engagement, and struggles with democracy and order because of insurgency and drug trafficking. However, Colombia's EIU score has risen since 2006, mainly as a result of improvements in the functioning of government, the electoral process, and civil liberties.

Numerous Colombian government institutions have a reputation for inefficient, corrupt, and bureaucratic management. Notable exceptions reportedly include the independent Bank of the Republic (Banrep; hereafter, Central Bank), the Ministry of Finance and Public Credit, and some other agencies responsible for economic policy formulation and judicial investigation and prosecution. As an example of the latter, President Uribe's independent attorney general (*fiscal*), Mario Iguarán Arana, earned the respect of human rights workers and average Colombians in 2007 for ordering high-level arrests on charges of collusion with paramilitaries. Although the military's public approval rating in Colombia in 2008 reportedly was about 80 percent because of counterinsurgency successes, the armed forces, too, have been in the spotlight in recent years for corruption at senior levels within the chain of command. Links between Colombia's various paramilitary groups and the armed forces continue to surface.

With U.S. aid contingent on fighting corruption, the Uribe government reportedly has been making improvements in these areas, but underfunded, key investigative agencies such as those of the attorney general, the comptroller general, and the inspector general face a major challenge. In addition, since May 2009, the paramilitary Black Eagles (Águilas Negras) have been waging a campaign of threats against the Human Rights Ombudsman's Office, two of whose staff members have been shot at, with one being wounded. A Human Rights Watch report released in October 2008 summed up the implications for Colombia of systemic corruption and human rights abuses as follows: "What is at stake in Colombia goes beyond the problem of how to find the truth and secure justice for past atrocities. At stake is the country's future: whether its institutions will be able to break free of the control of those who have relied on organized crime and often horrific human rights abuses to secure power." In an interview with *Semana* in June 2009, Christian Salazar Volkmann, representative in Colombia of the United Nations Office of the High Commissioner for Human Rights, pointed out that there have been at least 50,000 victims of disappearance in Colombia since the United Nations registered the first case in the country in 1973.

The focus of the second Uribe administration has been on both security and military aspects of the state of law and order in Colombia and promotion of international trade, including the ratification of a coveted free-trade agreement (FTA) with the United States. Other priorities involve fiscal and judicial reforms, including removing responsibility for prosecuting members of Congress from the Supreme Court and vesting it instead in the Attorney General's Office; and alternative development. The opposition's refusal to debate the Uribe government's reforms has diminished their prospects. The Uribe government's efforts to negotiate an FTA with the United States have stalled since mid-2007. There has been strong opposition in the U.S. Congress, which signaled its displeasure over the parapolitics scandal by postponing a vote on the FTA until after the administration of President Barack H. Obama took office in January 2009. The delay may have reduced the FTA's chances of approval, given the concerns of the U.S. Congress over Colombia's record on human rights and labor standards. According to Freedom House, more than 60 percent of all murders of trade unionists have taken place in Colombia. The National Union School (ENS), a labor-rights think tank in Medellín, reported that more than 2,500 Colombian union members have been murdered since 1986. The number of killings in 2007 dropped to 39 from 72 in 2006, but the ENS reported 41 killings in 2008.

Despite its best efforts, the FARC failed to sabotage Uribe's reelection in a landslide vote in the presidential election of May 2006 or to disrupt his inauguration on August 7 by launching a mortar attack on Nariño Palace that killed 21 people and wounded 70 others. The government adopted new counterinsurgency tactics in December 2007, using smaller-scale, more mobile military forces. According to a report by the government's National Planning Department (DNP), terrorist attacks dropped by 46.3 percent in Colombia in 2008, compared to 2006. However, the report found that comparing figures for 2007 and 2008 showed an increase of 9.8 percent in the number of attacks, as a result of an increase in terrorist incidents in the departments of Antioquia, Arauca, Cundinamarca, Guaviare, and Meta, as well as in the Distrito Capital de Bogotá.

The demobilization of 30,150 AUC paramilitaries was formally completed on April 18, 2006. According to *Cambio* magazine, by the end of 2008 a total of 49,000 armed combatants reportedly had been demobilized, including 32,000 former paramilitary group members and 17,000 former guerrillas. Of those numbers, 22,000 were enrolled in technical and vocational courses and about 9,800 were finishing elementary or high-school studies; the whereabouts of roughly 17,200 were unknown. An associate professor of political science at Kean University, New Jersey, who had interviewed many paramilitary members, Nazih Richani, asserted at Georgetown University on May 7, 2007, that the demobilization was more myth than reality and that the AUC command structure remained mostly intact. The director of the National Commission for Reparation and Reconciliation (CNRR) announced on April 28, 2009, that about 2,500 of the demobilized paramilitaries had rearmed, but the rearmament rate was only between 5 and 15 percent.

According to other authoritative sources, not only had the AUC's drug-trafficking networks continued operating, but they had retained an active armed wing, principally for the settling of scores and the protection of narcotics shipments. Carlos Salgado, the director of the humanitarian organization Peace Planet, told Notimex, the Mexican state press agency, on October 18, 2008, that the appearance of AUC redoubts in several areas shows that "paramilitarism is still alive." One such new group, operating in the northwestern part of Urabá and in the neighboring department of Córdoba, calls itself Gaitán Self-Defense Groups of Colombia (AGC). Although the AUC initially was able to demobilize largely on its own terms, most of the top well-known paramilitary leaders were extradited to the United States. On May 9, 2008, the Uribe government extradited AUC warlord Carlos Mario Jiménez (alias Macaco) to face drug-trafficking charges and on May 13 extradited an additional 14 AUC leaders for continuing to run their criminal networks from prison and failing to pay reparations to victims.

In addition to the aforementioned insurgent, paramilitary, and narco-terrorism threats, violence in Colombia often takes the form of kidnappings and homicides. Colombia has had some of the highest kidnapping and homicide rates in the world in recent decades. As of mid-2007, some 24,000 Colombians, including 2,700 children, had been kidnapped during the previous decade; 1,269 had died in captivity, and 3,143 were still being held according to *El Tiempo*. Guerrilla and paramilitary groups have been responsible for an estimated three-fifths of kidnappings, and common criminals for about two-fifths.

Colombia's homicide and kidnapping rates in major cities reportedly declined significantly under the two Uribe administrations, as a result of improved law enforcement, the government's offensive against the guerrillas, and demobilization of many paramilitaries. These declines allowed significant new foreign investment in Colombia, especially since 2006, and spurred sustained economic growth. At the end of 2005, Medellín, a city of 2.2 million people, had 755 homicides, significantly fewer than the annual figure of just over a decade earlier. Proportionately, Medellín's rate, which was 29 homicides per 100,000 inhabitants in 2006, was lower than that of some U.S. cities, such as Detroit. In 2006 the Colombian city with the highest homicide rate was Buenaventura on the Pacific coast at 144 per 100,000 people, or 408 murders, more than seven times the rate in Bogotá and more than four times that in Medellín. Although the urban homicide and kidnapping rates reportedly had abated, with the former down by 6.2 percent and the latter by 14.3 percent in 2008, compared with 2007, homicides, armed robberies, and extortion reportedly were on the upswing in the main cities in 2009.

Despite lower overall rates, political kidnappings and kidnappings for ransom by common criminals and guerrillas have remained frequent. Both criminal bands and the illegal armed groups have specialized in kidnapping for ransom, extortion, and robbery of businesses and civilians. The FARC and the ELN have also kidnapped or murdered numerous government officials, including members of Congress and the Supreme Court of Justice. On February 23, 2002, the FARC abducted its most high-profile hostage, Ingrid Betancourt Pulecio, a Liberal Party senator and presidential candidate of the Oxygen Green Party (PVO), along with her campaign manager, Clara Rojas. They were en route to a preannounced campaign visit to San Vicente del Caguán, Caquetá Department, where they intended to investigate the ending earlier that month of negotiations for peace talks between the government and the FARC. They entered the FARC-infested region, which had been serving as a 42,000-square-kilometer, demilitarized zone, despite an army warning.

The kidnapping of Betancourt, who has dual Colombian and French nationality, prompted Jacques Chirac, then-president of France, to immediately express his concern to Andrés Pastrana

Arango (president, 1998–2002). As a result of Betancourt's kidnapping, the European Union added the FARC to its list of terrorist organizations only two months later. Although Pastrana characterized Betancourt's kidnapping as akin to "kidnapping democracy," he rejected a FARC demand that a prisoner-exchange law be passed as a condition for releasing her. With the FARC being unwilling to engage in peace negotiations, Pastrana's successor, President Uribe, followed a no-negotiation strategy. The French government pursued all diplomatic options to win Betancourt's release, and Chirac again called for her release in June 2005 and January 2006. Ironically, the French government's campaign to free Betancourt only strained its relations with Colombia and convinced the FARC of her importance as a hostage. Consequently, the FARC decided to retain her indefinitely as a bargaining chip with the Uribe government, demanding the release from prison of 500 of its members in exchange for that of 59 military and political figures, including Betancourt and three Americans.

By the time of her kidnapping, Senator Betancourt was well known in Colombia and France as a courageous politician struggling against corruption (from early 1994 to early 2002). Her 2001 autobiography, *Rage au cœur*, was hailed in France—where it was a best seller—as the story of a crusader against corruption and injustice. Published in English in 2002 as *Until Death Do Us Part: My Struggle to Reclaim Colombia*, it is the remarkable story of an outspoken, young, Franco-Colombian woman's meteoric rise to the Senate of the Republic (Senado de la República) through sheer determination. Betancourt's bold use of political influence was not to enrich herself, as commonly done in Colombia, but to expose the endemic corruption at the highest levels of government. Translated into 20 languages, the Spanish version was the top-selling book in Colombia at the time of her kidnapping.

Betancourt was born in Bogotá on December 25, 1961, into one of Colombia's patrician families; her father, who died shortly after her kidnapping, was a revered Colombian minister of education and diplomat; her mother, a former Miss Colombia, became a leading social activist on behalf of Colombia's abandoned, homeless children and, in 1990, a senator. Although her parents regularly hosted prominent members of the Colombian and Latin American political and cultural elite (the latter included Fernando Botero, Gabriel García Marquéz, and Pablo Neruda), they disdained the corrupt Colombian oligarchy. Betancourt grew up in Paris, where she studied political science at elite universities and became a French citizen through her marriage to a French diplomat.

On August 18, 1989, assassins firing Uzis killed popular Liberal Party presidential candidate Luis Carlos Galán a few feet away from Betancourt's mother, who was Galán's campaign manager, at a campaign rally in southern Bogotá. Galán's fight against drug trafficking practically pre-ordained his assassination because he favored extradition of the traffick-ers. That murder, combined with her long-held desire to help improve the lot of ordinary Colombians, motivated Betancourt to give up the comfort and safety of life as a diplomat's wife and, with her two children, move back to Colombia a few months later. After working in the Ministry of Finance (now the Ministry of Finance and Public Credit) and the Minis-try of Foreign Trade (now the Ministry of Commerce, Industry, and Tour-ism), she launched an unconventional campaign to become a Liberal Party legislator with the aim of picking up Galán's banner, or at least restoring the political morality that he represented, for she felt compelled to confront corrupt elected officials. Starting without any money or pub-lic recognition but waging a brilliant, grassroots campaign, she ran on an idealistic, anticorruption platform and, to the surprise of the pundits, won election in March 1994 to the House of Representatives (Cámera de Rep-resentantes), with the most votes of any Liberal Party candidate.

Betancourt quickly overcame a media-supported campaign by dis-honest legislators to discredit her attempt to expose venality at the high-est levels of the administration of Ernesto Samper Pizano (president, 1994–98) and won credibility with the public, albeit at the cost of antagonizing corrupt politicians. Betancourt's two-week-long hunger strike in the legislative chamber and her documented and televised, but ultimately futile, exposure of presidential corruption further raised her standing with the public but earned her Samper's enmity. Her protest also made Betancourt and her family a target of death threats and an attempted assassination. In response to Samper's Teflon-like ability to deflect even documented evidence of corruption, Betancourt wrote a book, *Sí, sabia* (Yes, He Did Know), asserting that Samper knew that his campaign received millions of pesos from the Cali Cartel. An ensu-ing death threat forced her to flee the country with her family for the second time in six months. In 1997 Betancourt waged a lonely and per-ilous battle in the legislature in support of extradition of drug traffick-ers. Ironically, thanks to the support of the Samper administration, which sought to repair its tarnished image, extradition was reestab-lished later that year, after a constitutional amendment to provide for it.

As a senatorial candidate in the March 1998 legislative election, Betancourt founded the Oxygen Green Party, and she placed first, despite having 40,000 votes stolen from her by her Cali opponents. As senator, she subsequently campaigned for the Conservative Party's presidential candidate, Andrés Pastrana, after he agreed to champion her proposed anticorruption reforms. However, Pastrana reneged on his promise, making her more determined than ever to seek the presi-dency herself in 2002.

During her years of captivity (2002–8), Ingrid Betancourt became what María Jimena Duzán, a columnist for the weekly *Semana*, describes as "an icon of the resistance to the FARC." After her abduction, her family in Paris and the French press transformed her—somewhat inauspiciously—into a Colombian Joan of Arc. A more contemporary analogy is Aung San Suu Kyi, the Nobel Peace Prize–winning author of *Freedom from Fear* and longtime prisoner of conscience of the Burmese military regime, which denied her the prime ministership to which she was legitimately elected in 1990.

In Bogotá, however, the elite reportedly resented the global publicity over Betancourt's captivity, regarding her as just one of the thousands of irresponsible *secuestrados* (kidnap victims), who had allowed themselves to fall prey to criminal or guerrilla organizations. One of her fellow prisoners, a police officer, escaped in May 2007 after nine years in captivity, and he reported that Betancourt had been tortured and was kept chained by the neck for having tried to escape five times. The officer's first-hand report, which included news of the location of several groups of hostages in the departments of Guaviare and Vaupés, prompted President Uribe finally to order the military leadership to plan a rescue operation.

On November 29, 2007, the army intercepted three rebel emissaries in Bogotá and seized a letter from Ingrid Betancourt to her mother along with video footage of several of the hostages, including the three Americans. The despair and pain expressed by Betancourt in the letter and her haggard image, which at least provided long-awaited proof that she was still alive, awakened national and international conscience over the plight of the hostages and made her case, in particular, a cause célèbre. By 2008 the international condemnation over news of Betancourt's inhuman captivity apparently pressured the FARC into releasing to Venezuela's President Hugo Chávez Frias four key hostages, including Clara Rojas, on January 10 and four former Colombian legislators, among whom was Senator Luis Eladio Pérez, on February 27; all had been held since 2001–2. By subsequently barring Chávez from participating in efforts to reach a humanitarian agreement with the FARC, Uribe provoked another crisis in Colombian–Venezuelan relations.

The kidnapping industry in Colombia and the murder of any captives for whom ransom demands are not met (and even some captives for whom ransom has been paid) seem to epitomize the cruel contradictions of Colombian society. Tragically, almost a decade into the new millennium, Colombia's political and criminal violence has continued to eviscerate the country's great potential as one of the major South American countries. Despite the lower levels of violence associated with the internal conflict, drug trafficking, and common crime, they remain high by international standards. The many Colombians who marched against the FARC's hostage taking on February 4, 2008, in what was described as the largest demonstration in Colombia's history (at least 1 million people took part), showed the extent of popular outrage against this terrorist and criminal practice and the FARC itself.

In the first half of 2008, the FARC suffered even more spectacular blows, beginning on March 1, when the Colombian army attacked a FARC camp on the Ecuadorian side of the border in the remote Angostura jungle area. This action resulted in the death of Luis Édgar Devia Silva, alias Raúl Reyes, the FARC's second in command and the first member of its seven-member Secretariat (the group's highest command body) to be killed since the 1960s. Despite bellicose protests by Ecuador and Venezuela, the incursion revealed the extent of the FARC's international support network in more than 30 countries, particularly Venezuela and Ecuador. FARC ties with Peru's Túpac Amaru Revolutionary Movement (MRTA) were confirmed by 107 e-mail messages to or from the MRTA found in Reyes's computer files.

The death of Iván Ríos (nom de guerre of Manuel de Jesús Muñoz), the FARC's youngest Secretariat member, on March 6, 2008, was followed on March 26 by the death of its oldest, the septuagenarian and legendary but widely reviled Pedro Manuel Marín, alias Manuel Marulanda Vélez or Tiro Fijo (Sure Shot). Although most Colombians would like to forget Marín, Fernando Botero immortalized him in one of his paintings, depicting him as a rotund figure clad in camouflage uniform, holding an assault rifle and standing in a forest. Marín's successor, Guillermo León Sáenz Vargas, alias Alfonso Cano More, had been a student leader in the law school of the National University of Colombia in Bogotá and, despite coming from an intellectual background, was described by *Semana* as "uncompromising and dogmatic."

Extensive files found on three laptop computers seized from Reyes's headquarters caused enormous concern regarding the relations between the FARC and President Chávez and revealed broader support by Chávez for the FARC than previously known. For example, one e-mail, apparently sent by a Venezuela-based FARC commander, Rodrigo Londoño, alias Timochenko, to the FARC Secretariat in March 2007, describes meetings with Venezuelan naval intelligence officers. They offer the FARC assistance in obtaining "rockets" and help in sending a FARC guerrilla to the Middle East to learn how to operate them. In another e-mail dated early 2007, Luciano Marín Arango, alias Iván Márquez, describes meetings with Venezuela's military intelligence chief, General Hugo Carvajal, and another Venezuelan officer to talk about "finances, arms, and border policy." Carvajal offers to provide the FARC some 20 "very powerful bazookas," while another Venezuelan general at the meeting offers Venezuela's port of Maracaibo to facilitate arms shipments to the guerrillas. In reporting on a November 2007 meeting with Chávez at Miraflores Palace, two FARC leaders, Ricardo Granda and Iván Márquez, e-mail their Secretariat that Chávez gave orders to create "rest areas" and hospital zones for the guerrillas to use on the Venezuelan side of the border. In recent years, the FARC has established a major presence in the Sierra de Perija of Venezuela's western Zulia State, where it forcibly recruits and trains young members of indigenous tribes.

The setbacks inflicted on the FARC not only raised military morale but, according to a Gallup Poll, boosted the confidence of 75 percent of Colombians that the guerrillas could be defeated after all. A Gallup Poll taken in early March 2008 showed that Uribe's approval rating topped 84 percent, the highest since he took office, apparently as a show of solidarity in the wake of ostensible FARC denunciations by Ecuador, Nicaragua, and Venezuela, whose stances toward the FARC previously had been sympathetic.

In what was the most humiliating setback in the FARC's history and one of the world's most audacious and successful hostage-rescue operations, Minister of National Defense Juan Manuel Santos announced on July 2, 2008, the success of a 22-minute operation freeing 15 important hostages, including Ingrid Betancourt, being held in the Guaviare jungle. The rescued hostages also included three U.S. Department of Defense contractors—U.S. citizens Marc Gonsalves, Thomas Howes, and Keith Stansell—who had been captured when the FARC guerrillas shot down their Cessna while they were surveilling illicit coca and poppy crops on February 13, 2003; and 11 members of the Colombian military and police. In a press conference at the French Embassy in Quito on December 3, 2008, Betancourt explained that the earlier military raid on the FARC's Angostura camp allowed the rescue operation to succeed by disrupting communications between the FARC leadership and the commander who was holding the 15 hostages.

Operation Check, which involved the teamwork of 15 members of the army's Special Intelligence Force, was carried out by two unarmed helicopter pilots and several other undercover agents posing as pro-FARC humanitarian aid workers. The agents convinced the cell's leader that they had been instructed by senior FARC commanders to fly the 15 hostages to a new rebel camp in southern Colombia. The spectacularly successful operation established a new model for rescuing hostages. In contrast to many failed hostage-rescue operations that have relied exclusively on military force, it had intelligent civilian and military leadership, a stratagem based on audacity, cunning, cutting-edge communications technology, and, according to Agence France-Presse, intelligence support provided by France, Israel, and the United States. Paradoxically, the Colombian military achieved its most celebrated success using nonviolent means. The operation may prove to have been a decisive turning point in the FARC's four decades of warfare, for it exposed the group internationally as a terrorist organization. Moreover, the USB flash drives found on the two FARC jailers guarding the 15 hostages contained a trove of information regarding the service records of 351 guerrillas from the FARC's Eastern Bloc, including photographs of the subversives and their aliases.

In the weeks and months after her miraculous rescue, Betancourt became Colombia's most celebrated personality and one of the world's most famous women, transforming herself from liberated politician to global citizen, having taken up the cause of liberating the world's forgotten hostages. Awards bestowed on her in 2008 included France's Légion d'honneur and Spain's Premio Príncipe de Asturias. Although Betancourt reportedly lost some popularity by leaving Colombia (not surprisingly) three weeks after her liberation, she returned to Colombia from France in November 2008 to make a tour to protest against kidnapping, which included stops in the major South American capitals. The tour helped to focus regional and world attention on the continued captivity of approximately 3,000 hostages in Colombia. She pledged to do all she could to secure the release of the FARC's 28 political hostages in particular.

Having taken up residence in France, Ingrid Betancourt publicly ruled out running for president again in 2010. Uribe's popularity and third-term prospects could have dissuaded her from becoming a candidate, and she acknowledged concerns over the security risk that she would have faced. After her liberation, the FARC, reaffirming its status as a terrorist organization, declared Ms. Betancourt, who is a private Franco-Colombian citizen, a "military target." Moreover, Betancourt's public statements in 2008 indicated her disillusion with politics in Colombia, which she described as more about calculation, compromise, and corruption than about serving the public. Betancourt announced that she intended to spend most of 2009 rebuilding her life and writing a book about her harrowing ordeal as a FARC hostage.

Other signs in late 2008 that the government was making progress in the counterinsurgency war, against the FARC in particular, included a 40-percent diminishment in FARC-held territory and loss of urban networks; increasingly effective military actions against the insurgents; and a sharp drop in the number of FARC attacks. Furthermore, there was a considerable toll inflicted on the FARC by the army's offensive against the guerrillas' jungle rearguard (1,893 FARC fighters killed in

2007); a sharp drop in FARC morale and increasing FARC desertions (2,480 fighters in 2007 and more than 1,450 others in the first half of 2008); and as much as a 50-percent decline in FARC membership from about 18,000 to about 9,000.

Desperate for new recruits to fill their ranks depleted by desertions and casualties, the guerrilla organizations have been forcibly recruiting children averaging 11.8 years of age, according to Christian Salazar. Colombian authorities estimated in mid-2009 that the number of child warriors had grown from 11,000 in 2006 to between 14,000 and 17,000, about 50 percent of whom joined the FARC. According to the Human Rights Ombudsman's Office, 6,410 children had died in combat with the army between January 2000 and mid-2009.

In another indication that the government's rewards program was prompting more FARC members to defect, a 28-year-old FARC defector, Wilson Bueno Largo, alias Isaza, delivered former Congressman Óscar Túlio Lizcano, who had been held hostage by the FARC for more than eight years, to army troops in a jungle town in Chocó Department on October 29, 2008. Bueno was then allowed to emigrate to France, which had agreed to take in reformed FARC members not guilty of crimes. There were reports that Bueno received a US$400,000 reward or that Colombia provided him with a subsidy of 800 euros per month to live in France. In her new role as activist on behalf of FARC hostages and defectors, Ingrid Betancourt accompanied Bueno and his girlfriend on the flight from Colombia to France.

As the battered FARC becomes increasingly desperate in the face of overwhelming national sentiment against its continued existence, instead of making gestures to revive peace talks, it has been carrying out indiscriminate acts of urban terrorism. Since July 2008, the FARC under Alfonso Cano has committed several bombings in Bogotá and other cities, including one in Ituango, Antioquia, in August that killed seven pedestrians and wounded 51 others. That month it perpetrated more lethal car bombings in Cali, in which nine civilians were killed and 31 others wounded. One of those bombings destroyed 10 of 18 floors of Cali's Palace of Justice building. President Uribe cited the bombing of Cali's Palace of Justice as an example of narco-terrorism, and the military attributed it to a FARC faction called the Manuel Cepeda Vargas Group. The Cali police also blamed the group for assassinating, on August 11, 2009, the Cali prosecutor who was investigating this bombing. Three days later, two suspects who had been implicated were released from jail, leaving one perpetrator serving a 42-year prison sentence and another awaiting sentencing.

Minister Santos observed in March 2009 that the FARC had ceased guerrilla war for the time being and replaced it with terrorist bombings and attacks using antipersonnel mines against security and military forces. The minister's dismissal of the FARC's guerrilla capabilities may have been somewhat premature, however, because clashes between the FARC and the army have remained common. Evidence that the FARC is not a spent force and has been regrouping included its cross-border ambushes and killing of 17 soldiers in early May 2009 in the northeastern and southwestern border areas. Apparently, the FARC has adopted a tactic of operating out of border areas and carrying out relatively safe hit-and-run attacks. Indeed, practically all of the top FARC leaders, including Iván Márquez, were believed to be living in neighboring countries, particularly Ecuador and Venezuela. Only Secretariat members Alfonso Cano, Jorge Briceño Suárez (alias El Mono Jojoy), and Mauricio Jaramillo (alias El Médico) were known to be operating in Colombia.

Computer evidence found in a FARC camp in the first half of 2009 confirmed that Venezuelan officials were continuing to assist FARC commanders by providing weapons from Venezuela's military stockpiles, helping to arrange arms deals, and obtaining identity cards to move about in Venezuelan territory. The same Iván Márquez, citing talks with specific Venezuelan security officials, describes in one message to the FARC Secretariat the plan to purchase SA–7 surface-to-air missiles, Dragunov sniper rifles, and HF–90M radios in Venezuela in 2008.

The Colombian military tarnished its newly burnished image as a result of a scandal that began to emerge in September 2008. An investigation linked dozens of army personnel, including three generals, to an alleged army practice since 2002 of killing mostly homeless young civilian men in order to inflate the number of supposed insurgents or drug traffickers killed in combat by security forces. In 2002 the army commander, General Mario Montoya Uribe, himself was allegedly involved in covering up a case of what in Colombia is termed *false positives*. The scandal, which affected mostly the Bogotá-based 5th Division, revealed that civilian control of the military and security forces under President Uribe had not been as effective in respecting basic human rights as some Uribistas had claimed. Trying to remedy this lack of control and to repair the damage done to his own national standing, President Uribe on October 29, 2008, dismissed 25 army officers, including Montoya and two other generals and four colonels, over the extrajudicial executions of at least 11 civilians who disappeared from Bogotá in early 2008. He also announced in early November that every military unit down to the battalion level would have an appointed official to monitor allegations of abuse. Another casualty of the military purge, the army's 15th Mobile Counterinsurgency Brigade, which had been accused of extrajudicial executions by the U.S. Department of State's 2008 human rights report, was dismantled in January 2009. The 23rd Mobile Counterinsurgency Brigade, which replaced it, had 1,400 members who reportedly had received training in human rights. These actions did little to dampen the false-positives scandal. By May 2009, prosecutors had recorded 900 cases of extrajudicial killings, involving 1,708 victims (1,545 men, 110 women, and 53 minors). The number of implicated members of the security forces had grown to 1,177, of whom 15 were sentenced to 30 years of prison for disappearing 11 youths in the Bogotá district of Soacha.

Although most of the paramilitaries have demobilized officially, the challenge remains for the government to disband the criminal drug-trafficking networks. The government will likely continue talking with the ELN, despite the lack of significant progress to date. Prospects for peace talks with the FARC generally have been considered to be minimal, given that it has become more criminal and terrorist than political, thoroughly corrupted by years of narcotics trafficking, and seemingly averse to engaging in peace talks in good faith. However, the FARC could be forced to the negotiating table as a result of the mounting military pressure on it. Some observers believed that the only solution would require incorporating a demobilized FARC into the democratic system, as was done with the M–19. For example, in August 2008, the head of the Colombian government's peace commission, Luis Carlos Restrepo, said that the government believes it can advance demobilization negotiations with both the ELN and the FARC. In early September 2008, Ingrid Betancourt proposed opening "a political niche" to FARC guerrillas where they can act "in a scheme of political legitimacy."

In an apparent attempt to improve its extremely negative public image, the FARC released four hostages (three policemen and a soldier) on February 1, 2009, and former governor Alan Jara on February 3, after holding him for eight years. Senator Piedad Córdoba Ruiz mediated both releases. By the late spring, the intransigent FARC leadership did not appear to be serious about adopting the M–19 and AUC model of demobilization and political legitimacy. Instead, the FARC seemed bent on a fight-to-the-end strategy. A Gallup Poll suggested that the military successes achieved during 2008 had validated Uribe's Democratic Security and Defense Policy. However, the continuing stalemate in 2009 suggested that the government lacked the ability to defeat the FARC through only military means, at least in the near term.

In 2009 the Uribe government remained mired in scandals. In late May, the attorney general brought charges against the four former officials who had successively headed the Administrative Security Department (DAS) security service during 2002–8, accusing them of involvement in illegal wiretapping and surveillance of Supreme Court justices, journalists, NGOs, and opposition politicians. In addition, Uribe's two sons invested in land that subsequently soared in value after the government designated it part of a tax-free industrial zone. Another consideration was Colombia's relations with the United States. The U.S. Department of State expressed its opposition to a third term for Uribe. However, President Obama hosted a visit by Uribe in the spring of 2009 and surprisingly offered to support passage of the stalled FTA. After visiting President Obama at the White House on June 29, President Uribe expressed his optimism that Washington would support the FTA.

Except for the Middle East and Afghanistan, in 2009 Colombia remained the largest recipient of U.S. assistance, receiving a total of at least US$5 billion in Plan Colombia U.S. aid in the 2000–2008 period, including about US$582 million in aid in 2006, US$593 million in 2007, and US$422 million in 2008. Despite a declining trend, with US$420 million budgeted in 2009 and US$405 million in 2010, in August 2009, the Uribe government's political and military scandals did not appear to be jeopardizing Plan Colombia. Colombian–U.S. security cooperation was actually poised to expand substantially upon ratification of a 10-year military base "access" pact, formally called a Supplemental Agreement for Cooperation and Technical Assistance in Defense and Security between the Governments of the United States of America and the Republic of Colombia, or Defense Cooperation Agreement (DCA) for short. Ministerial representatives of both countries reached provisional agreement on the DCA in Washington, DC, on August 14.

Once formally ratified by both countries, the new DCA would allow the United States to lease access to seven Colombian military bases for U.S. logistical support in countering drug trafficking by cartels and guerrilla organizations. President Uribe approved the pact, but it still required authorization from Colombia's Senate, which must decide whether to "allow the transit of foreign troops through the territory of the Republic." In addition, the government is required to hear the consultative advice of the judiciary's Council of State on matters involving foreign troops and military aircraft or ships traversing Colombian territory or territorial waters. The Council of State was considering holding hearings on aspects of the agreement.

The DCA with Colombia will offset for the United States the expiration in November 2009 of an Ecuadorian–U.S. agreement allowing U.S. military personnel to use Ecuador's Manta Base as a Forward Operation Location (FOL) in the "war on drugs." Moreover, the DCA would significantly enhance the FOL concept by providing confirmed

U.S. access to five army and air bases, including Major General Alberto Pauwels Rodríguez Air Base at Malambo, near Barranquilla, Atlántico Department; Captain Germán Olano de Palanquero Air Base at Puerto Salgar, Cundinamarca Department; and Captain Luis F. Gómez Niño Air Base in Apiay, Meta Department. It would also provide for U.S. access to two naval bases: ARC Bolívar, Cartagena; and ARC Bahía Málaga, near Buenaventura on the Pacific coast. Two other military air bases that could be used are Lieutenant Colonel Luis Francisco Pinto Parra, also known as Tolemaida, near Melgar, Tolima Department; and Larandia in Caquetá Department. On mutual agreement, access could be granted to additional bases.

The DCA would also allow for the stationing of up to 800 U.S. military personnel and up to 600 U.S. civilian contractors at Colombian bases to support both drug-interdiction and counterterrorist missions in coordination with the Colombian military. These levels of U.S. military and associated personnel in Colombia are also governed by U.S. statute, and the U.S. Congress already had authorized these limits in October 2004, although the actual number of U.S. military personnel in Colombia in 2009 reportedly was only about 280.

The DCA would not allow U.S. personnel to engage in combat operations in the country, and the bases would remain entirely under Colombian jurisdiction and sovereignty. A Colombian national executive committee is to authorize the number and type of personnel and equipment deployed to each base. Furthermore, both parties agreed to a security protocol for the entry, overflight, and landing of aircraft, as well as the number of flights and the airports. According to the Colombian air force commander, the aircraft arriving at the seven bases would not be fighters but aircraft for tracking, logistics support, intelligence collection, and airborne surveillance of drug trafficking. Colombia's most important air base, at centrally located Puerto Salgar, would be the first to receive U.S. upgrading investment, totaling US$46 million.

In July news that the DCA was being finalized stunned the leaders of South America. Instead of a "new alliance of the Americas," as proposed by presidential candidate Barack Obama in 2008, South American leaders were suddenly confronted with the specter of what they initially perceived to be a militarization and expansion of the previous U.S. administration's failing "war on drugs." It appeared to them that Colombia would become a strategic platform for U.S. aerial intelligence surveillance of the region and possibly military intervention. For the Left, the DCA issue appeared to resurrect their image of Colombia as a U.S. "garrison state" like Israel.

Incensed over news of the Colombian–U.S military pact, the Venezuelan president, Hugo Chávez, immediately denounced it as a direct threat to Venezuela and himself in particular. Claiming that the accord could "generate a war in South America," Chávez vowed to strengthen his country's growing military buildup and announced that he had informed the Russian government, Venezuela's principal arms supplier, of his intention to double the number of tank battalions by buying dozens of T–72 main battle tanks and other military vehicles. Venezuela's earlier purchases since 2005 of US$4.4 billion worth of Russian arms had already generated concern in Bogotá about its neighbor's military buildup and its greatly superior air force. Moreover, since July 2009, Chávez has used bellicose rhetoric to spearhead a propaganda campaign in Latin America against the DCA, criticizing even its granting of immunity for U.S. personnel in Colombia—usually considered a bilateral matter between the two negotiating parties. Chávez has also portrayed the DCA as a U.S. conspiracy against Latin America designed to reestablish U.S. "imperial domination" in the region.

Addressing the Chávez-led campaign to isolate Colombia for its growing reliance on U.S. military and counternarcotics support, President Uribe pointed out at a multinational meeting held on July 23 in Santa Marta that "Colombia has never been an aggressor." Rather, he explained that "This agreement guarantees continuity of an improved Plan Colombia," and that it is aimed at fighting terrorism and drug trafficking. "These agreements are never made to create conditions to attack third-party states," he stated. "This is excluded from the text, the agreements themselves, and in practice." Uribe added that the pact would allow the implementation of "joint responsibility between both countries" under Plan Colombia.

In another attempt to counter Chávez's anti-Colombia campaign, President Uribe made a whirlwind tour of seven South American countries between August 4 and August 6 to explain the Colombian–U.S leasing agreement. Brazil and Chile then suggested that Bogotá's bilateral military agreements are a sovereign matter for Colombia. Although Argentina, Peru, and Uruguay also appeared to be mollified by Uribe's personal diplomacy, Argentina later that month announced its opposition to the DCA.

President Chávez sent his ambassador back to Bogotá in early August, but he noted that Venezuela's "relations with Colombia remain frozen" and "under review." Chávez had recalled his ambassador on July 28 because of a diplomatic row over the Uribe government's announced discovery of a Swedish antitank weapon and ammunition in a FARC camp that had been traced by serial numbers to official Venezuelan stockpiles. Chávez failed to provide a credible public explanation for how the FARC obtained the Swedish weapons from the Venezuelan army, and, according to the Uribe government, "Venezuela has provided no explanation whatsoever."

Nevertheless, Chávez's propaganda offensive against the DCA effectively eclipsed the FARC-related developments and the apparent clandestine support role played by Venezuela. Thus, Colombia, rather than the Russia- and Iran-allied Chávez regime, became the cynosure of regional concern and isolation. Calling the DCA a "declaration of war against the Bolivarian revolution," Chávez announced in late August that he would soon again be breaking diplomatic relations with Colombia.

In addition to his diplomatic and military threats, Chávez also began to use trade as a weapon to retaliate against the DCA. He ordered a freeze on bilateral trade with Colombia, beginning with the cancellation of imports of 10,000 cars made in Colombia, arranging instead to purchase that many vehicles from Argentina. Chávez also announced in August 2009 that Venezuela would stop all imports from Colombia in 12 months; he also cancelled preferential pricing for Venezuelan oil and oil derivatives for Colombia. Colombia's trade with Venezuela in this decade has been greatly to Colombia's advantage, according to the National Administrative Department of Statistics (DANE). In 2008 Colombian exports to Venezuela totaled US$6 billion, while Venezuelan sales to Colombia amounted to only US$1.2 billion. In the first five months of 2009, Venezuela was the leading market for Colombia's nontraditional exports, absorbing 33 percent of that category, followed by the United States, with 19.6 percent. In contrast, Colombia acquired from Venezuela only 1.8 percent of its total foreign purchases. Thus, exports to Venezuela have been vital to the Colombian economy.

Chávez's fanning of the rhetorical winds of regional war against Colombia appeared to have had the effect of rallying the support of Colombians for the DCA and President Uribe. A poll commissioned by the National Radio Network in July 2009 found that 55 percent of Colombians supported the agreement, while 36 percent opposed it. A tri-country poll taken in late August by Colombia's National Consultancy Center found that Uribe had a 69.1 percent favorability rating, as compared with 20.2 percent for Chávez and 23.4 percent for Ecuador's President Rafael Correa Delgado. Chávez's propaganda campaign against the Uribe government prompted Colombia's Roman Catholic Church to inject itself into matters of state by harshly criticizing the presidents of Venezuela and Ecuador, accusing Chávez and Correa of a complete lack of decorum in their treatment of Colombia. In late August, the National Federation of Merchants (Fenalco), an influential business guild, expressed its "total support" for Uribe's handling of relations with Venezuela and Ecuador, and said that "the highest interests of the country" came before "commercial conveniences." Some observers viewed Chávez's drive to cast the DCA as a military threat to the region as a way of supporting the FARC, in some ways his ally and surrogate.

The DCA is not without its critics in Colombia, who included Rafael Pardo Rueda, a former minister of national defense and a presidential candidate; members of the judiciary's Council of State; and some members of Congress. By allowing for a significantly increased U.S. military and counternarcotics role in Colombia and by providing immunity from Colombian laws to U.S. military personnel in Colombia, the DCA raised national sovereignty issues with some Colombians. Colombia's position reportedly is that legal immunity will be applicable only to U.S. troops and not the U.S. contractors and civilians to be hired to help implement the DCA. Basically, all immunity cases are to be handled under the terms of already existing bilateral agreements, such as the Mutual Defense Assistance Agreement of 1952 and the U.S. Military Missions in Colombia Agreement of 1975 (signed in Bogotá in October 1974). Moreover, U.S. military courts would not be allowed to operate on the bases. Nevertheless, negotiators reportedly decided to defer the controversial immunity issue to a future judicial cooperation agreement.

Some Colombian critics also expressed concern that the DCA would accentuate Colombia's already tense relations with neighboring Ecuador and Venezuela in particular, and risk further destabilizing and militarizing the region. Colombia and Ecuador have not had diplomatic relations since March 2008, when the left-wing government of President Correa withdrew its ambassador in protest of the Colombian army raid on a FARC camp located just inside Ecuadorian territory. Apparently in response to perceived cross-border aggression by Colombia, Ecuador increased its defense spending by buying 24 Brazilian fighter aircraft and six Israeli drones. Moreover, Ecuador denounced the DCA as a threat to regional stability. Despite the tense relations between Colombia and Ecuador, the Correa government, apparently alarmed by Chávez's chilling warning that "the winds of war were beginning to blow" across the region, announced in mid-August 2009 that it would not allow Chávez to draw Ecuador into a war with Colombia. Furthermore, both Colombia and Ecuador made efforts that month to reach a rapprochement, with the mediation assistance of the Carter Center.

In view of Chávez's continuing attempts to define the Uribe government's DCA with the United States as a threat to the region, on August 26 Colombia accused the Venezuelan leader of meddling in Colombia's internal affairs and proceeded to lodge a formal protest with the Organization of American States (OAS). Uribe succeeded in dampening the regional firestorm over the DCA by debating the agreement at a tense seven-hour summit of the Union of South American Nations (Unasur), held on August 27–28, 2009, in Bariloche, Argentina. Consisting of the 12 presidents of the member countries, Unasur is intended to serve as a regional interlocutor with the United States and the European Union.

Uribe explained to his fellow Unasur members that the DCA is limited to fighting narcotics trafficking and terrorism within Colombian territory and sharing tactical and operational intelligence as opposed to strategic intelligence. He also reminded them of Chávez's frequent military threats against Colombia and his campaign of intimidation. Although Uribe attempted to raise other regional concerns such as terrorism and military buildups by "certain neighbors," the meeting focused exclusively on the DCA. Realizing that the outcome of the summit would not be the cancellation of the DCA and that President Uribe was not there to renegotiate Colombia's bilateral agreement with the United States, the leaders of Argentina, Brazil, and Chile toned down their criticism of the DCA. The fact that Unasur did not officially condemn the DCA counted as a victory for Uribe. Nevertheless, most South American governments remained wary of the DCA. Exceptions included Peru, whose minister of defense discounted the notion that the DCA is a threat to South America. Following the Unasur meeting, those most critical of the DCA remained Bolivia, Ecuador, Paraguay, and Venezuela.

In a sign of the times, President Uribe returned from the Unasur summit ill with the H1N1 (swine) influenza. Colombia's National Health Institute (INS) confirmed the diagnosis. It was not yet known if Uribe contacted the virus in Argentina, which had many cases, or before he arrived there. According to the Ministry of Social Protection, Colombia had 621 confirmed cases of swine flu by the end of August 2009, including Uribe's, and 34 deaths, but the actual number of those infected with the virus was thought to be much higher. Two other high-level officials in the Uribe administration also contracted the H1N1 virus.

On the domestic political front, President Uribe asserted, in a late June 2009 interview with *Semana* magazine, that, "Today we have a nation with more trust." This strengthened trust, he explained, derives from his administration's policies of building democratic security, investor confidence based on social responsibility, and social cohesion based on liberties. Although the parapolitics, false-positives, and DAS-wiretapping scandals and the rampant extrajudicial executions and forced disappearances were symptomatic of a betrayal of the public trust, Uribe omitted any mention of them. As an example of the Uribe administration's tendency to gloss over scandals, in early May 2009 the outgoing minister of national defense replaced the civilian director of Military Penal Justice with an acting director, a colonel, who subsequently transferred 40 of its prosecutors, or 30 percent of the military judiciary's staff, who had been investigating the false-positives cases.

Against this backdrop of seeming abuse of the public trust, the appointment in late July 2009 of Gabriel Silva Luján, a close associate of Juan Manuel Santos, as the new minister of national defense was well received by Colombian politicians in general, who saw him as someone with the executive skills needed to manage the powerful ministry effectively. Trained at universities in Bogotá and Washington, DC, in economics and political science, Silva had served as Colombia's ambassador to the United States in the 1990s and had been serving as president of the National Federation of Coffee Growers (Fedecafé).

One of the first tasks of the new minister of national defense was to decide how to improve the defense of soldiers being investigated by the justice system, the number under investigation having ballooned. In 2009 Military Penal Justice had 17,000 unresolved cases; and the Attorney General's Office, 1,117. Until 2008, when Congress approved a law creating within the ministry a specialized Legal Defense Office (Defensoría) for the Public Force (the armed forces and National Police), these soldiers had to pay all their own legal expenses. This new Ministry of National Defense office is staffed with attorneys who provide free legal counsel to members of the armed forces facing Military Penal Justice courts. However, if a case begins with Military Penal Justice courts and then transfers to the Attorney General's Office, the ministry is required to continue its legal defense of the defendant in order to guarantee due process. As a result, the ministry is obligated to fund the defense of many military members who are, in some cases, eventually revealed to have been working with criminal networks. Thus, to some observers, it may seem paradoxical that the taxpayers should be financing the defense of military members indicted for murdering civilians, whether for the false-positives massacres in this decade or the Palace of Justice disappearances in 1985. In August 2009 a female civilian lawyer became director of Military Penal Justice. Another initiative launched by Minister Silva in his first month in office is called Plan Patria (Fatherland Plan), which is aimed at strengthening military and social efforts and state presence in the border areas. The idea was for Plan Patria to focus initially on La Guajira Department's border communities, which bear the brunt of unstable economic relations between Colombia and Venezuela.

In August 2009, President Uribe had to propose a list of candidates to replace the respected attorney general, Mario Iguarán Arana, whose four-year term expired at the end of July. During Iguarán's challenging term, he reactivated several investigations into the most serious crimes in the nation's history that had looked as if they would remain unsolved because of the statute of limitations. In the Palace of Justice case, the military commanders of the disastrous counterassault operation and Belisario Betancur Cuartas (president, 1982–86) were being investigated not so much for their responsibility for the resulting massacre as for their role, if any, in the disappearance, torture, and murder of eight employees of the Palace of Justice cafeteria, three female visitors to the cafeteria, and one female hostage-taker. Whether Iguarán's successor would be able to continue prosecuting these high-profile cases remained to be seen. The Supreme Court was supposed to elect the new attorney general on July 23 from the president's list of candidates. The leading candidate proposed by Uribe was Camilo Ospina Bernal, a former minister of national defense and more recently ambassador to the OAS, whose background was in administrative rather than penal law. However, the Supreme Court, apparently unimpressed, declared that it would take its time in making the important appointment in order to ensure that the candidates met the qualifications needed for the post.

The selection of Mario Iguarán's replacement as attorney general was particularly consequential because his successor would have to decide on how to handle no fewer than five scandals, several of which could compromise top government officials. These scandals included parapolitics, the DAS wiretappings, the assassination of Luis Carlos Galán, the false positives, and "FARC-politics." In the last case, a former presidential candidate and two journalists were being investigated in connection with several files found in Raúl Reyes's captured computers. In the parapolitics case, the new attorney general would have to decide whether to close the case or to summon former Senator Mário Uribe Escobar, cousin of President Uribe, to trial for his role in the scandal.

On August 14, 2009, the last day before the 20-year statute of limitations in Galán's assassination case expired, the Attorney General's Office ordered the arrest of General (ret.) Miguel Maza Márquez, the former DAS director, on a charge of ordering Galán's assassination. This was a stunning development because the drug cartels were generally assumed to have perpetrated the assassination, and, if supported by the evidence, it may illustrate once again how high drug-related corruption can reach into the security agencies. Maza's indictment prompted César Augusto Gaviria Trujillo (president 1990–94) to reveal publicly, after 20 years, that he had received an intelligence warning of a possible link between Maza and the Cali Cartel capos. Ernesto Samper Pizano (president, 1994–98) then faulted Gaviria for not making that information known earlier. With the drug cartels lurking like lobbyists behind government officials, the selection for the post of attorney general provided a likely indicator of whether the Uribe government was serious about overcoming Colombia's culture of impunity or was simply condoning it for reasons of political expediency.

Uribe's 2006 electoral mandate permitted him to remain in power until August 2010. As a first step toward a national referendum on amending the constitution to allow him the possibility of a third successive term as president, in November 2007 Uribe's allies began collecting 5 million signatures (well over the 1.4 million needed to initiate the proposal). Although the continuing parapolitics scandal weakened Uribe's political capital in 2007, the military successes against the FARC in 2008, particularly the rescue of Ingrid Betancourt and other hostages, and the generally favorable condition of the economy strengthened his popularity. Nevertheless, on October 29, 2008, the House of Representatives rejected a proposed constitutional amendment that would have allowed Uribe to seek reelection in 2010. Arguing the undemocratic nature of extending Uribe's time in office, the Liberal Party cited a letter in which Simón Bolívar said that "nothing is as dangerous as to allow the same citizen to remain in power a long time." Citing the need for continuity of his Democratic Security Policy, Uribe persevered with his third-term stratagem.

On May 19, 2009, the Senate approved by a vote of 62 to 5 a measure that could lead to a referendum on whether the constitution should be changed to allow Uribe to be reelected a second time. Whether this vote reflected the popular will was unclear because 30 percent of the 102-member body had resigned as a result of the parapolitics scandal and had been replaced by unelected officials, and only 20 senators attended the final debate on this issue. Moreover, the Senate's bill still had to be reconciled with the lower-house measure that would bar Uribe from seeking office again until 2014. Before a referendum could be scheduled, the Constitutional Court still had to ratify the proposal. Then 25 percent of Colombia's electorate, or 7.2 million voters, would have to approve it. However, resistance to his plan was significant in mid-2009. Sectors opposed to it included the Roman Catholic Church, the business community, and news media. Indeed, a growing concern in Colombia was that a constitutional amendment allowing Uribe the possibility of a third consecutive term would discredit him and put him in the same league as the leftist President Hugo Chávez of Venezuela. Foreign news media increasingly portrayed President Uribe as authoritarian. For example, the May 14, 2009, issue of *The Economist*, the British weekly magazine that usually praised President Uribe, was critical of a third term for him, suggesting that it would lead to an "autocracy."

On August 19, 2009, Uribe's prospects suddenly took on new life, when the referendum proposal received a majority vote in the Senate's Conciliation Committee and in the House of Representatives. The text then went to the Constitutional Court for review before going to the plenary Congress, where it had to be independently voted on in both the Senate and the House of Representatives. As expected, it easily passed the Senate, with 56 votes in favor and two against. On September 1, the House of Representatives voted to approve the referendum on the proposed constitutional reform by 85 votes against five, whereupon the project was sent to the Constitutional Court for review.

On September 17, 2009, the Supreme Court, in a 13-to-eight decision, took the unprecedented step of refusing to elect a new attorney general from the government's pool of candidates. Most justices decided that the proposed candidates did not meet the requirements of the post, which include, in particular, the credential of being a criminal attorney. As a result, filling the position, considered the second most important public post after the president of the republic, was expected to take several more months until this new power struggle between the judicial and executive branches could be resolved.

October 16, 2009

*　　　　*　　　　*

As Colombia began 2010, the country was facing challenging political and security issues in particular. The issue of naming a new attorney general remained unresolved, and the acting attorney general continued to serve. Meanwhile, academics and the courts welcomed a new proposal by the minister of interior and justice that these two areas should again be separate ministries.

Colombia's internal conflict appeared to be taking another turn for the worse. The impressive successes of Uribe's Democratic Security Policy in 2008 had led many Colombians to believe that the insurgency was at last about to end and that the AUC demobilization had tamed paramilitary violence. However, the New Rainbow Corporation (Corporación Nuevo Arco Iris), an NGO, reported that the effectiveness of the Uribe government's much-vaunted Democratic Security Policy had diminished during 2009, when the FARC regrouped in isolated areas of the Cordillera Central and along Colombia's borders with Ecuador and Venezuela. The FARC launched a new, more aggressive strategy, emphasizing attacks against small groups of servicemen, increased use of minefields, and manufacture of some of their own weapons. The

FARC increased the number of its offensive actions by 30 percent over 2008, and boosted its membership to 11,500. The ELN also appeared to be strengthening and becoming more active in its areas of operation near the Ecuadorian and Venezuelan borders.

According to the NGO, a continuous, seven-year counterinsurgency offensive and more than 2,000 pending prosecutions for extrajudicial executions were stalling the Military Forces, which reportedly had lost the initiative in various parts of the country. Military resources had declined, and casualties had increased, totaling an estimated 2,500 military deaths or injuries in 2009, many of them caused by antipersonnel mines. On December 21, 2009, the FARC kidnapped and murdered the governor of Caquetá Department. A new generation of ex-paramilitary criminal gangs was rapidly spreading throughout the country, including to the outskirts of Bogotá, Medellín, and a dozen other cities, and carrying out more violent actions than the FARC and ELN combined. In an apparent attempt to establish drug-smuggling corridors, these armed gangs were operating on key highways to Bogotá and its airport, Cartagena, and Urabá.

On the diplomatic front, relations between Colombia and Ecuador had normalized, but Colombian–Venezuelan relations remained tense. At the Copenhagen climate conference held in December 2009, President Uribe equated Colombia's counterinsurgency and counternarcotics struggles with the fight against deforestation. He pointed out that coca processing and trafficking in cocaine and lumber have been deforesting Colombia, threatening the country's biologically rich jungle and rainforests that cover 51 percent of the national territory. Therefore, he argued, cocaine-consuming countries have an obligation to provide financial support for efforts to combat deforestation. Just before the Andean Trade Promotion and Drug Eradication Act (ATPDEA) would have expired at the end of 2009, the U.S. Congress extended its benefits to Colombia for another year. However, the U.S. Congress had yet to ratify the free-trade agreement, which is an economic priority for Colombia.

January 21, 2010

*　　　　　*　　　　　*

It had seemed inevitable to many Colombians that President Uribe would somehow be a candidate in the May 30, 2010, presidential election and be reelected again. However, instead of the overwhelming public support that he received for his first reelection, scandals and skeptical public opinion tainted Uribe's never formally declared third presidential run. His chance to remain in power received its first significant setback on November 13, 2009, when the National Electoral Council (CNE) invalidated the petition of the Uribistas because the organizers had exceeded the legal limit of finance for the collection of signatures. The inspector general of the nation presented to the Constitutional Court on January 13, 2010, his opinion favoring the congressionally approved referendum on a constitutional amendment that would allow Uribe to run for a third successive presidential term, and some determined Uribistas began calling for the postponement of the May 30 election to permit the completion of the plebiscite process. In early February, their hopes were effectively quashed when a Constitutional Court justice (a Uribe appointee) filed a 434-page nonbinding opinion calling for the proposed referendum law to be overturned for legal and electoral reasons. The national registrar subsequently cast further doubt on the feasibility of holding a referendum on such short notice, even in the unlikely event that the Constitutional Court were to approve it. Finally, on February 26, the Constitutional Court brought the contentious referendum issue to a definitive close by ruling 7–2 against the proposed plebiscite, because both the bill and the legislative process that produced it were deeply flawed and unconstitutional. That Uribe graciously accepted the court's ruling distinguished Colombia's democracy from neighboring Venezuela's autocracy.

The court ruling vastly altered Colombia's political landscape by throwing the presidential election wide open. Political pundits and polls began reassessing the field of candidates in a new light, which no longer shone so brightly on the Uribistas. President Uribe was now seen as having marred his historical legacy. Instead of uniting his followers to ensure the continuation of his policies of democratic security, social cohesion, and investor confidence, he appeared to have clung to power, relying, moreover, on the same mechanism that Venezuela's Hugo Chávez used to make himself president for life, namely, a plebiscite. In this view, Uribe's unquenchable presidential aspiration only succeeded in fracturing the government coalition and eliminating any guarantee that he would be succeeded by one of his followers, notably Juan Manuel Santos.

In the absence of a united Uribista coalition, a rare uncertainty over who would become the next occupant of Nariño Palace preceded the March 14 legislative elections. Commentators predicted that the presidential race would be determined by whether or not Uribe's supporters could remain united in the congressional elections in a tacit alliance between the National Unity Social Party (PSUN) and the Conservative Party or whether Uribism would crumble. None of the leading presidential candidates looked strong enough to win outright in the first round on May 30. Rather, surveys indicated that party alliances would determine the winner of the runoff election in June.

As of March 10, the three most likely runoff candidates appeared to be: Sergio Fajardo Valderrama, the independent candidate of Citizen Commitment for Colombia (Compromiso Ciudadano por Colombia); Noemí Sanín Posada, an independent conservative with surprising runoff potential; and Juan Manuel Santos, the official standard bearer of the Uribe-allied PSUN. Other registered presidential candidates included centrist Rafael Pardo (Liberal Party), leftist Senator Gustavo Petro Urrego (Alternative Democratic Pole), and centrist Germán Vargas Lleras (Radical Change Party).

A relatively unknown but fast-rising candidate, Fajardo is a popular, charismatic, innovative, and independent former mayor of Medellín and a mathematics professor. In January 2009, he began informally organizing a Barack Obama–style, national grassroots campaign with the aid of the Internet and thousands of campaign volunteers. The only candidate seen as neither pro- nor anti-Uribe, Fajardo appeared to be surpassing Santos in some polls.

Sanín, who has held several ministerial and ambassadorial posts, resigned as ambassador to Britain to enter the presidential race. Favored by Conservative Party leader Andrés Pastrana, she was considered likely to be selected as the party's candidate on March 14. The Conservative and Green parties both planned to announce their presidential candidates on the same day as the legislative elections. The Green Party (Partido Verde) came into existence on October 2, 2009.

Santos had resigned as Uribe's minister of national defense in May 2009 in order to be able to qualify as a candidate. In contrast to Uribe, who had been a relatively provincial rancher, the U.S.-educated Santos is seen as well informed about how Washington operates. Before heading the ministry for three years, Santos, whose family were the main shareholders in *El Tiempo* until 2007, was a journalist and economist. Under his management, coordination between military and police forces improved, the services made the legitimate use of military force part of their war strategy, and the military scored major successes against the FARC. However, the period was also marked by the false-positives scandal. Running on the slogan "If not Uribe, Santos," Santos promised to build on Uribe's legacy. Although the early front-runner, Santos lacked Uribe's high public approval ratings and was not a shoo-in for the presidency. For example, *Semana* noted that a coalition of adversaries could derail Santos in the second round.

The economic and social challenges facing Colombia's next president were summed up by Roberto Steiner, director of the Foundation for Higher Education and Development (Fedesarrollo), in a March 1 interview with Cali's *El País*. Forecasting a slow economic recovery from the low point in 2009, Steiner pointed out the disadvantageous position that Colombia found itself in—trading heavily with countries with minimal economic growth but not with the rapidly growing Asian economies. He noted that Colombia's major problem is that it has the highest unemployment and informal employment rates in Latin America. Steiner explained that the country's pension and health-care systems cannot be adequately funded by payroll taxes, when 60 percent of people are working in the informal economy. Consequently, the country's health care is a benefit for all, paid by a few. Thus, Steiner emphasized the need to reform the tax code in order to fund these foundering systems and make the public debt sustainable again.

March 10, 2010   Rex Hudson

Chapter 1. Historical Setting

Top: An Amazonian indigenous geometric design, Archaeology Museum of the Casa del Marqués de San Jorge, Bogotá
Courtesy *Carlos Arturo Jaramillo Giraldo*, Murmullos del lenguaje Uik: La práctica del mopa mopa: De lo recolector a lo sedentario, *Medellín, 1986, 77*
Bottom: A Tolima-style indigenous geometric design
Courtesy *Museo del Oro, Banco de la República; Banco del Pacífico (Ecuador); and Casa de la Cultura Ecuatoriana Benjamín Carrión*, El oro de Colombia: Homenaje al Ecuador, *Quito, Ecuador, 1982, 82–83*

AT THE BEGINNING of the twenty-first century, Colombia exhibited social and economic indicators that, with few exceptions, were close to the Latin American norm. Yet forms of political and criminal violence plagued the country, with an intensity and duration that had few parallels in the region. Neither could many countries in Latin America or elsewhere in the developing world match Colombia's record of persistent, albeit imperfect, adherence to democratic forms and procedures. An examination of the historical path by which Colombia arrived at its present situation offers no easy explanation of these paradoxes but is a logical place to start.

The initial building blocks for the future Colombian nation were the same as for its Latin American neighbors: Amerindian peoples, European conquerors and colonizers, and Africans arriving as slaves. During three centuries of Spanish colonial rule, these elements were unevenly combined into a new multiethnic society. The Europeans and their descendants enjoyed a predominant share of political influence, economic wealth, and social prestige, while the Amerindians were assimilated or marginalized and inexorably reduced to subordinate status. The latter was also true of Afro-Colombians, even when they escaped from slavery. Yet for most of the colonial population, Spain's control was light, and it was maintained less by force than by the mystique surrounding the monarchy and by the influence of the Roman Catholic Church, which established a strong institutional base and acted as cultural and ideological arbiter.

Colombia played a preeminent role in the movement for independence in Latin America. Once independence was achieved, however, the country lapsed into relative obscurity, with a weak connection to the world economy and, for many years, scant progress in the development of infrastructure or public education. At the same time, peculiarities of the political system, notably the rise of strong and warring parties within a weak state, began to make themselves felt. Only with the rise of the coffee industry, in the late nineteenth and early twentieth centuries, did Colombia enter clearly on a path of economic modernization. Coffee likewise seemed, for a time, to usher in a phase of harmonious political consolidation. But by the mid-twentieth century, dysfunctional aspects of social and political development were increasingly evident as economic growth continued.

The successful transfer of power from one party to another by electoral means in 1930 and again in 1946—something that in much

3

of Latin America was still far from normal—seemed to confirm the maturity of Colombian democracy. Yet in both cases, the transfer was followed by outbreaks of violence in the backcountry. These revolts were relatively short-lived in the first case, but the latter was the start of what Colombians called La Violencia (The Violence), which would wrack the nation for roughly two decades and then give way to the leftist insurgencies that marked the last four decades of the century. The bitter antagonism between the entrenched Liberal and Conservative parties was a triggering mechanism in both 1930 and 1946, but the existence of deep rural poverty and illiteracy, despite rising gross domestic product (GDP—see Glossary) per capita and a modest beginning of social reform legislation, created an environment in which those antagonisms more easily found virulent expression. The same social problems, even though gradually diminishing, provided superficial justification for the violence of later guerrilla organizations.

Regular elections and formally constitutional government were interrupted only briefly, in the 1950s, yet the inability of the state to maintain public order throughout the country—indeed its virtual absence from much of Colombian territory—favored growth of the illegal drug industry in the final quarter of the century. That industry's combination with chronic political and criminal violence led to ever-greater disillusion with existing institutions. The adoption in 1991 of a new constitution aimed to make the political system more inclusive as well as to enshrine a long list of social guarantees. Although two of the irregular armed groups had earlier agreed to demobilize and pursue their objectives by legal political action, others wanted further concessions and assurances before doing the same. And the drug traffickers, of course, were more responsive to world market conditions, which remained favorable, than to any changes in the constitution. Nevertheless, the new constitution went into effect, and in the nation as a whole there was no lack of positive developments alongside the continuing traumas.

Early Colombia

It is not known when the earliest humans reached what is now Colombia. The oldest evidence of occupation, which is pending confirmation, dates from before 20,000 B.C., at sites in the central Andean highlands, but the first native peoples undoubtedly arrived earlier, coming presumably by way of the Isthmus of Panama. Over succeeding millennia, there were further migrations and mutual cultural influences between different geographic regions of Colombia and not just Central America but the Caribbean, coastal Ecuador, and

A stone divinity in San Agustín,
Huila Department
Courtesy Embassy of Colombia,
Washington, DC

the Amazon region. It is likely that settled, partly agricultural socie-
ties first arose in the northern Caribbean lowlands of Colombia by
the second millennium B.C. No single dominant native culture
emerged. Rather, most of the original Colombians belonged to one
or another of three major linguistic groups—Arawak, Carib, and
Chibcha—and comprised a patchwork of separate cultures and sub-
cultures. These indigenous peoples developed the cultivation of
yucca in the lower elevations, maize at middle altitudes, and potatoes in the highlands. They practiced ceramic pottery and other
crafts, with impressive achievements in the working of gold from
alluvial deposits. And by the time of the Europeans' arrival, they
generally displayed the beginnings of both social stratification and a
political system on the basis of chieftainships.

None of the native peoples developed a system of writing comparable to that of the Mayas, and much less would the Spaniards
encounter a native empire such as that of either the Aztecs or Incas.
By 1500 A.D., the most advanced of the indigenous peoples were
two Chibcha groups: the Taironas and the Muiscas. The Taironas,
who appear to have been fairly late arrivals from Central America,
inhabited well-organized towns connected by roads on the lower
slopes of the Sierra Nevada de Santa Marta in the far north of
Colombia, rising just to the east of Santa Marta, Colombia's oldest
city. Politically, they had progressed beyond the stage of local chieftainships, forming two larger, and rival, confederations. They were
also the only people to construct works of engineering such as stone
temples and stone-paved roads.

By contrast, the Muiscas—based in the present departments of
Cundinamarca and Boyacá in the Cordillera Oriental—lived in dwellings scattered through the countryside, and their temples and palaces

were of perishable materials. But Muiscas, of whom there were perhaps 600,000, were far more numerous than the Taironas and covered a wider territory, extending from the area of present-day Bogotá northeastward to Tunja and beyond. As in the case of the Taironas, Muisca local chiefdoms had consolidated into two separate confederations. The Muisca territory also included Laguna de Guatavita, site of the fabled ceremony of El Dorado, the gold-dusted dignitary who plunged into the crater lake along with a rain of golden offerings. More than any other native people, the Muiscas have served as a model for later ideas of Colombia's pre-Columbian civilization.

The Spanish Conquest and Colonial Society

Exploration and Conquest

The first Europeans to visit what is now Colombia were the crew of Alonso de Ojeda, who in 1499 led an expedition to the north coast of South America. It reached Cabo de la Vela, on the Península de La Guajira, but did not tarry, because these visitors were interested in trading for gold and pearls, not in colonization. As a member of Ojeda's expedition, Amerigo Vespucci was among the first to explore the Colombian coasts. Other early expeditions also came to trade, or to seize indigenous people as slaves for sale in the West Indies.

In 1510 Ojeda, having been named governor of the coast as far as Urabá in the west, returned to establish a settlement, named San Sebastián, on the Golfo de Urabá not far from the present border with Panama. Neither it nor other settlements in that vicinity survived long, although from them explorers struck out toward the Isthmus of Panama and elsewhere. A first permanent Spanish settlement on the Colombian coast was founded in 1525 at Santa Marta; it was close to the territory of the Taironas and would later serve as a base for conquest of the Muiscas. Before that took place, Pedro de Heredia, on January 14, 1533, had founded the city of Cartagena, farther west along the coast and with a magnificent harbor, thanks to which it became the principal port of the colony as well as a leading Spanish naval base in Caribbean waters.

Bands of Spaniards set out from Cartagena and Santa Marta for the exploration and conquest of both coastal lowlands and the Andean interior. In 1536 Gonzalo Jiménez de Quesada, a lawyer turned military commander who was comparable to Hernán Cortés, the conqueror of Mexico, or Francisco Pizarro in Peru, launched the most important of these expeditions. He headed inland up the Magdalena toward the land of the Muiscas, which he reached early in 1537 after losing more than half of his party to shipwreck at the mouth of the Magdalena and to disease, insects, and hunger on the march. After easily overcoming armed resistance, Jiménez de Quesada and his lieutenants occupied the entire Muisca territory and on August 6, 1538, founded the city of Santafé (present-day Bogotá, known as Santa Fe during the colonial period), as capital of the New Kingdom of Granada, as he called this new possession after his birthplace in Spain.

Jiménez de Quesada shortly found his control challenged by two rival expeditions converging on the same spot from different directions. One was led by Nikolaus Federmann, a German in Spanish service who arrived from western Venezuela, and the other by Sebastián de Belalcázar (or Benalcázar), a former lieutenant of Pizarro coming north from Quito who had founded Popayán and Cali on the way. Instead of fighting among themselves for the spoils of the Muiscas, the three conquistadors referred the matter to authorities in Spain, who, not wanting any one conquistador to become too powerful, placed a fourth party in charge instead. However, Jiménez de Quesada was granted other privileges and was one of those who continued the work of exploration and conquest. By the end of the century, most of the principal cities of today's Colombia already had been founded.

Colonial Government

After some initial improvisation, a definitive form of political organization took hold during the second half of the sixteenth century. The highest official was the captain general of New Granada, who from Santa Fe had oversight of all modern Colombia except the far southwest (Pasto and Popayán), which initially was administered from Quito in present-day Ecuador, and most of Venezuela except the area of Caracas. He shared superior jurisdiction with an *audiencia*, which functioned as both administrative council and court of appeal—separation of powers being foreign to the Spanish imperial system. At an intermediate level, the colony was divided into provinces headed by governors, whose titles and powers might vary. For example, because of Cartagena's strategic importance, its governor enjoyed a degree of military and other authority that most governors lacked. At the local level, the towns and cities had *cabildos* (municipal councils) in which positions were sometimes appointive, sometimes hereditary, and sometimes filled by election. Even in the latter case, elections were far from democratic, and it was only in town or city government that some element of direct popular participation could be found.

New Granada in the beginning formed part of the Viceroyalty of Peru, which was formed in 1544 and comprised all of Spanish South America plus Panama. However, subordination to the viceroy in Lima was mostly nominal, and in 1717–19 New Granada in its own right attained viceregal status, which it lost in 1723 but regained permanently in 1739. In its final shape, the Viceroyalty of the New Kingdom of Granada included Venezuela, Quito (now shorn of jurisdiction over Pasto and Popayán), and Panama. Venezuela became a captaincy general and as such conducted most affairs without reference to the viceroy, exactly as New Granada had done when attached to Peru, whereas Quito was a presidency and not quite so independent of the viceregal capital. Yet when even a fast courier would take weeks to travel from Santa Fe to Panama or Quito, officials in those outlying areas enjoyed substantial autonomy in practice. Exactly the same could be said of the viceregal administration at Santa Fe vis-à-vis the Council of the Indies and other officials in Spain who in principle exercised supreme executive, legislative, and judicial authority over all Spanish America. It was understood that sometimes an order from the mother country might be inapplicable in a given colony, whose top administrator could then suspend it while appealing for reconsideration—with a final decision likely to be years in coming, if it came at all.

Colonial Society and Economy

The highest officials in Spanish America were mostly natives of Spain, known as *peninsulares* because they came from the Iberian Peninsula. Spaniards also played a major role in commerce, especially at the wholesale level and in trade with Spain itself, whose government sought to keep all overseas trade a Spanish monopoly. But after one or two generations of European settlement, the principal owners of the means of production—landed estates, or haciendas, and mining concessions—were mostly criollos (Creoles), that is, persons of Spanish descent born in the New World. Even while recognizing the right of the Amerindians to keep land of their own, the Spanish monarchy claimed ultimate control over property in the conquered territory, and it rewarded many of the original conquerors with lavish land grants, which eventually passed to their children. In other cases, the early settlers and their descendants were allowed to buy land on favorable terms or simply helped themselves to what they found, assuming that through payment of the necessary fees they could later regularize their title.

Land in itself was of little use without people to work it, but there were a number of ways to obtain the needed labor. As in the other

Colonial entryway, Bogotá
Courtesy Embassy of Colombia,
Washington, DC

Spanish colonies, one device was the institution of the *encomienda* (see Glossary), whereby a specific group of Amerindians was "entrusted" to a Spanish colonist to protect them and convert them to Christianity in return for payment of tribute. This tribute often was paid in the form of labor, although that practice was generally against Spanish policy. Even when the Amerindians paid their tribute in money, the result was much the same, as they needed to work for the newcomers to obtain it. Although the *encomienda* never legally entailed a grant of land, in practice the Spanish *encomendero* (see Glossary) might well find a way to usurp the property of Amerindians entrusted to him. Spanish authorities gradually phased out the *encomienda* system, but Amerindians then paid tribute directly to the state, and they would still have to work to earn the money. Other systems of quasi-voluntary labor developed, too, while in early years some Amerindians were subjected to outright enslavement. Amerindian slavery was exceptional in New Granada and never took root there, but African slaves were soon being introduced, and although never as important to the overall economy as in Brazil or the West Indies, they became an appreciable part of the labor force in at least some parts of the colony.

Although the dominant criollos prided themselves on their Spanish descent, bloodlines in practice were often less pure than they might appear. In order to gain access to higher education, for example, it was technically necessary to prove one's *limpieza de sangre*, or "cleanness of blood," which meant not just European pedigree but

9

freedom from any trace of Jews, Muslims, or heretics in the family tree. However, both formal marriage and informal unions with the native population produced an ever-larger mestizo, or mixed European and Amerindian, population; by the end of the colonial period, this was the largest single demographic group (see Racial Distinctions, ch. 2). For most purposes, the population of mestizos was not clearly differentiated from that of criollos. Nevertheless, for a mestizo to enter the higher social strata and possibly marry the descendant of some conquistador, it did help to have a light complexion and some respectable economic assets, because upward mobility in colonial society was not easy to achieve.

It was even harder for someone of African or part-African descent to rise in society. The first African slaves to reach New Granada arrived with the conquistadors themselves because African slavery existed on a small scale in Spain. Greater numbers came later directly from Africa, to work in the placer gold deposits of the western Andes and Pacific slopes, landed estates of the Caribbean coastal plain, and assorted urban occupations. Few were to be found in the Andean highlands, and roughly the same relative distribution of Afro-Colombian people as in the eighteenth century continues to this day. Although at first all were slaves, the processes of voluntary manumission, self-purchase (with money slaves could earn by working on their own account), and successful escape into the backcountry produced a growing population of free blacks. Free and slave alike mixed with other ethnic groups, and some of the free—mainly *pardos* ("browns") of part-European ancestry—became small landowners, independent artisans, or lower-ranking professionals. But unlike mestizos, anyone with a discernible trace of African ancestry faced not just social prejudice but also legal prohibitions very roughly comparable to the jim crow laws that mandated segregation in the United States between 1876 and 1965. These laws were not always enforced, but they placed a limit on the advancement even of free *pardos*.

By the close of the colonial period, Amerindians accounted for less than a quarter of New Granada's total of roughly 1.4 million inhabitants. This change naturally reflected both the expansion of other demographic groups and the drastic fall in Amerindian numbers as a result of European diseases, mistreatment, and the widespread disruption of traditional lifestyles. In some peripheral areas, such as the Colombian portion of the Amazon basin, the Spanish had no incentive to establish effective control, and the ancestral modes of political and social organization remained in effect. In the central highlands and other areas of permanent Spanish settlement, however, the situation of the indigenous peoples was different. Imperial policy aimed to group them into villages where they would have their own local magistrates and would continue to own lands in common (*resguardos*—see Glossary) just as before the conquest, although under ultimate control of the Spanish and owing tribute to the crown itself or, especially in the first century of colonial rule, to individual Spanish *encomenderos*. In practice, the Amerindians were often irregularly stripped of their lands and compelled to labor for the newcomers. Willingly or not, they also adopted many aspects of European civilization, from chickens and iron tools to the Roman Catholic faith. In the Muisca heartland, all had become monolingual Spanish speakers by the end of the colonial period (in return contributing place-names and other terms to the speech of their conquerors).

Agriculture remained the principal activity of indigenous villages, the small farms of many mestizos or poor whites, and the large estates of the socially prominent. Products were the same as before the Europeans' arrival but with the addition of such novelties as wheat, which was consumed mainly by Spaniards and criollos. The hacienda owners also took particular interest in raising livestock. Whether cattle or crops, almost all of this production was for domestic consumption. Gold was the only significant export; it alone could support the cost of transportation from the interior to the seacoast, given the primitive state of internal transport networks. Theoretically, such tropical commodities as sugar could have been grown for export along the coastal plain, but New Granadan producers could not compete with the more developed plantation economies of Cuba or Venezuela. Hence, gold paid the bill for virtually all New Granada's imports, which were mainly for the upper social strata: wine and oil from Spain, cloth and other manufactured goods either from Spain or from other European countries by way of Iberia (or as contraband bypassing Spanish ports entirely). Coarser textiles and other handcraft items were made locally, however, and sometimes traded from one province to another. One example was the cotton cloth produced in the northeastern province of Socorro (present-day Santander Department). This industry featured the putting-out system, whereby an entrepreneur farmed out successive stages of the production process to local households. This system was widespread at the beginning of the Industrial Revolution in Europe and gave full or part-time employment to a significant number of criollos and mestizos.

Religion and Culture

The conversion of the indigenous population to Christianity was cited at the time as a guiding motive and justification for Spain's conquests in America and is cited still by traditionalists who reject the pervasive Black Legend of Spanish cruelty to the native inhabitants. In New Granada, proselytism was at least superficially a great success, with most of the native population quickly adopting the new religion. As elsewhere in America, the Amerindian converts did not necessarily abandon all previous beliefs or ascribe the same meaning to Roman Catholic rituals as did Hispanic Christians, but they conformed outwardly to those rituals, helped build churches and chapels, and showed the Roman Catholic clergy due respect. Spanish colonizers were sometimes annoyed when a priest or friar protested against mistreatment of the native population or of enslaved blacks, but they were eager to see the church established on a solid footing in the new lands and gave generously of their often ill-gotten gains to that effect. Likewise, the Spanish state, both from sincere conviction and from a realization of the church's value as an instrument of social control, helped endow the church with property, support its missionary activity, and, to the extent possible, suppress religious dissent. Extirpation of heresy and heretics, by burning as a last resort, was the special responsibility of the Spanish Inquisition, which had one of its three American headquarters (the least active of the three) at Cartagena. In the late colonial period, both state support and the missionary enthusiasm of the clergy tended to diminish, but by then the Roman Catholic Church was firmly entrenched as an institution, with roughly one priest or friar per 750 inhabitants, extensive property holdings, and additional wealth from investments, fees, and the compulsory payment of tithes by the faithful. That strong position would inevitably influence the course of Colombian history after independence.

Saints' portraits and other religious themes dominated colonial painting, including much popular art of the period, and religious festivals were regular occasions for public entertainment (commonly marked by drunkenness and rowdy behavior that the clergy disapproved of). Formal education was largely in the hands of the clergy, who controlled the only university-level institutions and were active at other levels too. The great majority of the population remained illiterate. For most of the colonial period, the literate were dependent on imported reading matter because the first press was set up in Santa Fe only in 1738, and the first real newspaper did not appear until 1791. However, the latter development coincided with a wider intellectual awakening to new currents in science and philosophy emanating from the European Enlightenment. A leader in this movement was José Celestino Mutis, a Spanish-born priest who settled in Santa Fe and won acclaim from European scientists for his work in studying botanical species of the viceroyalty.

Cathedral at Pasto, Nariño Department
Courtesy Embassy of Colombia, Washington, DC

Breaking the Spanish Connection

Antecedents of Independence

Several criollo disciples of Mutis would be active participants in the early nineteenth-century movement for independence. Not only scientific concepts but also ideas subversive of the existing political order managed to penetrate late-colonial New Granada, which was in principle an absolute monarchy. News of the American and French revolutions penetrated, too, and in 1793 a prominent member of the criollo elite, Antonio Nariño, printed in Santa Fe a translation of the French revolutionary "La Déclaration des Droits de l'Homme et du Citoyen" (Declaration of the Rights of Man and Citizen) of 1789. For this act, Nariño was arrested in 1794 and would spend much of his time in prison until the final independence movement began. It would seem that even at that early date he was hoping ultimately for outright independence, in which regard he was ahead of most New Granadans. Yet it occurred to more and more New Granadans, especially in the ranks of the educated minority, that the colonial regime was susceptible to improvement, even short of breaking all ties to Spain.

13

Political unrest reflected more than just the appearance of liberal and democratic ideas or the example of the British American colonies, which had demonstrated the feasibility of breaking loose from imperial control. Another contributing factor was the turn of events in Spain after the "Enlightened Despot," Charles III, was succeeded in 1788 by his son, the well-intentioned but weak Charles IV, under whom corruption and incompetence seemed the order of the day. Nor did the colonial population lack additional long-standing grievances, ranging from taxes and trade restrictions to the discrimination against native New Granadans in favor of those from the mother country in government appointments and other considerations. Of course, these grievances would be exaggerated by independence-period propagandists and by many later historians. For most people, taxes were more an annoyance than a crushing burden, and overseas trade was hampered more by the shortage of viable exports and lack of purchasing power for imports than by imperial regulations. Discrimination in appointments was rampant only at the highest levels, and the criollo upper class could influence the decisions and conduct even of peninsular appointees through social connections or, if need be, outright corruption. Moreover, different elements of the population sometimes disagreed on what was a grievance and what was not: people on the coast objected to barriers to the importation of cheap flour from the United States, whereas wheat growers in the highlands wanted stricter enforcement of the rules. Nevertheless, sources of discontent did exist, and any sudden aggravation could lead to violent protest.

Alongside lesser examples of rioting and protest in the late colonial period, one episode stands out: the Comunero Rebellion of 1781. The triggering mechanism was Spain's participation, as a traditional foe of England, in the very struggle that was bringing the British colonies their independence. Spain needed money for the naval base at Cartagena among other things, and the result was tax increases in New Granada along with irritating new controls to make sure the taxes were paid. Farmers and artisans in the province of Socorro demonstrated their defiance of these measures by destroying the liquor and tobacco belonging to state monopolies and establishing revolutionary committees (*comunes*), which took control of local administration. The movement spread beyond Socorro to much of New Granada, with the Comuneros demanding a rollback of the offensive tax measures. The protesters also made some unrelated demands designed to satisfy other complaints, such as that native New Granadans be given preference over Spaniards in official appointments. The *audiencia*, acting on behalf of the viceroy, who was in Cartagena overseeing defenses, gave an outward show of granting most demands, but as soon as it became possible to send military reinforcements from the coast into the interior, the movement quickly collapsed. A few leaders of last-ditch resistance were executed. At no point had the Comuneros proclaimed independence as an objective, and most likely few even considered the idea, but the rebellion underscored the existence of grievances and the potential for popular protest.

The Struggle for Independence, 1810–19

The trigger for the independence movement was the Napoleonic intervention in Spain in 1808 and resultant disarray of the Spanish monarchy. The French forces of Napoléon Bonaparte forced the abdication, first of Charles IV and then of his son and immediate successor, Ferdinand VII, who ended up a captive across the Pyrenees. A Spanish resistance movement arose to fight against the French and the intrusive authorities they imposed, and, with significant British help, it ultimately prevailed, but for some time most of Spain was in the hands of the French and their Spanish collaborators. And when the rump government that claimed to speak for what was left of free Spain—ostensibly in the name of the absent Ferdinand—claimed also to exercise authority over the American colonies, the response in New Granada, as elsewhere, was mixed.

The viceroy in Santa Fe, Antonio Amar y Borbón, sidetracked a first move in 1809 by criollo notables to form a governing junta that would rule in Ferdinand's name but enjoy virtual autonomy in practice. For their part, the leaders of Spain's struggle against Napoléon offered Spanish Americans token representation in their Central Junta and then in the Cortes, or Spanish parliament, which they were reviving after years of disuse. However, the Spanish Americans would be a small minority despite a population greater than that of Spain, and the Spanish offer did not diminish the ultimate authority that was to be exercised from Spain over the entire Spanish Empire. It therefore failed to satisfy the criollo lawyers and bureaucrats who aspired to greater control of their destinies (and higher positions for themselves), and with the future of the mother country itself still uncertain, new moves for local autonomy were inevitable. The year 1810 brought a series of mostly successful efforts to set up American governing juntas: in Caracas on April 19, in Cartagena not long afterward, and finally on July 20 in Santa Fe, where the viceroy was first made a member of the junta but soon was forced out.

Caracas and the rest of Venezuela, which had been little more than nominally subject to the viceroy, would go their own way until in the end Simón Bolívar Palacios, a son of Caracas, combined the independence movements of all northern South America. But neither did the towns and cities of New Granada proper agree to act in unison. The new authorities in Santa Fe, considering themselves natural successors to the viceroy, sought to establish under their leadership a government for the whole of the former colony. However, Cartagena and most outlying provinces refused to cooperate and in 1811 instead formed the United Provinces of New Granada, a league even weaker than the Articles of Confederation under which the rebellious British American colonies fought the American War of Independence. Insisting on the need for strong central authority, Santa Fe refused to join and instead annexed several adjoining towns and provinces to form the separate state of Cundinamarca, which before long was bogged down in intermittent civil warfare with the United Provinces. Even so, faced with Spain's refusal to offer meaningful concessions and bitter denunciation of all the Spanish Americans were doing, New Granada reached the stage of formally declaring independence, doing it piecemeal in the absence of an effective overall government: Cartagena led the way in 1811; Cundinamarca followed in 1813. To complicate matters further, still other parts of New Granada—notably Santa Marta on the coast and Pasto in the extreme south—remained loyal to the authorities in Spain and did their best to harass the revolutionaries.

Traditional historians dubbed the first years of the independence struggle the Patria Boba (Foolish Fatherland), both because of the patriots' disunity and because provincial legislatures wasted so much time on well-intentioned but impractical innovations. Elaborate declarations of citizens' rights, more on the French than the American model, are just one example. But a few of the measures were noteworthy: thus Antioquia Province began the process of abolishing slavery with a law of free birth, and Cartagena, which had one of the headquarters of the Spanish Inquisition, closed it down. Moreover, although political disunity was unfortunate, it faithfully reflected the fact that New Granada's population clusters, isolated by rugged topography and abysmal internal transportation, had really never had much to do with each other.

An outward appearance of unity was finally achieved in November–December 1814, when Bolívar, who owed the United Provinces a debt of gratitude for helping him militarily in Venezuela but was at the time a fugitive in New Granada, assumed command of an army that took Santa Fe and compelled Cundinamarca to join the confederation. Unfortunately, Ferdinand VII, having been returned to his throne as king of Spain in March 1814, was determined to restore the colonial status quo. Early in 1815, a major expedition of Spanish veterans under General Pablo Morillo set sail for America, landing first on the coast of Venezuela in April to mop up what remained of patriot resistance there. Its next target was New Granada. Correctly diagnosing the patriots' cause as hopeless because of their continuing dissensions, Bolívar decamped to the West Indies, to prepare for a better day. During August–December, Morillo's forces besieged Cartagena, starving it into submission, then advanced into the interior, where they restored Spanish rule in Santa Fe in May 1816.

The ease of the Spanish "reconquest" of New Granada in 1815–16 can be attributed not only to patriot divisions but also to weariness with the hardships and disruptions of wartime. Moreover, the pro-independence leadership, mainly drawn from criollo upper sectors of society, had generally failed to convince the popular majority that it had a real stake in the outcome. Although one patriot faction at Cartagena had succeeded in rallying artisans and people of color to participate actively on its side, more aristocratic rivals won local control, not only in Cartagena but also in all of the more populated regions of New Granada by July 1816. Yet restoration of the old regime was never complete. Some patriot fighters followed Bolívar into Caribbean exile to continue plotting, and others—including the man destined to become Bolívar's closest New Granadan collaborator and ultimate rival, General Francisco de Paula Santander y Omaña—retreated to the eastern plains (llanos), which became a republican sanctuary. Moreover, the financial exactions of the Spanish authorities together with revulsion against their tactics of repression, which included systematic execution of most top figures of the Patria Boba, turned feeling increasingly against them. Patriot guerrillas sprang up in many parts of the highlands.

Definitive liberation came from the direction of Venezuela under the leadership of Bolívar, who, by October 1817, had returned from the West Indies and occupied most of the Orinoco basin, an area encompassing one-fourth of Colombia and four-fifths of Venezuela. However, Bolívar had little success against Spanish units entrenched in Caracas and the Venezuelan Andes. In mid-1819, he therefore turned west toward New Granada, joined forces with Santander and other New Granadans who had taken refuge on the plains, and invaded the central highlands over one of the most difficult of Andean paths. On August 7, he defeated the Spanish in the Battle of Boyacá, which freed central New Granada, and three days later he entered Santa Fe, soon renamed Santa Fe de Bogotá. The battle had involved little more than 2,000 men on either side and was of short duration, but it destroyed the main Spanish force in New Granada and sorely damaged royalist morale. By the end of the year, patriot columns fanned out and occupied most of the rest of New Granada except the Caribbean coast and far southwest. Bolívar organized a provisional patriot government at Bogotá, naming Santander to head it. Then, in December 1819, he was in Angostura (present-day Ciudad Bolívar), temporary capital of patriot Venezuela, where at his behest the Venezuelan Congress (with the addition of a few New Granadan members) proclaimed the creation of the Republic of Great Colombia, comprising all the former Viceroyalty of New Granada.

Development of the Nation, 1819–1904

The Great Colombia Experiment, 1819–32

The Republic of Colombia founded by Bolívar is referred to retrospectively as "Gran Colombia," or "Great Colombia," to distinguish it from the smaller present-day Republic of Colombia. And it took almost four years for all the far-flung lands theoretically included to come under the Colombian flag. Bolívar's victory at the Battle of Carabobo, on June 24, 1821, delivered Caracas and virtually all the rest of Venezuela into his hands, except for the coastal fortress of Puerto Cabello, which held out another two years. The liberation of New Granada's Caribbean coast was completed when Cartagena fell to General Mariano Montilla's army in October 1821. In the following month, the Isthmus of Panama overthrew Spanish authority in a bloodless coup and then joined Colombia, ostensibly of its own volition, although Bolívar was prepared to take it by force if necessary. Bolívar assigned the task of extending Colombian rule to the Presidency of Quito (present-day Ecuador) to his lieutenant, Antonio José de Sucre, who went initially to the port of Guayaquil, where another local uprising had already deposed the Spanish authorities, and eventually won a decisive victory in the Battle of Pichincha, on the outskirts of Quito itself, in May 1822. The defeated royalist commander quickly surrendered the rest of the presidency to Colombia. The royalist army holding out at Pasto was now in an untenable position and surrendered, too. Guayaquil still posed a problem, for it had been operating as an autonomous city-state since its own rebellion against Spain, but Bolívar had no intention of allowing Quito's principal outlet to the sea to remain outside Colombia. In July, just days before he met in Guayaquil with the Argentine liberator José de San Martín, who was then serving as protector of Peru, which also had designs on Guayaquil, Bolívar's followers took control of the port city. A vote on joining Colombia was held, but the result was predetermined.

Simón Bolívar Palacios,
1783–1830, bust portrait,
artist unknown
Courtesy Prints and Photographs
Division, Library of Congress,
Washington, DC

The creation of Bolívar's Republic of Colombia was the only instance in which an entire Spanish viceroyalty remained united, even briefly, after independence. This unity resulted in large measure from the particular way in which independence was achieved in northern South America—by forces moving back and forth without regard to former colonial boundaries, under the supreme leadership of a single commander, Bolívar. It also reflected the conviction of Bolívar himself that the union brought together peoples whose sense of common destiny had been heightened in the recent struggle, plus a wealth of resources—the gold of New Granada, the agricultural economy of Venezuela, and the textile workshops of highland Ecuador—that were basically complementary. He likewise felt that only a large nation could gain respect on the world stage. However, he did not adequately weigh certain problems, of which perhaps most obvious was the lack of an integrated transportation and communication network: it was easier to travel from Caracas to Philadelphia or from Quito to Lima than from either one to Bogotá, which, by its central location, was the inevitable capital of the new nation. Although economies may have been complementary to some extent, interests were not necessarily compatible; the insistent demand of Ecuadorian textile makers for high protective tariffs was not what suited Venezuelan agricultural exporters. Neither did the common experience of Spanish rule and then the fight against it offset the stark social and cultural differences between, for example, the lawyers of Bogotá, the Quechua-speaking Amerindians of highland Ecuador, the *pardo* and

19

mestizo vaqueros of the Orinoco basin, and the planters of Andean Venezuela.

Nevertheless, in 1821 the young republic held a constituent assembly, known as the Congress of Cúcuta, which duly reaffirmed the union and went on to adopt a highly centralized system of government, under which the entire country was divided into provinces and departments whose heads were named from Bogotá. There were elected provincial assemblies, but with no meaningful power in local affairs. While eschewing federalism, the constitution of 1821 in some other respects revealed the clear influence of the U.S. model and was for the most part a conventionally republican document. It provided for strict separation of powers—too strict, in Bolívar's view, despite the fact that, like other early Latin American constitutions, it authorized sweeping "extraordinary" prerogatives for the executive to use in cases of emergency. Socioeconomic restrictions limited the right to vote to at most 10 percent of free adult males, but that was fairly standard procedure at the time. Citizens were guaranteed a list of basic rights that did not include freedom of worship, but neither were non-Roman Catholic faiths expressly forbidden, so that the question of religious toleration was left open to be dealt with later. At the same time, the Congress of Cúcuta itself equipped the new nation with a number of enlightened reforms: slavery was not immediately abolished, but provision was made for its gradual extinction by adopting nationwide the free-birth principle enacted earlier in Antioquia; likewise, Amerindians were relieved of the obligation to pay tribute or perform any kind of involuntary labor. Finally, the same Congress of Cúcuta elected Bolívar president and, because he was Venezuelan, provided regional balance by making the New Granadan Santander vice president.

In addition to acquiring a fine new constitution, the Republic of Colombia was the first Spanish American nation to obtain diplomatic recognition from the United States, in 1822; British recognition followed three years later. In 1824 Colombia even raised a foreign loan on the London market for the extraordinary sum of 30 million pesos (then equivalent to dollars). This consisted in part of mere refinancing of earlier obligations incurred during the independence struggle. It would prove impossible to maintain debt service, but the fact that the loan was even granted, on what for the time were quite favorable terms, attested to the prestige of Bolívar's creation.

Another sign of the Republic of Colombia's international prestige was the fact that it played host to Bolívar's Congress of Panama of 1826, which in the end accomplished little but was the first in a long line of Pan-American gatherings. Yet even before that meeting began, the fragility of the republic's unity was becoming apparent. The first serious crack came in Venezuela, where many people had been unhappy from the start with formal subjection to authorities in Bogotá, particularly when the head of government turned out to be the New Granadan, Vice President Santander, who became acting chief executive when Bolívar continued personally leading his armies against Spain. Indeed, Bolívar carried the struggle into Peru and stayed there even after the Battle of Ayacucho, won by Sucre in December 1824, put an end to serious royalist resistance. Venezuelans did have some real grievances, but equally important was the feeling that their present status was a step down from that of the colonial captaincy general, which for most purposes took orders (not necessarily obeyed) directly from Madrid. Thus, when General José Antonio Páez, the leading military figure in Venezuela, was summoned to Bogotá early in 1826 to answer charges against him in the Congress of the Republic (Congreso de la República), he refused to go, and most of Venezuela joined him in defiance. Both Páez and Santander looked for support to Bolívar, still absent in Peru, but he proved less interested in the immediate dispute than in the opportunity that the crisis seemed to offer to revamp Colombian institutions in a form more to his liking.

Bolívar knew that Venezuelan regionalism was not the only problem to be faced. There was similar, if less critical, unrest in Ecuador. The efforts of liberal-minded congressional representatives to subject the military more fully to civilian courts were seen by the latter as an affront. And much of the clergy resented legislation designed to curb church influence, such as measures closing small convents and promoting secular education. As a committed freethinker, Bolívar did not oppose the objectives of these first anticlerical measures, and as one who supported total abolition of slavery, he definitely opposed the campaign of slaveholders to water down the free-birth law passed by the Congress of Cúcuta in 1821. But he felt that many of the reforms adopted were premature, thus needlessly promoting unrest, and he assigned part of the blame to Vice President Santander, a man who had dropped out of law study to fight for independence but as chief executive surrounded himself with ardent young lawyers as helpers and advisers. What the country needed, in Bolívar's view, was a stronger executive, a less assertive legislature, and a partial rollback of overhasty reforms. He also hoped to see some form of a new constitution that he had drafted for Bolivia adopted in the Republic of Colombia. Its central feature was a president serving for life and appointing his successor. Some other features were highly liberal, but what attracted attention was the call for a life-term president, who in the Colombian case would obviously be himself.

Bolívar journeyed back from Peru to Colombia in September–November 1826. He found little real support for introducing his constitutional panacea, but he solved the Venezuelan rebellion by meeting with General Páez in Venezuela in January 1827 and pardoning him, as well as by promising to call a convention to reform the existing constitution in some way. That September Bolívar returned to Bogotá and resumed the presidency of Colombia. However, the Congress of Ocaña, which met in April–June 1828, ultimately dissolved with nothing accomplished. Bolívar then yielded to demands that he assume a personal dictatorship "to save the republic." It was a mild dictatorship, which had strong support from the military, especially the Venezuelan officers who dominated the upper ranks. He further enjoyed support from the church, which hoped that he would reverse recent anticlerical measures and was not disappointed. Although there was no clear-cut division along social lines, Bolívar's chief civilian supporters tended to come from long-established, aristocratic families, in effect his own class, whereas more of his opponents represented an emerging upper class of previously peripheral regions, such as Antioquia and eastern New Granada.

Santander, who came from one of those peripheral upper-class families, had since Bolívar's return aligned himself with the opposition and helped block progovernment initiatives at Ocaña. Once the dictatorship was established, he was given the option of diplomatic exile as minister to the United States, and he accepted, but before he could depart, some of his supporters attempted to assassinate Bolívar. The plot failed, and Santander, although not directly involved, was tried and condemned to death but instead was sent into nondiplomatic exile. In the aftermath, the dictatorship hardened, but opposition increased, especially when it became known that Bolívar's ministers were sounding out opinion at home and abroad on the possibility of recruiting a European prince to become king whenever Bolívar died or retired. Bolívar was not a party to the scheme, having gone south from Bogotá in December 1828 to deal with a local uprising and brief conflict with Peru. Yet he was blamed, and the monarchist intrigue caused the greatest backlash of protest in his native Venezuela, where a new revolt began before the end of 1829. This time Venezuela went all the way to secession.

In New Granada (the traditional name for the Colombian provinces carried over from the dissolved United Provinces of New Granada), there was virtually no support for an attempt to retain Venezuela by force. Instead, many New Granadans were happy to see the Venezuelans go. Under these circumstances, the more moderate elements of Bolívar's party took charge in Bogotá, even admitting some of the recently repressed Santanderistas to a share of power. Bolívar resigned the presidency, intending to go into voluntary exile, but in December 1830, before he could set sail, he died at Santa Marta on the coast. By that time, Ecuador had followed Venezuela's example to become an independent state.

Many of those who suffered repression during Bolívar's final dictatorship were slow to forgive, so that the division between his supporters and opponents foreshadowed, at least in part, subsequent party alignments in Colombia. Nevertheless, from his time to the present, virtually all Colombians have accepted his preeminence among the founders of the nation. Political liberals, including in due course the founders of the Liberal Party (PL), deplored most of what Bolívar did in that dictatorship but had no trouble finding things to approve in his earlier words and actions. Conservatives, naturally including founders of the Conservative Party (PC), tended to see the dictatorship as a necessary evil that Bolívar himself regarded as temporary, while emphasizing his consistent support for strong executive power and latter-day rapprochement with the church. Certain twentieth-century right-wing extremists lauded the dictatorship as a positive good, while present-day leftists claim him as forerunner and assert that they are striving to complete the work that he left unfinished. The leftists point to Bolívar's condemnation of slavery, rhetorical defense of Amerindian rights, and often keen analysis of social inequality in his statements to argue that he would have carried out a true social revolution if he had not been thwarted by selfish oligarchs, by which they chiefly mean the faction of Santander. Their analysis conveniently ignores the fact that Bolívar retained the support of the very cream of the traditional aristocracy. There is, in any case, a Bolívar for every conceivable ideological taste.

New Granada: Weak State, Strong Parties, 1832–63

In April 1830, an assembly meeting in Bogotá adopted a new constitution for the Republic of Great Colombia. It bore little resemblance to the one Bolívar drafted for Bolivia, even though he at one time had placed his hopes on this assembly to reform Colombian institutions in line with his ideas. The constitution of 1830 strengthened the executive and increased the presidential term (even if not to life) but was little different in fundamentals from that of 1821, and with the republic already in process of dissolution, it was an exercise in futility. The rump that was left of Great Colombia—present-day Colombia plus Panama—reconstituted itself as the Republic of New Granada (1832–58), and in 1832 it adopted another constitution closely following the 1821 model. The new charter slightly liberalized the conditions for suffrage and gave the provincial assemblies a limited right to enact ordinances on local affairs. One of its articles abolished the *fuero*, a royal charter bestowing special judicial privileges on the military. There was no similar action on the ecclesiastical *fuero* because the clergy was still too powerful to antagonize unnecessarily. But the prestige of the military had suffered in New Granada from overly close association with Venezuelan influence during Bolívar's Republic of Colombia. In addition, many top officers, being Venezuelan, had gone home after the collapse of the union. The military establishment was thus reduced in size and vulnerable, and its treatment in the first New Granadan constitution was a foretaste of the subordinate role it would continue to play in Colombian history.

The weakness of the military was a characteristic common among Colombian state institutions generally. The country's broken topography and primitive transportation made it difficult, if not impossible, to assert effective control in outlying areas. No cart roads existed anywhere outside the cities, and regular steam navigation on the Magdalena, the main artery connecting the coast with the interior, did not take hold until the 1840s. Improvements in transport infrastructure—or any ambitious governmental activity—would have cost money, which was not readily available, for the central administration operated on an annual budget of about one and a half pesos (still roughly equivalent to U.S. dollars of the time) per capita. Local governments had even smaller resources.

Fiscal poverty reflected, in turn, the underdeveloped state of the economy, in which the vast majority of the population labored farming crops, raising livestock for domestic consumption, or producing primitive handicrafts. Foreign trade per capita was the lowest among Latin America's larger countries, and this in itself was a major reason for fiscal poverty because customs duties were the leading source of revenue. New Granada began independent life with a single important export, gold, exactly as in the colonial era, but gold mining employed few people and had few linkages to the rest of the economy. Native, and some foreign, entrepreneurs looked intermittently for other exports that might stimulate wider economic growth, and these efforts led to a succession of speculative booms in tobacco, quinine, and certain lesser commodities. None would have lasting success until the expansion of coffee cultivation at the end of the nineteenth century and beginning of the twentieth; until then, with brief and partial exceptions, stagnation was the rule.

Only limited options were thus available when Santander (president, 1832–37) returned from exile to become the first elected president of New Granada (see table 2, Appendix). He was more cautious than in the 1820s in pushing liberal reforms, but he promoted education while holding down military expenditures. At the end of his term, Santander gave evidence of his legalistic bent by accepting the defeat of his chosen candidate and turning the presidency over to José Ignacio de Márquez Barreto (president, 1837–41), a former collaborator whom he now opposed. Most of their differences were minor, but Santander objected to Márquez's conciliatory gestures toward the former Bolivarian faction, with which he proceeded to share power once in office. When an assortment of malcontents rose up against Márquez in the so-called War of the Supreme Commanders (1840–42), Santander refused to give his blessing. However, most of his personal followers and the more intransigent liberals did back the uprising, and it became a watershed in the evolution of the Colombian political system. The threat to his government caused Márquez and moderate liberals who shared his views to tighten their alliance with the former Bolivarians, who in return gave crucial military support. Formal Liberal and Conservative parties did not exist until midcentury, but they were present in embryo in the forces arrayed on either side of this first of independent New Granada's civil wars.

Early conservative leaders, or Ministerials as they were called initially, were slightly more distinguished socially than their adversaries, and each faction was stronger in some regions than others, but there were no significant differences in economic interest or social policy. Neither faction was necessarily averse to economic liberalism. Differences revolved instead around constitutional and ecclesiastical issues. Having won the civil war, the Ministerials in 1843 adopted still another constitution, which strengthened central control over provincial authorities, whereas their opponents increasingly flirted with federalism. The Ministerials also invited the Jesuits, expelled from the Spanish Empire by Charles III, to return to New Granada, with a view to their playing a key role in secondary education and defending the country's youth against dangerous new doctrines. In this, they demonstrated their intention to forge a close relationship with the Roman Catholic Church, both from religious conviction and from a belief in its importance as a force for social and political stability. By contrast, their opponents hoped to resume the course of religious reform begun at the Congress of Cúcuta in 1821 and interrupted by Bolívar's dictatorship. Unfortunately for the Ministerials, however, in 1849 divisions in their camp allowed the opposition candidate, General José Hilario López Valdéz (president, 1849–53), to triumph. It was during this presidential campaign that the contending factions adopted definitively the terms Liberal and

Conservative and that the parties bearing those names can be said to have taken shape.

The victory of López and the Liberals can be attributed not just to the failure of government supporters to agree on a candidate but also to their alliance with artisan groups antagonized by the tariff legislation adopted during the administration of the last Ministerial president, Tomás Cipriano de Mosquera y Arboleda (president of New Granada, 1845–49; president of Colombia, 1861–63, 1863–64, 1866–67), which sharply reduced duties on imported manufactures. The alliance was strictly opportunistic, as López and the Liberal high command were not truly protectionist. They were lawyers, merchants, and landowners, much like their Conservative counterparts, and they had no stake in domestic manufacturing and in principle favored an opening to foreign trade. Yet the alliance held together long enough for the Liberals to enact a sweeping set of reforms. They again expelled the Jesuits, abolished the last vestiges of slavery and the colonial tobacco monopoly, authorized provincial assemblies to divide up Amerindian communal lands into private plots, reduced the standing army to a maximum of 1,500 men, and abolished libel laws for the printed (but not yet the spoken) word.

The capstone of this flurry of reforms was the constitution of 1853. It introduced for the first time unqualified freedom of worship and universal male suffrage, although the latter aroused misgivings among many Liberals for fear of clerical influence over the uneducated masses. The new constitution implemented a quasi-federalist system; it reversed the limitations on provincial authority contained in the constitutional reform of 1843, and provincial governors, although still regarded as agents in some sense of the national executive, were henceforth to be elected locally. The Liberal government did not, however, satisfy the protectionist demands of its artisan allies. New tariff legislation brought in a slight increase in import duties, but not enough to make a significant difference. Nor were thwarted protectionists the only source of political discontent. Conservatives, of course, had been unhappy all along, and in 1851 they launched a foolhardy rebellion. It was suppressed easily, but the more moderate or pragmatic elements of the Liberals were also convinced that ideologues in the Congress and administration were pushing their reform agenda too far and too fast, thereby undermining the foundations of law and order. A good many Liberal military officers took the same view, and on April 17, 1854, one of them, General José María Dionisio Melo y Ortiz, staged a coup d'état. The coup succeeded in overthrowing López's successor, José María Obando del Campo, who was president for the second time in 1853–54 and another Liberal general. The ousted president had been unhappy with the latest developments but too indecisive to do anything about them.

Melo ruled only about eight months, with the support of one faction of Liberals and of the artisans, who were particularly enthusiastic in his defense. Opposition came in the form of an alliance of Liberal and Conservative leaders, whose banner was the defense of constitutional legality but who at the same time rallied together in fear of the threat to social order posed by Melo's artisan allies. This partnership of ruling groups against their social inferiors would be cited repeatedly in the future, as a precedent for putative alliances of elite Liberals and Conservatives to thwart social change. By December 4, 1854, Melo's mild dictatorship had been defeated. Then, instead of restoring Obando, whom they distrusted, the victors formed a coalition government in which Conservatives increasingly gained the upper hand. When the next presidential election was held in 1856—the first to be decided by universal male suffrage—it was won by a civilian Conservative, Mariano Ospina Rodríguez (president, 1857–61). He defeated both the Liberal Party candidate and former President Mosquera, who renounced his previous associates to run as candidate of an improvised National Party that would soon be absorbed by the Liberal Party.

Official returns in the 1856 election would suggest that 40 percent of adult males participated. Undoubtedly, some of the votes tallied were fraudulent, but the results nevertheless demonstrated the extent to which the population had become aligned with one party or another. In the case of Conservatives, often the local priest recruited his flock on their behalf; or a local potentate of some sort—a leading landowner or a petty official—might recruit for either side. But no matter how initial allegiances took shape, they remained remarkably constant, passed down from generation to generation in such a way that small towns that voted Conservative or Liberal in 1856 were likely to be voting the same way a century later. Inherited party affiliation likewise generally determined on which side one participated or gave passive support in case of civil war. Although the reach of the state was limited, the parties blanketed the country, instilling in their adherents an instinctive loyalty that easily could trump obedience to a government of the opposite persuasion.

The extreme frequency of elections under the 1853 constitution, held at different times for all sorts of local and national offices, contributed to the early consolidation of party affiliations. And although the constitution did not introduce outright federalism, it was soon being amended to transform specific parts of the country into "states" with substantial powers of self-government. Panama, which had never felt much affinity with the rest of New Granada, was the first to receive such status, but other sections demanded and achieved the same, until in 1858 the ambiguous nature of the country's administration was tidied up by adoption of the first frankly federalist constitution. It was adopted during the Conservative administration of Ospina, whose party had been gradually warming to the idea of federalism, among other reasons because it seemingly guaranteed the Conservatives control of regions where they were strongest, regardless of who held power in Bogotá. However, before long the Liberals accused Ospina of failing to faithfully observe the new system and rose up in what would be the nation's only full-fledged civil war (as distinct from civil or military coup) to succeed in toppling a government. The war lasted from 1859 to 1862, and when it was over the provisional head of state was General Mosquera, now fully transformed into paladin of the Liberal cause.

A Failed Federalist Utopia, 1863–85

During the last stage of the civil war, in 1861, the Liberals changed the name of the country from Granadine Confederation (as in the 1858 constitution) to United States of New Granada (Estados Unidos de Nueva Granada, 1861–63). This action was followed by the adoption, in 1863, of another constitution that restored the name Colombia (more specifically Estados Unidos de Colombia, 1863–86) and took federalism to remarkable extremes. The new charter divided the nation into nine states, which could exercise any functions not expressly reserved to the central authorities. They could raise their own militias and, if they saw fit, issue their own postage stamps. They alone determined who had the right to vote, and more than half used this authority to retreat from the recent universal male suffrage, which had not worked out wholly to the Liberals' satisfaction. The constitution could be amended only by unanimous consent of all states. And the national president was elected on a basis of one vote, one state, for a period of only two years with no possibility of immediate reelection. This weakening of the presidential office resulted not just from theoretical considerations but also from the Liberals' real distrust of their current leader, Mosquera, whose undoubted ability was accompanied by a certain tendency toward megalomania.

The 1863 constitution took individual rights to similar extremes. Now there was no possible limit on the spoken word. In addition to abolishing the death penalty, the constitution guaranteed citizens' right to bear arms and to practice freedom of religion, at least in principle. However, the Liberals were not quite prepared to leave the Roman Catholic Church to its own devices, and therefore the charter endowed both national and state governments with vague supervisory authority in religious matters. Moreover, Mosquera had not waited for the constitution to be enacted before issuing decrees that yet again expelled the Jesuits, who had returned under Ospina's presidency, seized most church property, and (with certain exceptions) legally abolished the religious orders of monks and nuns.

The latest burst of anticlericalism was in part to punish the clergy for supporting the Conservatives in the recent civil war. It drove a further wedge of bitterness between the parties, and it consolidated the image of Liberal impiety among the Conservative rank and file. Had elections been free and fair, the Conservatives surely would have returned to power, for without much doubt they were the majority party at the time. Intent on staving off any such disaster, the Liberals engaged in rampant electoral manipulation. Nevertheless, the opposition was not totally excluded; much of the time it controlled one or two of the states, and it had some share of influence elsewhere by exploiting divisions in the Liberal camp. The ruling Liberals established a somewhat better record as far as basic civil liberties were concerned. And when Mosquera, who was reelected a last time in 1866, showed insufficient respect for constitutional technicalities, the Liberals summarily deposed him in May 1867. The Liberals also made a few attempts to promote social and economic development, despite the constitutional straitjacket in which they had placed the national authorities.

In Colombia, as throughout Latin America, publicists and politicians saw railroad construction as one key requirement. U.S. concessionaires had opened a first rail line, over the Isthmus of Panama, in 1856. In present-day Colombia, the first route was a short line completed in 1871, connecting the river port of Barranquilla with a point on the Caribbean to bypass the treacherous mouth of the Magdalena. Other railroads followed: most were short, supplementing river transport, and built by foreign entrepreneurs in return for subsidies and privileges granted by state or federal governments. For the federal authorities to be concerned with railroads at all, outside Panama, it was necessary to stretch the constitutional article restricting them to the promotion of interoceanic commerce. But they were well within their rights in 1878 in approving a concession for French interests to construct a canal across Panama, and in 1882 work actually began—which the French never finished.

Another area of earnest but limited accomplishment was education. The present National University of Colombia was founded in 1867. The need was much greater, however, in primary education, where little had been accomplished since the days of Santander; an illiteracy rate of more than 80 percent was an obstacle to almost any aspect of modernization. Accordingly, the Liberals in 1870 adopted a measure declaring primary education free and obligatory, as well as religiously neutral. New normal schools trained the necessary teachers, and experts from Germany imparted the latest pedagogical methods. However, this ambitious program required collaboration—not always forthcoming—between federal and state governments, and adequate resources were unavailable at either level. Thus, net progress was far from matching the contemporaneous push for popular education in Argentina. And although ecclesiastical backlash was a problem in Argentina also, it was much more severe in Colombia. Even though a provision existed for supplementary religious instruction to be offered by church representatives to children whose parents requested it, much of the clergy and devout Roman Catholic laity saw the Liberals' education initiative as heretical or worse.

Agitation over public education contributed to the outbreak of a brief but bitter civil war between Conservatives and Liberals in 1876. The government prevailed, but this was only one of an almost constant round of civil conflicts. Most were struggles for the control of particular state governments, pitting Conservatives against Liberals or simply different Liberal factions (with or without Conservative help) against each other; and the national authorities, taking a strict interpretation of states' rights, usually let the fighting run its course. Few people took part in general, casualties were few, and not much property was destroyed. However, the climate of insecurity clearly worked against the creation of new wealth. The state of public order thus contributed to a growing reaction against the Liberal regime, in which dissident Independent Liberals received support from the Conservatives and in 1880 saw their foremost leader, Rafael Núñez Moledo (president, 1880–82, 1884–86, 1887–88, 1892–94), elected to the presidency.

Núñez received further support from the artisans, to whom he offered and delivered a modest amount of tariff protection. He hoped to increase Colombia's options by stimulating domestic industry, and he also expanded the government's economic role through creation of a national bank. But the requirement of unanimity among the states for any amendment of the 1863 constitution thwarted his planned strengthening, or Regeneration, of the nation's political institutions—as in his slogan "Regeneration or Catastrophe!" After stepping down from the presidency at the end of his two-year term, he returned to office in 1884; and this time he had better luck. The doctrinaire Radical faction of Liberals, fearing he would try to change the constitution illegally, launched a preemptive revolt in 1885 that Núñez crushed, with massive help from the Conservatives.

Rafael Núñez Moledo,
(president, 1880–82, 1884–86,
1887–88, 1892–94), as illustrated
in Harper's Weekly *71 (1885): 52*
Courtesy Prints and Photographs
Division, Library of Congress,
Washington, DC

He then felt emboldened to declare that the constitution of 1863 had "ceased to exist."

Continuity and Change in Social Relations

Neither the rise and fall of federalism nor the frequent civil warfare had much impact on social structures. A federal system did provide more employment for politicians and officeholders than a strictly centralized one, thus continuing an expansion of opportunities of public service that began with independence. Yet it was hard to penetrate the upper strata without some formal education, which the vast majority still did not receive. In some Latin American countries (and to some extent during the independence struggle in Colombia), military prowess might be enough to propel an able individual of humble origin to positions of power, although not necessarily social esteem; but the weakness of the military institution made this a less promising path of advancement in Colombia. Once the veterans of independence died or retired, the generals of the civil wars tended to be lawyers or landowners who dabbled in fighting part-time.

The institutional reforms carried out since independence had done little to increase social mobility. The reform of most sweeping social significance might seem the abolition of slavery, but it was a gradual process, and there were no programs to help former slaves improve their material condition. The conversion of Amerindian communal land into private smallholdings, supposedly to imbue the recipients with a proper entrepreneurial spirit, apparently did not make much difference in most of the country. In the southwest, where the Amerindian presence was greatest, their objections caused state authorities to hold off implementing the policy. Neither did the series of commodity export booms, in products such as tobacco and quinine, have much impact on basic social structures, other than enriching some speculators and middlemen. However, one phenomenon of long-term significance during the mid-nineteenth century was the movement of settlers from Antioquia in the northwest into adjoining sections of the Cordillera Central. The traditional view of this process as one of homesteading by sturdy independent farmers was idealized, for speculators and intermediaries likewise found opportunities in colonization projects. Even so, campesino smallholders were the predominant settlers, who would eventually serve as the backbone of a new and more lasting industry, coffee.

Social as well as economic stagnation was still the rule, and most Colombians were illiterate, poorly housed, and all too subject to disease and early mortality, but they seldom went hungry. Vacant land was available for farming, and food of some sort was generally abundant. And in material—if not social—terms, class differences were less pronounced than they would become later. Members of the country's small upper and middle sectors could read and write and were proud of their lighter skins and (when possible) distinguished pedigrees, but by European standards their homes were meanly furnished, and the total assets even of the wealthiest were unimpressive. Moreover, because few luxury goods were produced locally, such commodities had to be brought from overseas and in most cases carried up the Magdalena, then over primitive mountain paths (sometimes on the backs of human carriers) before reaching their destination—at a vast increase over the products' original prices. This situation was beginning to change with such improvements as the introduction of steamboats on the Magdalena and the gradual accumulation of wealth from commerce or otherwise; meanwhile, to be rich in Bogotá was not the same as to be rich in Boston or Bordeaux.

Political Centralization and the Church–State Alliance

The Regeneration proposed by Rafael Núñez had much in common with the positivist program of order and progress in evidence elsewhere in Latin America during the late nineteenth century. Núñez was not a military man and avoided overt dictatorship, but he was prepared to make arbitrary arrests or close opposition newspapers when he felt the cause of order required such action. Above all, after declaring the constitution of 1863 null and void, he convoked a national council of delegates to draft a very different replacement,

*The National Cathedral on the
Plaza de Bolívar, Bogotá
Courtesy Inter-American
Development Bank
(David Mangurian)*

which was formally adopted in 1886 and would last more than 100 years—an exceptionally long life for any Latin American constitution. It exchanged the ultrafederalism of the 1863 charter for an equally extreme centralism, under which the president named the governors of the departments (as the former federal states were now called), and the governors in turn named all the mayors. Whatever party controlled the national presidency could thus control every departmental and municipal executive position in the country. The departments did have elected assemblies, but with very limited power. Naturally, the country could no longer be called the United States of Colombia but was now once again simply the Republic of Colombia, as it had been in the days of Bolívar. In addition, the sweeping definitions of individual rights in the old constitution were replaced by carefully restrictive wording in the new. The death penalty, abolished in 1863 as incompatible with the right to life, was reinstituted. Suffrage requirements were unified on a nationwide basis, and literacy was again required for national (not local) elections. The presidential term was lengthened, too, and with immediate reelection permitted. Núñez himself took advantage of these electoral changes to enjoy two more consecutive terms, one by vote of the constitutional convention and the other by popular election. But immediate reelection was subsequently forbidden again and was unavailable to any president until Álvaro Uribe Vélez (president, 2002–6, 2006–10) in 2006.

Although a religious freethinker himself, Núñez was convinced that to put law and order on a sound footing, it was necessary to end the conflict between clergy and anticlericals. In view of the institutional strength of the Roman Catholic Church and its hold on popular sentiment, he saw no way to do this other than by accepting the church's terms. The resulting religious settlement was contained partly in the new constitution itself and partly in a concordat signed with the Vatican the following year. There was no retreat from religious toleration per se, but the church was compensated for seizure of its properties, religious orders were legal again, and along with the restoration to the church of other miscellaneous privileges, the settlement provided that public education must be conducted in accordance with Roman Catholic doctrine. Divorce, which the Liberals had legalized, naturally was forbidden, and remarriages of divorced persons were retroactively annulled, even though the latter change affected Núñez himself.

As one more step toward the consolidation of order, Núñez hoped to overcome Colombia's bitter partisan rivalries by combining his Independent Liberals with like-minded Conservatives in a new National Party. In practice, however, many Independents drifted back to the main body of liberalism, incensed not only at the new constitution and religious concordat but at their members' almost total exclusion from power. They were denied all executive positions, and, thanks to the prevalence of fraud and intimidation, allowed to win the merest handful of seats in deliberative bodies. It was indeed ludicrous that only two Liberals could be found in the House of Representatives (Cámara de Representantes) as of the late 1890s. For their part, the Nationalists eventually became just another faction of the Conservatives, opposed by the self-styled Historical Conservatives, who tended to regard Núñez and Vice President Miguel Antonio Caro Tovar (acting president, 1894–98), who came to office on Núñez's death in 1894, as overly harsh politically and guilty of gross economic mismanagement. They complained of monetary inflation resulting from excessive issues of paper money and objected vigorously to an export tax introduced in 1895 on coffee, which was becoming an ever-more important export commodity but was trading in a world market of declining prices.

The War of the Thousand Days and Loss of Panama, 1899–1903

The combination of economic malaise and dissension within the Conservative camp emboldened Liberals to launch another uprising, starting on October 17, 1899, and lasting three years—hence called the War of the Thousand Days. It featured two massive engagements, the first won by the revolutionists and the second by government forces, after which the stalled conflict degenerated into desultory campaigning and some vicious guerrilla warfare. In the midst of it, a bloodless coup in Bogotá by the Thirty-First of July Movement, a coalition of Conservatives and Liberals, deposed Caro's successor in favor of his vice president, José Manuel Marroquín Ricaurte (president, 1900–1904), but this development did not help the Liberals, who finally had to accept defeat. By a conventional though unverifiable estimate, 100,000 persons died in combat or indirectly as a result of the war, in a population of about 4 million. The war battered the economy and reduced the government to bankruptcy, which it sought to overcome by a flurry of hyperinflation. The three years of war also distracted and weakened the government just when it was involved in critical negotiations with the United States over the projected Panama Canal. The definitive agreement that ended the conflict was the Treaty of Wisconsin, signed aboard a U.S. battleship of that name off the Panamanian coast on November 21, 1902.

After the failure of the French canal enterprise, it became apparent that the U.S. government was the entity best able to carry the project to a successful conclusion. The United States was certainly interested, provided it had total control of the strip of territory the canal would pass through, and the Colombian government entered into an agreement satisfying this condition even while civil war raged. The agreement was submitted to the Senate of the Republic (Senado de la República) in Bogotá after the war was over but there faced bitter opposition as an infringement of Colombian sovereignty. Despite warnings from Panama that the isthmus would secede if the agreement fell through, the Senate rejected it unanimously, unrealistically hoping to obtain better terms. Instead, Panamanian politicians in league with foreign canal promoters declared independence in November 1903, and the United States made clear that it would not allow Colombia even to attempt to retake the isthmus.

A New Age of Peace and Coffee, 1904–30

The Presidency of Rafael Reyes

General Rafael Reyes Prieto (president, 1904–9) became the leader of a country that had just gone through a ruinous civil war and humiliating loss of territory. A highly pragmatic Conservative, he accepted the main lines of Núñez's political and religious settlement. However, recognizing the pressing need to conciliate the defeated

Liberals, Reyes proceeded to anger hard-line members of his own party by taking Liberals into his administration and revamping the electoral system to guarantee the opposition a reasonable number of seats in Congress, department assemblies, and municipal councils. To do so, in 1905 he arbitrarily dissolved the overwhelmingly Conservative Congress and convoked in its place a national assembly, which voted to extend his presidential term from six years to 10. Reyes was also quite prepared to take high-handed measures against his critics, and there were leaders in both parties who either never supported him or ultimately turned against him. Nevertheless, the Reyes presidency inaugurated a period of general internal peace, broken by sporadic bursts of political violence mainly in the backcountry and at election time. This period lasted until 1930 and offers one argument against the notion that a propensity to violence is a defining trait of the Colombian national character.

Reyes had other accomplishments. He introduced a military reform designed to professionalize the armed forces and take them out of politics, importing a Chilean training mission to pass on lessons the Chileans had learned from similar German missions. To place Colombian finances on a solid footing, he made a settlement with foreign creditors over debts that had fallen into arrears and replaced depreciated pesos with sound new currency at a ratio of 100:1. He sponsored tariff legislation that gave more effective protection to manufacturing industries than Núñez had offered; one beneficiary was the nascent textile industry of Medellín. Not least, he energetically promoted more railroad construction and other public works.

The scope of Reyes's achievements was still limited, of course, by sheer lack of resources. During his presidency, the railroad network increased from 561 to 901 kilometers, which in percentage terms was a sharp increase, but unimpressive for a country of Colombia's size. In addition, public works contracts and other public programs gave rise to serious allegations, whether well-founded or not, of official corruption. Because the dominant sectors of Colombian society had always been wary of anything approaching one-man rule, if only because it limited their own opportunities for status and influence, the authoritarian tendencies that Reyes undoubtedly displayed were a further reason for the growth of opposition. What brought matters to a head in 1909 and induced him to step down, however, was a wave of indignation set off by his failed attempt to restore normal relations with the United States, through a treaty that provided a modest indemnity for Colombia while requiring Colombia to recognize the independence of its lost territory. Public opinion, at least in the major cities, was not yet ready for this step.

The fall of Reyes was triggered, in part, by street protests in Bogotá, but Congress chose an interim successor, after whom presidents were again chosen by regular elections. Until 1930, they were still Conservatives—even one who ran as a Republican with wide Liberal support—so that the entire era has come to be known as the Conservative Hegemony. Elections were not wholly free and fair, but neither were they a mere farce. Public order suffered minor disruptions here and there, yet no one tried to overthrow the government by revolution. Memory of the War of the Thousand Days was one reason for such forbearance. Another was the fact that, thanks to Reyes's reforms, opposition Liberals and dissident Conservatives could always count on some share of representation; indeed, much of the time, as under Reyes, members of both parties held administrative positions. Even so, political affairs only went so smoothly because the economy performed in such a way as to give ambitious individuals something else to think about and to relieve, slightly, the government's chronic penury.

The Growth of the Coffee Industry

The biggest economic success was the takeoff of Colombia's coffee industry. Coffee planting had grown steadily in the late nineteenth century. At the same time, the center of the industry was shifting westward, from the Cordillera Oriental to Antioquia and adjoining areas of *antioqueño* colonization. Here, the pattern of smallholdings was ideally suited to production of the higher grades of coffee in which Colombia came to specialize. Paradoxically, recurring crises of coffee overproduction in Brazil also helped, by causing the Brazilian government to undertake programs of crop reduction and price stabilization that in practice gave other nations, such as Colombia, an incentive to increase their output. Shipping problems and temporary loss of the German market hindered the advance of coffee during World War I, but in the mid-1920s it accounted for roughly three-quarters of Colombian export value, and Colombia was then the leading producer after Brazil. Colombia had no serious rival for that second-place ranking until the rapid rise of Vietnamese coffee production at the end of the twentieth century.

Although overshadowed by coffee and centered in a coastal enclave around the port of Santa Marta, bananas were another rising export commodity. The exploitation of petroleum deposits in the central Magdalena valley was also underway, initially for the domestic market, but by 1930 petroleum was being exported on a modest scale. The new textile mills clustered around Medellín were importers of cotton rather than exporters of finished cloth, but their growing importance was an indication of Colombia's belated and still somewhat limited entry into the industrial age. They at least found an expanding home market, including among campesino families who until the rise of coffee could seldom afford factory-made cloth. Like coffee growing, textile manufacturing was almost entirely in Colombian hands, whereas the Boston-based United Fruit Company controlled the banana trade, and U.S. and British firms had a stake in exploiting Colombian oil.

The fact that Colombia's leading export industry, coffee—with at least some presence in all parts of the country and multiple linkages to other segments of the economy—remained under native control tended to mute the appeal of economic nationalism, in which respect Colombia differed from much of Latin America. Total foreign investment remained low, mainly because foreign capitalists saw even greater advantages elsewhere. Yet most leaders of both parties were favorably disposed toward foreign capital, however much they might question the details of a concession or specific actions of a foreign company. For this reason, the Colombian government showed increasing interest in the very thing that led to Reyes's downfall: full normalization of relations with the United States, which supposedly would demonstrate to outside investors that a friendly climate awaited them.

Relations with the United States

The man most closely associated with this renewed push for a settlement with the United States was Marco Fidel Suárez (president, 1918–21). The career of Suárez, the illegitimate son of a campesino woman and a schoolteacher, is one indication that class divisions in Colombia have not been quite as rigid as often stated. Ideologically, he was a stalwart Conservative and Roman Catholic traditionalist, yet Suárez admired the more open society of the United States and believed that Colombia's progress depended on close relations with the leading hemispheric power. He therefore worked for ratification of a revised treaty that normalized relations with both the United States and Panama and provided for Colombia to receive a US$25 million indemnity from Washington. When Suárez perceived that political opposition to him stood in the way of a favorable vote, he resigned the presidency altogether, and under his interim successor the treaty was approved.

In the United States, the oil industry had been the main private interest pressing for the treaty, in the hope that Colombia would now resolve issues involving the exploitation of subsoil resources in a peaceful and friendly manner. That hope was only partially realized, but the indemnity amount, although a paltry sum for the United States, was equal to 10 times the total of Colombian bank reserves. Nor was it the only influx of new money during the 1920s, as Wall Street bankers were eagerly handing out loans during those pre-Great Depression boom years, and in Colombia national and departmental governments alike took advantage. The most obvious result was a splurge of public works: new government buildings, roads, and, above all, railroads, which in 1929 totaled 2,434 kilometers. The spending spree had a generally stimulative effect on the economy. In some areas, where workers were in high demand for construction projects, wages rose so sharply that landowners were hard put to recruit the hands they needed.

Decline of the Conservative Hegemony

The stimulus from loans and indemnity was not evenly spread. Outlying regions felt little impact, and neither was all the money wisely spent. Railroads were pushed through vote-rich Boyacá Department, when there was still no rail link or even a passable highway connection from Bogotá to the nation's second city, Medellín. Moreover, a good bit of money ended up in the pockets of well-connected businessmen and politicians as fees or contracting profits, giving rise to the inevitable suspicion (as earlier under Reyes) of official corruption, which in turn dimmed the prestige of the Conservative rulers.

A further complication was social and labor unrest, in part a renewal or continuation of the artisans' struggle during the previous century for job security and benefits. While Suárez was president, a tailors' demonstration in Bogotá against the importation of military uniforms led to several deaths at the hands of the Presidential Honor Guard in what has been termed a baptism of blood of the Colombian working class. On coffee estates in the upper Magdalena valley, there were also outbreaks as tenants and sharecroppers defied landlords who tried to prevent them from selling on their own account. That struggle was not a serious problem in the chief growing regions, where small proprietors prevailed, but it was a harbinger of future agrarian tensions. Above all, labor trouble broke out in two rising industries dominated by foreign capital—petroleum and bananas. Tropical Oil Company, a subsidiary of Standard Oil of New Jersey, which obtained concession rights in 1916, faced militant union organization and two massive strikes during the 1920s. Worse still was the banana strike of 1928 against United Fruit, in which soldiers fired on strikers and by official admission killed at least 13 of them.

Colombian governments were not wholly insensitive to social problems, enacting a limited workers' accident-compensation law and a few similar measures. But these laws were little more than tokenism, and the inability to think of anything better than harsh repression to deal with the banana strike was just one indication of the ruling Conservatives' lack of fresh ideas. The year after that strike, moreover, brought the first impact of the world economic depression, in the form of falling prices for Colombian exports and the drying up of possible foreign credit sources. With a looming economic crisis added to the accumulation of other problems, the Conservatives themselves were increasingly disheartened. Unable to overcome a deep internal division, they fielded two unsuccessful candidates in the presidential election of 1930, one representing moderate Conservatives and the other reactionary Conservatives. Capitalizing on the Conservative divisions, the Liberals returned to power for the first time in almost half a century.

Reform Under The Liberals, 1930–46

Enrique Olaya Herrera (president, 1930–34) was a moderate Liberal who had served as an envoy to the United States under the Conservatives before being elected president. To ease the transition, he established a coalition government, with Conservatives in his cabinet and elsewhere, and in Bogotá bipartisanship generally prevailed. In some parts of the country, however, Liberals who had been accumulating grievances (real or imagined) during the long Conservative ascendancy now seized the opportunity to take revenge. The result was spreading violence, especially in the eastern departments, which came under control in 1932 only when a border conflict with Peru over Leticia, a Colombian outpost on the Amazon, induced members of both Colombian parties to set aside hostilities in the cause of national defense. The dispute was settled by direct negotiations in 1934, when Peru recognized Colombian sovereignty over the port.

Colombia weathered the Great Depression rather successfully. More than half of the population was still rural and able to feed itself, while a sharp fall in coffee prices was partially offset by increased volume. The Olaya administration followed an orthodox policy of cutting expenses while at the same time raising tariffs, measures that both saved foreign exchange that would have gone to imports and stimulated domestic manufacturing. The government did not show great interest in fundamental social or economic reform, although it did more than previous Conservative administrations. New legislation established the eight-hour working day and explicitly guaranteed the right of labor to organize. Also, Colombia finally gave married women the same rights as their husbands to dispose of property, but suffrage for women remained a topic too hot to handle, as a result of both traditionalist Roman Catholic views on the role of women and Liberal fears that women would be too prone to vote as their priests suggested.

Olaya's successor, Alfonso López Pumarejo (president, 1934–38, 1942–45), was more receptive to the demands for change being put forward by labor activists, avant-garde intellectuals, and the recently founded Communist Party of Colombia (PCC), whose support he accepted, without giving it any formal share of power. He abandoned coalition government and grandly titled his program the Revolution on the March. His main service to organized labor was simply to reject any notion of using force (as the Conservatives had done) against strikers and to side instead with the workers in labor disputes. He sponsored the first agrarian reform law for rural workers, the effectiveness of which is still debated but which was a symbolic step of some importance. Above all, López presided over a set of constitutional amendments that reintroduced universal male suffrage, declared that property rights were limited by social rights and obligations—thereby legitimizing more extensive government regulation of the economy—and eliminated the previous constitutional provision requiring public education to be always in accord with Roman Catholic doctrine. The extension of suffrage was, if anything, a help to the Conservatives, who were strongest in rural areas where illiteracy was higher, but the business sectors of both parties expressed concern over the treatment of property rights. Even more controversial was the education reform of 1936, which, by outlawing racial and religious discrimination in education, helped to reopen the struggle between clergy and anticlericals that caused such strife in the previous century.

Many even in López's party felt that he was moving too fast. The Liberal candidate nominated to succeed him—and who won easily, with Conservatives abstaining on the ground that their opponents would not allow a fair vote—was a more moderate figure, Eduardo Santos Montejo (president, 1938–42). Partisan rancor briefly was put aside, but it soon returned, and it intensified once López won re-election to a second term in 1942. Distracted by the economic shortages resulting from World War II and by the demands of wartime cooperation with the United States, which Colombia had readily agreed to while Santos was president, López this time launched few reforms but still faced the hostility of those offended by his earlier policies. He even had to face one coup attempt by disaffected military; it was unsuccessful, but nevertheless alarming, because Colombia had for many years experienced nothing of the sort. Shaken by the political agitation surrounding him, López resigned from office before completing his second term.

A passionate Francophile, Santos had looked to the United States to help support both France and Colombia and the rest of the world against Adolph Hitler. The United States, for its part, as it first prepared for and then entered the war, was anxious to assist reliable friends on its southern flank. Hence, the tightening of formal U.S.–Colombian relations—while reflecting the growth of economic and cultural ties and even a sort of ideological affinity between Colombian Liberals and U.S. Democrats—also had much to do with developments on the larger world scene. Once the war began, Colombia gave full cooperation to the United States both before and after Pearl Harbor. The Santos administration never declared war, but it expedited the supply of strategic materials and supported all proposals for hemispheric defense collaboration made at inter-American gatherings. Wartime collaboration with the United States eventually reached the point of an outright declaration of war on the Axis, made after López had returned to the presidency and technically in retaliation for German attacks on Colombian shipping in the Caribbean.

Liberals liked to blame the vehemence of Conservative opposition on the supposed influence of European fascism, and undoubtedly Hitler and Benito Mussolini favorably impressed some Conservatives. More Conservatives felt an affinity with the Spanish variant of fascism under Francisco Franco. More important than foreign ideology, however, was the sheer frustration felt by Conservatives over their loss of power. The major parties were in fact rather evenly matched, although with the balance beginning to tip in the Liberals' favor (thanks to the advance of urbanization, among other factors). Conservatives insisted that they were the true majority and were denied the power they were entitled to by Liberal chicanery. After making this charge, Laureano Eleuterio Gómez Castro (president, 1950–53) emerged as the party's national leader and with vitriolic passion denounced everything done by the Liberal regime.

As if Gómez's relentless opposition were not enough, the Liberal leadership found itself attacked on another front by a dissident Liberal, Jorge Eliécer Gaitán. A gifted lawyer and orator of middle-class origin, Gaitán espoused a social democratic program not much different from López's Revolution on the March, but he assailed his party's establishment as involved in a tacit alliance with its Conservative counterpart to ward off real change. He appealed in particular to the social resentment of the middle and working classes against the mostly well-born and lighter-skinned figures who staffed the higher levels of government and of all the nation's institutions. When he presented himself as candidate for president in 1946, Gaitán carried Bogotá and several other large cities, while the Liberal machine was able to control most smaller Liberal strongholds and deliver their vote to the party's official candidate. The two Liberal contenders between them received a majority of the vote, but thanks to their division the winner was the Conservative, Luis Mariano Ospina Pérez (president, 1946–50).

Things Come Apart, 1946–58

La Violencia

The Liberals' fall from power because of a party split was an exact reproduction, with party roles reversed, of the Conservatives' defeat in 1930. What came next also eerily resembled earlier events. Ospina, like Olaya previously, chose to ease the transition by forming a coalition government, and at the upper levels this approach at first worked reasonably well. In the backcountry, things were different; only this time reempowered Conservatives provoked trouble by setting out to avenge themselves on Liberals—and to make sure the Conservative Party would not again be cast into opposition. Outbreaks of violence spread through much of the country, so that what came to be called La Violencia (The Violence) actually began in 1946 rather than (as is sometimes said) on April 9, 1948, the day that the assassination of Gaitán set off the orgy of rioting known as the Bogotazo. The riots were not limited to Bogotá, but that is where the greatest destruction and loss of life occurred.

The official investigation identified Gaitán's murderer as an unbalanced individual acting on his own, and this remains the most likely explanation, but the Liberal masses assumed that he had been struck down by a Conservative conspiracy. They proceeded to loot stores owned by the oligarchy in the hope that the government would fall. The Liberal top command, which had shortly before withdrawn its members from Ospina's coalition in protest over mounting carnage in the countryside, briefly shared the latter hope. But Ospina refused to resign, the army gradually regained control in Bogotá, and the Liberal leaders reluctantly rejoined the government for the sake of restoring order in time of crisis or, in the view of Gaitán's hardcore followers, to form a united oligarchic front against the demands of the people. Violence did diminish in the immediate aftermath of

April 9, but it built up again, particularly as the date for new elections drew near. Before the next presidential vote, the Liberals again left the government and at the last minute withdrew their candidate on the grounds that, in the climate of violence, no fair election was possible. The Conservative most hated by the Liberals, Gómez, thus won the presidency unopposed in 1950, but in such a way that most Liberals refused to regard him as a legitimate ruler.

Except for the Bogotazo, La Violencia was overwhelmingly rural. It was also vicious, with atrocities freely committed by Conservative police or vigilantes as well as by Liberal guerrillas, who received no formal endorsement from party directorates but enjoyed widespread sympathy. In certain enclaves of PCC strength, self-defense forces arose that would develop into communist guerrilla bands. Gómez himself, who took office in 1950, proposed a long-term solution to Colombia's problems in the shape of a constitutional reform project that would have retained some democratic forms but showed obvious borrowing from Franco's Spain. Making little headway against the violence, however, he steadily lost support even within his own party. On November 5, 1951, Gómez, because of his delicate health, temporarily ceded power to his minister of government, Roberto Urdaneta Arbeláez. Hours after Gómez resumed his presidency on June 13, 1953, military leaders loyal primarily to former President Ospina replaced Gómez with General Gustavo Rojas Pinilla (president, 1953–57). Beneath the veneer of military nonpartisanship, Rojas was close to the Ospinista wing of the Conservative Party.

Repressed Liberals and all but hard-core followers of Gómez greeted the 1953 coup with sighs of relief. A few Liberals joined the government, and many Liberal guerrillas accepted Rojas's offers of amnesty; for a time, the level of political violence subsided. However, Rojas made no serious effort to win over the guerrillas, and eventually violence picked up again; it was also changing. The original political conflict between Liberals and Conservatives became increasingly blurred by elements of economic competition and sheer banditry, using the party labels as banners to cover actions carried out for material gain. Rojas tried brute force against those who failed to accept his overtures, but without much success, and so the death toll kept climbing. By 1957 it had reached a cumulative total on the order of 175,000, in a population that had grown by 40 percent since 1946 to more than 14 million. Meanwhile, a string of Rojas's arbitrary actions—together with allegations of personal enrichment—eroded his support among both Liberals and Ospinista Conservatives. In May 1957, he was overthrown by another coup, organized by civilian leaders of both parties in conjunction with

Colonial architecture in Cartagena
Courtesy Lorenzo Morales

45

members of the business elite. A provisional military junta took his place but turned the government over to a sui generis bipartisan coalition the following year.

Growth Amid Mayhem

Death and destruction dominated news from Colombia during the years of La Violencia, but other things were happening, including steady economic growth—in 1945–55 the GDP increased at an annual rate of 5 percent. This growth was fueled in part by favorable world prices for coffee, still by far the leading export, which in the early 1950s for the first time pierced the dollar-a-pound barrier (and, of course, a dollar then was worth much more). The Conservatives' generally probusiness stance encouraged domestic and foreign investment, although the Conservatives were willing for government to take a hand in the development process when they considered it in the national interest. When the Tropical Oil Company's concession expired in 1951, a state corporation, the Colombian Petroleum Enterprise (Ecopetrol), took over production from its wells, but Tropical still shared in marketing. At roughly the same time, the government established a Colombian steel industry in the mining town of Paz de Río in Boyacá Department; private enterprise had not yet shown sufficient interest even though steel was deemed a necessary aspect of modernization. There was also a further increase in protective tariffs, representing a more explicit commitment to import-substitution industrialization than had been shown by the Liberals in the Great Depression years. During 1945–55, industrial output grew at 9 percent a year.

Among the obvious winners from higher import duties were owners of the Medellín textile factories, who were generally good Conservatives. The interest of workers in those same factories was a chief concern of the Union of Colombian Workers (UTC), which was founded in 1946 with government support and Jesuit advisers and grew rapidly in the industrial sector. The older Liberal and communist unions, whose main strength had been in transportation and services, suffered harassment if not outright repression. But governments of the period also introduced a few innovations in social policy intended to benefit the working class. The Conservatives produced a scheme of industrial profit-sharing as well as the first social security legislation, albeit initially with very limited coverage. For his part, Rojas established a state welfare agency, part of whose mission was to offer relief to victims of La Violencia; it bore some resemblance to the Eva Perón Foundation in Argentina, a similarity that became more pronounced when Rojas placed his daughter in charge of it. His flirtation with the model of Peronist Argentina was likewise evident in his sponsoring of a new labor confederation that ostensibly rejected Colombia's traditional partisan feuding in favor of a populist ideology similar to Perón's Justicialismo (Fairness). However, this last effort was not very successful, and by angering not only the existing unions but also the church, which had ties with the UTC, it contributed to his overthrow. More lasting achievements of Rojas were the introduction of television, in 1954, and the final adoption of suffrage for women, by vote of a largely handpicked assembly. Rojas named the first woman to a cabinet post, but he held no election in which women could exercise their vote—that happened only after he left office.

Another development of La Violencia was increased urbanization, reflecting not just the pull of industrial employment and other urban opportunities but also the flight of campesinos from strife-torn rural areas. By the end of the 1950s, Bogotá had finally surpassed 1 million in population, and secondary cities grew rapidly as well, so that Colombia continued to be an exception to the common Latin American pattern of a single primate city vastly overshadowing the rest. Altogether the urban population was now close to equaling that of the countryside. This shift meant that a greater percentage of Colombians would have access to education and social benefits and also that the pace of all sorts of change was likely to accelerate, with consequences difficult to foresee.

The National Front, 1958–78

Instituting the Coalition Government

Those who engineered the fall of Rojas were determined to cure their country of the partisan animosities that first produced La Violencia and then led, indirectly, to Rojas's rather mild dictatorship. Their solution was the National Front (Frente Nacional), a bipartisan coalition whose system of government was first approved by plebiscite and would last through four presidential terms. Liberals and Conservatives would alternate in the presidency while equally sharing cabinet posts and other appointive offices. Positions in Congress, department assemblies, and municipal councils were likewise allocated equally to the two parties until the return of unrestricted electoral competition in 1974. But the other key aspect of the National Front, the equal sharing of appointive positions—in which more was at stake because far more people were involved—was extended another four years, so that the system formally expired in 1978. Even after that, much of it remained in effect.

The power-sharing plan succeeded brilliantly in its primary objective: Liberals and Conservatives no longer had an incentive to fight each other, and many lost interest altogether in their ancient rivalry. Political violence diminished sharply, thanks not only to the elimination of traditional antagonisms but also to a combination of military action and social assistance in specific areas. Furthermore, the charge most commonly made against the arrangement, that it stifled democracy by totally excluding other parties, is not entirely accurate. Quite apart from the relative insignificance of other parties in Colombia up to that point, they could still take part in elections by presenting themselves as dissident factions of either major party and competing for a share of that party's quota of seats in Congress or some other body. The communists continued to compete, and occasionally win election, by the expedient of calling themselves Liberals on election day. Even more successful was the movement headed by Rojas on his return from temporary exile and known as the Popular National Alliance (Anapo). It ran candidates under *both* party labels, put a sizeable contingent in Congress, and nominated Rojas for president in 1970, for a term that under National Front rules had to go to a Conservative. Combining populist appeals to leftist nationalism and Roman Catholic traditionalism——a mixture of "vodka and holy water," one critic observed—he came close to winning a plurality, in a race against three more conventional Conservative candidates. According to his supporters and some others, Rojas did win, but backcountry chicanery deprived him of the presidency.

The alleged electoral fraud in 1970 seriously weakened perceptions of the National Front's legitimacy. The system also had certain undesirable and unintended consequences. The internal factions of each major party competed for their party's guaranteed share of offices in a way that was often unseemly even though it could never affect the balance between the parties, all of which tended to discredit the political system generally. Apart from the Anapo phenomenon, which with the declining health of Rojas soon petered out after the 1970 election, party politics simply became less interesting. Indeed, in some quarters there was outright revulsion against the existing regime, to the extent that a varied assortment of disaffected Colombians threw in their lot with the leftist guerrillas that began to make their appearance just as La Violencia wound down.

One guerrilla organization was the pro-Soviet Revolutionary Armed Forces of Colombia (FARC), an outgrowth of earlier communist self-defense forces that never made peace with Rojas and survived the military offensives launched against them by the National Front. The FARC remained a largely campesino force, whereas the National Liberation Army (ELN), inspired by the Cuban Revolution, attracted more urban students and professionals. A smaller group, the Popular Liberation Army (EPL), was of Maoist inspiration. These were only the most important guerrilla forces, but by the mid-1970s all had seemingly been contained in large but remote areas where the presence of the state had been close to non-existent and where the guerrillas were mostly out of sight and out of mind.

Sociocultural Changes

The strength of leftist guerrillas was due in part to disillusion with the social and economic achievements of the National Front; yet these were hardly negligible. Alberto Lleras Camargo (president, 1945–46, 1958–62) was the first president elected under its terms. In 1945–46 Lleras Camargo had filled out the term of Alfonso López on the latter's resignation, and he then gained international prestige as the first head of the Organization of American States (OAS). Lleras Camargo now pushed hard for a new agrarian reform law, which passed in 1961. The purpose of the measure was to defuse social tensions in the countryside, and although its main aim was to resettle the landless—or those whose plots were simply too small to support a family—on public land rather than break up existing estates, there was provision for the latter as a last resort. The main implementation, combined with some co-optation of campesino organizations, came during the presidency of Carlos Lleras Restrepo (president, 1966–70), a cousin of Lleras Camargo and easily the most vigorous of all National Front executives, who surrounded himself with eager young technocrats. If subsequent administrations had shown the same interest in the problems of the peasantry, it might have been harder for the new wave of leftist guerrillas to gain a foothold; unfortunately, such was not the case.

Progress in education was more striking. The plebiscite creating the National Front specified that henceforth at least 10 percent of the national budget should be devoted to education, and the target was regularly exceeded. One result was that the illiteracy rate, which had been almost 40 percent, fell in two decades to around 15 percent. Secondary enrollments doubled, admittedly from a very low level, during the 1960s alone. Such quantitative improvements were all the more notable in light of the rapid increase of population numbers and thus of those needing schooling. The annual rate of population increase reached a record 3.2 percent in the 1960s, and the figure would have been higher except for legal and illegal emigration to oil-rich Venezuela. Colombian officials were perfectly aware of the problem this posed for adequate provision of public services. They accordingly adopted family-planning programs, which were necessarily low-key because of disapproval both from Roman Catholic traditionalists and from leftists who claimed to see a U.S. plot to limit the number of proletarian antiimperialists. But the programs were successful—by 1980 the rate of increase was roughly 2 percent, one of the sharpest declines registered in any country.

Official promotion of family planning was one sign of the declining influence of what had once seemed an all-powerful Roman Catholic Church. Another was the return of legalized divorce, even if only for persons married in a civil, not a religious, ceremony. However, the church itself was changing. As in other Latin American countries, there was a segment of the priesthood that not only responded to the Second Vatican Council's call for renewal but also embraced the new tenets of liberation theology (see Glossary). In a few cases, this element carried disenchantment with the existing order to the point of joining hands with Marxist revolutionaries. One such priest was the charismatic Camilo Torres Restrepo, who after enlisting in the ELN died in combat in 1966. As a whole, the Colombian clergy was probably more conservative than the continental average. But it was lower-case "conservative," for the automatic identification of Roman Catholic clergy with the Conservative Party was a thing of the past. Also gone was the rabid anti-Protestantism that led a good many priests during La Violencia to urge on the faithful in attacks against the country's small Protestant minority, considered beyond the pale as both religiously heretical and politically Liberal. Now it even happened that Roman Catholic priests and Protestant pastors might amicably take part in the same civic events.

In economic policy, the National Front indulged in no lavish spending to court popular support and reward followers, as under Latin American populist regimes, but neither did it set off runaway inflation. Net growth was most of the time unspectacular, but it was at least uninterrupted. Governments did continue to promote import-substitution industrialization, of which one result was the definitive establishment of a Colombian automobile industry during the 1960s. But export promotion was not neglected, with tax rebates favoring the emergence of Colombia as the world's second-ranking (after the Netherlands) exporter of cut flowers. The flower industry was based primarily in the area around Bogotá, which offered both a favorable temperate climate and easy access to international air transport as well as a significant increase in employment opportunities for women. Other aspects of economic growth, along with the spread of education, likewise helped more women to find work outside the home, and there was even one more legal change in women's status when mothers were finally placed on the same footing as fathers in authority over their own children (see Family, ch. 2).

The slow but steady economic growth and the sociocultural changes that accompanied it did not meet everyone's expectations, of course, particularly given that the National Front had been launched amid quite unrealistic hopes and promises of all kinds. The contrast with neighboring Venezuela and with the developed-world scenes in movies or in the ever-more-widespread medium of television also contributed to disappointment, and certainly much remained to be done. Educational coverage expanded, but the quality was too often poor. Infrastructure was sorely inadequate. A railroad from Bogotá to the Caribbean was finally completed in 1961, but there was no integrated rail network, and that which the country had was soon deteriorating as officials concentrated on building highways, which still were far from meeting its needs. Per capita income increased, and inequality in income distribution tended to diminish, thanks in part to the greater educational opportunities and the effect on the labor market of slower population growth. Yet in absolute terms, income inequality remained high, with far too many Colombians living well below the poverty line. Poverty was less extreme in urban areas, where an ever-greater proportion of Colombians lived, than in the countryside, but in the cities it was also more visible.

The Contemporary Era, 1978–98

The agreement to share government positions equally between Liberals and Conservatives expired in 1978. However, there remained a constitutional requirement to give the runner-up party an "equitable" share of appointments, and the next president—a Liberal politician of Lebanese descent, Julio César Turbay Ayala (president, 1978–82)—interpreted this requirement as meaning that he should give Conservatives a quota proportionate to their share of elected members of Congress. That amounted to roughly 40 percent. With two Liberals splitting their party's vote next time around, a Conservative, Belisario Betancur Cuartas (president, 1982–86), succeeded Turbay and reverted to the system of the two parties each having a half share of appointments. Single-party rule reappeared only when Conservatives declined to accept the slice of patronage offered to them by Virgilio Barco Vargas (president, 1986–90), the Liberal elected after Betancur. Barco was not displeased, feeling that bipartisan government, by diluting responsibility, had contributed to the decline of public confidence in the political system; indeed, he did not really try very hard for Conservative collaboration. In practice, however, there was no sharp difference between Barco's administration and those preceding it, and neither were there any longer significant policy differences between the traditional parties. The religious question, once hotly fought over, had disappeared from politics. Both parties supported the relative fiscal orthodoxy that spared Colombia the hyperinflation and unmanageable foreign debt afflicting various regional republics; and both were willing to maintain macroeconomic stability even at the expense of further investment in infrastructure and social services. Thus, the radical left was not wholly unjustified in regarding Liberals and Conservatives as two branches of a single establishment party.

Popular election of mayors, provided for in a 1985 constitutional amendment, did not necessarily improve the quality of local government, where entrenched clientelism (see Glossary) and, in most places, extreme fiscal penury were hard to overcome. Even so, local elections were a step toward greater openness, allowing anyone to compete for positions to which incumbents formerly were appointed by the governors, who in turn were appointed by the president. Although Conservatives were shut out of Barco's cabinet, when the reform first went into effect they won the mayor's office in both Bogotá and Medellín (thanks to Liberal divisions), while a new Patriotic Union (UP) party, with informal ties to the revolutionary left, picked up 16 mayoralties (out of 1,009 nationwide).

The Rise of Drug-Trafficking Organizations

Neither changes in the distribution of cabinet posts nor the election of mayors had much effect on the increasingly negative popular perceptions of the political system, and another reason for this was the sudden rise of the illicit drug industry. In Colombia as elsewhere, illegal drugs were nothing new, but in the Colombian case the rapid expansion of the drug trade in the last quarter of the twentieth century had obvious destabilizing effects. The phenomenon first attracted attention in the 1970s, when the isolated mountain range just south of Santa Marta, the Sierra Nevada de Santa Marta, became the source of large amounts of marijuana grown for the United States market, but this was a short-lived boom. Production did not cease, but the Colombian product was competing against improved North American cannabis, and counternarcotics efforts likewise took a toll.

More serious was the emergence of Colombia in the following decade as the leading supplier of cocaine. Colombia was not at first a major producer of the coca plant and its coca paste derivative, which came principally from Peru and Bolivia, but Colombia had comparative advantages as processor and distributor. The country's location in the northwest corner of the continent meant that shipments could easily be made to either coast of the United States and to Europe. In addition, entrepreneurial skills were rather more developed in Colombia, most notably in Antioquia, where it further happened that the textile industry was facing hard times because of an increase in contraband imports. It is thus not altogether surprising that, in the 1980s, what was loosely termed the Medellín Cartel gained notoriety as the world's leading supplier of cocaine. Within that cartel, the key player was Pablo Escobar Gaviria, who was not just a gifted entrepreneur but also a second-string Liberal politician, local philanthropist, and employer of squads to kill both inconvenient rivals and public servants intent on enforcing the laws. The most eminent victims of the cartel and its associates were the Colombian minister of justice, Rodrigo Lara Bonilla, who was assassinated on April 30, 1984, and, five years later, the Liberal reformist Luis Carlos Galán, who was the odds-on favorite to succeed Barco as president in the next election.

The excesses of the drug barons inevitably provoked countermeasures by the Colombian authorities, with eager U.S. encouragement. Escobar himself was induced to surrender, on promise of lenient treatment, but still escaped from his comfortable prison, although police tracked him down and killed him on a Medellín rooftop as he attempted to flee in 1993. Yet even before his death, the Medellín Cartel had lost its preeminence, thanks to the rise of the rival Cali Cartel plus assorted minicartels and independent operators. Drug-processing laboratories continued to be raided, shipments intercepted, and the occasional member of the drug industry extradited to face charges in the United States, but the narcotics problem did not go away. In fact, certain new elements entered the picture. One was the rapid increase of coca cultivation in Colombia itself, which ultimately outstripped Peru and Bolivia in production. Another was the increasing involvement of leftist guerrillas as well as of the paramilitary groups that arose to combat them. These forces generally began by extorting protection money from growers, processors, and exporters but increasingly took a hand themselves, at least in processing and commercialization. And, by the 1990s, Colombia was becoming an important source of heroin from opium poppies, although the country's role in supplying heroin was far more limited than in cocaine.

Coca plantings and most processing laboratories were in areas of scant state presence, so the scope of the illicit drug industry was hard to estimate and susceptible to frequent exaggeration. One often read that the drug lords "controlled" Colombia, but they were not even interested in controlling most of what went on—only in staying alive, out of jail, and not extradited to the United States. Partly because of declining world coffee prices, illegal drugs came to surpass coffee in export value but did not outstrip mineral exports—petroleum, coal, and nickel—which in the late twentieth century were gaining new importance. Nor did the drug industry ever come close to coffee as a source of employment. The influx of dollars from drug sales contributed to an upward revaluation of Colombian currency, which inevitably had an adverse effect on the nation's legal exports. Drug dollars may have helped Colombia maintain its exemplary record of foreign-debt service, although it can be argued that even this apparent benefit was offset by a loss of revenues from legitimate business and by the increase in police and security expenditures. By purchasing protection from government officials as well as guerrillas or paramilitaries, primary figures in the industry fostered official corruption, and by their willingness to use violent intimidation when corruption was not enough, they further demoralized the weak criminal justice system.

The Spread of Leftist Insurgencies

Among the negative consequences of the illegal drug industry, the most serious was the impulse it gave to the advance of leftist guerrillas (and their paramilitary counterparts). The most notable sign of a resurgence of the revolutionary left after its low point in the early to mid-1970s was the rise of a new group, the Nineteenth of April Movement (M–19). Typically led by disenchanted middle-class professionals, the M–19 was ideologically more moderate than other guerrilla forces—more social democratic than Marxist—and it specialized in urban operations. One such was its seizure on February 27, 1980, of the Dominican Republic Embassy in Bogotá with a party of ambassadors within; the standoff ended peacefully, after 61 days, with the grant of safe-conduct out of the country for the terrorists and payment of an undisclosed ransom. The M–19 overreached itself on November 6, 1985, when it seized the Palace of Justice, also in Bogotá. The outcome of an army counterattack was the death of all but a few of the hostage takers and many hostages, including half of the Supreme Court of Justice. Weakened and discredited, the M–19 subsequently agreed with the Barco administration to lay down arms and enter legal political competition, which for a time it did with conspicuous success.

A few other guerrilla organizations, including the EPL, also entered into demobilization agreements, but not the ELN and the FARC. After being nearly defeated, the ELN made a striking come-

Plaza de Bolívar, Bogotá, before the destruction of the Palace of Justice (not visible) on November 6–7, 1985. Seen in the background on the right is the National Capitol; in the foreground on the right, the mayor's office; and on the far left, the National Cathedral.
Courtesy Embassy of Colombia, Washington, DC

back largely because of its success in extorting the German firm constructing a pipeline to transport the oil from newly developed fields in the llanos. When that work was finished, the ELN kept on extorting funds from oil-industry suppliers and contractors, local government agencies, and private citizens, in the latter case through the act or mere threat of kidnapping for ransom. It took to applying similar tactics against other industries and in other parts of Colombia, although, like the M–19, it avoided deep entanglement with illicit drugs. The FARC did not show similar restraint. By far the largest revolutionary organization, the FARC became larger still as it branched out from the extortion of ranchers and other commonplace ways of raising money to selling protection to coca growers and processors and, ultimately, entering the drug business on its own account. With its bulging war chest, it could import arms and recruit idle youths at far better pay than offered by army or police. The ELN and the FARC continued to operate mainly outside urban areas, but they committed acts of terrorism in the cities from time to time, and the growing epidemic of kidnapping brought the conflict home to middle- and upper-class Colombians, living almost exclusively in the cities, in a manner not before experienced.

The areas under effective guerrilla control were increasing, although they tended to be peripheral and thinly inhabited. Almost no part of Colombia was wholly safe from a sudden attack on the local police station or the abduction for ransom of some wealthy citizen or even of the less wealthy—crimes sometimes perpetrated by common criminals copying guerrilla methodology. The problem thus seemed to be getting worse, even though Colombia's GDP and most social indicators were generally improving, at least until the mid- to late 1990s. And popular support for the FARC and the ELN, which had once been around 15 percent in some opinion surveys, declined almost to the vanishing point thanks to the steady degradation of guerrilla tactics. The improvement in guerrilla finances was naturally one reason for the paradox. To some extent, moreover, Colombia was paying the price for its success over the years in containing military influence. The armed forces (including the National Police) simply lacked the personnel and equipment needed to root out political and criminal violence—both drug trafficking and leftist insurgency—over a vast expanse of poorly connected regions. Human rights abuses by government forces became all too common, yet the attachment of the country's rulers to democratic forms ruled out the frankly dictatorial response used against guerrilla movements in the Southern Cone countries of Argentina, Brazil, Chile, and Uruguay. Neither had the government, or the general public, taken the problem seriously enough—until it was already out of hand.

Some of the guerrillas' victims chose to take matters into their own hands, unleashing a spiral of counterguerrilla violence. This phenomenon first gained attention in the early 1980s, when members of the Medellín Cartel formed the group Death to Kidnappers (MAS), in response to the foolhardy seizure of one of their loved ones by the M–19, and landowners of the central Magdalena valley, tired of extortions, banded together to rid the area of radical troublemakers by fair means or foul. MAS and similar groups in different parts of the country, conventionally dubbed right-wing paramilitaries, made little distinction between guerrilla fighters and real or alleged sympathizers, and one result was decimation of the ranks of the UP, including assassination of its leader who had run for president in 1986 and its presidential candidate in 1990 (slain before the election). The paramilitaries were not right-wing in any ideological sense, for they were a mixed assortment united only by hatred of the guerrillas. Like the latter, they sold protection and extorted and, if not already part of the drug industry, became entangled with it; they generally did not kidnap, but they committed countless massacres of suspected guerrilla supporters. Despite their unsavory reputation, paramilitary forces in some areas developed an unacknowledged alliance with the army and National Police, which, according to critics, relied on them to do their dirty work and were certainly less inclined to crack down on them simply because they shared a common foe.

New Departures and Continuing Problems

In the view of many Colombians, the epidemic of multifaceted violence resulted in considerable part from the rigidity of the country's institutions. The existing constitution, dating back to 1886 and holding a record in Latin America for longevity, was seen as part of the problem. Accordingly, President Virgilio Barco agreed to the holding of a referendum, in May 1990, in which an overwhelming majority of voters approved the holding of a convention to reform the constitution. President César Augusto Gaviria Trujillo (president, 1990–94), the Liberal who a few weeks later succeeded Barco (and who reinstituted coalition government), moved quickly to convoke new elections for members of the Constituent Assembly. Some jurists seriously questioned the legality of the procedure, but the elections were held, albeit with a disappointingly high abstention. The eventual outcome was the constitution of 1991, easily the most democratic in Colombian history and also the most complicated.

The new charter further reduced government centralization, for example, by specifying that departmental governors as well as mayors should be elected, although the governors' independent authority was still less than in a truly federalist regime. It revamped the electoral system, required that the Senate be chosen by proportional representation on a nationwide basis, supposedly to counteract the evil influence of local bosses, and provided for special representation in Congress of the Amerindian and Afro-Colombian minorities. It contained a long list of sweeping individual rights, such as the right to work and special rights of children and adolescents. There was even the right not to be extradited to the United States, because an article prohibiting extradition of Colombian citizens was written into the text on the understanding that in return the drug lords would mend their behavior. A procedure of *tutela* was established whereby citizens whose rights had been abused could seek a writ of protection against the offending party. The new constitution also completed disestablishment of the Roman Catholic Church by dropping any reference to Roman Catholicism as the religion of the nation, placing all denominations on an equal footing, and extending the relegalization of divorce, timidly granted for couples in civil marriage in 1976, to cover religious unions as well.

There was something in the new constitution to please almost everyone, and in its immediate aftermath the mood of euphoria was such that some Colombians hoped that the FARC and the ELN, recognizing the constitution's democratic and egalitarian bent, would agree to lay down arms and pursue their objectives peacefully under its framework. Alas, no such thing happened. Neither did the drug problem go away; on the contrary, it returned to center stage when narco-traffickers made massive contributions to the campaign chest of Gaviria's successor, Ernesto Samper Pizano (president, 1994–98), and for his entire term he labored under the resulting cloud of distrust. The degree of administrative decentralization entailed onerous transfers of funds from the national treasury to the regions, taking money from other urgent needs and handing it to local politicians who did not always use it properly. The *tutela* device corrected some injustices, but at the cost of further clogging an overburdened legal system. Other articles of the constitution, too, either did not live up to expectations or had regrettable unintended consequences. Thus, before long the amendment provisions were put to use in changing one article or another, including, in 1997, the prohibition of extraditions, which had vastly annoyed the United States. The basic framework nevertheless remained in place, while Colombians settled down to argue over other things.

Drugs and guerrillas remained at the forefront of public discussion and debate, for both problems appeared resistant to all attempted countermeasures. A newer source of controversy was the Colombian version of the neoliberal and globalizing policies adopted in so much of Latin America, with strong urging from Washington and assorted international agencies, during the last decade of the twentieth century. Some steps toward a greater opening (*apertura*) of the economy occurred earlier, but President Gaviria was the leader who firmly committed Colombia to this path. Restrictions on foreign trade and investment loosened, at first gradually and then more abruptly, and the flow of foreign goods and capital duly increased, even though deficiencies in Colombian infrastructure limited the impact of policy changes. Privatization, another aspect of the neoliberal agenda, was also limited both because it was politically impossible for the government to divest itself of Ecopetrol, the preeminent state enterprise, and because in Colombia the public sector was not a particularly large employer.

The reduction in tariffs and elimination of numerous controls affecting foreign trade did have some clearly positive effects: for

A sculpture donated by Colombian artist Fernando Botero at the entrance to Bogotá's Parque La Esperanza on 26th Street Courtesy Lorenzo Morales

example, the availability of inexpensive foreign ingredients for chicken feed led to more protein in the Colombian diet. However, in Colombia as elsewhere greater opening to the world economy favored those with specialized training over unskilled workers, and, more broadly, capital as against labor, with a resultant increase in socioeconomic inequality. And while in the agricultural sector, those most affected by the competition of imports were large-scale commercial producers, some of the loudest protests against *apertura* came from the indigenous and Afro-Colombian communities, whose own production was not greatly threatened but who had borne much of the brunt of continuing rural violence and seized upon the evils of globalization as an effective way to publicize their other, quite justified, grievances and frustrations.

Colombia thus ended the twentieth century a land of many contradictions. A popularly elected government was in place, with no chance of being overthrown, yet unable to assert effective control over much of the nation's territory. Among Latin American nations, Colombia held a record for most consecutive years of economic growth——stretching back to the 1930s and uninterrupted until 1999——but a majority of its inhabitants lived in poverty, and income distribution remained highly unequal. Colombians such as Gabriel Garc a M rquez in literature, Fernando Botero in painting and sculpture, and several performers of popular music were esteemed throughout the Western world, but the standard image attached to the country was one of violence and criminality. Among Colombians

59

themselves, there was a steady stream of emigrants seeking greater opportunities and security in the United States or other developed-world destinations. Nevertheless, the human and material resources for a turn for the better were clearly present.

*　　　　*　　　　*

On pre-Columbian history, Gerardo Reichel-Dolmatoff's *Colombia indígena* is a masterful overview, of which an earlier version in English is titled simply *Colombia*. On the colonial era, there is Anthony McFarlane's *Colombia Before Independence: Economy, Society, and Politics under Bourbon Rule*, and for the independence period, Rebecca Earle's *Spain and the Independence of Colombia, 1810–1825*. For the nineteenth century, Frank Safford's *The Ideal of the Practical: Colombia's Struggle to Form a Technical Elite* covers considerably more than its stated topic of technical education; James E. Sanders's *Contentious Republicans: Popular Politics, Race, and Class in Nineteenth-Century Colombia* is a recent analysis covering the second half of the century, particularly in the southwest; Jaime Jaramillo Uribe's *El pensamiento colombiano en el siglo XIX* is a classic history of ideas; and José Antonio Ocampo's *Colombia y la economía mundial, 1830–1910* analyzes one critical aspect of economic development. Charles W. Bergquist's *Coffee and Conflict in Colombia, 1886–1910* covers politics and economics in the transition from nineteenth century to twentieth. James D. Henderson's *Modernization in Colombia: The Laureano Gómez Years, 1889–1965* takes the story to the 1960s, and John W. Green's *Gaitanismo, Left Liberalism, and Popular Mobilization in Colombia* examines an abortive but significant left-Liberal movement at midcentury. On La Violencia in the later 1940s and 1950s, Germán Guzmán Campos, Orlando Fals Borda, and Eduardo Umaña Luna's *La Violencia en Colombia: Estudio de un proceso social* has not been surpassed. The most recent developments are covered in several excellent compilations of contributed chapters, including Eduardo Posada-Carbó's *Colombia: The Politics of Reforming the State* and Cristina Rojas and Judy Meltzer's *Elusive Peace: International, National, and Local Dimensions of Conflict in Colombia*. Two readily available general surveys of Colombian history are David Bushnell's *The Making of Modern Colombia: A Nation in Spite of Itself* and Frank Safford and Marco Palacios's *Colombia: Fragmented Land, Divided Society*. The second edition of the 11-volume *Nueva historia de Colombia* edited by Jaramillo Uribe, with the assistance of Alvaro Tirado Mejía, Jorge Orlando Melo, and Jesús Antonio Bejarano, offers contributions on topical themes by Colombian and some foreign specialists. Economic history is surveyed by William Paul McGreevey's *An Economic History of Colombia, 1845–1930* and the collaborative *Historia económica de Colombia*, edited by Germán Colmenares and José Antonio Ocampo. Although it goes only to the 1960s, the historical review of political development in Robert H. Dix's *Colombia: The Political Dimensions of Change* remains useful. (For further information and complete citations, see Bibliography.)

Chapter 2. The Society and Its Environment

COLOMBIA IS KNOWN FOR ITS DIVERSE ethnicities and cultures and its tradition of producing world-renowned novelists and artists, as well as for its disparate and spectacular geography, ranging from beautiful Pacific and Caribbean coastlines to the three awe-inspiring Andean cordilleras that divide the country between the coastal lowlands and the expansive eastern plains (llanos) and the dense Amazonian jungle of the southeast. Perhaps because of its Andean topography and sociocultural diversity, national unity has long eluded this divided nation.

Supposedly unifying factors are a common religion (Roman Catholicism) and language (Spanish) and a long tradition of constitutional government, with varying degrees of political stability. Nevertheless, the society has low levels of solidarity and social trust; citizens are too wary of each other to develop enough social cohesion to build an effective and functioning state. Instead, some scholars characterize Colombians as extreme individualists who are heedless of the social effects of their actions. Rather than identify with the state, which is seen as an institution distant from the people and of benefit only to those in power who control it, most Colombians limit their social bonding to families and small social circles.

Extreme regionalism—fostered by the country's geographical and sociocultural divisions—historically has prevailed over national cultural and political unity and made Colombia one of Latin America's most regionalist nations. As Rafael Núñez Moledo, president in the late nineteenth century, observed, Colombia "is not a single nationality, but a group of nationalities, each one needing its own special, independent, and exclusive government." Even longtime residents of Bogotá, the country's capital, retain their original departmental identification. Colombia's traditionally low levels of national identification and regard for the rule of law, combined with sharp socioeconomic inequalities and political exclusion, have made the country a very fertile ground for breeding endemic violence, illegal narcotics trafficking, corruption, and other social ills.

The country's internal armed conflict has been fraught with social and environmental degradation, much of it resulting from cultivation of crops of coca (the plant that is processed for cocaine) and poppy (the flower from which heroin is derived). Another by-product of the internal conflict, which has included terrorizing of campesinos and other rural residents by the illegal armed groups, has been massive displacement of the rural population and its movement to *tugurios* (slums) in cities. This forced displacement reflects not only a shift away from agriculture but also a flight from guerrilla and paramilitary terrorism and problems associated with military operations and occupations of towns. Yet rampant criminal violence is even worse. It is hardly reassuring that scholars such as Eduardo Pizarro Leongómez have pointed out that between 80 and 90 percent of Colombia's homicides have resulted from criminal rather than political violence. The total number of uniformed insurgents and paramilitaries is probably well under 25,000, whereas perpetrators of criminal violence—most of it carried out with impunity—probably number in the hundreds of thousands.

Other serious social problems include widespread child labor, child abuse and child prostitution, and extensive societal discrimination against indigenous people and minorities. Post-traumatic stress disorder has been common and untreated, with many of its victims among the vast numbers of displaced people (*desplazados*), including children. Trafficking in women and girls for the purpose of sexual exploitation is a major criminal industry in Colombia. Although the country's laws mandate economic and social equality of women with men, women in Colombia nevertheless continue to suffer from sexism and extensive societal discrimination.

Some social advances appear more mixed than clear-cut. The autonomous Comptroller General's Office (Contraloría General de la República) estimated that between 50 and 60 percent of the population remained in poverty in 2005. The World Bank figure for 2005 was 52.6 percent. The administration of Álvaro Uribe Vélez (president, 2002–6, 2006–10) cited a lower estimate that the number of those living below the poverty line had fallen to 49.5 percent of the population from 57 percent in 2002. The estimate of the Economic Commission for Latin America was also lower, at 46.8 percent of the population in 2005. Government estimates of extreme poverty indicated a reduction from 26 percent of the population in 2002 to 15 percent in 2005. The field of education too showed mixed progress. Enrollment in basic and primary education rose from 9.6 million children in 2001 to 10.9 million in 2005, while the figures for tertiary education increased from 1 million to 1.2 million in the same period. However, enrollment in secondary education in 2004 was only 54.9 percent, while enrollment at primary schools included 83.2 percent of pupils in the relevant age-group. In short, despite being resource rich and broadly literate, Colombia remains socially divided and troubled.

Physical Setting

South America's fourth-largest and Latin America's fifth-largest country, Colombia measures 1,138,910 square kilometers (including insular possessions and bodies of water), or nearly the same size as France, Germany, and the United Kingdom combined. Of this total, land constitutes 1,038,700 km^2 and water, 100,210 km^2. Located in the northwestern part of South America, Colombia is bordered by the Caribbean Sea to the north and the North Pacific Ocean to the west. With a total of 3,208 kilometers of coastline, it is the only country in South America with littorals along both the Caribbean (1,760 kilometers) and the Pacific (1,448 kilometers). Colombia claims a 200-nautical-mile exclusive economic zone, a 12-nautical-mile territorial sea, and jurisdiction over the continental shelf to a 200-meter depth or to the depth of resource exploitation. Colombia has international borders with five nations: Panama, Venezuela, Brazil, Peru, and Ecuador (see fig. 2).

In addition to its mainland territory, Colombia possesses or claims a number of small islands in the Caribbean Sea, located 189 kilometers off the coast of Nicaragua and 640 kilometers from the Colombian coast. These islands include the Archipiélago de San Andrés, Providencia y Santa Catalina, which forms the country's smallest department with a total land area of about 44 km^2 (Isla de Providencia, 16 km^2; Isla de San Andrés, 26 km^2; and Isla de Santa Catalina, 2 km^2). The department has jurisdiction over the following small, uninhabited outcroppings of coral banks and cays in the Caribbean: Cayos de Roncador, 65 km^2; Banco de Serrana, 500 km^2; Banco de Serranilla (80 km^2), which is mostly lagoons, 1,200 km^2; and Banco de Quita Sueño, 400 km^2. Several small Colombian islands also lie off the Caribbean coast southwest of Cartagena. These include the archipelago of Isla del Rosario (8.4 km^2), which consists of 27 tiny coral islands southwest of Cartagena; Isla San Bernardo (24.4 km^2), which is located off the coast of Sucre Department; and Isla Fuerte (6.2 km^2), which is located off the coast of Córdoba Department. In the Pacific, Colombian territory encompasses Isla de Malpelo (measuring only 0.14 km^2) lying about 430 kilometers west of Buenaventura, a port city that handles the largest single share of the country's imports. Nearer the coast, a prison colony is located on Isla Gorgona, and lying off this island's southern shore is the even smaller Isla Gorgonilla.

Colombia has had territorial disputes with Nicaragua, Venezuela, and, at least technically, the United States. The issue of Nicaragua's alleged sovereignty rights over San Andrés, Providencia y Santa Catalina and 50,000 km^2 of the archipelago's surrounding Caribbean waters has occasionally produced diplomatic flare-ups. In December

Figure 2. Topography and Drainage

2007, the International Court of Justice at The Hague ratified the Treaty of Esguerra–Bárcenas of 1928, under which Nicaragua recognized Colombian sovereignty over the Archipiélago de San Andrés, Providencia y Santa Catalina, and Colombia recognized Nicaraguan sovereignty over the Costa de Mosquitos.

Under the Treaty of Quita Sueño, signed on September 8, 1972 (and ratified in 1981), the United States renounced all claims to the banks and cays of Banco de Quita Sueño, Cayos de Roncador, and Banco de Serrana without prejudicing the claims of third parties. The U.S. Senate ratified the treaty in 1981. In the meantime, in December 1979, the new Sandinista government, emboldened by the extended delay, revived Nicaragua's longstanding claim over the reefs, including Banco de Quita Sueño and Banco de Serranilla, as well as the Archipiélago de San Andrés, Providencia y Santa Catalina. Although the United States recognized Colombian possession of Cayos de Roncador, Banco de Serrana, and Banco de Quita Sueño in 1981, it claims two small island areas also claimed by Colombia. One is Banco de Serranilla, an atoll located about 130 kilometers north–northeast of Nicaragua; it has an abandoned military station used by the U.S. Marine Corps during the Cuban Missile Crisis and an active lighthouse. The other is Bajo Nuevo (also called the Petrel Islands), a small, uninhabited, grass-covered reef of 234 km^2 with some small islets. Claimed by the United States in 1856 under the Guano Islands Act, Bajo Nuevo became a U.S. military site. Although most of the "guano islands" claimed by the United States in the area of San Andrés, Providencia y Santa Catalina were ceded to Colombia in 1981, it is unclear whether that is the case with Bajo Nuevo, which is also claimed by Jamaica.

To emphasize its claimed sovereignty over San Andrés, Colombia began building up a naval presence on the island, including an arsenal of Exocet missiles. In 2001 Nicaragua pursued its claim in the International Court of Justice. In July 2002, the dispute flared up when Nicaragua began offering offshore oil concessions near the disputed waters and asked the court to validate its claim. The court ruled in December 2007 that a 1928 treaty awarding Colombia the archipelago was valid. However, the court also allowed Nicaragua's claim to the waters around San Andrés—rich in fish and, potentially, petroleum—to move forward.

Colombia's long-running dispute with Venezuela is over substantial maritime territory lying off the Península de La Guajira and in the Golfo de Venezuela, an area of potential petroleum wealth popularly referred to by Colombians by its colonial name of the Golfo de Coquibacoa. The dispute is theoretically being resolved through prolonged bilateral negotiations, although elements of national prestige continue to make it a major issue in both countries. The dispute has centered on control over the entrance to the Golfo de Venezuela. The key to establishing this control has been ownership of the Islas Los Monjes, a chain of three small rock outcroppings lying at the gulf's northern mouth. Although now owned by Venezuela, these islands are located in the relatively narrow maritime zone claimed by

Colombia. The latter projects its maritime boundary on the basis of Colombian ownership of 36 kilometers of the gulf's 748-kilometer coast (the remainder is Venezuelan territory). In April 2009, the Colombian government dismissed as speculation Caracas news reports that the dispute was nearly resolved.

Geology

As in the rest of South America, a combination of external and internal tectonic, volcanic, and glacial forces over the aeons formed Colombia's present-day geology. Island-like outcroppings in the eastern llanos are visible remnants of Precambrian times when Colombia consisted of metamorphic rocks. During the 332-million-year-long Paleozoic Era, which began 570 million years ago, the ocean again invaded Colombia's Andean zone, as subterranean volcanic eruptions in the western part of the country spouted lava. In the Triassic Period of the 143-million-year-long Mesozoic Era, which began 240 million years ago, the sea that occupied the Andean zone separated into two parts after the Cordillera Central rose. Large layers of sedimentary rock were deposited during the Jurassic Period, which ended with great igneous activity. During the Cretaceous Period, the sea to the east of the Cordillera Central extended to Putumayo in the south, while subterranean volcanic activity continued to the west of the Cordillera Central. During the 63-million-year-long Tertiary Period of the Cenozoic Era, which began about 65 million years ago, the seas withdrew from most of Colombia's territory, and enormous granite masses formed along the Cordillera Occidental. The three cordilleras began to take shape 12 million years ago. The Cordillera Occidental and the Cordillera Central form the western and eastern sides of a massive crystalline arch, which extends from the Caribbean lowlands to the southern border of Ecuador. The Cordillera Oriental, however, is composed of folded stratified rocks overlying a crystalline core.

Tectonic movement of the cordilleras continues today, as evidenced by frequent seismic activity. Indeed, Colombia remains part of the Ring of Fire, an active seismic area that surrounds the Pacific basin. The country is located where three lithospheric plates—Nazca, Caribbean, and South American—converge, and their movement produces different types of geologic faults. Almost all of the country's many earthquakes in recent centuries have occurred in the mountainous and coastal regions. Recent major earthquakes include those in Popayán on March 31, 1983, and in the nation's coffee-growing belt on January 25, 1999; and one on March 6, 1987, on the border with Ecuador, measuring 7.0 on the Richter scale. Recent earthquakes that struck Colombia's Pacific coast areas have included one accompanied by a tsunami in Tumaco, Nariño Department, on December 12, 1979, measuring 7.9 on the Richter scale, the largest in northwestern South America since 1942; another on November 15, 2004, with a magnitude of 6.7; and one on September 10, 2007, measuring 6.8. Although construction standards are high for new buildings in the main cities, smaller cities and rural zones are particularly vulnerable to earthquakes.

Geography

Colombia's most prominent geographical feature is the Andes, with its three nearly parallel, trident-like cordilleras that divide the country from north to south between the coastal areas to the west and northeast and eastern Colombia. Although geographers have devised different ways to divide Colombia into regions, Colombian geographers prefer to divide the mainland territory into five major geographic or natural regions: the lowland Caribbean and Pacific regions; the Andean region, which includes the high Andes Mountains, the intermontane high plateaus, and the fertile valleys that are traversed by the country's three principal rivers; the llanos region, lying to the east of the Andes Mountains and bordered on the east by the Orinoco; and the Amazonian region, which is the tropical rainforest (*selva*) south of the llanos and the Ariari and Guaviare rivers that includes but is not limited to Amazonas Department (see table 3, Appendix). Colombia also has a very minor, sixth, insular region consisting of Isla de Malpelo and the Archipiélago de San Andrés, Providencia y Santa Catalina.

Caribbean Lowlands

The Caribbean lowlands consist of all of Colombia north of an imaginary line extending northeastward from the Golfo de Urabá to the semiarid Península de La Guajira in the northern extremity of the Cordillera Oriental adjoining the Venezuelan border, an area bearing little resemblance to the rest of the region. The Caribbean lowlands form roughly a triangular shape, the longest side being the coastline. Most of the country's foreign trade in general moves through Barranquilla, Cartagena, Santa Marta, and the other port cities along the Caribbean coast. Inland from these cities are swamps, hidden streams, and shallow lakes that support banana and cotton plantations, countless small farms, and, in higher places, cattle ranches. The Caribbean lowlands region merges into and is connected with the Andean highlands through the two great river valleys of the Magdalena and the Cauca; it is the second most important region in economic activity. Most of the Caribbean lowlands population is

71

concentrated in the urban centers and port cities, especially Barranquilla, Santa Marta, Cartagena, and Valledupar.

Swamps separate the Caribbean lowlands from the base of the Isthmus of Panama. What is sometimes referred to as the Atrato swamp—in Chocó Department adjoining the border with Panama—is a deep marsh, about 100 kilometers in width, that for decades has challenged engineers seeking to complete the Pan-American Highway. This stretch where the highway is interrupted is known as the Tapón del Chocó. Environmentalists have warned that the thick jungle of the Darién region, a lush rainforest with one of the highest degrees of biodiversity in the world, provides an essential natural buffer zone between Colombia and Panama. Although the Tapón del Darién (Darién Gap) is currently protected in both countries by its national reserve status, powerful free-trade lobbies have been pressuring for paving the gap in the highway. The Norwegian Refugee Council, a private foundation known for accurate reports, stated in April 2007 that "paramilitary groups have displaced thousands of indigenous and Afro-Colombian communities such as the Emberá and Waounan people in northwestern Chocó to pave the way for projects such as a planned transoceanic canal, an inter-American highway, oil-palm plantations, and logging." Opponents argue that, in addition to its adverse regional environmental consequences, completing the highway gap will only provide an easier route for smuggling drugs through what will still be an effectively lawless area. In 2008–9 Colombian guerrillas were increasingly retreating into Panama's Darién region to seek refuge, smuggle drugs overland, and recruit indigenous Panamanian youth.

Pacific Lowlands

The Pacific lowlands consist of a narrow, sparsely populated, coastal region of jungle and swamp with considerable, but little-exploited, potential in minerals and other resources. Population density is no more than five inhabitants per square kilometer. The population is mostly (80 percent) black, with the remainder consisting of mestizos (mixed white European and Amerindian ancestry), mulattoes (mixed black and white ancestry), and whites. Buenaventura is the only port of any size on the 1,306-kilometer coastline, making it a popular corridor for illegal narcotics shipments. On the east, the Pacific lowlands are bounded by the Cordillera Occidental, from which numerous rivers run. Most of the rivers flow westward to the Pacific, but the largest, the navigable Atrato, flows northward to the Golfo de Urabá, making the riverine settlements accessible to the major Atlantic ports and commercially related primarily to the Caribbean lowlands hinterland. To the west of the Atrato rises the Serranía de Baudo, an isolated chain of low mountains that occupies a large part of the region. Its highest elevation is less than 1,800 meters, and its vegetation resembles that of the surrounding tropical forest.

Andean Highlands

The Andean highlands region includes three distinct cordilleras, which constitute 33 percent of the country's land area. The Andes divide into cordilleras near the Ecuadorian frontier. They extend northwestward almost to the Caribbean Sea and in the northeast toward Venezuela. Elevations reach more than 5,700 meters, and some mountain peaks are perennially covered with snow. The elevated basins and plateaus of these ranges have a moderate climate that provides pleasant living conditions and in many places enables farmers to harvest twice a year. Torrential rivers on the slopes of the mountains are the source of major hydroelectric power potential and add their volume to the navigable rivers in the valleys. On the negative side of the ledger, Colombia's mountains provide a place of refuge for illegal armed groups that are associated with the cultivation of illicit crops, such as coca and poppy.

The Cordillera Occidental, which extends from the Ecuadorian border to the Golfo del Darién, is the lowest and least populated of the three main cordilleras. Its western slope is not as steep as that of the Cordillera Oriental. Summits are only about 3,000 meters above sea level and do not have permanent snows. Few passes exist, although one that is about 1,520 meters above sea level provides the major city of Cali with an outlet to the Pacific Ocean. The relatively low elevation of the Cordillera Occidental permits dense vegetation, which on its western slopes is truly tropical. The eastern side of the Cordillera Occidental, however, is a sheer wall of barren peaks.

The Cordillera Central also begins at the Ecuadorian border, where several volcanoes are located, including the 4,276-meter Galeras, which erupted most recently in February and June 2009. The Cordillera Central is the loftiest of the mountain systems. Its crystalline rocks form an 800-kilometer-long towering wall dotted with snow-covered mountains, all of which are volcanoes. There are no plateaus in this range and no passes under 3,300 meters. The highest peak in this range, the Nevado del Huila, reaches 5,439 meters above sea level. The second highest peak, Nevado del Ruiz, erupted on November 13, 1985, and more recently on April 15, 2008. Like the Cordillera Occidental, the Cordillera Central at its northern end separates into two smaller sierras, or *serranías*, in the shape of two-pronged forks.

The Cordillera Oriental begins farther north, branching off from the Cordillera Central at Las Papas node, in the general area where the Caquetá rises. The length and width of the Cordillera Oriental make it the largest of the three Andean chains, although, with elevations generally between 2,500 and 2,700 meters, not the highest. Farther north, around Cúcuta, near the border with Venezuela, the Cordillera Oriental makes an abrupt turn to the northwest. The highest point of this range, the Sierra Nevada de Cocuy, rises to 5,493 meters above sea level. The northernmost region of the range is so rugged that historically it has been easier to maintain communications and transportation with Venezuela than with the adjacent parts of Colombia. Abutting the Caribbean coast to the east of Barranquilla rises the Sierra Nevada de Santa Marta, an isolated, lofty mountain system; its slopes generally are too steep for cultivation. This range, which is a detached continuation of the Cordillera Oriental, includes Colombia's highest point at Pico Cristóbal Colón (5,776 meters). The other branch of the Cordillera Oriental tapers out at the Península de La Guajira.

The intervening high plateaus and fertile valley lowlands are where about 95 percent of the Colombian population resides. This intermontane region is traversed mainly by three river systems: the Atrato, Sinú, and Magdalena. The Cordillera Occidental is separated from the Cordillera Central by the deep rift of the 1,350-kilometer-long Cauca valley, which has an elevation of 1,000 meters. The 1,013-kilometer-long Cauca, which is the major tributary of the Magdalena, rises within 200 kilometers of the border with Ecuador and flows through some of the best farmland in the country. After the two cordilleras diverge, the Cauca valley becomes a deep gorge all the way to the Caribbean lowlands, where the Cauca finally flows into the Magdalena.

Between the Cordillera Central and the Cordillera Oriental flows the Magdalena, which is considered a world-class river. It rises in southwestern Colombia about 180 kilometers north of Ecuador at an elevation of 3,685 meters, where the Cordillera Oriental and the Cordillera Central diverge. It runs for 1,612 kilometers through 18 of the country's 32 departments before reaching the Caribbean Sea, providing a major transportation artery and the only natural source of interregional connection. The Magdalena's spacious drainage basin, which covers 257,438 square kilometers, or 24 percent of Colombia, is fed by numerous mountain torrents originating at higher elevations. (As a result of global warming, the once-prevalent snowfields at these higher elevations are rapidly disappearing.) The Magdalena is generally navigable for 990 kilometers, from its mouth in Barranquilla as

The agricultural village of Villapinzón, Cundinamarca Department
Courtesy Inter-American Development Bank (David Mangurian),
Washington, DC
Characteristic red-tiled roofs in Boyacá Department
Courtesy Lorenzo Morales

far as the town of Neiva, deep in the interior in Huila Department, but is interrupted midway by the rapids of Honda in Tolima Department, from which it becomes Colombia's principal riverine outlet to the Atlantic. The largest of the intermontane valleys, the Magdalena valley has a very deep floor that runs no more than about 300 meters above sea level for the first 800 kilometers from the river's mouth, rising to about 400 meters over the rest of the Magdalena's length.

As much as 79 percent of Colombia's population, including that of the country's four largest cities, listed in order of population—Bogotá, Medellín, Cali, and Barranquilla, as well as Bucaramanga—is located in the Magdalena watershed. Thus, this basin has a high demographic density of 120 inhabitants per square kilometer. Bogotá is located in the Cundinamarca subbasin on the western side of the Cordillera Oriental, at an elevation of 2,650 meters above sea level. In the Cordillera Oriental, three large fertile basins and a number of small ones provide suitable areas for settlement and intensive economic production. To the north of Bogotá, on the densely populated plateaus of Chiquinquirá and Boyacá, are fertile fields, mines, and some of the large industrial establishments that produce much of the national wealth. Still farther north, in the department of Santander, the valleys on the western slopes are more spacious, and agriculture is intensive in the area around Bucaramanga. Finally, the Cordillera Oriental, which separates the Magdalena valley from the llanos, has on its eastern slope one of the most biologically rich areas on the planet, helping to make Colombia one of the world's 10 most biologically diverse countries.

Eastern Llanos and Amazonia

The vast llanos and jungle areas east of the Colombian Andes total about 631,000 square kilometers, or 54 percent of the country's area, but Colombians view the eastern regions almost as alien zones. Despite the extensive size of eastern Colombia, less than 3 percent of the total population resides in the nine eastern lowlands departments, with a population density of less than one person per square kilometer.

In the northern part of eastern Colombia, the eastern plains, also known as the llanos or Orinoco region, total about 310,000 km^2. This region is unbroken by highlands except in Meta Department, where the Macarena Sierra, a branch of the Andes, is of interest to scientists because its vegetation and wildlife are believed to be reminiscent of those that once existed throughout the Andes. Raising cattle is by far the most common economic activity in the piedmont areas of the llanos near the Cordillera Oriental. However, although the llanos region was traditionally used to raise cattle, it is now the main oil-producing region.

The southern half of eastern Colombia, measuring 315,000 km², consists of the *selva*, or Amazonia. This region was of little economic interest until the emergence of the cocaine trade and the expansion of tropical coca-growing areas. In the Amazon basin, population density is only 0.24 inhabitants per square kilometer.

Many of the numerous large rivers of eastern Colombia are navigable and, in the Amazonian region, are the principal means of transportation. The Ariari and Guaviare rivers divide eastern Colombia into the llanos subregion in the north and the *selva* subregion in the south. In the llanos region, the Guaviare and the rivers to its north drain northeast into the basin of the Orinoco, the largest river in Venezuela. The rivers to the south of the Guaviare flow southeast into the basin of the Amazon, which originates at an elevation of 4,300 meters near Pasco, at Lauricocha, a Peruvian lake.

Climate

Being situated on the equator, Colombia has a striking variety in temperatures, mainly as a result of differences in elevation. Temperatures range from very hot at sea level to relatively cold at higher elevations but vary little with the season. Breezes on the Caribbean coast, however, reduce both heat and precipitation. The habitable areas of the country are divided into three climatic zones: hot (*tierra caliente*), below 900 meters in elevation and with temperatures usually between 24°C and 27°C (a minimum of 18°C and a maximum near 38°C); temperate (*tierra templada*), 900 to 2,000 meters, with an average temperature of 18°C; and cold (*tierra fría*), from 2,000 meters to about 3,500 meters, with annual temperatures averaging 13°C. In the high, bleak, treeless mountain areas (usually referred to as the *páramos*) above 3,000 meters, there are very cold temperatures, often between -17°C and -13°C. Some of Colombia's mountains are perennially covered with snow and ice above 4,600 meters.

Average monthly minimum and maximum temperatures range from 9°C to 21°C in March (the hottest month) and 8°C to 19°C in July and August (the coldest months). At low elevations, temperatures may vary between 24°C and 38°C. Changes in these temperatures (not rainfall) determine the seasons. There are alternating dry and wet seasons corresponding to summer and winter, respectively, although in Colombia the dry summer (*verano*) and wet winter (*invierno*) do not coincide with the North American seasons of the same names.

About 86 percent of the country's total area lies in the hot zone. Included in the hot zone, and interrupting the temperate area of the Andean highlands, are the long and narrow northern valley extensions, including those of the Magdalena valley and the smaller Cauca valley. The tree line marks the approximate limit of human habitation. The temperate zone covers about 8 percent of the country. This zone includes the lower slopes of the Cordillera Oriental and the Cordillera Central and most of the intermontane valleys. The important cities of Medellín (1,487 meters) and Cali (1,030 meters) are located in this zone, where rainfall is moderate, and the mean annual temperature varies between 19°C and 24°C, depending on the elevation. In the higher elevations of this zone, farmers benefit from two wet and two dry seasons each year; January through March and July through September are the dry seasons.

The cold or cool zone constitutes about 6 percent of the total area, including some of the most densely populated plateaus and terraces of the Colombian Andes, such as Bogotá itself and its environs. The mean temperature ranges between 10°C and 19°C, and the wet seasons occur in April and May and from September to December, as in the high elevations of the temperate zone.

In Bogotá average temperature ranges vary little, for example, 10°C–18°C in July and 9°C–20°C in February. The average annual temperature is 15°C, and the difference between the average of the coldest and the warmest months is less than 1°C. More significant, however, is the average daily variation in temperature, from 5°C at night to 17°C during the day.

Precipitation is moderate to heavy in most parts of the country; overall average annual precipitation is 3,000 millimeters. The heavier rainfall occurs in the Pacific lowlands and in parts of eastern Colombia, where rain is almost a daily occurrence and rain forests predominate. Precipitation exceeds 7,600 millimeters annually in most of the Pacific lowlands, making this one of the wettest regions in the world, especially in Chocó Department, which receives an average annual rainfall of nearly 10,160 millimeters. Extensive areas of the Caribbean interior are permanently flooded, more because of poor drainage than because of the moderately heavy precipitation during the rainy season from May through October. In eastern Colombia, precipitation decreases from 6,350 millimeters in portions of the Andean piedmont to 2,540 millimeters eastward. In contrast, the Caribbean coastal La Guajira Department is the driest place in Colombia, with an average annual rainfall of only 254 millimeters.

Environment

In recent decades, Colombia has made important progress in protecting its environment, not only by enacting laws and adopting new policies, but also by establishing a system of national parks and forest reserves covering more than 25 percent of the country. Article 79 of the 1991 constitution establishes that "It is the right of the State to protect the diversity and integrity of the environment, conserve the areas of special ecological importance, and develop education to achieve these ends." A 1993 law created the National Environmental System and a Ministry of the Environment to manage it. Subsequently, the requirements for obtaining an environmental license before starting any new infrastructure project were tightened. Also in the early 1990s, the government created more than 200 specially protected zones, most of which are forest areas and national parks. In addition to promoting reforestation projects, the government adopted fiscal incentives for the use of alternative energy sources and imports to reduce carbon dioxide (CO^2) emissions.

Although Colombia's CO^2 emissions are relatively low, they grew by 40 percent in the 1990s. As a non–Annex I Party to the Kyoto Protocol, Colombia is not bound by specific targets for greenhouse gas emissions. According to the *Human Development Report 2007/2008* of the United Nations Development Programme, Colombia, with 0.7 percent of the world's population, accounts for 0.2 percent of global emissions—an average of 1.2 tons of CO^2 per person. These emission levels are below those of other countries of Latin America and the Caribbean.

In the late 1990s, research by the International Center for Tropical Agriculture (CIAT) in Colombia showed that deep-rooted African grasses that are prevalent in the llanos region have enormous potential for slowing the buildup of CO^2, a major greenhouse gas, in the earth's atmosphere. The ability of these grasses to store large amounts of carbon in the soil means they can slow the global warming that has been linked to atmospheric buildup of CO^2, according to CIAT researchers. Other harbingers of global warming include the spread of disease-carrying mosquitoes. *Aedes aegypti* mosquitoes that can carry dengue and yellow-fever viruses were previously limited to below 1,006 meters of elevation but recently appeared at 2,195 meters in Colombia.

Colombia's environmental protection measures have been weakened as a result of the Ministry of the Environment restructuring in late 2002, when the government renamed it the Ministry of Environment, Housing, and Territorial Development and gave greater priority to business interests. Despite the setbacks, environmentalists helped to pressure Álvaro Uribe Vélez (president, 2002–6, 2006–10) into vetoing a forestry law approved by Congress (Congreso de la República) in December 2005 that had favored commercial exploitation of forests.

Air and water pollution is a growing health problem in Colombia, with half of the population living in cities of more than 100,000 inhabitants. Air pollution exceeds acceptable standards in the industrial corridors of Bogotá–Soacha, Cali–Yumbo, Medellín–Valle de Aburrá, Sogamoso, and Barranquilla. Only about one-third of the country's 1,120 municipalities have adequate treatment systems for contaminated water. Of Colombia's cities in general, 20 percent lacked sewerage as of 2006, constituting a serious environmental problem for the country. Insufficient drainage in most built-up areas and the disposal there of garbage in natural channels have contributed to frequent urban flooding. The Bogotá, one of Colombia's most heavily polluted rivers, flows into the Magdalena at the port of Girardot, transporting chemical residues from the cut-flower industry and tanneries. Pollution of the Bogotá has severely affected its fish population. In the 1970s, the annual catch of fish in the river was some 70,000 tons, but in the 1980s this amount shrank to 40,000 tons, falling further in the 1990s to 20,000 tons, and by 2007, to only 8,000 tons.

The United Nations Food and Agriculture Organization ranked Colombia second in Latin America and seventh in the world in terms of average annual renewable freshwater resources. Nevertheless, nearly 12 million Colombians have no access to clean water, and 4 million have only limited access, such as a public faucet. According to a 2004 survey of the Residential Public Services Superintendency (SSPD), only 72 percent of those receiving public services had water of potable quality. In some places, the water supply system's pressure is not adequate, increasing the risk of bacterial contamination. Colombia's governmental Institute of Hydrology, Meteorology and Environmental Studies predicts that, absent corrective action, 69 percent of the Colombian population will suffer from a lack of clean water by 2025. According to government estimates, 65 percent of Colombia's municipalities could face water shortages by 2015 because of soil erosion.

Colombia's forests cover about half of its territory, and in November 2007 the country had 11.6 million hectares in protected areas of the National Natural Parks System, or more than 10 percent of the national territory. Nevertheless, the country's abundant rivers and streams have long been degraded as a result of guerrilla sabotage of oil pipelines and the use of chemicals in the coca-refining process. Illicit drug crops grown by campesinos in the national parks of the Sierra de la Macarena and Sierra Nevada de Santa Marta have contributed to deforestation and soil and water pollution. Herbicides and pesticides used to eradicate the coca crop have had an adverse impact on farmlands. Fumigation efforts have been criticized for harming the health of Colombians and Ecuadorians, killing legal crops along with the illegal ones, poisoning the soil and water, and jeopardizing the growing of legal crops in the future. Ironically, spraying reportedly has the least effect on coca, and farmers often can resow coca only six months after spraying. The Human Rights and Displacement Consultancy (Codhes), an authoritative non-governmental organization (NGO) that works with Colombia's *desplazados*, claimed in early 2006 that at least 17,000 people had been displaced (perhaps only temporarily) by United States–backed aerial spraying of coca plantations. The U.S. Department of State reported that 171,613 hectares of coca and poppy crops were fumigated in Colombia in 2006.

Spraying also has had significant diplomatic consequences. It has heightened border tensions with Ecuador, in particular because of claims that Colombian spraying in the border area has damaged Ecuadorian land and imperiled human health. The densest concentration of coca cultivation for the Revolutionary Armed Forces of Colombia (FARC) in Colombia is reportedly in Nariño, next to the Ecuadorian border. Ecuador has demanded that Colombia cease aerial spraying within 10 kilometers of the border. Although the Uribe government has insisted that spraying drug crops with the toxic herbicide glyphosate is harmless, Ecuador's protests forced the Colombian government to revert to manual eradication of coca bushes in 2007.

Also of concern to environmentalists is timber exploitation in the jungles of the Amazon region and Chocó Department, which are estimated to contain up to 10 percent of the world's known species of flora and fauna. Moreover, average reforestation rates are low compared with other Latin American countries with big timber industries. Mining activity and clearing of land for cultivation and converting it to pasture for cattle raising are other causes of deforestation. Increased mining of gold, marble, and emeralds in tributaries of the Magdalena, such as the Cauca basin, have resulted in rapid soil erosion and increasing sediment loads. All these factors have contributed to the Magdalena being one of the top 10 rivers in the world in terms of sediment load. Studies of the Magdalena basin and other assessments of land-cover change in Colombia have shown a clear correlation between forest loss and expansion of agricultural land. Deforestation in the Magdalena basin is estimated to be among the highest in the world. It is considerably higher than the national average, which was estimated at 1.4 percent per year between 1985 and 1995. The percentage of forest cover in the Magdalena basin was estimated to have declined from 46 percent in 1970 to 27 percent in 1990, at an annual deforestation rate of 1.9 percent. Between 1990 and 1996, total forest cover in the basin declined by 15 percent, for an average annual loss of 2.4 percent.

Race and Ethnicity

Indigenous Peoples

Present archaeological evidence dates the earliest human habitation of South America to as early as 43,000 B.C. Anthropologist Tom D. Dillehay dates the earliest hunter-gatherer cultures on the continent at almost 10,000 B.C., during the late Pleistocene and early Holocene periods. According to his evidence based on rock shelters, Colombia's first human inhabitants were probably concentrated along the Caribbean coast and on the Andean highland slopes. By that time, these regions were forested and had a climate resembling today's. Dillehay has noted that Tibitó, located just north of Bogotá, is one of the oldest known and most widely accepted sites of early human occupation in Colombia, dating from about 9,790 B.C. There is evidence that the highlands of Colombia were occupied by significant numbers of human foragers by 9,000 B.C., with permanent village settlement in northern Colombia by 2,000 B.C.

Colombia's indigenous culture evolved from three main groups—the Quimbayas, who inhabited the western slopes of the Cordillera Central; the Chibchas; and the Caribs. When the Spanish arrived in 1509, they found a flourishing and heterogeneous Amerindian population that numbered between 1.5 million and 2 million, belonged to several hundred tribes, and largely spoke mutually unintelligible dialects. The two most advanced cultures of Amerindian peoples at the time were the Muiscas and Taironas, who belonged to the Chibcha group and were skilled in farming, mining, and metalcraft. The Muiscas lived mainly in the present departments of Cundinamarca and Boyacá, where they had fled centuries earlier after raids by the warlike Caribs, some of whom eventually migrated to Caribbean islands near the end of the first millennium A.D. The Taironas, who were divided into two subgroups, lived in the Caribbean lowlands and the highlands of the Sierra Nevada de Santa Marta. The Muisca civilization was well organized into distinct provinces governed by communal land laws and powerful caciques, who reported to one of the two supreme leaders.

The complexity of the indigenous peoples' social organization and technology varied tremendously, from stratified agricultural chiefdoms to tropical farm villages and nomadic hunting and food-gathering groups. At the end of the colonial period, the native population still constituted about half of the total population. In the agricultural chiefdoms of the highlands, the Spaniards successfully imposed institutions designed to ensure their control of the Amerindians and thereby the use of their labor. The colonists had organized political and religious administration by the end of the sixteenth century, and they had begun to proselytize among the Amerindians.

The most important institution that regulated the lives and welfare of the highland Amerindians was the *resguardo* (see Glossary), a reservation system of communal landholdings. Under this system, Amerindians were allowed to use the land but could not sell it. Similar in some respects to the Native American reservation system of the United States, the *resguardo* has lasted with some changes even to the present and has been an enduring link between the government and the remaining highland tribes. As land pressures increased, however, encroachment of white or mestizo settlers onto *resguardo* lands accelerated, often without opposition from the government.

The government generally had not attempted to legislate in the past in matters affecting the forest Amerindians. During the colonial period, Roman Catholic missions were granted jurisdiction over the lowland tribes. With the financial support of the government, a series of agreements with the Holy See from 1887 to 1953 entrusted the evangelization and education of these Amerindians to the missions, which worked together with government agencies. Division of the *resguardos* stopped in 1958, and a new program of community development began to try to bring the Amerindians more fully into the national society.

The struggle of the indigenous people on these lands to protect their holdings from neighboring landlords and to preserve their traditions continued into the late twentieth century, when the 1991 constitution incorporated many of the Amerindian demands. New *resguardos* have been created, and others have been reconstituted, among forest tribes as well as highland communities. The 1991 constitution opened special political and social arenas for indigenous and other minority groups. For example, it allowed for creation of a special commission to design a law recognizing the black communities occupying unsettled lands in the riverine areas of the Pacific Coast. Article 171 provides special Senate (Senado) representation for Amerindians and other ethnic groups, while Article 176 provides special representation in the House of Representatives (Cámara de Representantes): two seats "for the black communities, one for Indian communities, one for political minorities, and one for Colombians residing abroad." Article

356 guarantees Amerindian territorial and cultural rights, and several laws and decrees have been enacted protecting them. Article 356 refers somewhat vaguely to both "indigenous territorial entities" and indigenous *resguardos*.

By 1991 the country's 587 *resguardos* contained 800,271 people, including 60,503 families. The general regional distribution of these *resguardos* was as follows: Amazonia, 88; llanos, 106; Caribbean lowlands, 31; Andean highlands, 104; and Pacific lowlands, 258. They totaled 27.9 million hectares, or about 24 percent of the national territory. Colombia today may have as many as 710 *resguardos* in 27 of the 32 departments.

Descendants of indigenous people who survived the Spanish conquest live primarily in scattered groups in remote areas largely outside the national society, such as the higher elevations of the southern highlands, the forests north and west of the cordilleras, the arid Península de La Guajira, and the vast eastern plains and Amazonian jungles, which had only begun to be penetrated by other groups in the twentieth century. The Amerindian groups differ from the rest of the nation in major cultural aspects. Nevertheless, although some continue to speak indigenous languages (about 80 Amerindian languages survive), Spanish, introduced by missionaries, is the predominant language among all but the most isolated groups.

Anthropological studies and political interests relating to Amerindian issues have generated data about the ethnic groups that exist in Colombia. More than 80 identified ethnic groups or tribes remain, scattered throughout the departments and national territories. According to the Dallas, Texas–based SIL International (previously known as the Summer Institute of Linguistics), in 2005 Colombia had 101 known indigenous languages that fell into 14 linguistic families; 80 were living languages, and 21 were extinct. The Páez (also known as Nasa Yuwes) constitute the largest ethnic group, with about 123,000 people. Although routed, the Páez survived the Spanish conquest by retreating to their rugged mountain homeland in Cauca Department in the southwest of the country. The Wayuus (also known as Wayús or Guajiros) make up the next-largest group, with 73,000 people living in the semidesert of the Península de La Guajira in the country's extreme north. The Páez form a patriarchal society, whereas the Wayuus have a matrilineal system that determines descendancy, inheritance, property, and residence. The 15,000-member Emberá group forms another important community, living in the humid jungle of the Golfo de Urabá region in Chocó Department in the west near Panama. These three communities account for 56 percent of Colombia's Amerindian population. The

A Wayuu woman at work in the salt reserves of
Manaure, La Guajira
Copyright Santiago Harker

other 44 percent is made up of 77 different groups, many of which are in Amazonia; among them are several families that some might consider tribes sharing some cultural characteristics. They may number about 50,000 people speaking a considerable number of languages. The Amerindians from the Sierra Nevada de Santa Marta are another important group and one that shows strong social cohesion. They include the Arhuacos, Armarios, Coguis, and Cunas.

Although all Amerindian peoples in Colombia have had some contact with outsiders, the degree and effect have varied considerably. Some tribes, such as the Makus, Chiricoas, Tunebos, and roughly 3,000 remaining members of the Yagua tribe in the Amazonia rainforest, have remained very primitive nomadic hunting and fishing groups. One of the more isolated and hostile Amerindian groups, the Motil ns, in the northeastern lowlands, have been known to greet missionary groups and oil company employees encroaching in their territory with poisoned arrows and darts. Yet other groups are settled farmers with well-developed handicraft industries, and some of the most successful tribes have developed effective methods of raising cattle. Nonetheless, it was long difficult for Amerindians to retain land that they traditionally held, especially in the highlands where the competition for cultivable land is keenest.

85

Even the indigenous people in Amazonia have not remained immune from Colombia's armed conflict. Also, assassins have singled out Wayuu leaders in northeastern Colombia. A few tribes, most notably the Paez in southern Colombia, have managed to drive out the armed intruders using nonviolent civil-resistance tactics involving large groups. However, across the country tens of thousands of Amerindians have become refugees. By the end of 2007, in order to escape forced recruitment by the FARC, 406 members of 10 ethnic groups, mainly in the Mitú area along the Vaupés in Amazonia, had fled into neighboring Brazil, raising the total number of Colombian refugees seeking refuge in Brazil's border region over the previous four years to 4,000. According to the United Nations, some of the smaller tribes are on the verge of disappearing.

Racial Distinctions

Colombia's population is descended from three racial groups—Amerindians, blacks, and whites—that have mingled throughout the last 500 years of the country's history. Some demographers describe Colombia as one of the most ethnically diverse countries in the Western Hemisphere, with 85 different ethnic groups. Most Colombians identify themselves and others according to ancestry, physical appearance, and sociocultural status. Social relations reflect the importance attached to certain characteristics associated with a given racial group. Although these characteristics no longer accurately differentiate social categories, they still help determine rank in the social hierarchy.

Colombia officially acknowledges three ethnic minority groups: the Afro-Colombian, indigenous, and gypsy (Rom, or Romany) populations. The Afro-Colombian population consists of blacks, mulattoes, and *zambos* (a term used since colonial times for individuals of mixed Amerindian and black ancestry). A 1999 resolution of the Ministry of Interior and Justice acknowledged the gypsy population as a Colombian ethnic group, although gypsies were not recognized in the 1991 constitution (unlike the Afro-Colombian and indigenous populations). Estimates vary widely, but the 2005 census found that the ethnic minority populations had increased significantly since the 1993 census, possibly owing to the methodology used. Specifically, it reported that the Afro-Colombian population accounted for 10.5 percent of the national population (4.3 million people); the Amerindian population, for 3.4 percent (1.4 million people); and the gypsy population, for 0.01 percent (5,000 people).

The 2005 census reported that the "nonethnic population," consisting of whites and mestizos (those of mixed white European and Amerindian ancestry, including almost all of the urban business and

Bogotá pedestrians of various ethnicities
Courtesy Lorenzo Morales

political elite), constituted 86 percent of the national population. The 86 percent figure is subdivided into 49 percent mestizo and 37 percent white.

The census figures show how Colombians see themselves in terms of race. The actual percentage of Colombians of primarily European ancestry may be closer to 20 percent, but many people may identify themselves as white when they actually belong in the mestizo category. In any case, more than half of Colombians are mestizo. Moreover, those recognized as white do not necessarily have direct Spanish lineage. Rather, their whiteness is attributed to their self-perception of being white. Indeed, according to the late Colombian anthropologist Virginia Gutiérrez de Pineda, whitening (*blanqueamiento*) is a recurrent practice for social climbing (hierarchized *mestizaje*). She explained that frequently the mix of blacks and Amerindians with whites produces a loss of black and Amerindian phenotypic features that facilitates the assimilation into the "white tree."

The various groups exist in differing concentrations throughout the nation, in a pattern that to some extent goes back to colonial origins. The whites tend to live mainly in the urban centers, particularly in Bogotá and the burgeoning highland cities. The populations of the major cities are primarily white and mestizo. The large mestizo population includes most campesinos of the Andean highlands where the Spanish conquerors had mixed with the women of Amerindian chiefdoms. Mestizos had always lived in the cities as well, as artisans and small tradesmen, and they have played a major part in the urban expansion of recent decades, as members of the working class or the poor.

According to the 2005 census, the heaviest concentration of the indigenous population (22 to 61 percent) is located in the departments of Amazonas, La Guajira, Guainía, Vaupés, and Vichada. The secondary concentrations of 6 to 21 percent are located in the departments of Sucre, Córdoba, Chocó, Cauca, Nariño, and Putumayo. Amerindian communities have legal autonomy to enforce their own traditional laws and customs. Despite its small percentage of the national population, the indigenous population has managed to obtain nearly a quarter of the country's land titles under the 1991 constitution.

The black and mulatto populations have largely remained in the lowland areas on the Caribbean and Pacific coasts and along the Cauca and Magdalena. The Afro-Colombian population is concentrated primarily (21 to 74 percent) in the department of Bolívar and in the lowland parts of Cauca, Chocó, and Valle del Cauca departments, with secondary concentrations (16 to 20 percent) in Atlántico, Cauca, Córdoba, Magdalena, Nariño, and Sucre departments. In the Chocó region, they have largely replaced the Amerindians and constitute about 80 percent of the population.

A minute percentage of the insular population originated in Scotland and Syria. The population of the Archipiélago de San Andrés, Providencia y Santa Catalina, which Colombia inherited from Spain after the Spanish had overcome an initial British settlement, is mostly Afro-Colombian, including several thousand *raizal* (those with roots) blacks. Despite the length of time during which Colombia has had jurisdiction over them, most *raizales* on these Caribbean islands have retained their Protestant religion, have continued to speak an English-based Creole as well as English, and have regarded themselves as a group distinct from mainland residents. Indeed, a nonviolent *raizal* separatist movement has been growing increasingly vocal in this archipelagic department.

Since independence both Amerindians and blacks have continued to reside on the outskirts of national life, as much because of their class and culture as their color. As a group, however, blacks have become more integrated into the national society and have left a greater mark on it for several reasons. First, they had been a part of Spanish society since the Middle Ages, whereas Amerindians were new to Spanish social structures. The Spanish had long possessed Africans as personal servants and did not find them as alien as the

Amerindians they encountered in the New World. Moreover, it was more difficult for the blacks to maintain their original culture because, unlike the indigenous people, they could not remain within their own communities and did not initially have the option of retreating into isolated areas. Moreover, the blacks came from different areas of Africa, often did not share the same language or culture, and were not grouped into organized social units on arrival in the New World. Despite slave revolts, no large community of escaped slaves survived in isolation to preserve its African heritage, as did the maroons in Jamaica.

Finally, despite their position on the bottom rung of the social ladder, black slaves often had close relations—as domestic servants—with Spaniards and were therefore exposed to Spanish culture much more than were the Amerindians. Thus, blacks became a part—albeit a peripheral one—of Colombian society from the beginning, adopting the ways of the Spanish that were permitted them and learning their language. By the end of the colonial period, the blacks thought of themselves as Colombians and felt superior to the Amerindians, who officially occupied higher status, were nominally free, and were closer in skin color, facial features, and hair texture to the emerging mestizo mix.

Many blacks left slave status early in Colombian history, becoming part of the free population. Their owners awarded freedom to some, others purchased their liberty, but probably the greatest number achieved freedom by escape. Many slaves were liberated as a result of revolts, particularly in the Cauca valley and along the Caribbean coast. The elimination of slavery began with a free-birth law in 1821, but total emancipation was enacted only in 1851, becoming effective on January 1, 1852.

Those blacks who achieved freedom sometimes moved into Amerindian communities, but blacks and *zambos* remained at the bottom of the social scale and were important only as a source of labor. Others founded their own settlements, mainly in unsettled lands of the Pacific basin where they were called *cimarrones* (maroons). Those regions were very unhealthy, inhospitable, and dangerous. A number of towns, such as San Basilio del Palenque in the present department of Bolívar, and Uré in southern Córdoba, kept the history of revolt alive in their oral traditions. In the Chocó area, along the Pacific, many of the black communities remained relatively unmixed, probably because there were few whites in the area, and the Amerindians became increasingly resistant to assimilation. In other regions, such as the Magdalena valley, black communities had considerable white and Amerindian admixtures.

Descendants of slaves have preserved relatively little of their African heritage or identification. Some place-names are derived from African languages, and some traditional musical instruments brought into the country by slaves are used throughout the country. Religion in the black communities remains the most durable link with the African past. Wholly black communities have been disappearing, not only because their residents have been moving to the cities but also because the surrounding mestizo and white populations have been moving into black communities. Eventual absorption into the mixed milieu appears inevitable. Moreover, as blacks have moved into the mainstream of society from its peripheries, they have perceived the advantages of better education and jobs. Rather than forming organizations to promote their advancement as a group, blacks have for the most part concentrated on achieving mobility through individual effort and adaptation to the prevailing system.

Afro-Colombians are entitled to all constitutional rights and protections, but they continue to face significant economic and social discrimination. According to the 2005 census, an estimated 74 percent of Afro-Colombians earned less than the minimum wage. Chocó, the department with the highest percentage of Afro-Colombian residents, had the lowest level of social investment per capita and ranked last in terms of education, health, and infrastructure. It also continued to experience some of the country's worst political violence, as paramilitaries and guerrillas struggled for control of the department's key drug- and weapons-smuggling corridors.

Population and Urbanization

Population Growth Trends

At the outset of the twentieth century, Colombia's population was only 4 million. By 1950, however, after growing by 2 percent annually in the 1940s, it had nearly tripled to 11 million. Between the late 1950s and the late 1960s, Colombia had one of the highest population growth rates not only in Latin America but in the world—more than 3 percent annually, peaking at 3.4 percent in the 1950s. Since then it has had one of the sharpest declines. A contributing factor was a quiet government-funded contraception campaign, which the Roman Catholic Church tacitly agreed to tolerate as long as the government did not promote it openly (see Demography, this ch.). According to the 2005 census, the population growth rate during 2001–5 was 1.6 percent. In 2008 it was only 1.4 percent and was predicted to remain at this rate through 2010.

With an estimated population of 45.3 million in early 2010, Colombia is the third most populous country in Latin America, after

A mestizo agricultural worker
Courtesy Inter-American Development Bank (David Mangurian),
Washington, DC
An Afro-Colombian man in front of a bicycle-repair shop
Courtesy Inter-American Development Bank, Washington, DC

Brazil and Mexico. According to the most recent national census conducted by the National Administrative Department of Statistics (DANE), the national population was 42,799,491 on June 30, 2005. This adjusted figure took into account geographical coverage omissions but did not include Colombians living abroad, who totaled 3,331,107. By 2015 the population is projected to total 53.2 million.

Estimates of national population density (inhabitants per square kilometer) have varied, ranging from 34.5 per km^2 to approximately 39 per km^2 in 2006, but population distribution throughout the country varies widely. By 2005 the most populated departments were Atl ntico in the Caribbean region (700 inhabitants per km^2) and Quind o (332 per km^2), Risaralda (248 per km^2), Valle del Cauca (205 per km^2), and Cundinamarca (98 per km^2) in the Andean region. The least-dense departments are those in the llanos, generally having between one and 12 inhabitants per km^2, and the departments in Amazonia, the least-populated region of Colombia, with less than one person per km^2.

Immigration

Colombia has experienced little foreign immigration since the colonial period. Spain discouraged the admission of non-Spaniards into its colonies. After independence, civil wars and a lack of economic prospects deterred immigration. Colombia has had the fewest non-Spanish immigrants relative to the size of its population, especially few non–Roman Catholic ones, of any of Spain's former colonies, with the possible exception of Bolivia. Thus, Spanish values have influenced Colombian society throughout its history. For instance, the 1886 constitution, which remained in force with some amendments until 1991, aimed at strengthening *hispanidad*, and some critics even argued that it attempted to replicate the Spain of Philip II (king of Spain, 1556–98). This constitution was very inhospitable to non-Spanish, non–Roman Catholic immigrants, because it allowed the Roman Catholic Church to monopolize many civil procedures and to control public education. It is also significant that Colombia is one of the countries where it is most difficult to obtain a work permit and to become a naturalized citizen. The spouse of a Colombian citizen, for example, can easily acquire a resident's visa, but that does not allow the person to work.

The country generally lacked a clear policy on immigration but never favored it on a large scale. Those who entered from abroad came as individuals or in small family units. After World War II, the country tried to encourage the immigration of skilled technicians, but immigration laws gave preference to persons who supposedly would not jeopardize the social order for personal, ethnic, or racial reasons. Germans, Italians, and some other educated foreigners found acceptance in the upper class and frequently married into the white group. Spanish immigrants—many of them until recently members of the clergy—continued to trickle into the country. Residents from the United States were mainly in business or missionary work and without intention to naturalize. The government began to organize immigration in 1953, ostensibly to settle underdeveloped regions of the country, and, in 1958, specified procedures for the admission of refugees. Little was done, however, to implement these measures.

During the early twentieth century, Colombia's Caribbean coastal region experienced immigration coming from Europe and the Middle East, mostly from Lebanon, Palestine, Syria, and Turkey. A second wave of immigrants from these countries took place during World War II. The Arab immigrants, mainly Maronite Christians from Lebanon, gradually began to settle inland, except for Antioquia. About 45 percent of the inhabitants of cities such as Barranquilla, Cartagena, Maicao, and Santa Marta have Arab ancestry. The country's Arab population, which reportedly numbers about 200,000, has produced several members of Congress and the 1978–82 president, Julio César Turbay Ayala, who is of Lebanese descent, as well as pop star Shakira.

Regionalism

The Spaniards who settled Colombia came shortly after seven centuries of warring with the Moors and from a region of Europe where medieval traditions remained strong. Traditional premodern Spanish values were not conducive to respect of central government laws or authorities, and the isolation of many of the descendants of the conquistadors allowed them to remain fairly autonomous from the central government and to maintain many of their independent, antigovernment traits. These historical factors help to explain why Colombia long remained remote from modernizing ideas and technologies.

As a country of five distinct mainland geographic regions, Colombia is, not surprisingly, highly regionalist. The Colombian state gradually took shape during the nineteenth century as a loose coalition of four semiautonomous regions: the central Andean highlands, greater Antioquia, the Caribbean coast, and greater Cauca. The latter included the city of Popayán, long known as a center of elitist literary culture. In more recent times, as during La Violencia and the rise of the illicit drug industry, regionalism was reinforced through significant rural–rural migration that extended into the "empty lands" (*tierras baldías*), where many settlements were established outside state control. A diverse geography and resultant regionalism thus exacerbate the lack of communal feelings among the masses and provide little basis for national cohesion within any of their social groups.

Even with rapid urbanization and modernization, regionalism and regional identification continue to be important reference points, although they are somewhat less prominent today than in the nineteenth and early twentieth centuries. Whatever their class, Colombians are identified by their regional origins, within which are relatively well-defined ethnocultural groups; each of these groups has distinctive characteristics, accents, customs, social patterns, and forms of cultural adaptation to climate and topography that have differentiated it from other groups. A highland inhabitant of Boyacá and Cundinamarca departments, which are dominated by urban mestizos of Spanish heritage and have an elitist literary culture, is called a *cundiboyacense*. Someone who is from Antioquia, Caldas, Quindío, or Risaralda departments, a region known for its egalitarian and independent traditions, is a *paisa*. Prominent *paisas* include

Belisario Betancur Cuartas (president, 1982–86), César Augusto Gaviria Trujillo (president, 1990–94), and President Álvaro Uribe, whose family moved to Antioquia when he was 10 years old. A resident of the ethnically diverse Caribbean or Pacific departments is a *costeño*. Colombia's Nobel Prize–winning novelist, Gabriel García Márquez, is a *costeño* (although he was educated in Bogotá), who fictionalized the Magdalena town of Aracataca as Macondo in his classic 1967 novel *Cien años de soledad* (One Hundred Years of Solitude). An inhabitant of Norte de Santander or Santander departments is a *santandereano*; inhabitants of these two departments tend to have more white than Amerindian blood and to share Venezuelan social characteristics, at least in the north. Someone from the llanos region is a *llanero*. And a resident of Cauca or Valle del Cauca, where most people are of Afro-Colombian or indigenous origin, is a *vallecaucano*. Residents of Huila and Tolima are also considered a separate group, as are residents of Nariño, but they are referred to by their departmental monikers.

Migration and rural or urban residence can also determine a person's status. A dark-skinned mulatto who because of wealth and prestige would be a member of the local elite in a rural area along the coast would not be so considered outside this region. Conversely, movement from a larger to a smaller town might enhance an individual's status. Usually, the only Colombians whose status is invariable are the national elite, Amerindians, and blacks (see Ethnic Groups, ch. 4).

Urbanization Trends

Unlike most of its Andean neighbors, Colombia is a nation of cities. It has a largely urban population and has had one of the highest urbanization rates of any Latin American nation. The transition of Colombia from a largely rural country to an urban one had occurred by the mid-1960s. By 1964 the rural percentage of the population had dropped to 47.2, from 61 percent in 1951. During the 23-year period from 1951 to 1973, the figures reversed, with the urban population increasing to 61 percent and the rural declining to 39 percent. Urban growth during 1951–73 was dominated by the growth of the four largest cities—Bogotá, Medellín, Cali, and Barranquilla—all of which were already large metropolitan areas of several hundred thousand people in 1951. The share of total population in these four cities quintupled from 5 percent in 1951 to 25 percent in 1973, compared with an increase in the total urban share of less than 50 percent during the same period.

In the new millennium, migration from rural to urban areas has continued to be prevalent. Although the rates of both population growth and urbanization fell during the 1980s, the proportion of the population living in urban areas increased from 57.5 percent in 1970 to 76.6 percent in 2005. Between 2000 and 2005, the urban population grew 2.1 percent. By some estimates, the urbanized population reached 78 percent in 2007.

By 2007 about 35 percent of the total population was concentrated in the four main cities. According to official Colombian statistics, the cities with more than 1 million inhabitants in 2007 were: Bogotá (7 million; Greater Bogotá, 8.2 million), Medellín (2.5 million; Greater Medellín, 3.4 million), Cali (2.1 million; Greater Cali, 2.7 million), and Barranquilla (1.1 million; Greater Barranquilla, 1.8 million). Bogotá remains smaller than five other Latin American cities: Mexico City, São Paulo, Buenos Aires, Rio de Janeiro, and Lima. According to the 2005 census, 16.4 percent of Colombia's 42 million people lived in Bogotá. Twenty-two other Colombian urban centers had populations of between 200,000 and 800,000. Among them are four medium-size cities with populations of more than 500,000: Cartagena, Cúcuta, Bucaramanga, and Soledad. Greater Bucaramanga actually exceeds 1 million inhabitants. According to a 2008 Central Bank study, the cities with the greatest inequality are Bogotá and Quibdó (the capital of Chocó Department), while those with the most even distribution of income are Pereira, Cali, Bucaramanga, Cúcuta, Cartagena, Barranquilla, and Santa Marta.

Population Displacement

During the twentieth century, specifically during La Violencia and at the end of the century, when the internal armed conflict intensified, violence generated massive rural–urban migrations and human displacements throughout the country's territory. The move to urban areas reflects not only a shift away from agriculture but also a flight from guerrilla and paramilitary violence. In recent decades, the insurgency and counterinsurgency have caused massive displacement of the rural population, accelerating migration to the cities. According to a 2007 report, *Drop by Drop: Forced Displacement in Bogotá and Soacha*, over the 2001–6 period Bogotá received an average of 93 displaced people, or 23 families, per day as a result of Colombia's internal conflict, and more than 235,000 people from 29 of the country's 32 departments sought refuge in Bogotá and neighboring Soacha, on the capital's southern edge. The majority (64 percent) of these refugees arrived from departments that surround Bogotá, such as Caquetá, Cundinamarca, Huila, Meta, and Tolima. Between 1985 and 2006, a total of 624,286 people, or 16 percent of all the displaced persons nationwide in the same period, took refuge in Bogotá.

Codhes noted that the FARC guerrillas and the United Self-Defense Forces of Colombia (AUC) right-wing militias were primarily responsible for the exodus. Roughly 53 percent of the displaced families who relocated to Bogotá and Soacha blamed the FARC for their current situation, while 34 percent held the paramilitaries responsible. Another 4 percent attributed their plight to the smaller pro-Cuban National Liberation Army (ELN) and the Maoist Popular Liberation Army (EPL). Of the displaced families, 3 percent accused the Colombian army, 4 percent pointed to unspecified other groups, and 2 percent said they had been victims of unknown perpetrators of violence. The same report warned that "there is concern over an eventual urbanization of the armed conflict in Bogotá and Soacha, where there have been reports of the presence of paramilitary groups, guerrilla bands, and the eruption of forms of violence, especially against young people and social leaders."

Colombia's *desplazados* are far less visible than those in countries such as Sri Lanka and Sudan because they settle in slums or shantytowns on the fringes of cities and society, interspersed among other indigent communities, instead of living in tented refugee camps. One salient effect of violence-induced migration is the loss of links between migrants and their original communities, which are often destroyed. Many rural–urban migrants lost whatever social links and constraints they had, and their predicament caused them in turn to be extremely resentful.

Among the essentially social—as distinct from politico-military or economic—effects of the illicit drug industry, the greatest was its contribution to two roughly opposite population movements. One of these involved people moving from towns and cities and established farming areas to seek work on the frontiers of settlement, where there are most coca plantings and processing laboratories. The other was made up of mostly poor rural Colombians, who became *desplazados* when driven from their homes as a result of the conflicts raging in the country and sought refuge in the larger cities or even in Panama, Ecuador, and Venezuela. In some cases, these people had been caught in the crossfire between guerrillas, paramilitaries, narco-traffickers, and armed forces. Others were escaping the attack or threatened attack of armed groups who rightly or wrongly accused them of giving aid to rival bands. Still others were forced off their land by criminal elements, commonly narco-traffickers, who coveted the land for themselves. Whatever the immediate cause of their predicament, population displacement constitutes one of the most critical social problems in Colombia today.

As of the end of 2007, more than 4.2 million Colombians had been internally displaced since 1985, according to Codhes (see table

4, Appendix). By United Nations High Commissioner for Refugees estimates, the number is 3 million, still the second highest population of internal refugees in the world, after Sudan. Many of these *desplazados* left areas where fighting intensified under Plan Patriota, a large government offensive against leftist guerrillas and drug traffickers (see United States–Colombia Security Cooperation and Plan Colombia, ch. 5). According to the 2005 census, 1,542,915 Colombians were victims of forced displacement between 1995 and 2005, but NGOs report that the actual number may be between 2 and 3 million. Codhes has estimated that about 1.5 million people have been displaced since the government of President Álvaro Uribe took office in 2002. Government figures on *desplazados* tend to be lower than those of Codhes, but since 2000 the yearly figures of both have become more similar as a result of methodological improvements.

When *desplazados* cross into a neighboring country, the problem is no longer essentially social or purely Colombian but becomes one of international relations. Whether or not the ultimate destination is within Colombia, it is impossible to say in what proportion of cases narco-traffickers are the ones forcing people to leave their homes, and some reports suggest that in the great majority of cases they are not directly involved. However, in light of their willing or unwilling financing of both guerrillas and paramilitaries, it is safe to conclude that the narco-traffickers, at least indirectly, share responsibility more often than not. Narco-traffickers' direct involvement is clearest when drug lords seek to accumulate land as both an investment and a means of acquiring social and political influence, because they often use force or the threat of force to evict the occupants. Eviction is facilitated if the current occupants lack clear title to the land, allowing the new tenants (or third parties in whom title is now vested) to claim that nothing irregular has happened and making it more difficult to seek redress.

An increase in the landownership concentration that was already a serious problem in Colombia is one result of the displacement process. Moreover, a common pattern is to convert former cropland to pasture, which is easier to manage and increases the rate of eviction of prior inhabitants. But a particularly notorious example has been the taking of lands in the far northwest (Chocó primarily) that had been claimed as ancestral homeland by Afro-Colombian communities, and introducing plantations of palm trees for the extraction of exportable oil. The Afro-Colombians theoretically could have stayed on as hired hands, but most became *desplazados* instead.

The Uribe administration has demobilized thousands of paramilitary fighters under legislation that includes provision for the victims of their abuses to obtain reparations, such as the return of lands illegally taken from them (see Peace Processes, ch. 5). There have been repeated instances, however, of violence and intimidation used to prevent victims from denouncing the perpetrators; even when formal petitions for redress are presented, the task of investigating and acting upon them is so overwhelming that for most victims the prospects of success are highly questionable. Nor would even successful claimants necessarily want to return to the scene of their misfortune. Thus, for most *desplazados* the displacement is likely to be permanent. They join the ranks of those already subsisting in the informal sector of the economy and continue to place an added strain on urban social services. The deficiencies in education and health care are inevitably compounded in the process (see Health and Welfare; Education, this ch.).

Emigration

A large emigration wave also has limited population growth. Many Colombians have been fleeing the civil conflict and economic difficulties. Some of those who left the country reportedly have begun to return, but most who fled are illegal immigrants where they have sought sanctuary, and only a fifth, at most, are registered at Colombian consulates. It is thus difficult to estimate total numbers, but it appears that owing to problems of security and unemployment, a total of 1.2 million Colombians abandoned the country during 2000–5 and have not returned. According to the 2005 census, more than 3 million Colombians were living abroad, but other estimates suggest that the actual number could exceed 4 million, or almost 10 percent of the country's population.

External migration is primarily to Ecuador, the United States, and Venezuela. In 2003 North America was the destination for 48 percent of Colombian emigrants; Latin America and the Caribbean, 40 percent; Europe, 11 percent; and Asia, Oceania, and Africa, 1 percent. The population movement in recent years toward North America and Europe in particular has been motivated in some cases by the threat of violence but more typically by the search for greater economic opportunity. Colombians living abroad—1.5 million of whom departed during the economic downturn between 1996 and 2002—have had a positive effect on the balance of payments thanks to remittances to family and friends at home. But external migration to the United States or Europe has represented a definite loss of talent and energy because migrants to the developed world tend to be better educated and in the prime of working life. Some estimates would have roughly half the physicians trained in Colombia during certain years, at great expense to fellow Colombian taxpayers, now working in the United States. Then, too, there are communities (as in Mexico, for example) that have been so drained of young workers that they find themselves dependent on the flow of remittances. Several municipalities in the vicinity of Pereira in western Colombia, hard hit by troubles in the coffee industry and the competition of cheap Asian labor in garment exporting, exemplify the latter phenomenon.

Demography

The Colombian experience is remarkable for the abruptness and magnitude of the declines in fertility and mortality after 1966. Between then and 2000, total fertility fell by about 45 percent. A variety of factors combined to produce the decline, and, as in most countries, fertility patterns varied widely among Colombian socio-economic groups, whose composition shifted substantially during the period. In the late 1960s, for example, Colombian women living in rural areas who had not completed primary education had a total fertility rate of eight children, compared with 3.4 children for urban women with at least a full primary education.

Family-planning programs did not initiate the rapid fertility decline, because such programs started after its onset. Nevertheless, Colombia's well-organized family-planning programs helped to keep the population growth rate down. Information about contraceptives and use of them increased rapidly after 1969, when the government began to support family planning. In that year, the Liberal Party (PL) administration of Carlos Lleras Restrepo (president, 1966–70) began providing subsidized family-planning services in local health centers through the maternal- and child-health program of the then Ministry of Public Health. In 1972–73 the Conservative Party (PC) government of Misael Eduardo Pastrana Borrero (president, 1970–74) extended services to postpartum cases in about 90 hospitals throughout the country. Urban areas had substantially more access to family planning than rural areas, most of it through the private sector in urban areas; overall, private entities provided as much as 50 percent of the services. The government also subsidized the cost of contraceptives. Between 1969 and 1976, according to one survey, the proportion of women with knowledge of contraceptives rose from 51 to 72 percent. By 1976 about 95 percent of married women had this knowledge, and 59 percent were using contraception, compared to 34 percent in 1969. The drop in the birthrate since the mid-1960s has been among the most dramatic experienced in any country, falling from 44.2 births per 1,000 in 1960 to 19.9 per 1,000 population in 2008, according to an unofficial estimate.

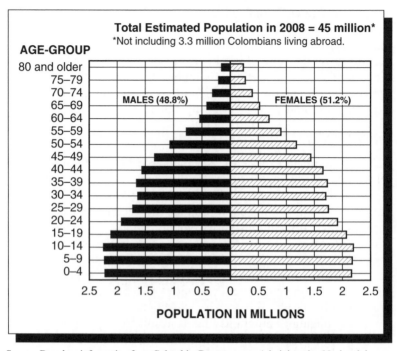

Source: Based on information from Colombia, Departamento Administrativo Nacional de
Estadística, "Censo General 2005: Datos desagregados por sexo" [2005 General Cen-
sus: Data Disaggregated by Sex], *Boletín* (Bogotá), http://www.dane.gov.co; and U.S.
Census Bureau, Population Division, International Data Base, http://www.census.gov.

Figure 3. Population Distribution by Age-group and Sex, 2008

Beginning in the 1980s, other changes have taken place relating to
family size, age distribution, gender, marital status, education levels,
and economic activity of heads of family. The average family size
fell 20 percent from 5.1 in 1979 to 4 in 2000. In 1960 each woman
had on average seven children, a figure that fell to five in the 1970s,
four in the 1980s, three in the 1990s, and to 1.9 in the first years of
the new millennium, according to the Economic Commission for
Latin America and the Caribbean and the Latin American and Caribbean Demographic Center. The 2005 census found that approximately 66.7 percent of Colombian homes had four or fewer persons,
and the average number was 3.9. It also determined that 44.9 percent
of Colombians were single, 23 percent were married, and 23.1 percent were living together as unmarried couples. These trends reflect
the new social and cultural roles of women and their increased education, which have changed their expectations.

According to the World Health Organization, Colombia's infant
mortality rate (under one year of age) declined from 68 per 1,000

live births in 1970 to 19.5 in 2008, the under-five mortality rate dropped from 105 per 1,000 live births in 1970 to 26 in 2008, and annual estimates for life expectancy at birth during the 2000–5 period averaged 72.3 years. The latter figure for 2008 was 72.5 years. Overall life expectancy at birth in 2008 was 72.5 years (males, 68.7 years; females, 76.5 years). In 2006 the adult mortality rate per 1,000 population between 15 and 60 years of age was 176 for males and 87 for females. Not surprisingly, in a country as violent as Colombia, men are twice as likely as women to die prematurely. The greater number of male homicide victims accounts for the significant differences in the probability of dying for men and women.

Colombia has a relatively young population; the median age in 2008 was estimated at 26.8 years (25.9 years for males and 27.8 years for females). Less than 6 percent of the population is older than 64 years; less than 30 percent, under 15 years of age; and 77 percent, under age 45. According to the 2005 census, 48.8 percent of the population was male and 51.2 percent female (see fig. 3).

Social Strata Division

Since the sixteenth century, Colombian society has been highly stratified, with social classes generally linked to racial or wealth distinctions, and vertical mobility has been limited. The proportion of white ancestry has been an important measure of status for the mixed groups since the colonial era. In the nineteenth century, Colombia's rugged terrain and inadequate transportation system reinforced social and geographic distance, keeping the numerically superior but disunited masses fragmented and powerless. The nascent middle class lacked a collective consciousness, preferring to identify individually with the upper class. Except in certain instances of urban artisans and some Amerindian communities, the elite was the only social group with sufficient cohesion to articulate goals and make them known to the rest of the society. In the twentieth century, the society began to experience change, not so much in values or orientation as in broadening of the economic bases and an expansion of the social classes. Improvements in transportation, communications, and education—coupled with industrialization and rapid urban growth—opened Colombian society somewhat by expanding economic opportunities. These advances, although mixed, have continued during the first decade of the present century.

The many terms for color still being used reflect the persistence of this colonial pattern and a continuing desire among Colombians to classify each other according to color and social group. These terms also cut across class lines so that persons at one level define themselves as being racially similar to those at other levels. The confusion over clas-sification has affected most Colombians because most of them do not define themselves as being white, black, or Amerindian, which are dis-tinct and mutually exclusive groups, but as belonging to one of the mixed categories. In addition to racial and wealth factors, Colombia's classes are distinguished by education, family background, lifestyle, occupation, power, and geographic residence. Within every class, there are numerous subtle gradations in status. Colombians tend to be extremely status-conscious, and class identity is an important aspect of social life because it regulates the interaction of groups and individuals. Social-class boundaries are far more flexible in the city than in the countryside, but consciousness of status and class distinctions contin-ues to permeate social life throughout Colombia.

The upper class is very successful in maintaining exclusivity and controlling change through a system of informal decision-making groups called *roscas*—the name of a twisted pastry. Such groups exist at different levels and across different spheres and are linked hierarchically by personal relationships. Their composition varies according to level—municipal, departmental, or national—but each group tries to include at least one powerful person from every sphere. A *rosca* is a vitally important system in both the social and the political context because it is at this level of interaction that most political decisions are made and careers determined. Only as a mem-ber of such a group can an individual be considered a member of the upper-middle or upper class. Indeed, the listed names of past presi-dents reflect how power has remained the purview of a small number of elite families instead of a meritocracy (see table 2, Appendix).

The official strata division provides another look at social classes. A 1994 law provides "an instrument that allows a municipality or dis-trict to classify its population in distinct groups or strata with similar social and economic characteristics." The law was framed this way to establish cross-class subsidies that would help those in the lower strata pay for utilities. Housing characteristics, such as a garage, a front yard, and quality of the neighborhood, are the main criteria used. Depending on the diversity and quality of housing, there could be six strata: level one is lower-low, two is low, three is upper-low, four is medium, five is medium-high, and six is high. Most cities have all six, but there are towns that have only three. This national classifi-cation identifies groups with similar socioeconomic characteristics. Although strata are not a direct reflection of social class, they provide useful information beyond income measures.

The lower-middle class, constituting the bulk of the middle class, comes primarily from upwardly mobile members of the lower class. A large number are clerks or small shopkeepers. Many have only a precarious hold on middle-class status and tend to be less concerned with imitating upper-class culture and behavior than with making enough money to sustain a middle-class lifestyle. Such families tend to be just as concerned as those at higher social levels with giving their children an education. Many hope to send at least one of their children through a university, regardless of the financial burden.

In 2007 Colombia had an abundance of families that belonged to the middle-class sector of society and were struggling between the need to survive and the desire to give their children a good education. Government agencies such as DANE and the National Planning Department (DNP) refer to Colombia's middle class, which constitutes about 30 percent of Colombians, as "stratum three." The generous subsidies that the state once granted to stratum three have been gradually dismantled, and as a result millions of Colombians have had to live in hardship from day to day, forced to take out loans to make ends meet. According to DANE, the policy of creating social strata in Colombia is "a technical tool for categorizing the population...mainly for the purpose of charging for public services," which, in the case of stratum three, do not include government subsidies in the majority of cases. A majority of the 31 programs managed by the Social Action Agency focus on strata one and two and on displaced persons.

The great majority of the population (89 percent) lives in strata one, two, and three, and on that basis, even if not by other criteria, is considered poor. Strata four, five, and six house only 6.5 percent, 1.9 percent, and 1.5 percent of the population, respectively. In other words, only about 10 percent of the population lives in dwellings that are well built and located in well-developed neighborhoods with access to good utility services.

The overlap between these official strata and social class is not perfect. It is possible to find very high-income people living in stratum three and some stratum-six residents who have strong affinity with the lower classes. There are several reasons for these coexisting disparities, the main one being perhaps the strong upward mobility allowed by the illegal-drug industry wealth that did not necessarily lead to a change in self-perception. The living expenses of this group of drug traffickers are very high, but they retain some of the cultural identity, education, and self-perceptions of the lower classes.

Family

The Colombian family traditionally has been an extended one, that is, a wide circle of kinship consisting of several generations. However, the decline of the patriarchal extended-family structure is apparent in urban society, as increased geographic and social mobility weakens kinship ties and offers greater independence to young people. Despite frequent claims that the "family is disappearing," what has happened is a change in family structure and the public illusions about it. The nuclear family that the state and the Roman Catholic Church have promoted since independence has changed as culture and society have changed. The new society has pushed for changes in legislation about inheritance, spousal rights, and the rights of women and children. Families at the bottom of the social ladder are adversely affected by geographic dislocation and are increasingly less cohesive. They continue to be characterized by a large number of consensual unions and matriarchal households.

Social changes caused by industrialization, urbanization, political reforms, changes in labor markets, and modernization accelerated family change by the mid-twentieth century. Such changes are evident in today's family legislation. For example, a 1982 law granted equal rights and obligations (including inheritance rights) to all children: legitimate, extramarital, and adoptive.

Traditional elements of trust and mutual dependence among relatives, no matter how distant the relationship, are still strong. The already large circle of family relationships is extended through the institution of *compadrazgo* (see Glossary), a complex form of ritual kinship linked to Roman Catholic notions of baptismal godparenthood. Ties with relatives and *compadres* (godparents) continue to be important in political and business activities and provide the person of low status with a wide circle of mutual assistance.

The nuclear family unit in general continues to be authoritarian, patriarchal, and patrilineal. Legal reforms have extended equal civil and property rights to women, but tradition dominates male–female relations, and roles and responsibilities in marriage are still relatively clear-cut. In the lower class, in which the father is frequently not a permanent member of the household, the mother often assumes the role of chief authority and family head, but in all other cases the father unquestionably occupies this position. Within the household, the wife is considered the husband's deputy and the chief administrator of domestic activities. Her first duty is to bear and raise children. She is also expected to keep the household running smoothly and efficiently. In her relations with her husband, she traditionally is supposed to be deferential, thinking of his wishes and needs before considering her own.

Men of the upper and middle class have always been paternal and protective toward their dependents, trying to shelter their wives and children from undesirable outside influences. The activities of women were for many years severely circumscribed because of the male concern for the honor and virtue of the wife and unmarried daughters. Women in the upper and middle classes traditionally were not permitted to work outside the home except for volunteer work.

In the upper and middle classes, the social life of women, particularly of unmarried young women, was limited to home, school, church, and well-chaperoned parties and dances. Today, with those same unmarried young women going to university, partying without chaperones, and enjoying career options of their own even if they do marry, the situation is fast changing; it simply has not evolved quite as far as in North America and Europe.

Far fewer restrictions traditionally applied to lower-class or lower-middle-class women than to upper-class women. Formal chaperonage was always impossible to maintain because of family instability, economic need, the frequent absence of the husband and father, and moral standards differing somewhat from those of the upper social levels. The lower-class woman usually has had to be employed and contribute her salary to the family's subsistence or work in the fields beside her male relatives. Her economic contribution has given her a degree of equality. The husband's and father's control over her has been further limited by the matrilocal nature of much lower-class life—the custom for a husband to live with his wife's family.

There are, increasingly, exceptions in urban society to the traditional concept of a woman's role. Many women in the middle and upper social levels are well educated and may pursue careers in many fields; the availability of relatively inexpensive domestic service is a factor favoring this trend. Indeed, Colombian women are considered among the most politically active in Latin America. Many of them hold high elective or appointive offices. One prominent example is Noemí Sanín Posada, who began her distinguished career as a lawyer and businesswoman and, since the 1980s, has held ministerial portfolios and ambassadorships (she became Colombia's ambassador to the United Kingdom in 2008); she has also run for president twice (in 1998 and 2002). At the same time, women who engage in these activities are considered exceptional by the general population. Most upper-class and upper-middle-class women do not take on full-time work after marriage but rather devote themselves primarily to their homes, families, and church groups.

The Roman Catholic Church is the single most important force affecting marriage and family life, and Roman Catholic marriage is recognized as the ideal and the preferred legal, social, and sexual basis of the family. Nearly all formal marriages take place within the church, and most other turning points in the life of the individual family member are marked by religious rites. However, in 1973 a new agreement replaced the 1887 concordat with the Holy See, opening the way for increased acceptance of civil marriages. Regardless of the increasing acceptability of civil weddings, most middle-class and upper-class families still try to provide their children with the most elaborate church wedding they can afford.

Despite the efforts of the church to encourage legal marriage within the lower class, people in this group generally regard a religious marriage as a heavy social and economic burden. Thus, both the religious and the civil marriage ceremonies are commonly forgone in the lower-class, consensual union. In rural communities with traditional lower-class standards, formal marriage is regarded as neither important nor essential. Although other kinds of union are more prevalent within the lower class, Roman Catholic marriage often connotes superior social status and prestige.

Some Colombians, especially those in the middle class, regard marriage as one of the best means of facilitating upward social mobility, and conversely members of the upper class are generally reluctant to marry persons of lower social position. With the increasing independence of young people and the declining authority of the family, marriages between relatives have become less common, but intermarriage between families of similar aristocratic background is a custom that most young people still honor.

The institutions of marriage and family are ruled by a combination of nineteenth-century civil code and twentieth-century constitutional law. The 1873 Civil Code, which has undergone many changes since 1932, has governed relations between couples and spouses and between parents and their children. Equality between husband and wife in personal relations within marriage was achieved only by the 1974 Civil Code reform; until then there was a legal requirement for women to obey their husbands. Until 1970 women had to take their husbands' last names. Today, according to a 1988 decree, wives can choose whether to add it, but if they so choose, the husband's name has to be preceded by the preposition *de*. Today, both parents have authority over their children, which was a paternal prerogative until 1968. Article 42 of the 1991 constitution establishes several norms for the family based on parental equality.

Divorce in Colombia has also increased. After decades of debate, in 1976 Colombia adopted a divorce law permitting the dissolution of the civil marriages entered into by non–Roman Catholics or by Roman Catholics who simply defied clerical directives. Non–Roman Catholics and Roman Catholics who officially renounce their faith have the alternative of civil marriage. Until the 1991 constitution changed the matrimonial regime, divorce was not allowed for

Roman Catholic marriages. Under subsequent regulations, a legal or de facto separation of more than two years was accepted as grounds for divorce. Then, on June 9, 2005, the Congress approved the Express Divorce Law in an effort to eliminate paperwork and delays, which previously took an average of six weeks and required the services of a judge and lawyers. Under the new law, the two parties need only appear before a notary public and do not require a lawyer.

Prenuptial agreements are rare. Under the Civil Code, net-worth increases that occur during the marriage are divided between husband and wife, and each spouse has control over his or her assets and their yields. When a marriage dissolves, the net-worth increases that were created during the marriage are distributed in accordance with civil law.

Traditionally, Colombia's family structure was rigidly hierarchical and male-dominated, giving men economic power over women. However, as a result of judicial changes made in the 1960s and advances in women's participation in the labor market, this power has been drastically reduced. Today, the average marital relationship is more egalitarian. Article 43 of the 1991 constitution gives men and women equal rights and specifically recognizes a female head of household. Parents now share power over their children, and even the latter participate in some decisions. Since the 1980s, data on household composition and the economic activities of their members are more available, and female heads of households have become more visible. Indeed, households headed by single women increased from 27 percent of all households in 1979 to 31 percent in 2000. Nevertheless, the nuclear family is still dominant, accounting for almost 60 percent of Colombian families in 2000, according to DANE.

These modernization trends in the composition of the family have been more evident in the cities than in rural areas. In Bogotá the new family forms and the new roles of their members are more acceptable than in the rest of the country. In Antioquia Department, for example, and the southwest region of the country, strong religious and patriarchal traditions are intertwined with the new family dynamics.

Income Distribution

In recent years, Colombia has achieved respectable if unspectacular economic growth—an average rate of 4.75 percent per year during the twentieth century as a whole, or 2.3 percent in per-capita terms; yet the benefits have not been shared equally. Just how unequal the distribution has been depends on the study methods and indicators chosen. Economists with ties to Colombia's amorphous "establishment"—a catchall term conventionally used without precise definition to refer to business and government leaders, wealthy families, and members of such presumably influential groups as the church hierarchy—tend to paint a brighter picture than do independent academics. Nevertheless, there is general agreement on the broad outline.

Despite fluctuations from year to year and significant differences between urban and rural sectors, it is clear enough that income distribution has been highly skewed in favor of the wealthiest Colombians at the expense of the lower and middle social strata. Using the Gini Coefficient (see Glossary) as a standard measure of inequality, averages of some widely varying estimates from 1970 to 2007 range from 0.49 (at the lowest, in 1990) to 0.58 (four years later, in 1994), with 0.59 the result for 2007. All these estimates are far removed from the point of perfect equality, which would be 0.0, and the highest is a bit high even for Latin America, the region of the world most renowned for uneven income distribution. (By contrast, most developed European nations tend to have Gini coefficients between 0.24 and 0.36, whereas that of the United States is above 0.4). Another approach is to compare the proportion of total income received by the top 10 percent or so of the population with that received by the bottom 10 percent. Here again there is fluctuation, but a clear picture of inequality emerges: during the final decades of the twentieth century, the share going to the top decile went from 12.14 times that of the bottom 10 percent in 1978 to 11.50 in 1988 but rose again to 14.38 in 1999.

Vast numbers of Colombians must be classified as "poor," by any possible measurement, and the inequality of income distribution appears resistant to major change, yet the official poverty index—based on the number of households whose income amounts to less than the cost of two "basic" food baskets—has been falling steadily if not precipitously. The same is true of the standard measure of "indigence," defined as income not even equal to one such basket. In rural poverty and overall indigence, there was a slight increase during the economic recession at the turn of the century, but by 2005 the overall poverty index had declined about 8.0 points to 46.8 percent of the population, and the overall indigence index had fallen about 6.5 points to 20.2 percent of the population.

The reduction in poverty resulted primarily from economic growth rather than specific antipoverty programs, although increased education spending was a factor that certainly helped, for example, by preparing unskilled Colombians to move up to, at least, semi-

A hillside urban tugurio *in Medellín*
Courtesy Inter-American Development Bank (David Mangurian),
Washington, DC

skilled employment. In the 1990s, the Colombian economy underwent a series of adjustments that diminished some of the formal protections enjoyed by labor and increased the premium for skilled workers. For much of that decade, world conditions were also, on balance, unfavorable, and unemployment in the late 1990s reached a peak of more than 20 percent. Even when economic growth resumed in the early 2000s, unemployment declined somewhat but remained a serious problem, while many of the new jobs created were lower paying and less likely to carry benefits than those that had been lost.

The gap between upper and lower social strata is, of course, nothing new; however, qualitatively it is greater now than at independence, when the material comforts and luxuries of a Colombian aristocrat were comparable to those of a middle-class English person. Thanks to the development of the Colombian economy itself and to the greater ease of importing whatever that economy does not produce, wealthy Colombians can now quaff the best French wines and pamper themselves with fancy cars and electronic gadgetry almost as easily as in Europe or North America. In 2007 one also could read of a booming trade in first-class air tickets to Paris. At the same time, thanks to advances in both transportation and communications and to the proliferation of mass media, the stark differences in living standards between the highest and lowest social strata are more visible than they had been, fueling social discontent. And one factor still limiting conspicuous consumption by wealthy Colombians is the fear of drawing the attention of kidnappers.

Rural Poor and Urban Poor

Although statistical measurements of income distribution and poverty vary, they all show that the worst poverty is in rural areas. The rural poor, however, fall into distinct categories, one key differentiating factor being access to landownership. The *minifundistas* who do own land, located particularly in rugged Andean areas not suited to large-scale crop farming or cattle grazing, may not have enough land to support their families and thus need to accept occasional outside employment to supplement their income. That income is not much different from, indeed often less than, that of day laborers. Nevertheless, they enjoy higher social status than sharecroppers or tenants, and their situation is hard to compare with that of landless workers because they themselves produce part of what they consume. Coffee growers were hard hit by the fall in the price of coffee after the 1970s and increasingly have turned to different crops (including coca) or to other employment. As for the rural workers wholly dependent on wages, their incomes increased notably in the 1970s as a result of the spike in world coffee prices during those years, as well as the growing urban employment that pulled agricultural workers into the cities and thereby lessened the supply of labor in the countryside. Since then, there have been fluctuations in coffee prices, without, apparently, much basic change.

In urban areas, the living conditions of organized industrial workers might cause them to be classified as poor in a developed country, yet they form a labor elite in Colombia. They are also a declining proportion of the urban labor population because of the slow pace of manufacturing growth and an increasing tendency of industrial firms to contract out part of the production process. The result has been an increase in low-paid, nonunion, often part-time employment. Construction work is an attractive alternative, but a volatile one. In any case, the greatest numbers of urban poor are people with little or no education, who can be found in service work and retail trade, including the large informal economy, where people do odd jobs or sell things from their homes and at street corners, without observing official regulations, and, of course, without regular access to social benefits. Among the most desperate are the millions of *desplazados*. Ending up in the cities as they usually do, these migrants from rural

Colombia generally start their urban life in makeshift housing and, at best, marginal employment. Particularly in the Caribbean coastal region, families of the urban poor, *desplazados* or not, tend to be headed by a single parent, almost always a woman, who is at a disadvantage as she juggles domestic and outside work responsibilities. In the cities, however, at least it is easier than in the countryside to increase total household cash income by combining the earnings of several family members.

Income Effects of Narco-Trafficking

The complexity of the changes in income distribution can be illustrated by looking at the impact of a particular activity, such as narco-trafficking. The rise of the illicit drugs industry has obviously created thousands of new jobs in cultivating, processing, and exporting, of which the greatest number are in cultivating the coca plant. Workers may be hired hands or independent farmers, often on new frontiers of settlement, where the weakness or absence of legal authority favors the activity. Earnings are as much as double what they could be in the production of legal crops, even though, for coca growers, income is still probably less than that of the average construction worker. At the same time, the investment of illicit-drug profits in construction projects and the like has created new jobs, for urban workers especially. By mid-2008, U.S. government alternative-development initiatives were supporting the cultivation of more than 238,000 hectares of legal crops; more than 291,000 families in 18 departments had benefited from these programs, according to the U.S. Department of State.

Any income advantage for the growers of illicit crops is offset in whole or in part by the higher cost of living in most production areas and by the relative inaccessibility of social services. Moreover, the income received by cultivators is much less than that accruing to processors, whose earnings are comparable to those of midlevel professionals. Official Colombian sources calculate that members of the narco-trafficking elite of exporters earn 20 times as much as those categorized as regular "employers." Income distribution in the production and sale of illicit drugs is therefore even more skewed than in the economy as a whole. The net contribution of narco-trafficking to the overall income pattern is not great, but it still must be counted as one more negative aspect of the illicit drug industry.

Health and Welfare

Resources and Organization

Health care in Colombia was long sharply divided between the practice of formal medicine and the popular or folk medicine that was the only care available to a majority of the population. The Roman Catholic religious orders originally ran the hospitals, and they still play a part, but both private secular institutions (including both those that charge and charitable ones) and the state have assumed a steadily larger share of the burden. Medical care at for-profit hospitals in the major cities today is comparable to that found in the United States or Western Europe; indeed, patients have even come from across the Atlantic for treatment at Bogotá's noted eye clinic, La Clínica Barraquer; and Diego Armando Maradona, the Argentine soccer legend, had a successful gastric bypass in Cartagena. But for most Colombians, the picture is somewhat different.

In 2005 Colombia had approximately one physician for every 1,000 inhabitants, which is a little more than half as many as in Chile. Although a somewhat respectable number by Latin American standards (1.5 per 1,000 average in 2005), Colombia's average was well below the Organisation for Economic Co-operation and Development (OECD) average of 3.1 per 1,000 in 2006. To train its physicians, Colombia has 35 medical faculties (not to mention additional health-care training programs in other institutions), though quite a few of the faculties are of marginal quality, and many medical students go abroad for at least part of their training. However, despite the assorted guarantees of health care as a fundamental right of all citizens that were written into the 1991 constitution—and in line with the maldistribution of so many other goods and services in Colombia—there is an excessive concentration of physicians in the major cities. The same is true of the availability of hospital beds, a category in which Colombia, with 1.1 beds per 1,000 inhabitants in 2003, is not much better off than some of the poorest Latin American countries and is outclassed even by Paraguay.

Both national and local authorities play an important role in the health-care system, and in the provision of local services such as potable water and sewerage, the role of the national government has been primarily that of facilitator. Departmental governments have long operated lotteries, ostensibly for the support of medical and other welfare programs. But with positions in the lottery administrations often awarded as political spoils rather than for technical competence, misuse of the funds collected has been all too common. Municipal governments, for their part, mostly lack sufficient funds and expertise to make much difference, although they deserve some credit for the increase in the number of homes having piped potable water and sewer connections. In the major cities, the coverage of the water and sewerage systems is now almost universal, with private enterprise since the 1990s also deserving some of the credit for improvement. In the main cities, 97 percent of households have adequate water supplies, and 92 percent have sanitation.

The involvement of private firms in water supply and sewerage led not just to better quality of service and greater efficiency but also to some sharp rate increases. However, the impact on poorer Colombians was minimal because the country for some time had a policy of charging higher utility rates to upper-income consumers in order to subsidize the service provided to poor families. In rural Colombia, unfortunately but not surprisingly, much remains to be done; as of 2004, potable water reached only 72 percent of homes—slightly down from 1990—and significantly less than a nationwide figure (by one calculation) of 93 percent. Sewerage connections reached 54 percent of rural homes, as against an estimated 86 percent nationwide.

From 1953 until late 2002, the government had a Ministry of Public Health, but it merged along with the Ministry of Labor and Social Security into the Ministry of Social Protection. Thus, the organization that formerly had ministry status is now known as the National Superintendency of Health (SNS), an entity of the Ministry of Social Protection. Various other agencies whose missions, often poorly coordinated, touch on aspects of public health are also under this ministry. Whether through the SNS or through the ministry's other official agencies, such as the Colombian Family Welfare Institute, the national authorities have conducted vaccination campaigns, worked to control communicable diseases, and provided food subsidies to improve the nutrition of poor children. An overriding objective, strongly supported by international agencies as an essential part of any overall national development plan, has been to bring health benefits to as many Colombians as possible. For this purpose, the government has worked to expand the coverage offered through two other entities of the Ministry of Social Protection: the Social Security Institute (ISS) and the National Social Pension Fund (Cajanal). Cajanal serves state employees, as do certain pension or welfare funds catering to particular groups of state employees such as the police, military, and railroad workers.

The ISS has provided a measure of health insurance for private-sector employees, thus supplementing plans offered by various private organizations. Since 1954 a notable example of the latter has been the network of Family Compensation Funds (CCFs). Since the 1960s, the

113

CCFs have been authorized to provide a broad range of benefits that are financed through a percentage of affiliated firms' payroll costs. The benefits include payment for treatment at hospitals and other health-care facilities, vacations at resort hotels, and funding for attendance at cultural or educational programs; but the beneficiaries are chiefly the employees of large firms in major cities—obviously they do not include people in the informal sector of the economy. Another economic association (*gremio*) that is a health-care provider is the National Federation of Coffee Growers (Fedecafé), which serves essentially the coffee-growing regions. Yet, by the 1980s there were still a great many Colombians with no coverage at all. Moreover, since the care offered even to those who do have access is often of poor quality, many middle-income and well-to-do Colombians opt to take out individual prepaid medical insurance policies.

In an effort to bring some order into the existing patchwork of state and private programs, the administration of César Gaviria in 1993 sponsored the ambitious reform measure known as Law 100. Like other neoliberal initiatives of that government, the aim of the law was to carve out a larger role for private enterprise in medical insurance (and also in pension benefits). It established two basic forms of subscription, which between them were supposed to cover the entire population, as enrollment was obligatory. One form is the contributive regimen, whereby individuals with sufficient means join health insurance companies (EPS), which are basically fund administrators, receiving the quotas paid by members and then contracting with health-care providers (IPS) for services to their affiliates as needed. The other basic division is the subsidized regimen, for those unable to pay a full monthly quota, in which state subsidies help cover the payments due from members, with the money going to Administrators of the Subsidized Regime (ARS), which like the EPS contract with providers to meet members' needs.

Some further changes have been made since 1993, but the basic program set forth in Law 100 remains in effect. In 2007 DANE reported that 78 percent of the population had access to the health-care system. However, all this was achieved with some deterioration in quality of the care given, for the government made a deliberate decision to sacrifice the latter to the extent necessary to maximize coverage. Longer waiting times for appointments and procedures are just part of the problem; many of those enrolled in the subsidized program, especially in rural districts, simply do not have reliable access to modern diagnosis or treatment. The program generates many complaints, not just over the quality of care but also over numerous instances of administrative confusion, inefficiency, and outright corruption. Many of these complaints are only to be expected in dealing with a new and rather complex program. Public hospitals have been hard hit, as they no longer receive direct financing from the state but must compete for patients and then be paid by an EPS or ARS for services rendered. Moreover, the ARS, as it turns out, often set up their own clinics and other care providers, bypassing the existing hospitals.

Health expenditures as a percentage of total gross domestic product (GDP—see Glossary) rose sharply: from 2.6 percent in 1993, they already had reached 4.7 percent in 1997, as a result of the higher quotas and other payments made by users as well as an increase in public expenditures. The latter rose from a meager 1.3 percent of GDP in 1990–91 to almost 6 percent in 2003. Clearly, however, deficiencies remain in the health-care system, despite the extended coverage. A report in 2004 suggested that the proportion of patients served adequately by the system declined from 84 percent in 1997 to 77 percent in 2003. The decline resulted from the closure of hospitals and other health-service institutions because of financial difficulties that have been blamed on both the structure of the new system and misuse of funds. The system's resources also suffer from a high level of evasion, estimated at around one-third of all contributions due. The government passed a reform in 2006 aimed at reducing inefficiency and corruption in the provision of services (particularly for low-income groups) by increasing competition; at the same time, it raised employers' contributions. Any final assessment of the impact of Law 100 will have to recognize at least a quantitative improvement in health coverage since the law was enacted, but there will be continuing disagreement as to whether even greater improvement might have occurred under a different system. Meanwhile, for critics of the government and of all neoliberal privatization measures, Law 100 has become a favorite example of everything wrong in Colombia today.

Current Health Overview

Although income distribution has been resistant to change, and decline in the poverty index has been at times erratic, there are a number of clear indications of improving conditions of life for the Colombian population in recent decades. The Human Development Index (HDI)—devised by United Nations experts to present a more balanced picture of well-being than strictly economic measurements—shows Colombia in 2005 with a ranking of 75, or somewhat better than the median, among all 177 countries thus measured. This result cannot be considered satisfactory, but it does reflect a process of slow but steady improvement that could be seen even in the first half of the twentieth century, though the pace has increased markedly since 1950.

People in the poorest regions and social strata suffer most from preventable diseases, such as gastrointestinal disorders and certain respiratory ailments, and they are the most likely to suffer from some form of malnutrition—if not from lack of calories, then from an excess of the sugar, starch, and cholesterol-prone fats in the Colombian diet. But they are relatively less afflicted by the degenerative and chronic diseases typical of urban and higher-income groups, such as coronary ailments and cancer. Nationwide, an increase in the latter diseases is related simply to a declining birthrate and increasing life expectancy, so the Colombian population is steadily aging; with an increasing percentage of Colombians over 45 years of age, the impact of geriatric issues must inevitably increase.

It is also true that Colombia's record in the reduction of infant mortality from 35.2 per 1,000 live births in 1990–95 to 19.5 in 2008 is mediocre by Latin American standards. Maternal deaths are likewise high, at 1.3 per 1,000 births in 2005 as against 0.3 for Chile. Many of these maternal deaths are the result of induced abortions, performed outside the formal health system because of traditional religious and legal sanctions; only in 2006 was abortion finally legalized, and then only in very special cases. On the whole, it appears that health improvements have been least evident for infants and children, for while the infant mortality rate was 19.5 per 1,000 live births in 2008, the overall death rate was an estimated 5.54 deaths per 1,000 population. Roughly a third of Colombian children suffer from anemia. And a fifth of the infant and child deaths are linked either to diarrheal or respiratory ailments or to other diseases associated with lack of pure water and poor sanitation and living conditions—all more typical of rural areas. The benefits of better medical care and living conditions are thus concentrated both in the upper age-groups and in urban environments. And many of the adult deaths are the result of such social pathologies as homicide and vehicle accidents. In the 1990s, homicide became for a time the leading single cause of mortality in Colombia, reflecting not just the impact of political violence and the illicit drug industry but also other social problems and generally poor standards of law enforcement.

Tropical diseases, including malaria, are endemic still in certain areas; indeed, the currents of internal migration to or from the less-developed tropical hinterland have helped spread not just malaria but also yellow fever, which had once been considered almost extinct. In addition to cerebral malaria, parasitic diseases such as leishmaniasis are still endemic in lowland and coastal areas. The incidence of sexually transmitted diseases is also high. Human immunodeficiency virus/acquired immune deficiency syndrome (HIV/AIDS) is a growing problem, although Colombia was slow to recognize its importance, and for some years, the number of reported cases was undoubtedly far less than the actual total. As in various other countries, reluctance to face the issue is due in part to cultural factors, including a strong rejection of homosexuality. By the beginning of the twenty-first century, there was more willingness to see HIV/AIDS as a threat to the nation's health, and estimates of the affected population are more reliable. With an infection rate of approximately 0.6 percent for the 15–49 age-group, the situation in Colombia remains less critical than in certain Caribbean countries and Brazil but still troublesome.

One other public-health problem that has often received less than its due share of attention is drug addiction. No doubt many Colombians were inclined to minimize the adverse effects of the illicit drugs industry as long as the consumers were in some foreign country, but addiction also became a health issue at home, even if less serious than in the main export markets. At the end of the twentieth century, cocaine users as a percentage of the population were roughly half as numerous in Colombia as in the United States. From an early date, traffickers had made use of low-quality coca paste not suitable for the export trade by dumping it on the domestic market, where, combined with tobacco or other substances, it became *bazuco*, the Colombian equivalent of crack cocaine. However, addiction did not remain a problem simply of the lower social classes but spread to the middle and upper strata just as in North America, based on the use of a more refined cocaine. For the benefit of Colombian consumers, the Constitutional Court declared that possession of small personal dosages must be allowed even if large-scale trafficking is not. However, the administration of President Álvaro Uribe and conservative elements generally have sought to maintain penalties for personal use, and the issue remains unresolved.

The Pension Conundrum

The Colombian social security system has long been an egregious example of an inordinately complex and unfair redistributive mechanism that takes from the poor to give to the middle class and wealthy. For much of the twentieth century, Cajanal, created to administer benefits for different categories of state employees, and the ISS, created to offer retirement coverage to a small number of private-sector employees, were institutional landmarks, but for a minority of Colombians. In 1993 new legislation authorized the establishment of private funds based on the Chilean model, in which pensions are financed from individual accounts into which both employees and employers make direct contributions, and the primary role of the state is to supplement pensions of the lowest earners.

The 1993 reform resulted in large part from the previous disarray and gross inequity in retirement benefits. A multiplicity of funds offered pensions that often bore no relation to the contributions made by the employees and their employers (public or private), so that general tax revenues covered more than three-quarters of the total cost of pensions. Because a majority of Colombians were still not covered—most obviously those in the informal sector, but a great number of others as well—many of the poor who themselves lacked coverage were subsidizing through their taxes retirees from the upper social strata, most of whom were actually covered. Moreover, the retirement ages—originally set at 55 for women and 60 for men—took no account of the fact that Colombians were now living longer. The worst abuse concerned the special pension regimes for particular groups of employees—teachers, the military, members of Congress, and so forth—which often had scandalously high payouts. In principle, the rate of payroll contributions was to have been raised steadily, but this did not happen, so that the total cost of pensions for the Colombian treasury was rapidly becoming unsustainable.

The César Gaviria administration made the first serious effort to reform pensions as a key part of Law 100. The reform did not eliminate the ISS but gave workers the option of having what in effect were individual savings accounts, administered by private funds that would eventually pay the pension benefits. However, the state still promised to provide whatever was needed in order for the pensions of low earners to meet a minimum standard. For anyone who chose to remain with the ISS retirement system, contributions were increased moderately, as was the number of weeks required to work and contribute in order to earn a pension. The law provided for retirement ages to rise to 57 for women and 62 for men, effective in 2014. As things turned out, there was a rush to join the private system, which came to have approximately 5 million workers affiliated (albeit with only half as many contributing at any given moment) as against 2 million in the ISS. But many special retirement funds for privileged groups remained in operation, and under the terms of the law some of its provisions would not take full effect until 2013.

In 2005 a new reform again raised contributions, reduced the period for changes to take effect, and made other adjustments. Some unreasonably high entitlements still exist, and the jurisprudence of the Constitutional Court, which tends to favor litigants with a vested interest in preexisting arrangements, poses a continuing threat to the effectiveness of reforms so far accomplished (see The Judiciary, ch. 4). By 2005 the cost to the state of ISS pensions, together with retirement benefits for which Cajanal is responsible and pensions for those enrolled in the separate special retirement systems, amounted to 30 percent of total tax receipts—all going to 3 percent of the Colombian population. That last figure will inevitably increase, as more people subscribe to a pension and as more retire. In 2008, however, a system both fiscally supportable and socially equitable was still a long way off (see The Pension System, ch.3).

Religion

Religion no longer plays as important a role in Colombian society as it once did, and neither does the Roman Catholic Church, despite close ties to the state and a firm hold on popular sentiment and belief. Church–state relations do not add fuel to political disputes as they did from the mid-nineteenth century to the mid-twentieth century, when heated arguments over such topics as the role of religious orders and the alleged hostility or subservience of political leaders toward high clerics were among the factors spurring Liberals and Conservatives to civil war. Such issues have not been resolved, but they are no longer so controversial. Judging from the steadily falling birthrate, Colombians pay little attention to the church's condemnation of artificial birth control—and indeed it is unlikely that the main reason for previous high rates of population increase was strictly theological. Similarly, priests complain that nowadays few come to confession, whereas not too long ago, at least during Holy Week, one could see long lines in front of the confessionals.

However, the church does not lack influence. Colombians (especially women) are more religiously observant than a majority of other Latin Americans, as measured by attendance at mass and similar indicators. The institutional church, if not all-powerful, is still a significant force in national life. Although Martin Scorsese's controversial 1988 film, *The Last Temptation of Christ*, could not be shown in Colombia for some years because of its seeming disrespect for fundamental tenets of the Christian religion, in 2008 such a restriction on people's right to view what they wanted would have been almost unthinkable.

Opinion polls continue to show a higher degree of public confidence in the Roman Catholic Church than in politicians, journalists, and other institutions. Moreover, not only do the great majority, almost 90 percent, of Colombians still consider themselves Roman

Catholics, but also the Roman Catholic Church maintains a far more impressive institutional structure than any other religious body in the country. The Colombian Roman Catholic Church is divided administratively into 77 dioceses, of which 13 are archdioceses headed by archbishops. Eleven others are technically classified as apostolic vicariates; 12 of them are located in remote areas, but one is the Ministry Ordinariate of Colombia. The archbishop of Bogotá is just one of three Colombians who, by appointment of the pope, belong to the College of Cardinals. The Colombian Episcopal Conference (CEC) represents the hierarchy as a whole. The Roman Catholic priesthood numbers, in total, about 8,000, including roughly 5,700 parish priests and 2,300 who belong to religious orders. There are also slightly more than 1,000 unordained brothers in religious orders and more than 17,000 Roman Catholic sisters. The ratio of Roman Catholic priests to total population, at one in 5,575, is not really adequate to meet the needs of the church but is among the highest in Latin America, and, unusually for the region, members of the clergy are predominantly Colombian natives.

The church further maintains an extensive network of schools to educate the children of its members and any others whose parents care to send them, although they might well need to pay tuition. The CEC even has its own department of education to coordinate education policy and to defend church interests in the field of education. Both regular clergy and religious orders operate universities, including the Jesuits' Javeriana University in Bogotá, which is one of the country's finest. Technically speaking, lay persons run other institutions of higher education that have close ties to the church, in some cases through organizations, such as Opus Dei. The church also continues to operate charitable institutions, such as orphanages and hospitals—alongside programs of social welfare and action that often receive additional support from other sources, including state agencies.

Just as in other aspects of social and cultural life, there are important differences in religious faith and practice from one class or geographic region to another. Upper-class Colombians, with few exceptions, expect to be married in and buried from a Roman Catholic church, have their children baptized, and treat first communion as an important rite of passage. However, in between these family landmarks and the principal festive occasions of the church calendar, they are not always faithful in their religious practice. The intellectual elite, as in so much of the Western world, is largely agnostic, although its members may still observe some of the formal ceremonies out of a respect for cultural tradition, to satisfy more devout family members, or simply for the festive value of the events. The upper-middle class tends to be more observant, and the same can be said

A religious artifacts store, Bogotá
Courtesy Lorenzo Morales

of the peasant populations in Antioquia, the eastern highlands, and certain other regions, commonly with an admixture of folk religion that the ordained clergy may not be quite sure whether to accept as harmless or try to root out. Among rank-and-file lay Roman Catholics, an emphasis on prayer and ritual acts to gain the intercession of the Virgin and saints, in solving immediate problems, takes precedence over the finer points of doctrine and church teaching. But be that as it may, in almost any Colombian small town, the parish church, facing the main plaza, overshadows all other buildings, and the priest is a figure to whom the inhabitants look for more than just spiritual leadership. Indeed, he is likely to be involved even in various state-sponsored social and development programs.

The Colombians who are least observant of official Roman Catholicism are the rural and urban population groups of the Caribbean and Pacific lowlands, where the presence of the institutional church is weakest. Moreover, because free unions and households headed by women tend to outnumber conventional family units in the lowlands, a formal Roman Catholic church marriage is more the exception than the rule. Religious belief nevertheless remains strong, but again with a major strain of folk religion, including elements drawn from the African heritage of so many coastal inhabitants.

Church, State, and Society

The Colombian Roman Catholic clergy had and still has the reputation of being more conservative, politically and theologically, than Latin American clergy in general. During the 1960s and 1970s, following the Second Vatican Council, the church in Colombia, as elsewhere, felt the need to modernize its outlook and at the same time work for the amelioration of social problems. Indeed, a recognizable minority of the Colombian clergy was attracted to the tenets of liberation theology (see Glossary), while also espousing a more rapid pace of social and economic change. A fraction of this minority actually joined the guerrillas, Camilo Torres Restrepo being the best-known example. However, although Father Camilo, who was killed in battle in 1966, became a leftist folk hero, his actions and those of the few others who chose the same path served to discredit the liberationist movement within the clergy, whose only supporter within the hierarchy was Bishop Gerardo Valencia Cano of Buenaventura. The latter's death in a plane crash in 1972 was a serious blow, after which the radical movement among the Colombian clergy attracted steadily less attention. The elevation of John Paul II to the papacy further assured that orthodox clerical and lay figures would fill key positions. And with a moderate liberal democracy as the country's political system, it was easy for the bulk of the Colombian clergy to be politically conformist while tending to pastoral duties. In fact, starting at the time of the bipartisan National Front (1958–78), the Roman Catholic Church as a whole in Colombia assumed what can only be described as a remarkably low profile.

Naturally, there were exceptions. The Research and Public Education Center (Cinep), for example, a think tank based at the Javeriana University, churned out reports highly critical of Colombia's social system (although without giving any express comfort to advocates of violent revolution) and thereby earned a reproof from the hierarchy. Yet toward the end of the century, there was a modest increase of political and other activism that is hard to categorize under the usual labels. The clergy led a successful campaign to make sure that the 1991 Constituent Assembly did not omit mention of God in the preamble to the new constitution, and it has continued to lobby against any form of legalized abortion, euthanasia, or recognition of homosexual partnerships. On these issues, liberal and conservative clerics and lay leaders are for the most part united, in defense of traditional morality. At the same time, however, though with slightly less unanimity, the church has participated in various efforts to facilitate peace in the country's internal conflicts (with certain bishops even engaging in direct negotiations with guerrilla fronts) and in campaigns for the defense of human rights.

Things changed again after President Uribe launched his Democratic Security Policy, which reduced the emphasis on searching for a negotiated peace with the guerrillas in favor of more active resistance to the insurgency (see Internal Armed Conflict and Peace Negotiations, ch. 4; Democratic Security Policy, ch. 5). He received strong if not quite uncritical support from Pedro Rubiano Sáenz, the cardinal-archbishop of Bogotá, and from most but definitely not all of the Colombian church hierarchy. Representatives of all political persuasions in Colombia could thus find reasons from time to time to condemn clerical involvement in politics. Likewise, the clergy has suffered its share of outrages and assassinations inflicted by both guerrillas and paramilitaries, including the murder of two bishops by the guerrillas.

Divorce is an issue that reflects as well as anything the ambiguities and also long-term decline in the power of the church and of traditional religious values (see also Family, this ch.). Divorce became legal in Colombia in 1976, but with a glaring exception: Roman Catholic Church weddings could be dissolved only by ecclesiastical annulment. However, the pressure to obtain such annulments grew steadily, as did social acceptance of de facto separations and of foreign divorces that technically had no validity in Colombia. At least in the cities, the act of shedding or changing spouses no longer drew much attention. That in the 1990 presidential election, the Conservative Party, once a stalwart champion of Roman Catholic values, nominated a divorcé, Rodrigo Lloreda Caycedo, who was remarried to a divorcée, was symptomatic of the change in attitude (but the Liberal Party easily won the election). Finally, the 1991 Constituent Assembly declared that all marriages are subject to the civil law and can therefore be legally terminated.

Although the assembly did not remove the mention of God from the constitution and vigorously rejected a move to legalize abortion, it underscored the increasing secularization of Colombian society, not just by its handling of divorce but also by omitting any reference to Roman Catholicism as the national religion. The constitution now guarantees strict legal equality of all religious denominations. A few years later, the Constitutional Court would put an end to the traditional yearly ceremony consecrating the republic to the Sacred Heart of Jesus. In May 2006, the same court, meeting beneath the crucifix that adorns the wall of its chamber, declared that abortion cannot be prohibited in extreme cases, such as following incest or rape. Despite protests by the clergy and traditionalists, with threats to excommunicate any doctor who carried out such an operation, the decision was not subject to appeal, and the first legal abortions in Colombian history soon took place.

The Growth of Protestantism

Until recently, Colombia's Protestant churches—taking that label in a broad sense to include denominations that might prefer to be categorized simply as evangelical or Pentecostal—played no significant role in national life. Formal religious toleration and the first Protestant (Presbyterian) missionary activity date back to the mid-1800s, but roughly 100 years later Protestants still comprised less than 1 percent of the total population. Even such small numbers often suffered severe repression during the years of La Violencia; their experience attracted attention and sympathy to the Protestant groups and actually seems to have won them new members. However, their main growth has occurred since the 1960s, associated with the rapid social and cultural changes taking place in the country that among so much else weakened habitual allegiance to Roman Catholicism. During this process of expansion, the role of North American and European Protestant missionaries became steadily less important, as Colombians took over the leadership of congregations and other religious bodies; indeed, some of the current evangelical and Pentecostal denominations are of purely Colombian origin.

The growth of Protestantism in Colombia is still less than in many other Latin American countries, but Protestants now make up about 10 percent of the population. The denominations with longstanding roots in Colombia, such as Presbyterians and Methodists, have not been the main beneficiaries of growth. Instead, as in Latin America generally, the most explosive expansion has been that of the churches commonly called Pentecostal—even if the Pentecostal movement was slower to take hold in the Colombian case—with others classified simply as evangelical having moderate growth. The older, established denominations have their greatest strength within the middle sectors of society, whereas the Pentecostal churches, whose style of worship has something in common with the emotional and magical aspects of Latin American popular Roman Catholicism, have had notable success in attracting upwardly mobile members of the working and lower-middle classes. Protestant churches of one sort or another are to be found in all parts of the country, including some traditional Amerindian communities formerly regarded as a special preserve of the Roman Catholic religious orders. The Protestants have built schools, just as the Roman Catholic Church has done, and some denominations are deeply involved in social services, for nonmembers as well as their own congregations. In 1989 a broad range of Protestant churches joined forces to create the Evangelical Confederation of Colombia, which does not include every denomination but does to a large extent speak for the Protestant churches generally.

More unusual was the creation of explicitly evangelical political parties to take part in elections for the 1991 Constituent Assembly: the Christian Union and the Christian National Party. Presenting a joint ticket, they elected two of the 70 members of the assembly, and one of their delegates was named to head a key committee. Their participation, however, was for the most part narrowly focused on the issue of religious liberty and legal equality of all denominations, and the final constitutional text ostensibly satisfied these demands. From the Protestant standpoint, there did remain a few objectionable vestiges of the Roman Catholic Church's previous official status, in the appointment of chaplains for official institutions such as the police, military, or hospitals, and in certain other areas, but these matters were satisfactorily resolved by a decree of Ernesto Samper Pizano (president, 1994–98), in 1998. For the rest, the Colombian Mennonites and a few other Protestant churches became deeply involved in movements for the defense of human rights and for a peaceful solution to the country's armed conflicts, and activists have suffered injuries and death in the process. Protestant parties also have continued taking part in elections, with occasional success. However, various other Protestant groups are resolutely apolitical, and since the time of the Constituent Assembly, the Protestant community has not made its weight felt on major national issues in the way that the Roman Catholic Church does through the CEC or otherwise.

Other Religious Expressions

Religion in Colombia of course consists of more than Roman Catholics and Protestants and interaction between the two. African and Amerindian religious rites and beliefs have survived among the Afro-Colombian and Amerindian populations, generally in some combination with Christian elements. Indeed, there are distinct congregations that expressly identify themselves in terms of syncretism.

There is a small Jewish community, most of which has its origin in the limited and restricted immigration of European Jews during the second quarter of the twentieth century. By 2005 the community numbered only about 4,200, down from about 25,000 in the 1980s. Many emigrated because criminal and terrorist groups targeted the relatively well-off Jewish community for kidnappings for ransom.

Colombia likewise has Muslim citizens, some of them the product of Middle Eastern immigration, even though most of the Syrians and other Arabs who came to Colombia were Christian; others are the result of proselytizing initiated by a follower of Malcolm X from the United States among Afro-Colombian communities of the Pacific coast. Lebanese—usually referred to as Turks (*turcos*) or Syrians because they came from the Christian Lebanese part of Syria that formerly belonged to Turkey—are active in commerce, particularly in the port cities of Barranquilla, Buenaventura, and Cartagena. Some Lebanese married into the Wayuu indigenous population. Estimates of Colombia's Muslim population range from an improbable low of 10,000 to a likely 200,000.

Education

Although individual Colombians have excelled in literature and other fields of intellectual endeavor, the country is not renowned for the quality of its public and private educational institutions. With a few temporary exceptions, public education of the lower-income masses has not received high priority. Over the years, formal education instead catered to the middle and upper social strata, with emphasis on preparing their children for the more prestigious professions (law in particular). As good an indicator as any of the lack of broad educational achievement was a persistently low rate of adult literacy, albeit close to the norm for Latin America. Roughly a third of Colombians 15 years of age or older could read in 1900, and the rate barely exceeded one-half of the population in 1930. Moreover, as late as 1950 only 1 percent of Colombians received exposure to university-level training. Almost all of them were males because only since the 1930s had women been allowed to enter Colombian universities.

Basic Education

Under the 1991 constitution, the basic education cycle is free and compulsory for all Colombian children between the ages of five and 15 and consists, at a minimum, of one year of preprimary education (kindergarten), five years of primary school, and the first four years of secondary education. However, the schooling offered does not always meet these guidelines, especially in rural areas. Primary education is provided for children between six and 12 years of age. For those who have completed the primary cycle successfully, secondary education lasting up to six years is theoretically available. Following completion of a first cycle of four years, secondary

*A classroom scene at a primary school in the mountain town of Armenia,
the capital of Quindío Department, where an earthquake killed
1,000 residents on January 25, 1999
Courtesy Inter-American Development Bank (Daniel Drosdoff),
Washington, DC*

pupils may pursue a further two years of study, leading to the bacca-
laureate examination.

All standard indicators show significant advances over the last half-
century in providing Colombians with at least the bare minimum of
skills required to function effectively as members of contemporary society. At the most basic level, adult literacy, Colombia has done even better than Cuba, where the campaign to extirpate illiteracy was justly
celebrated but began from a much higher starting point. By the beginning of the twenty-first century, the rate of illiteracy had fallen (naturally
depending on the definition used) to 8 percent, still more than twice the
figure for Cuba or for Argentina but better than Brazil (above 12 percent) and of an order wholly different from the figure at mid-twentieth
century. Also positive was the trend in coverage of primary education,
whether gross coverage (the relation between total school attendance
and the population of primary school age) or net coverage (referring
only to the attendance of children actually of primary age). The former
of these two measurements went from 43 percent in 1950 to 87 percent
in 1970 and, after relapsing in the 1980s because of fiscal crises and
other distractions, reached 110 percent at the beginning of the twenty-
first century. By the latter date, net coverage—that is, disregarding the

127

older or younger children who were nevertheless enrolled in primary grades—came to approximately 90 percent. Less striking was the increase in the actual years of schooling received by Colombians now older than 15 years of age, from an average of slightly more than five at mid-twentieth century to somewhere still between five and six years in the 1980s. Naturally, this figure reflects among other things the fact that many present-day Colombians had already reached adulthood before the recent increase in educational opportunity.

The statistics on literacy and primary coverage also need qualification, as they obscure significant regional and social differences. In major cities, literacy is close to universal, and net coverage in the primary grades is not far behind. In rural Colombia, the picture is different. Some rural families simply live too far from the nearest school, while others still do not see the benefits to be gained by formal schooling. Another factor of equal or greater importance is the failure of local authorities in many places to provide sufficient schools and adequately staff them with teachers—whether for sheer lack of resources, inefficiency, or outright corruption. The national government itself oversees all education in Colombia and provides most of the funding for public schools, whether directly from the Ministry of National Education or in the form of revenue transfers to departments and municipalities as required by the constitution of 1991. However, as a result of the decentralization begun in the 1980s and accelerated under the terms of the 1991 constitution, the ministry now shares control of the schools with regional and local bureaucracies, frequently beholden to entrenched political machines, whose record of performance varies widely. Considerable confusion as to responsibilities in educational administration continues, even though the 1994 Education Law put the Ministry of National Education ultimately in charge of public and private education.

For most of the time since independence, it is safe to say that although the state took the chief responsibility for primary education and for universities, private schools (religious and otherwise) were dominant at the secondary level. Moreover, because the private schools charged tuition, which most Colombians could not pay, secondary education functioned as a bottleneck that severely limited upward mobility. Today, the picture is somewhat different, as far as secondary and higher education are concerned, but the state is, if anything, even more dominant in the primary sector.

In public primary education, there have been some promising advances, such as the introduction in the 1970s of the New School (Escuela Nueva) program, which features the establishment of multi-grade rural schools emphasizing parent participation and modern, flexible teaching methods; some schools in this program have out-performed urban schools in test scores. There are also some highly questionable private schools set up in improvised quarters by enter-prising citizens with no particular educational training—known in Colombia as *colegios de garage*, or garage schools—the term *colegio* as used in Colombia covering a much wider gamut than the English *college*. Nevertheless, the overall quality of private education is in most cases superior to public. And there is an even greater differ-ence, perhaps, in the prestige of attending one or the other, so that domestic servants, for example, will sometimes undergo real hard-ship for the sake of sending a child to a private *colegio*.

The superiority of private schools results in considerable part from the same factors—inadequate resources and mismanagement of those available—that still limit overall public education coverage, especially in rural areas (where virtually all schools are public). Although all public-school students are supposed to receive free textbooks, that does not always happen in practice. Despite consider-able progress since the 1960s, when rapid expansion of the school system was just getting underway and the shortage of qualified teachers was extreme, there are still some teachers whose formal education extends barely beyond the grades they are teaching. Fur-ther improvements are at times made more difficult by the strength of the Colombian Federation of Educators (Fecode), which is the largest labor union in the country. Fecode has been unhappy with the government's recent emphasis on decentralization, finding it easier to exert pressure at the national level; and it tends to resist anything that might resemble a purge of ineffective classroom teachers.

In percentage terms, the expansion of secondary education since the mid-twentieth century is even more impressive than that of pri-mary schooling, from gross coverage of less than 5 percent in 1950 to 35 percent in 1980 and 70 percent by the century's end. Although dif-ferent methods of calculation may give higher or lower figures, the trend is unmistakable. Noteworthy also is the changing balance in enrollments, between public and private institutions. Whereas private schools had long absorbed a majority of secondary students, by 2000 some two-thirds were enrolled in state schools. This shift, together with the quantitative increase in secondary education, means that the secondary level is no longer quite the bottleneck impeding upward mobility that it once was. At the same time, a significant number of students from families of lesser means received aid from the state or certain private sources so that they could attend private institutions.

Secondary schools of any variety are overwhelmingly located in urban areas, however, and the private institutions, although now enrolling a minority of secondary students, continue to offer generally higher-quality training (as well as conferring more prestige). Some state schools, it is true, match the standards of the better private schools, while in the private sector there are *colegios de garage* offering secondary as well as primary classes. Nevertheless, private institutions are still at the apex of the education system, especially those associated with particular foreign communities such as the Colegio Anglo-Colombiano or the Colegio Nueva Granada. The latter, established in Bogotá on the model of a U.S. preparatory school, caters both to resident North Americans and to Colombians hoping to send their sons or daughters to a university in the United States. Many upper-class Colombians do go abroad, to Europe or North America, for university education.

University, Technical, and Vocational Education

The Colombians who go on to higher education in their own country are both far more numerous than before and faced with a remarkably increased range of institutions to choose from. Today Bogotá alone hosts 113 main tertiary education institutions. By 2000 the percentage of Colombians attending a university or other institution of higher education had risen to 22 percent. Net coverage or attendance of university-age students was lower, but a majority were now women. Until the 1940s, students could go to the National University of Colombia and a few other state universities in the rest of the country; to a network of normal schools and teacher-training institutes; and to a few private universities, such as the Javeriana University in Bogotá and the Pontifical Bolivarian University, of more recent foundation, in Medellín. In the immediate postwar period, these institutions were joined by the University of the Andes (Uniandes), founded in Bogotá in 1948 as a nonsectarian, nonpartisan institution designed to provide higher education on the model of the better North American private universities. It enjoyed critical support from the business community and from moderate elements of the two political parties. With a select student body, small classes, and well-qualified professors, it soon consolidated a reputation—inside and outside Colombia—as the country's most distinguished institution of higher learning. Today Colombia has 30 public universities (seven national and 23 departmental).

The explosive growth of private universities came a bit later, beginning in the 1960s, as a result of the excessive politicization of the National University of Colombia and other public universities, whose students seemed at times more interested in demonstrating for left-wing causes than in studying. By no means were all students

One of many new public libraries in poor sections of Bogotá, the El Tunal Public Library has 6,826 square meters of space and a capacity for 110,000 volumes. Courtesy Lorenzo Morales

political activists, but when serious unrest of any sort caused a university to be closed for a length of time, as repeatedly happened, all students suffered. The closures offered opportunities to new private universities, ranging from substandard *universidades de garage* to others that sought to emulate the rigorous standards of Uniandes, such as the University of the North in Barranquilla. Private universities are now much more numerous than public ones and enroll the largest share of the university-age population. Of the main private universities, 14 are Roman Catholic and 26, nonsectarian. Both public and private institutions are now endeavoring, with varying degrees of success, to adapt the U.S. model of higher education to Colombian circumstances. There has been a significant general advance of studies in economics, engineering, and business administration at the expense of studies in law and medicine, while pure and applied natural sciences have continued to lag.

Colombia also has a variety of technical and vocational institutions that mostly operate at the secondary level but sometimes extend into higher education, which in Colombia tends to be broadly defined. They include secretarial schools (mainly private), regional normal schools, the National Apprenticeship Service (Sena), the National Institutes of Diversified Intermediate Education (INEMs), and assorted others. Sena, established in 1957 and supported by levies on larger business enterprises, provides courses to upgrade the skills of industrial and other workers and to improve the training of supervisors as well, but in recent years, it has become increasingly involved in technical and technological training. Since 1969 the INEMs, some of which are really excellent, have provided some training similar to that offered by Sena, along with general education courses. Both Sena and the INEMs have made a positive contribution, not simply to the advancement of education as such but also to Colombian economic development.

Continuing Problems

The most obvious deficiency of the education system is that despite recent progress, and efforts to achieve universal coverage at the primary level, provision at all levels still lags behind that of many Latin American countries, to say nothing of the developed-world standards that Colombia aspires to achieve. This lag is compounded by the continuing gap in access to education among regions and social classes and by the poor quality of so much of the education on offer from primary through university levels. Public spending on education in 2005 came to 4.5 percent of GDP, a higher figure than for Argentina and Chile but still lagging behind the standards of countries belonging to the OECD. By comparison, Colombian government expenditures on education in the 1999 budget represented 19.7 percent of total spending.

Social Movements

From a societal as well as purely economic standpoint, the most important structural problem facing Colombia today is clearly the high rate of inequality, which ultimately also accounts for most of the shortcomings in health care and education. Among critical problems, the plight of the *desplazados*, which is hard to deal with and difficult for some Colombians to comprehend, is the most urgent. But other members of Colombian civil society have sought to confront these and other challenges with everything from ad hoc mobilizations to new formal organizations, all these activities being conventionally lumped together under the broad heading of "social movements." New movements, focusing on human rights; the environment; or issues of ethnicity, gender, and sexual orientation now preoccupy Colombians, alongside older issues, such as the student, labor, and peasant movements (see Other Parties and Political Movements, ch. 4).

As in other Latin American countries, the university students' movement in Colombia enjoyed special prestige because of the supposed idealism of its young members. Since the dissolution in the 1960s of the National University Federation, students have lacked one primary nationwide organization and instead have gathered in congeries of separate student organizations along political, regional, gender, or ethnic lines, or following some other particular orientation. Since the 1970s, there has been a decline in radical activism on university campuses, even though it certainly has not disappeared. However, student groups can still make their weight felt. Student marches, most involving secondary students from private institutions, helped convince the government to convoke the 1991 Constituent Assembly. And any serious project to reform the public universities can be counted on to bring forth a slew of protest demonstrations that may or may not abort the proposal.

Organized labor, for its part, reached a high point in membership during the National Front era, when the unions enrolled approximately 15 percent of those Colombians who might potentially have joined one. Since then, however, there has been a steady decline, which the unification in 1986 of most of the labor movement under the banner of the United Workers' Federation (CUT) was unable to stem. By 1990 membership had fallen to 8 percent, although total numbers had not changed much because of the increase in population. The proportion today would be about 5 percent, with most unionized workers concentrated in the public sector. Along with the decline in membership, strike actions have become less frequent and the role of organized labor in politics less significant. The election of former CUT leader Luis Eduardo ("Lucho") Garzón as mayor of Bogotá in 2003 might have seemed to mark a labor revival, but his victory was more a personal triumph and that of a promising new, leftist party.

One frequent explanation given for the declining fortunes of organized labor is that the state and private business interests have worked hand in hand to undermine the unions' strength. There have been cases in which the former Ministry of Labor (now part of the Ministry of Social Protection) too readily declared a given strike illegal, which presumably had the further effect of deterring some other unions from trying to use the strike weapon. This explanation also highlights instances of murder and other violence against union activists, in which respect Colombia has the unenviable distinction of leading all Latin American nations by a wide margin. To be sure, state security agents or employers' hit squads do not necessarily orchestrate these attacks, however much government critics like to imply that they do. More important, in any event, as a cause of organized labor's decline, are changes in the economy, such as the relative decline of industries in which organized labor once was strong (Colombian railroads being here an extreme example) and the high unemployment, particularly since the mid-1990s, which weakened labor's bargaining power. Reduced union strength is another feature that Colombia shares with other countries in the modern world. Moreover, a host of other social movements strongly support the causes that labor holds dear, such as the defense of its own organizers or opposition to neoliberal economic policies (see also Labor Unions, ch. 4).

The main peasants' organization, the National Association of Peasant Land Users (ANUC), had its peak in the early 1970s, when it enrolled 40 percent of the economically active agrarian population, but from that peak the organization suffered a far more precipitous decline than the labor unions. A contributing factor was the advance of mechanized commercial agriculture at the expense of more labor-intensive traditional farming, but a greater problem was the mere fact that the countryside was the main arena of the armed conflicts being waged in Colombia. Peasant leaders and followers were caught in the crossfire of guerrillas, paramilitaries, and armed forces, while even those who tried desperately to distance themselves from the parties in conflict were liable to come under suspicion as sympathizers of a given armed band and suffer violence at the hands of its adversaries. ANUC itself, under intense pressure from both the government and its supporters and the leftist guerrillas, was torn by dissension and split into two main branches, neither of which could speak with unquestioned authority on behalf of Colombian peasants. Indeed, the fragmentation continued, although the splinter groups still were able to stage protests against human rights abuses and demonstrations in favor of land redistribution.

Agrarian protests often were staged in coordination with groups representing the indigenous population, among them the Cauca Regional Indigenous Council, itself formed in 1971 under ANUC auspices. The Amerindian movement was not immune to the tug and intrusions of opposing political forces, but with ethnic identity as an organizing principle, its members were strongly inclined to avoid entanglement as far as possible in the quarrels of non-Amerindians. Lack of agreement led to disunity among those who thought in terms of a Colombia-wide indigenous community, those who identified primarily with a subnational ethnicity (or "tribe," as non-Amerindians might put it), and others who chose to emphasize the strictly local level. But whatever sense of identity the Amerindians preferred, it was inevitably sharpened in reaction to the unwelcome presence of non-Amerindian armed bands on or adjacent to their lands. Moreover, an umbrella organization, the National Indigenous Organization of Colombia (ONIC), was founded in 1982. In addition to providing some coordination among different sectors of the Amerindian movement, ONIC has sought to represent indigenous interests generally in dealing with the Colombian state and also through participation in certain government programs.

The Amerindian communities were awarded a special quota of representation (two out of 70 seats) in the 1991 Constituent Assembly, and the resulting new constitution provided for special treatment in future elections. The constitution likewise guaranteed indigenous communities the secure possession of ancestral lands and respect for traditional customs. Central to their agenda since then has been the demand that these provisions be properly implemented; to that end, their organizations have made effective use of both lobbying and judicial action. Indigenous communities also have taken part in some campaigns of highly marginal significance to their own interests, such as when they joined demonstrations against a proposed free-trade treaty with the United States. Most noteworthy, however, has been their struggle against the depredations of guerrillas and paramilitaries, as well as opposition to unwelcome attention from the nation's security forces. In certain well-publicized cases from the Cauca region especially, this has taken the form of a Gandhian kind of unarmed civil resistance.

The Afro-Colombian population is several times larger than the Amerindian but, with the main exception of certain isolated communities, has less of a sense of distinct identity. It has been more open to assimilation and has long enjoyed legal equality with other Colombians. Nevertheless, Afro-Colombians are naturally aware of de facto inequalities, and in the closing decades of the twentieth century, black intellectuals took the lead in demanding greater recognition; one of them, novelist Juan Zapata Olivella, even made a symbolic run for the presidency in 1980. In the new constitution, Afro-Colombians, like Amerindians, are guaranteed political representation and respect for their lands and traditions, although in practice few took the step of explicitly identifying themselves as members of an Afro-Colombian community in order to take advantage of the special voting jurisdiction created for them. Both within and outside the political system, Afro-Colombians continued denouncing instances of mistreatment, many of them by-products of rural conflict, or apparent land grabs by narco-paramilitaries at their communities' expense.

A somewhat special case is that of the *raizal* population of the Archipiélago de San Andrés, Providencia y Santa Catalina, which feels threatened by an influx of mainland Colombians and by increasing attention from the authorities in Bogotá that results at least in part from a desire to show the flag in Colombia's territorial dispute with Nicaragua. Some have gone so far as to raise a call for independence, although such an aim is scarcely practicable, not least because the *raizales* are no longer an actual majority of the islands' population.

The concerns of indigenous and Afro-Colombian communities coincide with those of "green" activists, who are mostly urban-based, in defense of the environment against the degradation inflicted by guerrillas, paramilitaries, and the state itself. Two obvious examples are the pollution of streams and rivers by the favorite guerrilla tactic of blowing up oil pipelines, and the government's aerial spraying of coca plantings with herbicides, the long-term effects of which are subject to debate, but which inevitably spill over onto legal crops as well. Then there are all the common environmental problems that stem from activities of modern civilization, whether the building of roads through pristine natural settings or the inadequate disposal of used chemical inputs (a practice particularly associated with the illicit drugs industry). Colombia can boast a comprehensive body of regulations designed to protect the environment, but the bureaucratic machinery and even the will to enforce them are often lacking. Strong U.S. support for aerial spraying has resulted in an unusually broad swathe of anti-U.S. protesters when demonstrations against the policy have been held, and these are no doubt partly responsible for the erratic stop-and-go application of spraying. Yet the environmental effects of armed conflict pose an even greater challenge, and one impossible to fully meet while the conflict drags on (see Environment, this ch.).

The women's movement, for its part, would seem already to have achieved its main objectives: women's right to vote came late to Colombia (in 1954), but even before the constitution of 1991, women had obtained, in effect, full formal equality with men. Women have been well represented in appointive positions up to and including the ministries of communications, national defense, and foreign relations, although their representation in Congress remains low; and they still do not have the full reproductive freedom that activists identify with an unrestricted right to abortion. In practice, however, women's groups in recent years have been concerned above all to protest the prolongation of armed struggle in the country, the violation of human rights, and, in particular, the widespread violence against women not just as part of armed conflict but also in the home and neighborhood, where not all ordinary males have taken to heart the notion of equality between the sexes.

Gender issues also are involved in one of the newest social movements of all, that of the LGBT (lesbian, gay, bisexual, and transgender) community, whose members have become increasingly vocal in their demands for respect and for access to such things as the partner benefits normally extended only to those in heterosexual relationships. So far, there has been little progress on the matter of benefits, but the Sunday following June 28 has become the date of an annual gay pride parade in Bogotá that would have been unthinkable in 1990. Nothing else, perhaps, so forcefully symbolizes the ongoing changes from a society steeped in Roman Catholic tradition to one that increasingly takes its cues from the global media—and from the spirit of renovation sanctioned for better or worse by the 1991 constitution.

*　　　　*　　　　*

Raymond Leslie Williams and Kevin G. Guerrieri's *Culture and Customs of Colombia* provides a general introductory overview of Colombian society, including topics beyond the scope of this chapter, such as social customs, daily life, and the arts. Alberto Gerardino Rojas's *Colombia: Geografía* is a particularly useful reference source. On environmental issues, the most comprehensive and informative source is *Environmental Priorities and Poverty Reduction: A Country Environmental Analysis for Colombia*, edited by World Bank staffers Ernesto Sánchez-Triana, Kulsum Ahmed, and Yewande

Awe. The Web site of the National Administrative Department of Statistics (DANE) at http://www.dane.gov.co/censo/ is the reference for demographic findings of the Colombian census of 2005, although nonregistered users have only very limited access to DANE data. Carmen Elisa Flórez Nieto's *Las transformaciones sociodemográficas en Colombia durante el siglo XX* is a general discussion of sociodemographic changes in Colombia during the twentieth century. *Gota a Gota: Desplazamiento forzado en Bogotá y Soacha* is a recent in-depth report on displacement, especially as it has affected Bogotá, by the Consultancy for Human Rights and Displacement (Codhes) and Bogotá's Migrants' Care Foundation (Famig) of the Arquidiócesis de Bogotá. Peter Wade's *Blackness and Race Mixture: The Dynamics of Racial Identity in Colombia* is a good English work on race and informal discrimination in Colombia. For an official report on the country's ethnic diversity, the best source is *Colombia, una nación multicultural: Su diversidad étnica*, by DANE.

Dated but still useful scholarly works in English on Colombian society include T. Lynn Smith's *Colombia: Social Structure and the Process of Development*, which provides an overview of the profound changes in the country's traditional agrarian social structures during the twentieth century up to the mid-1960s, and Orlando Fals-Borda's *Peasant Society in the Colombian Andes: A Sociological Study of Saucio*, a classic case study of the impact of modernization on Colombia's rural communities in the 1950s and early 1960s. Virginia Gutiérrez de Pineda's *La familia en Colombia: Trasfondo histórico* provides an excellent overview of the evolution of family structures.

Albert Berry and Miguel Urrutia's *Income Distribution in Colombia* explores how the benefits of Colombia's rapid economic growth after World War II were distributed by regions and strata in the mid-1970s, whereas Urrutia's *Winners and Losers in Colombia's Economic Growth of the 1970s* revises and updates his earlier work with Berry through the end of the decade. Recent standard works on income distribution and related issues are Alejandro Gaviria Trujillo's *Los que suben y los que bajan: Educación y movilidad social en Colombia* and Armando Montenegro and Rafael Rivas's *Las piezas del rompecabezas: Desigualdad, pobreza y crecimiento*. For monographic chapters on all aspects of recent Colombian development, one may turn to the multivolume *Nueva historia de Colombia* edited by Alvaro Tirado Mejía. On public-health conditions and trends since the 1990s, *La salud está grave: Una visión desde los derechos humanos* by Víctor de Currea Lugo, Mario Hernández Alvarez, and Natalia Paredes Hernández is informative. Daniel

Levine discusses the changing role of the Roman Catholic Church in Colombia in the twentieth century in *Religion and Politics in Latin America: The Catholic Church in Venezuela and Colombia*. For more recent developments as well as broad and detailed analyses on the evolution of religion in Colombia, one may consult the work edited by Ana María Bidegaín and Juan Diego Demera Vargas, *Globalización y diversidad religiosa en Colombia*, and Bidegaín's *Historia del cristianismo en Colombia: Corrientes y diversidad*. Rebecca Pierce Bomann's *Faith in the Barrios: The Pentecostal Poor in Bogotá*, covers its subject well. The basic reference on education is Aline Helg's *La educación en Colombia*; a more recent overview is provided in an article by Alfredo Sarmiento Gómez, "Equity and Education in Colombia." (For further information and complete citations, see Bibliography.)

Chapter 3. The Economy

FOLLOWING A LONG TRADITION of heavy state intervention in and active management of the Colombian economy, the end of the 1980s and the beginning of the 1990s were years of wide-ranging, market-oriented reforms aimed at promoting private-sector participation, enhancing trade, improving the performance of the financial sector, and making labor and product markets more efficient. A new constitution enacted in 1991 also had broad implications for the economy, in particular for monetary and fiscal policy, through the establishment of an independent Bank of the Republic (Banrep; hereafter, Central Bank) and the promotion of fiscal decentralization.

These changes have made present-day Colombia a more diversified national economy and better integrated with the world economy. The service sector has continued increasing its proportion of the nation's gross domestic product (GDP—see Glossary). Mineral exports and remittances have become an important source of foreign exchange. The country's longtime dependency on revenue from coffee has significantly diminished. National and foreign private-sector entrepreneurs now have greater involvement in the provision of public services and in the exploration and exploitation of natural resources. Domestic consumers have gained access to greater varieties and qualities of a wide range of goods and services. In the meantime, the government has strengthened its role as a market regulator.

The heavy burden on the fiscal accounts that resulted from implementing fiscal decentralization led to a significant increase in the vulnerability of the economy to international shocks. Together with a very unsettled domestic security situation, these shocks severely complicated and delayed the achievement of several of the goals expected from the broader market-oriented reforms. As a result, the second half of the 1990s was a period of diminished and more volatile growth, including, in 1999, the first and only recession since 1931. Overall, the years between 1995 and 2000 were a period of disappointing economic performance and deterioration of many social indicators.

During 2000–7 achievements in domestic security, a more prudent fiscal policy, and a more benign international environment allowed the economy to recover, unemployment to shrink, and economic prospects to improve. Inflation decreased from more than 30 percent per year in 1990 to 5.7 percent per year in 2007, a level close to that of developed countries. By 2005 Colombia ranked as a lower middle-income country, with a per capita income of US$2,735 and with a GDP that was the fifth largest in Latin America, behind Brazil, Mexico, Argentina, and

Venezuela. Still, Colombia remains a nation with very high poverty levels—49.5 percent in 2005, according to the government of Álvaro Uribe Vélez (president, 2002–6, 2006–10)—and with one of the most uneven income distributions in Latin America and the world.

Economic History, 1819–1999

Growth and Structure of the Economy, 1819–1989

Colombia first became an exporting region in the sixteenth century, under the Spanish system of mercantilism (see Colonial Society and Economy, ch. 1). Spanish imperial rule defined much of Colombia's social and economic development. The colony became an exporter of raw materials, particularly precious metals, to the mother country. With its colonial status came a highly structured socioeconomic system based on slavery, indentured servitude, and limited foreign contact. Colombia's contemporary economy, based on coffee and other agricultural exports, did not emerge until after independence in 1819, when local entrepreneurs were free to capitalize on world markets other than Spain.

Although colonialism fostered minimal domestic economic growth, small entrepreneurial efforts began to take shape, so that by the nineteenth century well-defined economic enterprises existed. The economy at that time was based primarily on mining, agriculture, and cattle raising, with contributions also by local artisans and merchants.

Socioeconomic changes proceeded slowly; the economic system functioned as a loosely related group of regional producers rather than as a national entity. Land and wealth were still the privileges of a minority. Forced labor continued in the mines, and various labor arrangements existed on the haciendas, such as sharecropping and low-wage labor. In each case, those owning the land benefited excessively, whereas those working the land remained impoverished.

In the late nineteenth century, tobacco and coffee export industries developed, greatly enlarging the merchant class and leading to population expansion and the growth of cities. The concentration of economic activity in agriculture and commerce, two sectors that focused on opening channels to world markets, continued slowly but steadily throughout the nineteenth century.

Following the War of the Thousand Days (1899–1902), Colombia experienced a coffee boom that catapulted the country into the modern period, bringing the attendant benefits of transportation, particularly railroads, communications infrastructure, and the first major attempts at manufacturing (see A New Age of Peace and Coffee,

1904–30, ch. 1). The period 1905–15 has been described as the most significant growth phase in Colombian history, characterized by an expansion of exports and government revenues, as well as an overall rise in the GDP. Coffee contributed most to trade, growing from only 8 percent of total exports at the beginning of the 1870s to nearly 75 percent by the mid-1920s. Beyond its direct economic impact, the expansion of coffee production also had a profound social effect. In sharp contrast to mining and to some agricultural products such as bananas, which were grown on large plantations, coffee production in Colombia historically developed on very small plots of land. As a result, it generated an important class of small landowners whose income depended on a major export commodity. Unprecedented amounts of foreign capital found their way into both private investment and public works during this period because of the strong performance of coffee and other exports.

The rapid growth and development of the economy in the early twentieth century helped to strengthen the country so it was largely resistant to the Great Depression that began in 1929. Colombia continued to produce raw materials, and, although coffee prices collapsed during the Depression, output continued to expand. Nonetheless, social and economic improvements were uneven.

The expansion of the coffee industry laid the groundwork for national economic integration after World War II. During the course of the postwar expansion, Colombia underwent a distinct transformation. Before the 1950s, because of the steep terrain and a relatively primitive transportation network, local industries that were only loosely linked to other regional businesses dominated the manufacturing sector. Improved transportation facilities, financed directly and indirectly by the coffee industry, fostered national development. Greater economic integration soon became evident with the heavier concentration of industry and population in the six largest cities. Coffee's success, therefore, led ultimately to a reliable transportation network that hastened urbanization and industrialization.

In addition to coffee production, economic expansion of both the rest of the industrial sector and the services sector took place in two distinct stages. From 1950 until 1967, Colombia followed a well-defined program of import-substitution industrialization, with most manufacturing startups directed toward domestic consumption that previously had been satisfied by imports. After 1967 planners in both government and industry shifted the economic strategy to export promotion, emphasizing nontraditional exports, such as clothing and other manufactured consumables, in addition to processed coffee.

From 1967 to 1980, the Colombian economy, and particularly the coffee industry, experienced sustained growth. Because of severe weather problems affecting the world's largest exporter, Brazil, coffee prices reached unprecedented levels in the mid-1970s. High prices prompted an important expansion in coffee production in Colombia. This expansion involved a significant increase in the harvested area and, more importantly, the introduction of a high-yielding coffee variety. In just over a decade, Colombia's coffee production doubled. The expansion of production and exports boosted the income and purchasing capacity of the thousands of households involved in coffee cultivation, thereby increasing consumption rapidly and allowing the GDP to expand at an average annual rate of more than 5 percent during this period. Strong export earnings and a large increase in foreign-exchange reserves were the most noticeable results of this economic expansion. At the same time, the Central Bank had to use a variety of policies and instruments at its disposal in order to prevent inflation from accelerating.

Most of the second half of the twentieth century, at least until the late 1980s, saw Colombia's economy being managed in a reasonably conservative way. By all accounts, and contrary to most other countries in the region, the government did not indulge in populist macroeconomic policies. The fiscal accounts were never seriously out of balance, and, as a result, public debt remained at comfortable levels. Foreign finance flowing to the region diminished significantly at the beginning of the 1980s, and Colombia was the only major Latin American economy that did not default on or restructure its public debt. This prudent policy stance resulted in rather stable if modest economic performance, despite a wide range of international shocks, including shifts in the prices of coffee and oil, the international debt crisis, and swings in the economic performance of its main trading partners.

In the 1980s, the government played a simultaneous role as a legislator, regulator, and entrepreneur, particularly in the provision of public utilities and in the exploitation of major natural resources, such as oil and coal. Colombia also used diverse trade-policy tools, such as tariffs and quotas, in order to promote import substitution, supplemented after 1967 by export promotion and economic diversification. To encourage exports, a competitive exchange rate became a centerpiece of macroeconomic policy, together with several export subsidies, including tax exemptions and subsidized credit. The initial export-promotion strategy did not include import liberalization as one of its components. A prominent feature of the export-promotion strategy was that the Central Bank stood ready to vary the fixed but adjustable exchange rate to compensate for domestic inflation, in order to maintain the competitiveness of domestic producers. As a result, the exchange rate became indexed to the rate of inflation, and it did not take long for a vicious circle to develop, one in which inflation fed into the exchange rate and vice versa. Consequently, and notwithstanding a tradition of prudent fiscal policies, for a long period Colombia was characterized by a moderate, albeit stable, rate of inflation. Widespread indexation mechanisms, particularly for wages, public utilities, and mortgage-interest rates, blurred most income-redistribution effects generally associated with inflation.

The financial sector became highly regulated, and the Central Bank established a range of subsidized credit lines. The government intervened heavily in the foreign-exchange markets by setting prices and controlling access to foreign exchange. The Central Bank had a monopoly over the purchase and sale of all foreign exchange. Traders had to surrender export proceeds to the bank, and importers had to meet all their foreign-exchange requirements through the Central Bank. Consequently, a black market for foreign exchange emerged, which would eventually be the vehicle of choice to bring back to Colombia part of the proceeds flowing from the sale of illicit drugs in the United States and Europe. Strict regulations also governed international capital flows, and foreign direct investment became highly regulated. International agreements among the Andean Community of Nations (see Glossary) members prohibited foreign investment in the financial sector.

Because the fiscal position remained broadly under control, Colombia managed to service its foreign debt during the debt crisis of the 1980s. Average growth was not very high, but, unlike other regional economies, no sharp recession occurred either. Likewise, inflation was stable at moderate levels. On the negative side, in the late 1980s Colombia had grim prospects for productivity growth. The expansion of the labor force and increases in the capital stock engendered economic growth, but both factors were exploited very inefficiently. The government and the international financial institutions, especially the World Bank, concluded that the lackluster performance and bleak prospects for productivity growth to a great extent reflected the economy's inadequate exposure to foreign competition and the prevalence of government intervention in the economy. In addition, the increasing internal conflict, in which guerrilla groups, paramilitaries, and drug cartels were major players, had negative economic effects, primarily by displacing legal and productive agricultural activities. The insecurity fostered huge investments in sectors inconducive to economic efficiency, such as low-density cattle raising on some of Colombia's most productive land, and created a very unfavorable environment for domestic and, especially, foreign investors.

Thus, in common with other developing countries, particularly in Latin America, the late 1980s and early 1990s in Colombia were years of major changes. Some of the changes, particularly at the initial stages of the reform process, were geared toward enhancing competition and making several markets more efficient. These changes included meaningful trade liberalization in 1989 and labor, financial, and foreign-exchange reforms beginning in 1989 and 1990 (see Macroeconomic Policies and Trends, this ch.).

The 1990s: A Decade of Economic Reform

In 1991 the country elected a Constituent Assembly in order to write a new constitution that would replace the 1886 charter. The drive toward this major change was not related to economic issues. Rather, it took place within a complex political scenario, including a peace process with the Nineteenth of April Movement (M–19) guerrilla group and the debate over how to bring major drug lords to justice.

Important provisions in the 1991 constitution would have lasting effects on the economy, particularly the articles that aided the over-arching goal of facilitating progress toward long-awaited peace and political reconciliation. Of particular importance were the promotion of fiscal decentralization and the social role of the state. The aim of fiscal decentralization was to complement the process of political decentralization that had been initiated in the mid-1980s, with the popular election of city mayors. The social role of the state was deemed a necessary supplement to recent economic reforms, in order to ensure that the benefits resulting from these reforms would reach the vast majority of the population. The manner in which these critical issues were eventually handled had profound implications for the constant increases in public expenditure. Inasmuch as the growth in government outlays was not matched by increases in taxes or other government revenue, the fiscal provisions in the constitution had a negative effect on the public debt. The new constitution also made the Central Bank independent, with a mandate to strive for a low and stable rate of inflation.

Between 1989 and 1992, Colombia went through an unprecedented period of change in economic policy and institutions. These reform processes, which might not seem particularly ambitious when compared with other experiences in Latin America, were rather exceptional within Colombia, given the country's long tradition of moving very slowly and cautiously on reforms. One set of policies—including trade liberalization, labor and financial sector reform, and Central Bank independence—was geared toward promoting trade and competition, enhancing flexibility, and increasing productivity. Another set of policies—especially fiscal decentralization and the constitutionally mandated social role of the state—was mostly driven by political and social considerations. In the context of a favorable international environment, these principles served the country well until 1995. However, after 1996 several factors conspired to make the two sets of policies somewhat inconsistent and quite costly. Furthermore, the reform momentum had largely evaporated, so that several of the identified policy inconsistencies were not addressed.

Colombia enjoyed a fairly good economic performance in the first half of the 1990s because of an initial increase in public spending, and the wealth effect resulting from increased oil production, which, however, peaked in 1999, and a greater role for the private sector. However, continuous fiscal deficits led to higher public debt, and the increases of both private and public foreign debt made the country vulnerable to negative international shocks. Furthermore, a profound political crisis emerged because of allegations that drug traffickers had partially financed the presidential campaign of Ernesto Samper Pizano (president, 1994–98; see Public Administration, ch. 4). The political crises that ensued had two serious consequences for economic policy. On the one hand, the government tried to enhance its popular support through initiatives that were very costly in fiscal terms, including significant wage increases for civil servants, particularly for members of the very powerful teachers' union. On the other hand, the government's ability to engage the Congress of the Republic (Congreso de la República) in meaningful reform vanished. As a result, a much-needed push to enhance public revenues, including thorough changes to the tax code, did not happen.

Unsurprisingly, in the midst of the Asian and Russian economic crises of the late 1990s, Colombia had its first economic recession in more than 60 years. The exchange rate came under severe pressure, and the Central Bank devalued the exchange-rate band twice. The sudden stop in international lending led to an abrupt adjustment in the current account, which meant a large contraction in aggregate demand. Increases in international interest rates together with expectations of devaluation of the peso (see Glossary) caused rises in internal interest rates, contributing to the contraction of GDP. The recession and the bursting of a real-estate bubble also resulted in a major banking crisis. The savings and loan corporations were especially affected. The government took over a few private financial institutions and forced others to close. Public banks and private mortgage banks were hard hit, and the subsequent government intervention to aid some of the distressed financial institutions added pressures on public expenditure.

In late 1999, the government and the Central Bank undertook a major policy decision: the exchange rate would be allowed to float and be determined by market forces, and the Central Bank would no longer intervene in the foreign-exchange market. Inasmuch as this change in policy came when confidence in the peso was very low, there was a distinct possibility that the currency would weaken to an extent that could make foreign debts—both of the government and of the private sector—unpayable.

To prevent such an event from occurring, Colombia signed a three-year extended-fund facility arrangement with the International Monetary Fund (IMF) in order to boost confidence in the economy, prevent the exchange rate from collapsing once it was allowed to float, and return economic reform to the agenda, with fiscal sustainability and inflation control. This agreement, with minor variations, was extended twice and served as an important guiding framework for economic policy making, particularly in reestablishing Colombia's reputation as a fiscally sound economy, a long-standing positive tradition that was lost in the 1990s. Signing the extended-fund facility with the IMF demonstrated that the government and the Central Bank were willing to make needed major policy decisions. In the context of the agreements with the IMF, the Central Bank allowed the exchange rate to float in 1999 and concentrated on reducing inflation. The government also introduced several tax-enhancing reforms and partial reforms of the public pension system, amended the fiscal decentralization regime, strengthened the financial system, and once again privatized several financial institutions that the government had taken over during the crises.

Economic Structure and Sectoral Policies

During the late 1980s and early 1990s, Colombia needed to foster productivity by enhancing the economy's exposure to foreign competition, make the labor market more efficient, strengthen the financial sector, and reinforce the role of the government as a regulator. Economic policy did not generally promote certain sectors at the expense of others. To reach its policy objectives, the government adopted several reforms at the sector and the aggregate macroeconomic levels. Important developments, including the collapse of the international coffee agreement and the discovery of significant oil reserves, also played a key role in reshaping the structure of the Colombian economy. Thus, the structure has changed quite significantly in the late-twentieth and early twenty-first centuries, in line with developments in other middle-income countries. In 1945 agriculture represented 47 percent of the nation's GDP, services 27 percent, industry 22 percent,

Highway traffic, Medellín
Repaving a street in Bogotá
Courtesy Inter-American Development Bank
(David Mangurian, top; Daniel Drosdoff, bottom), Washington, DC

151

and mining 4 percent. Since then the nation has gone from a predominantly agricultural economy with a nascent manufacturing sector to one dominated by the services sector (see fig. 4).

Agriculture

The share of agriculture in GDP has fallen consistently since 1945, as industry and services have expanded. However, Colombia's agricultural share of GDP decreased during the 1990s by less than in many of the world's countries at a similar level of development, even though the share of coffee in GDP diminished in a dramatic way. Agriculture has nevertheless remained an important source of employment, providing a fifth of Colombia's jobs in 2006.

The most relevant policy instrument affecting the recent evolution of the agricultural sector has been the price bands that Andean countries introduced to protect agriculture in the context of the trade-liberalization program of the early 1990s. According to the mechanism, when international prices decrease, import tariffs increase and vice versa. These price-band ranges remain, despite domestic controversy regarding the level of protection that they provide. This is mainly because of pressure from interest groups and because of the difficulties in identifying clearly the impact on international prices of the subsidies and internal supports given to producers in the developed world.

Public policy toward the agricultural sector also has included the establishment of subsidized sources of credit. Since 1990 such mechanisms have included the Fund for the Finance of the Agricultural Sector (Finagro). Other policy instruments have included minimum price guarantees, import quotas, subsidized credits and tax exemptions, campaigns to promote consumption, incentives for new investments and for forestry plantations, and more recent exchange-rate or currency-hedging options.

In 2006 Colombia's most important agricultural products were cattle, accounting for 45 percent of agricultural output; coffee, 9.5 percent; fruits, 15.2 percent (including plantains, 5.2 percent; and bananas, 2.8 percent); rice, 4.9 percent; flowers, 4.2 percent; vegetables, 4.1 percent; and other agricultural products, 17.1 percent. This composition has remained basically the same since 1992, except for an increase in the share of cattle and fruits, and a decrease in the share of coffee.

Cattle

Cattle raising is the most widespread agricultural activity in Colombia, accounting for 74 percent of Colombia's agricultural land in 2005. Nevertheless, cattle traditionally were not a particularly important or consistent net export for Colombia, and coffee's dominance within the country's agricultural exports remains largely unchallenged.

Perhaps the most significant sectoral change in modern times was the creation of the National Livestock Fund (FNG) in 1993, administered by the Association of Colombian Stockbreeders (Fedegan). That fund has generated resources to tackle five major issues: sanitation, commercialization, research and development (R&D), training, and promotion of consumption. Although progress has been made on all five fronts, perhaps the most remarkable achievements have occurred in sanitation. A national program of vaccination against foot-and-mouth disease began in 1997. In 2009 the World Organization for Animal Health declared the country free of foot-and-mouth disease by vaccination. Significant progress also has been made in vaccination for brucellosis. These sanitation achievements are of major importance in increasing market access for Colombia's cattle exports.

Coffee

Coffee historically has been a major factor in the Colombian economy. Since the middle of the twentieth century, however, its relative importance has been decreasing, largely as a natural outcome of the country's development process. The increase in the share of the services sector, as the nation has developed, corresponded to the reduction of coffee in both GDP and exports. Whereas in 1985 coffee exports represented 51 percent of total exports in value terms, they represented less than 6 percent in 2006. However, the relative decline in coffee's share of both GDP and exports should not imply that coffee has ceased to be a determining factor both in economic and social terms. The livelihoods of an estimated 566,000 families, some 2.3 million Colombians, depend entirely on coffee.

The two most important increases in coffee's international price per pound since 1821 occurred after the signing of the Inter-American Coffee Agreement of 1940 and the International Coffee Agreement of 1963. Such real price peaks occurred in 1954 and 1978, inducing increased production, enhancing inventories, and leading eventually to lower real coffee prices.

In 2003 coffee registered a price of US$0.60 per pound, its lowest price since 1821, because of the collapse of the International Coffee Agreement of 1989, the expansion of production in Vietnam, and the reallocation of production in Brazil toward the northern milder areas. Moreover, between 1999 and 2002 Colombia shifted from being the second-largest to the third-largest producer of coffee in the world, behind Brazil and Vietnam.

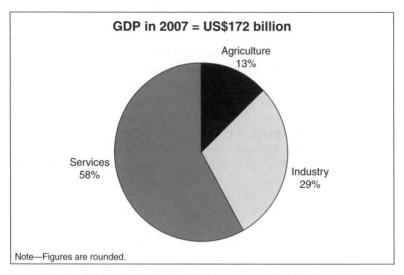

GDP in 2007 = US$172 billion

Agriculture
13%

Services
58%

Industry
29%

Note—Figures are rounded.

Source: Based on information from Colombia, Departamento Administrativo Nacional de
Estadística, http://www.dane.gov.co.

Figure 4. Gross Domestic Product by Sector, 2007

These developments in international markets mean that since 2002 Colombia has restructured the institutional management of coffee. There have been significant changes at the National Federation of Coffee Growers (Fedecafé), one of the country's most traditional and important business organizations, which is owned and controlled by 500,000 farmers who cultivate coffee on small farms. Before 2002 Fedecafé had a large and diverse investment portfolio in shipping, airlines, and the financial sector. Since the reforms, Fedecafé has pursued three objectives: commercialization and output-purchase guarantees; stabilization of coffee growers' income; and advancement of coffee institutions by funding R&D, improving the coffee growers' managerial skills, safeguarding Colombian coffee brands in international markets, and developing special coffees. Fedecafé launched the Juan Valdez coffee shops in Bogotá in 2002 and in the United States in 2004. By 2008 it had more than 70 stores, including at least 60 in Colombia, eight in the United States, and others in Spain and elsewhere in South America (Chile and Ecuador). Through the Juan Valdez coffee shops, Colombia is trying to expand its involvement in coffee consumption, not limiting itself to selling coffee beans to be roasted abroad and later sold at the retail level, but rather attempting to capture part of the coffee retail market itself, where most of the profits are made.

Bananas

Colombian bananas (excluding plantains) are another export success story, in this case despite the violence that has long affected the producing regions. Banana exports, which amounted to about US$525 million in 2006, are the third-largest legal agricultural export of the country, behind coffee and flowers. In 2005 Colombia was the tenth-largest producer, with 2.5 percent of the world's banana output, and the third-largest exporter, with 8 percent of the world's exports after Ecuador and Costa Rica. Output for export, mainly of the Cavendish Valerie variety, is highly productive compared to international standards. The Urabá region in Antioquia and the northeast of Magdalena Department are the main areas producing bananas for export. Chiquita Brands International, Dole Food Company, and Del Monte Fresh Produce are among the most important banana-marketing companies in Colombia.

The main destination of Colombia's banana exports is the European Union (EU), and the second is the United States. Given the importance of the EU's banana market for Colombia and for Latin America, the outcome of the continuing disputes at the World Trade Organization (WTO) with regard to quotas and tariffs is a major issue to this sector. In November 2007, the WTO ruled against the dramatically increased duties imposed by the EU on its imports of Colombian bananas in January 2006.

About 9 percent of Colombia's banana output is destined for the domestic market, and 70 percent of this production is located mainly in the departments of Valle del Cauca and Tolima. Production for domestic consumption is not as sophisticated in technological terms as that for export markets. Producers and exporters are organized in several associations, of which the best known is the Association of Colombian Banana Producers (Augura). Plantains are less important than bananas as a Colombian export but have a larger output share, representing 5.2 percent of agricultural GDP in 2006.

Flowers

Cut-flower production represented 4.2 percent of agricultural GDP in Colombia in 2006, generating 94,000 direct jobs and 80,000 indirect jobs, and it is estimated that about 1 million Colombians depend on income generated by the growth of flowers. Women account for 60 percent of the workers in the flower industry, and their terms of employment are favorable in light of Colombia's overall labor markets. Nevertheless, working conditions, which may include exposure to pesticide spray, are far from ideal. Flowers are produced by 300 companies on 600 farms, 20 percent of which are owned by foreign investors, located mainly in the Bogotá savanna and the Rionegro region in the department of Antioquia. Most of the production consists of roses, carnations, mini-carnations, and chrysanthemums.

The flower sector is an example of Colombian entrepreneurship in international markets, with little government involvement. Colombia has long been the second-largest cut-flower exporter in the world, behind the Netherlands, and continues to be the largest flower exporter to the United States. Colombia's flower exports in 2004 amounted to US$704 million, making flowers the country's second most valuable legal agricultural export, behind coffee and ahead of bananas and sugar. After the United States, which receives 82 percent of Colombia's flower exports, the second-largest market for Colombia's flowers is the EU, with 9 percent.

The Colombian Association of Flower Exporters (Asocolflores) represents Colombian flower producers and exporters on trade policy and legal issues, mainly with the policy makers of Colombia, the United States, and the EU. Asocolflores also addresses sectoral issues, such as transportation, market intelligence, and R&D.

Sugar

Sugar production, which represented 2.5 percent of agricultural GDP in 2004, is concentrated in Valle del Cauca Department and is based on sugarcane output. Colombia has about 1,200 sugarcane producers, 14 sugar mills, and about 53 confectionary firms, the sector is one of the most productive for sugar in the world.

The domestic market is highly protected through the Andean Price-Band System (see Glossary), and thus, domestic prices are higher than international prices, which has hurt consumers and producers using sugar as an input. In order to avoid extra sugar costs for the domestic confectionary industry competing in the international markets, a joint program between domestic confectioners and the sugar producers began in 1993, allowing the confectionary firms access to sugar inputs for its exports at more competitive prices.

About half of Colombia's sugar output is exported, one-quarter is used for domestic consumption, and the rest is sold as an input to the industrial sector. Colombia is the seventh-largest exporter of raw sugar in the world and the fifth-largest exporter of refined sugar, with exports of US$369 million in 2006. The main export destinations for Colombian sugar are the Andean countries, the United States, and Russia.

Government policies aimed at lowering dependence on fossil fuels and reducing pollution have boosted the production of ethanol derived from sugars. Vehicles have been using ethanol mixed with gasoline in Colombia's major cities since 2005. Thus, several sugar mills have begun to build ethanol distilleries, and it now appears that about 40 percent of sugar exports will be redirected to ethanol production by around 2010.

Thirteen of the 14 Colombian sugar mills are members, along with a group of sugarcane producers, of the Association of Sugarcane Growers (Asocaña), an influential business group. The Colombian Association of Sugarcane Producers and Suppliers (Procaña) also represents sugarcane producers, and the Sugarcane Research Center of Colombia (Cenicaña) has made a positive contribution to Colombia's sugarcane productivity.

Palm Oil

Oil-palm tree fruits, soybeans, cottonseeds, and sesame seeds are the main sources of Colombian vegetable oils. Colombia is a net importer of all of its vegetable oil needs except for oil-palm tree fruits, which grow in many regions of the country, including the departments of Meta, César, Santander, Nariño, and Magdalena.

Palm-oil production was highly protected in the 1980s, but less so thereafter. An import tariff and a price band have remained as protection mechanisms. The way the oil-palm tree industry operates is closely tied to the existence of a price-stabilization fund, which equalizes the higher domestic price with the lower export price, as a tool to promote palm-oil exports.

Output of palm oil tripled between 1990 and 2006, putting Colombia among the world's top-five producing countries and making the country the largest producer in the Americas, although with a world-market share of only 2 percent in 2006. Production of palm oil is expected to increase further because it is an important component in Colombia's biodiesel industry, which began in 2008. It has been estimated that Colombia can produce biodiesel more efficiently than the United States and Europe, but further improvements are required because Colombia's biodiesel production is still not as efficient as that of world leaders Indonesia and Malaysia. The government nevertheless expects the demand for biodiesel to increase fourfold between 2008 and 2019, so there are plans to expand oil-palm tree cultivation from 330,000 hectares in 2007 to 1 million hectares, with partial funding from the U.S. Agency for International Development (USAID). This planned increase in the production of oil-palm trees is both an alternative to the extensive use of land for cattle and its use for growing illegal crops, and a source of employment for former members of illegal armed groups. However, the latter have sometimes displaced ethnic minority communities in taking over their land.

Mining and Energy

Minerals—in particular coal, oil, and natural gas, but also emeralds, gold, and nickel—have played an important role in Colombia's GDP and foreign trade in the last 20 years. Accounting for only 1.4 percent of GDP and 13 percent of total exports between 1980 and 1984, minerals represented about 5 percent of GDP and 42 percent of total exports in 2006. The minerals industry has compensated to a certain extent for the decreasing role of agriculture and has expanded the importance of commodities for the economy as a whole. Colombia is the world's leading source of emeralds, and illegal mining is commonplace. However, production of precious minerals is small-scale despite high international prices for minerals such as gold.

Coal

Colombia's coal output has increased consistently from 4 million tons in 1981 to 65.6 million tons in 2006, when it contributed 1.4 percent of the world's coal production. In 2006 Colombia accounted for 81 percent of the total coal production in Central and South America. Furthermore, 94 percent of Colombia's coal is of very good quality and is classified as hard, with high heat-generating capacity. Coal has been Colombia's second-largest export since 2001.

The largest coal mines—and the ones that generate the most exports—are located in the north of the country, in the departments of La Guajira and César. Cerrejón is considered to be one of the largest open-pit coal mines in the world. There are also smaller coal mines scattered throughout the rest of the nation.

Since 2000 government participation in the production of coal has been decreasing, and there has been a shift to private domestic and foreign investors. Major changes have occurred in the institutional framework of the coal industry in recent years. In particular, in 2000 the government sold the stakes that Colombia Coal (Carbocol), a state-owned company, had in Cerrejón, and the new mining code introduced in 2001 led the government to concentrate on its role as regulator through the Ministry of Mines and Energy.

Oil

Colombia became an oil exporter in the mid-1980s and has remained so, as a result of policy changes made in 2003. Colombia exports about half of its production, most of it to the United States. Although the share of oil in GDP has remained between 2 and 4 percent since 1990, its share of total Colombian exports has been between 20 and 30 percent since 1995, and it has generated important revenues for the nation's public finances. In 2006 oil and derivatives accounted for 26 percent of total exports (18.6 percent for oil and 7.4 percent for derivatives). Oil is particularly important because of its fiscal implications, which cut across several dimensions.

The state-owned Colombian Petroleum Enterprise (Ecopetrol) is an important exporter and a highly profitable concern. The government also subsidizes gasoline and other fuels by selling them locally at a price below the comparable international market price, and this subsidy is channeled through Ecopetrol. In 2004 rough estimates suggested that while the central government was running a fiscal deficit of about 5 percent of GDP, Ecopetrol was producing—net of taxes and domestic subsidies—a surplus close to 3 percent of GDP. In addition, domestic fuel subsidies had a fiscal cost of between 1 and 2 percentage points of GDP.

Since 1974 Colombia has applied a system of association contracts, in which the profits from oil exploration are divided in half between the national government and private investors, both national and foreign. Within that framework, Colombia's oil production increased significantly in 1986, when the Caño Limón oil field began operating, and was further enhanced in 1995, when production began in the Cusiana and Cupiagua oil fields.

A higher tax on oil production came in 1989, with further taxes on oil companies' profits in 1994. These measures, unfriendly to private investors, played a key role in reducing the rate of exploration. As a result, oil reserves, which increased 600 percent at their peak between 1978 and 1992, have been declining since then. Similarly, oil production, which increased more than 400 percent between 1979 and 1999, when it peaked at 838,000 barrels per day (bpd—see Glossary), began a period of decline, totaling an estimated 529,000 bpd in 2006.

In 1999 this loss of private investors' interest led to a reduction in the share of the income accrued by the state, from 50 percent to 30 percent of the total oil income. In 2000 the government modified the royalties system, with variable coefficients based on output and ranging from 5 percent to 25 percent. Although the tax system changed to encourage exploration, private-sector investment has been slow to rebound, among other reasons because the oil sector has been a direct target of insurgent groups. Although no new major discoveries have been announced and no new capacity was expected to be produced before 2010, oil production increased in 2008.

The outlook for the oil supply is complex because of the trend of decreasing oil reserves and the sharp increase in international oil prices in 2008. The government was considering a variety of options to ensure an appropriate supply of energy for the nation as a whole. In 2003 important changes in oil policy were introduced that led to an increase in exploration, production, and reserves of oil and gas. Among those changes is the separation of state roles: Ecopetrol assumed a role as an operator with greater autonomy and more ability to compete. The new National Hydrocarbons Agency (ANH) became a resource administrator. A contingency tax should give the government a share of profits when prices of oil are higher than a given threshold price. Compressed natural gas, biodiesel, and ethanol are also being promoted as options to increase the nation's domestic supply of energy resources.

In 2007 Ecopetrol began a public stock offering in order to finance its growth, increase accountability, and improve its capacity to compete with other oil companies. In the initial sale of 10.1 percent of the firm, almost 500,000 Colombian investors bought shares in the company, which was listed on the Colombian stock exchange that same year and is expected to sell an additional 9.9 percent of its shares before the end of the decade. As Colombia's largest firm, Ecopetrol should provide a significant boost to the overall level of transactions on the Colombian stock exchange.

Natural Gas

Colombia's production of natural gas in 2007 was entirely for domestic consumption, when it amounted to 7.7 billion cubic meters, or 0.3 percent of world output. In 2005 Colombia had an estimated 4 trillion cubic feet of commercial natural gas reserves that should last until about 2022. This natural endowment has been used since the 1990s, and monopolies on the Atlantic coast and in the eastern plains (llanos) control production. Several firms provide transport, although two—National Gas Company of the Atlantic Coast and the Colombian Gas Company—control the main pipelines. Except in Medellín, where the local public utilities company, Medellín Public Companies, distributes gas, distribution is generally by private firms. Coverage for residential use of natural gas in 2002 was 80 percent in Barranquilla, 70 percent in Bucaramanga, 60 percent in Bogotá, and 30 percent in Cali. Because of its high cost, the availability of natural gas in rural areas tends to be limited.

Industry

The share of industry in GDP has shifted significantly in the last few decades. Data from the World Bank show that between 1965 and 1989 the share of industry—including construction, manufacturing, and mining—increased from 27 percent to 38 percent of GDP. However, since then the share has fallen considerably, down to approximately 29 percent of GDP in 2007. This pattern is about the average for middle-income countries.

The spirit of the 1991 constitution led to reform of the Industry and Commerce Superintendency (SIC) in order to foster competition and protect consumer rights by strengthening its capacity to prevent monopolistic activities and promote competition and market access. Offenses against free competition, collusion, and abuses of market power were defined, and the SIC gained the capacity to sanction individuals and firms for violations. The changes also strengthened a period of trade liberalization, increasing the degree of competition in domestic markets after a long period of import-substitution industrialization and export-promotion policies (see Trade Policy and Trade Patterns, this ch.).

Before 1990 it was common to have subsidized sources of credit for industries, mainly through the Central Bank, the Industrial Development Institute (IFI), and the Export Promotion Fund (Proexpo). Financial subsidies declined significantly at the end of the 1980s and the beginning of the 1990s. Although the role of the Central Bank as promoter of industry transferred to the IFI in 1992, in 2003 the IFI entered into liquidation. In 2002 the Ministry of Foreign Trade merged with the Ministry of Development and became the Ministry of Commerce, Industry, and Tourism. The government created Proexport Colombia, an export-promotion agency, and Proexpo became the Foreign Trade Bank of Colombia (Bancoldex), an export-import bank that now provides financing alternatives for Colombian producers of all sorts in commerce, industry, and tourism.

Colombia has not had a significant tradition of R&D. In 2003 the country spent only 0.3 percent of its GDP on R&D. In 2004 public institutions and universities spent more than 80 percent of all the resources devoted to R&D, while private firms and private research centers invested less than 20 percent.

The National Association of Industrialists (ANDI), the country's most important entrepreneurial organization, represents more than 650 member firms from a variety of sectors, including the manufacturing, financial, agro-industrial, and services sectors. Since its creation in 1944, ANDI has been actively promoting the strengthening and competitiveness of private enterprise, state-owned companies, and public organizations. In addition to taking a leading role among manufacturing organizations in Colombia, ANDI actively lobbies the executive and legislative branches of government. Besides representing its members at regional, national, and international levels, ANDI is also a leader among business organizations in Colombia.

Construction

Colombia's construction sector has represented between 5 and 7 percent of GDP and between 5 and 6 percent of total employment in recent decades. About 60 percent of the population owns homes. However, financial intermediation (see Glossary) in the housing industry traditionally has been low by world standards; total mortgages were 5 percent of GDP in 2008 and have never been more than 11 percent of GDP. Because of Colombia's strong rural–urban migration, more than 70 percent of the population lives in urban areas, but serious problems in housing quality, size, and access to public services have created a housing deficit estimated at more than 40 percent. For many years, governments have played a major role in the promotion of social-interest housing. In order to foster construction, in 1972 the government introduced the Unit of Constant Purchasing Power (UPAC). Based on it, a mortgage system in which debts and interest payments originally were indexed to inflation came into being and was quite successful in the 1970s and 1980s. The UPAC increased private savings and thus the resources available to finance mortgages, boosting the construction sector.

The construction sector boomed between 1990 and 1994 because of a combination of factors, including greater competition and fewer restrictions in the financial markets, increased capital inflows, relaxed regulation and supervision of financial institutions, and a loose monetary policy. The resulting housing-price hike, with increases of 70 percent in real terms between 1990 and 1994, also led to significant mortgage expansion during those years.

With the financial market reforms at the beginning of the 1990s, mortgage companies faced stiffer competition from other financial institutions, and, in order to compete on equal terms, demanded the indexation of the UPAC to prevailing interest rates. Moreover, as real interest rates increased sharply in the second half of the 1990s, among other things as a response to the Asian and Russian economic crises when the value of housing assets began falling, many mortgage holders were exposed to negative equity, eventually losing their homes.

The lack of demand and the excess supply of houses precipitated a sharp fall in real prices. In 1998 house prices had dropped to 1991 levels. This situation further depressed the quality of mortgages and loan guarantees in general, leading to a bust in the housing market between 1997 and 2000. The UPAC was replaced in 2000 by the Real Value Unit, which is indexed—just as the UPAC initially was—to inflation rather than to interest rates. Since then there has been a slow recovery of housing prices and an even slower recovery of mortgage volume.

Upscale hillside housing in the north of Bogotá
Courtesy Lorenzo Morales
A cobblestoned street in Bogotá
Courtesy Inter-American Development Bank, Washington, DC

Innovations in housing finance have included Colombian Titling, an institution that turns mortgages into capital-market instruments in order to improve the liquidity of mortgage lenders. Such instruments also improve the matching between the duration of loans and the commitment of resources received by mortgage-lending institutions. Colombian Titling is part-owned by several domestic financial groups, as well as by the International Finance Corporation, an organization of the World Bank Group.

Infrastructure construction in recent years has focused on electricity projects and urban mass-transportation systems. Because of fiscal constraints, the government has promoted greater involvement of the private sector in maintaining and developing infrastructure.

The production of cement and other nonmetallic building products, which have a share of 4 percent in manufacturing output and employment, is closely linked to the changes in the construction sector. In Colombia cement output is highly concentrated, with three main economic groups controlling more than 90 percent of total output. The cement sector survived the housing crises between 1996 and 2000 by reorienting production toward export markets, including the United States. As a result, in 2003 Colombia provided 5 to 6 percent of U.S. imports of cement and clinker.

Manufacturing

A key feature of Colombian manufacturing has been the high concentration of location and ownership. Some 30 percent of output in 2005 was produced in Bogotá, 15 percent in Medellín, 11 percent in Cali, 7 percent in Cartagena, and 5 percent in Barranquilla. Thus, these five cities produced 68 percent of the nation's total manufacturing output.

Three main Colombian economic groups control a significant share of manufacturing output: the Antioquia Entrepreneurial Group (GEA) focuses on food products, as well as cement, energy, and finance; the Santo Domingo Group, on beer, soft drinks, and other investments; and the Ardila Lülle Organization, on soft drinks, sugar, and other related businesses. Manufacturing output in chemicals, motor vehicles, and paper is concentrated in multinational firms. Public-sector manufacturing consists mainly of oil refineries and alcoholic drinks. Colombia has three official sizes of smaller companies: micro (those with fewer than 11 workers), small (with 11 to 49 employees), and medium (with 50 to 199 employees). These smaller firms produce 28 percent of Colombia's output and hire 46 percent of the workers in manufacturing. In 2006 the most important manufacturing sector by value of output was refined petroleum products, followed by chemicals and chemical products, beverages, basic iron and steel products, and milled and prepared animal-food products.

In 2005 the most important manufacturing sector for employment was textiles and clothing, followed by chemicals and chemical products, plastic products, cement and other nonmetalic goods, and beverages. Colombia's textile industry represented 9 percent of output and 23 percent of employment in manufactures in 2005, although the share in output has been falling steadily since 1990. Between 2001 and 2003, Colombia was a net importer of textile inputs, while it was a net exporter of apparel. The United States is the main export market for Colombian textiles and apparel, followed by the members of the Andean Community and Mexico. The sector has been one of the main beneficiaries of the Andean Trade Preference Act and the Andean Trade Promotion and Drug Eradication Act. The United States extended these trade preferences to Colombia and other Andean countries because of their continuing fight against the production and distribution of illegal drugs. Colombia's designer clothing is a segment of the industry that has received international recognition in recent years.

Colombia's chemical industry is composed mainly of petrochemicals and agrochemicals. The petrochemical industry includes plastics, synthetic fibers, paint, and rubber. Petrochemical production accounted for 27 percent of manufacturing GDP and 10 percent of manufacturing employment in 2005. However, Colombia imports more than double the quantity of petrochemicals and agrochemicals that it exports. The United States is the main source of Colombian imports, while the Andean countries are the main destination of Colombian exports in this sector.

Two main economic groups have had control of the largest shares in the beverages market, which in 2005 represented 9 percent of manufacturing GDP and 3 percent of employment in manufacturing. The Ardila Lülle Organization is the largest producer of soft drinks and the Santo Domingo Group, of beer. The Santo Domingo Group had a controlling stake in Grupo Bavaria, the tenth-largest beer company in the world, until SABMiller acquired a major interest in Bavaria in 2005, in a deal worth US$7.8 billion. As a result of this merger, the Santo Domingo group obtained a 15-percent share in SABMiller (see Business Associations, ch. 4).

In 2005 paper, paper products, lithography, and printing accounted for about 7 percent of Colombia's manufacturing output and 8 percent of manufacturing employment. Input production of pulp and paper is highly concentrated in a few firms, while book publishing is more dispersed. Colombia is a net importer of pulp and paper and has been a net exporter of printed products for many years.

Vehicle assembly and vehicle components represent 2 percent of manufacturing GDP and employment, and those shares have been falling in recent years. Colombia has automobile-assembly plants linked to Chevrolet (the market leader), Renault, Mazda, and Toyota; motorcycle-assembly plants have links to Kawasaki, Yamaha, and Suzuki. Vehicle assembly represents 70 percent of this subsector's GDP, while vehicle components represent 30 percent. Since 1990 there has been greater international competition in vehicle assembly, leading to increases in the number of available vehicle brands and models. Overall, Colombia is a net importer of vehicles, mainly from Japan, the United States, and South Korea. Its main export markets are the Andean countries, especially Venezuela and Ecuador.

Services

The services sector dominates Colombia's GDP, contributing 58 percent of GDP in 2007, and, given worldwide trends, its dominance will probably continue. The sector is characterized by its heterogeneity, being the largest for employment (61 percent), in both the formal and informal sectors.

Commerce

The share of commerce in Colombian GDP fluctuated between 10 and 12 percent in the period 1994–2006, very similar to the share of commerce in developed countries, which tends to be about 11 or 12 percent of GDP. Data from the National Administrative Department of Statistics (DANE) show that commerce has provided around 25 percent of total employment, more than half of which is in the informal sector and the remaining one-quarter in the formal sector (see The Informal Economy, this ch.).

In the last few years, Colombia has seen the appearance of large retail establishments, as has happened in other developing countries, and as occurred in many developed countries some years ago. Such large retail establishments, boosted by trade and investment liberalization, have included national companies such as Olímpica and Éxito's Carulla Vivero. They have also included international firms such as Casino, which in 2007 became the major shareholder in Éxito, and Carrefour (France), Makro (the Netherlands and South Africa), and Falabella (Chile). Although the process of creating large retail establishments may be far from complete, it has already resulted in increased concentration in the retail business, the beginning of own-brand developments, and technological improvements in information. It also has shifted some market power from producers to large retailers.

Public Utilities

At the end of the 1980s, public services in Colombia were of low quality; the charges made to consumers were determined politically and were insufficient to finance the operation of those services. Furthermore, the cost structures were highly inefficient. A deficient legal framework and the monopolistic role played by the state since the beginning of the twentieth century created this unfortunate situation.

The constitution of 1991 gave private initiative a major role in providing public utilities and allowed the government to regulate the sector. The government made improving the provision of public utilities to the vulnerable sectors of society a key goal. These general objectives became the responsibility of the Public Utilities Regime, which provides for increasing coverage, promoting privatization of utilities, developing a tariff regime, and giving consumers a supervisory role. The regime created three regulatory commissions (for electricity, telecommunications, and water and sanitation) and an organization for the promotion, supervision, and control of competition called the Residential Public Services Superintendency (SSPD).

A typical restaurant, open to the streets and passersby,
in Bogotá's Candelaria district
Market stands such as this one are found in towns throughout Colombia.
Courtesy Lorenzo Morales

As a result of the reforms, which naturally generated resistance in certain sectors of society, particularly among union workers, provision of all services has improved significantly. For example, between 1990 and 2003 electricity coverage increased from 80 to 95 percent of the population; drinking water, from 67 to 87 percent; sewerage, from 50 to 72 percent; and local telephone service, from 8 to 22 percent. Natural gas service began in the mid-1990s, and coverage increased from 20 percent in 1997 to 35 percent of the population in 2003. One possible explanation for the comparatively low coverage in natural gas is that expanding its rural availability is very expensive. The quality of ancillary services has risen, and today it is possible to pay most public-utility charges by phone or Internet.

Throughout the process, rates for most public utilities, including drinking water and electricity, have gone up in real terms. This increase in charges has meant lower dependency on public funds to cover the cost of supplying these services. It also has meant that consumption has fallen as a result of the higher prices, delaying the need for further investments in order to increase installed capacities of different services. Some rates also have gone down, as in the case of waste collection for multiple users (for example, buildings or housing complexes), and of international phone calls. Despite these improvements, there is a need for much more progress in improving the regulatory framework, fostering competition, reducing production costs, and allowing consumers to benefit more from some of these efficiency gains.

Electricity

Before 1990 public monopolies provided electric service. As a result of significant expansion of electricity-generation capacity between 1970 and 1990—financed mostly by foreign loans—and the inefficiencies in the provision of this service, by 1990 about one-third of the nation's public foreign debt was associated with the electricity sector. The debt originated not only from mismanagement but also from the cost of replacing the electric-power infrastructure sabotaged by the guerrillas. In 1992, as a result of severe drought, Colombia resorted to electricity rationing.

The reforms of the 1990s broke down this monopolistic structure by encouraging the participation of private enterprise in the generation, transmission, and distribution of energy and by creating the Energy and Gas Regulatory Commission (CREG). CREG has regulated natural monopoly stages, such as transmission and distribution, through price caps, while competition has played an increasing role in generation and commercialization. Interconnection with Andean and Central American countries is presently being considered as a means of improving competition and providing better protection against future rationing in the region.

Potable Water and Sewerage

In 2000 the Water and Basic Sanitation Regulatory Commission (Cra) formalized the requirements for public and private companies to provide drinking water and sewerage. The main objectives were to promote competition and new investments, while increasing transparency and reducing regulatory risk.

As private companies—foreign and national—have taken over water-supply services in various Colombian cities, charges have increased, and the financial deficit in the provision of drinking water has been reduced from 45 to 10 percent. As prices have increased, consumption has decreased by at least 13 cubic meters a month per household to 16.9 cubic meters a month per household in 2004.

This reduced consumption in response to higher prices has generated efficiency gains by lowering expansion requirements and variable costs. Increased efficiency also has brought about a smaller workforce and reduced the number of employees for every 1,000 subscribers in major cities. For example, between 1995 and 2000, the number of employees per 1,000 subscribers dropped from 6.8 to 3.7 in Barranquilla, and from 3.2 to 2.3 in Bogotá.

Waste Collection

Bogotá began transferring responsibility for waste disposal to private firms even before the existence, since 1994, of the SSPD. Since then private participation in waste disposal has increased. The SSPD has more than 500 waste-collection firms registered, about 20 percent of which are private. Approximately 80 percent of the users of waste-disposal services regarded the service as good. Public campaigns and economic incentives exist to increase public awareness of the need for recycling, and some progress has been made, but there is still a long way to go in promoting its environmental benefits.

Tourism

Colombia has major attractions as a tourist destination, such as Cartagena and its historic surroundings, which are on the United Nations Educational, Scientific, and Cultural Organization (UNESCO) World Heritage List; the insular department of San Andrés, Providencia y Santa Catalina; and Santa Marta and the surrounding area. Fairly recently, Bogotá, the nation's capital, has become Colombia's major tourist destination because of its improved museums and entertainment facilities and its major urban renovations, including the rehabilitation of public areas, the development of parks, and the creation of an extensive network of cycling routes. With its very rich and varied geography, which includes the Amazon and Andean regions, the llanos, the coasts, and the deserts of La Guajira, and unique biodiversity, Colombia also has a major potential for ecotourism.

In the early to mid-1990s, international tourism arrivals in Colombia reached nearly 1.4 million per year. Although they decreased by more than half thereafter, they have recovered at rates of more than 10 percent annually since 2002, reaching 1.9 million visitors in 2006. Tourism usually has been considered a low-growth service industry in Colombia because of internal violence, but in 2006 the country earned US$2 billion from international tourism. Tourists visiting Colombia from abroad came mainly from the United States (24.5 percent), followed by Venezuela (13.4 percent), Ecuador (9.1 percent), Spain (6.4 percent), and Mexico (4.9 percent). Approximately 90 percent of foreign tourists arrive by air, 10 percent by land transportation, and a tiny share by sea.

The recovery of tourism has been helped by the Democratic Security and Defense Policy of Álvaro Uribe Vélez (president, 2002–6, 2006–10) and the so-called tourist caravans (*caravanas turísticas*), in which military forces provide reinforced protection on previously scheduled days to roads reaching major holiday attractions. The Democratic Security Policy, as it is known, is aimed at reestablishing control over all of the nation's territory, fighting illegal drugs and organized crime, and strengthening the justice system (see Internal Armed Conflict and Peace Negotiations, ch. 4; Democratic Security Policy, ch. 5). The government also has been working toward generating a significant recovery in international tourism through Proexport Colombia, the public export-promotion agency.

Transportation and Telecommunications

Colombia's geography, with three cordilleras of the Andes running up the country from south to north, and jungle in the Amazon and Darién regions, represents a major obstacle to the development of national road networks with international connections. Thus, the basic nature of the country's transportation infrastructure is not surprising.

In the spirit of the 1991 constitution, in 1993 the Ministry of Public Works and Transportation was reorganized and renamed the Ministry of Transportation. In 2000 the new ministry strengthened its role as the planner and regulator within the sector.

A street vendor at the entrance to a plaza in Cartagena
Courtesy Lorenzo Morales

Air Transportation

Colombia was a pioneer in promoting airlines in an effort to overcome its geographic barriers to transportation. The Colombian Company of Air Navigation, formed in 1919, was the second commercial airline in the world. It was not until the 1940s that Colombia's air transportation began growing significantly in the number of companies, passengers carried, and kilometers covered. In the early 2000s, an average of 72 percent of the passengers transported by air go to national destinations, while 28 percent travel internationally. One notable feature is that after the reforms of the beginning of the 1990s, the number of international passengers tripled by 2003.

In 1993 the construction, administration, operation, and maintenance of the main airports transferred to departmental authorities and the private sector, including companies specializing in air transportation. Within this process, in 2006 the International Airport Operator (Opain), a Swiss-Colombian consortium, won the concession to manage and develop Bogotá's El Dorado International Airport. In addition to El Dorado, Colombia's international airports are Palo Negro in Bucaramanga, Simón Bolívar in Santa Marta, Ernesto

Cortissoz in Barranquilla, Rafael Núñez in Cartagena, José María Córdova in Rionegro near Medellín, Alfonso Bonilla Aragón in Cali, Alfredo Vásquez Cobo in Leticia, Matecaña in Pereira, Gustavo Rojas Pinilla in San Andrés, and Camilo Daza in Cúcuta (see fig. 5). In 2006 Colombia was generally reported to have a total of 984 airports, of which 103 had paved runways and 883 were unpaved. The Ministry of Transportation listed 581 airports in 2007, but it may have used a different methodology for counting them.

Perhaps the most significant infrastructure development since 1990 has been the construction of the new José María Córdova International Airport, which provides services for large commercial aircraft flying to and from Medellín. Another important new asset is the second runway at El Dorado International Airport. Avianca has been the airline with the largest market share in Colombia of both national and international flights; it held 36 percent of the domestic market and 44 percent of the international passenger market in 2003. In that same year, Aero República, founded in 1993 with a lighter labor structure than Avianca and competing low prices, already held one-quarter of the local market. In 2003 American Airlines held 11 percent of the international passenger market, followed by Copa Airlines, with 9 percent; and Continental Airlines and Iberia, with 4.5 percent each. In 2003 international air cargo had a much larger share of the total (77 percent) than national cargo (23 percent), a trend that has been reinforced with the greater opening of the economy.

Because of difficult times in the air industry at the beginning of the twenty-first century and complex internal problems within the firms, Colombia's main airlines—Avianca, SAM, and ACES—have made a cooperative effort to survive. However, the final outcome of the strategy involved the disappearance of ACES and the takeover of Avianca by a Brazilian entrepreneur in 2004. Moreover, in 2005 Copa Airlines acquired a majority shareholding of Aero República. Since then both companies have modernized their fleets and expanded and improved their services.

At the end of 2007, and after major restructuring within the established airlines, EasyFly, Colombia's first low-cost airline, began service, focusing initially on the domestic market. The company began with domestic shareholders owning two-thirds of the firm, and foreign investors owning the remaining shares. As a result of an open-skies policy and a bilateral air transport agreement between the countries, signed in the last quarter of 2007, a significant increase in flights between Colombia and the United States, and of airlines covering such routes, was expected.

Inland Waterways

Before the twentieth century, Colombia's rivers offered the main means of transportation, mostly linking regions with the Atlantic coast, and the means by which vast parts of the country had contact with the outside world. Colombia has four major basins around the Magdalena, Amazon, Orinoco, and Atrato rivers (see Geography, ch. 2). Overall, the country has 24,725 kilometers of inland waterways, 74 percent of which are navigable. Of the navigable waterways, 39 percent allow for permanent major navigation, while 23 percent allow for temporary major navigation. Inland waterways have been consistently underutilized in Colombia. For example, in 2002 only 3 percent of total cargo and only 5 percent of passengers were transported by inland waterways.

Colombia's main river, the Magdalena, still provides services for transportation, although stiffer competition from rail transportation and especially from roads has meant that the Magdalena has specialized in transporting high-volume and low-cost-per-unit-weight goods. In 2002 hydrocarbons transported on the Magdalena represented 80 percent of the total cargo transported via inland waterways. The main transshipment ports on the Magdalena are La Dorada, Puerto Salgar, Puerto Berrío, Barrancabermeja, Estación Acapulco, and Gamarra. The main specialized ports along that river are Imarco (for cement) and Barrancabermeja (for hydrocarbons). A second interoceanic canal system, to be built by dredging the Atrato and other rivers and digging short access canals, has been proposed periodically over the years but had not materialized by 2009.

Ports

Seaports traditionally have been Colombia's gateway for international trade. In the 1950s, the main ports—all publicly owned and operated—were Buenaventura, Barranquilla, Cartagena, and Santa Marta. Major changes occurred after the port reforms of 1991, when the public organization in charge of ports was abolished, and private agents were given authorization to build, operate, and maintain ports.

Because ports have been and are the main entry and departure point for international trade, their development has been linked closely to trends in exports and imports. The production of bananas in the Urabá region in the mid-1960s and the expanded exports of coal and oil in the mid-1980s led to the privately funded construction of some specialized ports. For example, on the Caribbean coast, the need for a coal-export port resulted in the construction of Puerto Bolívar, and

Figure 5. Transportation System, 2008

Mamonal serves as the principal outlet for hydrocarbons and fertilizers shipped up the Magdalena.

Between 1999 and 2003, about 96 percent of Colombia's export volume went through ports; 3 percent by road; and 1 percent by air. Some 57 percent of the tonnage exported was of coal. And of the total number of tons of imports, 89 percent was moved through ports, 10 percent on roads, and 1 percent by air.

Railroads

Colombia's transport system developed at the end of the nineteenth century with the construction of a rail network, aimed initially at connecting regions with the Magdalena and Cauca rivers. The rail system contributed to the development of the coffee industry, and the growth of the coffee industry encouraged the development of the rail network.

However, Colombia never managed to complete its rail network, and technical incompatibilities prevented the nation from making better use of the existing railroads. The development of Colombia's road system also hampered further improvements in rail services. In recent decades, rail services have tended to specialize. For example, a specially designed railroad transports coal from the mine at Cerrejón. Certain lines also remain active, such as the one between Bogotá and Sogamoso, where major steel and cement industries are located. In 2006 Colombia had 3,304 kilometers of rail, of which almost 2,000 kilometers had service managed by private companies; the remainder were inactive. With the exception of 150 kilometers of standard gauge, most of the rail lines are narrow gauge.

Road Transportation

Colombia's road system originated in the first half of the twentieth century. Transport by rail or river used to be oriented toward exports, imports, and communication with the outside world. The road network, in contrast, was designed to improve communications across the country and locally. Road transport has had the largest volume increase of the main forms of transportation, while train and river transport lag far behind. This disparity can be explained partly by the country's topography, the increasing size of Colombia's internal market, and by the road network being designed for domestic convenience. Other reasons for the faster development of road transport are the flexibility of road systems and some mistakes in railroad- and river-transport policy.

As of October 2008, Colombia had 164,257 kilometers of roads, of which 13,467 kilometers, or about 8 percent, were paved, according to the National Institute of Highways. Of the paved roads, 55.5 percent were in good condition, 30.3 percent in bad condition, and 14 percent in very bad condition (the remaining minute percentage was considered in very good condition). Some 8,787 kilometers of Colombia's paved roads were designated as part of the national highway network, of which 46.9 percent were considered in good condition, 33.2 percent in regular condition, 19.5 percent in bad condition, and the remaining 0.4

percent in very bad condition. The remaining 150,790 kilometers of unpaved roads were secondary and tertiary roads, of which 42.3 percent were considered to be in regular condition, 36.6 percent in bad condition, 20 percent in good condition, and the remaining 1 percent or so in very good condition.

The country has six major highway networks, three of which (*troncales*) run from south to north on either side of the Cordillera Central and alongside the Cordillera Oriental. The Western Highway (forming part of the Pan-American Highway) begins at the border with Ecuador and passes near Cali on its way north through Medellín to the Caribbean coastal city of Cartagena. The Magdalena Highway separates from the Western Highway near Popoyán, passing by Neiva all the way to Ciénaga, near Santa Marta, and the Central Highway runs north from Bogotá to Cúcuta and the border with Venezuela and on northwest to Valledupar and Cartagena.

The fourth, fifth, and sixth major highway networks (*transversales*) run east–west. The Caribbean Highway, which begins at Paraguachón, on the Venezuelan border in La Guajira Department, runs through the northern Caribbean lowlands, circumvents the Sierra Nevada de Santa Marta, and passes by Santa Marta, Barranquilla, and Cartagena all the way to Turbo in Antioquia Department. Another highway runs from Bogotá to Medellín, and a third horizontal link goes from Puerto Gaitán in the eastern llanos (Meta Department), passes through Villavicencio, Bogotá, and Cali, and ends in Buenaventura on the Pacific coast.

The Darién rainforest, also known as the Atrato swamp, prevents the Pan-American Highway from linking Colombia and Panama. Located in Chocó Department adjoining the border with Panama, it is a deep swamp about 100 kilometers in width that has challenged engineers for years. The highway is interrupted for 100 kilometers, terminating on the Colombian side a few kilometers beyond the Río Atrato at Lomas Aisladas, near Guapá, and on the Panamanian side at Yaviza. Planning efforts to remedy this missing link in the Pan-American Highway began in 1971, with the help of U.S. funding, but halted in 1974. Another effort to build this part of the road began in 1992 but was also abandoned. Among its benefits, the project would allow transportation by road throughout the Americas, reducing costs and promoting the trade of goods and services. Among its problems are environmental and health issues, including the theory that the Darién rainforest has prevented the spread of cattle diseases into Central and North America, and cultural concerns primarily for the Chocó and Cuna indigenous peoples. As a result, bridging the gap in the Pan-American Highway is a project that remains in the planning stage.

The issue resurfaced in 2005, when President Uribe strongly advocated the construction of the highway through the Darién. However, a coalition of indigenous groups, environmental activists, and business and political leaders in Panama apparently succeeded in pressuring the Panamanian government not to endorse the Colombian proposal. In any case, as of January 2006 Panama and Colombia were planning to build an electricity transmission line to link their power grids through the Darién rainforest, a project that would require cutting a path at least 40 meters wide through virgin jungle. However, that project also has stalled.

Growing fiscal constraints have led to fostering private enterprise, and private companies have been granted leases to maintain highways since the mid-1990s. In 2009 major projects with private-sector participation planned for the near future included the tunnel to cross the central branch of the Andes in La Línea and the highways between Bogotá and Cajamarca, which would improve mobility between Bogotá and the southern, central, and western regions of the country. When the 8.5-kilometer-long La Línea Tunnel opens around 2013, it is expected to save heavy vehicles 80 minutes and private automobiles 40 minutes off the previous route by connecting the departments of Tolima and Quindío. These new highway projects include one that will link Bogotá with Buenaventura, the main Colombian port on the Pacific Ocean. Other projects with private participation include the Bogotá–Santa Marta Highway, linking the capital city with the Atlantic coast, and the Bogotá–Sogamoso Highway, connecting Bogotá with the department of Boyacá.

Bogotá still had major and long-lasting traffic congestion in 2007, because the number of private and public vehicles exceeded the capacity of the street infrastructure. In order to overcome the problems generated by a whole range of market failures, including perverse incentives for bus owners and drivers, poorly defined property rights of streets and sidewalks, and environmental pollution and congestion, Bogotá has a massive new transport system called Trans-Milenio. It is an integrated bus rapid-transit system, using dedicated lanes for articulated buses, stations and terminals adapted for large-capacity buses, and fare-integrated operations with smaller buses on the outskirts of the city. The city grants contracts to private companies that provide and operate the buses in this system, and fees are based on distance traveled. In 2009 the TransMilenio network was far from complete, so it was too early to fully assess its impact. Still, in 2001, only two years after TransMilenio began operations, the duration of the average trip in Bogotá decreased from 44 minutes to 35 minutes, while the average speed of cars increased from 27 kilometers per hour to 32 kilometers per hour.

The TransMilenio system has become a reference point for similar future projects, both in Colombia and abroad, mainly because of its cost-effectiveness compared to alternatives such as underground metro systems. Currently, these massive transport systems are also in development for Barranquilla, Bucaramanga, Cali, Cartagena, Medellín, Pereira, and Soacha. The systems include financial support from the national government as long as the local authorities demonstrate the financial capacity to support the project during construction and operation. In 2008 Samuel Moreno Rojas took office as major of Bogotá with a popular mandate to build a metro line. In 2009 this proposed project and its links to the other elements of the capital city's public transport system, including TransMilenio and a future regional train plan, were still under review.

Telecommunications

In the first half of the 1990s, several reforms promoted competition in telecommunications by allowing both private and public firms to provide service. They included the introduction of the framework for cell-phone operations in 1993 and the creation, in 1994, of the Telecommunications Regulatory Commission (CRT).

Before the reforms, the company known as Telecom had a monopoly on national and international long-distance calls. After the reforms, two more firms provided service—Orbitel and the Bogotá Telephone Company (ETB). In 2003 Telecom went into liquidation, and a new firm, Colombia Telecommunications, also with the acronym Telecom, took over its businesses.

The number of telephone landlines per 1,000 people increased from 70 in 1990 to 180 in 2002. As of 2007, Colombia had fewer than 8 million fixed telephone lines. Since 1990 many value-added services have been introduced in telecommunications, including answering service, caller ID, conference calls, call waiting, call transfer, abbreviated dialing, and more. Cell phones were introduced in Colombia in 1994. Initially, two companies provided mobile-phone service (Comcel and Bellsouth), and subsequently Tigo (formerly known as Ola) became a provider following decisions on the bids for personal communications service (PCS), a digital mobile-phone technology. Tigo is a consortium that includes ETB and the Medellín Public Companies (EPM). Since 2006 Millicom International Cellular, a European multinational company, has held a majority shareholding in Tigo. These operators are free to compete in pricing. In December 2007, Colombia had 32.3 million active cell-phone users, two-thirds of them served by Comcel. According to the SIC, the Colombian mobile market reached 40.7 million subscriptions at the

*Bogotá's innovative TransMilenio mass-transportation
system uses dedicated lanes for articulated buses.
Courtesy Lorenzo Morales*

end of 2008, bringing the penetration rate to 91 percent. The data showed a growth rate of 20 percent for mobile subscriptions, higher than the 14 percent increase reported for 2007. Colombia also has a mobile communication services company, Avantel, based on another mobile-phone technology called trunking.

Colombia obtained its direct connection to the Internet on June 4, 1994, after a joint effort made by several local universities through a process that had begun in 1990. By the end of 2007, Colombia had as many as 12.1 million Internet users. Thus, 23 percent of the population had access to the Internet—above the world average of 19 percent—and the government is determined to increase this access share in a significant way in the next few years. Of those connected, about 80 percent were households, and the rest were corporate subscribers; moreover, 80 percent of Internet users had dedicated access. Wireless connections, although still not widespread, were increasing at a very significant rate by 2007, almost doubling each year. Trade through the Internet had begun, including financial services, news services, retail shopping, and a variety of other exchanges and services. The government has also accelerated the automation of a wide range of information, procedures, and services, such as tax payments, through the central Gobierno en Línea (Government Online) Web site. In 2008 Colombia had an estimated Internet penetration rate of 32.3 percent and broadband penetration rate of 3.9 percent.

Television broadcasting began in 1954 as a publicly provided service. However, financial difficulties led to a private-public partnership arrangement in the mid-1960s, in which the private sector was allowed to program and produce television materials, while the state kept control of the stations. In the mid-1980s, the government authorized regional channels and leases for subscription channels. In 2008 Colombia had five national channels. Caracol Television, S.A., and National Radio Network (RCN) were private channels, and three (Canal Uno, Señal Colombia, and Señal Institucional) were state operated. There was also a range of regional, local, and community channels. Colombia also had 76 registered providers of cable television services and one television company broadcasting by satellite (DIRECTV). In 2008 bidding opened on a license for one additional private channel.

Radio broadcasting began in 1929, and since 1933 Colombia has had various private firms providing the service, along with the public stations and, since 1997, community-based broadcasting companies. A variety of broadcasting companies and programs exist. Among the major broadcasting companies are Caracol, in which the Spanish investment group Prisa has a majority stake; RCN; Olympic Radio Organization (ORO); and Todelar Radio.

In 2004 almost two-thirds of the nation's 1,292 radio stations broadcast in frequency modulation (FM), while the rest broadcast in amplitude modulation (AM). Of the 167 public-interest broadcasters, most served municipalities, the armed forces, universities, and indigenous groups.

Financial Regulation and Financial Markets

At the end of the 1980s, Colombia's financial system was small, overregulated, and highly specialized, and it encompassed several state-owned institutions. For the most part, the gap between the interest charged by banks for loans they made and the interest paid by the banks for the deposits they received—the so-called intermediation spread—was high. This situation resulted from banks being rather inefficient, with high administrative costs in relation to assets, high taxes on financial intermediation, and a less-than-competitive environment. Thus, the productive sector had limited access to relatively expensive domestic credit, while access to foreign credit was highly constrained.

In the 1990s, reforms under the administration of César Augusto Gaviria Trujillo (president, 1990–94) promoted competition, creating a more efficient financial system that would support the transformation of Colombia's productive sector. The new measures eased the entry of firms into the financial sector; improved regulation; and encouraged bank business by simplifying mergers, conversions, and breakups and by allowing foreign investment. The reforms also privatized several public banks, liberalized interest rates, and changed the emphasis of the financial markets from specialization to a system of multipurpose banking. They also allowed the international best-practice standards for the financial sector—known as Basel rules—to be applied along with enhanced supervision by the Banking Superintendency. In addition, Gaviria's reforms reduced reserve requirements, which were no longer used as primary monetary policy tools; and encouraged financial institutions to participate in the foreign-exchange market and offer a wider range of products.

These measures improved competitiveness so that new banks could enter the market more easily, but they also increased the size of banks and the capital backing of financial institutions. Eventually, however, the positive effects of greater competition were neutralized by the higher risk caused by a poorer economic performance and the subsequent deterioration in the creditworthiness of finance companies. Intermediation spreads therefore remained at a high level.

181

Throughout the 1990s, the financial sector grew, as measured by total credits to both the public and the private sector, from 24 percent of GDP in 1988 to 41 percent of GDP in 1999. A sharp increase in capital inflows fueled this growth. In the late 1990s, and as a result of a combination of adverse exogenous shocks, including the Asian and Russian financial crises, a weak fiscal position, and an end to the boom in the housing market, the economy suffered a deep recession, and the banking sector underwent a severe crisis. Total credit allocation as a share of GDP diminished significantly and in 2003 had levels of 35 percent—similar to those of 1993—despite the substantial increase in public borrowing since 1997.

The financial crisis of the late 1990s affected mainly the public financial institutions, which were less efficient and had invested in lower-quality loans, and the savings and loan corporations, locally called CAVs, which had loans supported in housing assets that had shrunk significantly in value after the boom years. As a result, the financial system had large losses between 1998 and 2001. The depth of the financial crisis was due in part to the cyclical nature of financial regulation, which was lax during economic booms and strict during economic recessions.

In response to the financial crisis, the government took prompt and effective but fiscally expensive action. New regulations in 1999 meant that commercial banks could absorb the former mortgage institutions. These strict regulations during the crisis were because the government needed to reduce the financial sector's risk exposure from the boom in the first years of the 1990s and particularly to help public financial entities and the mortgage owners. Between 1998 and 2000, the worst years of the crisis, the loans of private financial institutions were of higher quality than those of public financial institutions and the CAVs. However, not all policy interventions strengthened the financial sector. In 1999 the weak fiscal position forced the government to introduce a financial transaction tax, initially a temporary tax at a rate of 0.2 percent, increased to a permanent 0.3 percent in 2000, and increased further to 0.4 percent in 2004.

Colombia's Banking Superintendency developed the Credit Risk Management System (SARC) so that there would be systematic supervision to evaluate credit risk. Institutions such as the IMF have acknowledged SARC as a pioneering effort in financial supervision. By using statistical techniques, an appropriate technological platform, and different levels of internal and external controls, SARC improves the quality of data.

As the economy slowly recovered from the recession, and the different policy measures began to take effect, the health of the finan-

Bogotá's new financial district on 72^d Street
Courtesy Lorenzo Morales

cial sector improved quite significantly. In a financial-stability report published in mid-2004, the Central Bank acknowledged that the financial system showed highly satisfactory indicators of profitability, credit, and liquidity risk. In 2005 public and private banks, both domestic and foreign, were all delivering healthy profits. This recovery allowed the government to sell back to the private sector several financial institutions. Despite these improvements, financial institutions still had a very high exposure to public-sector debt, on average a third of their assets.

Some of the changes introduced in the 1990s have contributed to the development of Colombia's capital markets, which are now much more sophisticated than a decade ago. The increasing role of the domestic market in the financing of the public deficit, the creation of private pension funds, and the securitization of mortgage-backed loans all have contributed to such development. In 2004 pension funds had accumulated assets equivalent to 12 percent of GDP, half of it invested in Colombian public debt. However, the loss of investment grade in 1999 during the recession meant that important funds, such as the California Public Employees Retirement System (CalPERS), the largest pension fund in the United States, have not been allowed to allocate funds in Colombia. As a result of CalPERS not investing in Colombia, other institutions that base their decisions on the CalPERS restricted list of countries where funds can be invested also held back.

To strengthen the operating basis of Colombia's capital markets, in 2005 a new law gave the Capital Markets Commission greater power as a regulator and allowed the government to produce a legal framework setting out the main rules that apply to the capital markets. These steps were designed to improve the transparency of financial information, clearing and settlement, protection of investors, and sanctions. At the end of 2005, the banking and capital markets superintendencies merged into the Colombian Financial Superintendency (SFC or Superfinanciera). In 2006 Colombian capital markets were stronger than they had been between 1995 and 1998, when Colombia had investment grade, although there is still a long way to go in their development.

In 2007 Colombia had 60 financial establishments: 16 banks, 33 leasing and finance corporations, and 11 public specialized institutions. In 2006 domestic banks held approximately 80 percent of the financial-sector assets and foreign banks, 20 percent. The largest Colombian investor was the Luis Carlos Sarmiento Angulo Organization. Other major domestic entities included the Agrarian Bank of Colombia, which is publicly owned and provides financial services to the rural sector, with more than 700 offices nationwide; Banco Caja Social Colmena (BCSC); Bancolombia, which has various foreign affiliates, such as the Bancolombia financial group in El Salvador; and Davivienda. Foreign multinational institutions included Citibank and Spain's Banco Bilbao Viscaya Argentaria (BBVA) and Banco Santander.

Trade Policy and Trade Patterns

In the 1990s, speculative import delays and significant private capital flows—within a crawling-peg system (see Glossary)—fueled domestic inflation and forced acceleration of the removal of trade barriers. In response, policy makers adopted decisive measures to promote trade liberalization. During that period, the percentage of tariff-free goods in total imports rose from 67 to 76, average tariffs declined from 34 to 12 percent, and a simplified tariff structure operated with just four tariff levels (0 percent, 5 percent, 10 percent, and 15 percent).

Colombia and other Andean nations received unilateral and preferential Generalized System of Preferences (GSP) access to the European Community (later the EU) in 1990 in recognition of their fight against illegal drugs. These countries also received preferential GSP access to the United States in 1992 for the same reasons, in a program that became known as the Andean Trade Promotion and Drug Eradication Act. Both the European and the U.S. preferential schemes are unilateral and subject to periodic appraisal and renewal.

Colombia also participates in a number of regional trade agreements. It signed a free-trade agreement with Chile in 1993; Mexico, Colombia, and Venezuela formed a regional agreement known as the G–3 (for Group of Three) in 1994; Colombia was a founding member of the Andean Pact, which became the Andean Community in 1997; and in 2004 Colombia negotiated a free-trade agreement with the members of the Common Market of the South (Mercosur—see Glossary). In 2007 Colombia signed a free-trade agreement with the Northern Triangle of Central America (Guatemala, Honduras, and El Salvador). In February 2006, the negotiation of a free-trade agreement between Colombia and the United States called the United States–Colombia Trade Promotion Agreement was finalized, and it was signed on November 22 of that year. The agreement—similar to the pact signed by the United States with Peru and with the Central American countries—liberalized most trade between the two countries and dealt with issues including foreign direct investment, competition policy, property rights, workers' rights, and environmental protection. Although the Colombian Congress and Constitutional Court initially approved the agreement and a reform protocol in 2007, the actual adoption of such an agreement was pending the approval of the U.S. Congress.

Colombia began negotiations in 2007—along with Peru—for a free-trade agreement with Canada and the European Free Trade Association (Iceland, Liechtenstein, Norway, and Switzerland). Together with the Andean Community, Colombia also started free-trade negotiations with the EU. Furthermore, Colombia has committed to the Free Trade Area of the Americas (FTAA). On the multilateral front, Colombia approved the Uruguay Round of the General Agreement on Tariffs and Trade (GATT) in 1993 and was a founding member of the World Trade Organization in 1995.

Commodities traditionally have dominated the composition of Colombia's exports. However, the pattern has changed over the past five decades. Coffee, which represented about 85 percent of Colombia's total exports in 1959, represented less than 6 percent in 2006—less than the share that it had in the 1870s. Oil and coal have become Colombia's two major export products, representing, respectively, 18 percent and 12 percent of the nation's total exports in 2006. The so-called nontraditional exports (new export products other than coffee, oil, coal, and nickel), which constituted 30 percent of total exports in 1970, increased their share to about 52 percent of total exports by 1991 and have fluctuated around that level to date. Overall, and despite its dependence on commodities, Colombia's export basket is today more diverse than in 1990. The main exported manufactures include chemicals and refined oil products, processed foods, basic metallurgical products, clothing, and vehicles.

In 2006 the United States was the destination of 40 percent of Colombian exports; Venezuela received 11 percent; Ecuador, 5 percent; Mexico and Peru, 3 percent each; and Germany, Japan, and Belgium, 2 percent each. These eight countries were the destination of 68 percent of Colombia's total exports. The fact that the United States is Colombia's most important trade partner explains why the negotiation of the free-trade agreement with the United States has been a major economic and political issue for Colombian officials and for many of the nation's main pressure groups. In order to enhance security and improve efficiency in its trade with the United States, Colombian export companies have been allowed to participate in the Customs–Trade Partnership Against Terrorism program of the U.S. Customs and Border Protection agency.

In 2006 some 25.5 percent of Colombia's exports were from the Caribbean coast, that is, the departments of Atlántico, Bolívar, César, Córdoba, La Guajira, Magdalena, and Sucre, as well as Colombia's Caribbean department of San Andrés, Providencia y Santa Catalina; 16.9 percent were from Bogotá and Cundinamarca Department; 12.9 percent were from Antioquia; and 7.4 percent were from Valle del Cauca Department.

Colombia's import bill rose by 26 percent to US$30.1 billion in 2006. Of these imports, 80 percent consisted of capital goods and industrial raw materials and inputs, and 20 percent of consumption goods. In that same year, the United States provided 26 percent of Colombian imports; China and Mexico, 9 percent each; Brazil, 7 percent; Venezuela, 6 percent, Germany and Japan, 4 percent each; Ecuador, 3 percent; and Spain, 1 percent. These nine countries were the source of 69 percent of Colombia's total imports.

Foreign Investment Regulation and Outcomes

Before the reforms of the 1990s, foreign direct investment (FDI) was highly restricted both nationally and within the Andean Pact. During those years, FDI was not allowed in principal financial services, infrastructure, and public utilities, although Colombian governments exercised some discretion. The change in the economic model that occurred in the 1990s led to a range of policy measures to foster FDI, simplify its procedures, and remove impediments to investment in specific sectors, except for national security or serious environmental concerns. The Colombia Investment Corporation, a national FDI-promotion agency, came into being and later merged with Proexpo. Colombia became a member of the Multilateral Investment Guarantee Agency and the International Centre for Settlement of Investment Disputes, in order to establish political risk-management mechanisms.

Colombia's FDI increased from an annual average US$2.4 billion between 1994 and 2004 to an annual average US$8.5 billion between 2005 and 2007. In 2005 the United States had the largest share of FDI in Colombia with 16.3 percent, followed by Spain and the United Kingdom with 12.2 percent each, and Panama with 10.4 percent. The tax havens in the Caribbean, such as the British Virgin Islands and the Cayman Islands, have been significant sources of outward FDI for Colombia. FDI to these tax havens may be explained to some extent as investment by Colombian citizens using front companies as tax-evasion maneuvers, or as wealth-protection measures, given the high levels of violence and insecurity that have prevailed in Colombia for many years.

Between 1994 and 2007, the leading sectors attracting FDI were manufactures, mining, petroleum, financial services, and transport and communications. Increasing oil prices worldwide and domestic requirements have meant that there has been an increasing interest on the part of foreign investors in the exploration of new oil fields and in the production of biodiesel and ethanol in Colombia.

FDI patterns from the United States were led by financial services between 1993 and 2000, represented by investment companies such as Citigroup and Liberty Mutual Insurance, and the sector accounted for 21 percent of all inflows from the United States. Telecommunications and information technology played a major role between 2001 and 2004, with companies including Dell, Oracle, Computer Associates, Sun Microsystems, and others responsible for 65 percent of all FDI inflows from the United States. In 2007 General Electric bought a 39 percent share of a large bank, Colpatria Red Multibanca (Colpatria Multibank Network).

Among the most important FDI transactions by firms not from the United States are the merger between Grupo Bavaria and SABMiller, which has been followed by new investments in its beer business; and the acquisition of a controlling share in Casa Editorial El Tiempo (CEET), which owns Colombia's largest newspaper, with a significant investment in CEET's associated television channel, CityTV, by the Spanish Grupo Planeta. The Spanish Grupo Fenosa has made major investments in electricity generation. French and Chilean companies have also been important foreign investors in Colombia.

Foreign-investment funds have been able since 1991 to invest in Colombia through their portfolios. The Colombian assets of these funds increased to more than US$1 billion between 1996 and 2000, then depreciated steadily, and by 2003 had fallen to less than US$700 million. In order to minimize the effects of speculative financial flows on exchange-rate volatility, since December 2004 such investments must remain in Colombia for at least one year.

Foreign investments by Colombian companies have increased significantly in the last two decades, from US$59 million in 1992 to more than US$1 billion since 2005. They have invested, for example, in cement producer group Argos and the ceramics and plumbing Corona Group in the United States; the Corona Group in Mexico; the Peruvian state oil company Ecopetrol; the Grupo Empresarial Interconexión Eléctrica S.A. in Brazil, Panama, and Peru; Compañia Nacional de Chocolates in Peru and other Latin American countries; and the Bancolombia financial group in El Salvador. A wide range of smaller Colombian firms are also making investments abroad in sectors such as apparel and fashion design, food products, and restaurants.

Illegal Drugs

The illegal drug problem appeared in the 1970s, intensified in the 1980s, and has continued unabated since then. The Colombian government has tried many different policies since 1990 to fight the illegal drug trade. Gaviria put his administration's policy emphasis on countering narco-terrorism—the combination of illegal drug businesses and terrorism. After the 1991 constitution banned extradition, the government adopted a program allowing major traffickers to do jail time in Colombia in return for lenient sentences, and eventually a group of drug lords headed by Pablo Escobar Gaviria took part in it. As there was clear evidence that justice was neither thorough nor impartial, the government attempted to transfer Escobar away from the comfortable so-called prison that he had built for himself near Medellín; Escobar and several of his associates escaped. This situation forced the Colombian government to make major efforts to capture, dead or alive, key figures of the Medellín Cartel. Eventually, several of those drug lords were put back into prison, or, like Escobar, were killed. After serious allegations that the Cali Cartel had financed his presidential campaign, Ernesto Samper's administration captured the heads of the cartel, reestablished extradition in 1997, and introduced court powers in order to allow the state to take possession of properties obtained with funds from illegal activities.

The 1990s were years of significant increase in the area of coca-crop cultivation, from 40,100 hectares in 1990 to 163,300 hectares in 2000. The 1990s also saw the start of opium-poppy cultivation, with a production area in 1994 of 15,000 hectares. Besides, the Cali and

*Growing to a height of two or three meters, the coca shrub
is a member of the family* Erythroxylaceae. *Its leaves
contain cocaine alkaloids, a basis for cocaine.
The opium poppy, of the family* Papaveraceae, *is an annual
herb cultivated in Colombia for heroin production.
Courtesy Narcotics Affairs Section Office, U.S. Embassy, Bogotá*

189

Medellín cartels were gradually replaced by the Revolutionary Armed Forces of Colombia (FARC) and the United Self-Defense Forces of Colombia (AUC) as major players.

To confront these issues, the administration of Andrés Pastrana Arango (president, 1998–2002) designed a largely U.S.-financed program called Plan Colombia, which has been in operation since then. Plan Colombia strengthens the state presence in drug-producing regions and is combined with a range of social and environmental measures. Given that a significant amount of illegal drugs leaves Colombia by sea, in 1997 Colombia and the United States signed a maritime agreement to strengthen procedures and cooperation in coordinating maritime interdiction. In 1999 the two countries also signed a bilateral air interdiction agreement with resources from the Air Bridge Denial program. According to local authorities, both of these interdiction programs have contributed significantly to restriction of the flows of illegal drugs out of the country.

Recent policies and eradication programs have contributed to reducing the production areas of drug crops. For example, in 2006 the production area of coca crops fell to 78,000 hectares; the opium-poppy production area fell to 1,023 hectares; and the number of illegal processing labs destroyed rose from 317 in 1999 to 2,217. Furthermore, the government of President Álvaro Uribe initiated procedures for bringing to justice the main leaders of the AUC and in 2008, when several of them would not cooperate with the program, for extraditing them to the United States. The FARC also lost in 2008 three members of its seven-member Secretariat, including FARC founder Pedro Antonio Marín (also known as Manuel Marulanda Vélez, or "Tiro Fijo"—Sure Shot). Many of the other members of the AUC and the FARC have been killed, captured, or have demobilized through specially designed programs.

Despite many efforts, reductions in production areas have been accompanied by increases in productivity. As such, the United Nations Office on Drugs and Crime (UNODC) estimated that in 2006 the potential coca production of Colombia passed from 463 metric tons in 2001 to 610 metric tons in 2006. Even allowing for changes in measurement methodologies, these numbers are a sign of concern about the effectiveness of the policies adopted so far. According to UNODC, in 2006 Colombia supplied 62 percent of the world's cocaine; an estimated 67,000 households were involved in coca farming; and 83 percent of cultivation took place in the departments of Putumayo, Caquetá, Meta, Guaviare, Nariño, Antioquia, and Vichada.

Colombia has been the main supplier of cocaine and an important supplier of heroin to the U.S. market, and a major supplier of these drugs to the EU. The importance of Colombia as a supplier of illegal drugs, however, does not necessarily mean that Colombia as a whole has profited from such trade. Data gathered by U.S. authorities show that a significant share of the revenues generated by this illegal trade accrues mainly at the retail level and remains in developed countries because the price of cocaine increases dramatically during the commercialization process. It has been estimated that the retail price in the United States is 200 times the price paid for the equivalent product at the farm level in Colombia and eight times the price received by whoever makes the wholesale export into the U.S. market. Inasmuch as retail sales in the United States are undertaken mainly by persons who are not Colombian nationals, most of the profits from the drug trade go to foreigners. Furthermore, the profits generated in consumer countries that do end up in the hands of Colombian nationals are not necessarily transferred back to Colombia, at least not entirely. Although the annual value of processed cocaine and other exported illicit drugs is believed to exceed US$5 billion, only about one-half of this amount actually returns to Colombia. Despite counternarcotics efforts since the mid-1980s, drugs are currently as available as ever, of better quality, and at lower prices.

The economic effect of the illegal drug trade also includes the distortional effects that foreign-exchange revenues from such activities have on legal production of goods and services. Furthermore, drug proceeds foster corruption, fund contraband and money laundering, jeopardize political stability, and weaken institutions. They have also stoked Colombia's internal conflict. Recent estimates indicate that Colombia's GDP growth rate has been diminished by about 2 percent per year because of the deleterious effect that the drug-fueled internal conflict has had on investment and productivity. The overall effect of drug trafficking on the Colombian economy remains negative even though certain sectors, particularly the housing industry in certain cities, may have received a boost from this illegal activity. According to the Ministry of Agriculture and Rural Development, between 1995 and 2006 the share of illicit drugs in GDP fell (see The Rise of Drug Trafficking Organizations, ch. 1; Drug Trafficking and the Origins of Paramilitarism, ch. 5).

Macroeconomic Policies and Trends

Until the end of the 1980s, Colombia was widely acknowledged as a remarkably stable economy in the Latin American context, characterized by moderate inflation and growth. The country's public finances and foreign debt were in good health, and exchange-rate policy was based on a crawling-peg system, supported by a wide range of exchange controls.

Following international trends, at the beginning of the 1990s Colombia began a conscientious effort to reduce inflation. Likewise, the government decided to remove many of the inefficient and inequitable exchange-rate controls. Both of these goals led to a series of institutional changes and policy adjustments. However, at the same time that new measures came in to boost the private sector, the 1991 constitution brought about important changes that called for additional fiscal expenditure. In the absence of adequate compensatory taxes and spending controls, the increased spending eventually weakened the fiscal position and made the economy more vulnerable to exogenous shocks. The pledge to reduce inflation was quite costly to GDP growth, given a weak fiscal position and the shock effects of the Asian and Russian crises of the late 1990s. Following a deep recession and financial crises in 1999, Colombia had low and stable inflation in 2006 and 2007 and some improvement in its fiscal policy stance, for which a close engagement with the IMF is partly responsible. In 2004 Colombia became the second Latin American nation—after Uruguay—to sell bonds denominated in local currency in international markets. It also has reduced the share of external debt in total public debt to about 35 percent in 2006 and increased the average duration of its loans. However, Colombia can still be characterized as a vulnerable economy, with a high public-debt burden of about 52 percent of GDP in 2006, higher than the 43.3 level it had in the crisis year of 1999.

Monetary Policy and Inflation

From 1963 until 1991, a monetary board headed the Central Bank. Its members included the ministers of finance, agriculture and livestock, and economic development and the director of the Institute of Foreign Trade. The control of the executive branch over monetary policy meant that there were constant pressures to use monetary policy to promote certain sectors of the economy. This configuration resulted in an average rate of inflation of 20 percent between 1963 and 1990.

Under the 1991 constitution, the Central Bank is the authority in charge of monetary policy, including the role of lender of last resort for financial institutions, and responsible for management of the country's exchange rate and foreign reserves. More importantly, the 1991 constitution also gives the Central Bank significant autonomy from the executive. A board of directors headed by the minister of finance and public credit replaced the monetary board. Six board members elect the bank's general manager for a four-year term. The five other board members are appointed by the president of the republic for four-year terms. Every four years, the government may change two of the appointed board members and must reappoint the other three. No member may serve for more than three terms. Loans from the bank to the government and to the nonfinancial private sector are severely restricted.

The new constitution establishes that the Central Bank's mandate is to guard price stability and that its policies have to be made in coordination with overall economic policy. The 1991 charter gives the Central Bank political and financial autonomy, but the Central Bank has to present a biannual report on its activities to Congress to ensure accountability. Despite sporadic debates about the objectives, structure, operation, and independence of the Central Bank, since the reforms were introduced in 1991, Colombia has managed to reduce its inflation rate from 32.4 percent in 1990 to 4.5 percent in 2006. However, the trend had been slightly reversed by 2008, a year in which inflation reached 7.7 percent.

Normally, reducing inflation comes at a price, and for Colombia the price was especially high in 1999, when the Asian crisis affected its economy negatively, while the country was vulnerable because of its public and foreign debt burden. In that year, GDP fell 4 percent, and unemployment reached levels of almost 20 percent.

Since 1999, and in the context of a floating exchange rate, monetary policy has been formulated through an inflation-targeting framework. Accordingly, the Central Bank establishes an inflation target for the year and an indicative target for the medium term. The intermediate target for monetary policy is the Central Bank's overnight interest rate. Therefore, and contrary to its pre-1999 practices, the Central Bank no longer announces targets for monetary aggregates. As part of the inflation-targeting structure, the Central Bank now issues quarterly inflation reports, a most valuable source for analysis and data on macroeconomic developments in Colombia.

Exchange-Rate Policy and the Balance of Payments

After the collapse of the gold standard in 1931, the Central Bank began controlling transactions in foreign exchange, maintaining different exchange rates and relatively free international movements of capital. However, a 1967 law gave the Central Bank a monopoly on all foreign-exchange transactions made in the official foreign-exchange market, introduced the crawling-peg system of gradual devaluations, and unified the exchange rate. In order to make those changes operational, the bank implemented a wide range of capital controls.

In 1991 the government abolished the 1967 law as part of Colombia's promarket reforms and removed many restrictions on capital movements. It also allowed the exchange rate to float within a band—informally until 1994, formally until 1999. In that year, the large public and private foreign debt made the country vulnerable, and speculative attacks led the Central Bank to twice devalue the foreign-exchange band and then to allow the exchange rate to float, once a precautionary three-year extended-fund facility had been agreed with the IMF. However, the bank reserved the right to intervene in the foreign-exchange market, with a range of fairly transparent and publicly known instruments, in accordance with its policy objectives.

Significant devaluations of the Colombian peso occurred in 2002 and 2003 with the floating exchange rate. Following international patterns, between 2004 and 2007 the Colombian peso experienced both significant nominal and real appreciation against the U.S. dollar. This appreciation caused groups involved in exports to press government officials and the Central Bank to design measures to alleviate their position. These pressures demonstrated, at least in part, that by 2004 Colombian entrepreneurs were still not properly prepared to live under a floating exchange-rate system and rarely used financial-coverage mechanisms to protect themselves against fluctuations in the exchange rate.

A careful analysis of the real exchange-rate index shows that in 2007 the Colombian peso was quite overvalued, compared to its patterns since 1990, and that it was about 10 percent stronger compared to 1994. The net foreign reserves expressed in total debt payments within the next year increased substantially from 0.9 in 1999 to 1.6 in 2006, a level considered a sign of a healthy balance of payments.

Since the early 1990s, Colombia's balance of payments has shown some consistent patterns. Exports have grown in line with imports. Colombia consistently has been a net importer of services, especially in transport, travel, insurance, finance, entrepreneurship, and construction. Colombia also has had negative net-factor income, with outlays consistently above revenues, mainly on interest payments, profits, and dividends, as would be expected given the increase in foreign debt and foreign-investment inflows that occurred during the period. The growing importance of remittances as a source of foreign exchange is a fairly new and striking feature of the Colombian economy, resulting from the high emigration levels that occurred in the second half of the 1990s in response to the persistent violence and the economic crisis of 1999. Remittances to Colombia rose from US$745 million in 1996 to US$3 billion in 2003, equivalent to 90 percent of the nation's exports of oil and its derivatives, the country's largest exports.

Despite the growing importance of remittances, Colombia has had a negative current account since 1993, resulting largely from the public sector's fiscal imbalance. The exceptions were the recession years (1999 and 2000), when there was a lack of international finance sources for Colombia in the midst of the Asian and Russian financial crises.

The current-account deficit of recent years has been financed, except in 1999, with long-term financial inflows, such as FDI and long-term loans. These net long-term financial inflows have more than compensated for the net short-term financial cash outflows that have prevailed. Mirroring the current-account deficits, Colombia has reported a financial and capital-account surplus throughout the period. International reserves also generally have increased, most significantly in 2007, reaching record levels of more than US$20 billion and representing about eight months of current imports of goods.

During the debt crises of the 1980s, Colombia avoided foreign-debt rescheduling processes and was widely acknowledged as the Latin American country with the best creditworthiness. However, the unprecedented increase in public debt experienced in the country between 1990 and 2000 and generated by the country's structural fiscal imbalance was accompanied by a large increase in foreign debt in both the public and the private sectors. This development was a key factor in the economic crises of 1999, as financial markets regarded Colombia as a vulnerable emerging market because of its high public- and foreign-debt exposure.

The share of the private sector's foreign debt reached 19 percent of GDP in 1999 but by 2006 was estimated to have dropped to 10 percent of GDP. The public-sector foreign debt as a share of GDP reached 30 percent in 2003 but declined to 15 percent of GDP in 2007. By May 2008, Colombia had US$45.7 billion in total foreign debt.

Fiscal Policy and Public Finances

The introduction of the 1991 constitution led to a rise in Colombia's public-sector expenditure from 20.4 percent of GDP in 1990 to 33.7 percent of GDP in 2001. In 2002 government expenditure was 31 percent higher than the average in Latin America. The decentralization process that began in the 1970s and accelerated under the new constitution largely explained the higher government spending.

Decentralization transferred funds from the central government to the territorial entities—departments, special districts, and municipalities—through several mechanisms. The decentralization of funds, however, was not accompanied by devolution of discretion in spending these resources. The constitution and some subsequent legislation restricted the use of the resources and left the departmental governments very limited in their expenditure decisions. Furthermore, and perhaps more importantly in view of its adverse fiscal implications, the central government continued to undertake certain expenditure responsibilities that should have devolved to the regions, including health, education, and infrastructure.

The constitution established that the territorial entities' share of central government revenues had to increase from 26 percent in 1993 to 46.5 percent in 2002. Along with the greater resources, territorial entities increased their indebtedness throughout the 1990s. The debt of departments and departmental capitals increased from 0.9 percent of GDP in 1990 to 2.8 percent of GDP in 1999. Their higher revenues and the lack of effective budgetary controls encouraged the increase in regional debt. Instruments such as the cofinance funds, which operated until 1998 and were designed to concentrate additional funds from the central national government to finance projects at lower levels of government, also facilitated fiscal irresponsibility. Although the Education Compensation Fund (FEC) was created in 1997 to promote efficiency in education, it eventually became a bailout mechanism for the regions, increasing the perverse incentives even more.

Colombia's untenable pension system further complicated the country's fiscal problems. In the latter part of the 1990s, Colombian policy makers became increasingly aware of the growing fiscal burden that the existing pension plans posed for public resources. Such pension payments increased from 0.8 percent of GDP in 1990 to 3.5 percent in 2003. In order to address the problem, a series of pension reforms has taken place (see The Pension System, this ch.).

Another source of pressure on Colombia's public revenues introduced by the 1991 constitution was the creation of the Constitutional Court as the legal entity in charge of preserving the integrity and supremacy of the constitution (see The Judiciary, ch. 4). The Constitutional Court's opinions are final, and its actions generally have been geared to ensuring that all constitutional provisions granting rights to the people are actually enforced. The Constitutional Court has made a literal interpretation of broad policy goals, such as "the right to fair wages" or "the right to decent housing," and in so doing has in effect ordered the government to satisfy those rights, regardless of the availability of fiscal resources. The more salient decisions of the Constitutional Court include the retroactive indexation of the wages of public-sector workers to maintain purchasing power and the extension of the fourteenth monthly wage (*mesada* 14), an additional payment (on top of the thirteenth monthly wage known as *prima*), originally designed to equalize unbalanced pension payments of certain workers (at a cost that has been estimated at 14 percent of the nation's GDP). In addition, the court ordered the recalculation of mortgage payments, which generated regressive income distribution by not differentiating among debtors on the basis of wealth or indebtedness.

These decisions have created tension between policy makers and the court. Policy makers point out that the Constitutional Court is not democratically elected and determines expenditures arbitrarily with no provision for the revenues to fulfill them. The members of the Constitutional Court claim that the executive and legislative powers have not built a minimum legal capacity for their own use and have not provided the court with enough resources for it to be in a position to make accurate judgments.

The structural imbalance in public finances created since 1991, because of legal restrictions on increasing fiscal revenues at the same pace as public expenses, generated persistent fiscal deficits and subsequently a dramatic increase in public debt compared to most of the twentieth century. Thus, while between 1950 and 1990 total central-government debt averaged 13 percent of GDP, debt rose from 14 percent of GDP in 1995 to 54 percent in 2003.

Colombia was traditionally a country with low levels of debt, and its public debt was awarded investment grade in 1995, but the serious deterioration in economic health led to the downgrading of its investment status in 1999 and to successive standby agreements with the IMF between then and 2006. These agreements reflected a commitment toward structural reform and macroeconomic and financial stability, limiting the short-run temptations that had led successive governments to postpone resolution of fiscal problems.

New requirements made departments and municipalities face their budget constraints and improve their efficiency and transparency. The new constitution and subsequent laws restricted their ability to increase their debt and limited the capacity of the central government to bail them out. Transfers became centralized under the General Participation System, consisting of the funds that the central government is constitutionally required to transfer to the regions. In 2001 transfers to departments and municipalities were temporarily capped until 2008, and in 2007 further reforms made transfers more consistent with a sounder and sustainable long-term fiscal policy.

These reforms have generated substantial savings to the central government and will continue to do so, while still ensuring enough resources to reach universal coverage in the near future in primary and secondary education and in health. They will also contribute to the improvement in the quality of those services, and in the provision of drinking water and sewerage services.

To help finance the increasing public expenditures, Colombia has had a significant number of tax reforms since 1990 and a range of other measures taken by the government to start addressing fiscal problems. The tax-reform process has been so intense that some analysts have identified more than 10 significant fiscal reforms between 1990 and 2007. One reason for the repeated fiscal reforms and the almost insoluble fiscal imbalances is the greater political participation of Congress. Although congressional involvement fosters democracy, it hinders agreement. Other reasons are the lack of party discipline and the strong incentives for each administration to transfer responsibility for problems to its successor. This gradual approach to fiscal reform has resulted in a complex tax system, with regressive taxes, such as a tax on financial transactions, a high marginal income tax, and a small value-added tax (VAT) levied on a restricted set of goods. The Colombian VAT regime has many rates and exemptions, as well as a broad range of exemptions to income tax, which increases unnecessarily the administrative burden of tax collection.

Although Colombia had held most of its public debt in foreign markets, it has increasingly been placed with internal sources in order to mitigate the vulnerability of the country to significant changes in the exchange rate induced by foreign shocks and to avoid high appreciation of the exchange rate. As of 2006, about 65 percent of total public debt was being held domestically. During 2007 and in the midst of economic recovery and overall improvements in the finances of the public sector, Colombia's credit rating was upgraded, and it was likely that the country as a whole would soon recover investment grade.

On balance, the macroeconomic reforms of the 1990s were well intentioned but ill conceived in some cases and contradictory in others, particularly in demanding increasing social responsibility from the state but without the necessary increase in public revenues. Moreover, the Constitutional Court's decisions increased government expenditures and weakened some revenue-generating tax reforms. The combination of these factors led to more severe fiscal problems. Constitutionally mandated low inflation, competitive real exchange rate, and opening of the economy to trade in goods and services, while liberalizing the capital account, were somewhat conflicting policies. Their timing has had some unwelcome results, such as a long period of revaluation of the real exchange rate.

Labor, The Informal Economy, Social Spending, and Pensions

Throughout the twentieth century, Colombia achieved important improvements in human development and social protection. For example, between 1900 and 2008 life expectancy increased from 37 to 72.5 years, and infant mortality fell from 204 per 1,000 live births to 19.5. According to the World Bank, by 2004 illiteracy had dropped from 58 percent to about 8 percent, poverty had declined from 92 percent to 52.6 percent, and income per capita had increased more than ninefold to US$5,515, at purchasing-power parity (PPP) in current international dollars. Nevertheless, the second half of the 1990s was a period of disappointing results overall for social indicators. The first decade of the twenty-first century has been a period of sluggish recovery. The social impact of Colombia's economic policy has been transmitted mainly through the labor markets, welfare expenditure, and the pension system (see also Health and Welfare, ch. 2). By 2008 illiteracy had fallen to 7 percent and GDP per capita had risen to US$6,958 (at PPP).

Labor Markets

Demographic factors have shaped the Colombian labor force. In the last few decades, it has been characterized by fairly stable participation of men and increasing participation of women, an increase in rural–urban migration, and an increase in the average age of the population as a result of a longer life expectancy and a decrease in the size of families. Another important feature of the Colombian labor force is that qualified workers—understood as those workers who completed secondary education—who at the beginning of the 1990s represented less than 40 percent of the urban labor force, represented almost 60 percent of the labor force at the beginning of 2006.

System rigidities and nonwage payments of about 50 percent of the basic wage are other important characteristics of Colombia's labor markets. Such nonwage payments include holidays, pensions, health-care insurance, lay-off compensation, and labor-risk insurance. They also include contributions to family-welfare programs through the Colombian Family Welfare Institute, public workforce training programs through the National Learning Service, and family compensation programs through nonprofit entities called Family Compensation Funds (CCFs). The state has allocated CCFs the role of granting subsidies and services to lower-income families with resources coming from a contribution paid by employers and equivalent to 4 percent of the basic wages paid. Studies since 2000 have shown that nonwage payments in Colombia are close to the levels of developed countries and are among the highest in Latin America and the world.

Colombia has not had particularly strong labor unions, and membership has decreased from 13 percent in 1965 to less than 5 percent in 2005 (see Labor Unions, ch. 4). The three principal unions, in descending order of importance, are the United Workers' Federation (CUT), the General Confederation of Democratic Workers (CGTD), and the Confederation of Colombian Workers (CTC). These labor unions, the employers, and the government have bargained formally over wages for many years, especially at the end of every year. And between 1996 and 2006, Colombia's minimum wage increased 24 percent in real terms, despite record levels of unemployment, the worst recession in decades, and no significant improvements in labor productivity. A nominal 7.7 percent rise in the minimum wage came into effect in January 2009. Although Colombia's minimum wage is modest, its increases are important because they are a reference for wage increases in other segments of the labor market.

The Colombian demand for labor has been influenced by the technological changes that originated in the reforms of the 1990s, mainly through the opening of the economy, which led to an increase and an upgrade in the capital stock, an increase in the demand for higher skills, and a decrease in the demand for lower skills. In 1990 a labor-market reform reduced the cost of firing a worker, increased the range of alternatives to hiring workers, and brought down the nonwage payments to about 43 percent of the basic wage. However, the social security and health reform of 1993 increased payroll contributions from 43 percent to 53 percent of the basic wage, more than reversing the earlier savings of nonwage costs.

In the short term, perhaps the most important occurrence in Colombia's labor markets was the sharp increase in the unemployment rate from 1994 to 2000, when it reached record levels of almost 20 percent. The high unemployment was closely linked with the recession, which was accompanied by an increase in the participation of women and youngsters in the labor force, as households attempted to diversify their income sources. It was also accompanied by a deterioration in the quality of employment, measured by the size of the informal sector and the extent of underemployment.

The increases in labor costs, however, both through minimum wage and nonwage payments, had a more lasting impact on Colombia's labor markets. The average unemployment rate between 1984

A seamstress in Bogotá
Courtesy Inter-American Development Bank (Daniel Drosdoff),
Washington, DC
Flower vendors on the sidewalk at the entrance to Bogotá's main cemetery
Courtesy Lorenzo Morales

and 2006 was 12.4 percent, which is very high by world standards. The average unemployment rose from 11.4 percent between 1984 and 1989 to 14.9 percent between 2001 and 2006 (with a change in measurement methodology in the latter period). The increase in the average level of unemployment has been accompanied by an increase in the variance of unemployment. Recent studies show that in Colombia unemployment hits women and young workers, mainly those with only secondary education, the hardest. Unemployment also increases as the level of income falls, affecting primarily the poorest groups of the population.

The recovery of the economy meant that by 2006 some improvements in the labor markets had occurred, notably a fall in the rate and duration of unemployment, an improvement in the quality of employment, and an increase in the number of jobs for young workers. The benefits of the 2002 labor reform were still under scrutiny, and it was too early to judge its full effectiveness. The aim of this reform was to reduce employment costs and labor-market rigidities and to promote the hiring of apprentices and vulnerable groups of society. It also introduced an unemployment subsidy financed through a further increase in the nonwage costs. Nevertheless, the high level of unemployment remained one of Colombia's most serious economic and social problems.

The Informal Economy

The high rigidities in the country's labor markets and the high nonwage costs mean that Colombia has a large informal economy. Although employment in the informal sector had decreased until 1996, the recession of 1999 and the sharp increase in forced displacement because of the internal conflict reversed this trend. Between 2000 and about 2006, the informal economy accounted for some 50 percent of total GDP and 60 percent of employment in the cities. Although informal employment in the rural sector has not been as well documented as in urban areas, some estimates indicate that in rural areas it has been as high as 90 percent of total employment.

Within cities and towns, the most important informal-sector work is in services (75 percent of such employment), followed by industry, with 16 percent, and construction, with 6 percent. Informal-sector workers are most likely to be in the younger and older segments of the population. About 90 percent of employees under 18 years of age and 74 percent of employees older than 55 years of age work in the informal sector. The informal sector involves women more than men as a result of the later entry of women into the labor force, the preference of women for more flexible working conditions, and outright discriminatory practices by formal-sector employers. Also, informality becomes less likely the larger a company is and the greater the number of years that it has operated.

Estimates suggest that in 2005 male workers in the informal sector could earn approximately 52 percent less than what they would have earned in the formal sector, while female workers earned about 60 percent less working in the informal sector than in the formal sector. In that same year, an estimated 14 percent of informal workers made contributions toward retirement pensions, while 46 percent had some form of health coverage.

Given the large size of the informal economy in Colombia, it is not surprising that this sector has been very heterogeneous. Informal workers can be classified in three groups: direct subsistence, informal salaried, and small entrepreneurs. A study of the urban informal sector in employment has shown that these groups have different patterns of behavior. Whereas the number of direct-subsistence workers has tended to increase in recessions and to decrease in economic booms, the number of informal salaried workers and small entrepreneurs has tended to decline in recessions and to rise in economic booms.

Social Expenditure

During the 1990s, Colombia saw an increase of more than 50 percent in its public spending, particularly in social spending. Health and education each increased their shares of resources from 4 percent of GDP in the early 1990s to 8 percent of GDP in the latter part of the decade. Perhaps the main achievement was the increase in health-insurance coverage. In 1993 some 25 percent of the population was affiliated with some health-care insurance system, as compared with 53 percent of the population in 2000. Moreover, in 1993 the poor had no health-care coverage, whereas in 2000, about 55 percent of the poor did.

Progress in education has not been so encouraging. Public expenditure on education increased 500 percent between 1995 and 2000, while coverage for primary (110 percent because of the participation of over-aged students in primary education), secondary (82 percent), and tertiary education (20 percent) were hardly affected. Studies have shown that a significant portion of the increase in expenditure went to raise the wages of teachers, and that during the 1990s real public-sector wages increased 70 percent. Studies also have shown that teachers' wages increased 8 percent per year more than other public-sector workers, mainly because of changes in rankings and pension benefits. Public-sector teachers traditionally have not been evaluated, and promotion has been based on seniority rather than performance. Furthermore, between 1993 and 1997 public expenditure on education was not a key determinant of educational quality.

A positive aspect in education has been the growing national and international recognition of the success of the New School programs for rural education that developed across the country during the 1970s and the 1980s. These programs are characterized by the use of very flexible plans that allow students to make progress according to their own capabilities and restrictions, reducing the dropout rate and improving results. International reports have shown that Colombia is the only Latin American nation in which students from the rural New School program obtain better grades in mathematics and language than students from urban areas outside the largest cities (see Education, ch. 2).

Despite the sharp increase in public spending, in the mid-1990s the poverty and extreme-poverty rates began to worsen for the first time in many years. Social assistance programs (excluding education, health, and pensions) received about 1 percent of GDP during the same period, although the spending share tended to increase slightly when the economy was doing well and to decrease slightly in leaner times. Despite the large number of reforms carried out in the 1990s, spending on social assistance programs stagnated during those years.

The deterioration of the poverty indicators in recent years led in 2004 to a heated debate on the measurement of this variable. Regardless of the different arguments in the measurement debate, poverty remains one of the main economic problems in Colombia, and it is perhaps its major challenge for the near future. In 2007 Colombia ranked 75 out of 177 countries in the Human Development Index rankings from the United Nations Development Programme.

Colombia's conservative management of the economy and its remarkable economic stability had served for many years as a social safety net. However, when the 1999 recession occurred, the country had no structured safety net in place to alleviate the impact of the recession on poverty and the subsequent high unemployment. The incumbent national government tried to respond to the social crisis, creating a number of family, youth, and employment programs, initially designed to be temporary, to support the most vulnerable members of society. Not surprisingly, though, the response to the social crisis was very slow.

One major problem has been the lack of focus of social spending. Some 40 percent of Colombia's social spending is for pensions, but the system covers very few of the retired population and does not reach the most vulnerable sectors of society. Programs target formal-sector workers, as does the minimum wage, ignoring the informal-sector workers, who are by definition more vulnerable. Lack of focus also has been a problem with the main welfare program, the System for the Identification and Selection of Beneficiaries of Social Programs (Sisben). Information is outdated, the program does not reach enough people, and there are serious doubts about what data should be gathered, as well as how data should be used to target different social groups.

The results of a check on the percentage of poor households outside the poverty trap that benefit from social spending in Colombia—known as inclusion errors—confirm how such spending has serious focus problems. For example, the errors in inclusion have been estimated at 93.9 percent in pensions, 76.3 percent in family-compensation companies, 72.6 percent in higher education, and about 48 percent in most public services.

Another problem has been the inefficiency and weakness of social protection programs as a result of their dispersion and the duplication in some of their functions. And finally, the lack of consistent and broad information on social spending remains a handicap in attempting to evaluate the effectiveness of the wide range of existing programs and in planning a coherent social network.

The increase in public expenditure that led to a very significant increase in public debt reduced the margin for countercyclical expenditure (that is, increasing expenditure in bad times and reducing it in good times). Consequently, the 1999 recession caused the loss of about 10 years of improvements in social indicators. Given the increase in the volatility of economic indicators that has occurred since 1990, a recent World Bank study has highlighted the role of sound macroeconomic policies in alleviating poverty. The country's greater macroeconomic volatility also implies that Colombia's social safety net requires measures to protect transient vulnerability.

Another problem has been the increase in forced displacement in Colombia. Although data on this problem are subject to controversy, different sources acknowledge that such displacement averaged about 150,000 victims per year between 1985 and 2004 (see table 4, Appendix). Forced displacement has increased significantly since the mid-1990s, reaching peak levels of about 400,000 victims in 2001; even though the level diminished between 2005 and 2008, it remains very high (see Population Displacement, ch. 2).

Major deficiencies remain in child care, sanitation, health care, and insurance for adverse events such as those generated by the internal conflict, economic recessions, and natural disasters. Tertiary education also has low coverage, but it is expensive, and public expenditure on it tends to be regressive for income distribution. Given Colombia's fiscal constraints, improving access to credit for tertiary education remains a major future challenge. In 2009 Colombia still needed a social protection system that is better targeted, more focused, well financed, and with the capacity to operate in a countercyclical way. Furthermore, Colombia has one of the worst income distributions in the world. Although income distribution has improved in the twenty-first century, its inequality is another challenge for Colombia to add to the difficulties posed by poverty (see Income Distribution, ch. 2).

The Pension System

Pensions in Colombia began as a pay-as-you-go system, with more than 1,000 pension funds created since 1946 for public-sector workers, which meant that pension conditions were determined in a dispersed and isolated manner. The pay-as-you-go model for private-sector workers began in 1967 and was supplemented in 1990 by the establishment of a parallel and fully funded private-pension system. A 1993 reform allowed for the creation of individual savings accounts. As a result, the country now has a very complex pension structure, making it hard to establish accurate measures of the extent and efficiency of coverage.

For many years, pension contributions were very low compared to benefits, and the number of years required for contributions was also low—about 20 years, and as low as 10 years in some cases. Life expectancy in Colombia has increased, but the retirement age has not increased in proportion and is currently 55 years for women and 60 years for men and set to increase in 2014 to 57 years for women and 62 years for men.

Colombia's pension system has a solidarity component in which workers with sufficiently high incomes make contributions to a solidarity pension fund, thereby contributing to ensure minimum pensions for low-income workers covered by the system and subsistence payments to elderly and low-income citizens, who are not covered at all. Overall estimates suggest that the government subsidizes about 70 percent of pension payments from public funds, and the accumulated pension debt is more than 160 percent of GDP.

The system has low coverage, with only 25 percent of Colombians of retirement age actually receiving a pension. It also has been estimated that 94 percent of pension payments go to people who are not poor. The high share of pension payments financed from public funds means that about 40 percent of Colombia's social expenditure is spent on badly targeted pensions with low coverage.

Because of these flaws, there have been several pension reforms since the beginning of the 1990s, but none have solved Colombia's pension problems, mainly because of the high political cost of pension reform. Even after Congress approved tough measures, the Constitutional Court reversed some of them—decisions that have entailed fiscal costs of more than 17 percent of GDP. An important and recent pension reform was Law 1 of 2005, which, among other provisions, eliminated one of the two extra monthly payments and created a mechanism to control pensions obtained unlawfully. It also established that most privileged pension regimes will be active only until 2010—except for the president and the armed forces—and that future agreements between labor unions and employers will not be allowed to set conditions different from those stated in the law.

Approximately half of all those paying into pensions now do so through the fully funded pension system created in 1990 and composed of the so-called Pension Funds Administrators (AFP). The fully funded private pension system does not have as many weaknesses as the pay-as-you-go system. By definition, the former's funding is collected retroactively, and it too involves a solidarity component. However, the transition from the pay-as-you-go system to the fully funded system has been a financially challenging process, involving high fiscal costs. The latter arise mainly because the pay-as-you-go system lost a significant amount of (young) contributors but retained most of the workers who were closer to retirement. In short, many observers regard Colombia's pension system as Colombia's most serious fiscal problem (see The Pension Conundrum, ch. 2).

Outlook

After experiencing a severe downturn in the second half of the 1990s, Colombia began forcefully addressing many of its most pressing problems in 2000. Since Álvaro Uribe became president in 2002, in addition to implementing the Democratic Security Policy, the government also has attempted to improve respect and protection of human rights and to involve the international community in the process of reestablishing peace, law, and order in the country. During this period, there has been improvement in indicators such as reductions in the number of guerrilla attacks in urban areas, the number of homicides and kidnappings, and the amount of land devoted to the production of illegal crops. There also have been increases in the amount of traffic on intercity highways and a reduction in attacks on the electric-power grid and oil pipelines. Although all these indicators have generated an improved social, political, and economic environment, it is not entirely clear yet whether such improvements will be sustainable in the long term.

As a result of these strategies, in the early twenty-first century the deteriorating trend in the fiscal accounts has been reversed, and the public-debt burden has been reduced. Likewise, economic growth has picked up significantly from its depressed levels of the late 1990s to 7.5 percent per year in 2007, the highest growth rate in 30 years, although growth has not yet remained at a high enough level for long enough to provide adequate employment to a growing population. Thus, unemployment, while lower than in 1999, is still quite high (9.9 percent in 2007), and poverty indicators, though improving, are still at very high levels. Notwithstanding the progress in recent years, many challenges remain, including the need to create the conditions to reduce poverty further and to improve income distribution.

Among the most important economic achievements of the last 15 years are the reduction in the rate of inflation to single digits, close to the levels prevailing in developed countries. This was no small achievement for a country that had sustained moderate two-digit inflation for almost 30 years. Other achievements include an improved allocation of resources in some sectors, such as electric energy and fuel, and the greater quantity, quality, and variety of goods and services available to Colombian nationals thanks to the increasing activity of the private sector as entrepreneur and of the state as a market regulator. Economic diversification has been impressive and not easily matched by other countries in the region. In only a few decades, Colombia went from an economy heavily dependent on coffee to a country with a fairly diversified export base. Even at extraordinarily high prices, oil, the leading export, accounted for just 26 percent of total exports in 2006.

Although the economy has recovered its momentum, many challenges lie ahead. In particular, Colombia's potential rate of GDP growth must increase substantially if there is to be a meaningful and lasting reduction in the still very high levels of poverty. Enhancing the rate of potential GDP growth will imply challenges in several areas, including strict adherence to macroeconomic discipline, further progress on the structural reform agenda, and continued improvements in security. The main challenge to maintaining macroeconomic stability has to do with fiscal policy. Although the share of public debt over GDP has begun to fall, it remains high. Thus, fiscal and pension reforms will be key challenges in the next few years. Changes to the tax code, a reduction in revenue earmarking, a better distribution of expenditure responsibilities among levels of government, and a continuous updating of the reach of the pension system to better reflect demographic changes will be integral elements of any strategy to maintain sound public finances.

Colombia will also have to continue striving to become a more diversified economy, better integrated to international markets. In that vein, and besides taking an active part in all multilateral trade negotiations, the government is planning to broaden the scope of its preferential trade agreements, benefiting from the progress made during the negotiation of a free-trade agreement between Colombia and three other Andean countries and the United States.

Important progress has been made in recent years, yet there is ample room for further improvements in the business environment. Colombia's government remains legislator, regulator, and entrepreneur in several sectors, such as oil and public utilities. These roles, which sit ill together, have developed despite some effort to create more transparency. Steps include the creation of the National Hydrocarbons Agency (ANH) and the sale of Colombia Coal (Carbocol). Despite some progress, there is much to be done in further improving the business environment, including developing the capital market, simplifying and stabilizing the tax regime, and strengthening and consolidating the financial sector.

Colombia will need greater integration with the world economy and further infrastructure development: better roads and improved ports and airports. In particular, better highways will be needed to connect Bogotá and other major cities and regions, other internal connections, and to link Colombia to Venezuela and Ecuador, and better local roads within the country. Colombia also needs improved options and infrastructure to reach Panama, Peru, and Brazil. The construction of the tunnel at La Línea remains a major challenge, currently being addressed, but making better use of Colombia's rivers for transportation and optimizing the possibilities of its railroads are changes that remain necessary.

Clearly, enhancing physical capital will not be enough, and Colombia also will need to increase its human capital significantly. This challenge, which is not unique to any country, becomes even more pressing in a more highly integrated global economy. Even though Colombia has increased education funding and equity, improvements in efficiency are sorely needed. The application of international standardized tests is not generalized; the development of bilingual public education is in very early stages; and significant resources for tertiary education subsidize supply, rather than the removal of credit constraints on students on the demand side.

Improvements in information on (and focus, coverage, and efficiency of) Colombia's social protection policies remain major challenges as well, despite the natural institutional barriers that operate under any democratic regime, and that are particularly strong in this area. Improving the quality of information in general will be a major challenge because it is not uncommon to find divergence in the data provided by different institutions, such as the World Bank and DANE.

Consolidation of peace and minimal security conditions within the country will be important to restore consumer and investor confidence across all sectors of the economy, and a boost for international tourism as a source of foreign exchange. As such, a major question is whether President Uribe's Democratic Security Policy, which so far has yielded a short-term boost to the national morale as a result of its major breakthroughs—such as the submission to justice of the main paramilitary leaders; the deaths of three members of the FARC's Secretariat in the first half of 2008; and the death, capture, or demobilization of many of the other members of the AUC and FARC—can become a nonpartisan and permanent policy, delivering long-lasting results.

In 2005 the Colombian government proposed a long-term program to commemorate the second centenary of independence in 2019. The program outlines long-term goals for 2019 and policies to significantly increase annual per capita income and to drastically reduce poverty, indigence, and unemployment. The process of achieving such goals is expected to eradicate illiteracy for people between the ages of 15 and 24, and to vastly increase Internet usage with broadband access, expand seaport capacity, and increase public areas for people living in urban centers. Whether these goals can be achieved over several presidential terms, without a national political commitment, remains to be seen.

*　　　　*　　　　*

Germán Colmenares and José Antonio Ocampo's *Historia económica de Colombia* is a classic presentation of Colombia's economic history, revised in 2007 and covering the period from the beginning of the colonial era up to 2006. *An Economic History of Colombia, 1845–1930* by William Paul McGreevey is another well-known economic history book. James Robinson and Miguel Urrutia's *Economía colombiana del siglo XX: Un análisis cuantitativo* is very well-documented, focusing on the twentieth century. Mauricio Cárdenas Santa-María's textbook *Introducción a la economía colombiana*, which examines Colombia's economic policies and institutions, using both theory and data, is a useful reference, especially on labor markets, pensions, and the informal economy.

For a fairly contemporary analysis of a broad range of topics related to Colombia's economic activity and proposals for the future, mostly from international analysts, a valuable source is *Colombia: The Economic Foundations of Peace*, edited by Marcelo M. Giugale, Oliver Lafourcade, and Connie Luff. *Institutional Reforms: The Case of Colombia*, edited by Alberto Alesina, provides an overview of the major issues in Colombian politics and economics by highly qualified national and international researchers, with a broad range of proposals to improve the institutional operation of the country. Álvaro Pachón and María Teresa Ramírez's *La infraestructura de transporte en terrestre Colombia durante el siglo XX* is an invaluable source on transportation. Hugo López and Jairo Núñez's *Pobreza y desigualdad en Colombia: Diagnóstico y estrategias* is an up-to-date and encompassing reference for analysis and policy recommendations on poverty and inequality.

These organizations and government entities have Web sites that are useful sources of documents and statistics on a wide range of areas of interest in Colombia: the Central Bank, the National Administrative Department of Statistics (DANE), the National Planning Department (DNP), the Economic Commission for Latin America and the Caribbean (ECLAC), and the World Bank. The reports of the Central Bank to Congress (http://www.banrep.gov.co) are key sources of information on current economic affairs, with a solid technical background and focus on monetary and exchange-rate issues. The National Association of Financial Institutions (ANIF), the Economic Development Studies Center (CEDE), and the Foundation for Higher Education and Development (Fedesarrollo) are think tanks that generate useful information on a wide range of topics. World Development Indicators Online at http://web.worldbank.org is the World Bank's annual compilation of data about development.

A site that is useful for petroleum data is British Petroleum's "Statistical Review of World Energy 2008" at http://www.bp.com/productlanding. do?categoryId=6929&contentID=7044622. The Economist Intelligence Unit's annual *Country Profile: Colombia* is a good source for updated summaries and statistics regarding the country's economy. The Proexport Web site at http://www.proexport.com.co/ is a useful source of information on international trade-related issues and foreign investment. For information related to Colombia in general and to the public sector in particular, the Government Online Web site at http://www. gobiernoen-linea.gov.co provides access to a broad range of institutions and information. (For further information and complete citations, see Bibliography.)

Chapter 4. Government and Politics

Top: An indigenous geometric design, C. Jaramillo Collection, Pasto
Bottom: An indigenous geometric design, private collection, Pupiales
Courtesy Carlos Arturo Jaramillo Giraldo, Murmullos del lenguaje Uik:
La práctica del mopa mopa: De lo recolector a lo sedentario, *Medellín,*
1986, 87, 89

THE COEXISTENCE OF FORMAL DEMOCRACY and prolonged internal warfare constitutes the distinguishing feature of the Colombian political system. Political violence in Colombia is largely attributed to a complex history of political exclusion, repression of opposition groups, social and economic inequality, absence of the rule of law, and drug trafficking.

When César Augusto Gaviria Trujillo (president, 1990–94) took office, Colombia was also in the midst of a campaign of narco-terrorism (see Glossary) inaugurated by the country's drug cartels in order to impede the extradition of their leaders to the United States. In August 1989, gunmen hired by the Medellín Cartel had assassinated Liberal Party (PL) presidential candidate Luis Carlos Galán. For Gaviria, narco-terrorism—and the social, economic, and political costs associated with it—constituted a primary threat to Colombia's democracy. The government subsequently enacted a plea-bargaining provision, under which those individuals accused of drug-related crimes would receive reduced jail sentences in exchange for their voluntary surrender and confession of their crimes. Nearly a year later, the Constituent Assembly, under significant pressure from the country's drug-trafficking cartels, voted to prohibit the extradition of Colombian citizens altogether.

The Constituent Assembly was convened in 1991, partly because it appeared that the National Front (Frente Nacional, 1958–78), a bipartisan power-sharing arrangement created to end violence and conflict between the PL and the Conservative Party (PC), had failed to resolve the economic and social problems at the root of the country's ills. Indeed, some observers have noted that power sharing between the Liberals and the Conservatives had become part of the problem. The 1991 constitution, which replaced the 1886 charter, aimed to restore the legitimacy of the political system by expanding citizens' basic rights, increasing the participation of civil society in various decision-making processes, incorporating previously marginalized groups, including indigenous and black communities, and bringing illegal armed factions, such as the Nineteenth of April Movement (M–19), into the political fold. Although the new charter formally enhanced channels of political inclusion, in practice many of Colombia's structural problems remained intact.

The 1991 constitution coincided with the implementation of a neoliberal economic model in Colombia. Neoliberalism (see Glossary) facilitated an economic opening, reduced inflation, and helped rationalize the bureaucratic structure of the state. However, as elsewhere in Latin America, Colombia's introduction of this model brought a weakening of the judicial and legislative branches and a strengthening of the executive branch in order to facilitate approval of the measures needed to implement the model. In addition, by concentrating macroeconomic planning in the hands of a small circle of technocrats, Colombia's neoliberal policies have constrained the effective participation of civil society. Neoliberal reform and the policy of economic opening that accompanied it produced several negative social and distributive outcomes, including increased underemployment and informal-sector employment, poverty, and inequality. An acute crisis in agriculture, largely a result of the neoliberal program, made poverty in rural areas, where armed violence is largely concentrated, particularly pronounced.

Optimism surrounding the new charter gradually gave way to skepticism regarding the country's future, further fueled by economic uncertainty, alarming levels of political violence and human rights abuses, and weakening law and order. This situation was aggravated by the questionable circumstances surrounding the 1994 presidential election campaign of Ernesto Samper Pizano (president, 1994–98), who allegedly received financial contributions from the Cali Cartel. A drawn-out series of accusations and denials concerning this allegation polarized the country and irrevocably damaged the legitimacy and credibility of the Samper administration.

On assuming office, Andrés Pastrana Arango (president, 1998–2002) took charge of a country plagued by a deep economic recession, high levels of corruption, the intensification of the internal armed conflict, and a flourishing narcotics trade that increasingly involved illegal armed groups. Pastrana pledged to put an end to the war by negotiating with the country's two main guerrilla organizations, the Revolutionary Armed Forces of Colombia (FARC) and the National Liberation Army (ELN). He also actively sought out international support in resolving the country's crisis. During the Pastrana administration, U.S. financial assistance to Colombia rose to approximately US$500 million annually, largely for the antinarcotics effort. Following the end of the peace process with the FARC in early 2002, Pastrana portrayed the organization as a terrorist group, thereby inserting the Colombian internal armed conflict into the United States–led "war on terror." Consequently, Washington lifted restrictions associated with its aid package to Colombia in order to contribute to counterinsurgency efforts.

Álvaro Uribe Vélez (president, 2002–6, 2006–10) was the first presidential candidate in Colombian history to win a majority vote in the first round of elections. In both the 2002 and 2006 elections, Uribe won on a hard-line platform, promising to win the war against the insurgents and terrorism in general. A cornerstone of Uribe's security strategy has been his Democratic Security and Defense Policy, or Democratic Security Policy, through which he has declared an all-out war against terrorism. Close relations with the United States and a strong antiterrorist stance have characterized his foreign policy. In contrast to his first term, Uribe's second term has been marked by a number of challenges and setbacks related to the demobilization of Colombian paramilitary groups, the negotiation of a humanitarian exchange with the FARC guerrillas, links between the armed forces and drug-trafficking groups, and growing tensions with the U.S. Congress, which has taken issue with the Uribe government's human rights record. In particular, the U.S. Congress has been concerned over Colombia's "parapolitics" scandal, which began in 2006 and was still a preoccupation three years later and which implicated dozens of members of the Congress of the Republic (Congreso de la República) in supporting paramilitary activities in the country.

The Governmental System

The Executive

As in most Latin American countries, strong presidential government characterizes the Colombian political system. The president of the republic is the chief of state, head of government, supreme administrative authority, and commander in chief of the armed forces. For about a century, until 2005, the president was elected for a nonrenewable four-year term. The Congress then passed legislation authorizing reelection for a single consecutive term, and the Constitutional Court approved it in October 2005. This new legislation made possible the reelection of Álvaro Uribe for a second term in May 2006. The vice president is elected on the same ticket as the president and succeeds him or her in the event of the president's death, illness, or resignation. The president of the republic must be more than 30 years of age, Colombian by birth, and a legal citizen of the country. The national government also includes the ministers and the directors of the administrative departments (see fig. 6). At the departmental level, the executive branch includes the governors, the mayors, and the heads of various public establishments, including superintendencies, and state industrial and commercial companies.

The President of the Republic

The president oversees the executive branch and exercises appointive powers to freely select the cabinet and the directors of all administrative

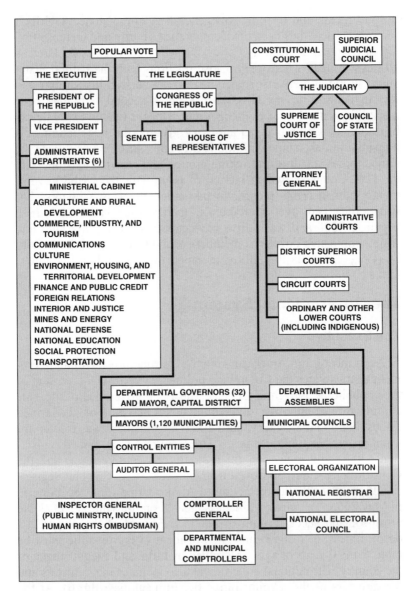

Figure 6. Structure of the Government, 2009

agencies. As head of government, the president, in consultation with the cabinet, is responsible for maintaining law and order and declaring a state of internal commotion, a state of emergency, a state of external war, with the consent of the Senate of the Republic (Senado de la República), or a state of exception. A state of emergency can be a state of social emergency, a state of ecological emergency, or a state of economic emergency. As chief of state, the president is also responsible for establishing national macroeconomic policies and signing treaties with other nations, with the consent of the Congress. The 1991 constitution (Article 189) also authorizes the president, as commander in chief of the armed forces, to defend national sovereignty, territorial integrity, and constitutional order, as well as guarantee the conditions required for the exercise of public rights and freedoms. The vice president replaces the president during temporary or permanent absence and may be appointed by the president to any office in the executive branch or to any other special assignment. During recent years, the office of the vice president has been particularly involved in advising national agencies on issues related to human rights and, to a lesser degree, the illegal drug trade. From early 1990, a series of presidential advisories (*consejerías presidenciales*) have briefed the president on specific issue areas, including international affairs.

In addition to administrative powers, the president enjoys considerable legislative authority. On request, the Congress may grant the president extraordinary powers to create laws on specific matters not necessarily related to problems of public order. Additional legislative powers are derived from the government's constitutional role in presenting legislation and from its responsibility for drafting the national development plan and overseeing economic policy.

The 1886 constitution authorized the president to invoke a state of siege, under which the president could issue legal decrees and suspend laws that contravened the maintenance of public order. In practice, declarations of a state of siege did not distinguish between cases of external warfare and internal armed conflict and could be prolonged indefinitely. The 1991 constitution, in contrast, establishes clear differences between a state of external war and instances of internal commotion, while also preserving the concept of the state of social emergency contemplated in a constitutional reform adopted in 1968. Article 215 of the 1991 constitution provides for a state of emergency.

Under Article 212, the Senate must authorize a declaration of a state of external war, and the executive must inform the Congress regularly as events occur and must report the specific content of the decrees issued. The Congress has the right to modify or reject these presidential decrees. In cases of disruptions in public order that threaten the security of the state or society, Article 213 empowers the president, with the approval of the cabinet, to declare a state of internal commotion for a 90-day period, during which time the president acquires legislative decree powers. The Senate can authorize two extensions of the state of internal commotion. However, given that the constitution also stipulates in Article 214 that constitutional control of state authority is to remain in effect throughout the duration of these exceptional states, and that any suspension of human rights and fundamental liberties is expressly prohibited, the Constitutional Court must certify that the state of internal commotion does not violate the constitution. As a result, during the Gaviria government and for the first time in Colombian history, Congress overturned a declaration of a state of internal commotion. It also declared unconstitutional President Uribe's second request in mid-2003 for an extension of a state of internal commotion.

The Superior Council on National Defense and Security (CSSDN), formed by the executive branch in 1992, is an advisory body on defense and security matters. Chaired by the president, the CSSDN counts as its members the minister of national defense, the general commander of the armed forces, the director general of the National Police, the director of the Administrative Security Department (DAS), the minister of interior and justice, the minister of foreign relations, and the heads of two congressional committees—constitutional affairs and defense and international relations. The CSSDN advises on the planning and execution of defense and security policy and is responsible for coordinating the various civilian and military entities involved in national security.

Ministries

The ministerial cabinet coordinates and implements government policy. In December 2002, several ministries merged as part of the Uribe government's plan to modernize the public administration apparatus. The Ministry of Interior (previously the Ministry of Government) and the Ministry of Justice and Law became the Ministry of Interior and Justice. The Ministry of Foreign Trade (created by the 1991 constitution) and the Ministry of Economic Development became the Ministry of Commerce, Industry, and Tourism. The Ministry of Labor and Social Security and the Ministry of Health merged into the Ministry of Social Protection. And the Ministry of Environment, also created by the 1991 constitution, became the Ministry of Environment, Housing, and Territorial Development. Since 2007 there has been some talk of once again dividing the two components of both the Ministry of Interior and Justice and the Ministry of Social Protection, but neither ministry has reverted to its former organization.

The ministries are responsible for drafting legislation in their respective areas and for maintaining communications between the president of the republic and the other branches of government. In addition to the ministries already mentioned, there are ministries of Agriculture and Rural Development; Communications; Culture (created in 1997, following intense political debate concerning its relevance); Finance and Public Credit; Foreign Relations; Mines and Energy; National Defense; National Education; and Transportation.

The ministries have varying degrees of influence or importance depending on their respective budgets, the particular issue areas they address, their role in an administration's policies, and the personal relationship of each minister with the president. Based on these factors, the ministries can be ranked in three basic groups, corresponding to high, intermediate, or inferior levels of significance. Among those exercising high levels of influence, the Ministry of Interior and Justice carries considerable political weight because of its role in managing relations between the executive branch and the Congress, the country's regional departments and municipalities, and the judiciary. The intensification of the Colombian internal armed conflict and the increased role of the United States in matters related to the war have led to the ascendency of the Ministry of National Defense in both domestic politics and foreign relations (see Ministry of National Defense, ch. 5). The Ministry of Finance and Public Credit and the Ministry of Commerce, Industry, and Tourism also are relatively powerful, given their roles in economic planning and foreign trade, respectively. And the Ministry of Foreign Relations, although exercising little tangible influence on crucial issues, such as relations with the United States, security, drugs, human rights, and trade, has formal responsibility for conducting the country's external affairs and thus continues to enjoy a high to intermediate level of importance.

Administrative Departments

A series of executive-branch administrative departments came into being following a 1945 constitutional reform in order to professionalize specific governmental and public services and to separate them from the politically driven environment characterizing the ministeries. Unlike the ministries, these departments do not represent the president politically, and their primary objective is to formulate and adopt governmental policies, programs, and projects corresponding to their given sectors. In 2009 the six departments included the Administrative Department of the Presidency of the Republic (DAPR), the lead agency; the Administrative Department of the Public Function (DAFP); and the National Administrative Department of Economic Solidarity (Dansocial), which is headed by former M–19 guerrilla and senator Rosemberg Pabón Pabón. The other three departments were the National Planning Department (DNP), the National Administrative Department of Statistics (DANE), and the Administrative Security Department (DAS). Technocratic expertise provided by such agencies, in particular by DNP, has enabled the executive to increase its legislative capacity vis-à-vis the Congress, which lacks the specialized knowledge required to develop complex, technical legislation, particularly on budgetary and economic matters. However, their semiautonomous, apolitical nature also means that administrative agencies operate with relative independence. Such independence occasionally has led to conflict with the president or specific ministers. For example, the director of DANE resigned in September 2004, alleging that the office of the president had pressured him to delay the release of a joint DANE–DNP study on perceptions of citizen security in the country's principal cities. The study apparently contradicted executive-branch statistics indicating that the Democratic Security Policy had achieved significant success. A second DANE director resigned in September 2007 under similar circumstances.

Territorial Government

Organization and Administration

Colombia's territorial and administrative organization encompasses departments, districts, municipalities, and indigenous entities (see Special Jurisdictions, this ch.). The constitution recognizes 32 administrative departments (including nine new ones, which formerly had been four intendancies and five commisaryships), plus the Distrito Capitál de Bogotá (see fig. 1). The primary function of a department is to coordinate and promote local and departmental development. In 2007 Colombia had 1,120 municipalities (up from 1,096 in 2005), four of which are categorized as a district mayoralty (*alcaldía distrital*) because of significant population or cultural or economic importance: Bogotá (the national capital), Barranquilla, Cartagena, and Santa Marta. Unlike the departments, the number and size of municipalities are subject to administrative change.

At the departmental and municipal levels, the governor and the cabinet secretary, and the mayor and the cabinet secretary, respectively, administer local government. Each department has a popularly elected departmental assembly. The assembly may range from 11 to 31 members, who complete four-year terms. The head of the departmental administration is the governor, who is also popularly elected for a four-year, nonrenewable term. Each municipality (or district) also has a popularly elected administrative body, the municipal council (or district council), with a membership ranging from seven to 21. The mayor, elected by popular vote for a nonrenewable, four-year term, heads the municipal administration. Large cities such as Bogotá also are subdivided into localities governed by administrative boards, whose members are popularly elected. Each one also has a local mayor, who is appointed by the mayor of the city. The Uribe government was planning to introduce a bill that would allow for the immediate reelection of local officials.

During the last year of the presidency of Belisario Betancur Cuartas (1982–86), a law strengthened local government in Colombia by authorizing the direct election of mayors and other steps designed to achieve greater decentralization. Increasing civic protest in the mid-1980s against political corruption and inadequate public services at the local level had led to the adoption of these measures. A number of administrative functions previously controlled by the central government transferred to the local level, although the scarcity of resources, lack of technical and administrative skills, and low level of social participation made decentralization difficult to implement.

The 1991 constitution accelerated and enhanced the process of devolution by identifying decentralization, departmental autonomy, and citizen participation as three fundamental principles of the administrative organization of the country. The popular election of governors and municipal mayors, previously appointed by the president of the republic and departmental governors, respectively, gave Colombian citizens under the 1991 constitution a direct means of intervention in the control and execution of local public affairs. Departments and municipalities for the first time had the right to exercise self-government, to administer their own taxes, and to receive and spend state income.

To this end, legislation provided for a series of resource transfers from the national level to the departments and municipalities to finance the provision of education and health services, particularly for the poorest sectors of the population. State social spending grew from 8.2 percent of gross domestic product (GDP—see Glossary) in 1990 to 14.4 percent in 1998, slightly surpassing increases in total public spending. Spending on education, health, and water and sewerage services increased in many departments. However, in 2000 President Andrés Pastrana signed an extended-fund facility fiscal-adjustment agreement with the International Monetary Fund, in which the Colombian government promised to reduce regional monetary transfers. Consequently, the executive branch presented a constitutional reform bill that the Congress approved in 2001. In June 2007, the legislation on transfers changed again. Opposition parties, labor unions, indigenous groups, and representatives of other social sectors have proposed a referendum on reforms of the articles of the constitution related to local transfers, arguing that the cutbacks in the general system of participation have been overly severe. These opposition groups, including the Liberal Party and the Alternative Democratic Pole (PDA), demanded the return of the old transfers regime, which fixed the funds distributed to regions to the increase in the national government's current income. The Uribe government warned that if the reforms won approval in a proposed referendum, then new taxes would have to be created, requiring another new tax reform (see Fiscal Policy and Public Finances, ch. 3).

Special Jurisdictions

Local justices of the peace have a special jurisdiction created by the 1991 constitution. These judges are ordinary members of a given community, who are appointed by civic and popular organizations on the basis of their familiarity with the area's problems and their social prestige. Justices of the peace are common individuals without any legal training; they do not charge for their services; they conduct oral, informal hearings on everyday, local matters; and their rulings are based on considerations of equity according to the needs of the community. The presence of justices of the peace nationwide has improved local processes of conciliation and conflict resolution and has provided the country's communities with important tools for solving their own conflicts expeditiously and in accord with their own social practices.

The constitution explicitly recognizes the collective rights of Colombia's indigenous and Afro-Colombian communities. It grants them seats in the Congress, requires the state to consult with tribal groups before exploiting natural resources located in their territories, and grants indigenous territories (*resguardos*) municipal status, enabling them to administer their own resources. The constitution recognizes the right of indigenous authorities to exercise judicial functions within their respective territories, as long as specific norms and procedures corresponding to the preservation of indigenous practices and customs do not violate the constitution or other Colombian law. Legal decisions made by the *resguardo* authorities have the same weight as those made by ordinary judges. In practice, however, legal norms pertaining to issues of public order normally have legal priority over the protection of indigenous practices and customs, particularly when these are considered to protect a constitutional value superior to the principle of ethnic and cultural diversity, such as the protection of life or property.

Clientelism

Before 1991 the departments were the cornerstone of a spoils system used by regional Liberal and Conservative political bosses to reinforce their local power. Clientelism (see Glossary), or the private appropriation of public goods for political gain, has been particularly entrenched at the regional and local levels in Colombia, where state resources, jobs, and bureaucracies traditionally have been apportioned in exchange for political loyalty. The incapacity of the Colombian state, until only recently, to exercise a physical presence in vast portions of the national territory and its unresponsiveness to popular needs explain why clientelism has been a primary source of political adhesion and legitimacy in Colombia. The 1991 constitution acknowledges the right to local direct elections and seeks to counteract the danger of abuse of fiscal and administrative autonomy in departments and municipalities (particularly increased access to public finances and bureaucracy by regional political entities) by making elected officials more accountable.

Following the start of direct mayoral elections in 1988, the presence of "outsiders," that is, political parties and movements unaffiliated with the Liberal or Conservative parties, grew considerably at the local level. Such movements achieved important victories in the 1988, 1990, and 1992 local elections, and in 1994 outsiders actually won the mayoralties of many of Colombia's larger cities, including Bogotá. This trend has continued. However, in smaller cities and municipalities where clientelistic practices have been much more prevalent, the Conservative and Liberal parties have maintained local power.

Decentralization in Colombia coincided with the unprecedented growth of the membership and territorial presence of the FARC and the ELN. The municipality became a key area in which these groups pursued the military, economic, and political strategies that accompanied this expansion; the insurgents saw local decentralization and autonomy as offering new opportunities for influence in both rural and urban areas. Between 1986 and 2000, for example, the active guerrilla presence at the local level grew from 400 to approximately 650 municipalities. In 1994 the FARC had 105 operations in 569 municipalities, compared with only 17 combat fronts operating in remote areas of the country in 1978. By 2006 the FARC operated on 60 to 80 fronts with a total fighting force of up to 16,000 members (see Internal Armed Conflict, ch. 5). By the end of 2008, however, the FARC was down to about 9,000 members, according to some reports.

The guerrilla organizations have particularly wanted to penetrate local administrative and governmental institutions. The FARC and the ELN target those municipalities managing important economic resources derived from oil, coal, gold, bananas, and coffee, and, from the mid-1990s, coca leaf, given their potential for creating revenues for the guerrillas and their significance for the national economy. Armed clientelism, consisting of the hiring of guerrilla sympathizers in public offices, the retention of a percentage of their salaries, the assignment of public-works contracts, and the enforcement of local "taxes" in exchange for guerrilla services, became the preferred means of exercising influence.

The success of this form of clientelism has been largely dependent on the delivery of tangible goods to those municipalities experiencing a guerrilla presence. However, contrary to the traditional spoils system, guerrillas also practice violence and intimidation against the local population to achieve their goals. According to the Colombian Federation of Municipalities (Fedemunicipios), 69 mayors were murdered between 1998 and 2007, when another 102 mayors were kidnapped, and many others were simply forced to resign. During the October 1997 elections, 75 municipalities had no candidates for mayor, 20 lacked candidates for the city council, and 18 had no candidates for either because of pressures exerted by the guerrillas.

The paramilitary groups in Colombia also experienced phenomenal expansion. Between 2000 and 2004, their numbers grew from 5,000–6,000 to approximately 13,500, and they gained an active presence in 35 percent of the national territory. Given that one of the stated objectives of the paramilitaries was to eliminate the country's guerrilla organizations, those municipalities in which the guerrillas had gained dominance became susceptible to paramilitary violence and to the same types of armed clientelism practiced by their enemies. For example, of 1,071 municipalities that existed in 2002, Fedemunicipios reported that illegal armed groups had threatened more than half the mayors, some of whom were still under threat.

In mid-2007 the New Rainbow Corporation, a nongovernmental organization (NGO), in collaboration with three private Bogotá universities and a think tank, the Democracy and Security Foundation, released a report on municipal and departmental elections held between 2000 and 2006 that questioned their transparency in 950 municipalities (equivalent to 86 percent of the national territory) because of the infiltration of illegal armed groups and irregularities such as the extensive purchase of votes. The electoral risk maps published by this coalition of organizations and the United Nations Development Programme during the 2007 electoral process suggested that in 576 municipalities local elections continued to be threatened by the violent actions of both guerrillas and demobilized paramilitaries. This electoral observation mission also registered 29 homicides of candidates, 8 kidnappings, 23 attacks, and 91 threats.

The Legislature

Colombian legislative authority resides in a bicameral Congress, consisting of the Senate and the House of Representatives (Cámara de Representantes). Members of Congress are popularly elected for four-year terms beginning on July 20 and can be reelected indefinitely. Candidates are selected from multiple-name lists corresponding to members of specific political parties or movements. The Council of State can remove members of Congress from office for misconduct, the existence of conflicts of interest, or absenteeism (see The Judiciary, this ch.). The next candidate on the respective congressional member's electoral list fills the vacancy resulting from such action.

Congress meets twice annually, from July 20 until December 16 and from March 16 to June 20. The president of the republic also may convene Congress for extraordinary sessions to deliberate on legislation presented by the government. Each house has a president and two vice presidents, who are elected for a one-year, nonrenewable period starting July 20, and a general secretary elected for two years. Members of each house are assigned to one of seven permanent committees (*comisiones*) that conduct the first round of debates on all legislative proposals. Each committee has a president and a vice president who preside over its debates. The internal regulations of the Congress also provide for some additional subcommittees.

The joint responsibilities of the two houses include proposing, interpreting, reforming, and repealing legislation; reforming the constitution; approving the national development plan; approving and rejecting international treaties; determining the general internal demarcation of the national territory and the national administrative structure; granting extraordinary decree powers to the president; and establishing the legal national currency. This last responsibility does not, however, permit the Congress to interfere in the making of national currency policy by the Central Bank. Congress also has responsibility for granting amnesties or general pardons for political crimes, establishing the salary regime in the public sector, and regulating public education.

The Senate consists of 102 members, who must be more than 30 years of age, Colombian by birth, and legal Colombian citizens. The Senate's functions include accepting the resignation of the president or the vice president of the republic, trying government officials that the House of Representatives accuses of misconduct, approving the promotion of high-ranking military officials, and granting the president a temporary leave of absence. Other functions include approving the passage of foreign troops through the national territory, authorizing the government to declare war on another nation, electing from lists presented by the president the members of the Constitutional Court and the Council of State, and electing the inspector general.

Members of the House of Representatives, who numbered 166 in 2009, must be more than 25 years of age and legal Colombian citizens. The total number of representatives is fixed according to the national population census. In addition to electing the human rights ombudsman (*defensor del pueblo*), the House of Representatives is responsible for electing the judges of the disciplinary branch of the judiciary, studying and approving the budgetary and treasury general accounts, investigating high-level goverment officials, and pressing charges of misconduct.

After a legislative initiative is presented in either house of Congress, it is published in the *Diario Oficial*, and the president of the respective house refers it to one of the seven committees and designates one of its members to present the bill. If approved by the committee in the first debate, the bill goes to a plenary session of the same house, where it can be approved, rejected, or modified. Bills that have been approved by the plenary session proceed to the other house, where they undergo the same process. Differences between the specific contents of each house's version of a bill go to conference for resolution. Once approved by the two houses, the bill goes to the president of the republic. If the president objects to the bill on constitutional or political grounds, it is returned to Congress. If absolute majorities of both houses approve the bill again, it is sent either to the Constitutional Court (if the presidential objection was for constitutional reasons) or directly to the president, who must sign the bill without further objections.

Although, historically, political dynamics within the Congress have mirrored the country's bipartisan system, driven mainly by clientelism and party accommodation, political parties in Colombia have experienced high degrees of fragmentation and disorder internally. They generally have low identification with the party platform and ideology, low levels of party discipline in legislative and voting practices, and low degrees of articulation of regional, local, and national policies. Institutionalizing an opposition strategy within the legislature is improbable, given the erratic nature of voting patterns. For example, dissident factions within the government party often exercise opposition, while sympathetic sectors within supposedly oppositional parties regularly collaborate with the government. The growing presence after 1991 of "independent" parties and political movements claiming to represent an alternative to the Liberal Party and the Conservative Party has altered this situation very little. How-

Plaza de Bolívar and the National Capitol,
seat of the Congress of the Republic
Courtesy Lorenzo Morales

ever, on specific matters perceived to directly affect the interests of
distinct parties and movements, temporary political alliances at
times operate effectively.

Concern over the functional deficiencies of the Congress as well
as over its lack of public legitimacy was a key factor leading to the
new constitution in 1991. Although the basic structure of the legislative branch remained the same, several significant changes occurred.
These included the creation of special voting districts to guarantee
the representation of ethnic and other minorities as well as the
Colombian diaspora, stricter rules on conflicts of interest for congressional members, the partial reduction of corruption through the
elimination of institutionalized parliamentary pork barrels (*auxilios
parlamentarios*), and the grant to both houses of the right to greater
political control over government action through a vote of censure.

Notwithstanding such modifications, the Congress still lacks a
dynamic legislative role or fiscal power, while its independence
from the executive branch is relatively limited for a number of reasons. Firstly, executive leverage in negotiations with the Congress,
in particular when issues of vital interest to the government are at
stake, continues via bureaucratic prerogatives and political favors.
Secondly, the motion of censure, although in principle guaranteeing

congressional oversight, has never been applied successfully to any government official. An attempt in May 2007 to censure the minister of national defense arose from the government's illegal phone tapping of the political opposition, journalists, academics, and civil society representatives.

Congress initiates more bills than the executive branch; however, the latter is much more effective in obtaining support for its bills, and thus more legislation initiated by the executive is passed into law. The legislature is also poorly equipped to modify the content of budget and treasury bills presented by the executive, given the complex nature of such initiatives, the lack of technical expertise of most legislators, and the absence of congressional research units.

High rates of turnover exist among members of Congress, particularly in cases where the political machinery of the traditional parties or clientelism continue to be prevalent. The elimination of the alternate system in 1991 gave way to even higher rates of rotation, because legally rotation can take place until the entire number of candidates on a given electoral list has occupied the same congressional post. Congressional rotation occurs for several reasons: it allows multiple individuals to obtain sizeable congressional pensions, it works as political payoff for votes obtained by candidates occupying different levels on the electoral lists, and it helps position these candidates politically for future congressional elections. Absenteeism is also a chronic problem and often prevents voting on legislative proposals.

The Electoral System

The National Registrar of Civil Status (RNEC), or National Registrar's Office, and the National Electoral Council (CNE) are responsible for the electoral process in Colombia. The first institution, which is headed by the judicially selected national registrar of civil status for a four-year term, organizes the elections. The second counts the popular vote and oversees compliance with the laws regulating political parties and movements. Congress elects its nine members for four-year terms.

In order to vote, a citizen must be at least 18 years old and must register to vote in his or her assigned municipal district during dates preceding scheduled elections that are established by the National Registrar's Office. Voter registration normally occurs in the same localities where people will cast their votes during the elections or in the immediate vicinity. Colombians living abroad vote at the Colombian embassies or consulates nearest to their place of residence. In order to vote, they must have a valid passport and be registered as electors either abroad or in Colombia, but not both.

Congressional and presidential elections take place every four years within two months of each other. The constitution prohibits the two elections from occurring simultaneously. Every four years, local and departmental elections are held to elect governors, mayors, council members, assembly members, and local administrators and must be held on dates other than the presidential and congressional contests. Local and departmental elections also may not be held simultaneously. A simple majority vote decides gubernatorial and mayoral races.

Given historically high voter-abstention rates, a law to stimulate voter participation passed in 1997. It provides those who vote with a 10-percent reduction in the annual fees if they are students enrolled in public institutions of higher education and one day off work for people who are public-sector employees.

The election of the president usually requires two rounds of voting, unless one of the candidates obtains an absolute majority in the first vote. Since 1991, when this measure was adopted, the only candidate to win the presidency in the first round of elections has been Álvaro Uribe. In the event of a second round, one of the two candidates obtaining the highest number of votes in the first round is elected president by a simple majority.

Since 1932 congressional elections have been conducted using proportional representation. The 1991 constitution stipulates that 100 senators be elected nationwide and two more be chosen by the country's indigenous groups. The 32 departments and the Distrito Capitál de Bogotá elect the members of the House of Representatives. Each district, irrespective of its population size, elects two representatives, and an additional representative is apportioned for each 250,000 inhabitants or fraction above 125,000 after the first 250,000. Of the 33 electoral districts existing in 2008, three are large in size (with more than 10 representatives), six are medium (ranging from six to 10 representatives), 12 are small (between three and five representatives), and 12 have the minimum number of two representatives. A special provision created by the constitution also enables indigenous ethnic groups, Afro-Colombians, and Colombians residing abroad to elect a total of up to five representatives.

Senatorial elections, which are based on a single nationwide electoral district, have led to the underrepresentation of those departments with small populations. In 2005, for example, 13 out of 33 electoral districts had no senator in the congressional term that ended in 2006. In contrast, the method used to elect the members of the House of Representatives tends to overrepresent the smaller departments.

Candidates appear in a given order on lists corresponding to different political parties and movements. The constitution prohibits laws that regulate the internal organization of political groups, so the general tendency has been for each party and movement to sponsor as many candidate lists as possible in order to win more seats in the Congress. Congressional seats are distributed to candidates in the same order that their names appear on their respective electoral lists. The electorate used to vote for a given list. However, a political reform law approved by the Congress in 2003 grants voters the right to exercise a preferential vote, meaning that in future elections they will have the option of selecting a specific candidate on an electoral list or designating a general vote for a list in the order in which the candidates' names appear.

The electoral quotient and residuals (Hare) method was used until 2003 to determine the winners of the elections for the House and the Senate, with the quotient obtained by dividing the total number of valid votes by the number of seats to be distributed. For example, if the quotient was 20,000 votes and a given list obtained 30,000, the first candidate on the list won the seat and the remaining 10,000 votes competed for a second seat. During the congressional elections of 1994, 1998, and 2002, fewer than 15 electoral lists (less than 10 percent of the total number) obtained enough votes to elect their first candidate through the quotient, meaning that most congressional seats were apportioned among those lists with the highest residuals below the electoral quotient. The system was criticized because it rewarded candidates winning low numbers of votes by granting them residual congressional seats, encouraged atomistic electoral behavior on the part of political parties and movements that presented many lists in order to win as many residual seats as possible, and affected the proportionality of the system. The 2003 political reform approved the use of the d'Hondt method, or highest-average method, in future elections (see Political Party Reform, this ch.). The new law allows each political party or organization to present only one list of candidates and lets voters choose the candidate of their preference, independently of the order of a given list. Congressional seats will be distributed accordingly.

The issue of campaign financing, which has both public and private origins, has been a particularly sensitive one in the Colombian context. The constitution obliges the state to contribute funding to electoral campaigns depending on the number of votes obtained and stipulates a limit to campaign expenditures and the maximum amount that any private interest may donate to a specific party or movement. The National Electoral Council supervises campaign expenditures, sets the total limits and permissible amounts for individual contributions, and apportions public funding according to the number of votes obtained by each group in an election. In practice, however, oversight is lax, providing considerable leeway for private interests to contribute large donations to specific campaigns (see Corruption, this ch.). In addition to the regulation of political campaign contributions, a law of electoral guarantees went into effect in June 2007. In order to guarantee higher levels of fair play, the law limits the right of those holding political office to open new government contracts and spend state funds four months before elections are held. It also provides a certain amount of government financing of the presidential campaigns of candidates whose parties obtain more than 4 percent of the votes for the Senate.

The Judiciary

Although the suspension of rule of law happened formally only once, during the dictatorship of Gustavo Rojas Pinilla (1952–57), the frequent use of the state of siege during the subsequent three decades led to significant restrictions of many constitutional rights and principles. The existence of martial law and militias that applied their own forms of law and justice in many parts of the country meant that parallel systems tended to erode the credibility and effectiveness of the judicial branch.

In the early 1980s, the members of the judicial branch began coming under increasing attack by drug-trafficking, paramilitary, and guerrilla organizations, undermining judicial administration and the ability to conduct important investigations. The creation of the Attorney General's Office (Fiscalía General de la Nación) strengthened the penal justice system. Constitutional interpretation, previously the mandate of the plenary committee of the Supreme Court of Justice, became the responsibility of the new Constitutional Court installed in February 1992. The judicial branch is divided into four distinct jurisdictions.

The 1991 constitution also instituted a series of reforms in the judicial branch that modified its administrative structure and the application of constitutional oversight, transformed the penal system, recognized alternative mechanisms for resolving legal disputes, and introduced measures to protect the constitutional rights of the population. Basic rights were expanded primarily through a tutelary mechanism called a *tutela*, or writ of protection, which allowed citizens whose rights had been abused to seek redress against an offending party.

Notwithstanding such measures, the judicial branch continues to be plagued by an absence of concrete modernization policies, insufficient financial resources, extended judicial delays, poor conviction records, lack of personnel, and bureaucratic conflict among the judicial bodies. As an example of the latter, although the Supreme Court is the final arbiter on matters of civil law, the fact that all *tutelas* against civil legal sentences must be submitted to the Constitutional Court for their eventual revision has led to constant rifts between these two courts. On various occasions, the Constitutional Court has overturned sentences decreed by the Supreme Court. The administration of justice continues to be precarious: for every 100 homicide cases, an average of 10 suspects are arrested, and usually only one is found guilty and sentenced. General impunity levels are nearly 97 percent.

Supreme Court

The 23-member Supreme Court is the highest judicial body in charge of the country's civil jurisdiction. It acts as the court of final appeal; judges the president of the republic and other high executive-branch officials accused of wrongdoing; investigates and judges members of Congress; judges other government, diplomatic, and military officials; and reviews international agreements. It is divided into four chambers—agrarian and civil, constitutional, criminal, and labor. The Supreme Court administers a series of lower courts at the departmental and municipal levels and receives appeals on cases originally presented to them. District superior courts constitute the maximum judicial authority at the regional level. Circuit courts operate at the municipal level and handle cases involving large sums of money and matters of considerable political importance. The lower court system also consists of ordinary courts with jurisdiction over civil, commercial, criminal, family, labor, and land cases; justice of the peace courts with jurisdiction over minor civil and criminal matters; and authorities of indigenous territories with jurisdiction over indigenous communities.

The Supreme Court elects its own justices, who serve nonrenewable, eight-year terms, from a list of candidates presented by the Superior Judicial Council (CSJ). The court elects the attorney general from a list of candidates proposed by the president of the republic, it selects two of the six judges of the CSJ administrative chamber, and it proposes one name for the list of candidates from which the Senate elects the judges of the Constitutional Court. The Supreme Court submits one of the names on the list of candidates from which the Senate elects the inspector general of the nation, and the Supreme Court pro-

View of the rebuilt Palace of Justice from behind the statue of Simón Bolívar. Photographs on the façade depict the 11 Supreme Court justices murdered during the terrorist assault and military counterattack that destroyed the old building on November 6–7, 1985.
Courtesy Lorenzo Morales

poses the list of candidates from which the Council of State elects the auditor general of the republic, who monitors the budget of the comptroller general of the republic and the territorial comptrollers and reports annually to the Congress, the Supreme Court, and the Council of State. The Supreme Court's constitutional functions include reviewing the decisions of superior courts, trying the president of the republic and high-level public officials, and investigating and trying any member of Congress accused of wrongdoing.

A particularly sensitive issue that falls within the Supreme Court's jurisdiction is the approval of extradition requests, which have risen in number during the past 10 years. Since 2003 alone, 400 Colombian nationals have been extradited to the United States. Although requests presented by the United States for the extradition of drug traffickers constitute the bulk of all cases, the fact that Colombia has a weak immigration-control apparatus also makes it a haven for foreigners seeking to escape from international police and justice. Supreme Court justices also spend a considerable amount of their time resolving cases of *tutelas*, which by law must receive priority attention, creating backlogs of several years in the handling of other matters. In September 2006, the Supreme Court's decision to investigate allegations that a group of politicians from the Atlantic coast had signed an agreement with the right-wing paramilitary United Self-Defense Forces of Colombia (AUC) to "recreate the Republic," the Santa Fe de Ralito Agreement of July 15, 2003, boosted the court's legitimacy and judicial clout (see Peace Processes, ch. 5). Since the inception of this scandal, the nine justices of the court's criminal branch have handled all cases collectively in order to safeguard their decisions against undue political influence from the government, implicated politicians, or illegal groups.

Council of State

The 27-member Council of State oversees the legality of the administrative process, advises the government on administrative issues, and resolves conflicts between the public sector and society. More specifically, the Council of State serves as the supreme tribunal of administrative disputes; reviews the constitutionality of decrees issued by the national government that are not under the jurisdiction of the Constitutional Court; acts as the highest consultative body of the government on administrative matters; rules on the transit of foreign troops, warships, or military aircraft through the national territory; prepares and presents constitutional and other legislative reforms; and reviews cases concerning the status of members of Congress accused of crimes. The Council of State, which is also the plenary body, is divided into three chambers (government, consultation and civil service, and administrative litigation). The Council of State selects its own judges for eight-year, nonrenewable terms from lists presented by the CSJ. As the supreme administrative tribunal, the Council of State hears complaints against the government and public officials. The Supreme Court also holds power of judicial review over the constitutionality of some administrative decrees that do not fall under the jurisdiction of the Constitutional Court. A law passed in 1998 led to the creation, at least on paper, of a series of department-level administrative courts and judges that the Council of State supervises. However, by late 2009, they had not yet begun operating.

Superior Judicial Council

Prior to 1991, judges were elected directly by the country's judicial bodies themselves, but the judicial branch was functionally subordinate to the executive branch in administrative and budgetary terms. The CSJ has responsibility for administering and regulating the judicial system and came into being in an attempt to grant this branch of the government greater administrative and budgetary autonomy. The 13 members of the council are elected for nonrenewable, eight-year terms. The CSJ is divided into two chambers. The administrative chamber comprises six judges, who are elected by the Council of State (three judges), the Supreme Court (two), and the Constitutional Court (one). The jurisdictional discipline chamber consists of seven judges elected by the Congress from a list presented by the government. The administrative chamber's primary functions include responsibility for the judicial branch's budget, determining the structure and personnel of the distinct judicial bodies and courtrooms, presenting lists of candidates for the Supreme Court and the Council of State, and administering the judicial career service. The jurisdictional discipline chamber investigates allegations of misconduct on the part of the members of the judiciary.

Constitutional Court

The nine-member Constitutional Court defends the constitution, and its decisions are binding on all other national judicial bodies. The Senate elects the court's judges for eight-year, nonrenewable terms from a list established by the Council of State, the Supreme Court, and the president of the republic, each of which proposes one candidate. The Constitutional Court's judicial functions include ruling on the constitutionality of laws, administrative and legislative procedures, constitutional reform proposals and popular referenda, and legislative decrees issued by the president. The court also reviews the decisions of other courts regarding *tutelas* of citizens' fundamental rights and rules on the constitutionality of international treaties. More specifically, it oversees the integrity and supremacy of the constitution by deciding on complaints of unconstitutionality made by citizens, the constitutionality of holding a referendum or establishing a constituent assembly to reform the constitution, the constitutionality of laws and national plebiscites, and the constitutionality of legislative decrees and other bills proposed by the government, *tutelas* that relate to the national interest, and international treaties and laws.

Since its creation in 1992, the Constitutional Court has issued judgments on a wide variety of highly sensitive political, economic, and social matters. Given that its decisions are binding on the other sectors of the judicial branch and the government, Constitutional Court pronouncements frequently generate considerable levels of public controversy. Until recently, cyclical conflict among the court members, other judges or judicial employees, and the other branches of government contrasted with the high levels of credibility that it enjoyed with the Colombian public, which viewed the Constitutional Court as an independent body that interpreted and applied the 1991 charter in a progressive manner. However, the court has become more conservative on key political, social, and economic matters; for example, its decision to approve the immediate reelection of Álvaro Uribe was widely criticized on legal grounds. In 2007–8 its impartiality came under question as a result of the appointment of its newest member, the former legal secretary of the president's office. In 2009 six more members were expected to be appointed to the court, leading to fears that it may lose its independence.

Attorney General's Office

The Attorney General's Office is an independent judicial organ with the primary roles of investigating criminal offenses and prosecuting the accused. It consists of the attorney general, an assistant attorney general, delegates to other judicial entities, and departmental and municipal offices. Specialized national investigative units also exist in particularly sensitive areas, including human rights, corruption, money laundering, and drug trafficking. The Supreme Court elects the attorney general for a four-year, nonrenewable term from a list established by the president of the republic.

On January 1, 2005, a new Code of Criminal Procedure took effect in Bogotá and the Colombian coffee zone and began to be gradually applied throughout the whole country during 2008. The new code passes some investigatory responsibility to penal judges instead of the Attorney General's Office. The accusatory system, which replaces the Napoleonic Code, is based on the U.S. Penal Code in that it introduces an oral hearing into the process. Although it is too soon to evaluate the effects of this shift on the administration of justice, there is widespread consensus that the new system requires more and better-trained investigators, for which the United States has provided active support.

Public Administration

The 1991 constitution specifically identifies two control entities with administrative and budgetary autonomy—the Comptroller General's Office and the Public Ministry. They are state institutions that do not belong to any of the three branches of government, and both have offices at the national, departmental, and municipal levels.

The Comptroller General's Office (Contraloría General de la República) exercises fiscal control over state expenditures based on criteria of efficiency, economy, equity, and environmental cost. The comptroller is elected by the plenary of the Congress for a four-year, nonrenewable period from a list presented by the Constitutional Court, the Supreme Court, and the Council of State. Fiscal control is selective in that, although all state institutions are subject to scrutiny, only a certain number are chosen for examination in a given period. The budget of the comptroller general of the republic and departmental and municipal comptrollers is monitored by the auditor general of the republic, who is elected for a two-year term by the Council of State from a list of candidates proposed by the Supreme Court.

The Public Ministry, a noncabinet-level ministry, promotes respect for human rights, defends the public interest, oversees compliance with the law and legal sentences, and investigates disciplinary misconduct by public officials and employees in general, including members of the state security forces. The inspector general of the nation (*procurador general de la nación*) directs the Public Ministry and has the primary function of overseeing the correct conduct of state employees. The Senate elects the inspector general for a nonrenewable term of four years.

The Human Rights Ombudsman's Office (Defensoría del Pueblo) operates under the direction of the Inspector General's Office within the Public Ministry, and its primary function is to oversee the promotion, exercise, and defense of human rights throughout the national territory. The House of Representatives elects the human rights ombudsman for a four-year, nonrenewable period from a list presented by the president of the republic.

Given acute problems of public order and systematic violation of human rights in the country, the human rights ombudsman has been involved in particularly sensitive aspects of Colombian political life since the creation of this position in 1991. The ombudsman has issued a number of reports, including denunciations of violations of the human rights of ethnic minorities, forced displacement and humanitarian crises in Colombia, the public health effects of the aerial fumigation of illicit drug crops, and public health conditions in the jails.

District and municipal ombudsmen (*personerías*), supervised by the ombudsman of Bogotá, are responsible for defending fundamental rights and other community interests, such as environmental matters and public services at the local level. The public role exercised by the ombudsmen is very important, given that they are in direct contact with local populations that are affected by the internal armed conflict. *Personerías* cooperate with the human rights ombudsman in promoting respect for human rights, implementing human rights policies, intervening with local authorities when the fundamental rights of the citizens in their respective districts are being violated, and reporting human rights abuses. Their function appears to complement the local system of conflict resolution provided by the justices of the peace.

Political Dynamics

The Weakening of the Bipartisan System

The dominance of the Liberal and Conservative parties, their entrenchment in local personalistic, clientelist networks, and a system of representation based on special interests have been traits of the Colombian political landscape since the midnineteenth century. Traditionally, both parties have lacked discipline and failed to build intermediate party organizations capable of linking local and regional political processes with national-level entities.

The National Front power-sharing agreement in place between 1958 and 1978 weakened the two-party system, because it led to fragmentation of the two parties and reduced their capacity for interaction with the national population. Urbanization and modernization had the additional effects of eroding traditional party loyalties and highlighting the incompetence of Liberals and Conservatives alike in responding to basic social needs.

The 1991 constitution attempted to correct many of the political distortions of the bipartisan system by facilitating the creation and operation of new political parties and movements, reducing previous barriers to political participation, and granting Colombian citizens new rights to engage more actively in this process. However, the electoral system remained unchanged, and intraparty competition, fragmentation, and the presentation of multiple electoral lists belonging to the same party or movement continued. In the 1994 congressional elections, the Liberal Party alone presented 134 lists for the Senate and 293 lists for the House of Representatives. Between 1991 and 2002, the total number of electoral lists that competed for seats in the Senate and the House grew by approximately 45 percent and 55 percent, respectively.

Notwithstanding the crisis of the traditional parties, since 1991 the Liberal Party and, to a lesser degree, the Conservatives have maintained a significant presence in the Congress and in departmental and local governments. Whereas in 1991 and 1994 the Liberals won more than 50 percent of the seats in the Senate, their share shrank to 48 percent and 28 percent in 1998 and 2002, respectively. During this same period, on average the Conservatives won approximately 20 percent of the congressional seats. Both parties performed poorly in the 2006 congressional elections, although the two adopted

*Álvaro Uribe Vélez
(president, 2002–6, 2006–10)
Courtesy Embassy of Colombia,
Washington, DC*

opposite strategies in order to counteract their waning political influence. The Conservative Party allied itself with the pro-Uribe coalition in the Congress, while the Liberals began to exercise political opposition, often in alliance with the left-leaning Alternative Democratic Pole (PDA). At first glance, this downward trend continued in the 2007 municipal and departmental elections. The Liberal Party took only 200 municipalities and nine governorships, compared to 222 and 18, respectively, in 2002, while the Conservatives won the same number of municipalities and only five governorships. However, the total number of votes accrued nationwide and the number of candidates elected to departmental assemblies and municipal councils indicated that both parties performed well. The two parties received the highest shares of the vote—the Liberals took 21.6 percent of the total vote and the Conservatives, 18.6 percent—suggesting that they continue to have strong support in many parts of the country.

Other Parties and Political Movements

One outcome of the decline in the prestige of the two main parties has been the upsurge of politicians who claim to be independents. Noemí Sanín Posada, whose political career has been characterized by close collaboration with the Conservative Party, ran for the presidency in 1998 as an outsider, but, ironically, members of the political and economic elite supported her. Both Andrés Pastrana and Álvaro Uribe competed as independent candidates in the 1998 and 2002 elections, respectively, and won the presidency on political platforms critical of the Conservatives and the Liberals. Ingrid Betancourt Pulecio, a presidential candidate who was kidnapped by the FARC on February 22, 2002, founded an "antipolitical" party, the Oxygen Green Party (PVO), which had sponsored her bid for the presidency.

A second, related outcome has been the massive regrouping of traditional politicians into new political parties and movements. Such is the case of the Citizens' Convergence, the Democratic Colombia Party (PDC), the National Unity Social Party (PSUN), or Partido de La U, the Radical Change Party (PCR), and Team Wings Colombia (Equipo Alas Colombia). What distinguishes these new parties from the traditional parties is their lack of a single ideological base and their loose internal coherence. Indeed, most constitute marriages of political convenience and demonstrate unity that is largely grounded in loyalty to President Álvaro Uribe. In the 2006 congressional elections, this strategy allowed the pro-Uribe coalition to win an absolute majority in the legislature. One year later, the 2007 local and departmental elections also yielded favorable results for the coalition—18 governorships and 714 mayoralities—although these newer parties obtained fewer votes overall than the Liberals or the Conservatives.

The 1991 constitution was largely successful in broadening the Colombian political spectrum. Above all, the explicit recognition of ethnic, sociocultural, and religious diversity in the constitution's conceptualization of the nation encouraged indigenous and religious groups to participate more actively in political life. Modifications in the electoral system led to a proliferation of new political candidates of varied origins. The aim of partial state funding for political campaigns was to create at least minimal conditions of equality between the newer movements and the two traditional political parties, and to isolate both from potentially corruptive influences. There were new guarantees of equal access to electoral information and to media campaign coverage.

The results of such modifications were telling. In the 1998 congressional elections alone, more than 80 parties and movements presented candidates. Between 1991 and 2002, the total number of political groups that occupied a seat in one or both of the chambers of Congress increased from 23 to 62.

The creation of a special indigenous district electing two members to the Senate and of a special ethnic district electing up to five members to the House of Representatives is largely responsible for the growing political participation of Colombia's indigenous communities. Although no one political organization articulates the interests of the country's entire Amerindian population, three movements, the Indigenous Authorities of Colombia (Aico), the Indigenous Social Alliance (ASI), and the Colombian Indigenous Movement (MIC), have occupied seats in the Congress since 1991. Indigenous candidates also have established temporary political alliances in order to influence presidential and gubernatorial races, and to gain additional seats in the Congress.

At the regional and local levels, the three indigenous movements have achieved significant victories in elections for municipal councils, departmental assemblies, governors, and mayors. In the 1994 elections, in addition to winning a list for the Cauca Departmental Assembly, the ASI presented 10 lists for various municipal councils, of which eight were elected. In 1997 the ASI and Aico successfully elected 152 council members, along with eight assembly members and 13 mayors. In 2000 Cauca elected an indigenous governor for the first time, while one-quarter of the members elected to that department's assembly also were representatives of the indigenous community.

In the 1998 and 2002 elections, the country's Afro-Colombian communities also elected delegates for the seats to which they are entitled via the special minority voting district in the House of Representatives. A total of 23 candidate lists competing for two seats in 2002 indicated the extreme levels of disaggregation characterizing Afro-Colombians. Colombians residing abroad, another community represented in the special district in the House, presented 28 lists that same year.

By contrast, two alternative political parties, Democratic Action M–19 (AD M–19) and the National Salvation Movement (MSN), simply disappeared from the political scene after achieving impressive political victories in the early 1990s. In the 1990 presidential election, these two parties, representing former rebels of the Nineteenth of April Movement (M–19) and a dissident faction of the Conservative Party, won 23.9 percent and 12.6 percent of the popular vote, respectively. In the case of the AD M–19, this result was particularly noteworthy, given the assassination of the group's initial candidate, Carlos Pizarro Leongómez, prior to the election and his replacement by its lesser-known member, Antonio Navarro Wolff. However, after winning 26.9 percent of the total popular vote in elections for the Constituent Assembly in 1991, the AD M–19 received 9 percent in the 1991 congressional elections, 3 percent in 1994, and vanished in 1998. Several of its members, including Senator Navarro Wolff and Deputy Gustavo Petro Urrego, continue to occupy congressional seats but are affiliated with other political movements. Following MSN leader Álvaro Gómez Hurtado's assassination in November 1995, the MSN disappeared altogether, suggesting that it was essentially Gómez's personal electoral vehicle and was never intended to be an alternative to the Conservative Party.

During the latter half of the 1980s, the FARC-sponsored leftist Patriotic Union (UP), founded in 1985, obtained highly impressive electoral success at the departmental and municipal levels, and reasonable levels of representation in the Congress. However, between 1985 and 1996 the UP's members, including presidential candidate Bernardo Jaramillo Ossa in 1990 and Senator Manuel Cepeda Vargas in 1994, were victims of a systematic purge—approximately 3,000 were murdered. Consequently, the UP presence in the Colombian political system became marginal after the mid-1990s. In 1993 the Inter-American Commission on Human Rights received a complaint filed on behalf of the families of more than 1,000 UP members killed, on grounds that the Colombian state had been negligent in preventing and investigating the alleged murders. In 1997 the case came before the commission, which recommended that the state reach a friendly agreement with the families, but conciliation between the sides has been impossible. While the case continued before the commission, in August 2007 the Attorney General's Office reopened hundreds of cases related to the UP murders. Testimonies provided by several paramilitary leaders under the Justice and Peace Law have also helped to clarify their participation, as well as that of drug-trafficking organizations, in specific killings.

Authentically independent outsiders also have achieved important electoral victories as a result of growing public criticism of traditional parties and conventional politics. Unlike Noemí Sanín, with whom he ran as the vice presidential candidate in the 1998 elections, Antanas Mockus Sivickas, twice mayor of Bogotá (1992–96 and 1996–2000), has developed his public career far removed from Colombia's political establishment. In order to do so, he has appealed consistently to the electorate's dislike of traditional political practice with provocative campaigns that demand little funding but have a highly visible impact. The Christian-based Independent Movement of Absolute Renewal (MIRA) has also achieved substantial recognition, earning two seats in the Senate and one in the House of Representatives in 2006, along with local-level positions of less importance. Former labor leader Luis Eduardo Garzón ran for the presidency in 2002 on an antipolitics platform and gained a considerable portion of the popular vote. His supporters included the Social and Political Front (FSP), a broad leftist coalition that includes the Communist Party of Colombia (PCC) and several labor movements, human rights and peace activists, indigenous leaders, and other progressive parties and movements. A significant number of congressional candidates affiliated with the FSP also won seats in the Senate and the House of Representatives. Three FSP candidates, Antonio Navarro Wolff, former Liberal Party member Samuel Moreno Rojas, and former Constitutional Court justice and 2006 presidential contender Carlos Gaviria Díaz, were elected to the Senate with more than 100,000 votes, placing them third, fourth, and fifth, respectively, in the tally of votes.

Many FSP affiliates went on to create a larger leftist coalition within the Congress in 2003 called the Democratic Alternative (AD). In the 2003 departmental and municipal races, Garzón mobilized the political capital he had acquired in the 2002 presidential election to create a distinct political movement, the Independent Democratic Pole (PDI), whose membership supported Garzón's successful candidacy for the mayoralty of Bogotá, as well as the bids of several other candidates in some of Colombia's largest cities, including Medellín, Barranquilla, and Cali. In the second half of 2005, the AD and the PDI merged to create the PDA and agreed to choose a single candidate for the 2006 presidential election.

Recent electoral successes by the PDA in the Congress and at the departmental and municipal levels have posed interesting challenges to the old system. The outcome of the 2006 congressional and presidential elections suggests that this trend will continue. In the legislative elections, the PDA obtained approximately 10 percent of the popular vote for the Senate and 5 percent for the House of Representatives. The presidential race, although resulting in a landslide victory for President Álvaro Uribe (62 percent of the popular vote), gave PDA candidate Carlos Gaviria an impressive 22 percent of the popular vote, in comparison with only 12 percent obtained by Liberal Party candidate Horacio Serpa Uribe. In the 2007 elections, PDA candidate Samuel Moreno succeeded in holding on to the Bogotá mayoralty (and the party won 19 other mayoralties), notwithstanding the strong track record of his opponent, the former mayor Enrique Peñalosa Londoño, and President Uribe's active campaign against Moreno in the days preceding the election. The total number of votes accrued by the party nationwide suggests that its political base continues to expand.

Political Party Reform

Since the 1991 constitutional reform, two of the most visible characteristics of the Colombian party system have been the many internal divisions of the country's two traditional parties and the formation of a significant number of alternative parties and movements that also exhibit high degrees of fragmentation. Colombia's bipartisan system thus has been severely weakened, but establishing a multiparty system has been extremely difficult. The new political options have failed to translate into greater responsiveness to community needs, given the extreme fragmentation of political parties and the subsequent absence of solid political majorities. Furthermore, with several notable exceptions, the myriad new movements that have surfaced in Colombia since 1991 engage in many of the same practices that characterize the dominant political culture, specifically clientelism and personalism, and therefore their emergence has had little impact on the political landscape.

In order to address these problems, the Congress finally approved a political reform in 2003 that brought in the d'Hondt system, which requires a minimum of 2 percent of the total vote to obtain representation in the Senate, and a minimum of 50 percent of the electoral quotient to obtain seats in the House and other bodies. Under this new system, each party or movement may present only one list of candidates in an election, the minimum requirements for constituting a legal political party have been raised, participation in multiple parties is prohibited, party discipline in the legislature is compulsory, and the preferential vote replaces the closed-list system. In the 2006 congressional elections, this new set of rules led to a smaller number of electoral lists—14, which was well down from 2002—with fewer candidates each and to the creation of several new political parties, most notably, the National Unity Social Party and the Radical Change Party, both supportive of President Uribe.

The political reform was at first relatively successful in enforcing unified party action in the Congress, departmental assemblies, and city councils, and in reducing the number of political parties operating in the country. However, the October 28, 2007, departmental and municipal elections posed a relative setback, given that legislation allowing write-in candidates led many to bypass the new electoral law, resulting in a surge in the numbers of political parties and movements competing for political office to 244.

Corruption

The 1991 constitution adopted a series of articles designed to strengthen the state's capacity to punish corrupt practices, and it established new rules to regulate political activities. Anticorruption measures have been relatively effective in punishing corrupt public practices and making them more transparent. Since 1991 the Council of State has removed 42 members of Congress from office and investigated more than 300 additional members. Between 2001 and 2004, the Attorney General's Office investigated more than 3,000 public officials, many of whom it charged with misconduct or abuse of power. By 2006 the Supreme Court had ruled on the charges against approximately 300 high-ranking officials of crimes against the public administration.

Notwithstanding these efforts, corruption continues to be widespread in Colombia, especially at the local level. The persistence of clientelism, the lack of accountability between branches of government and between government and society, the general deterioration of political institutions, and the presence of drug-trafficking organizations and illegal armed groups largely account for pervasive malfeasance. Administrative corruption, consisting of the illegal private use of public monies and goods, is the prevalent abuse. The primary types of administrative corruption in Colombia include bribery, favoritism in public contracts, the use of political influence to obtain public office, and the contracting of public-works projects that are either useless to the community or never completed. Fiscal losses due to such wrongdoing have been considerable.

In 1994 the attorney general initiated Case 8,000, which revealed the extent to which corruption had penetrated the highest levels of political power. At the center of the case were allegations that the presidential campaign of Ernesto Samper had received financial contributions from the Cali Cartel. The attorney general presented formal charges against a number of members of Congress over the funding of their campaigns and other high-level government officials also accused of receiving monies from drug-trafficking groups. Although the House of Representatives formally absolved Samper in June 1996, many other public servants and businesspeople were charged with being involved financially with the drug cartels. Case 8,000 was a clear indication that the measures adopted by the 1991 constitution were inadequate to prevent the illegal funding of electoral campaigns.

The Colombian political system suffered another devastating blow in September 2006, when the Supreme Court began investigating allegations that significant numbers of politicians from the Atlantic coast and elsewhere had formed alliances with paramilitary groups. One month later, the attorney general formally accused Jorge Noguera Cotes, former director of the Administrative Security Department, of collusion with the paramilitaries while in office. In early 2007, the minister of foreign relations, María Consuelo Araújo, had to resign following the detention of her brother, Senator Álvaro Araújo Castro, and the filing of charges against her father, as a result of their involvement in the parapolitics scandal. By April 2008, 33 appointed and elected officials had been jailed awaiting trial, while another 62 members of Congress had become official suspects. The list included a former minister, a serving minister, and a cousin of President Uribe. These tainted officials also included congressional deputies, senators, mayors, governors, and assembly and council members, many of whom belong to the political coalition that supports President Uribe. Five of the groups associated with this paramilitary alliance in the Congress—Colombia Alive, Citizens' Convergence, Democratic Colombia Party, Living Colombia Movement (MCV), and Team Wings Colombia—had the majority or all of their legislators linked to the scandal.

Societal Institutions

The Church

Traditionally, Colombia's Roman Catholic Church has been one of the most powerful and conservative in Latin America. However, the 1991 constitution's explicit recognition of religious, ethnic, and sexual heterogeneity and diversity as the basis of the nation reduced the church's influence on the state. Moreover, the charter stipulates a strict separation of the church from the branches of political power and proclaims that religious education is not a requirement in public schools. The extensive growth of other religious communities in the last decade, most notably Protestant evangelism, gradually has eroded Catholicism's base, although the Roman Catholic Church itself continues to enjoy high approval ratings in public opinion.

In many respects, the Roman Catholic Church continues to be very conservative. The church hierarchy has virulently opposed efforts to legalize abortion, euthanasia, and stem-cell research in Colombia and has been critical of the government's sex-education and birth-control policies. Nevertheless, members of the clergy also have been visibly active in seeking solutions to many of the most vexing problems faced by the country today, including the armed conflict, poverty and inequality, and the drug trade. In August 1995, the president of the Colombian Episcopal Conference created the National Reconciliation Commission (CNN), an independent body seeking ways to resolve the warfare and facilitate negotiations between the state and the armed groups. The commission's membership represents all sectors of Colombian society and includes academics, politicians, human rights defenders, journalists, businesspeople, and labor union representatives.

In addition to supporting international humanitarian law, the church has expressed profound concern over the fate of the displaced population. Many clergy members also have highlighted the need to attend to problems of poverty and inequality as a precondition for peace. In those regions in which the economic survival of the rural community depends primarily on coca cultivation, bishops have opposed intrusive strategies such as aerial fumigation to eradicate illicit crops.

In the many regions of Colombia in which rebel groups, in particular the FARC, operate, members of the church have actively defended community rights and have taken measures to protect local populations against abuses committed by guerrillas. The fact that the church has become one of the most visible critics of armed political violence in the country has converted its members into political targets, in particular of the FARC. Since 2002 armed groups have killed a dozen or more priests a year. According to Justice, Peace and Nonviolent Action (Justapaz), a religious NGO, in 2006 alone 15 religious leaders were killed, nearly 100 received death threats, and six priests were kidnapped (see Religion, ch. 2).

News Media

Although Colombian law enshrined freedom of expression and of the press before 1991, the new charter reformulated the constitutional bases of press freedom by prohibiting censorship, and by directly linking freedom of expression with freedom of information. However, extralegal restrictions on the media continue to be significant. The government attempts to manipulate information and to influence media reports by using family, personal, or political relations. The important clout of Colombian economic groups in the media industry and the increasing acts of violence against members of the press by guerrillas and paramilitaries have placed considerable limitations on the media.

The ownership structure of Colombian mass media has shifted significantly since 1980. In particular, national radio, television, and newspaper conglomerates controlled by the country's principal economic groups have replaced local media chains. Today, control over most Colombian media is divided among three multimedia companies: Caracol Televisión, S.A. (Caracol), National Radio and Television of Colombia (RNC), and Casa Editorial El Tiempo publishing company. Grupo Bavaria and the Santo Domingo family owned Caracol (comprising a private television network, a radio station, and Bogotá's *El Espectador* newspaper) until 2003, when the Spanish communications firm Prisa acquired a majority stake in it. The Ardila Lülle Oranization owns RNC, consisting of the other private television network and a chain of radio stations broadcasting throughout the country. And the Casa Editorial El Tiempo, long owned by the politically and economically influential

Santos family, controls Bogotá's local television channel, CityTV, several magazines, music stores, and, until recently, the largest daily national newspaper, *El Tiempo*, with a circulation of around 265,000 on weekdays and twice that number on Sunday. In August 2007, the Spanish Grupo Planeta obtained majority ownership of *El Tiempo*.

Colombia has approximately 25 regional newspapers, including several with a daily circulation of more than 50,000 copies. Those with the largest circulation outside Bogotá are Medellín's *El Colombiano* (90,000 on weekdays), *El Heraldo* (Barranquilla and the Atlantic coast, with 70,000 on weekdays), and *El País* (Cali, with 60,000 on weekdays). Some of the larger regional newspapers have bought up the smaller ones. For example, Bucaramanga's *Vanguardia Liberal* is currently the owner of several other dailies, including *El Pueblo* (Pereira), *El Universal* (Cartagena), and *El Liberal* (Popayán). In addition to daily newspapers, several weekly news magazines, most notably, *Semana* and *Cambio*, with circulations of approximately 150,000 and 20,000, respectively, are major sources of political analysis and debate. Since the parapolitics scandal was uncovered in 2006, the media have devoted much attention to this issue.

The concentration of media ownership in Colombia has had a substantial homogenizing effect on coverage of specific national and international issues. The daily newspaper with the highest circulation nationally is *El Tiempo*, with a weekday circulation of at least 300,000, rising to about half a million for the Sunday edition. The oldest newspaper in Colombia, *El Espectador*, a daily publication, became a weekly in September 2001 but returned as a daily in May 2008, with a weekday circulation of 50,000 and a Sunday circulation of 250,000. In October 2008, *El Espectador* became one of the three major newspapers around the world to host the *New York Times* new weekly news supplement. Only two television news programs, "Noticias Uno" and "CM&," offer alternatives to the coverage provided by Caracol and the National Radio Network (RCN). And three large, private radio chains share control over the majority of AM and FM stations: Caracol, RCN, and family-owned Todelar Radio.

The concentration of media ownership, the continuing armed conflict, and the impunity of perpetrators of crimes against journalists have acted to limit freedom of expression and opinion in Colombia. According to the Inter-American Press Society (SIP), Colombia is one of the most dangerous countries in the world in which to practice journalism, along with the Philippines and Iraq. During the 1997–2007 period, more than 114 journalists were murdered. In August 1999, gunmen murdered nationally famous comedian and radio journalist Jaime Garzón in Bogotá. Since 2000 assassins have

The Art Museum of the Central Bank in Bogotá's Candelaria district
Courtesy Lorenzo Morales

killed 11 journalists because of their reports related to the drug traffic, paramilitary organizations, and corruption. In 2004 alone, two journalists were killed, three were kidnapped, 28 injured, and 25 threatened. Self-censorship practiced by journalists perceiving or actually receiving threats has also constrained media reporting.

Colombian Interest Groups

Traditionally, clientelist practices and the closed nature of the Colombian political system largely constrained the development of national interest groups distinct from those directly related to the country's political and economic elites. In the 1980s, Colombia's participation in the cocaine industry facilitated the consolidation of powerful illegal organizations, in particular the Medell n and Cali cartels, which began to exercise systematic influence over government decisions through bribery and assassination. For example, the 1991 Constituent Assembly, under violent pressure from the drug-trafficking organizations, voted to prohibit the extradition of Colombian nationals, although this decision was overturned during the Samper administration. In the 1990s, the prevalent use of armed force in clientelism also resulted in further manipulation of the political process at all levels. Following the 2002 congressional elections, paramilitary leader

Salvatore Mancuso Gómez went so far as to claim that where the United Self-Defense Forces of Colombia had a substantial social and military presence, the group had successfully elected the candidates it supported.

However, the institutionalization of assorted mechanisms of democratic participation and of political and fiscal decentralization by the 1991 constitution led to positive modifications in the political environment, given that citizens gained greater opportunities to participate in the discussion of local, regional, and national issues. As a consequence, since the early 1990s the role of a variety of new social and political movements has expanded considerably (see Social Movements, ch. 2). Growing citizen participation has taken place within an adverse domestic context, characterized by extreme inequality and poverty and the continuation of the internal armed conflict. Many interest groups have focused on issues related to these problems. A large majority of Colombia's NGOs collaborate with international counterparts and receive some type of funding from them.

Nongovernmental Organizations

In the late 1990s, Colombia's internal crisis spurred greater international involvement in numerous issues in the country, including law and order, human rights, humanitarian protection, the environment, and community development. Some of the most visible international organizations were Amnesty International, Doctors Without Borders, Human Rights Watch, International Peace Brigades, International Red Cross, and Save the Children; most of them have established links with local civic organizations.

The number of international and domestic nongovernmental organizations operating in Colombia has expanded exponentially since 2000. Although the activities of these organizations are extremely diverse, NGOs working in the areas of development, forced displacement, gender issues, human rights, and conflict have been particularly significant. In 2004 there were approximately 1,300 national NGOs registered with the Colombian Chamber of Commerce. The Colombian Confederation of NGOs, an umbrella organization created in 1989, seeks to mediate between approximately 1,000 Colombian NGOs and regional federations and national and international organizations. The confederation also nurtures linkages between groups specializing in the same issues throughout the country. The National Network of Development and Peace Programs (Redprodpaz) is another national network grouping together about 15 different regional peace and development programs.

In the areas of armed conflict, forced displacement, and human rights, the most visible NGOs, both nationally and internationally, include the Alternative Social Development Association (Minga), the Research and Public Education Center (Cinep), the Colombian Commission of Jurists (CCJ), the Consultancy for Human Rights and Displacement (Codhes), and the New Rainbow Corporation. Their research on these topics has been largely incorporated into the reports of significant international and foreign governmental agencies, including the Organization of American States (OAS), United Nations (UN), and U.S. Department of State.

In many regions of Colombia characterized by a precarious state presence and acute levels of poverty, NGOs have played key roles in publicizing and defending the social, economic, and political demands of local communities. The intensification of the internal armed conflict in the mid-1990s led to increased violence against and intimidation of NGO representatives, particularly in those areas under dispute between guerrillas and paramilitaries. Between 1996 and 1998, there were 29 killings of human rights workers, while 17 sought asylum in third countries. During 2000–2005, at least 48 NGO activists were either assassinated or disappeared. Eleven human rights workers were killed in 2008.

In response to this situation, as well as to the growing stigmatization that Colombian NGOs have been subjected to by both paramilitaries and the Colombian state, approximately 90 organizations created the Colombian Platform for Human Rights, Democracy, and Development (Plataforma Colombiana de Derechos Humanos, Democracia y Desarrollo). In the second half of 2003, this group published a controversial report entitled *The Authoritarian Jinx* (*El embrujo autoritario*), documenting the deteriorating human rights situation, the growing impunity of the military, greater involvement of the civilian population in the internal armed conflict, and the existence of an intimidation campaign against human rights activists. Following the report's indictment of the Uribe administration, which was not nearly as severe as its title suggests, Uribe accused national and global NGOs working in the country of being terrorist sympathizers. The offices of several human rights organizations were searched illegally, and a number of NGO activists were detained or arrested on charges of aiding terrorists. The international community has criticized such actions harshly as placing NGO representatives at greater risk. Notwithstanding significant organizational advances in the past decade, Colombian NGOs also continue to contend with the dispersed, fragmented character of local peace, human rights, and development initiatives, and the limited impact of civic initiatives in Colombian politics.

Ethnic Groups

Colombia's national population includes about 80 indigenous groups located throughout the country and a large number of Afro-Colombian communities, many of which inhabit the Atlantic and Pacific coastal regions and the islands of San Andrés, Providencia, and Santa Catalina. Indigenous groups comprise approximately 3.4 percent of the total population and Afro-Colombians, 10.5 percent. Hundreds of organizations represent these groups locally and regionally. At the national level, the National Indigenous Organization of Colombia (ONIC) and the Indigenous Authorities of Colombia (Aico) represent nearly all of Colombia's indigenous population. The Cimarrón Movement and the Platform of the Black Communities (PCN) are the main umbrella organizations representing Afro-Colombian communities.

One of the major goals of the Constituent Assembly was to open the Colombian political system to broader representation, and the indigenous population achieved a direct voice through the participation of ONIC. The 1991 constitution evinced recognition of Colombian ethnic minorities in measures to promote their participation in the political system, primarily through the creation of special indigenous and ethnic congressional districts, and by acknowledging their cultural and territorial rights. Indigenous groups have been represented in Congress since later that year. Following the electoral successes of the indigenous movement, Colombia's black communities also achieved political representation in the Congress in 1998.

Access to land and preservation of land rights, considered a basic cultural right by indigenous and Afro-Colombian communities alike, have been central to the activities of both groups. Although Afro-Colombians account for 90 percent of the inhabitants of Chocó Department, they own only 10 percent of the land, primarily as a result of earlier legislation that designated the Pacific basin as a reservation zone and limited access to individual and collective land ownership. In 1993 constitutionally mandated legislation recognized the Afro-Colombian community's right to collective property within its ancestral territories and to individual property within the Pacific basin's cities. Some progress has been made in complying with the Colombian state's constitutional obligation to ensure respect for Afro-Colombians' territorial, economic, and cultural rights, and by 2005 more than 100 land titles had been granted. However, the active paramilitary presence in and around Chocó has lent itself to the systematic, violent reappropriation of newly granted titles by the paramilitaries. In other regions of the country, ethnic minorities have been especially hard-hit by the extremely high concentration of landownership; 1.4 percent of landowners in the country hold 65.4 percent of the total land.

More than 90 percent of the Afro-Colombian population in Chocó continues to lack access to basic public services, and 80 percent endures inhuman, overcrowded housing. The black residents are extremely vulnerable to armed violence and forced displacement. Illegal armed groups have murdered disproportionately high numbers of indigenous and black community members and leaders. Approximately one-quarter of the total number of displaced persons in the country are of indigenous or African descent. In 2003 alone, more than 40,000 Afro-Colombians and 2,800 members of indigenous groups became displaced.

Although displacement is highly correlated with the internal war, the fact that Colombia's Pacific lowlands comprise one of the five most biodiverse regions in the world has led to the proliferation of agro-industrial megaprojects that also have competed with the local population in the struggle to control land. A similar problem arose in the case of the U'wa Amerindians, who conducted a highly visible, drawn-out legal battle against Royal Dutch Shell and Occidental Petroleum between 1992 and 1997 over their attempts to engage in oil exploration and extraction on U'wa communal lands. Although the U'wa secured the withdrawal of those two companies, the tribal struggle continues as the Colombian Petroleum Enterprise (Ecopetrol) and Spain's Repsol YPF seek to drill on their land.

Colombia's ethnic groups have increased their political and social participation, and they have explored new forms of collaborative action. Indigenous and Afro-Colombian movements also have frequently linked up with the country's rural organizations, including the National Campesino Council (CNC) and the National Agrarian Coordinator (CNA), in protest over the acute social problems that plague Colombia's rural population, including government neglect, aerial fumigation of coca crops, and violence by armed groups. Nevertheless, ethnic- and rural-based interest-group activity continues to be relatively weak and uncoordinated, largely because of the territorial dispersion of activists and the diversity of their claims, the repressive effects of violence, and the lack of adequate state protection for legitimate social protest (see also Race and Ethnicity, ch. 2).

Labor Unions

The Colombian labor movement represents only a small percentage of the country's workforce and has rarely played an active role in national politics. Since the early 1990s, the scope of labor unions decreased even further, given the perpetration of violence against them and the implementation of economic liberalization policies. Nevertheless, between 1991 and 2004, Colombia continued to experience an average of one mobilization, strike, or protest per month. Judicial and legislative authorities often have disregarded the right to strike and the right of association. For example, the Constitutional Court ruled that workers in the education, health, telephone, and electric-power sectors had only a limited right to strike, because of the fundamental entitlement of all Colombian citizens to these services. Notwithstanding constitutional recognition of the need to establish tripartite negotiations among labor, employers, and the state, in practice the Constitutional Court makes crucial decisions such as the establishment of the minimum wage. Labor leaders also have been accused regularly of sympathizing with guerrilla organizations. During the Samper administration, leaders of the Workers' Social Union (USO), which represents workers in the oil industry, were arrested on charges of rebellion.

In 2007 the labor movement accounted for between 5 and 6 percent of the economically active population. Traditionally, it consisted of three central organizations: the United Workers' Federation (CUT), representing 75 percent of the unionized workforce, equivalent to 550,000 affiliates; the General Confederation of Democratic Workers (CGTD); and the Confederation of Colombian Workers (CTC). These three organizations, which were involved in different labor sectors of the Colombian economy, merged to create the National Unitary Command (CNU), which has led labor union efforts to influence Colombia's development plans and the general budget, as well as education, social security, labor reform, and pension policies. Attempts by the labor movement to participate in Colombian political life reached their peak in 2002, when a former president of the CUT, Luis Eduardo Garzón, ran for the presidency. Although Garzón lost the presidential election, he was elected mayor of Bogotá a year later.

Like other nonelite interest groups, Colombian labor unions have been victims of systematic violence. Between its creation in 1986 and 2001, some 3,500 members of the CUT were murdered. The majority of these killings have been attributed to paramilitary groups. Notwithstanding the demobilization of most of the paramilitaries, 78 union leaders were murdered in 2006. As of November 2007, there were 26 murders of union members during the year, indicating a considerable decline since the peak in 1996 of 275 murders. Violence against unionized labor has concentrated in the areas most characterized by acute armed conflict, abundant natural resources, and disputed territorial control between guerrillas and paramilitaries,

*Bogotá's 50-story Colpatria Tower, Colombia's tallest building,
is illuminated at night with multicolored Xenon lights.*
Courtesy Lorenzo Morales

including Antioquia, Bolívar, César, Córdoba, Magdalena, Norte de Santander, Santander, and Urabá (see Labor Markets, ch. 3).

Business Associations

At least 200 business associations exist in Colombia today, a more than twentyfold increase since the 1950s. They vary in size, specificity, geographical coverage, and longevity. The oldest Colombian business associations have existed for more than 100 years. They include the Society of Colombian Farmers (SAC) and the National Federation of Coffee Growers (Fedecafé). Several associations, such as the National Association of Industrialists (ANDI), which was formed in the 1940s, and the SAC, cover a significant portion of the national economy and represent various smaller industrial and agricultural associations. Groups such as the Association of Colombian Sugarcane Growers (Asocaña) and the Colombian Association of Flower Exporters (Asocolflores) are geographically limited to Valle del Cauca and the plains surrounding Bogotá, where sugarcane and flowers are mainly grown.

The National Business Council (CGN), founded in 1991, speaks for the most important business associations representing each sector of the Colombian economy. The members of the council account for approximately 60 percent of national production, even though only 16 associations are members. The original purpose of the CGN was to support César Gaviria's attempt to liberalize the Colombian economy and diversify the country's commercial relations.

Independent economic conglomerates also exercise significant political and economic influence, given their size and their importance for the national economy. The most important ones are the Ardila Lülle Organization (soft drinks, beer, textiles, media, and sugar); the Santo Domingo Group (beer, financial and insurance services; the media; and, until the recent sale of the national airline, air transportation); the Sarmiento Angulo Organization (construction, financial and pensions sectors, and telecommunications); and the Antioquian Syndicate (construction, the financial and insurance sectors, cement, and foodstuffs), which was the result of a concerted effort to pool business capital in its department in order to fend off potential outside competitors.

Colombian business has been relatively active in regional economic integration efforts and in issues related to the internal armed conflict. Inspired by the Mexican business sector's effective participation in the negotiations leading up to the North American Free Trade Agreement (NAFTA), various business associations participated as advisers to the Colombian delegation's negotiations at the Group of Three (G–3) talks with Mexico and Venezuela during the early 1990s. The Colombian business groups also were involved in their country's talks concerning the Free Trade Area of the Americas and the bilateral free-trade agreement, called the United States–Colombia Trade Promotion Agreement, which Colombia began negotiating with the United States in 2004. However, the U.S. Congress halted progress on the bilateral agreement because of the parapolitics scandal and still had not approved it by November 2009. Several business leaders also participated in the Colombian government's negotiating team during peace negotiations with the FARC. Despite these initiatives, the business sector is highly divided, making collective action extremely difficult.

Internal Armed Conflict and Peace Negotiations

Following nearly four decades of internal war, the Belisario Betancur administration (1982–86) attempted unsuccessfully to negotiate peace agreements with Colombian armed groups. The administration of Virgilio Barco Vargas (president, 1986–90) resumed peace efforts, and some rebel organizations viewed the proposal to convoke a national constituent assembly in a positive way, as an opportunity to participate in political reform. The example set by the M–19, the first group to lay down its arms, was followed by four others, which signed peace agreements during the Barco and Gaviria governments. During this period, approximately 3,720 guerrillas demobilized. However, neither the FARC nor the ELN, two of Colombia's oldest and largest guerrilla organizations, signed accords.

In the mid-1990s, internal armed conflict changed significantly because of Colombia's altered role in the drug trade and the intensification of the war. The dismantling of the Medellín and Cali drug cartels during the Gaviria and Samper governments gave way to fundamentally different drug-trafficking organizations, characterized by greater horizontal dispersion and low-profile tactics. Guerrilla (primarily FARC) and paramilitary units that became more directly involved in drug-related activities filled an important portion of the void created by the disappearance of these two cartels. Colombia also replaced Bolivia and Peru as the primary producer of coca leaf between 1996 and 1997. Manual-eradication campaigns in the latter two countries, the successful rupture of the air bridge that previously facilitated the illegal transport of Bolivian and Peruvian coca leaf to Colombia, and a fungus that wiped out a large percentage of Peru's coca crops pushed coca cultivation into areas of southern Colombia controlled by the FARC.

During this same period, the FARC expanded its territorial base and its personnel, and it achieved financial autonomy through increased kidnapping, extortion, and involvement in the early stages of the drug chain. Between 1996 and 1998, the rebels won a series of impressive victories that led many to suspect that the military balance had shifted in their favor. In turn, paramilitary groups, formed in the 1980s to combat the increasing threat of the guerrillas, joined together in 1995 to form the AUC, in order to gain military strength and political recognition.

The intensification of violence and combat, the legitimacy crisis surrounding Ernesto Samper's presidency, and the climate of lawlessness and government paralysis in Colombia fed popular support for new efforts to negotiate peace with the illegal armed groups. The most visible expression of that support was the Citizens' Mandate for Peace, a ballot initiative presented by different sectors of civil society in the 1997 mayoral and gubernatorial elections that received 10 million votes in favor of negotiations with the guerrillas.

Although the Pastrana administration began peace negotiations with the FARC, the process suffered from dramatic reversals. During the approximately 1,100 days that talks lasted, negotiations were frozen on six different occasions for reasons related to either paramilitary or FARC demands, acts of violence committed by the FARC, and the management of a demilitarized zone the size of Switzerland that the government created in order to hold the talks. Civil–military relations became strained as a result of Pastrana's perceived leniency in handling the zone. When the talks finally ended in Feburary 2002, it became clear that the FARC had used the zone to hide kidnap victims, conduct arms transactions, and organize military attacks on neighboring areas. Although the Colombian government also initiated peace talks with the ELN in 1999, these, too, were unsuccessful.

Pastrana's peace efforts yielded extremely disappointing results. Peace remained elusive, and extrajudicial killings, massacres, population displacements, and kidnappings continued to escalate. Although U.S. military aid provided through Plan Colombia helped reinforce the Colombian military, the FARC also drew attention to the weakness of the Colombian state by attacking local police stations, threatening government officials, attacking infrastructure, and strengthening its presence in rural cities. Notwithstanding Pastrana's promise to combat paramilitarism in the country, the AUC, too, experienced unprecedented growth during his administration. Paramilitary strength increased from 5,000–6,000 combatants in 2000 to approximately 12,000–15,000 in 2004, their territorial presence mushroomed, and their public acceptance grew.

Álvaro Uribe's election in the first round of the 2002 presidential race signaled an important shift in the Colombian political climate, mainly because his campaign was based on hard-line war rhetoric. Since he took office in August 2002, Uribe's Democratic Security Policy has focused on combating the illegal use of arms and the drug traffic, and reestablishing state control over the national territory. Specific measures include the enlargement and modernization of the armed forces, increased taxation in order to finance the war effort, the use of local informants, and recruitment of peasant soldiers. Many of these policies took effect during the state of internal commotion declared by Uribe on August 12, 2002, which expired in May 2003.

Although the Democratic Security Policy emphasizes military and security strategy within the parameters established by the law, in practice the Uribe government has found it difficult to reconcile the search for public order with the protection of fundamental rights and freedoms. International institutions, such as the UN and the European Union (EU), and numerous human rights organizations have expressed concern that many measures adopted by the Uribe government in fighting illegal armed groups may be incompatible with international humanitarian law. They particularly criticized an anti-terrorist statute presented by the government, given that it proposed to limit fundamental rights provided in the constitution, such as Article 15's "freedom of personal and family intimacy" and Article 310's "right of movement and residency," to give the police and the military extraordinary search and detention powers, and to grant judicial police powers to the military. However, on August 30, 2004, the Constitutional Court ruled the statute unconstitutional. In addition, recent annual human rights reports issued by the U.S. Department of State, the UN, and some international NGOs maintain that the Uribe government, although successful in reducing human rights violations in the country, has failed to completely sever links between members of the armed forces and paramilitary groups and to effectively punish officials involved in human rights violations and corruption.

Government negotiations with the AUC have been another key aspect of President Uribe's domestic policy. In late November 2002, the AUC announced a unilateral cease-fire to demonstrate its willingness to lay down its arms. On July 15, 2003, the government and the paramilitaries signed the Santa Fe de Ralito Agreement, whereby the AUC agreed to demobilize its forces gradually and lay down its weapons by the end of 2005. Following nearly another year of discussion of the terms of this process, formal talks began in May 2004. The government set up a zone consisting of 368 square kilometers in Santa Fe de Ralito, Córdoba, to relocate demobilized paramilitaries and conduct the talks, and an Organization of American States (OAS) mission came to verify this process. Between November 2004 and December 2005, more than 20 AUC groups amounting to more than 13,000 fighters demobilized, in addition to the demobilization of nearly 1,000 members of the paramilitary Cacique Nutibara Bloc (BCN) in November 2003.

Despite considerable progress in paramilitary demobilization, the process has been highly controversial. One of the most significant obstacles is that the paramilitaries are responsible for approximately 70 percent of the human rights violations committed in Colombia. A second obstacle derives from the AUC's direct involvement in drug trafficking, which has created internal divisions between those favoring and those opposing links with the drug business. Before the negotiations formally began in mid-2004, several AUC leaders critical of such links, including paramilitary leader Carlos Castaño Gil, were either killed or disappeared. The United States requested the extradition of four members of the AUC's negotiating team between 2003 and 2004 (see Current National Security Panorama, ch. 5).

Since 2003 several legislative proposals for the punishment of crimes of violence or combat have been presented to the Congress. For example, the Justice and Peace Law came into effect in late December 2005. However, it has been strongly criticized by an important group of Colombian legislators, NGOs, and politicians, and by international bodies for its perceived leniency to paramilitaries guilty of human rights violations. The law also has been faulted for the lack of justice and compensation provided to the victims of such crimes, and for its neglect of the problem of drug trafficking. In particular, the law allows relatively lenient sentences for paramilitary members who confess their crimes and protects them from extradition, and it lacks concrete measures for extricating former paramilitaries from the drug trade. Because of these shortcomings, in May 2006 the Constitutional Court declared several of the law's articles unconstitutional.

Several days after his second inauguration, in August 2006, President Uribe gave demobilized paramilitary leaders an ultimatum, demanding their compliance with the Justice and Peace Law as a precondition for avoiding extradition to the United States. Subsequently, nearly all of them were captured and incarcerated. The demobilization process has resulted in significant reductions in the country's rates of homicide, abduction, and forced displacement. Nevertheless, the Colombian Commission of Jurists claimed that paramilitaries, demobilized or active, had killed more than 3,000 civilians from December 1, 2002, through July 2006. Moreover, in

*Ingrid Betancourt Pulecio,
a former senator, shortly after
being rescued on July 2, 2008,
from six years of FARC captivity
Courtesy National Army, Ministry of
National Defense, Colombia*

February 2008 the Consultancy for Human Rights and Displacement reported that the 2007 displacement rate of 305,996 people constituted a large increase over 2006 and was the highest figure since 2002. In 2006 both the Colombian human rights ombudsman and the UN Office of the High Commissioner for Human Rights reported a rise in complaints of human rights violations and extrajudicial executions committed by the Colombian security forces. In most cases of extrajudicial killings, which occurred in 21 of the country's departments, civilians were portrayed as having died in combat, and the crime scene had been altered.

Attempts to conduct a humanitarian exchange of prisoners with the FARC have met with less success than the demobilization process. Since early 2006, the Colombian government and the guerrillas have discussed the possibility of such a negotiation. However, the government has consistently rejected FARC demands that the Andean towns of Florida and Pradera, located in the southeastern part of Valle del Cauca Department, be demilitarized in order to facilitate the exchange. In May 2007, this process received a push from French president Nicolas Sarkozy, who petitioned the Uribe government to release captured FARC leader Rodrigo Granda so that he could act as intermediary. In addition to freeing Granda on June 4, President Uribe announced the unilateral release of imprisoned guerrillas, apparently as a gesture of goodwill. However, on June 18, 2007, the FARC reportedly murdered 11 of the 12 assemblymen from Valle del

Cauca who were kidnapped in 2002. This incident provoked a massive protest in July 2007, when millions of Colombians marched to demand that the government and the FARC negotiate in order to liberate all kidnapping victims. In August the government appointed Liberal senator Piedad Córdoba Ruiz to facilitate the humanitarian exchange and invited Venezuelan president Hugo Chávez Frias to act as mediator. However, President Uribe interrupted the process in mid-November 2007 following several disagreements between him and Chávez concerning the latter's role, including a meeting between Chávez and FARC leader Luciano Marín Arango ("Iván Márquez") in Caracas. Nevertheless, in February 2008 the FARC released six political hostages to Chávez. Uribe easily topped that feat in July when a daring rescue operation freed Ingrid Betancourt, three U.S. hostages, and 11 military and police members.

Foreign Relations

General Foreign Policy Traits

The particular nature of Colombia's political system and the country's relations with the United States have been the main determinants of the nation's foreign policy. The major features include: the amount of power vested in the president, the traditional Liberal–Conservative consensus on foreign policy, the personalized nature of Colombian foreign relations, the degree of fragmentation in the formulation of foreign policy, the centrality of international law, a pro–United States outlook, a low international profile, and lack of popular influence or interest.

As is the case in most Latin American countries, the concentration of power in the hands of the president, the absence of a true separation of powers, and the marginal role played by the legislature in international matters historically have granted the executive a significant degree of autonomy in foreign policy. The Ministry of Foreign Relations is formally responsible for the planning and execution of the country's international relations. In addition, the president has a consultation mechanism, the presidential Advisory Commission on Foreign Relations (CARE), composed of all former elected presidents and several other members appointed by Congress and the president. This commission advises the executive on diverse international issues of strategic importance. The original purpose of CARE, founded in 1914, was to forge a consensus between the Liberal and Conservative parties over Colombia's negotiations with the United States following the independence of Panama. CARE has thus been important in nurturing the bipartisan consensus on foreign policy that has remained intact throughout most of the country's history.

The extreme personalization of the Colombian political system, along with its powerful presidency, has allowed for a marked distinction between the formal structure of the country's foreign policy apparatus and the actual execution of external affairs, which have tended to revolve around a small network of individuals directly associated with the president of the republic. In practice this situation has resulted in varying foreign policy orientations, depending on the idiosyncracies of the administration of the time, and the absence of consistent, long-term state policies.

Colombian foreign policy has been fragmentary, partly because of the perceived inefficacy of the Ministry of Foreign Relations in conducting the country's external affairs and the politicization of the foreign service. Traditionally, this ministry's activities have been concentrated in two areas: the resolution of territorial and border disputes and the conduct of conventional diplomacy in international organizations. However, the changing nature of international and domestic politics and the inability of the ministry to exercise effective coordination of the country's external affairs have led to the creation of parallel public posts, and the ascendance of alternative institutions involved in the formulation and execution of foreign policy.

The practice of conventional diplomacy by the Ministry of Foreign Relations has sometimes been driven more by the consistent application of the basic principles of international law than by specific political goals. The loss of Panama in the early twentieth century and the subsequent national humiliation led Colombian policy makers to view international law as the principal means of guaranteeing the country's sovereignty and territorial integrity. Nevertheless, the strict application of juridical principles has at times led to political inconsistency. Following the onset of the Falklands–Malvinas War in 1982, for instance, Colombia abstained, along with the United States, from voting on the application of the Inter-American Treaty of Reciprocal Assistance in support of Argentina. This decision, based entirely on legal considerations, marginalized the country from its Latin American neighbors, with which Colombia was supposedly seeking to build stronger ties.

Another central characteristic of Colombian foreign policy is the country's alignment with the United States, both in economic and political terms. Following the independence of Panama, Colombia began to seek the satisfaction of its foreign policy objectives through a close affiliation with the United States. In addition to becoming a passive recipient of U.S. policy, the country's insertion into broader international relations became strongly conditioned by its links with Washington.

The lack of public input and interest in international relations has been marked in Colombia. After the loss of Panama, for many years the country adopted an inward-looking, isolated stance in relation to the rest of the world. For the vast majority of the population, the nearly continuous existence of civil conflict since the late 1940s has compounded this historical predisposition, given that the challenges inherent in Colombia's external affairs seem to pale in comparison with the domestic situation.

Primary Doctrines of Foreign Policy

Colombia's foreign relations have tended historically to reflect two conflicting views of the country's place in the world. One position is that its peripheral, subordinate status allows marginal leeway in foreign policy and warrants strict alignment with the hegemonic power, the United States. The opposite view is that the diversification of foreign relations, in combination with more active participation, would increase Colombia's negotiating power and create relative margins of autonomy in its relations with the United States.

The tendency to align Colombia's interests with those of Washington is widely known as the *respice polum* doctrine—the term implying an attraction toward the "polar star" of the north, the United States. In practice, this principle has consistently led the country to adopt a pragmatic position of economic and political subordination to the United States. In exchange for its loyalty, the country normally has expected to receive substantial economic, political, and military assistance from the United States.

Periodically, however, Colombia also has oriented its foreign policy toward Latin American neighbors and other nations, with the goal of diversifying its international relations—the *respice similia* doctrine. Following this principle, Colombia at times has sought greater interaction with its Latin American neighbors, as well as increased leeway vis-à-vis the United States.

Beginning in the early 1980s, both the *respice polum* and the *respice similia* doctrines came to be used interchangeably, and Colombian foreign policy began to alternate between the two, depending on the administration, issue, and circumstances in question. This pendular swing largely resulted from the growing impact of domestic factors on the country's foreign policy, including the end of the National Front power-sharing agreement, decreasing political consensus, intensification of the armed conflict, growing political and social unrest, and escalation of the drug problem.

The foreign policy of the Barco administration in the late 1980s, for example, alternated between the two principles described.

Although Barco asserted Colombia's independence in relation to the United States, primarily by stressing diversification of the country's foreign relations through foreign economic diplomacy and regional economic integration, he also initiated a war against drug-trafficking organizations, a move that aligned the country with Washington's policy. The election of César Gaviria in 1990 marked the continuation of many strategies implemented during the Barco administration. In particular, President Gaviria stressed Colombia's foreign economic relations over domestic politics as a means of asserting greater autonomy and an enhanced international negotiating capacity. However, Gaviria's drug policy strayed considerably from the U.S. position.

Foreign Policy Decision Making

The constitution gives the president of the republic responsibility for the conduct of foreign policy. Despite the existence of foreign relations committees in the Senate and the House of Representatives, the Congress plays only a marginal role in making foreign policy. The Ministry of Foreign Relations is responsible for carrying out the country's external relations, for coordinating the individual governmental institutions involved in international affairs, and for resolving disputes and inconsistencies that arise between different institutional policies.

Although Colombia has had a career foreign service since the late 1960s, a considerable percentage of diplomatic posts abroad are allocated to noncareer individuals based on political considerations. In 2004 political appointees occupied more than 60 percent of Colombia's diplomatic positions. Since President Uribe assumed office in 2002, the media and the political opposition have been highly critical of his systematic use of diplomatic posts to reward support for the government's political initiatives, particularly because he came to power on an anticorruption platform. Control by political appointees over the great majority of high-level posts in the country's embassies and consulates has led to considerable inconsistency in the development of foreign-policy strategies.

The 1991 constitutional reform also included efforts to modernize public administration. One result of this process was the creation of the Ministry of Foreign Commerce (currently, Ministry of Commerce, Industry, and Tourism) and the Ministry of Environment (currently, Ministry of the Environment, Housing, and Territorial Development), responsible for Colombian foreign economic policy and environmental policy, respectively. International relations offices also came into existence in the great majority of the other ministries. The result of these changes was to shift Colombia's international relations even further into the domain of the president, to marginalize the Ministry of Foreign Relations from the most strategic areas of foreign-policy decision making, such as foreign trade and relations with the United States, and to obstruct the effective coordination of Colombia's foreign affairs. Although the advisory bodies played a considerable role in executive decision making and the management of particularly sensitive domestic and foreign-policy issues during the Barco, Gaviria, and Samper administrations, they were dismantled during the Pastrana government.

The intensification of the internal armed conflict and its entanglement with the drug trade in the mid-1990s gave the Ministry of National Defense, the military, and the National Police greater discretion in determining the country's foreign policies in matters involving the war against drugs and insurgents. The Ministry of Foreign Relations, which lacked sufficient relevant expertise, thus became further marginalized from crucial aspects of the country's international relations.

Diplomatic Relations

International Institutions

Colombia has been an active member of the UN and the OAS since their creation in the midtwentieth century and also has actively participated in a large number of other international institutions, including the Nonaligned Movement (NAM). During the Samper administration, Colombia held the NAM presidency. Samper aimed to improve the country's international image and visibility, diversify its political and commercial relations, and increase its international negotiating power. On all of these counts, Samper's efforts proved insufficient to overcome U.S. opposition.

In relations with the UN and the OAS, the foreign policy prerogatives since 1991 have been the drug problem, the armed conflict, and the human rights crisis. Colombian strategies have included insistence on the shared responsibility of the international community in combating drug trafficking, defense of the government's human rights policy, and engagement of global support for domestic objectives such as development and peace. Colombia has participated as a nonpermanent member of the UN Security Council on two occasions in recent years, in 1989–90 and 2001–2. During the first period on the council, the Colombian government criticized the U.S. invasion of Panama in December 1989 and promoted the peaceful resolution of Iraq's invasion of Kuwait on August 2, 1990, also known as the Iraq–Kuwait War, that ultimately escalated into the Gulf War in

Minister of National Defense Juan Manuel Santos Calderón resigned in order to qualify as a potential presidential candidate in the 2010 election. Courtesy Colombian presidential Web site

1991. In the second period, which coincided with particularly close relations with the United States, Colombia consistently voted as Washington would have wished. In 2003 Colombia was one of the few countries in Latin America and the world to support President George W. Bush's decision to invade Iraq. In UN General Assembly debates on the Middle East, Colombia consistently has favored the creation of a Palestinian state.

Throughout the 1990s, consecutive Colombian presidents reiterated the international community's responsibility for increased consumption of illegal substances and its duty to assist Colombia in confronting drug trafficking. One concrete result of such efforts was the approval of the Andean Trade Preference Act (1991) in the United States and the Special Cooperation Program in Europe (1990), which were designed to assist drug-producing nations in the Andean region to diversify their commercial relations. The UN General Assembly held extraordinary sessions on the drug problem in 1998, incorporating the principle of joint responsibility. In the OAS, similar measures aimed to counteract the unilateral nature of U.S. counternarcotics policies. In particular, the OAS started a multilateral evaluation mechanism within the Inter-American Drug Abuse Control Commission (CICAD) to ascertain member governments' compliance with jointly established antidrug goals.

The Samper government introduced significant changes to Colombia's human rights policy, which traditionally had ignored the existence of systematic violations. Between 1994 and 1995, Samper explicitly acknowledged that grave violations of human rights occurred in Colombia, promoted the Geneva Convention Protocol II, and accepted the state's responsibility in the 1988–90 massacres of nearly 100 people in Trujillo. In 1996 the Colombian government acknowledged the binding nature of Inter-American Commission on Human Rights rulings and agreed to open a national branch of the United Nations Office of the High Commissioner for Human Rights. Since 1998 this office has issued yearly reports, which the Colombian government has criticized, that have become increasingly critical of the country's human rights situation.

Andrés Pastrana emphasized a "diplomacy for peace" initiative to engage foreign support for the peace process that the Colombian government began with the FARC in 1999. The basic assumption of this policy was that human rights and international humanitarian law violations would subside once peace was achieved in Colombia, and, thus, that international assistance should concentrate mainly on the peace effort. Notwithstanding Pastrana's attempts to internationalize the peace process, the government was reluctant to request international mediation and the creation of a UN peace mission. Only when the process was near collapse did Colombia accept the special UN envoy as intermediary, but the envoy was ultimately unsuccessful in preventing the breakdown of the talks. The Uribe administration's relations with the UN have been tense. President Uribe has unsuccessfully sought out greater UN involvement in the internal armed conflict, mainly because the UN secretary general has insisted that all parties to the conflict and not just the government must request any measures taken to resolve the war. The UN also has been highly critical of the Uribe government's failure to comply with many of the recommendations of the Colombian Office of the High Commissioner for Human Rights for improving human rights standards in the country, and on several occasions the government has accused UN officials of being terrorist sympathizers.

The United States

Beginning in the 1980s, the salience of the drug issue in Colombia's relations with the United States reinforced the dependent relations between the two countries and crowded other issues off the agenda. Notwithstanding the willingness of previous governments to collaborate with the U.S. "war on drugs," the terror campaign that the Colombian drug cartels adopted in order to impede their extradition to the United States led the Gaviria administration to focus its drug policy on domestic objectives rather than those established by Washington. The mid-1992 escape from prison of Medellín Cartel leader Pablo Escobar Gaviria, ultimately killed in December 1993, led to increasing U.S. apprehension over the effectiveness of Colombia's drug strategy (see United States–Colombia Security Cooperation and Plan Colombia, ch. 5).

The bilateral relationship experienced a severe breakdown following the scandal over Samper's presidential campaign. The United States began to refer openly to Colombia as a "narco-democracy" and a "narco-state," and U.S. policy toward the country became markedly aggressive. In June 1996, Samper's U.S. visa was revoked, and direct relations with the Colombian president ceased altogether. However, the National Police, the Attorney General's Office, and other institutions maintained close ties with the U.S. government throughout this period and often acted independently of the Colombian executive. Although the Samper government consistently complied with Washington's antinarcotics policy, the United States, in its annual ratings of Colombia's cooperation in counternarcotics efforts, decertified the country in 1996 and 1997.

U.S. ostracism of Samper had significant domestic and international effects. Domestically, it forced the Colombian government to vigorously embrace the U.S. counternarcotics strategy while eroding Samper's internal credibility. Internationally, Colombia became identified as a pariah state, with significant political costs for the country's foreign policy. During his entire presidency, Samper received only two official state visits by heads of state—those from Venezuela and Ecuador. Ten of Samper's 12 international trips were taken in his capacity as president of the Nonaligned Movement, not as president of Colombia.

The election of Andrés Pastrana in 1998 appeared a prime opportunity for reestablishing a cooperative tone in the bilateral relationship. Before his inauguration, Pastrana met with President William Jefferson Clinton in Washington. One of Pastrana's primary goals was to press for an "opening" of the bilateral agenda beyond the issue of drugs. During Pastrana's first official visit to the White House in late October 1998, Clinton made an explicit pledge to support the Colombian peace process, and to work with international institutions to mobilize resources to support this objective. The United States also stepped up its military assistance to Colombia, which reached US$289 million in 1999, compared with only US$67 million in 1996. The increased funding was spurred by the deteriorating security situation and extensive drug trafficking.

Growing skepticism among key U.S. officials regarding the viability of the peace process led to an important shift in the Colombian government's foreign policy strategy. In particular, Plan Colombia, presented to the U.S. Congress in late 1999, addressed the drug problem instead of the peace process in order to secure U.S. support. Colombia's strategy was successful in that the aid package approved for 2000–1 amounted to more than US$1 billion. Of that funding, 80 percent consisted of military assistance for the "war on drugs," and 20 percent was for social and economic assistance related to alternative development (see Glossary), the administration of justice, human rights, and peace.

The Pastrana government's termination of the peace process with the FARC in February 2002 placed Colombia squarely within Washington's post–9/11 counterterrorist efforts. Although President Pastrana had never publicly referrred to the guerrillas as terrorists, he made this association explicit when he announced his decision to call off the peace talks. Colombia's insertion into the George W. Bush administration's global "war on terror" intensified following Álvaro Uribe's inauguration. The effect of the September 11 terrorist attacks in the United States and the end of the peace process with the FARC was to lift the previous strict distinction of U.S. drug policy between counternarcotics and counterinsurgency. This distinction had restricted all U.S. aid to Colombia to use in drug-producing regions. With the lifting of this restriction, all U.S. aid received under Plan Colombia could now be used in both counternarcotics and counterinsurgency (now called counterterrorism). Counternarcotics assistance already disbursed through Plan Colombia became available for Colombia to use in its counterterrorism efforts. And in its 2003 budget proposal, for the first time since the end of the Cold War, a U.S. administration requested military funding for activities unrelated to the drug war in Colombia, including monies to train and equip Colombian army brigades to protect the Caño Limón–Coveñas oil pipeline. Between 2001 and 2005, aid to Colombia averaged approximately US$500 million per year. Beginning in 2004, a portion of this total was used to finance Plan Patriota, the largest Colombian military offensive against armed groups in the country's history.

Increased U.S. military assistance to Colombia between 2000 and 2005 led to greater U.S. involvement in the country's internal conflict. However, extremely close bilateral ties established during this period did not eliminate altogether sources of tension in Colombian–U.S. relations. The Uribe government's negotiations with the paramilitaries are a particularly sensitive issue, given these groups' links with drug trafficking and outstanding U.S. extradition requests for several AUC members. Although the human rights situation showed some improvement, the persistence of high levels of violations and the Colombian government's failure to sever links between paramilitaries and members of the military and to punish military officials charged with human rights crimes also continue to be problematic areas.

After the November 2006 congressional elections in the United States, the tone of bilateral relations changed dramatically. Democratic control of both houses of the U.S. Congress led to greater levels of scrutiny over U.S. military aid to Colombia, higher levels of skepticism toward the existing counternarcotics strategy, and increased demands on President Uribe over human rights, particularly in relation to the murders of labor union activists. Two results of the changing political climate within the United States were the postponement of the congressional vote on the free-trade agreement (FTA) with Colombia and the readjustment of the 2008 aid package to favor social and economic assistance over military aid. In early 2009, however, President Barack H. Obama tasked the Office of the U.S. Trade Representative with addressing unresolved issues surrounding the Colombia FTA.

Latin America

Close ties with the United States have tended to overshadow Colombia's relations with the rest of the world, including its Latin American neighbors. Nevertheless, regional relations normally have been cordial, with the exception of long-standing border disputes with Venezuela and Nicaragua, and more recently with Ecuador. Colombia has signed free-trade agreements with Chile, Mexico, and Venezuela. Since the early 1990s, the country has had a strong bilateral trade agreement with Venezuela, its second-largest trading partner. The Uribe administration favors extending these bilateral trade agreements across the hemisphere.

The adoption of the *respice similia* doctrine between the late 1960s and the early 1980s contributed to the establishment of further links with similar, nearby countries, to more active participation in regional organizations, and to efforts to create institutionalized frameworks to nurture relations with regional counterparts. In addition to attempts to strengthen the Andean group, President Barco, with his Venezuelan counterpart, Carlos Andrés Pérez, initiated an ambitious program of integration in Feburary 1989, designed to expand the scope of bilateral relations beyond the border disputes that traditionally had dominated. Colombia and Ecuador formed a similar bilateral border commission several months later. The G–3, also formed in 1989, primarily had the goal of increasing political and diplomatic cooperation among Colombia, Venezuela, and Mexico.

The explicit reference in the 1991 constitution preamble to Colombia's commitment to promoting Latin American integration signaled a tentative shift in the country's perception of its role in the subcontinent. President Gaviria's Latin American policy stressed regional dynamics and diversification of Colombia's foreign relations as part of a larger economic liberalization strategy. As well as continuing President Barco's policies, under Gaviria Colombia also nurtured relations with the Caribbean, assumed the leadership of the Association of Caribbean States (ACS), and formed border commissions with Brazil in 1993, Panama in 1993, and Peru in 1994.

During the first half of the 1990s, the border commissions contributed to more productive relations with Colombia's closest neighbors, the expansion of its bilateral regional agenda, and considerable reductions in tensions with neighbors, particularly Venezuela. However, heavier emphasis on traditional border security in the mid-1990s and mixed success in implementing methods of handling shared problems at the border tended to reduce the border commissions' effectiveness and importance. More importantly, the intensification of the Colombian armed conflict between 1996 and 1997 led to the prioritization of security issues in Colombia's relations with its neighbors.

Although armed guerrillas have long been present on Colombia's borders, their presence there began to increase during the second half of the 1990s. In addition, movement beyond the borders became more frequent, as well as isolated skirmishes between Colombian groups and national forces from neighboring countries, and incidents of violence involving local border populations. The increased U.S. military presence in Colombia—following the approval of Plan Colombia in 2000—became a major cause for alarm in Brazil, Venezuela, and Ecuador, given their fear of growing U.S. intervention in the region. All five countries bordering Colombia (Brazil, Ecuador, Panama, Peru, and Venezuela) adopted varying degrees of border militarization in order to protect themselves from the spillover effects of Plan Colombia, mainly the increased numbers of displaced persons fleeing from armed violence, the growing presence of armed groups on the border, and environmental and public health problems caused by aerial fumigation of illegal crops.

The regional foreign policy focus of presidents Pastrana and Uribe has consisted largely of requesting that neighboring countries express their solidarity with Colombia's internal crisis. The Pastrana government's strategy of seeking out Latin American support for

A FARC guerrilla of the 53d Front with a South African grenade launcher, somewhere in southern Cundinamarca Department
Courtesy David Spencer Collection

both the peace process with the FARC and for Plan Colombia met with limited success, particularly given the region's wariness of U.S. involvement in Colombia. Uribe has insisted on the need for stronger regional initiatives to combat terrorism and has consistently sought the support of Latin America in declaring illegal armed groups, particularly the FARC, terrorists. On both counts, he, too, has been relatively unsuccessful. Aside from a series of diplomatic statements expressing regional support for Colombia's fight against terrorism, neighboring countries have been reluctant to publicly identify the FARC as terrorists, mostly because they disagree with President Uribe's portrayal of the Colombian crisis as a terrorist war and not an armed insurgency, and because they are averse to further involvement in the internal war. Colombia's emphasis on terrorism in its foreign policy increasingly contrasted with the foreign policies of several neighboring countries that had attempted to distance themselves from the counterterrorist and security policies of the George W. Bush administration, with which the Uribe government strongly identified.

Within this worsening climate of regional relations, Colombia's bilateral relations with Venezuela and Ecuador have been by far the most tense. Given the growing complexity of the border region, the increased presence of illegal armed groups, and the many outstanding problems characterizing Colombian–Venezuelan relations, cooperation between President Uribe and President Hugo Chávez of

Venezuela was close to impossible until 2005, particularly over security. In addition to strong ideological differences, a lack of mutual
trust between the two leaders has characterized the relationship.
Chávez views the Uribe government as part of a Colombian oligarchy that supports the Venezuelan opposition, and as an ally of the
former Bush administration, which was consistently critical of
Chávez. Colombia has suspected that President Chávez maintains
close relations with the guerrillas, a situation that reached a tipping
point in December 2004, when FARC leader Rodrigo Granda was
apprehended on Venezuelan territory and secretly moved to Colombia for official capture. Following the withdrawal of the Venezuelan
ambassador in Colombia and the temporary suspension of bilateral
trade relations, the Colombian government offered an unofficial
apology. Recognizing the importance of the bilateral relationship to
both countries, the two presidents worked to restore mutual confidence and were largely successful, vide Chávez's role between 2005
and 2008 as mediator in the humanitarian exchange with the FARC.

Tensions between Colombia and Ecuador revolve mainly around
the fumigation of coca crops in the border region—particularly the
alleged public-health problems and environmental damage it
causes—and the presence of Colombian illegal armed fighters who
commit acts of violence in Ecuadorian territory. In contrast to
Colombia's relations with Venezuela, a similar rapport does not exist
between presidents Uribe and Rafael Correa Delgado, nor do the two
countries enjoy adequate degrees of mutual confidence (see International and Regional Security Relations, ch. 5).

Europe

Colombia's relations with Europe, although long-standing, have
been of secondary importance compared to its relations with the
United States and within the region and have mostly been limited to
trade and investment flows. However, in the years following 1990
several factors converged to increase the relevance of both bilateral
and multilateral relations with the continent. First, approval of the
Special Cooperation Program in Europe, in addition to economic liberalization and diversification of Colombia's foreign economic relations, led to considerable growth in trade and investment, thus
strengthening Colombian interdependence with Europe. Second, the
prioritization in the early 1990s of issue areas in Europe that were of
lower priority to the United States, including human rights, development, and the environment, led to increased efforts on the part of
Colombia to consolidate its political relations with the continent. In
addition to government interaction, a significant number of Colom-

bian NGOs began to work directly with specific European official and private-sector organizations. Third, the internationalization of the Colombian armed conflict in the late 1990s led to growing European involvement in peace and humanitarian assistance efforts in the country. Lastly, interregional negotiations between the Andean Community of Nations (see Glossary), of which Colombia has been an active member, and the EU have opened additional forms of multilateral interaction.

Europe's involvement in Colombia grew noticeably during the Pastrana administration as a result of the president's efforts to internationalize solutions to the country's armed conflict. The Colombian government sought to counteract the excessive weight of military factors in the Plan Colombia package by requesting social, development, and diplomatic assistance from Europe. Initial European participation in the peace effort was clouded precisely by skepticism concerning Plan Colombia, seen as a U.S.-inspired counternarcotics strategy with some objectionable aspects such as aerial spraying of coca crops.

In 2000 Europe declared explicit support for the peace process and government efforts to seek a negotiated settlement (notwithstanding substantial reservations) while simultaneously rejecting U.S. intervention in Colombia. European governments participated in peace talks with both the FARC and the ELN guerrillas, while total European contributions for peace, humanitarian assistance, and development efforts during the Pastrana and the first Uribe administrations amounted to approximately 350 million euros. This level of support made Europe the principal source of international cooperation funding in Colombia.

Colombia's relations with Europe deteriorated following the termination of the peace talks with the FARC and Uribe's electoral victory. The EU has been critical of the Uribe government's hard-line counterterrorist language, is suspicious of its Democratic Security Policy, and has systematically criticized its human rights record and its stigmatization of NGOs accused by Uribe of supporting terrorists. Europe also has been unwilling to support negotiations with the paramilitaries, because of the lenient treatment that they stand to receive when they lay down their arms and the lack of adequate reparations and justice for the victims of human rights abuses committed by them.

A July 2003 meeting, held in London by Colombian and European government officials, NGOs, and representatives of the UN, made European assistance contingent on Colombia's compliance with a series of 24 UN recommendations for improving the country's human rights situation. The London declaration also was celebrated

widely in Colombia as a step forward in securing European cooperation. However, the Uribe government's failure to comply with many
of the UN's recommendations has constituted a serious obstacle to
progress. Uribe's antiterrorist discourse received a tepid reception
during his official visit to Europe in the first half of 2004.

Several developments within Europe itself also account for the
state of Colombian–European relations. The replacement of right-
winger José María Aznar as Spanish prime minister by the socialist,
José Luis Rodríguez Zapatero, in early 2004, prompted Spain to distance itself from Colombia while seeking closer diplomatic relations
with ideologically sympathetic Latin American leaders in Brazil and
Venezuela. In addition, the expansion of the EU's membership in
2004 and later, and continuing debate concerning its constitution,
has drawn the continent's attention closer to home. French president
Nicolas Sarkozy's interest in Colombia and a proposal to exchange
FARC prisoners for Ingrid Betancourt was directly related to domestic pressures to free the former presidential candidate, who is also a
French citizen, from FARC captivity.

Asia

In comparison to other Latin American countries, Colombia's
relations with Asia traditionally have been weak, notwithstanding
their formal commencement in the early twentieth century, in the
case of Japan. Unlike Chile, Mexico, or Peru, Colombia also has
been slow to strengthen its links with this part of the world, in particular with China, in the post–Cold War period.

Barco initiated diplomatic outreach with two visits to Asia in
1987 and 1989, followed by a visit by Gaviria to Japan in 1994 and a
tour to China, South Korea, and Indonesia by Samper in 1996. In
1994 the Pacific Basin Economic Council and the Pacific Economic
Cooperation Council accepted Colombia as a member. Although the
Samper government lobbied hard for Colombian admittance to the
Asia–Pacific Economic Cooperation (APEC), in 1998 this organization decided to freeze its membership for a period of 10 years, to
concentrate on achieving its main goal of promoting economic dyna-
mism and growth among its members.

Japan continues to be Colombia's primary trade and investment
partner in Asia, although current levels of interaction are low, given
visa requirements for Colombian travelers to Japan and what is perceived by Japanese investors as an unfavorable business climate in
Colombia. However, private-sector interest in China has grown considerably during the past five years. In 2003 about 400 representatives of the Colombian private sector participated in the Guangdong
Sheng Fair, the most important commercial fair in China. In contrast

to the private sector, Colombian diplomatic coverage in Asia has been reduced, with the closing of embassies in Thailand, New Zealand, Australia, and Indonesia, and of the consulate in Singapore in 2003. In April 2005, President Uribe, accompanied by a commission composed of more than 25 government representatives, 140 private-sector representatives, and 40 university presidents, conducted an official visit to China and Japan. Additionally, following the end of APEC's freeze of new country members in December 2006, the Colombian government requested that the other members of the institution support its application for membership.

Outlook

The Colombian political system continues to pose a major paradox. The country has been able to maintain formal democracy and relatively successful levels of economic, political, and social development notwithstanding the existence of prolonged armed conflict, humanitarian crises, human rights violations, drug trafficking, corruption, and social and economic inequality. Colombia's political future is largely tied to this contradiction. Indeed, as one of the few countries in Latin America with an uninterrupted democracy for nearly 50 years, Colombia has state institutions that can be considered fairly robust and stable.

The stated goal of President Uribe's Democratic Security Policy is precisely to put an end to the internal armed conflict while reinforcing democratic governance, yet the Uribe administration's "war against terrorism" has tended to undermine fundamental constitutional rights and guarantees, while stigmatizing certain sectors of Colombian and international society. These include local and global human rights organizations, ethnic communities, labor unions, journalists, and international institutions such as the Office of the High Commissioner for Human Rights, which have been critical of Uribe's leadership. Negotiations with the paramilitaries, although a fundamental component of peace, threaten to pardon heinous human rights crimes committed by these groups with inadequate reparations for the victims. Of equal concern are the paramilitaries' close ties with the drug trade.

The Uribe government's hardhanded strategy earned it high domestic approval and the support of the George W. Bush administration in the United States, which regarded the Colombian president as a key ally in the region. However, the U.S. Congress and opposition political groups within Colombia, including the Liberal Party and the Alternative Democratic Pole, have become increasingly critical of the Colombian president. The country's political future will depend largely on the outcome of the parapolitics scandal and the internal armed conflict. Although the Uribe government has argued at home and abroad that the ties between politicians and paramilitaries came to light as a result of the Democratic Security Policy, the fact that several Uribe appointees and numerous members of the government's political coalition in the Congress, including the president's cousin, have been accused of or are under investigation for such links does not sit well among the Colombian president's critics.

The formal participation of former paramilitaries in political activities, which is forbidden by law until they confess their crimes and serve their sentences, will also have profound effects on Colombian politics. One of the most acute problems during the 2006 and 2007 elections was precisely that of paramilitary influence in electoral campaigns. In addition to their legal and illegal participation in the electoral process, paramilitary penetration of public institutions, in particular outside Colombia's larger cities, poses a considerable threat to the democratic state of law.

It is feasible that informal talks with the ELN guerrillas—begun in October 2005 in Cuba—will eventually culminate in a peace agreement. However, peace negotiations with the FARC are unlikely in the short term. Given the high-profile role of the United States in the Colombian conflict, the evolution of U.S. policy toward negotiations with the paramilitaries, Plan Colombia, and the war against terrorism will also continue to influence the country's political scenario. The outcome of the 2008 U.S. presidential election might have seemed likely to lead to renewed criticism from Washington of President Uribe's handling of a number of issues, from human rights to the parapolitics scandal. Surprisingly perhaps, Colombia–United States relations appeared not to be especially strained during the first eight months of the administration of President Barack H. Obama. Neither did the approval by the Colombian Congress of Uribe's referendum proposal, which could allow him to run in the 2010 presidential election, appear to have any adverse impact on Colombia's relations with the new U.S. administration. President Uribe's bid for a third term depended on the outcome of the Constitutional Court's review of the referendum proposal and other political factors affecting his decision.

*   *   *

Frank Safford and Marco Palacios offer an interesting sociological and historical discussion of Colombia's spacial fragmentation and the subsequent difficulties that the country has encountered in constructing the nation-state in *Colombia: Fragmented Land, Divided Society.* An exhaustive analysis of political violence in Colombia can be found in *Violencia política en Colombia: De la nación fragmentada a la construcción del estado* by Ingrid Bolívar, Fernán E. González, and Teófilo Vásquez. *El conflicto, callejón con salida: Informe nacional de desarrollo humano para Colombia,* a UNDP multiauthor report edited by Hernando Gómez Buendía, offers a particularly useful study of the development of the armed conflict in Colombia and the distinct avenues available for its peaceful resolution. Ann C. Mason and Luis Javier Orjuela's volume, *La crisis política colombiana: Mas que un conflicto armado y un proceso armado de paz,* conducts a thorough examination of the Colombian crisis, including studies of the origins and construction of the state, the evolution of the armed conflict, the development of national and local political dynamics, and the role of global factors. In *Una democracia asediada: Balance y perspectivas del conflicto armado en Colombia,* Eduardo Pizarro Leongómez discusses the protracted nature of the armed conflict in Colombia and its effects on the development of political and social dynamics in the country. A useful analysis of judicial power in Colombia is provided by *El caleidoscopio de las justicias en Colombia: Análisis socio-jurídico,* a two-volume study edited by Boaventura de Sousa Santos and Mauricio García Villegas. The contributors analyze the transformations in the judicial system introduced by the 1991 constitution and their primary strengths and weaknesses.

In *Síntesis,* the National University of Colombia's Institute for Political Studies and International Relations (IEPRI) publishes excellent annual analyses of Colombia's principal political, social, and economic phenomena. *OASIS,* also published yearly, by the Externado University of Colombia, provides analyses of Colombian foreign policy that address a diverse range of issue areas and geographic regions. Martha Ardila, Diego Cardona, and Arlene B. Tickner's volume, *Prioridades y desafíos de la política exterior colombiana,* provides a comprehensive analysis of Colombia's foreign relations during the decade up to 2002. (For further information and complete citations, see Bibliography.)

Chapter 5. National Security

Top: An indigenous geometric design, C. Jaramillo Collection, Pasto
Bottom: An indigenous geometric design, Museo Zambrano, Pasto
Courtesy Carlos Arturo Jaramillo Giraldo, Murmullos del lenguaje Uik: La práctica del mopa mopa: De lo recolector a lo sedentario, *Medellín, 1986, 79, 81*

COLOMBIA'S NATIONAL SECURITY situation is the most complex in Latin America. A protracted armed conflict, chronic criminal and political violence, and an illegal drug industry that supplies 80 percent of the world's cocaine have combined to create a security predicament of multiple dimensions. Colombia has an established tradition of political violence, as evidenced by the War of the Thousand Days (1899–1902), the period of sectarian violence called La Violencia (1946–58), and the internal armed conflict since the 1960s. Nevertheless, the country's security scenario in the first decade of the twenty-first century involves a multifaceted maze of threats, human rights violations, and diverse forms of violence. Colombia's security problems are largely internal in nature, and yet they are also part of complex transnational dynamics related to global markets for illicit drugs and small arms.

Following a failed peace process with the Revolutionary Armed Forces of Colombia (FARC) in the late 1990s, the government pursued a two-pronged counterinsurgency strategy. It called for eradicating the insurgency by means of a military offensive designed to defeat the guerrillas, or at least to force them into negotiations, and continuing the "war on drugs" to seek elimination of the insurgents' primary source of financing. This policy was implemented with significant U.S. military assistance dedicated to the aerial fumigation of coca crops and military training. Plan Colombia later evolved into a more comprehensive counterinsurgency and counterterrorism posture with an increased U.S. military presence committed to strengthening Colombia's armed forces and their fighting ability. Since 2003 the government has also engaged in negotiations with the right-wing paramilitaries to achieve their disarmament and demobilization. Although the administration of Álvaro Uribe Vélez (president, 2002–6, 2006–10) has improved Colombia's security situation, negotiations with the FARC have remained deadlocked, and the process of demobilization of paramilitaries also has been fraught with difficulties.

The Military

Historical Background

Colombia's current armed forces had their origins in the militia organized in 1811 by a rebellious league called the United Provinces of New Granada (see Breaking the Spanish Connection, ch. 1). The force—composed of poor, uneducated, campesino volunteers—was divided into infantry and cavalry units trained by a senior officer corps. The constitutional charter of 1811 assigned the power to raise and organize the army to the nascent Congress, which proved supportive of the military. Spanish military structure and traditions were adopted and plans laid for the creation of an academy to regularize military training. Many key military leaders died during the first phase of the war for independence that lasted from 1810 to 1816, and their troops gradually came under the command of Simón Bolívar Palacios.

Unlike the military of several Latin American countries, the Colombian forces played a subordinate role during the first few decades of the nineteenth century. A strong antimilitarist tradition emerged in the postindependence period among the nation's civilian leaders, who wanted to prevent the military from becoming an autonomous power. The country's two-party system, which limited the leading party's power to establish absolute control over the military, also held military influence in check. It was customary for the opposing party to raise its own army. Government opposition to the development of a strong professional military led to the transformation of the armed forces in the 1860s into a sort of Colombian national guard as well as to the creation of official state-level militias with marked sectarian loyalties.

When factional fighting subsided in the 1880s, the government approved the first laws governing the military and defined its constitutional responsibilities of providing for domestic order and external defense. The constitution of 1886 also called for a program of universal male conscription, which was not enforced until the early twentieth century. These measures encouraged limited progress in military discipline and morale. However, the 1899 revolt by the Liberal Party (Partido Liberal), which marked the start of the War of the Thousand Days, set back these military-reform efforts (see The War of the Thousand Days and Loss of Panama, 1899–1903, ch. 1).

Modernization of the Military

A government campaign to revitalize the country following the civil war included plans for the reorganization and modernization of the armed forces. Although there were concerns over border tensions with Venezuela, efforts to modernize the military at the start of the twentieth century were motivated by an interest in creating a nonpartisan, professional, and, above all, apolitical military. The reforms had two main objectives: to subordinate the armed forces to civilian authority and to purge the military of the political rivalry between supporters of the Liberal Party and those of the Conservative Party

(Partido Conservador). The centerpiece of the first military reorganization that began in 1907 was the establishment of education centers to provide nonpartisan training in doctrine, tactics, and technology. Chilean military officers trained in the Prussian tradition developed the curricula in the newly founded Military Cadet School (Esmic), the Superior War College (Esdegue), and the Naval Cadet School (Enap). The first Military Aviation School (Emavi) began operating in 1921 as the flight school of the newly established Colombian Air Force (FAC). In 1933 Emavi moved from Flandes, Tolima, to its present location in Cali and, in the late 1950s, named itself after Marco Fidel Suárez (president, 1918–21). The second military aviation school, the Army Aviation Branch School (Escuela de Arma de Aviación del Ejército), also opened in 1921. Meanwhile, the government widened the conscription base and set new standards for salaries and promotions.

After this flurry of reform activity, official interest in the armed forces began to wane. On December 6, 1928, the government called on the army to suppress a banana workers' strike against the United Fruit Company (see Decline of the Conservative Hegemony, ch. 1). The army's use of extensive and indiscriminate force in that incident, in what came to be known as the "massacre of the banana workers," raised doubts as to the military's professionalism. During the 1932–34 border conflict with Peru over Leticia, Colombia had serious problems with military readiness, which spurred increases in ground forces and military spending in the 1930s.

The Role of the United States

The United States played a major role in the modernization of the armed forces in the second half of the twentieth century. The first U.S. military adviser in Colombia counseled the National Navy in the defense of ports and arms procurement during the conflict with Peru over Leticia. In 1938 a U.S. naval mission arrived, charged with planning for the defense of the Panama Canal in case of German aggression. This mission was followed in the 1940s by the construction of air and naval bases on Colombian territory and Colombia's participation in the Inter-American Defense Board. Military cooperation entered a new phase in 1950 with Colombia's decision to support the United Nations (UN) action in Korea by sending an infantry battalion and a warship in 1951. With the Colombian battalion attached to a U.S. infantry regiment, the Korean theater represented another opportunity for Colombian troops to receive training from their U.S. counterparts. In 1952 the Military Assistance Agreement between the United States and Colombia established a U.S. mission in Colombia's Ministry of War, and Colombian officers began training in counterinsurgency operations at the U.S. Army School of the Americas in the Panama Canal Zone. Two years later, Colombia founded the first counterguerrilla-training center in Latin America, followed in 1960 by the establishment of the organization that later became the Superior Council on National Defense and Security (CSSDN).

Partisanship and the Armed Forces

Efforts to modernize the armed forces remained thwarted by the persistent partisanship of certain segments of the military. Despite efforts to depoliticize the forces, many high-ranking officers remained loyal to the Conservative Party, whereas the lower ranks were more partial to the Liberal Party. In 1944 disgruntled mid-ranking officials attempted to overthrow Alfonso López Pumarejo (president, 1934–38, 1942–45) for his reformist political agenda. Although the coup attempt failed for lack of support by the military command, the action suggested that the military's restraint from political involvement was deteriorating.

In the late 1940s, the military abandoned any pretense of neutrality when the Conservative government of Luis Mariano Ospina Pérez (president, 1946–50) openly employed the army to harass the Liberal opposition. Conservative officers received favorable treatment in terms of salaries and promotions, whereas many of their Liberal counterparts were discriminated against, cashiered, or sent to fight in Korea. This split echoed a broader rupture within Colombia's law and order institutions, as the police in Bogotá aligned themselves with the Liberal Party, whereas rural police were loyal to the Conservatives. The principles of modernization and professionalism in the military were dealt a severe blow following the assassination of presidential contender Jorge Eliécer Gaitán in 1948, when the army was called out to help defend Bogotá after the police sided with the rioters protesting events.

In 1953, at the height of La Violencia, Colombia's military leaders overthrew the archconservative Laureano Eleuterio Gómez Castro (president, 1950–53), placing General Gustavo Rojas Pinilla (president, 1953–57) in power. Despite having engineered the only successful coup d'état since the War of the Thousand Days, the military command was reluctant to accept Rojas's efforts to involve the services in political affairs. Although he dubbed his administration the "government of the armed forces," opposition by military leaders forced Rojas to jettison plans to create a political support group directed by the army chief of staff. In the midst of growing tension with top military leaders, Rojas transferred certain powers from the

General Command to the Ministry of War and the army's General Staff.

Colombia's armed forces were strengthened overall during the Rojas dictatorship. Troop strength more than doubled in the 1950s to 32,000 soldiers, and reforms with lasting repercussions included the reorganization of the National Police under the direct control of the military. In addition to implementing a one-year obligatory military service, Rojas created the Military Industry (Indumil) as an autonomous company to manage the domestic production of weapons and ammunition, established two new training schools, including the Tolemaida training base modeled after Fort Benning, founded the Military Club for officers, built the military hospital, and created the military's National Administration Center.

In 1957 the military again intervened in politics. Dissatisfaction with the internal situation, rising popular discontent, and growing concern that corruption charges against the general would further tarnish its image led the army to overthrow Rojas in a bloodless coup. His successor ruled with a military junta that one year later turned power over to the first National Front government (see The National Front, 1958–78, ch.1).

Organizing for Counterinsurgency

During the four administrations of the National Front, the military largely submitted to civilian power and respected the political status quo, vindicating the professional reputation of the armed forces. Attempts by the military to become more active in national politics were sporadic and not widely supported. This shift in the military's attitude to its role in relation to the civil government was closely linked with national security developments beginning in the 1960s. The evolution of a counterinsurgent, anticommunist posture to meet the growing guerrilla threat not only shaped the strategic evolution of the armed services but also became a unifying ideological force for the military, replacing Liberal and Conservative loyalties. Consensus regarding the new internal enemy allowed the military finally to overcome the factionalism that had been the principal obstacle to achieving a modern and professional force since Colombia's founding. Changing the name of the Ministry of War to the Ministry of National Defense in 1965 reflected the military's modernizing trend, although army officers still controlled the ministry.

Military organization and operations became increasingly responsive to the necessities of irregular warfare. The first mobile brigade and elite counterguerrilla force began operating in the 1960s, and the army restructured into divisions in the late 1980s. Among the institutional reforms enacted by the administration of César Augusto Gaviria Trujillo (president, 1990–94), the most significant was the creation of a civilian Ministry of National Defense that established political authority over security and defense affairs, restricting the autonomous power of the military. In the late 1990s, the changing nature of the internal conflict was the impetus for a major military reform that consisted of increases in personnel, resources, territorial presence, and intelligence capabilities. Significant defeats at the hands of the FARC between 1996 and 1998 and a general deterioration in public order were apparently due to the military's still-inadequate preparation for irregular warfare and a posture that was dispersed, static, and defensive. The population held the military in low regard because of a poor human rights record and a passive attitude to paramilitarism. At the turn of the century, Colombia implemented important reforms in military doctrine and institutional structure emphasizing a force that was professional and mobile, with an effective offensive capacity supported by air transport and air combat, and with improved intelligence and advanced combat technology. The reforms of the administration of Andrés Pastrana Arango (president, 1998–2002) included a troop buildup, additional divisions, and the mobile brigades, as well as the creation of the army's first aviation brigade.

Although the military was one of the least-respected institutions in Colombia in the 1990s, with only a 34-percent favorable rating with the public in 1994, by 2003 it had an 82-percent public approval rating. The surge in popularity resulted from a combination of the increase in military successes and expanded territorial coverage of the armed forces, the army's recovery of the demilitarized zone from the FARC, and the popularity of Álvaro Uribe's get-tough policy (see Current National Security Panorama; National Security Doctrines and Policies, this ch.).

Constitutional Authority

The 1991 constitution establishes the president of the Republic of Colombia as the head of state, head of government, and commander in chief of the armed forces, which include the National Police. According to Article 189, the president's functions in the area of defense and security are to direct foreign relations and, as commander in chief of the Armed Forces of the Republic (Fuerzas Armadas de la República), to direct the Public Force (Fuerza Pública), protect public order, lead military operations during war, and defend the country's external security. Article 216 defines the Public Force as being composed of the Military Forces (Fuerzas Militares) and the National Police. Article 217 establishes that the Military Forces are permanent and made up of the army, navy, and air force, whose collective mission is to defend Colombia's sovereignty, territory, and constitutional order. The constitution also establishes the executive's authority in the matter of states of exception. It is within the president's legal mandate to declare a state of external war (Article 212) to respond to foreign aggression, defend Colombia's sovereignty, meet the requirements of a war in which Colombia is involved, or reestablish internal order. A state of internal commotion grants exceptional powers to the executive when the ordinary powers of the National Police are inadequate to maintain public order. Article 213 permits this state of internal commotion to be declared for a period of 90 days and to be renewed twice. A declaration of war (Article 212) and a state of emergency (Article 215) require cabinet and Senate authorization.

The 1991 constitution, like its predecessor, stipulates that the Military Forces and National Police are nondeliberative. The armed forces are legally prohibited from political activity, and personnel have no right of assembly for political purposes. Citizens in active police and military service also have no right to vote.

Organization of the Armed Forces

As commander in chief, the president appoints the minister of national defense (see fig. 7). One of the most significant reforms of the Gaviria presidency was changing the head of the ministry from a military to a civilian post, breaking a practice that had been uninterrupted since 1953, and in 1991 Rafael Pardo Rueda became minister of national defense. The Ministry of National Defense directs the military and police forces by formulating and implementing defense and security policies. The general commander of the Military Forces of Colombia, the highest-ranking military position (held by General Freddy Padilla de León in late 2009), has maximum authority for the planning and strategic management of all operational and administrative matters and exercises a legal mandate over the armed forces through the minister of national defense, the second in command after the president. In practice, however, the president has routinely issued orders directly to the general commander.

The General Command of the Military Forces consists of the commander and his General Staff, the Advisory Group, and offices of the inspector general, general adjutant, strategic planners, and legal advisers. The Supreme Military Tribunal (TSM), which is headed by the general commander of the Military Forces, also reports to the General Command, but its judgments in some cases may be appealed to the Supreme Court of Justice. Directly under the General Command are the deputy commander and the Joint General Staff, with the

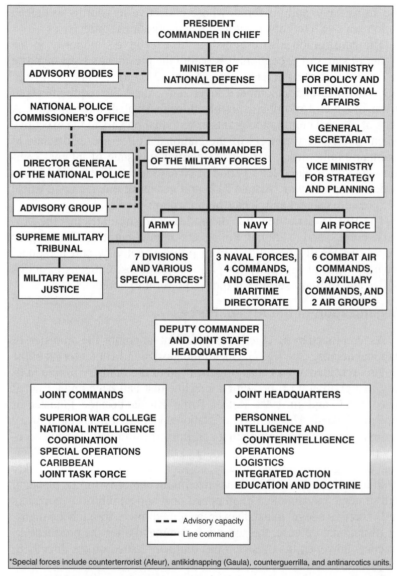

Figure 7. Organization of the Ministry of National Defense and the Public Force, 2009

directorates for general military health, administration and finance, the United Action Groups for Personal Freedom (Gaula), as well as the Commercial Arms Control Department, and the five joint commands (see Joint Commands, this ch.). The General Command exercises direct authority over the three military services, and each service commander is in direct line of command. The deputy commanders of each service are also the chiefs of staff, who together constitute the Joint Chiefs of Staff and report directly to the General Command, rather than being part of the chain of command. The chairman of the Joint Chiefs of Staff assists the General Command in the coordination of operational and administrative affairs of the three services and the Urban Counterterrorist Special Forces Group (Afeur). Roughly paralleling the U.S. military, the Joint Chiefs of Staff is divided into six departments, or headquarters (*jefaturas*), for personnel (J–1), intelligence and counterintelligence (J–2), operations (J–3), logistics (J–4), integrated action (J–5), and education and doctrine (J–6).

The establishment of the joint command structures represented an important step toward the implementation of a major reform of the Colombian military modeled on the command structure of the U.S. Armed Forces. Five joint commands under the general commander of the Military Forces are those of the Superior War College, National Intelligence Coordination, Special Operations, Caribbean, and Joint Task Force. The Joint Task Force Command includes Joint Task Force Omega (Fuerzas de Tarea Conjunta Omega), which was created in 2003 by recruiting the best 15,000 troops in the military. Initially created to support Plan Patriota, it began supporting Plan Consolidación (Consolidation Plan) on December 10, 2006. Headquartered at Larandia Air Force Base in Caquetá Department, Omega's mission is to engage in counterinsurgency operations, especially against the FARC and its leaders.

The Military Forces have been gradually introducing a sweeping organizational change, which calls for replacing the current structure with five joint operational commands: Pacific (covering the western coastline and Ecuadorian border); Caribbean (north coast and Panamanian border); Eastern (frontier with Venezuela); Central (the Andean heartland of Colombia); and the existing Joint Task Force Omega, expanded to cover the southeast, including the borders with Peru and Brazil. The new organization is designed to encourage closer cooperation among different branches of the military and to ensure dedicated resources of troops and naval and air assets in all zones. However, as of mid-2009 it appeared that the proposed new organization had been either only partially implemented or possibly further modified.

The Superior Council on National Defense and Security, formed by the executive branch in 1992, is an advisory body on defense and security matters. Chaired by the president, the CSSDN counts as its members the minister of national defense, the general commander of the Military Forces, the director general of the National Police, the director of the Administrative Security Department (DAS), the minister of interior and justice, the minister of foreign relations, and the heads of two congressional committees—constitutional affairs and defense and international relations. The CSSDN advises on the planning and execution of defense and security policy and is responsible for coordinating the various civilian and military entities involved in national security.

Ministry of National Defense

The Ministry of National Defense is responsible for the administration and planning of security and defense policy. The ministry manages administrative functions related to policy execution, including the defense budget, ministry personnel, and military procurement contracts. In coordination with the president and the military command, the institution has definitive responsibility for the formation of national security and defense strategies. The ministry also works with the Ministry of Foreign Relations in the negotiation of international agreements on national security and is responsible for presenting bills to the Congress of the Republic (Congreso de la República) that relate to defense.

Reporting to the minister of national defense are the General Secretariat, which is responsible for internal management, including the ministry's budget, human resources, legal matters, anticorruption programs, and veterans' affairs; the Vice Ministry for Policy and International Affairs, which also serves as the ministry's liaison with the presidency, Congress, other ministries, and the press; and the Vice Ministry for Strategy and Planning. Both the military and the National Police are fully integrated into the Ministry of National Defense. Reporting up through the General Command are the commanders of the three military services and the joint commands. The director general of the National Police is also under the direct authority of the ministry, as is the National Police Commissioner's Office.

Various advisory bodies also report directly to the minister of national defense. These include the Joint Advisers of the Military Forces and the National Police, the Advisory Council on Military Justice, the National Council Against Kidnapping, the Superior Health Council of the Military Forces and the National Police, the Administrative Development Committee, the Internal Control System Coordinating Committee, and a Human Resources Commission. Also under the auspices of the ministry is the Superintendency of Guard Forces and Private Security Companies (SVSP). This semi-autonomous agency, headed by a lawyer, monitors and inspects the several hundred guard forces of companies and the approximately 3,500 private security companies. The SVSP operates in close cooperation with the National Police. The ministry additionally supervises the activities of a large number of entities that do not depend on it financially, including the Nueva Granada Military University, the military and police retirement funds, the Central Military Hospital, the Military Club, and Indumil.

Military Services

Military personnel are under the authority of the general commander of the Military Forces. The General Command headquarters, as well as those of the three services, are located in the ministry's complex in Bogotá. The military reserves are made up of those who have fulfilled their military service, retired officers and noncommissioned officers (NCOs), and civilians who have undergone special reservist training. According to London's International Institute for Strategic Studies (IISS), in 2008 Colombia's Military Forces were made up of 267,231 active personnel (army, 43,013 career active-duty plus 183,339 conscripts, for a total of 226,352; navy, 23,515 plus 7,214 conscripts, for a total of 30,729; and air force, 10,150). The IISS total does not include naval aviation, 146; and marines, 14,000. The ability to mobilize the reserve force is considered limited.

The Army

The effective combat strength of the National Army (Ejército Nacional) is considerably less than that suggested by the total strength figures. Despite having a total of 226,352 members in 2008, well over half of the army, or 128,818 personnel in early 2009, could not legally be used for combat duty because they were serving their obligatory military service. In 2008 the army ranks included approximately 7,000 officers and 26,000 NCOs.

The general commanding the army is assisted by a staff consisting of a chief of army operations and an inspector general. The army deputy commander is also the army chief of staff. This general oversees the directorates of planning and information and coordinates operations, logistics, human development, and education and doctrine.

Various special units are under the direct authority of the General Command of the Military Forces. The 3d Colombian Battalion, an infantry unit comprising 31 officers, 58 NCOs, 265 soldiers, and some civilians, is assigned to the multinational observer force in the Sinai Peninsula. Between 120 and 150 Colombian soldiers are likely to have joined the Spanish contingent deployed in Afghanistan by the end of 2009. The Aviation Brigade is made up of a helicopter battalion, an aircraft battalion, and the army's aviation school. The Army Aviation School (EAE), originally known as the Army Aviation

Branch School, has been part of the brigade since 2003. The EAE moved from Tolemaida to Bogotá's El Dorado International Airport in 2004. The army's air capacity has expanded by more than 300 percent since 1999 as a result of aircraft contributions by Plan Colombia, even though the army's fleet size has remained fairly constant (see table 5, Appendix). The Counternarcotics Brigade with four separate battalions, created as a part of Plan Colombia, also reports directly to the commander of the army.

By October 2007, the army had 20 mobile brigades, each containing four counterguerrilla battalions of approximately 375 personnel each, with the capacity to undertake special missions in any part of the national territory and to engage in night operations. Six of these counterguerrilla units are special infantry battalions trained to operate in high-altitude zones frequently utilized by insurgents as strategic corridors. The first high-mountain battalion succeeded in driving the FARC out of its traditional stronghold in the Sumapaz region to the south of Bogotá. The Rapid Deployment Force (Fudra) is an elite counterinsurgent unit made up of the 1st, 2d, and 3d mobile brigades with their own transport capacity and air support.

In 1996 the army formed the United Action Groups for Personal Freedom (Gaula), an elite force dedicated to combating kidnapping and extortion. There are 16 army Gaula units throughout the country, each composed of individuals trained to carry out rescue operations of kidnap victims and to dismantle criminal organizations. The Gaula units also include members of the DAS, the Technical Investigation Corps (CTI), the crime scene unit, and the Attorney General's Office (Fiscalía General de la Nación). Plan Meteoro (Meteor Plan) units, which President Uribe founded in 2002 in order to reestablish security on the country's roads and provide protection to motorists, also came under the General Command of the Military Forces.

In 2007 the army had seven divisions assigned to territorial regions. The divisions are organized into brigades, which in turn comprise some 320 battalions. The 1st Division is headquartered in Santa Marta and has jurisdiction over the northern departments of Atlántico, Magdalena, La Guajira, César, Bolívar, Córdoba, Sucre, Antioquia, and northern Chocó. This division has five fixed brigades, with regional headquarters in Barranquilla (the 2d), Medellín (the 4th), Valledupar (the 10th), Montería (the 11th), and Carepa (the 17th). The 4th Mobile Brigade, with three counterguerrilla battalions and two Afeur units, is also assigned to this divisional jurisdiction.

The 2d Division operates out of Bucaramanga and has responsibility for Santander, Northern Santander, Arauca, parts of Antioquia, parts of Bolívar, and the southern region of César. The division has three brigades in Bucaramanga (the 5th), Puerto Berrío (the 14th),

*Soldiers from a Plan Meteoro company after arriving in Mocoa,
Putumayo Department. Since their formation in 2002, seven Plan Meteoro
companies have practically eliminated highway violence and
have also assisted in counternarcotics operations.*
Courtesy David Spencer
*An army special jungle group training in
Facatativá, Cundinamarca Department*
Courtesy Narcotics Affairs Section Office, U.S. Embassy, Bogotá

297

and Arauca (the 18th). Various special units also operate in this division, including the 2d Artillery Airborne Defense Battalion, the 5th and 22d mobile brigades with a total of nine counterguerrilla battalions, the Plan Meteoro 3d Company, and two Afeur units.

Cali is home to the 3d Division, based in Quindío, Risaralda, Caldas, Valle del Cauca, Cauca, Nariño, and southern Chocó. It is composed of the 3d Brigade, based in Cali, the 8th Brigade in Armenia, and the 29th Brigade located close to Popayán. Also in this jurisdiction are the 6th and 14th mobile brigades, six counterguerrilla battalions, the 9th Afeur unit, and the Plan Meteoro 4th Company.

The 4th Division is headquartered in Villavicencio and operates in Casanare, Guaviare, Guainía, Vichada, Caquetá, Vaupés, the extreme southern territory of Cundinamarca, southern Boyacá, and the eastern areas of the departments of Cauca and Meta. It has two brigades, the 7th, based in Villavicencio, and the 16th, which operates out of Yopal. The Eastern Specific Command, also assigned to this division, is based in Puerto Carreño. Special units in the 4th Division's jurisdiction include the 7th and 9th mobile brigades, with 12 counterguerrilla battalions and two Afeur units, the 31st Combat Company for Support Services, and the Plan Meteoro 5th Company.

The 5th Division is assigned to Bogotá, with jurisdictional control over Cundinamarca, Tolima, Huila, and Boyacá. It is composed of the 1st Brigade in Tunja, the 6th Brigade in Ibagué, the 9th Brigade in Neiva, and the 23d Brigade in Bogotá. The 8th Mobile Brigade, six counterguerrilla battalions, the 1st, 2d, 3d, and 4th Afeur units, and the Plan Meteoro 6th Company are also part of the 5th Division.

The 6th Division is headquartered in Florencia, Caquetá Department (12th Brigade). Its other brigades are located in Mocoa, Putumayo Department (27th Brigade); Leticia, Amazonas Department (26th Brigade); Santana, Putumayo (13th Mobile Brigade); and the Counternarcotics Brigade in Larandia, Caquetá. This division operates in the departments of Amazonas, Putumayo, and Caquetá, as well as in a few municipalities in Cauca and Vaupés. The 6th Division also includes the 12th Afeur unit and the Plan Meteoro 7th Company, and it has additional brigades serving with the Southern Naval Force in Puerto Leguízamo on the Putumayo and the 6th Airborne Combat Command (6th Cacom) in Tres Esquinas, Caquetá.

Finally, the 7th Division is responsible for Antioquia, Córdoba, Sucre, and Chocó and is based in Medellín. Created in 2005 to cover territory previously under the 1st Division's jurisdiction, the 7th Division provides more autonomy to operations conducted in the northwest region of the country. This division encompasses the 4th Brigade stationed in Medellín; the 11th Brigade, which covers Carepa, Chigirodó, and Montería; the 14th Brigade in Puerto Berrío; and the 17th Brigade based in Maporita. The 11th Mobile Battalion is also assigned to the 7th Division.

The Navy

In 2008 the National Navy (Armada Nacional) had a total of 30,729 personnel, plus about 14,000 marines and 146 naval aviation personnel. The navy operates in three naval forces and four commands. The naval forces are the Caribbean Naval Force, the Pacific Naval Force, and the Southern Naval Force. The latter consists of the Southern River Fleet, which controls and guards the Caquetá and Putumayo rivers. The first of the four commands is the Marine Infantry Command, which operates on land along the Caribbean and Pacific coasts, on the island territories, and on the country's rivers, where its amphibious capabilities can support the naval forces as needed. The second command is the Coast Guard Corps Command, which operates two task forces, one along the Caribbean coast and one along the Pacific coast. The third is the Naval Aviation Command, which is equipped with some small airplanes and helicopters. The fourth is the Specific Command (Comando Específico) of San Andrés and Providencia; it consists of the General Headquarters of the Specific Command, Naval Base No. 4, and a unit attached to the Caribbean Naval Force.

Although the navy has maintained its traditional mission of defending the nation's maritime waters, the evolution of the internal conflict during the 1990s also led to the development of new objectives. The navy not only participates in antinarcotics activities through the detection and interception of boats suspected of drug trafficking, but its Marine Infantry Command also became directly involved in the counterinsurgent effort through a buildup on the nation's coastal and internal waterways. The navy also has two Gaula units.

The commander of the navy is assisted by a chief of naval operations and an inspector general. The Marine Infantry Command and seven headquarters (*jefaturas*) report directly to the navy's deputy commander. Naval Education oversees the Enap, the Naval School for Noncommissioned Officers (ENSB), and the Marine Infantry School (EFIM). Logistics Operations is responsible for the four largest naval bases, in Cartagena, San Andrés, Málaga, and Puerto Leguízamo on the Río Putumayo. Naval Operations commands the Caribbean Naval Force, the Pacific Naval Force, the Southern Naval Force, the Coast Guard Corps Command, and the Naval Aviation Command. Other *jefaturas* include Plan Orion, naval intelligence, naval matériel, and human development.

The commander of the navy's Marine Infantry Command is advised by the marines' chief of staff. The Marine Infantry Command has three brigades and one Riverine Task Group that patrol a total of

16,000 kilometers of rivers and coastline and are under the operational authority of the chief of naval staff; two are coastal and riverine brigades, and one is a counternarcotics brigade. The 1st Marine Infantry Brigade has three marine infantry rifle battalions, two counterguerrilla battalions, and one command and support battalion that conduct operations in 46 municipalities in Córdoba, Sucre, and Bolívar. Based in Buenaventura, the 1st Marine Infantry Riverine Brigade consists of five battalions that cover the coastal regions in the departments of Nariño, Cauca, Valle, and Chocó. The 2d Marine Infantry Riverine Brigade is based in Bogotá and has battalions stationed throughout the country on the Atrato, Magdalena, Arauca, Meta, Guaviare, Caquetá, and Putumayo rivers. All six Nodriza PAF–III riverine patrol craft are assigned to this brigade, including one on the border with Ecuador. Each of these heavy, Colombian-built, counterinsurgency ships is equipped with a small hospital, four M–60 machineguns, and a helicopter and can accommodate up to 200 soldiers. The Riverine Task Group operates out of Puerto Leguízamo in Putumayo and is responsible for the border waterways with Ecuador on the Putumayo and with Peru on the Amazon, as well as the Caquetá, Orteguaza, and Caguán. The Marine Infantry Command also has its own training center and a Logistics Support Command. The marines have their own BTR–80A armored personnel carriers.

The two task forces of the Coast Guard Corps Command operate on the Pacific and Caribbean coasts. The Caribbean task force, under the command of the Caribbean Naval Force, maintains five stations based in La Guajira, Santa Marta, Cartagena, Coveñas, and Turbo. The Pacific task force is under the operational authority of the Pacific Naval Force and maintains stations in Buenaventura and Tumaco. An eighth Coast Guard station is located in Leticia on the Amazon. The Naval Aviation Command conducts logistical support missions for the navy.

The navy's General Maritime Directorate is responsible for Colombia's maritime policies and programs, the Merchant Marine, and maritime signals. It also manages port authority for ship registration and titles and the development of research and maritime cartography. The Corporation for Science and Technology for the Development of the Naval, Maritime, and Riverine Industry is in charge of the shipyards in Mamonal and Boca Grande, near Cartagena. This entity is responsible for the design and construction of the Coast Guard's fast patrol craft and riverine supply vessels (see table 6, Appendix).

The Air Force

The Colombian Air Force (FAC), the smallest of the armed services, had a total of 10,150 personnel in 2008. This total included up to 2,000 conscripts. The commander of the air force is assisted by a staff made up of a chief of air operations, an inspector general, and a council of former commanders. The deputy commander, in addition to being the chief of staff, coordinates the FAC's nine directorates: air operations, intelligence, logistics operations, aeronautic education, air base security and defense, logistics support, human development, judicial, and health. The FAC deputy commander also coordinates the service's Directorate of Health.

In addition to the conventional mission of protecting Colombian airspace, the air force is involved in both antinarcotics and counterinsurgent operations. The FAC has primary responsibility for aerial interdiction, which includes detection, interception, and neutralization of aircraft used in drug-trafficking activities. The air force also plays a key role in counterinsurgent operations through direct aerial bombing, air-fire assistance to ground troops, and troop and matériel transport using a wide range of aircraft (see table 7, Appendix).

The basic unit of the air force, the Combat Air Command (Cacom), is responsible for air operations in a specific geographic area. Aircraft can be deployed or loaned to a different Cacom, as needed. The air force has six Cacom units and two training schools. The 1st Cacom is assigned to the Captain Germán Olano de Palanquero Air Base in Puerto Salgar, Cundinamarca, and operates six squadrons; its mission is air defense and combat training. The 2d Cacom is headquartered in the Captain Luis F. Gómez Niño Air Base in Apiay, Meta, and operates four squadrons; it is responsible for counterinsurgency and offensive operations. The 3d Cacom is located at the Major General Alberto Pauwels Rodríguez Air Base at Malambo, near Barranquilla, Atlántico, and operates two squadrons; it conducts search-and-rescue and maritime patrol operations along the Caribbean coast. The 4th Cacom is located at the Lieutenant Colonel Luis Francisco Pinto Parra Air Base in Melgar, Tolima, and operates five helicopter squadrons; it is dedicated to tactical support operations and training. The 5th Cacom is assigned to the Brigadier General Arturo Lema Posada Air Base in Rionegro near Medellín, Antioquia, where it operates one helicopter group and conducts search-and-rescue, transport, and heavy-helicopter support operations. The 6th Cacom is located at the Captain Ernesto Esguerra Cubides Air Base in Tres Esquinas, Caquetá, and operates two squadrons; it is devoted to counterinsurgency operations. In addition, the air force has a Military Air Transport Command (Catam), based at Bogotá's El Dorado International Airport; an Air Training Command (CAE), based at the Emavi in Cali; and an Air Maintenance Command (Caman), based in Madrid.

The air force also has two air groups, which are smaller units than the Cacoms and do not have their own operational aircraft. The Eastern Air Group (Gaori) is located in Puerto Carreño, Vichada, and is the launching base for joint operations in the Vichada, Arauca, and Vaupés region. The Caribbean Air Group (Gacar) is based on Isla de San Andrés. Gacar's mission includes the strategic and tactical patrol of airspace and island and coastal areas and support for the navy in its search-and-rescue missions. The FAC's training schools include the Marco Fidel Suárez Military Aviation School (Emavi) in the Cali suburb of Santiago de Cali, where officers receive instruction, and an NCO school (Esufa) in Madrid, Cundinamarca. The other schools are the Aeronautics Military Institute (IMA), which is part of the Superior War College, and the Helicopter School of the Public Force (Ehfup) in Melgar.

Joint Commands

In 2003 the services took the first step toward a significant organizational restructuring, prompted by the difficulties in conducting missions that involved more than one service and by delays in responding to insurgent actions. Joint commands that will oversee personnel and resources from each of the services, assigned to different geographical designations, will replace the conventional configuration.

This model, based on the organizational arrangement of the U.S. military, resulted in the first experimental joint command in 2003, the Joint Task Force Omega, which directed the joint operations of Plan Patriota in the southern regions of Colombia and now supports Plan Consolidación. The formation of the Caribbean Joint Command followed in 2005, and it directly manages 20,000 personnel and logistics resources in eight departments along the Atlantic coast and in Antioquia. The chiefs of both of these joint commands are army generals.

Despite uncertainty in 2009 about the extent of progress in planned military restructuring, various other joint operations have been held by the armed forces. These include actions by the amalgamated navy's 40th and 50th marine infantry riverine battalions with the 18th and 28th brigades of the army, which operate in the east of the country. The formation of the Decisive Action Force, a special rapid-deployment force composed of the 16th, 17th, and 18th mobile brigades, a high-mountain battalion, two Plan Meteoro units, two counterguerrilla battalions, and an operative command, is another positive step

Conscription and Military Service

According to Article 216 of the 1991 constitution, "all Colombians are bound to bear arms when public necessity so requires, in order to

One of the military's Bell 212 helicopters after refueling at Perales Airport, on the outskirts of Ibagué, Tolima Department
Courtesy Narcotics Affairs Section Office, U.S. Embassy, Bogotá

defend the independence of the nation and the country's institutions." The Military Service Law of 1993 stipulates that all Colombian males between 16 and 18 years of age must present themselves for military service. In practice, the ages of conscripts may range from 15 to 24, and they may serve in the Military Forces or the National Police. Military service for those who have completed secondary education (*bachilleres*) lasts for a year; for others, it is 18 to 24 months.

Although previous legislation explicitly exempted women from obligatory military service, the 1991 constitutional provision permits women to volunteer for any of the armed services, including the police, and stipulates that they may be conscripted into service if national security so warrants. Barred from active combat, women's military service is restricted to logistical support or administrative, social, and cultural functions. In 2007 the number of women serving in the army totaled 3,900.

Permanent exemptions are granted to priests, physically or mentally handicapped individuals, and members of indigenous communities who reside within established reserves. Peacetime exemptions are granted to individuals who can prove themselves to be essential for the support of their families, including only sons and married men cohabiting with their spouses. Anyone who has been divested of political rights on account of criminal activities may not be conscripted. There is no conscientious-objector status. Deferments are granted to high-school and university students, including those studying to enter the priesthood, men who already have a brother fulfilling obligatory military service, and prisoners. Once the reason for the deferment expires, the individuals in question must report for service or otherwise resolve their military obligation.

Those who receive a peacetime exemption, whether barred because of a psychological or physical incapacity, or, although fit to serve were not drafted because the service lottery did not select them, must pay a special tax in lieu of performing military service. Every Colombian male more than 18 years of age has to resolve his military duty, either through fulfilling obligatory service or through being exempt from doing so. Such an exemption usually involves a monetary payment. Only then are adult males issued a military reservist card (*tarjeta de reservista*) that is evidence of resolution of status and signifies that the individual could be called into the reserves in case of a national emergency, up to age 50. This card is an indispensable public document for Colombian men. A 1995 decree requires presentation of the card in order to register professional titles, to engage in contracts with public entities, and for employment in the public sector.

Despite legislatively mandated military service, only about 30,000 to 40,000 of an estimated 350,000 to 450,000 eligible male youths are drafted annually. Once the military establishes its personnel needs, a lottery system selects those to be conscripted. Starting in 1997 during the Pastrana administration, the number of conscripts began to decline as the ranks of professional soldiers increased. This trend has accelerated during the Uribe administrations, with the ratio of conscripts to professional soldiers decreasing significantly. The government's goal is for mandatory military service to be eliminated once the number of professional soldiers reaches 100,000. By July 2007, the level had reached 76,000.

Serious social inequalities continue to plague Colombia's conscription system. The informal rules of the lottery arrangement are such that a higher percentage of rural, uneducated youths are drafted. In addition, the special tax paid by young men not called up varies according to family income, serving as an incentive to grant exemptions to draft-age males from relatively wealthy families. Although there is a legislative review of the measure, its underlying premise of differentiated payments is not being modified. The purchase of exemptions from the military by families whose sons have been selected by the lottery is also widespread. This practice also discriminates against youths from the lower social strata. Any male not called up, but unable to pay the tax, has to perform service in order to fulfill his military obligation. Furthermore, poor, rural draftees bear a disproportionate share of active fighting because conscripted high-school graduates, who are likely to be urban and more affluent, are exempt from combat service.

The Military Service Law establishes that unmarried, male citizens between the ages of 16 and 23 are eligible for regular enlistment as NCOs or officers. As in the case of conscripts, enlisted men have to pass physical and psychological tests. It is common practice for individuals to enlist in the NCO corps upon completion of obligatory military service.

Military Education System

The military education system plays a critical role in the formation of a professional officer corps in all branches of the armed services. With the exception of officers trained in medicine or law, all commissioned officers are graduates of one of the three service academies.

The José María Cordova Military Cadet School (Esmic), the army's training academy located in Bogotá, represents the backbone of the military's professional education system. The school's program ranges from three to five years, depending on the need to graduate troops for active service. On completing the training phase, the student obtains the rank of second lieutenant and a degree in military sciences. The school also grants degrees in business administration, law, civil engineering, and military physical education.

The Naval Cadet School (Enap), established in Cartagena in 1938, is an accredited four-year university. Cadets pursue professional degree programs in naval mechanical engineering, electronics, physical oceanography, maritime administration, and naval sciences. Enap graduates also become officials in the Marine Infantry Command and the Merchant Marine. Navy cadets spend nearly one year of the four-year program at sea on the navy's sail-training ship, the frigate *Gloria*. The air force's Marco Fidel Suárez Military Aviation School (Emavi) was founded in Cali in 1933 and like Enap is an accredited four-year university. On completion of the program, graduating second lieutenants gain a diploma in mechanical engineering or in aeronautical administration.

The requirements for admission to the service academies include being a Colombian citizen by birth, having completed—or being in the final year of—secondary school, being between 16 and 20 years of age, being unmarried, and having no children. In addition to the medical, psychological, and physical examinations that candidates must pass before admission, family members are interviewed, and a security background check is performed. Emavi also requires its applicants to be males. Admission to Enap has height requirements: at least 1.68 meters tall in the case of men and 1.62 meters tall in the case of women. Emavi additionally requires special entrance examinations in mathematics, physics, and general culture.

Postacademy professional training is increasingly a requirement for a successful military career. The Lancers School at the military base in Tolemaida provides three to six months of training in counterinsurgency strategy and tactics, equivalent to the U.S. Army Rangers School. This course, although no longer required for promotion to first lieutenant, remains highly prestigious and is frequently attended by members of foreign militaries. All of the branches of the army—infantry, cavalry, artillery, engineering, logistics, and intelligence—additionally operate their own application schools, which offer six-month training programs required for promotion to the rank of major. Majors in the army and air force and lieutenant commanders in the navy are eligible to attend a six-month Staff Course at the Superior War College (Esdegue), which is required for promotion. A one-year course taught at Esdegue, known as the Higher Military Studies Course (CAEM), also is required of army and air force colonels and navy captains before they are eligible for promotion to general officer or flag rank. The course emphasizes the formulation of national security policy and analysis of national and international affairs. Esdegue also offers a one-year Comprehensive Course of National Defense (Cidenal). Attended mainly by public and civilian officials, Cidenal provides basic information on the military's mission and organization, as well as familiarizing civilian personnel with the military's perspectives on national policy. The course is a requirement for promotion from the rank of colonel to brigadier general in the National Police, and officers in the Higher Military Studies Course usually also take Cidenal.

A select number of Colombian officers receive advanced training in special programs for foreign military personnel offered by the U.S. military's professional schools. Colombian military officials and soldiers receive special instruction in counterinsurgent tactics and assault operations, antiterrorist and antinarcotics operations, the detection of land mines, operational planning and implementation, evacuation techniques, and first aid. The majority of U.S. military personnel in Colombia in 2006 were instructors training Colombian aircraft and helicopter pilots and mechanics. Plan Colombia programs also provide advice on the design of curricula for advanced programs at Esdegue in the areas of security, conflict, and terrorism.

ARC Gloria, *the navy flagship, is used for training.*
Courtesy Colombia Tourism Office

NCOs are trained in the Sergeant Inocencio Chincá Military School for Noncommissioned Officers in Tolemaida, Tolima. The training program lasts 18 months, and graduates qualify as military sciences technicians. Continuing instruction and retraining of professional soldiers take place at the Training School for Professional Soldiers (EFSP), established in 2000 in Nilo, Cundinamarca. Training lasts from three to six months. Individuals may enter the school either directly or after having first fulfilled obligatory military service. Aspirants to the NCO corps must pass screening by a board of officers and preparatory exams. On meeting these minimum physical and testing requirements, the individual is appointed to the lowest NCO grade. With additional training, NCOs may be promoted further. In 2003, with the assistance of the U.S. Southern Command, Colombia created the rank of command sergeant major, with the aim of strengthening senior enlisted ranks. NCOs promoted to command sergeant major had first passed an intensive 11-week training and leadership course.

The Military Judiciary

Military Penal Code

As part of the Ministry of National Defense, the military judiciary falls under the executive branch rather than under the judicial branch. In an effort to correct failings of the military judiciary, including the lack of transparency and accountability, the government adopted a new Military Penal Code in August 2000. The reformed system denies unit commanders the power to judge subordinates and provides legal protection for service members who refuse to obey illegal orders to commit human rights abuses. The reformed code excludes torture, genocide, and forced disappearance from the military criminal jurisdiction and stipulates that such crimes be tried in civilian courts.

Under Article 221 of the constitution, military courts have jurisdiction over offenses committed by members of the Public Force (the military and National Police forces) on active duty, in accordance with the prescriptions of the Military Penal Code. These military courts are composed of members of the Public Force on active duty or in retirement.

Military Penal Justice

Military Penal Justice, an agency of the Ministry of National Defense, tries cases involving active-duty members of the armed forces. The military justice system consists of 44 military courts of Military Penal Justice and the Supreme Military Tribunal or military appeals court. The Supreme Court of Justice serves as an additional appeals court in cases of prison sentences of six years or more. According to the U.S. Department of State, military judges preside over courts martial without the presence of juries. The accused have the right to counsel, and witnesses may be called. Representatives of the civilian Inspector General's Office must be present at military trials.

Conflicts between Military Penal Justice and civil jurisdictions normally have involved cases of human rights violations and, to a lesser degree, corruption in the military ranks. The Constitutional Court has ruled that serious human rights violations should not be tried under Military Penal Justice. Although cases continued to be tried there, given the slowness with which the Attorney General's Office transfers specific cases to the civil jurisdiction, the military justice system has greatly increased its cooperation with civilian justice counterparts; for example, it has expedited the transfer of more than 600 human rights cases from military justice to the civilian system. In late 2005, it was estimated that nearly 16,900 cases awaited trial in the military justice system, and, despite improvements, it remains overloaded.

Although the attorney general has the power to dismiss convicted officers from service, high-ranking military officials accused of human rights violations and brought to trial rarely have been convicted. A number of cases absolved by Military Penal Justice and then tried by the Inter-American Court of Human Rights have resulted in decisions against the Colombian state. During Álvaro Uribe's consecutive terms in power, more than 150 officers and 300 soldiers have been dismissed because of links with drug-trafficking groups. In 2006 Congress passed new legislation to bring Military Penal Justice under the jurisdiction of the judicial branch and to reform the Military Penal Code. As of mid-2009, however, the office remained part of the Ministry of National Defense, headed by a colonel appointed by the minister.

Uniforms, Ranks, and Insignia

Colombian military personnel wear uniforms in three general categories: full-dress, dress, and the service uniform. The army's full-dress attire consists of a midnight-blue jacket and sky-blue trousers, the air force full-dress uniform is midnight-blue, and the navy's formal dress is a full-white uniform. All full-dress uniforms have piping on the trousers. The army's dress uniform is dark green, the air force's is midnight-blue, and the navy's dress uniform is full-black. All three services use a camouflage field uniform, and the navy additionally has a khaki tropical-service uniform. There are no significant differences between the officer and NCO uniforms. Hot-weather uniforms differ by a short shirt-sleeve length.

In 2006 the army updated its forest-type uniform for a so-called digital- or pixel-model camouflage design. The new uniforms are made only in Colombia, and only Colombian Military Forces may use them. The army uses two types of camouflage uniform—one for the jungle (*selva*), which is used by most soldiers; and the other for the desert, which is used by troops deployed to La Guajira Department and the Colombian Battalion assigned to the Sinai. With these sartorial changes, the troops now have more comfortable uniforms made of material that permits the application of mosquito repellent and minimizes bacterial concentration.

The rank structure for all services closely parallels that of the U.S. military, with some exceptions (see fig. 8; fig. 9). Army and air force officer rank insignia are shown in gold on shoulder boards. General ranks use stars with 10 identical points that resemble suns. Insignia for army enlisted personnel consist of yellow, blue, and red chevrons placed with their vertices down at the bottom of the right sleeve. Air force enlisted insignia are in gold. Navy officer and cadet insignia are indicated in gold on shoulder boards or sleeves. Navy enlisted insignia consist of gold markings worn on the outer left sleeve of the

	SUBTENIENTE	TENIENTE	CAPITÁN	MAYOR	TENIENTE CORONEL	CORONEL	BRIGADIER GENERAL	MAYOR GENERAL	TENIENTE GENERAL	GENERAL
ARMY COLOMBIAN RANK	SUBTENIENTE	TENIENTE	CAPITÁN	MAYOR	TENIENTE CORONEL	CORONEL	BRIGADIER GENERAL	MAYOR GENERAL	TENIENTE GENERAL	GENERAL
U.S. RANK TITLES	2D LIEUTENANT	1ST LIEUTENANT	CAPTAIN	MAJOR	LIEUTENANT COLONEL	COLONEL	BRIGADIER GENERAL	MAJOR GENERAL	LIEUTENANT GENERAL	GENERAL
AIR FORCE COLOMBIAN RANK	SUBTENIENTE	TENIENTE	CAPITÁN	MAYOR	TENIENTE CORONEL	CORONEL	BRIGADIER GENERAL	MAYOR GENERAL	TENIENTE GENERAL	GENERAL
U.S. RANK TITLES	2D LIEUTENANT	1ST LIEUTENANT	CAPTAIN	MAJOR	LIEUTENANT COLONEL	COLONEL	BRIGADIER GENERAL	MAJOR GENERAL	LIEUTENANT GENERAL	GENERAL
NAVY COLOMBIAN RANK	TENIENTE DE CORBETA	TENIENTE DE FRAGATA	TENIENTE DE NAVÍO	CAPITÁN DE CORBETA	CAPITÁN DE FRAGATA	CAPITÁN DE NAVÍO	CONTR-ALMIRANTE	VICE-ALMIRANTE	ALMIRANTE	ALMIRANTE DE 4 SOLES
U.S. RANK TITLES	ENSIGN	LIEUTENANT JUNIOR GRADE	LIEUTENANT	LIEUTENANT COMMANDER	COMMANDER	CAPTAIN	REAR ADMIRAL LOWER HALF	REAR ADMIRAL UPPER HALF	VICE ADMIRAL	ADMIRAL

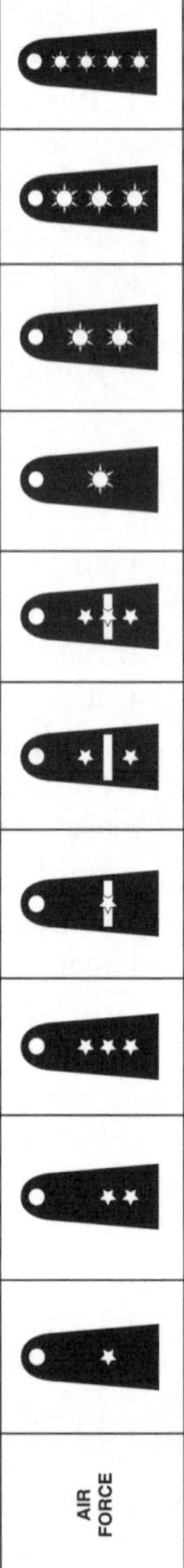

Note—U.S. equivalents represent ranks of relatively comparable authority and are not necessarily the corresponding ranks for protocol purposes.

Figure 8. Officer Ranks and Insignia, 2009

COLOMBIAN RANK	CABO TERCERO	CABO SEGUNDO	CABO PRIMERO	SARGENTO SEGUNDO	SARGENTO VICEPRIMERO	SARGENTO PRIMERO	SARGENTO MAYOR	SARGENTO MAYOR DE COMANDO	SARGENTO MAYOR DE COMANDO CONJUNTO
ARMY									
U.S. RANK TITLES[1]	PRIVATE (E-1)	PRIVATE (E-2)	PRIVATE 1ST CLASS	CORPORAL/SPECIALIST	SERGEANT	STAFF SERGEANT	SERGEANT 1ST CLASS	MASTER SERGEANT	SERGEANT MAJOR/COMMAND SERGEANT MAJOR
COLOMBIAN RANK	NO RANK	AEROTÉCNICO	TÉCNICO CUARTO	TÉCNICO TERCERO	TÉCNICO SEGUNDO	TÉCNICO PRIMERO	TÉCNICO SUBJEFE	TÉCNICO JEFE	TÉCNICO JEFE DE COMANDO/TÉCNICO JEFE DE COMANDO CONJUNTO
AIR FORCE									
U.S. RANK TITLES	AIRMAN BASIC	AIRMAN	AIRMAN 1ST CLASS	SENIOR AIRMAN	STAFF SERGEANT	TECHNICAL SERGEANT	MASTER SERGEANT	SENIOR MASTER SERGEANT	CHIEF MASTER SERGEANT/COMMAND CHIEF MASTER SERGEANT
COLOMBIAN RANK	NO RANK	MARINERO SEGUNDO	MARINERO PRIMERO	SUBOFICIAL TERCERO	SUBOFICIAL SEGUNDO	SUBOFICIAL PRIMERO	SUBOFICIAL JEFE	SUBOFICIAL JEFE TÉCNICO	SUBOFICIAL JEFE TÉCNICO/SUBOFICIAL JEFE TÉCNICO DE COMANDO CONJUNTO
NAVY[2]									
U.S. RANK TITLES	SEAMAN RECRUIT	SEAMAN APPRENTICE	SEAMAN	PETTY OFFICER 3D CLASS	PETTY OFFICER 2D CLASS	PETTY OFFICER 1ST CLASS	CHIEF PETTY OFFICER	SENIOR CHIEF PETTY OFFICER	MASTER CHIEF PETTY OFFICER/COMMAND MASTER CHIEF PETTY OFFICER

[1]U.S. equivalents represent ranks of relatively comparable authority and are not necessarily the corresponding ranks for protocol purposes.

[2]The ranks of the marine infantry are similar to navy enlisted ranks, but their insignia are red on black, rather than gold on black, and show a right-tilting anchor crossed by a rifle.

Figure 9. Enlisted Ranks and Insignia, 2009

coat, jumper, or shirt (depending on the uniform), halfway between the top shoulder seam and the elbow.

Defense and Security Spending

State resources for military and police spending in Colombia are determined according to the same procedures followed for all other spending items in the national budget. Spending items are public, voted on by Congress, incorporated into the national budget, and subject to control by the Comptroller General's Office (Contraloría de la República) and other civilian oversight agencies. Annual budgets are prepared based on the objectives and programs defined by each administration's national development plan. The first time that defense and security objectives appeared in this planning document was in the first year of the presidency of Ernesto Samper Pizano (1994–98). Budget preparation for defense takes place in the first half of the year, with input from the Ministry of National Defense Planning Office, the Ministry of Finance and Public Credit, and the National Planning Department (DNP) in the case of procurements. Before July 20 of each year, a spending bill goes to the Congress, and prior to September 15 the Senate (Senado) and the House of Representatives (Cámara de Representantes) decide on specific appropriations. After final congressional and then presidential approval, the spending bill takes effect on January 1. Modifications to the federal budget are permissible, and defense and security items frequently receive additional appropriations in the second half of the fiscal year.

Spending on defense and security in Colombia grew steadily during the 1990s, because of redoubled efforts against the guerrillas and illicit drug activities. In 1999 dollars, Colombia spent on average US$2.15 billion annually during the 1990s, placing fourth after Brazil, Argentina, and Mexico in defense spending among Latin American countries. As a percentage of gross national product (GNP), Colombia's defense spending increased from 2.3 percent in 1990 to 3.2 percent in 1999, contradicting a global trend of reductions in defense outlays. Defense spending in 1999 as a percentage of GNP was higher than the developed-country average (2.3 percent), the developing-country average (2.7 percent), and the Latin American average (1.5 percent). Defense spending in Colombia in 1999 was second in Latin America only to Ecuador, which in the same year spent 3.7 percent of GNP on defense and security. As a percentage of overall government spending, defense and security outlays throughout the 1990s remained constant at 15.9 percent. From 2001 to 2005, Colombian spending on defense grew more than 30 percent after inflation, from US$2.6 billion to more than US$3.9 billion.

In 2006 the portion of GNP dedicated to defense and security amounted to 4.0 percent, nearly double what it was in 1990, and 12.6 percent of the overall national budget went to the same sector. Between 1999 and 2005, Plan Colombia, which contributed to improving national capabilities against drug trafficking and terrorism, was jointly financed by US$3.4 million from Colombia's national budget and US$2.8 million by the U.S. government. In 2007 Colombia spent US$5.7 billion on national security and defense. Of this total, 71 percent went to the Military Forces and 29 percent to the National Police. Spending was broken down as follows: 53 percent on personnel, including pensions; 14 percent on internal transfers; 23 percent on operating expenses; and 10 percent on procurements. This distribution indicated excessive spending on operations and pensions, with relatively little invested in acquisitions, modernization, or research and development. Of the 10 percent spent on procurement, 64 percent went to armaments and war matériel, 11 percent to maintenance and transport, 9 percent to communications and intelligence functions, and 7 percent to new infrastructure. The remaining 9 percent was spent on information, health services, human resource training, and welfare.

The government has compensated for its defense budget shortfalls with additional funding, including funds derived from departmental or municipal governments, the armed forces' own security-related businesses, the "wealth tax" that raised more than US$800 million between 2004 and 2006, and annual U.S. military aid in the form of "foreign military financing" and financial assistance from counternarcotics initiatives. In 2007 the Colombian government announced a new tax on wealthy Colombians. The expectation is that this wealth tax will generate up to US$3.6 billion between 2007 and 2010.

Law Enforcement

National Police

Colombia's first national police force of 450 men originated in 1891 with the assistance of a *commissaire* (commissioner) from France's national police, primarily to maintain law and order in Bogotá. The present-day executive-level ranking system of the National Police reflects the French influence. Over the ensuing decades, the police became active participants in Colombia's partisan struggles. During La Violencia, the national character of the police was diluted as local forces were organized and directed by caciques. The first attempt to reconstitute the police as a national, centralized entity occurred during the military government of Rojas

Pinilla, when the police force was moved from the jurisdiction of the Ministry of Government to that of the Ministry of National Defense. In 1962 the National Police came into being, assuming centralized administrative and operational control over the multiple, individual forces that had previously operated in the country's departmental divisions. Along with the successful nationalization of the force, the National Police also aspired to reassert its autonomy from the military, although it remained within the Ministry of National Defense with a marked military character.

The militarization of the National Police deepened when it entered the "war on drugs" in the 1980s as the country's primary antinarcotics body. The police force also was drawn into counterinsurgency operations as conflict dynamics and drug activities became intertwined, and as the irregular armed groups increasingly targeted police posts in conflict zones. By the early 1990s, in the face of soaring crime rates, the National Police came under sharp criticism for having lost sight of its primary function of protecting the civilian populations in urban areas, and for the high levels of institutional corruption. A series of reform efforts throughout the 1990s aimed to transform the military identity of the National Police by increasing civilian controls, scaling back on rural security, and reemphasizing conventional urban crime prevention functions. The National Police's public standing improved significantly in the wake of this restructuring, although the force will likely continue to play some military role in Colombia's future.

According to Article 218 of the 1991 constitution, the National Police is a "permanently armed civilian force responsible for the nation, and whose primary objective is to uphold the necessary internal conditions for the full exercise of public rights and liberties, so that Colombian citizens can live in peace." Like the military, the National Police is part of the Ministry of National Defense, and the minister exercises formal operational command. In practice, the president of the republic maintains direct communication with the director general of the National Police.

In 2008 the National Police had 136,097 personnel plus a mounted rural paramilitary force of between 8,000 and 10,000 members. During the 1970s and most of the 1980s, the service had fairly constant personnel numbers, but it doubled in size from 1988 to 2007. The director general of the National Police is a general with a permanent staff that includes a chief of planning and an inspector general. Next in the chain of command is a deputy director who oversees individual directorates, each run by a brigadier general.

A November 2006 decree partially modified the structure of the Ministry of National Defense and reorganized the National Police. It divided the National Police into eight regions and created eight operational directorates (citizen security, carabineros and rural security, criminal investigation, police intelligence, antinarcotics, protection and special services, antikidnapping and antiextortion, and transit and transportation) and six support directorates (schools, incorporation, personnel, administration and finance, health, and social welfare).

At the national level, the police are further organized according to the country's administrative divisions. Each of the 32 departments has a departmental police command that supervises personnel assigned to the various districts, stations, substations, and police posts throughout the jurisdiction. There are an additional three municipal police commands in the country's largest cities—Bogotá, Cali, and Medellín. The departmental and municipal commanders depend administratively on the central operational and support directorates of the National Police but coordinate local operations with governors and mayors, who have constitutional authority to supervise police commands. Police commanders have the rank of colonel or lieutenant colonel. The Transit and Transportation Directorate oversees all patrol agents and transit police in urban areas, including those that staff the Immediate Care Centers (CAIs), which provide neighborhood police services in large municipalities. Approximately 70 percent of police personnel are concentrated in urban centers, and most of these are patrol officers. As this distribution suggests, the primary police function is to provide security in urban areas. The National Police, like the army and the navy, has a Gaula unit to counter kidnappers.

The Carabineros and Rural Security Directorate supervises the Mounted Police, or Carabineros Corps, a rural paramilitary police force resulting from the 1993 reform to patrol and maintain public order in conflict zones and in the national parks. Despite its reestablishment in 1993, the Carabineros Corps is actually Colombia's oldest police force, created by a law of May 18, 1841. Beginning in 1936, a Chilean mission helped to professionalize the corps. In 2006 there were 9,800 Carabineros officers, located principally in rural areas and trained in irregular conflict and in the rescue of hostages. Units of the Mobile Squadron of Mounted Police (Emcar), which operate in 120-member squadrons, were formed in 2004 as a part of President Álvaro Uribe's Democratic Security and Defense Policy (usually referred to as Democratic Security Policy) to provide extra support for police activities in conflict areas. Special Carabineros Corps units also provide backup to urban police during public events or civil protests.

By 2004 each of the nation's 1,096 municipalities had a police station or substation. This 100-percent police coverage was maintained through late 2007, when the number of municipalities had increased to 1,120. Redeploying personnel to towns where police had been withdrawn in the 1990s, in conjunction with the increased Carabineros Corps units, is a key aspect of President Uribe's strategy to regain control of the countryside. Nevertheless, this policy is controversial because isolated agents with no police or military backup are the frequent targets of guerrilla violence. The strategy additionally raises concern about the overlapping functions of the Military Forces and the National Police in counterinsurgency. The National Police also continues to play a central role in Colombia's "war on drugs." The Antinarcotics Directorate of the National Police coordinates the eradication of illicit crops, by both aerial fumigations and manual uprooting, and collaborates in the interdiction of drugs and chemical supplies for processing drugs.

In 2006 the National Police budget of US$1 billion covered personnel expenses, general operational expenses, government transfers, and, to a lesser extent, procurement and modernization. Of that budget, 63 percent was apportioned to personnel, 19 percent to general expenses, 15 percent to transfers, and 3 percent to procurements. Military and police procurement expenses were similar, because of the military missions that the Mounted Police undertook in rural areas.

The National Police fleet of aircraft is second only to that of the FAC (see table 8, Appendix). Its aircraft and helicopters are used in antinarcotics operations, provide logistics support for police operations, and transport police personnel. The bulk of the National Police transport inventory is composed of motorcycles, trucks, vans, and other vehicles.

The National Police maintains its own professional education system, separate from that of the Military Forces. Of about 20 police schools, the main educational institution is the General Santander Police Cadet School (ENP) in Bogotá, an accredited four-year university that offers programs in police and criminal administration, technical programs in police studies, police communications, and aeronautic maintenance. The academy additionally offers graduate degrees in criminal investigation, vehicle accident investigation, security, and police service. The National Police also operates 12 other training units throughout the country, where agents and traffic patrol units receive instruction. The Police Justice and Investigation School is located in Sibaté, Cundinamarca. The Mounted Police operates two specialized training programs in its schools: the National Carabineros School located in Facatativá, Cundinamarca; and the Carabineros School of Vélez Province, in Vélez, Santander.

Antiriot police in Bogotá
Courtesy Lorenzo Morales

Police officer ranks are similar to those of the army, but the insignia differ. The ranking system in the National Police is a quasimilitary structure with three career tracks as in the army: superior officers (generals, colonels, lieutenant colonels, and majors), subordinate officers (captains, lieutenants, and second lieutenants), noncommissioned officers (sergeant majors, master sergeants, sergeants, and corporals), and police agents, who correspond to the army's rank and file. A fourth rank, intended since 1993 to fuse subordinate officers and agents into a single category, has yet to be implemented fully. The insignia of generals in the National Police are the same as for the military. They have stars with 10 identical points that resemble suns. Police majors, lieutenant colonels, and colonels use one, two, or three bars, respectively, separate and surrounded by two laurel branches joined in a semicircle. Lieutenants and second lieutenants are identified by two and one stripes, respectively.

Overseeing the National Police is the National Police Commissioner's Office (OCNP), which is also under the Ministry of National Defense. Created by a 1993 law, the OCNP serves as an intermediary between the citizenry and the National Police. Under a 2000 law, the National Police adopted an executive-level rank and insignia system for members of the OCNP. It allows National Police NCOs to become OCNP agents after taking certain courses at the ENP. Headed by a commissioner (*comisario*), the OCNP ranks also

317

include those of *subcomisario, intendente jefe, intendente, subintendente,* and *patrullero.*

The OCNP has a national, departmental, and municipal organization paralleling that of the National Police. The president appoints the National Police commissioner to a nonuniformed position requiring qualifications similar to those of a Supreme Court justice. The commissioner is responsible for overseeing the operational and disciplinary actions of the police and guaranteeing the fulfillment of the constitution and the law by means of prevention, vigilance, control, and the peaceful resolution of conflicts. The commissioner's duties include analyzing citizen complaints against the police, proposing policies and institutional improvements, supervising internal disciplinary control, ordering and monitoring penal investigations against police members, ensuring that police activities are within the legal framework, and presenting an annual report to Congress. In late 2009, the exact status of the OCNP was unclear.

Administrative Security Department

Another key law enforcement organization is the Administrative Security Department (DAS). The DAS is the state's primary intelligence agency and has a national role similar to that of the Federal Bureau of Investigation in the United States. Founded in 1960 by Alberto Lleras Camargo (president, 1945–46, 1958–62) to replace the Colombian Intelligence Service, which had been associated with abuses and repression during La Violencia, the DAS mandate is to produce intelligence for the state, with an emphasis on information about threats to national security. Nevertheless, DAS involvement in a variety of policing functions not directly related to intelligence has made the organization a de facto parallel police service.

According to a 2000 decree, the DAS mandate is to provide a wide range of intelligence, security, and police-related services to the national government. Its primary functions relate to domestic and foreign intelligence gathering, the performance of counterintelligence activities, and the investigation of crimes against the internal security of the state. It assists the executive in policy formulation and in decisions affecting security. The DAS exercises judicial police functions, maintains all crime records and judicial files of citizens, manages all migration matters of both Colombian citizens and foreigners, administers the citizen registration and identification system, and provides protection services to high-ranking government officials and to individuals whose security is at risk. The DAS is also the national office of the International Police (Interpol).

The director of the DAS is a civilian appointed directly by the president. In addition to being aided by a secretary general and a deputy director, the director's support staff includes the offices of planning, legal counsel, communication and press, disciplinary control, and special protection. The organization is divided into two general directorates for intelligence and operations. Intelligence comprises five subdirectorates, including analysis, operations, human resources, counterintelligence, and technological development. The Operations Directorate has four subdirectorates, including strategic investigations, Interpol, alien affairs, and antikidnapping. The capital city of each department has its own section of the DAS. These sections each oversee about 20 security and operational units in municipalities with operational and strategic importance throughout the department's territory. In 2007 the DAS had an operating budget of US$118 million and approximately 7,000 employees throughout the country, an increase of approximately 10 percent in personnel since 1990.

The Superior Intelligence Academy, located in Bogotá, provides training for intelligence officials and detectives. The academy additionally offers courses required for the advancement of officials and detectives, as well as induction and training programs for all DAS personnel.

Since 2005 a series of institutional crises has shaken the DAS. Evidence of paramilitary penetration of the entity first emerged after the DAS chief of intelligence was accused of corruption involving drug traffickers and paramilitaries. Jorge Noguera Cotes, DAS director from 2002 to 2005, was arrested in 2007 after he had resigned his position and been assigned to a diplomatic post; he was charged with electoral fraud, leaking information to the paramilitaries, and having links with paramilitary leader Rodrigo Tovar Pupo, alias Jorge 40. This episode not only seriously damaged the credibility of the organization but also had negative implications for U.S. support for President Uribe, who had named Noguera to the position and had repeatedly expressed confidence in his innocence. After Noguera was found guilty of the charges, María del Pilar Hurtado became the first female director of the DAS in August 2007. However, she, too, was implicated in the scandal and resigned on October 24, 2008, and the president appointed her deputy to lead the DAS.

Judicial Police

The 1991 constitution, Article 250, stipulates that the Attorney General's Office must direct and coordinate the activities of all state entities with either permanent or temporary judicial police facilities. In

2004 the Attorney General's Office, the Directorate of the Judicial Police and Investigation (Dijin) of the National Police, and the DAS had permanent judicial police powers. The principal responsibility of Dijin is to carry out criminal investigations and to assist in the technical preparation of criminal cases. Dijin's role in the process of discovery is essential to judicial rulings in the new accusatory penal system in Colombia. Although Dijin is organizationally under the National Police and reports to it, the Attorney General's Office also directs and coordinates the activities of the judicial police with all state agencies. Thus, there may be some overlapping control over Dijin activities by the National Police and the Attorney General's Office. There are additionally a wide variety of other state organs with some judicial police authority within their organizations, including the Comptroller General's Office, transit authorities, national and regional directors of the National Jail and Penitentiary Institute (INPEC), the directors of security personnel, mayors, and police inspectors.

The National Institute of Legal Medicine and Forensic Sciences is the primary entity responsible for assisting the Attorney General's Office in criminal investigations and providing technical and scientific evidence. The DAS, the Technical Investigation Corps, and Dijin all maintain separate forensic laboratories. National and foreign private laboratories, as well as public and private universities, also provide scientific-technical support. The multiplicity of training centers in judicial police functions, which results in a lack of standardization in academic programs, technical training, and procedures, is a problem for all the entities involved. To address this concern, the Uribe administration proposed the establishment of a Central School of Judicial Police in its 2002–6 Development Plan, as well as the strengthening of the Dijin School of Criminal Investigation and Forensic Science.

The U.S. Department of Justice and the U.S. Agency for International Development (USAID) have assisted Dijin in achieving its reform goals. The International Criminal Investigative Training Assistance Program (ICITAP) spearheads training and reform initiatives oriented to developing specialized investigative units to improve coordination and cooperation among all entities involved in the investigative process. These ICITAP writs, composed of prosecutors, forensic specialists, paralegals, judicial police, and specialized government personnel, focus on money laundering and asset forfeiture, human rights, and anticorruption. ICITAP also works with the Colombian government in standardizing Dijin training by designing a unified investigative pilot program, from which 51 judicial police graduated in 2003. In 2004 ICITAP helped prepare Dijin for the accusatory trial system with specialized training in crime-scene management. The U.S. Office of Overseas Prosecutorial Development, Assistance, and Training also participated in a reform of Colombia's four forensic laboratories aimed at standardizing forensic protocols and procedures.

Penal System

Colombia's penal system established laws that are applicable to both citizens and aliens who commit crimes defined by the Penal Code of 2000. The primary categories of crimes, classifiable as felonies or misdemeanors, include crimes against persons, property, individual liberties, or state security; political crimes, including rebellion and sedition; and sex crimes. In 2003 the majority of convictions were for crimes against property, followed by crimes against persons.

The maximum prison term allowable under 2005 legislation is 50 years for a single crime and 60 for multiple crimes. The 2000 code establishes two forms of punishment: detention (usually meaning imprisonment) and fines. Terms of confinement for criminal conduct are served in a maximum-security penitentiary or a prison facility. House arrest is common for white-collar crimes and for offenses committed by public officials. A Penal Code for Minors establishes separate courts, sentences, and juvenile detention centers. The Code of Criminal Procedure provides for the rights of defendants and also stipulates the detention of accused individuals prior to trial in the case of serious offenses. The death penalty was abolished in 1910.

Colombia's extradition laws, which permit citizens to be tried in foreign jurisdictions, have been a source of national controversy since the 1980s. The assassination of the minister of justice in 1984 and the ensuing wave of terrorism and violence against judges, politicians, and journalists was a strategy by the Medellín Cartel to pressure the state to ban extradition to the United States. The campaign succeeded, at least for the short term, and extradition was prohibited in 1987. However, Virgilio Barco Vargas (president, 1986–90) canceled this policy two years later following the killing of presidential candidate Luis Carlos Galán. The policy reversal led to an all-out assassination and bombing operation by the so-called Extraditables that lasted until 1991, when a constitutional ban on extradition was enacted in an effort to stem narco-terrorism. Extradition was subsequently reestablished in 1997, and in 2004 Colombia extradited the first guerrilla insurgents for drug trafficking to the United States.

The National Jail and Penitentiary Institute (Inpec) runs the country's 139 national prisons and is responsible for inspecting municipal jails. Although part of the Ministry of Interior and Justice, Inpec has an independent budget and administrative decentralization. Inpec

321

personnel do not have permanent general investigative authority, although the Attorney General's Office does have the power to grant them such authority for specific purposes.

In November 2007, the capacity of the country's prison system was 52,555 inmates, yet the prison population was 63,000, about 6 percent of whom were female. This total was more than double the number of prisoners incarcerated in 1984. Nevertheless, the overcrowding rate of nearly 18 percent in 2006 was an improvement compared with nearly 40 percent overcrowding in 2005. Other serious problems include poor training of many of Inpec's 14,000 prison guards and administrative staff, a lack of security, corruption, and an insufficient budget.

Colombia's high crime rate and the backlog of cases are the primary causes of the overcrowding. Alternative punishment mechanisms for those convicted of minor offenses should reduce the prison population. Only individuals arrested for crimes that carry more than a four-year sentence and who are considered flight risks are held in jail before trial. Judges may suspend prison terms for those convicted of minor crimes that carry a sentence of less than three years. In the case of sentences between three and four years, judges routinely order house arrest. Much longer prison terms exist for serious crimes, such as kidnapping for ransom, extortion, terrorism, and drug trafficking.

Colombia's prison system is organized geographically into six regional directorates: Bogotá (central), Cali (western), Barranquilla (northern), Bucaramanga (eastern), Medellín (northeastern), and Pereira (Old Caldas). There were six maximum-security prisons in the country in 2007, of which the Penitenciaría de Cómbita in Boyacá was one of the best known because of the drug traffickers incarcerated there. Smaller penitentiaries are located in Barranquilla, Ibagué, Manizales, Medellín, Palmira, Pamplona, and Pasto. There are prison facilities for women in the major cities. An agricultural penal colony is located at Acacías, Meta. Each judicial district and municipality also operates its own jail. The majority of prisoners convicted or awaiting trial are detained in facilities in large municipalities. Juvenile reformatories for youths aged 14 to 18 are located at Bogotá and Dagua. Imprisoned insurgents are incarcerated with regular criminal detainees in many of the penitentiaries. Occasionally, captured guerrillas are grouped together as a protective measure. Guerrillas historically have been imprisoned for rebellion or treason, although a 1991 constitutional reform permits their prosecution and trial for criminal acts.

The 1991 constitution also instigated a significant reform of the Colombian justice system and penal process. The legal modification introduced a hybrid penal system, combining elements of both inquisitory and accusatory models in order to make the penal process more efficient and more compatible with modern concepts of justice and democracy. Nevertheless, the predominantly inquisitory aspect was preserved amid concerns that the accusatory system was too weak for the scale of Colombia's criminal problems. The inquisitory system is largely written, partially private, and limits participation by the accused. Likewise, under this system, the Attorney General's Office not only investigates crimes but also participates in judicial decisions. These problems led to concerns regarding the ability of the Colombian penal system to adequately comply with constitutional guarantees and deliver justice.

In 2004 a new law provided for the conversion of the penal system from the mixed model to an entirely accusatory arrangement. The new system took effect in January 2005 and introduced the procedures of oral arguments and trials open to the public. The conversion process has not been without its problems, and full transition to the new model will take some years to complete. Nevertheless, the accusatory system is expected to deliver justice more speedily and to limit the role of the attorney general to the investigation of crimes, the process of discovery, and the presentation of material evidence. A new judicial police was established for the purpose of unifying all criminal investigations and bringing about central control. The National Institute of Legal Medicine and Forensic Sciences works directly with the Judicial Police and the Attorney General's Office in the collection and verification of state's evidence in criminal trials. Since 2003 USAID's program on democracy has provided technical assistance and training in the penal system reform, funded the establishment of 28 oral trial courtrooms, and trained judges in oral trials, legal evidence, and procedures.

By 2007 the system had succeeded in speeding judicial processes in cases involving in flagrante delicto. However, there were serious problems with other types of cases that demand an investigation, and the new accusatory system had made no significant difference in cases of organized crime, personal lawsuits, or corruption.

National Security Background

Colombia's national security experience following independence consisted of persistent domestic unrest and civil conflicts that culminated in the devastating War of the Thousand Days at the end of the nineteenth century. International security affairs took on more importance with the secession of Panama in 1903, followed by a border war with Peru (1932–34) and territorial disagreements with Venezuela.

Sectarian violence in the 1950s diverted Colombia's attention from its deepening security relations with the United States and its commitment to a new hemispheric security structure at the end of World War II. In conjunction with the guerrilla movements that had their origins in the period of La Violencia (1946–58), the subsequent development of drug trafficking and paramilitarism submerged Colombia in its current domestic security crisis.

Nineteenth-Century Civil Unrest

Colombia's earliest security challenges in the postindependence period were entirely internal in nature. In the nineteenth century, there were recurring ideological disagreements that split political elites into rival camps that resorted to armed conflict to settle differences and determine the exercise of power. The first significant civil war was the War of the Supremos, or Supreme Commanders (1840–42), which pitted the proto-Conservative government against the more liberal federalist model of government. This was followed by the Conservative rebellion in 1851 and a military coup in 1854. Civil war broke out again in 1859, when Liberals declared their opposition to the Conservative regime. The resulting Liberal Rionegro constitution of 1863 sparked another period of fighting, during which Liberals and Conservatives engaged in some 40 local conflicts and several major military battles. The conspiracy of May 23, 1867, brought radical Liberals to power, putting an end to four years of chronic instability, yet prompted a Conservative armed rebellion in Tolima and Antioquia that was suppressed by the government. When Conservative-leaning Rafael Núñez Moledo (president, 1880–82, 1884–86, 1887–88, 1892–94) was reelected in 1884, Liberals started an armed uprising against the government that spread throughout much of the country.

By century's end, the two main parties had splintered into multiple factions, each promoting a particular political and economic agenda. Liberal militants inspired by the earlier reformist policies of Francisco de Paula Santander y Omaña (president of New Granada, 1832–37) started another rebellion against the government in 1899 that became the War of the Thousand Days. After an early defeat, the Liberal army persisted in a desperate strategy of guerrilla warfare that dragged on for two more years. The defeated Liberals finally sued for peace after nearly three years of fighting and more than 100,000 deaths. One of the most violent conflicts in Colombia's history, the War of the Thousand Days ushered in a new century, having devastated much of the country.

International Security Affairs

International security affairs took on more prominence in the twentieth century, starting with the secession of the department of Panama in 1903. What began as a local rebellion in the Panamanian province turned into an international incident when U.S. Navy gunships intercepted Colombian soldiers sent to suppress the revolt. After the Colombian Senate refused to approve the Hay–Herrán Treaty, which would have granted Washington permission to construct a canal across the isthmus and to gain effective authority over the territory surrounding the canal, President Theodore Roosevelt took advantage of both the insurrection and the Colombian government's weakness in the aftermath of the War of the Thousand Days to intervene. Having encouraged separatist sentiments and militarily supported the revolutionaries, the United States moved quickly to grant diplomatic recognition of Panama following the new government's declaration of independence in November 1903. Almost immediately, a treaty was signed that granted the United States, in perpetuity, exclusive control over the Canal Zone. The subsequent payment of US$25 million to the Colombian government as compensation for the loss of its territory did little to assuage national resentment or to repair U.S.–Colombian relations.

Colombia also was involved in various border disputes with its immediate neighbors in the first half of the century. The most significant of these was with Peru over control of the Amazon town of Leticia. The first treaty that established the boundary according to the colonial demarcation placed the outpost in Colombian territory, although Peru continued to press its claim to the land. Four subsequent treaties designed to solve the dispute did not end repeated military skirmishes over the territory. In 1932 about 300 armed Peruvian civilians seized Leticia in protest of the 1922 agreement. Colombia's mobilization of troops to retake the town prompted Peru's military invasion. Open fighting in the Amazon basin between the armies resulted in 850 deaths. A League of Nations commission resolved the conflict in 1934 through a resolution that returned the disputed area to Colombia.

Acrimonious territorial disputes centered on the Península de La Guajira also characterized the Colombia–Venezuela relationship, although there was never open conflict. The Pombo–Romero Treaty of 1842 initially established Colombian sovereignty over the territory. The persistence of conflicting claims led in 1891 to Spanish arbitration, which awarded territory to each country but failed to demarcate the entirety of the shared frontier. The Santos–López Treaty of 1941 finally settled the boundary issue, granting most of the Península de La Guajira to Colombia. Nevertheless, uncertainty regarding the extension of the maritime boundary into the Golfo de Venezuela remained a contentious issue between the countries, and it nearly erupted into open warfare in the late 1980s.

During World War II, Colombia broke diplomatic relations with the Axis powers after the attack on Pearl Harbor on December 7, 1941, and later declared war against Germany following a 1943 submarine attack that destroyed a Colombian schooner. As the war entered its final stage, along with 19 other nations Colombia signed the Act of Chapultepec in March 1945, the first multilateral collective security treaty in the Western Hemisphere that provided for consultation in the event of an attack on an American state. In 1947 Colombia entered into the Inter-American Treaty of Reciprocal Assistance, known as the Rio Treaty, which mandated a policy of collective defense against possible communist aggression. Closely aligned with U.S. geopolitical and security interests, Colombia also participated in the Korean War, contributing an infantry battalion and a warship.

La Violencia and the Emergence of Insurgency

Although partisan fighting following the end of 16 years of Liberal rule was already threatening to destabilize the nation in 1946, the assassination of Liberal leader Jorge Eliécer Gaitán in 1948 and the ensuing political violence that engulfed the country transformed Colombia's national security. The murder initially sparked massive rioting in Bogotá that resulted in the deaths of 2,000 people. To this day, what came to be known as the Bogotazo has remained the largest urban riot in the history of the Western Hemisphere. The greatest disturbances during La Violencia occurred in the countryside, however, where the Liberal–Conservative civil war is estimated to have claimed more than 200,000 lives. Swept up in the ideological furor and exploited by political parties, Colombia's security forces were ineffective at reestablishing order. The cacique-controlled police in rural areas were active agents for the Conservative cause, whereas the police in Bogotá supported the Liberals. The army remained loyal to the Conservative Party. The hard-line Conservative President Gómez brutally suppressed Liberal resistance in the countryside in the early 1950s and increasingly relied on the military to crush his political opposition, further corrupting the already highly politicized armed forces.

General Rojas seized power in 1953 in the first successful military coup in a century. Rojas achieved some early success in reducing the fighting in the countryside, as many responded to an offer of political amnesty in exchange for abandoning the violent struggle. Nevertheless, the partisan conflict continued because of the proliferation of armed bands dedicated to local criminal enterprises or involved in self-defense activities. Indeed, at the height of the internal conflict, approximately 20,000 members of illegal armed groups operated throughout the country, some of whom had established their own "independent republics" in remote regions. Self-defense organizations composed of campesino rebels loosely affiliated with the outlawed Communist Party of Colombia (PCC) represented a strong pocket of resistance to the government's amnesty program. Military offensives in the 1950s increasingly targeted these campesino vigilantes, especially in the central coffee-growing regions (see Things Come Apart, 1946–58, ch.1).

The FARC, long Colombia's most important insurgent movement, had its origins in this midcentury period of political violence as an organization that provided protection to campesino communities in southern Tolima and the Sumapaz region of Cundinamarca. As the National Front regime of 1958–78 reconstructed the state and sought to reestablish centralized authority in remote regions, it increasingly clashed with campesino movements striving for land rights and local autonomy. After providing protection to rural populations in local struggles during La Violencia, various groups evolved into more mobile and offensive guerrilla movements in response to the state's counterinsurgency strategies. One such group, headed by the campesino Pedro Antonio Marín, also known as Manuel Marulanda Vélez and Tiro Fijo (Sure Shot), first established itself as the Armed Southern Bloc in 1964. The radicalization of his organization occurred in reaction to Operation Marquetalia, a massive counterinsurgency action by the army in May and June of that year. In July 1966, during the bloc's second conference, the group announced its reconstitution as the FARC, an armed resistance movement associated with the PCC. Throughout the 1970s, the FARC slowly expanded by consolidating its campesino base of support in remote areas with little or no state presence.

During the 1980s, the FARC developed into an independent, well-established guerrilla movement with its own political agenda and military doctrine. It more than tripled in size, with action spreading from 10 fronts to more than 30, and expanded into new areas of influence throughout the national territory. Paradoxically, peace discussions with the government of Belisario Betancur Cuartas (president, 1982–86) in the mid-1980s fortified the FARC in two ways: the guerrilla organization gained recognition as a legitimate political movement, and the three-year truce permitted a steady buildup and expansion. The FARC also gained strength in the second half of the

1980s by its disassociation from the PCC. Both the decimation of the Patriotic Union (UP), the FARC's political party, by paramilitary violence between 1985 and 1996 and the collapse of the Soviet Union in 1991 led to a reduced emphasis on the FARC's Marxist ideology and a corresponding emphasis on its identity as an armed guerrilla force. The FARC's increasing strength at the end of the 1980s was facilitated by its first tentative alliances with drug traffickers who had pushed into areas under guerrilla influence, offering new sources of financing (see Other Parties and Political Movements, ch. 4).

The evolution of the FARC from its loose Marxist roots happened at the same time as a number of other guerrilla organizations inspired by the Cuban Revolution also developed in Colombia during the National Front period. The most influential of these, the National Liberation Army (ELN), was an urban-based movement founded by university students that gradually became a rural guerrilla group with close ties to radical urban networks. Divided by internal class and ideological conflicts, the ELN did not become a serious threat until the 1980s, when, under the leadership of the priest Manuel Pérez Martínez, the organization grew rapidly following the discovery of oil in Arauca. Extorting oil companies not only transformed its financial base but also contributed to ELN expansion as it gained influence among local populations affected by socioeconomic dislocations caused by oil exploration.

Other guerrilla movements that shaped Colombia's internal security scenario during the 1970s and 1980s included the Quintín Lame Armed Movement (MAQL), which was based in the indigenous community in Cauca; the Popular Liberation Army (EPL), based in the northern regions of Urubá and Alto Sinú; and the urban Nineteenth of April Movement (M–19). The M–19 became notorious first for its armed occupation of the embassy of the Dominican Republic in 1980, during which it held many diplomats hostage for 59 days, and later for its dramatic 1985 seizure of the Palace of Justice, which ended with the deaths of half of the Supreme Court justices, scores of civilians, and all but two of the guerrillas involved in the takeover. The organization demobilized soon after, forming a political party whose members participated in the mainstream political process.

Drug Trafficking and the Origins of Paramilitarism

The twin developments of drug trafficking and paramilitarism further compounded Colombia's internal security problems in the 1980s. By the early part of the decade, trade in cocaine had replaced Colombia's involvement in marijuana cultivation and smuggling. Following a highly successful aerial fumigation campaign against cannabis by the administration of Julio César Turbay Ayala (president, 1978–82), traffickers turned to the more lucrative business of processing coca paste imported from Bolivia and Peru and then exporting finished cocaine. The major cartels that emerged in Colombia during the 1980s in Medellín and Cali were initially involved exclusively in cocaine processing and trafficking. As the cocaine business flourished, with income from trafficking tripling throughout the decade to US$4.5 billion, drug money penetrated the country's most important public institutions, including the police, Congress, and the justice system, as the cartels sought to maintain their enormous wealth, influence, and resulting privileges. The cartels' response to the state's efforts to limit their activities brought about nearly a decade of violence and terror. From the assassination of Minister of Justice Rodrigo Lara Bonilla in 1984 and through the murder of Galán in 1989, the drug interests perpetrated a narco-terrorist campaign against the government, politicians, and journalists, and the related violence threatened to destabilize the national government. As domestic conditions and crackdowns in Peru and Bolivia reduced coca production there in the late 1980s, coca-leaf cultivation began to shift to Colombia, sparking the widespread purchase of cultivable land by criminal organizations involved in drug trafficking.

Colombia's paramilitary groups emerged in the 1980s at the intersection of the drug-trafficking phenomenon and the leftist insurgency. The first paramilitaries were urban vigilante groups in the employ of drug cartels in the early 1980s, the most notorious of which was Death to Kidnappers (MAS), which retaliated against guerrillas who kidnapped cartel family members. Parallel developments in the countryside involving the guerrillas were another factor that drove paramilitarism. The FARC's territorial expansion and the early electoral successes of its UP party following peace talks with the Betancur administration led large landowners and ranchers to begin forming local security forces to defend themselves. They argued that the state was ineffective in protecting their interests and maintaining order in rural areas; the resulting self-defense militias first appeared in the middle Magdalena valley.

The arrival of drug lords, who were becoming large landowners themselves, in the middle Magdalena in the mid-1980s, compounded land struggles between the left-wing insurgents and agrarian interests. Private militias proliferated to protect cocaine-processing laboratories, and eventually coca cultivations. By the late 1980s, in collaboration with military units, the self-defense groups adopted progressively more offensive and violent strategies against the guerrillas and leftist sympathizers who threatened their increasingly independent territorial domination. Paramilitaries openly targeted civilian politicians from the UP, approximately 3,000 of whose members were assassinated. The paramilitaries also unleashed a wave of political violence against journalists, campesino associations, labor leaders, politicians, and regional government functionaries. Nevertheless, the perception that the military was ineffective at combating the guerrillas and protecting the rural population from the growing insurgent threats of extortion and kidnapping strengthened local support for these so-called self-defense forces. With roughly 1,800 adherents in the late 1980s, these groups rapidly spread from the middle Magdalena region to Córdoba and Urabá, where they continued to unleash a reign of criminality and lawless violence. The growing direct involvement of paramilitaries, as well as guerrillas, in drug activities would be a key ingredient in the downward spiral in the next stage of Colombia's security situation (see The Contemporary Era, 1978–98, ch. 1).

Current National Security Panorama

Colombia limped into the 1990s, destabilized by the growing strength and lethal convergence of its three primary security threats: the FARC guerrillas, the right-wing paramilitaries, and the drug traffickers. Despite the successful demobilization of the M–19 and some smaller guerrilla groups, Colombia's primary insurgent movement continued its territorial expansion and organizational growth and improved its offensive capabilities. The paramilitary groups, which had been largely left alone, or in some cases nurtured, by the authorities, also increased in strength through the unification of their disparate groups into the United Self-Defense Forces of Colombia (AUC). At the same time, the paramilitaries and the guerrillas filled the void left by the collapse of the drug cartels in the early part of the decade. The expansion of these illegal armed groups and the intensification of the conflict coincided with the explosion of the illegal drug business in Colombia, which provided both left and right with an incomparable source of independent financing.

Internal Armed Conflict

Colombia's internal conflict underwent a dramatic escalation during the 1990s. Both the FARC and the paramilitaries increased their personnel, armaments, organization, and territorial presence. Confrontations with state security forces increased, and the proportion of the civilian population affected by direct actions or hostilities among the armed groups grew exponentially. The extent of the FARC buildup during the previous decade became obvious following the army's

*A young officer communicates with his superiors while on a
counterguerrilla patrol near San José del Guaviare, Guaviare Department.
Courtesy David Spencer
Two counterguerrilla soldiers of the 7th Brigade pause
after a successful operation, Apiay, Meta Department.
Courtesy David Spencer*

attack against the FARC headquarters in Casa Verde in 1990. The
guerrillas responded with the largest offensive in their history, made
possible by a new ability to conduct well-organized, large-scale, military operations. By 1995 the FARC had approximately 7,000 members
in 60 fronts, up from 32 fronts in 1986. Likewise, the number of guerrilla actions committed the same year increased fourfold to more than
600, consisting of attacks on police stations and villages with a police
presence, ambushes of military units, and sabotage of infrastructure.
Between 1996 and 1998, the FARC launched a series of direct assaults
against army units and bases in the south of the country, resulting in a
total of 220 soldiers dead and 242 captured. In one spectacular operation, the FARC even took control of the military base in Mitú, near the
Brazilian border.

The insurgent movement expanded into much of the national territory, particularly in coca-growing regions and areas of strategic
importance for national security and the economy. The insurgents
spread into border areas with neighboring countries and increased
their influence in urban centers. The FARC also took advantage of the

three-year peace process with the government of Andrés Pastrana (president, 1998–2002) in the late 1990s, using the demilitarized sanctuary (*zona de despeje*) to train combatants, harbor kidnapping victims, and improve its finances. As a result, peace negotiations were aborted in 2002. By 2006 the FARC had an estimated 60 to 80 fronts, with a total fighting force of approximately 16,000.

The ELN also continued to play a role, albeit an increasingly minor one, in Colombia's conflict dynamics. Eschewing the drug trade until about 2005–7 limited the ELN's military growth and thus its capacity for attacks on security forces. Instead, the ELN dedicated itself to sabotage of the energy and oil infrastructure in Arauca. Starting in 1999, the ELN began to carry out mass kidnapping operations, including hijacking an airplane with its passengers and crew and abducting all the Sunday worshippers in a church. The ELN grew from approximately 2,000 combatants at the start of the 1990s to 4,500 by the end of the decade. Hard hit by the paramilitaries and the security forces, it was estimated to number 3,300 combatants in 2004.

The growth of paramilitary organizations and their geographical expansion paralleled that of the FARC during the 1990s. A radical anticommunist agenda framed their strategy of using violence and terror to subdue or expel local populations sympathetic to the left, and to drive out any FARC presence. The paramilitary groups in Córdoba and Urabá were infamous for their indiscriminate massacres and torture of civilians up until the late 1990s, and they were responsible for the majority of human rights violations committed in Colombia. Multiple independent paramilitary movements united under the umbrella of the AUC in 1997, permitting greater coordination, growth, and advancement of their political agenda. The number of AUC combatants grew from only 1,800 in 1990 to an estimated 13,500 in 2004.

The critical ingredient in the conflict's expansion and intensification during the 1990s was the explosion in domestic coca production and the involvement of the FARC and the paramilitaries in different facets of drug cultivation and trafficking. Harvesting coca leaves had been a relatively small-scale business in Colombia. As it became harder to obtain coca base from neighboring countries, the new baby cartels—smaller and more independent organizations that replaced the Cali and Medellín cartels, such as the Norte del Valle Cartel, now considered Colombia's most powerful drug syndicate—dedicated themselves to shifting coca cultivation to Colombia. With only 14 percent of the global coca-leaf market in 1991, by 2004 Colombia was responsible for 80 percent of the world's cocaine production. The 13,000 hectares of coca in Colombia in the mid-1980s had ballooned to 80,000 hectares by 1998. By 2007 the coca-cultivation hectarage had increased to 99,000.

Drug-related activities became the principal source of income for the illegal armed groups, funding 50–70 percent of both the AUC and the FARC actions. According to the United Nations Development Programme, of the FARC's average annual income of US$342 million, US$204 million derived from the drug business. Drug-related enterprises were considered responsible for some US$190 million of the AUC's US$286 million average annual income. The FARC initially took part in production, processing, transportation, and extortion of protection payments, although it had diversified into drug trafficking by the early 2000s. The AUC appeared to control directly 40 percent of the drug-trafficking business. Whereas the paramilitaries engaged in direct drug trafficking, the FARC now preferred drugs-for-arms swaps. Armed groups dominated the country's major coca-growing regions. Paramilitaries had a presence in 86 of the 162 municipalities where coca was cultivated, and half of the FARC's 60 to 80 operational fronts participated in either coca or poppy cultivation and trade. Bitter territorial fighting between the AUC and the FARC to control regions dominated by coca cultivation and the drug business were a key feature of the conflict, although occasional incidents of pragmatic, strategic cooperation between them in narcotics operations demonstrated the complex dynamics of the Colombian conflict. The intimate relationship between drug trafficking and the armed conflict led to the formation of Plan Colombia, and eventually to a change in policy regarding the use of U.S. drug-control resources for antisubversive activities (see United States–Colombian Security Cooperation and Plan Colombia, this ch.).

The intensification of the internal conflict following the failed negotiations with the FARC in 2002 dashed the nation's hopes for peace. After the FARC retreated to remote bases, it resumed military offensives by trying to retake strategic corridors. It also increasingly resorted to terrorist acts, one of the most significant of which was the bombing of the Club Nogal in Bogotá in February 2003. This change of tactics could be interpreted variously as a sign of the guerrilla movement's strength and urban penetration or of its military weakness.

The character and aspirations of these illegal armed groups continue to generate debate. The United States considers them outright terrorists (vide their inclusion in the U.S. Department of State's terrorism list); many others see them as common criminals, or purely politically motivated insurgents or counterinsurgents. The FARC, ELN, and AUC display a mix of all these elements. They commit acts of terrorism, with the FARC, in particular, accused of increasingly resorting to terrorist acts. The groups engage in a range of criminal activities, including drug cultivation and trafficking, kidnapping, and extortion; yet they also maintain political agendas and have some base of social support. All the armed groups, both on the left and on the right, have established certain sociopolitical structures and gained autonomous authority in their respective zones of influence, effectively substituting for the state, with rudimentary systems of justice, conflict resolution, and political participation. The FARC continues to espouse a broad socialist political agenda and militant opposition to the Colombian government, even though the likelihood of its gaining national power through armed revolution is virtually nil. The FARC remains committed to territorial control and to local power, with an eye toward maximizing political gains in eventual negotiations. The paramilitaries seek status as legitimate political representatives in regional and national politics. Various paramilitary groups entered negotiations with the government in 2003, seeking legal pardon for their criminal activities and human.rights abuses in exchange for their complete demobilization and an entry into the political process. Having gained local support for their anti-insurgent platform and restoration of public order, the paramilitaries have achieved some success at penetrating national political institutions, as attested by the parapolitics scandal of 2006 (continuing in 2009). In mid-2008, at least 33 regional and national elected politicians were jailed awaiting trial, accused of collusion with the paramilitaries, while another 62 members of Congress were official suspects (see Corruption, ch. 4).

Human Rights

Colombia's internal conflict has caused the Western Hemisphere's worst humanitarian crisis. Civilians bear the brunt of the conflict, in which the warring parties commit serious and extensive breaches of human rights and act in disregard of international humanitarian law. Although the situation improved after 2002, the overall human rights panorama in Colombia continues to be cause for grave concern. In pursuit of their military objectives of dominating coca regions and controlling strategic corridors for the transport of drugs and arms, the illegal armed groups have increasingly targeted civilian populations. Credible threats of direct attacks or massacres, as well as the risk of violence from military confrontations between the FARC, the AUC, and the armed forces, forcibly displaced about 220,000 people in 2006, raising the total of internally displaced civilians since 1985 to 3.7 million. Women, children, indigenous populations, and Afro-Colombians are especially vulnerable to displacement. By 2006 some observers considered the paramilitaries to be responsible for 50 percent of displacements and the FARC for 25 percent.

Massacres, assassinations and extrajudicial executions, torture, abductions, forcible recruitment, the use of child soldiers, land-mine maiming, terrorism, and attacks on villages routinely target Colombia's civilian population. Although the situation remained very grave in 2007, important improvements in many indicators suggest progress is being made in the area of security, according to the U.S. Department of State's 2008 *Country Reports on Human Rights Practices: Colombia.*

In 2008 Colombia experienced 37 confirmed mass killings (defined by the government as killings of four or more persons), in which 169 people were killed. Although this was a 32-percent increase from 2007, it was a significant reduction in the annual number of victims since 2002, attributed principally to the sharp decrease in AUC violence following demobilization. Political assassinations are a particularly virulent tool in Colombia's conflict; mayors, congressional representatives, and candidates for political office are frequent targets. In 2006 the country had 153 politically related murders, including of one mayor and four former mayors. Many others were forced from office and banished from their towns by threats of violence, replaced by illegal armed actors who exercised de facto rule. In the first six months of 2006, more than 70 Colombians were "disappeared" forcibly, down significantly from 1,358 for the entire 2002 calendar year, but 23 percent more than during the same period of 2005. In 2006 an average of three persons a day, both civilians and soldiers, fell victim to land mines and other improvised explosive devices placed by the FARC and ELN across Colombia, a more than sevenfold increase from 2000. The figure was down to two persons per day in 2008. FARC attacks on villages continued to fall significantly during 2006, as did the group's previously indiscriminate use of gas-cylinder bombs against villages, which resulted in high civilian casualties. In 2005 an estimated 11,000 child combatants were serving in the various irregular groups in Colombia, approximately 80 percent of them abducted by the FARC or the ELN.

Until 2006 Colombia had the highest kidnapping rate in the world. During the 30-year period ending in 2006, almost 29,000 people were kidnapped for ransom, and on average seven kidnappings occurred daily from 1999 to 2002. Kidnapping for ransom is an important source of income for both the FARC and the ELN, and illegal armed groups commit approximately 60 percent of both extortive and political kidnappings. By 2006 this rate had decreased to two kidnappings per day, down nearly 76 percent from 2002. This reduction is attributed largely to the reduced kidnapping activity by the FARC, even while the participation of common criminals in such abductions grew. Of the 687 recorded kidnappings in 2006, which included children, 282 were for ransom. In 2007 the

FARC still held more than 750 people captive, while the ELN continued to hold 410 people. More than 4,000 people are still considered as disappeared. Between 1997 and 2007, more than 622 kidnapped Colombians died in captivity.

Besides extortive kidnappings, politically motivated kidnappings by the guerrillas continued to be a serious concern in 2008. Approximately 50 kidnapped victims were still being held by the FARC as potential bargaining chips with the government, among them politicians and members of the Colombian armed forces. The political hostages had included former presidential candidate Ingrid Betancourt Pulecio, who was kidnapped in 2002 while campaigning, and three American citizens kidnapped in 2003 while working as drug-control contractors with the U.S. military; they and 11 other hostages were rescued in a spectacular blow to the FARC in 2008. Colombia's minister of foreign relations in 2008, Fernando Araújo Perdomo, had been held by the FARC for more than six years until his daring escape in 2007. The June 2007 massacre of 11 assembly members from Valle del Cauca, who had been kidnapped by the FARC in 2002, underscored fears for the future of hostages whose value is measured in terms of their political bargaining weight.

Human rights abuses attributed to Colombia's military and security forces were acknowledged publicly for the first time during the Samper administration. International pressure by the United Nations and the Inter-American Commission on Human Rights, the linkage of U.S. military aid with Colombian human rights compliance, and reforms in the military penal system have contributed to improvements in the military and police human rights record since the late 1990s. According to the United Nations Office of the High Commissioner for Human Rights in Colombia, violations by the security forces are considered low, and all state agencies have made considerable efforts to increase their compliance with human rights norms. However, credible allegations of serious violations continued to be reported by this office in 2006. In addition to extrajudicial killings, security forces committed 32 known acts of torture in the first half of 2006 and 74 in the first half of 2008, a 46-percent increase compared with the first six months of 2007. To the extent that military participation in human rights abuses has declined, the paramilitaries, followed by the guerrillas, have increasingly replaced security forces as perpetrators of such violations.

Violence and Crime

Although the internal conflict is at the core of Colombia's acute security crisis, multiple forms of violence and criminality also pose grave risks to domestic order. No other country formally at peace registers Colombia's level of violence. Homicides, kidnappings, violence against journalists and activists, social cleansing (based on class and socioeconomic factors), and the systematic use of violence in the commission of property crimes underscore the country's security crisis. Criminal and social violence are frequently intertwined with conflict dynamics and drug cultivation and trafficking, with the majority of homicides and kidnappings taking place in municipalities where at least one of the principal illegal armed groups is present. Urban gangs, vigilante groups, and the notorious *sicarios*, or juvenile hired assassins, are also responsible for much of the violence in association with criminal, guerrilla, and paramilitary organizations, often through the extralegal application of security and justice.

Colombia's kidnapping rate has declined significantly in recent years. Although the majority of abductions are attributed to the illegal armed movements, common criminals account for the remaining 40 percent of kidnappings. In most cases, delinquents sell their captives to the guerrilla or paramilitary armies, creating a complex web of kidnapping.

The presence of organized crime and its links to drug trafficking, guerrilla and paramilitary movements, death squads dedicated to social cleansing, and high levels of impunity are all correlated with the homicide rate in Colombia, once the highest in the world. After having doubled throughout the 1980s, the homicide rate reached its peak of 70 homicides per 100,000 inhabitants in 1991 and then dropped from 28,500 cases in 2002 to 17,500 cases in 2006. This figure contrasted sharply with the Latin American average of only 17 in the late 1980s. The average homicide rate of 61 per 100,000 people in the 1990s increased in the early 2000s, then fell approximately 20 percent in 2003, because of the Democratic Security Policy and the paramilitary demobilization process. It was estimated that 5,000 of the 28,500 homicides committed in 2002 were directly related to the conflict.

Certain sectors of society, including the press, human rights workers, intellectuals, teachers, and labor leaders, are especially vulnerable to violence by both the left and right. In 1999 the Colombian government created a special Human Rights Unit within the Attorney General's Office to investigate violence against journalists and also implemented a Journalist Protection Program. Colombia has had the highest homicide rate against the press in the hemisphere, with 114 journalists murdered during the 1997–2007 period. In 2003 alone, five journalists were murdered, 11 kidnapped, and 31 threatened. However, no journalists were murdered in 2008, despite 72 death threats during the year. Human rights activists also are particular targets, with 73 murdered between 1996 and 2002 and 11 in 2008. The paramilitaries are considered responsible for the majority of these acts. Labor is also vulnerable to right-wing violence; an estimated 1,800 union members were killed between 1993 and 2003. Violence against labor was down sharply in 2004 as paramilitaries began the process of negotiation with the government. Unionized teachers are also often victims of Colombia's political violence, suffering 60 assassinations and 13 disappearances in 2005–6. In 2008 some 55 percent of all union members who were killed were teachers.

National Security Doctrines and Policies

Colombia's national security doctrines and policies evolved primarily in response to the threats posed by the insurgency and illicit drugs. Military plans to defeat or eliminate these problems lay at the core of the country's security policy. In the case of the guerrilla movements, the aim of counterinsurgency strategies first implemented in the 1960s was a military solution to what was considered an illegitimate armed challenge to the state. The inefficacy of this strategy led to various efforts in the 1980s and 1990s to seek a peaceful, negotiated solution to the armed conflict. When the last of these initiatives failed in 2002, Colombia readopted an exclusively military approach to the guerrilla problem. Drug trafficking also played a vital role in shaping security policies in Colombia, first in the 1980s with the rise of narco-terrorism, and later because of the increasing reliance on drug-related activities by both the guerrillas and the paramilitary organizations. In the early twenty-first century, all of these elements form part of a complex and paradoxical national security policy: the government is engaged in an all-out military campaign to defeat the FARC and the drug traffickers, at the same time that it aggressively pursues peace negotiations with the paramilitary organizations.

Counterinsurgency Strategies and Emergency Decrees

Colombia's military orientation since the 1940s reflected the Cold War anticommunist agenda that prevailed throughout South America. National security doctrines to counter growing internal challenges from the left were first elaborated in Brazil and Argentina, and soon dominated military institutions across the continent. Colombia's national security doctrine developed in the 1950s in response to rural self-defense units, which by the 1960s had evolved into guerrilla organizations engaged in irregular warfare against the state. This counterinsurgency posture coincided with changes in military institutions that began in the second half of the twentieth century, and with strengthening ties between Colombia and the United States in defense and security matters. Military assistance, counterinsurgency instruction of Colombian officials by the U.S. Army, and the creation of a national counterinsurgency training center were all precursors to the development of Colombia's first counterguerrilla strategy launched in 1960.

Plan LASO (Latin American Security Operation) was a direct offshoot of Colombia's national security doctrine and the counterinsurgent tactics learned from the U.S. military. With financing from the Kennedy administration, Colombia sought to use the plan to wipe out the guerrillas by applying the counterinsurgency doctrines employed by the United States in Vietnam. At the same time, the aim was to win the support of the civilian population through social and economic projects implemented by the army. In this regard, a key aspect of security thinking was economic development as a social defense against communism, as embodied in the Alliance for Progress ideology. The balance at the end of the five-year Plan LASO was mixed, however: some rural outlaw groups were eliminated, but others such as the FARC merely moved to outlying regions of the country where there was little or no state presence. Indeed, the radicalization of the FARC and its conversion into an offensive revolutionary movement were in large measure attributed to Plan LASO.

Two developments shaped national security policy in the immediate wake of Plan LASO. First, counterinsurgency became the centerpiece of the military's security strategy. Training and equipment acquisitions became oriented toward combating the guerrillas, and all the army's operative units developed into counterinsurgency companies. A National Intelligence Board, which reported to the military command, came into being in 1967 in order to develop intelligence and counterintelligence functions related to combating the guerrillas. The government intended a new National Defense Statute to improve coordination between the country's defense and civilian authorities.

Despite these reforms, counterinsurgency efforts in the late 1960s and through the 1970s failed to make much headway against the growing guerrilla threat. Divorced from broader state policies and political considerations, security strategy was largely in the hands of the army and remained of a strictly military nature. Colombia also increasingly relied on the implementation of states of emergency to respond to the internal situation. Constitutional provisions authorized the president to implement emergency measures, including legislation, in case of situations of extreme public disorder or war. Executive emergency decrees provided cover for summary executions, permitted the trial of citizens by military courts, and granted the military authority over the civilian population. In 1978 President Turbay made permanent certain facets of what had until then been considered extraordinary measures with a new security statute. By granting even greater autonomy to the Military Forces and loosening civilian controls over security matters, this legislation was sharply criticized for the systematic military abuses it engendered.

Peace Processes

Growing concern over the failure of counterinsurgency, the military's excessive autonomy over national security, and the escalation of repressive authoritarian responses to the internal conflict during the Turbay administration all led to consideration of a negotiated solution in the government's political agenda. Breaking with Colombia's national security paradigm, President Betancur announced his intention to seek peace with the country's various armed insurgent groups and declared that civilian authorities would manage negotiations. The ambitious peace policy involved the establishment of a commission to initiate dialogues with the guerrillas, a congressionally approved amnesty law, a rehabilitation plan, a series of public works projects in conflict zones dominated by the insurgents, and a commitment to strengthening the role of the National Police in maintaining public order. Significantly, both the FARC and the M–19 reached tentative agreements with the government in 1984. The success of the peace initiative was short-lived, however. The FARC was unable to sustain a viable political movement, and the M–19 broke the truce and took over the Palace of Justice on November 6, 1985.

Despite these setbacks, President Barco refused in the mid- to late 1980s to abandon the pursuit of a negotiated solution with the two principal guerrilla organizations, continuing efforts to demobilize insurgents, increasing resources for conflict zones, and creating the new position of presidential peace adviser. Indeed, the political commitment to reach a peace agreement with the guerrilla groups took on more urgency, as the drug cartels and narco-terrorism emerged as the country's new security priority in the mid-1980s. The government's 1988 peace initiative culminated in the demobilization of the M–19 and the participation of many of its leaders in the political process. The continuing threat posed by the FARC and the drug-trafficking groups, however, kept the military option very much on the table, and the strategic and operational autonomy of the armed forces intact.

The administration of President Gaviria represented a turning point in the early 1990s in Colombia's management of its national security strategies. With a series of far-reaching reforms, including the designation of the Ministry of National Defense as a civilian department, security ceased to be controlled exclusively by the armed forces as nonmilitary institutions gained a central role in the security decision-making process. For the first time, security entered the sphere of state policy, which allowed the government greater latitude in pursuing political solutions to the armed conflict and facilitated the demobilization agreements with the minor Renewed Socialist Movement (MSR) and various militia groups in Medellín. The government again failed, however, to reach an agreement with the FARC on a proposal to include guerrilla leaders in the 1991 Constituent Assembly in exchange for their demobilization. This failure, in conjunction with the political fallout from Pablo Escobar Gaviria's escape from prison in 1992, again led to the declaration of successive states of emergency to deal with the country's growing security crisis. In 1993 the government passed a public order bill that permanently legalized some of the more moderate aspects of the state of emergency provisions. Ironically, the same administration that wrested control over security policy from the military in the end resorted to the traditional formula of a military approach combined with emergency measures to restore domestic order.

In an effort to jump-start negotiations in the face of the FARC's impressive advances in the 1990s, President Pastrana accepted a bold proposal by the FARC to demilitarize five municipalities in an extensive territory in the department of Meta. Simultaneously, the military also withdrew from a smaller area in northern Colombia for the purpose of engaging in peace talks with the ELN. Both negotiations were fraught with difficulties and controversy because of the continuation of guerrilla attacks on state infrastructure and criminal activities such as kidnapping and coca cultivation while the talks were taking place. With suspicions high regarding the sincerity of the guerrillas' commitment to peace, and with doubts as to the proficiency of the government's negotiating skills, the process with the FARC was particularly contentious. When the government called off the talks and redeployed troops in February 2002 after a series of flagrant provocations by the FARC, including the assassination of a congressman and the hijacking of a commercial airplane, once again Pastrana declared a state of exception, followed by a new 2002 defense and security bill that granted the military judicial powers. Thus, Colombia arrived at the beginning of the new century with a somewhat contradictory track record in counterinsurgent security policy, alternating between the two extremes of political dialogue and the application of military force, which tended toward excesses sanctioned by emergency decrees.

The latest attempt at a peace process involved negotiations with a number of paramilitary fronts. By 2007 approximately 35,000 paramilitary combatants had participated in a national demobilization program established in the agreement between the government and the AUC signed on July 15, 2003, in Santa Fe de Ralito. The goal was to dismantle the entire AUC apparatus by the end of 2006, although serious difficulties remained regarding the demobilization process, the reabsorption of AUC members into civil society, and the nature of the judicial treatment of paramilitary leaders, who demanded pardons in exchange for demobilizing. Concerns were widespread that perpetrators of some of the worst atrocities committed during the conflict would receive excessively lenient punishments, that drug-trafficking operations would not be dismantled, and that the paramilitary command structures and political influence would remain intact.

Antidrug Strategies

The earliest antinarcotics efforts in Colombia in the 1970s occurred within the same counterinsurgency framework that guided security strategy, consisting of military offensives in marijuana- and coca-growing areas. Following the assassination of the minister of justice by drug traffickers in 1984, the military justice system expanded to cover not only guerrilla activities but also crimes committed by cartel members. At the same time, the military implemented forced eradication of coca crops and aerial fumigation.

The drug phenomenon became more complex, violent, and destabilizing by the mid-1980s, and Colombia responded with institutional measures to combat what was increasingly seen as a narcoterrorist threat to national security. Not only did the Barco administration pass the first antiterrorist statute, but the DAS and Ministry of Justice emerged as key players in the state's fight against drug trafficking and related criminal activities. One of the most significant developments was the shift in responsibility to the National Police for counternarcotics operations, as the military preferred to concentrate on its counterinsurgent priorities. An elite unit within the National Police also took charge of pursuing death squads, paramilitary groups, and drug organizations.

The Gaviria administration was the first to employ judicial incentives to combat the drug-trafficking threat. Invoking national security interests, the 1991 constitutional ban on extradition aimed at weakening the assassination and bombing campaign by the extraditables against the government. Reduced sentences and a prohibition on extradition to the United States were intended to encourage crim-

A soldier stands guard while coca crops are fumigated. Courtesy Narcotics Affairs Section Office, U.S. Embassy, Bogotá

inals to turn themselves in, which would eventually lead to the dismantling of the country's drug cartels. The Gaviria government also created an elite search unit of both police and military agents, originally to hunt down Pablo Escobar following his escape from prison, and later to pursue the country's other drug traffickers.

Under the Samper government, antinarcotics strategies broadened and the military reentered the "war on drugs." Samper not only reinstated Colombia's extradition laws but also stiffened sentences for drug-related crimes. A new search unit was established to hunt down the Cali Cartel, and an antinarcotics strategy led to increased fumigation of illicit coca crops. Military operations targeted destruction of the drug business infrastructure in the southern part of the country where coca cultivations dominated. With the installation of a radar system from the United States in Vichada, aerial interdictions began against suspected narco-trafficking flights.

United States–Colombia Security Cooperation and Plan Colombia

Although the hardening of Colombia's antidrug policies stemmed from the upsurge of political violence and terrorism perpetrated by the drug-trafficking organizations in the 1980s, the escalation of the U.S. "war on drugs" became a key factor in Colombia's national security orientation in the late 1990s. The Pastrana administration, while negotiating with the insurgents, also aggressively pursued international aid to help finance alternative counternarcotics policies, as well as to support institutional reforms, state building, trade relations, and the peace process itself. Early backing by the Clinton administration for Pastrana's comprehensive peace initiative stopped abruptly when the FARC murdered three American activists for indigenous rights in 1999. U.S. skepticism over the demilitarized zone and political negotiations with the FARC led to a shift in emphasis in Colombia's request for assistance in its counternarcotics efforts and military aid.

Following an intensive diplomatic campaign, in 2000 the U.S. Congress approved a US$860 million aid package to reduce the cultivation and production of drugs, largely through the aerial spraying of coca crops. The goal was to reduce coca cultivation by 50 percent in five years. Although there were also provisions for judicial reform, human rights, and democratic strengthening, 74 percent of the aid package, known as Plan Colombia, was earmarked for strengthening the military and the police and improving their antinarcotics capacity. Most of this aid went to the acquisition of intelligence-gathering equipment, vehicles, and helicopters; the creation of a new counternarcotics brigade; professional training; and the enhancement of military bases at Larandia and Tres Esquinas, both in Caquetá Department, and Tolemaida in Cundinamarca. The centerpiece of Plan Colombia's strategy was a push into southern Colombia by the 2,300-strong mobile brigade, followed by the massive fumigation of coca crops in Putumayo Department.

Two years later, another appropriation of US$400 million was part of a wider strategy called the Andean Regional Initiative, which placed the "war on drugs" within a regional context. The most significant change in this new round of U.S. legislation, however, was that U.S. military funding in Colombia broadened from counternarcotics activities to include counterinsurgency and counterterrorism. As the U.S. global posture took shape post–September 11, Colombian criminals and insurgents alike were increasingly viewed as terrorists. The lines between counternarcotics and counterinsurgency strategies became blurred, as it became evident that both the guerrilla and paramilitary movements were directly involved in the drug business. This change allowed U.S.-aided military units to actively pursue the FARC, ELN, and paramilitaries, led to the arrival of U.S. Special Forces to train Colombian soldiers in counterinsurgency and in the protection of the pipelines of U.S. oil companies, and permitted the sharing of nondrug intelligence.

The expansion of the U.S. mission in Colombia from a "war on drugs" to a "war on terror" had two immediate effects. It contributed to the intensification of Colombia's military campaign against the

FARC and triggered Colombia's reframing of its armed conflict and the illegal drug business according to the antiterrorist logic. With a new reading of Colombia's security situation as a terrorist threat, President Uribe became a top supporter of the U.S. "war on terror." Colombia gained an additional US$105 million of mostly military assistance in 2003 under the emergency supplemental bill for the war in Iraq, and the cap on U.S. troop numbers rose from 400 to 800 in 2004. U.S. military training reached 13,000 Colombian personnel in 2003, up from 2,500 in 1999. Finally, U.S. intelligence and logistical provisions supported the implementation of Plan Patriota, a large-scale, multiforce, counterinsurgency offensive of 17,000 Colombian troops in the country's southern region meant to be the beginning of the end of the guerrilla insurgency. Plan Patriota was replaced in 2006 by Plan Consolidación, intended to uproot the territorial control that the FARC still exerts upon the southern departments of Caquetá, Cauca, Guaviare, southern Meta, and Putumayo, and to combat drug trafficking in these regions. Financing came in part through a special war tax levied in December 2006 on the wealthiest individuals and companies in Colombia, which should raise US$4 billion between 2007 and 2010.

U.S. congressional criticism of military assistance to Colombia grew in 2005–6, owing to the poor results from aerial fumigation and persistent concerns about the Uribe government's leniency with the paramilitaries, and aggravated by incidents of corruption by U.S. troops in Colombia. Given the Uribe administration's overall security performance, however, and Colombia's role as one of the George W. Bush administration's strongest Latin American allies in Washington's global "war on terror," U.S. military assistance to Colombia rose to US$772.2 million in 2005. The U.S. Congress approved military and police aid totaling US$733.8 million in 2006.

After the November 2006 U.S. elections, in which Democrats gained control of both houses of Congress, Colombia began to lose its status as the darling of Latin America, and United States–Colombia relations suffered serious setbacks. As the voices of criticism in the U.S. Congress grew increasingly vociferous over what was perceived as a failing antidrug strategy, a series of scandals in Colombia led to a plummet in Washington's support for the Uribe administration in 2007. Charges of paramilitary collusion against a number of Colombian congressional representatives loyal to President Uribe's political party, together with incidents involving the army's ties to paramilitary groups and its role in the massacre of an elite police and antidrug unit, seriously damaged Uribe's reputation and resulted in the entire aid package to Colombia being called into question by the Democratic majority. A bill passed in the U.S. House of Representatives in June 2007 reduced the portion of U.S. aid destined for military assistance from 80 percent to 55 percent.

Democratic Security Policy

Frustrated by a steadily worsening security situation and the failure of Pastrana's peace negotiations with the FARC, Uribe rode to victory in the 2002 presidential election on a "get-tough" platform. Amid the new "war-on-terror" framework, increased U.S. military involvement, and a closely managed military strategy, Uribe made law and order his priority. These elements came together in his administration's Democratic Security Policy, a broad and ambitious policy package designed to provide internal security within a framework of democratic protections and guarantees. The policy's main strategic objective was to change the military balance of power in the armed conflict in order to defeat the guerrillas, or to force them to negotiate on terms favorable to the government. Achievement would come through the strengthening of the armed forces, the reestablishment of military control over the totality of Colombian territory, the eradication of drug crops, and the elimination of illegal armed groups, all supported by expanded military cooperation with the United States. The Uribe government allocated the U.S. aid to significantly increasing the number of professional foot soldiers, retaking control over strategic corridors from the guerrillas, and creating militias of peasant soldiers, additional mobile brigades, and new high-mountain battalions. The military offensive against the guerrillas also targeted the paramilitary combatants. The armed forces sought to improve their professionalism and compliance with international human rights standards, as well as mobility, readiness, and intelligence capabilities.

Lasting and comprehensive security was understood as going beyond military victory over the illegal armed groups. Uribe's Democratic Security Policy broke with previous military doctrines by incorporating institutional protections of citizens' rights (*tutelas*), guarantees of justice, and the rule of law as essential components in a comprehensive, viable vision of security. By improving governance and strengthening confidence in public institutions and democracy, state legitimacy would be enhanced at the same time that nondemocratic alternatives would become discredited.

These objectives notwithstanding, government policy continued to favor military protection of public order over institutional strengthening. Early in Uribe's first administration, a state of emergency that temporarily granted judicial powers to the military, special powers for security forces, and the application of security measures to noncombatants generated concerns about possible misuses of government power. Improvements in most security indicators in Colombia in 2003–4 suggested that Uribe's approach had made important gains, although questions remained about the government's interpretation of the conflict as a struggle against terrorism, and about the prospects for long-term success of a military strategy to defeat the 45-year-old insurgency at the expense of dealing with fundamental social and economic problems.

President Uribe's plan included the formation of legally recruited platoons of campesino soldiers; they would perform their obligatory military service by serving on guard duty around previously unguarded municipalities in support of the police and regular troops. By August 2004, more than 8,000 campesino soldiers had been recruited and trained. The military program for the second half of 2006 provided for 32,376 campesino soldiers. By 2009 the actual number of trained campesino soldiers in the armed forces totaled 25,202. Nevertheless, analysts believe that it would take years to make any significant progress in reducing the territory held by the illegal armed groups.

According to official figures, the military campaigns within the framework of the Democratic Security Policy accounted for a 35 percent decrease in attacks against infrastructure. They also resulted in the state's regaining control of key rivers such as the Atrato, Caguán, Caquetá, Guaviare, and Guayabero; the seizure of 153 tons of cocaine; the eradication of 223,000 hectares of illicit plantations; and the destruction of 2,000 laboratories for coca processing.

The Uribe administration's military offensive has had a significant effect on the FARC's fighting force. By early 2008, as a result of sustained military operations in regions traditionally controlled by the insurgents and improved intelligence capabilities, the number of FARC combatants had been reduced from a high of between 18,000 and 21,000 to approximately 10,000, a number that may have declined further by 2009 to less than 8,000. The number of guerrilla fronts was generally estimated at between 60 and 80 at most.

Negotiations in 2007–8

The various illegal groups involved in Colombia's internal security problems have required the government to pursue separate peace agendas with the FARC, the ELN, and the paramilitaries, each with very different mechanisms and results. The most significant progress toward a negotiated solution has been with the paramilitaries.

The Justice and Peace Law of 2005 formalized the paramilitary demobilization process that had been established in 2003. This provision

offered release from prison, reduced sentences, and other judicial concessions to paramilitaries in exchange for demobilization, surrendering
arms, and confessing all crimes committed as a way of providing reparation to the victims' families. Compliant paramilitary combatants not
accused of human rights violations or war crimes would not be imprisoned. Those accused of such crimes would receive a maximum of eight
years in prison, including exemption from extradition to the United States
under charges of drug trafficking.

When the process ended in August 2007, approximately 32,000
people claiming to be members of the AUC had demobilized, handing in more than 15,000 weapons, explosives, and pieces of communications equipment. Most analysts agree that the process has
produced positive results insofar as a significant number of paramilitary leaders are now in prison or in reintegration programs. Nevertheless, the volume of demobilized individuals far surpasses the
estimated number of AUC paramilitary combatants, raising concerns
that drug traffickers and other criminals have co-opted the demobilization program in order to avoid legal prosecution, or that campesinos were seeking access to the social and monetary benefits that the
Justice and Peace Law provides. Either way, the government's ability to control the process has been seriously questioned. The disparity between the number of decommissioned weapons and the
number of demobilized combatants has also led to speculation that
many paramilitaries have stashed arms for future use. The most serious concern about the demobilization process is that it has been
unable to guarantee the complete dismantling of the paramilitary
infrastructure. By 2007 more than 3,000 supposedly demobilized
individuals had been recruited by 22 newly formed paramilitary
groups that continue to vie for control of the territories abandoned by
the AUC, especially in drug-trafficking corridors. This new generation of paramilitarism is principally active in the Caribbean and
Pacific coastal regions.

The demobilization process has also produced significant political
fallout in Colombia. The confessions of paramilitary leaders involved
in the truth and reconciliation process have compromised many
elected politicians and regional leaders. In one particularly dramatic
episode, the computer records of the paramilitary leader Rodrigo
Tovar Pupo, known as Jorge 40, revealed the names of 11 congress-
men who had signed an accord with the paramilitaries in 2001, in
which they committed themselves to supporting a new political order
in Colombia, presumably founded on values held by the AUC (see
Internal Armed Conflict and Peace Negotiations, ch. 4).

The Justice and Peace Law also provided for the creation of a new
National Commission for Reparation and Reconciliation (CNRR) in

A unit of the navy's Marine Infantry Command patrols the Guaviare, which divides the eastern llanos from the Amazonian jungle.
Courtesy David Spencer

2005. In 2006 the CNRR recommended forms of reparation to the victims of paramilitary violence and atrocities, established regional offices to attend to the victims, and started a program to investigate disappearances. Nevertheless, the nongovernmental organization (NGO) community has been critical of the CNRR, alleging a lack of effective reparation mechanisms.

After more than 25 years of intermittent talks, a formal peace process with the ELN had its start in December 2005 in Havana. The talks were preceded by the release from prison of ELN leader Gerardo Bermúdez, alias Francisco Galán, and his confinement to a *casa de paz*, or peace house, established by the government in Medellín for the purpose of facilitating peace discussions with leaders of civil society and the international community. Eight rounds of talks during 2006–7 took place with Mexico in the role of facilitator, and a more formal dialogue was held with the participation of Norway, Spain, and Switzerland. Although the ELN's military capability has been curtailed by Uribe's security policy, the armed group has continued its military operations, including bombings of pipelines and energy towers, assassinations, and kidnappings. Disagreements on the conditions for a cease-fire and the role of the international mediators have thwarted progress in the talks, which thus far have

349

produced no tangible results. Although the process had not formally broken down in 2008, the peace initiative has been at an impasse. Having repeatedly refused to have any contact with the government while Álvaro Uribe is in office, the FARC has minimized possibilities for a viable peace process. The government for its part has opted for a military offensive against the guerrillas and has not actively sought the resumption of peace talks. The lesson learned from the Pastrana administration is that negotiating with the FARC is a losing formula, and that a military solution is possible. At the same time, the Uribe government has pursued parallel strategies to its military approach designed to contribute to the overall weakening of the FARC organization. Such policies include incentives for unilateral demobilization through the benefits of the Justice and Peace Law to FARC deserters and cash payments to people whose information contributes to the capture or killing of FARC leaders. In 2007, for the first time in the history of the internal conflict, more FARC members deserted than were killed in combat. By early 2008, the number of demobilized guerrilla combatants had grown to 11,320, and an additional 3,461 guerrillas demobilized during 2008.

Despite the apparent irreconcilability of their positions, the government and the FARC continued to have regular communications in 2007 on a humanitarian agreement that would liberate several hundred guerrillas from prison in exchange for the release of members of the armed forces and political figures who had been held in captivity by the FARC for more than five years. To negotiate the conditions of the trade and effect the actual exchange, the FARC demanded a demilitarized zone in the south of the country, which the government firmly rejected. The Uribe administration also insisted that freed guerrillas not return to the FARC or engage in any subversive activity. The humanitarian agreement drew the attention of the international community, motivated by the plight of the kidnapped victims and an interest in moving forward a peace process in Colombia. France, Spain, and Switzerland offered to serve as mediators, while French president Nicolas Sarkozy was actively involved in attempts to reach an agreement between the government and the FARC for the liberation of former presidential candidate Ingrid Betancourt, who is also a French national. In late 2007, the Colombian government granted permission to Venezuelan president Hugo Chávez Frías to hold talks with the FARC in order to facilitate an agreement. However, this mediation effort was short-lived. Dissatisfaction with President Chávez's refusal to abide by the previously agreed terms of mediation led the Colombian government to terminate his role in November 2007.

International and Regional Security Relations

Agreements and Treaties

Colombia is involved in a number of international security instruments, especially in the Western Hemisphere, and is a member of its principal collective security agreement. In the face of a perceived communist threat following the end of World War II, in 1947 Colombia participated in founding the Inter-American Treaty of Reciprocal Assistance (Rio Treaty), which stipulates collective defense in the event of military aggression by an extrahemispheric power. Additionally, Colombia is a founding member of the Organization of American States (OAS—see Glossary), the regional organization responsible for determining when the Rio Treaty's collective security provisions should be implemented, and is bound to the peaceful settlement of disputes among signatory nations by the American Treaty on Pacific Settlement, or Bogotá Pact, of 1948. Colombia also supports a number of the inter-American conventions on arms trafficking; drugs; conventional, chemical, and biological weapons; and terrorism. Colombia participates in the OAS Committee on Hemispheric Security and supports its initiatives on antiterrorism, transregional crime, and confidence- and security-building measures. Colombia also ratified the Inter-American Human Rights Convention in 1978, and the Inter-American Court of Human Rights made a series of important rulings ordering reparations for victims of human rights abuses or violations of due process by Colombia's security forces.

In 1972 Colombia signed the Treaty for the Prohibition of Nuclear Weapons in Latin America, or Treaty of Tlatelolco, which prohibits the introduction of nuclear weapons into the region. The country also became a signatory to the Treaty on the Non-Proliferation of Nuclear Weapons in 1986.

Colombia and the OAS entered into an agreement in January 2005 that established a special OAS mission in Colombia to observe the paramilitary demobilization process. OAS activities include verification of the cease-fire, demobilization and disarmament, and the reintegration of combatants, as well as the proposal of confidence-building measures. The United Nations, for its part, decided to suspend its special mission in Colombia in April 2005 after five years of involvement in diverse efforts to help end the country's conflict.

Colombia is a signatory to the Rome Statute, which established the International Criminal Court. In 2002 the government was granted the statute's Article 124 exception, exempting Colombia from the court's jurisdiction for seven years from the date of signing the treaty. Colombia argued that this temporary exclusion would facilitate future peace negotiations and act as an incentive to armed groups to negotiate within that time period. In order to avoid losing its U.S. military aid, in 2003 Colombia also accepted the Article 98 agreement with the United States, which stipulates that it pledges not to seek the prosecution of U.S. military personnel and other citizens in the International Criminal Court for human rights crimes.

Regional Relations

Closer to home, the internal conflict has had a direct impact on Colombia's security relations with neighbors in the Andean region, as well as with bordering Brazil and Panama. Some 6,000 kilometers of shared boundaries through mostly remote, ungoverned territory have contributed to the regionalization of a conflict conventionally assumed to be domestic. Certain aspects of the Colombian conflict cross international borders, such as criminality and population displacement, and conditions and activities in the region in turn have aggravated Colombia's situation. Andean leaders routinely accuse Colombia of making insufficient efforts to contain the conflict, which is considered the driving force behind regional instability. Bogotá, for its part, blames neighboring governments for turning a blind eye to the inflow of illegal arms and outflow of illegal drugs through Colombia's ports, as well as to narcotics-related money laundering. Recurrent recriminations and high levels of political instability in all the Andean states are obstacles to effective regional security cooperation in the early 2000s.

Venezuela

Colombian–Venezuelan security relations are the most complex and conflictive of the region. President Chávez openly sympathized with the FARC's political platform, and Caracas is routinely accused of providing material support and haven to the FARC in Venezuelan territory. Chávez's ideological empathy with Colombia's guerrilla movements was tested in 2004 following a series of incidents involving the FARC, the ELN, and paramilitaries in Venezuelan territory, one of which resulted in the deaths of five Venezuelan soldiers. In 2004 Colombian police extralegally captured and then transported to Colombia a FARC leader resident and naturalized in Venezuela, causing a near rupture in diplomatic relations. Although Colombia and Venezuela maintain a binational border commission, security cooperation is poor.

In addition to tensions directly associated with the internal armed conflict in Colombia, the territorial dispute over maritime waters in the Golfo de Venezuela continues to plague bilateral relations. In the

1960s, the disagreement revolved around control over access to the Golfo de Venezuela and the Islas Los Monjes, a chain of three islands located at the gulf's northern mouth. Although the islands themselves are minuscule, ownership permits control over a 200-nautical-mile circumference around them. Thus, by gaining recognition of a rightful claim to the islands, Colombia would gain control over a substantial maritime territory in the Caribbean Sea that extends into the gulf, including waters suspected of having significant oil reserves. Following several unsuccessful attempts in the 1970s and 1980s to come to an agreement on the border, Colombia anchored a warship in the disputed waters for 10 days in 1987. The mobilization of both countries' armies and air forces suggested that the countries were dangerously close to war. The situation defused after Venezuela's military buildup in the border area prompted Colombia's withdrawal.

Colombia and Venezuela also traditionally have viewed each other as a potential military rival in the region. Venezuela's stronger military capacity increased in 2005 through the acquisition of 10 Russian helicopters and Spanish transport airplanes, patrol boats, and assault rifles. Venezuela attributes the buildup to the Colombian situation and to the potential threat posed by the U.S. regional military presence. Colombia, for its part, has accused Venezuela of starting an arms race and creating a military imbalance in the region.

Ecuador

Colombia's internal conflict has dominated its relations with Ecuador. Ecuador increasingly has been concerned during the early 2000s by the growing presence of paramilitary and FARC units in the Ecuadorian border region and the criminality and violence this presence has engendered. There have been confirmed cases of kidnapping and extortion in all the Ecuadorian provinces that border Colombia. Coca regularly crosses the border to Ecuador, either for direct export or for processing, and then usually reenters Colombia as cocaine for export. Although the expected surge of refugees into Ecuador because of Plan Colombia's fumigation policy did not occur, there were approximately 6,300 Colombian refugees on Ecuadorian soil in 2003 and an estimated 600,000 Colombian citizens who lived there irregularly. In response to what is seen as the Colombianization of the country, the Ecuadorian government increased its troops and patrols of the border region and restricted its traditional open-border policy in 2001. The Ecuadorian government has opted for a modus vivendi with Colombian illegal armed groups in the border area, whereas Bogotá has accused Quito of being too tolerant of what it considers terrorist organizations. President Rafael Correa

Delgado denounced the effects of aerial fumigations of coca crops in the Ecuadorian border areas and advocated manual eradications. Following a temporary suspension of aerial spraying, the Colombian government resumed it in December 2006, triggering an immediate condemnation from Ecuador. The two presidents reached an agreement in 2007, in which Colombian authorities agreed to inform their Ecuadorian counterparts before every aerial fumigation, in order to allow a special commission from Ecuador to verify that glyphosate was not reaching Ecuadorian territory.

Colombia's relations with neighboring Ecuador and Venezuela came to a crisis point in early 2008 as a consequence of Colombia's bombing of a FARC camp in Ecuadorian territory that killed the FARC second in command, Luis Édgar Devia, also known as Raúl Reyes, as well as an Ecuadorian citizen. Venezuela and Ecuador responded by terminating diplomatic relations with Colombia, accusing it of violating Ecuadorian sovereignty. Colombia, for its part, denounced the direct ties between each government and the FARC. Information recovered from Reyes's computer files pointed toward political and financial support from the Correa and Chávez governments to the FARC, in addition to face-to-face meetings with ministers from the Correa cabinet. Tensions were calmed through an OAS ministerial meeting in March 2008.

By January 2009, Colombia had reinforced its border with Ecuador. Colombia brought 27,000 army, navy, and air force members to its side of the border and a Nodriza riverine craft to patrol the San Miguel and Putumayo rivers 24 hours a day. However, the two countries agreed to reestablish diplomatic relations by November 15, 2009.

Panama

Of all the neighboring territories, Panama is the most vulnerable to the volatility of Colombia's security. Both the FARC and the paramilitaries openly operate along the 225-kilometer-long border through the remote jungles of the isthmus of Darién. These armed groups routinely cross into Panamanian territory for provisions and relaxation; and they also have engaged in combat and attacked villages for collaborating with the guerrillas or the paramilitaries, as the case may be. A strategic transit point for arms and drug smuggling, the border region is not only fiercely disputed by armed groups but also plagued by Colombian and Panamanian criminal organizations. The high levels of insecurity are compounded by the lack of a Panamanian military to defend its border, and by a police force with insufficient capacity to effectively patrol the region. A 1999 agreement between the Colombian and Panamanian naval forces strength-

A FARC guerrilla having lunch at a camp in Cundinamarca Department
Courtesy David Spencer Collection

ened maritime and border controls, and in 2002 Panama passed a resolution that allowed U.S. law enforcement agencies to conduct antidrug operations within Panama. Nevertheless, Colombia and Panama do not have a binational border commission, such as Colombia maintains with Peru and Venezuela.

Brazil

Despite an enormous shared border area that is a haven for criminal groups and insurgents, the possible expansion of the conflict into national territory is not Brazil's primary concern. Rather, regional trade, integration, and technical cooperation dominate Brazil's agenda with Colombia. Security relations were strained by the Colombian military's unauthorized use of a Brazilian military base during a 1998 operation to recover the town of Mitú, which had been taken over by the FARC. Brazil initially had concerns over Plan Colombia and the implications of U.S. military involvement in Colombia for its own sovereignty. Brazil prefers a more measured and somewhat distant diplomatic position regarding Colombia, citing its potential role as a peace facilitator as the reason for refusing to declare the FARC a terrorist group. It also considers the Colombian conflict an internal matter—external interference in which would constitute a violation of Colombia's sovereignty. Brazil's concern over the Colombian situation is more related to criminality, in particular the growing drug and arms smuggling through the jungle that spans the two countries, and the soaring crime rates and drug use in Brazilian cities. Although Brazil has shown a preference for unilateral measures to respond to the growing insecurity in the Amazonian border region, bilateral security cooperation and the exchange of intelligence and information between the countries have increased in recent years. The two governments signed several security accords in 2007, and commercial relations showed a slight improvement over previous years.

Peru

The Colombian–Peruvian relationship is the least tense in the region and is marked by the greatest levels of security cooperation. Peru's concern is limited to the possible increase in coca cultivation in Peru as a result of Plan Colombia's crop-eradication efforts at home. Despite a slight increase in coca plants in Peru in 2002, the much-feared balloon effect did not materialize. Colombia, for its part, is concerned that Peru's political instability might permit a repeat of the Vladimiro Montesinos scandal of 1999, in which the head of Peru's intelligence service arranged a shipment of Jordanian arms to the FARC. Bilateral security mechanisms put in place in the 1990s established defense and police collaboration on river and air interdiction. A 2001 agreement on security and judicial cooperation against terrorism, corruption, and illegal drug trafficking was followed in 2002 by the creation of a bilateral defense working group.

Nicaragua

Another regional geopolitical worry for Colombia relates to the contested sovereignty of the Archipiélago de San Andrés, Providencia y Santa Catalina, located off the Caribbean coast of Nicaragua. In 1979 the Sandinista government renewed historical claims to the islands, charging that the 1928 Treaty of Esguerra–Bárcenas, which granted Colombia jurisdiction, was invalid because Nicaragua had signed the agreement under pressure from the United States. Colombia responded by dispatching a naval task force, a squadron of Mirage fighters, and 500 marines to the islands and constructing a new base to serve as headquarters for the Caribbean Naval Command. During the 1980s, the presence of Nicaraguan fishing boats irritated Colombia, although there was no real threat of open conflict. Nicaragua's interest in oil exploration near the archipelago led to renewed interest in the islands, and in 2001 Nicaragua instituted proceedings with the International Court of Justice (ICJ) at The Hague, requesting recognition of its jurisdictional claim to the islands and the fixing of a single maritime boundary and

*Three FARC guerrillas using a laptop computer at a
temporary camp in Cundinamarca Department
Courtesy David Spencer Collection*

economic zone between the two countries. After the Nicaraguan government granted four foreign oil companies a license to drill in its offshore oil fields within several kilometers of the islands in 2003, Colombia claimed the concessions were in its maritime waters and threatened to use force if drilling commenced. Colombia argued that the ICJ had no competence to resolve the dispute, given that both countries had signed a legally binding agreement, whereas the ICJ resolves border disagreements only where there is no previous agreement. The preliminary hearings phase ended in August 2007, and that December the ICJ ratified the Treaty of Esguerra–Bárcenas, under which Nicaragua recognized Colombian sovereignty over the islands, and Colombia recognized Nicaraguan sovereignty over the Costa de Mosquitos (see Foreign Relations, ch. 4).

Outlook

Mixed signs for Colombia's security appeared in 2008. On the positive side, a series of unexpected and rather extraordinary events related to the FARC in the first half of the year suggested the possibility that the Western Hemisphere's longest-running internal armed conflict could be entering a critical last stage. Although the FARC has proved itself to be remarkably resilient over the years, recent developments point to the guerrilla organization's unmistakable weakness and fracturing. In the span of a few short months, a cross-border bombing raid of a guerrilla camp in Ecuador killed Luis Édgar Devia, also known as Raúl Reyes, the FARC's second in command; Secretariat member Manuel de Jesús Muñoz, alias Iván Rios, was murdered by one of his own security guards, who then turned himself in; the highest-ranking female commander in the FARC, Elda Neyis Mosquera, alias Nelly Ávila Moreno and Karina, surrendered along with a close collaborator; and the FARC founder and leader of near-mythic proportions, Pedro Antonio Marín, died of a supposed heart attack in his jungle hideout. On top of these major setbacks for the FARC, on July 2, 2008, a spectacular operation by the Colombian military, which freed 15 victims of political kidnappings, including Ingrid Betancourt and the three U.S. military contractors held captive for five and six years, respectively, was the strongest blow to date. All these events taken together not only point to incontrovertible deterioration in the FARC command structure but also to a devastating blow to the organization's cohesion and morale. It is likely that the steady flow of guerrilla deserters will only accelerate, as the FARC leadership, discipline, communications, and logistics capabilities continue to deteriorate.

The parallel story to this apparent implosion of the FARC is the success of the government's military approach and its Democratic Security Policy in dealing with the internal conflict. The Uribe administration's strategy of giving priority to a military offensive over negotiations with the FARC has shown undeniable results, reinforcing President Uribe's long-held position that a military victory over the FARC is possible. At the same time, the Military Forces' recent wave of successes over a much-discredited subversive organization has contributed to a renewed confidence by the public in Colombia's military.

It is quite premature, however, to claim that the FARC has been defeated. It retains substantial military capability and financial resources from drug-related activities. The group also still had in its power in late 2009 numerous civilians, public figures, and members of the armed forces to use as bargaining chips with the government. Although the FARC has clearly been routed in certain traditional areas of control such as Antioquia, Caldas, Risaralda, southern Cundinamarca, and parts of Chocó, in the southern regions of Colombia it continues to have an important presence and capacity for military actions. It is doubtful that the FARC, having endured for so many years, will simply fade away. More violence and acts of terrorism are expected, in part as a way of attempting to demonstrate its continued power and relevance. At the same time, given its proven capacity for hunkering down in remote jungle and mountainous areas of the country and playing a defensive waiting game with the government, the FARC may be trying to outlast President Uribe, whose term expires in 2010.

Given the apparently irreversible disintegration of the FARC's hierarchy and control and communications, which have been exposed by recent events and by the personal testimonies of deserters, a more likely scenario is the organization's fracturing. While some guerrilla fighters will follow the lead of those who have deserted, other units will break off and pursue autonomous guerrilla warfare in isolated regions of the country, or establish alliances with smaller subversive groups, including the ELN. Still other fronts will turn entirely to criminality, joining forces with narco-traffickers and reconstituted paramilitary groups.

The implications of these developments for a negotiated settlement to the Colombian conflict are mixed. On the one hand, President Uribe has stepped up calls on the FARC to release all kidnapped victims and make an historic peace with the Colombian government. Military pressure on the FARC will continue unabated until it demonstrates interest in a negotiation. The international community has joined Colombia in this effort. Not only has global public support for the FARC plummeted following recent events and Ingrid Betancourt's eloquent denunciation of its inhumane practices in the name of a leftist struggle, but also political sympathy for the Colombian insurgents has all but evaporated in Latin America. Venezuela's President Hugo Chávez, who in 2008 praised the FARC's struggle and called on the international community to grant the guerrilla organization belligerent status, is now urging the FARC to disarm and continue its political activities within the parameters of Colombia's democratic institutions. Even Fidel Castro of Cuba publicly denounced the FARC's kidnapping practices.

An optimistic view of the FARC's hard-line new leader, Guillermo León Sáenz Vargas, alias Alfonso Cano More, is that, as a university-educated ideologue, he will be concerned with trying to reestablish the FARC's political legitimacy, be more cognizant of changing global conditions that do not favor the FARC's violent struggle, and advocate abandoning criminal and terrorist activities, which would bode well for political negotiations with the government. At the same time, the FARC leadership may accept that they have lost their leftist struggle and that the time for negotiation has arrived. Nevertheless, the antipathy between President Uribe and the FARC is well known. The guerrillas have repeatedly refused to consider any peace discussions with the Uribe administration and insisted on another demilitarized zone as a precondition for a humanitarian exchange. The new balance of power between the FARC and Colombia's Military Forces is such that the government is hardly likely to consider any real power-sharing arrangement. A peace process that is little more than a surrender, however, will not be especially attractive to the FARC, which continues to espouse its goal of exercising political power. The window of opportunity for reaching a negotiated settlement to Colombia's conflict may also be short-lived because of the FARC's partial disintegration and fractures. The collapse of the guerrilla organization's central command and the simultaneous creation of multiple, autonomous illegal armed groups would foil chances to establish a decisive and lasting peace in Colombia.

Negotiations with the paramilitaries are, on the other hand, proceeding apace. Although there are many uncertainties regarding the judicial treatment of individuals accused of some of the worst human rights violations, the generally successful demobilization of AUC fighters and dismantling of paramilitary structures would represent an important step toward ending Colombia's internal conflict. A legal framework has been established for paramilitary disarmament and reintegration into civilian life—an attempt to reconcile the competing goals of peace and justice. However, the approved bill has elicited severe criticism, including accusations of being too generous to the illegal groups. The success in the implementation of the law is also threatened by the insufficient capacity of the Colombian judicial system to expedite the number of cases and to determine whether the demobilized fighters had complied with the requirement to confess their crimes. At the same time, there was mounting evidence in early 2008 that many demobilized paramilitaries had regrouped in autonomous criminal organizations dedicated to narco-trafficking, while others maintained their criminal operations during incarceration.

In early 2008, the Colombian government decided to suspend the judicial benefits offered to most of the high-ranking AUC leaders who participated in the process, arguing that they had continued to commit crimes from prison following their demobilization. President Uribe signed an executive order that led to the unexpected extradition of 14 paramilitary leaders to the United States to be tried on drug-trafficking charges. They included Salvatore Mancuso Gómez; Francisco Javier Zuluaga, alias Gordolindo; Diego Fernando Murillo Bejarano, alias Don Berna; and Rodrigo Tovar Pupo. This action effectively placed the paramilitary leaders beyond the reach of the Colombian justice system, raising concerns about the impossibility of trying these persons for crimes against humanity under the Justice and Peace Law in Colombia.

A wild card in the future of the Colombian conflict remains cocaine. Even with redoubled fumigation efforts, it appears highly unlikely that coca cultivations can be entirely eradicated by this method, leaving intact the illegal drug trade, which sustains Colombia's internal conflict. In 2008 the annual report of the United Nations Office on Drugs and Crime indicated that in 2007 some 99,000 hectares in Colombia were cultivated with coca plants, the same as 2002 levels. A key element in this dynamic is external demand for cocaine, most of which originates in the United States and Europe. Unless drug use in the advanced industrialized countries declines, and as long as its illegality maintains the incentives associated with black-market trading, it is unlikely that drug cultivation and trafficking in Colombia will go away entirely. The strengthening of Colombia's rural economy and the implementation of alternative development (see Glossary) and crop-substitution programs are also needed to discourage cultivation of coca.

The Colombian Military Forces, with U.S. military assistance, have made significant progress against the insurgent threat. In January 2007, the Colombian government launched the Strategy to Strengthen Democracy and Social Development. Known as Plan Colombia II, this six-year program will continue the successful strategies and consolidate the results of its predecessor plan and achieve the steady transfer of responsibility for the plan to Colombia. Its components include the "wars on drugs and terror," improved human rights, justice reform, free-market trade, social development, assistance for the internally displaced population, and the disarmament, demobilization, and reintegration into society of armed combatants.

Institutional weakness and persistent poverty and inequality also are correlated closely with the violent ruptures in Colombian society. Fragile state institutions and poor socioeconomic conditions for much of Colombian society continue to aggravate the conditions that gave rise to the internal conflict and contribute to illegality. Violence and privatized systems of justice undermine the state's capacity to govern effectively, to establish a monopoly on the legitimate use of force, and to provide security, justice, social services, and sustainable growth. A viable, comprehensive security agenda in Colombia requires not only the establishment of public order and protection for citizens, but also enhancements in both the institutional and socioeconomic aspects of national life. Military progress against the insurgent movements and the pervasive drug problem is a necessary but insufficient condition to achieve genuine national security. In that regard, the shift in U.S. aid to Colombia for 2007–8 toward social programs was a promising development.

There is cautious optimism about the possibility for peace in Colombia despite persistent obstacles. The challenge for the government is to articulate its military successes against the FARC and important gains in public security into a broad-based platform of political, social, and economic inclusion and justice. After three failed peace processes, a government campaign that has brought the guerrilla organization to the lowest point in its 45-year history, and the loss of its domestic and international support, the FARC for its part faces the choice between clinging to a futile struggle or embracing an historic opportunity to end Colombia's internal conflict and facilitate the transition to a postconflict stage.

*   *   *

There is an abundance of material available on Colombian national security, which encompasses a wide variety of thematic issues. Among the most authoritative Spanish-language sources on military and defense are *Estado y Fuerzas Armadas en Colombia: 1886–1953* by Adolfo Leon Atehortúa and Humberto Vélez; *Fuerzas Armadas y seguridad nacional* by Cesar Torres del Río; Russell W. Ramsey's *Guerrilleros y soldados*; and Andrés Villamizar's *Fuerzas Militares para la Guerra: La agenda pendiente de la reforma militar*. English-language sources include *Colombian Army Adaptation to FARC Insurgency* by Thomas Marks and Richard L. Maullin's *Soldiers, Guerrillas and Politics in Colombia*, which continues to offer a solid overview of the military. Francisco Leal Buitrago's *La seguridad nacional a la deriva: Del frente nacional a la posguerra fría* is the definitive source for the evolution of Colombia's national security policy. María Victoria Llorente's chapter "Demilitarization in Times of War: Police Reform in Colombia," in *Public Security and Police Reform in the Americas*, edited by John Bailey and Lucía Dammert, is most informative on the National Police. On the formation of the FARC, Eduardo Pizarro Leongómez and Ricardo Peñaranda's *Las FARC (1949–1966): De la autodefensa a la combinación de todas formas de la lucha* is the best reference. Alfredo Rangel Suárez analyzes the guerrilla movement today in *Las FARC–EP: Una mirada actual*. A general overview of the rise of the leftist insurgent phenomenon can be found in Pizarro's chapter "Revolutionary Guerrilla Groups in Colombia," in Charles W. Bergquist, Ricardo Peñaranda, and Gonzalo Sánchez Gómez's volume, *Violence in Colombia: The Contemporary Crisis in Historical Perspective*, and also in Gonzalo Sánchez Gómez and Donny Meerten's *Bandits, Peasants and Politics*. Mauricio Romero offers an analysis of the development of paramilitarism in *Paramilitares y Autodefensas, 1982–2003*, the arguments of which can also be found in English in the article "Changing Identities and

Contested Settings: Regional Elites and the Paramilitaries in Colombia," in the *International Journal of Politics, Culture, and Society*. The literature on the Colombian conflict, insurgency, and violence is immense. Rafael Pardo Rueda's survey study *La historia de las guerras* provides a comprehensive historical overview of war and conflict in Colombia since independence. The current internal conflict is showcased in diverse studies, including Charles W. Bergquist, Ricardo Peñaranda, and Gonzalo Sánchez Gómez's volume *Violence in Colombia, 1990–2000: Waging War and Negotiating Peace*; Camilo Echandía Castilla's *El conflicto armado y las manifestaciones de violencia en las regiones de Colombia*; Alfredo Rangel Suárez's *Colombia: Guerra en el fin de siglo*; Malcolm Deas and María Victoria Llorente's volume *Reconocer la guerra para construir la paz*; and Paul H. Oquist's classic *Violence, Conflict and Politics in Colombia*. The political economy aspects of the conflict are explored in Nazih Richani's *Systems of Violence: The Political Economy of War and Peace in Colombia*, as well as by Rangel Suárez in his 2000 *Journal of International Affairs* article "Parasites and Predators: Guerrillas and the Insurrection Economy of Colombia." Christopher Welna and Gustavo Gallón discuss the human rights dimension of the Colombian conflict in *Peace, Democracy, and Human Rights in Colombia*, and Winifred Tate's *Counting the Dead: The Culture and Politics of Human Rights Activism in Colombia* is also pertinent to this subject.

Good sources on diverse aspects of contemporary forms of political violence include Malcolm Deas's "Violent Exchanges: Reflections on Political Violence in Colombia," in David Apter's *The Legitimation of Violence*; Mauricio Rubio's *Crimen e impunidad: Precisiones sobre la violencia*; Herbert Braun's *Our Guerrillas, Our Sidewalks: A Journey into the Violence of Colombia*; and Jaime Arocha, Fernando Cubides, and Myriam Jimeno's volume, *Las Violencias: Inclusión creciente*. Colombia's experiences with peace processes are explored in Harvey Kline's *State Building and Conflict Resolution in Colombia, 1986–1994*; *Armar la paz es desarmar la guerra: Herramientas para lograr la paz*, by Álvaro Camacho Guizado and Francisco Leal Buitrago; and Mark W. Chernick's "Negotiated Settlement to Armed Conflict: Lessons from the Colombian Peace Process."

Francisco E. Thoumi's *Drogas ilícitas en Colombia: Su impacto económico, política y social* and María Clemencia Ramírez, Kimberly Stanton, and John Walsh's "Colombia: A Vicious Circle of Drugs and War," in *Drugs and Democracy in Latin America*, edited by Coletta Youngers and Eileen Rosin, are informative on the national security implications of drug trafficking. Finally, recent studies of the interconnections of drug trafficking, U.S. national security, and U.S.–Colombian security relations include Ingrid Vaicius and Adam Isacson's working paper "The War on Drugs Meets the War on Terror"; Russell Crandall's *Driven by Drugs: U.S. Policy Toward Colombia*; and Ted Galen Carpenter's *Bad Neighbor Policy: Washington's Futile War on Drugs in Latin America.* (For further information and complete citations, see Bibliography.)

Appendix

Table 1. Metric Conversion Coefficients and Factors

When you know	Multiply by	To find
Millimeters...........................	0.04	inches
Centimeters	0.39	inches
Meters	3.3	feet
Kilometers..........................	0.62	miles
Hectares............................	2.47	acres
Square kilometers.....................	0.39	square miles
Cubic meters	35.3	cubic feet
Liters	0.26	gallons
Kilograms............................	2.2	pounds
Metric tons..........................	0.98	long tons
....	1.1	short tons
....	2,204	pounds
Degrees Celsius (Centigrade)	1.8 and add 32	degrees Fahrenheit

[1] The following special weights and measures are also used in Colombia: *libra*=0.5 kilograms; *carga*=125 kilograms; *arroba*=12.5 kilograms; *vara*=79.8 centimeters; *quintal*=50 kilograms; *cuadra*=80 meters; *saco*=62.5 kilograms; and *fanegada*=0.64 hectares.

Table 2. Presidents of Colombia, 1819–2010

Term	President(s) and Party Affiliations
REPUBLIC OF GREAT COLOMBIA, 1819–32	
1819–28	General Simón Bolívar Palacios (1819–28, and dictator, 1828–30)
1821–27	General Francisco de Paula Santander y Omaña (acting)
1830–31	Joaquín Mariano Mosquera y Arboleda
1831	General Rafael José Urdaneta Farías (by military coup)
1831–32	General Domingo Caycedo Santamaría, General José María Obando del Campo, and José Ignacio de Márquez Barreto (vice presidents and acting presidents)
REPUBLIC OF NEW GRANADA, 1832–58	
1832–37	General Francisco de Paula Santander y Omaña
Early Conservatives (Ministerials)	
1837–41	José Ignacio de Márquez Barreto
1841–45	General Pedro Alcántara Herrán y Zaldúa
1845–49	General Tomás Cipriano de Mosquera y Arboleda
Early Liberals	
1849–53	General José Hilario López Valdéz (Liberal Party—PL)
1853–54	General José María Obando del Campo (PL)
1854	General José María Dionisio Melo y Ortiz (PL; by military coup)
1854–55	José de Obaldía y Orejuela (PL; acting president)
Conservative Interval	
1855–57	Manuel María Mallarino Ibargüen (Conservative Party—PC; acting, to complete Obando's term, elected vice president)
1857–58	Mariano Ospina Rodríguez (PC)
GRANADINE CONFEDERATION, 1858–61	
1858–61	Mariano Ospina Rodríguez (PC)
1861	Juan José Nieto Gil (PL), Bartolomé Calvo y Díaz de Lamadrid (PC), and Julio Arboleda Pombo (PC)

Table 2. Presidents of Colombia, 1819–2010 (Continued)

Term	President(s) and Party Affiliations
UNITED STATES OF NEW GRANADA, 1861–63	
A Liberal Era	
1861–64	General Tomás Cipriano de Mosquera y Arboleda (now PL; provisional president by victory in civil war, then elected to the office by constitutional convention)
UNITED STATES OF COLOMBIA, 1863–86	
1864–66	Manuel Murillo Toro (PL)
1866–67	General Tomás Cipriano de Mosquera y Arboleda (PL)
1867–68	General Santos Acosta Castillo (PL; by coup that overthrew Mosquera)
1868–70	General José Santos Gutiérrez Prieto (PL)
1870–72	General Eustorgio Salgar (PL)
1872–74	Manuel Murillo Toro (PL)
1874–76	Santiago Pérez de Manosalbas (PL)
1876–78	José Bonifacio Aquileo Parra Gómez (PL)
1878–80	General Julián Trujillo Largacha (Independent PL)
1880–82	General Rafael Wenceslao Núñez Moledo (Independent PL)
1882	Francisco Javier Zaldúa (PL)
1882–84	José Eusebio Otálora Martínez (Independent PL; as presidential designate, completed term of Zaldúa, who died in office)
1884–86	General Rafael Wenceslao Núñez Moledo (Independent PL / Nationalists)
REPUBLIC OF COLOMBIA, 1886–Present	
1886–87	José María Campo Serrano (acting)
1887	José Eliseo Payán Hurtado (acting)
1887–88	General Rafael Wenceslao Núñez Moledo
1888–92	Carlos Holguín Mallarino (acting)
1892–94	General Rafael Wenceslao Núñez Moledo (acting)
1894–98	Miguel Antonio Caro Tovar (PC / Nationalists; as vice president, completed term of Núñez, who died in office)
Conservative Hegemony	
1898–1900	Manuel Antonio Sanclemente Sanclemente (PC / Nationalists)
1900–1904	José Manuel Marroquín Ricaurte (PC / Nationalists; as vice president, completed Sanclemente's term when the latter was overthrown by coup in 1900)
1904–9	General Rafael Reyes Prieto (PC)
1909	Jorge Holguín Jaramillo (PC, acting)
1909–10	General Ramón González Valencia (chosen by Congress to fill out the term of Reyes, who resigned)
1910–14	Carlos Eugenio Restrepo Restrepo (PC / Republican Union)
1914–18	José Vicente Concha Ferreira (PC)
1918–21	Marco Fidel Suárez (PC)
1921–22	Jorge Holguín Jaramillo (PC; as presidential designate, completed the term of Suárez, who resigned)
1922–26	Pedro Nel Ospina Vásquez (PC)
1926–30	Miguel Abadía Méndez (PC)

Table 2. Presidents of Colombia, 1819–2010 (Continued)

Term	President(s) and Party Affiliations
Liberal Reformers	
1930–34	Enrique Olaya Herrera (PL)
1934–38	Alfonso López Pumarejo (PL)
1938–42	Eduardo Santos Montejo (PL)
1942–45	Alfonso López Pumarejo (PL)
1945–46	Alberto Lleras Camargo (PL; as presidential designate, completed term of López, who resigned)
Conservative Rule during La Violencia	
1946–50	Luis Mariano Ospina Pérez (PC)
1950–53	Laureano Eleuterio Gómez Castro (PC)
1951–53	Roberto Urdaneta Arbeláez (PC, acting)
1953–57	General Gustavo Rojas Pinilla (by military coup)
1957–58	Major General Gabriel París Gordillo (chair, military junta)
The National Front	
1958–62	Alberto Lleras Camargo (PL)
1962–66	Guillermo León Valencia Muñoz (PC)
1966–70	Carlos Lleras Restrepo (PL)
1970–74	Misael Eduardo Pastrana Borrero (PC)
1974–78	Alfonso López Michelsen (PL)
Contemporary Era	
1978–82	Julio César Turbay Ayala (PL)
1982–86	Belisario Betancur Cuartas (PC)
1986–90	Virgilio Barco Vargas (PL)
1990–94	César Augusto Gaviria Trujillo (PL)
1994–98	Ernesto Samper Pizano (PL)
1998–2002	Andrés Pastrana Arango (PC)
2002–6	Álvaro Uribe Vélez (PL / independent)
2006–10	Álvaro Uribe Vélez (PL / independent)

Table 3. Natural Regions of Colombia (by Department)[1]

Natural Region	Department
Amazonia.....................	Amazonas, Caquetá, Guainía, Guaviare, Putumayo, Vaupés
Andean highlands[2]..............	Antioquia, Arauca, Bolívar, Boyacá, Caldas, Caquetá, Cauca, César, Córdoba, Cundinamarca, Huila, Magdalena, Meta, Nariño, Norte de Santander, Putumayo, Quindío, Risaralda, Santander, Tolima, Valle del Cauca
Caribbean lowlands.............	Atlántico, Bolívar, César, Córdoba, La Guajira, Magdalena, Sucre
Eastern llanos.................	Arauca, Casanare, Cundinamarca, Meta, Vichada
Insular[3]......................	Archipiélago de San Andrés, Providencia y Santa Catalina
Pacific lowlands................	Cauca, Chocó, Nariño, Valle del Cauca

[1] Departmental boundaries of the natural regions may overlap.
[2] Also includes Distrito Capital de Bogotá (not a department).
[3] Also includes Isla de Malpelo (not a department).

Source: Based on information from Alberto Gerardino Rojas, "Regiones Naturales" (a map), *Colombia: Geografía*, Bogotá, 2001, 25.

Table 4. Annual Estimates of Displaced People in Colombia, 1985–2007

Year	Consultancy for Human Rights and Displacement (Codhes)[1]	Social Solidarity Network (RSS) / Social Action of the Colombian Government
1985–94.......................	720,000	7,886[2]
1995–99.......................	1,123,000	86,734
2000..........................	317,375	287,064
2001..........................	341,925	347,663
2002..........................	412,553	414,814
2003..........................	207,607	211,203
2004..........................	287,581	199,965
2005..........................	310,387	217,773
2006..........................	221,638	201,623
2007..........................	305,966	284,055
Cumulative total.................	4,248,032	2,258,780

[1] A nongovernmental organization.
[2] No information available for 1994.

Source: Based on annual data on Colombian displacement from Consultancy for Human Rights and Displacement (Codhes), http://www.codhes.org; and Internal Displacement Monitoring Centre, http://www.internal-displacement.org.

Table 5. Major Army Equipment, 2009

Type and Description	In Inventory
Light tanks/reconnaissance vehicles	
EE–9 Cascavel	123
M–8 Greyhound (antiriot vehicle)	6
M–8 Greyhound (with 1 TOW[1] missile)	8
M1117 Guardian	39
Armored personnel carriers	
BTR–80.	80
EE–11 Urutú	56
RG–31 Nyala.	4
TPM–113 (M–13A1).	54
Armored utility vehicles	
M–20.	8
Artillery	
Towed artillery	
105mm M–101	86
155mm 155/52 APU SBT–1	15
Mortars	
81mm M–1	125
107mm M–2	148
120mm Brandt	210
Antitank guided weapons	
TOW missiles (including 8 self-propelled)	18
Recoilless launchers	
106mm M–40A1	63
Rocket launchers	
66mm M–72 LAW	15+
73mm RPG–22	n.a.[2]
89mm M–20	15
90mm C–90C	n.a.
106mm SR–106	n.a.
Air defense guns	
12.7mm M–8/M–55	18
35mm GDF Oerlikon	21
40mm M–1A1 towed	21
Helicopters	
Observation	
OH–6A Cayuse.	6
Support	
Mi–17–1V Hip	8
Mi–17–MD	9

Table 5. Major Army Equipment, 2009 (Continued)

Type and Description	In Inventory
M–17–V5 Hip	5
Utility	
K–MAX	5
UH–1H–II Huey II......................	30
UH–1N Twin Huey	20
UH–60L Black Hawk....................	35
Aircraft	
Electronic Warfare	
Beechcraft Super King Air B–200	2
Transport	
Antonov AN–32........................	1
B–727...............................	9
Beechcraft C–90.......................	1
Casa 212 Aviocar (Medevac)...............	2
CV–580	1
PA–34 Seneca.........................	2
Rockwell Turbo Commander...............	2
Utility	
Cessna 208B Grand Caravan	2
Training	
Utva–75	5

[1] Tube launched optically wire guided.
[2] n.a.—not available.

Source: Based on information from International Institute for Strategic Studies, "Colombia," *The Military Balance, 2010* (London) 110, no. 1 (February 2010): 75.

Table 6. Major Naval Equipment, 2009

Type and Description	In Inventory
Submarines	
Pijao (German T–209/1200)[1]	2
Intrepido[2]	2
Principal surface combatants	
Corvettes	
With guided missiles[3].....................	4
Patrol and coastal combatants	
Coastal patrol craft	
Reliance offshore patrol vessel..............	1
Espartana (ex-Spanish Cormoran)	1
Lazaga	2
Pedro de Heredia (former U.S. tug) with one 76mm gun...................	1

Table 6. Major Naval Equipment, 2009 (Continued)

Type and Description	In Inventory
Quitasueño fast patrol craft ex-U.S. Asheville-class with one 76mm gun.	1
Toledo patrol craft	2
Jaime Gómez inshore patrol craft.	2
José María Palas swiftships 105.	2
Castillo y Rada swiftships 110	2
Point inshore patrol craft	4
Riverine patrol craft	
Andromeda (ex-Piranha)	11
Arauca.	3
Delfin	20
Diligente.	4
LPR–40 Tenerife.	9
Nodriza PAF–111 with Bell 212 or 412 helicopters	6
Río Magdalena	11
Rotork.	2
Amphibious	
Mechanized landing craft	1
Morrosquillo utility landing craft.	7
Logistics and support	
Hydrographic survey vessel	1
Oceanographic research vessel.	2
Hospital ship.	1
Transport.	1
Sea-going buoy tender	1
Training (sail)[4].	1
Naval aviation	
Aircraft	
Transport	
C–212 Medevac	1
Cessna 208 Caravan	2
Maritime patrol	
PA–31 Navajo	1
CN–235–200 Persuader	2
Utility	
Cessna 206	4
PA–31 Navajo	1
Helicopters	
Antisurface warfare	
AS–555SN Fennec	2

Table 6. Major Naval Equipment, 2009 (Continued)

Type and Description	In Inventory
Utility	
Bell 212............................	1
Bell 412............................	4
BK–117.............................	1
Bo–105	2

[1] Each diesel-electric submarine with eight single 533mm torpedo tubes with 14 surface-and-underwater target heavy-weight torpedoes for antisubmarine warfare.
[2] Italian SX–506, special forces delivery (midget submarines).
[3] The four frigates—*Almirante Padilla, Antioquia, Independiente,* and *Caldas*—are each equipped with one Bo–105 utility helicopter, two B515 ILAS–3 triple 324mm antisubmarine torpedo launchers, each with an A244 light-weight torpedo, two quad—eight, in effect, each with one MM–40 Exocet tactical surface-to-surface missile—and one 76mm gun.
[4] The training ship *Gloria* is a three-mast Spanish Bricbarca sailing vessel built in 1968 with a capacity for 125 sailors. Still in use, the ship visited Shanghai and Manila in June–August 2009.

Source: Based on information from International Institute for Strategic Studies, "Colombia," *The Military Balance, 2010* (London) 110, no. 1 (February 2010): 76.

Table 7. Major Air Force Equipment, 2009

Type and Description	In Inventory
Aircraft	
Fighter ground attack	
A–37B/OA–37B Dragonfly	10
EMB–312 Tucano	12
EMB–314 Super Tucano (A–29)	25
IA–58A Pucará.........................	3
Kfir C-2, C–12[1]	20
Kfir TC–7[1]	4
Mirage 5 COAM[2].......................	5
Mirage 5 CODM[2].......................	2
T–37C................................	4
Electronic intelligence	
Ce–208	2
Forward air control	
OV–10A Bronco	7
Special operations	
AC–47T Fantasma	8
Reconnaissance	
Aero Commander.......................	3
B–300 Super King Air	2
SA–2–37A/SA–2–37B....................	6
Surveillance	
Ce–650 Citation IV	5
C–26B................................	4

Table 7. Major Air Force Equipment, 2009 (Continued)

Type and Description	In Inventory
Transport	
Arava 201	1
B–737	1
B–727–700	1
B–707	1
B–767ER	1
Ce–208	1
Ce–550	1
C–130B Hercules	4[3]
C–130H Hercules	3
C–90 King Air	1
C–26 Metro.	3
C–95 (EMB–110P1)	2
C–295M	4
C–212	4
CN–235M	3
Do–328	3
F–28T	1
Queen Air B65	2
Training	
AC–47T	8
Ce–310R (multiengine training).	2
T–27 Tucano.	13
T–34M Turbo Mentor.	9
T–37 Tweet.	6
T–41 Mescalero	10
Liaison	
B–300 Super King Air (Medevac)	2
Ce–185 Floatplane	1
Ce–210	2
Ce–337G/H.	2
Ce–401	1
Ce–404	3
PA–31 Navajo.	2
PA–31T Navajo	1
PA–42 Cheyenne	1
PA–34 Seneca.	4
PA–44 Seminole.	1
Turbo Commander 1000.	2

Table 7. Major Air Force Equipment, 2009 (Continued)

Type and Description	In Inventory
Helicopters	
Attack	
MD–500MD Defender.....................	1
MD530MG Escorpion	4
H369HM.............................	7
Sikorsky/Elbit AH–60L Arpia III	14
Utility	
Bell 212 Rapaz..........................	8
H500C	8
H500M...............................	2
UH–1B Uroquois	2
UH–1H..............................	6
UH–1H Iroquois.........................	6
UH–60Q..............................	2
Training	
Bell 206B	11
H500C	2
H500ME..............................	1
Bell 212	1
Transport	
UH–1P Huey II..........................	7
Bell 212 Twin Huey......................	12
Bell 412HP/SP	2
UH–60A Black Hawk	8
UH–60L Black Hawk (on order)	8

[1] The Kfirs are in one squadron; being upgraded to C–10 and C–12; 13 more on order. The first four Kfirs were received in June 2009, but one subsequently crashed while being tested.
[2] The Mirages are in one squadron.
[3] Plus four in storage.

Source: Based on information from International Institute for Strategic Studies, "Colombia," *The Military Balance, 2010* (London) 110, no. 1 (February 2010): 76.

Table 8. Major National Police
Aviation Equipment, 2009

Type and Description	In Inventory
Aircraft	
Air Tractor AT–802	6
Ayres 52R	3
Caravan 208	5
Caravan 208B	1
Cessna C–152	3
Cessna 206	5
C–26SA227–AC	4
C–26B	2
King Air C–99	1
DC–3	1
King 200	2
King 300	1
OV–10A Bronco	5
Turbo Truck	1
DHC 6 Twin Otter	2
Transport	
Basler Turbo–67	11
Utility	
Gavilián 358	12
Helicopters	
Utility	
Bell 206B	3
Bell 206L LongRanger	7
Bell 212	12
Bell 412	1
Hughes 500D	2
MD 500D	2
MD–530F	1
UH–1H Iroquois/ UH–1H–II Huey II	25
UH–60L Black Hawk	7

Source: Based on information from International Institute for Strategic Studies, "Colombia," *The Military Balance, 2010* (London) 110, no. 1 (February 2010): 77.

Bibliography

Chapter 1

Abel, Christopher. *Política, iglesia y partidos en Colombia, 1886–1953.* Bogotá: Fundación Antioqueña para los Estudios Sociales / Universidad Nacional de Colombia, 1987.

Appelbaum, Nancy P. *Muddied Waters: Race, Region, and Local History in Colombia, 1846–1948.* Durham, North Carolina: Duke University Press, 2003.

Avellaneda Navas, José Ignacio. *The Conquerors of the New Kingdom of Granada.* 1st ed. Albuquerque: University of New Mexico Press, 1995.

Bergquist, Charles W. *Coffee and Conflict in Colombia, 1886–1910.* Durham, North Carolina: Duke University Press, 1978.

Bergquist, Charles W., Ricardo Peñaranda, and Gonzalo Sánchez Gómez, eds. *Violence in Colombia: The Contemporary Crisis in Historical Perspective.* Wilmington, Delaware: Scholarly Resources Books, 1992.

Berquist, Charles W., Ricardo Peñaranda, and Gonzalo Sánchez Gómez, eds. *Violence in Colombia, 1990–2000: Waging War and Negotiating Peace.* Wilmington, Delaware: Scholarly Resources Books, 2001.

Braun, Herbert. *The Assassination of Gaitán: Public Life and Urban Violence in Colombia.* Madison: University of Wisconsin Press, 1985.

Bushnell, David. *The Making of Modern Colombia: A Nation in Spite of Itself.* Berkeley: University of California Press, 1993.

Bushnell, David. *The Santander Regime in Gran Colombia.* Newark: University of Delaware Press, 1954. Reprint. Westport, Connecticut: Greenwood Press, 1970.

Colmenares, Germán, and José Antonio Ocampo, eds. *Historia económica de Colombia.* Bogotá: Presidencia de la República, 1997.

Deas, Malcolm D. *Del poder y la gramática: Y otros ensayos sobre historia, política y literatura colombianas.* 1st ed. Bogotá: Tercer Mundo Editores, 1993.

Deas, Malcolm D. "The Fiscal Problems of Nineteenth-Century Colombia." *Journal of Latin American Studies* (London) 14, no. 2 (November 1982): 287–328.

Delpar, Helen. *Red Against Blue: The Liberal Party in Colombian Politics, 1863–1899.* Tuscaloosa: University of Alabama Press, 1981.

Dix, Robert H. *Colombia: The Political Dimensions of Change.* New Haven: Yale University Press, 1967.

Earle, Rebecca. *Spain and the Independence of Colombia 1810–1825.* Exeter, United Kingdom: University of Exeter Press, 2000.

Farnsworth-Alvear, Ann. *Dulcinea in the Factory: Myths, Morals, Men, and Women in Colombia's Industrial Experiment, 1905–1960.* Durham, North Carolina: Duke University Press, 2000.

Fluharty, Vernon Lee. *Dance of the Millions: Military Rule and Social Revolution in Colombia, 1930–1956.* Pittsburgh: University of Pittsburgh Press, 1957.

González, Fernán, S.J. "La guerra de los mil días." In *Las guerras civiles desde 1830 y su proyección en el siglo XX.* Bogotá: Museo Nacional, Memorias de la II Cátedra Annual de Historia "Ernesto Restrepo Tirado," October 22–24, 1997, 1998.

Green, John W. *Gaitanismo, Left Liberalism, and Popular Mobilization in Colombia.* Gainesville: University Press of Florida, 2003.

Guzmán Campos, Germán, Orlando Fals Borda, and Eduardo Umaña Luna. *La Violencia en Colombia: Estudio de un proceso social.* 2d ed. Bogotá: Ediciones Tercer Mundo, 1963–64.

Hartlyn, Jonathan. *The Politics of Coalition Rule in Colombia.* Cambridge: Cambridge University Press, 1988.

Helg, Aline. *Liberty and Equality in Caribbean Colombia, 1770–1835.* Chapel Hill: University of North Carolina Press, 2004.

Henderson, James D. *Modernization in Colombia: The Laureano Gómez Years, 1889–1965.* Gainesville: University Press of Florida, 2001.

Jaramillo Giraldo, Carlos Arturo. *Murmullos del lenguaje Uik: La práctica del Mopa Mopa: De lo recolector a lo sedentario.* Medellín: Editorial Lealon, 1986.

Jaramillo Uribe, Jaime. *El pensamiento colombiano en el siglo XIX.* 1st ed. Bogotá: Editorial Temis, 1964.

Jaramillo Uribe, Jaime, ed. *Nueva historia de Colombia.* 2d ed. 11 vols. Bogotá: Planeta, 1998.

Kalmanovitz, Salomón. *Economía y nación: Una breve historia de Colombia.* 3d ed. Bogotá: Centro de Investigación y Educación Popular / United Nations / Siglo Veintiuno Editores, 1988.

Kline, Harvey F. *Colombia: Portrait of Unity and Diversity.* Boulder, Colorado: Westview Press, 1983.

König, Hans-Joachim. *En el camino hacia la nación: Nacionalismo en el proceso de formación del estado y de la nación de la Nueva Granada, 1750–1856.* Bogotá: Banco de la República, 1994.

LeGrand, Catherine. *Frontier Expansion and Peasant Protest in Colombia, 1850–1936.* Albuquerque: University of New Mexico Press, 1986.

Londoño de la Cuesta, Juan Luis. "Brechas sociales en Colombia." Pages 118–22 in Jaime Jaramillo Uribe, ed., *Nueva historia de Colombia*. 2d ed. Vol. 8. Bogotá: Planeta, 1998.

Lynch, John. *Simón Bolívar: A Life*. New Haven: Yale University Press, 2006.

Maingot, Anthony P. "Social Structure, Social Status, and Civil–Military Conflict in Urban Colombia, 1810–1858." Pages 297–342 in Stephen Thermstrom and Richard Sennett, eds., *Nineteenth-Century Cities: Essays in the New Urban History*. Papers presented at Yale Conference on the Nineteenth-Century Industrial City, New Haven, 1968. New Haven: Yale University Press, 1969.

McFarlane, Anthony. *Colombia Before Independence: Economy, Society, and Politics under Bourbon Rule*. New York: Cambridge University Press, 1993.

McGreevey, William Paul. *An Economic History of Colombia, 1845–1930*. Cambridge: Cambridge University Press, 1971.

Moreno de Ángel, Pilar. *Santander*. 1st ed. Bogotá: Planeta, 1989.

Museo del Oro, Banco de la República; Banco del Pacífico (Ecuador); and Casa de la Cultura Ecuatoriana Benjamín Carrión. *El Oro de Colombia: Homenaje al Ecuador*. Quito, Ecuador, 1982.

Ocampo, José Antonio. *Colombia y la economía mundial, 1830–1910*. 1st ed. Mexico City: Siglo Veintiuno Editores, 1984.

Ospina Vásquez, Luis. *Industria y protección en Colombia, 1810–1930*. Medellín: E.S.F., 1955.

Palacios, Marco. *Between Legitimacy and Violence: A History of Colombia, 1875–2002*. Trans., Richard Stoller. Durham, North Carolina: Duke University Press, 2006.

Palacios, Marco. *Coffee in Colombia, 1850–1970: An Economic, Social, and Political History*. Cambridge: Cambridge University Press, 1980.

Park, James. *Rafael Núñez and the Politics of Colombian Regionalism, 1863–1886*. Baton Rouge: Louisiana State University Press, 1985.

Phelan, John Leddy. *The People and the King: The Comunero Rebellion in Colombia, 1781*. Madison: University of Wisconsin Press, 1978.

Pinto Nolla, María. *Galindo: Un sitio a cielo abierto de cazadores-recolectores en la Sabana de Bogotá (Colombia)*. Bogotá: Banco de la República, Fundación de Investigaciones Arqueológicas Nacionales, 2003.

Posada-Carbó, Eduardo. *The Colombian Caribbean: A Regional History, 1870–1950*. Oxford, United Kingdom: Clarendon Press, 1996.

Posada-Carbó, Eduardo, ed. *Colombia: The Politics of Reforming the State*. London: University of London, Institute of Latin American Studies, 1998.

Randall, Stephen J. *Colombia and the United States: Hegemony and Interdependence.* Athens: University of Georgia Press, 1992.

Rappoport, Joanne. *The Politics of Memory: Native Historical Interpretation in the Colombian Andes.* Cambridge: Cambridge University Press, 1990.

Rausch, Jane M. *Territorial Rule and the Llanos Frontier.* Gainesville: University Press of Florida, 1999.

Reichel-Dolmatoff, Gerardo. *Colombia indígena.* 1st ed. Bogotá: Editorial Colina, 1998.

Reichel-Dolmatoff, Gerardo. *Orfebrería y chamanismo: Un estudio iconográfico del Museo del Oro.* Medellín: Editorial Colina, 1988.

Rippy, J. Fred. *The Capitalists and Colombia.* New York: Vanguard Press, 1931.

Rojas, Cristina. *Civilization and Violence: Regimes of Representation in Nineteenth-Century Colombia.* Minneapolis: University of Minnesota Press, 2002.

Rojas, Cristina, and Judy Meltzer. *Elusive Peace: International, National, and Local Dimensions of Conflict in Colombia.* 1st ed. New York: Palgrave Macmillan, 2005.

Roldán, Mary. *Blood and Fire: La Violencia in Antioquia, Colombia, 1946–1953.* Durham, North Carolina: Duke University Press, 2002.

Sáenz Rovner, Eduardo. *Colombia años 50: Industriales, política y diplomacia.* Bogotá: Universidad Nacional de Colombia, Sede Bogotá, 2002.

Safford, Frank. *The Ideal of the Practical: Colombia's Struggle to Form a Technical Elite.* Austin: University of Texas Press, 1976.

Safford, Frank, and Marco Palacios. *Colombia: Fragmented Land, Divided Society.* New York: Oxford University Press, 2002.

Sanders, James E. *Contentious Republicans: Popular Politics, Race, and Class in Nineteenth-Century Colombia.* Durham, North Carolina: Duke University Press, 2004.

Silva, Renán. *Los ilustrados de Nueva Granada, 1760–1808: Genealogía de una comunidad de interpretación.* Medellín: Banco de la República/ Fondo Editorial Universidad EAFIT, 2002.

Sowell, David L. *The Early Colombian Labor Movement: Artisans and Politics in Bogotá, 1832–1919.* Philadelphia: Temple University Press, 1992.

Stoller, Richard. "Alfonso López Pumarejo and Liberal Radicalism in 1930s Colombia." *Journal of Latin American Studies* (London) 27, no. 2 (May 1995): 367–97.

Thermstrom, Stephen, and Richard Sennett, eds. *Nineteenth-Century Cities: Essays in the New Urban History.* Papers presented at Yale Conference on the Nineteenth-Century Industrial City, New Haven, 1968. New Haven: Yale University Press, 1969.

Thoumi, Francisco E. *Illegal Drugs, Economy, and Society in the Andes.* Washington, DC: Woodrow Wilson Center Press; and Baltimore: Johns Hopkins University Press, 2003.

Tirado Mejía, Álvaro. *Aspectos sociales de las guerras civiles en Colombia.* Bogotá: Instituto Colombiano de Cultura, 1976.

Uribe Urán, Víctor M. *Honorable Lives: Lawyers, Family, and Politics in Colombia, 1780–1850.* Pittsburgh: University of Pittsburgh Press, 2000.

Urrutia, Miguel. *The Development of the Colombian Labor Movement.* New Haven: Yale University Press, 1969.

Urrutia, Miguel, ed. *40 años de desarrollo: Su impacto social.* Bogotá: Banco Popular, 1990.

Wade, Peter. *Blackness and Race Mixture: The Dynamics of Racial Identity in Colombia.* Baltimore: Johns Hopkins University Press, 1993.

Zamosc, León. *The Agrarian Question and the Peasant Movement in Colombia: Struggles of the National Peasant Association, 1967–1981.* New York: Cambridge University Press; and Geneva: United Nations Research Institute for Social Development, 1986.

Chapter 2

Aagesen, David. "People in Nature: Wildlife Conservation in South and Central America." *Environmental History* 10, no. 4 (October 2005): 795–97.

Abel, Christopher. *Health Care in Colombia c.1920–c.1950: A Preliminary Analysis.* London: University of London, Institute of Latin American Studies, 1994.

Acevedo Carmona, Darío. *La mentalidad de las élites sobre la violencia en Colombia, 1936–1949.* Bogotá: Instituto de Estudios Políticos y Relaciones Internacionales / El Áncora Editores, 1995.

Alesina, Alberto, ed. *Institutional Reforms: The Case of Colombia.* Cambridge: MIT Press, 2005.

"América Latina y el Caribe: Estimaciones y proyecciones de población, 1950–2050." *Boletín Demográfico* (Santiago, Chile: Comisión Económica para América Latina), no. 73 (January 2004): 67–72.

Arboleda Mora, Carlos Angel. "Tendencias de la religión hacia el futuro: Conclusiones de una investigación entre los universitarios del área metropolitana de Medellín." In Ana María Bidegaín and Juan Diego Demera

Vargas, eds., *Globalización y diversidad religiosa en Colombia*. 1st ed. Bogotá: Universidad Nacional de Colombia, Facultad de Ciencias Humanas, 2005.

Archila Neira, Mauricio. "Los movimientos sociales en la encrucijada de comienzos del siglo XXI." Pages 266–84 in Francisco Leal Buitrago, ed., *En la encrucijada: Colombia en el siglo XXI*. Bogotá: Universidad de los Andes, Centro de Estudios Sociales e Internacionales / Grupo Editorial Norma, 2006.

Beltrán, William M. *Fragmentación y recomposición religiosa del campo religioso en Bogotá*. Bogotá: Universidad Nacional de Colombia, 2002.

Beltrán, William M. "La diversificación del cristianismo en Bogotá." Pages 263–73 in Ana María Bidegaín and Juan Diego Demera Vargas, eds., *Globalización y diversidad religiosa en Colombia*. 1st ed. Bogotá: Universidad Nacional de Colombia, Facultad de Ciencias Humanas, 2005.

Berry, Albert, and Jackeline Barragán. "Winners and Losers from the Illicit Drug Industry in Colombia." Pages 119–52 in Cristina Rojas and Judy Meltzer, eds., *Elusive Peace: International, National, and Local Dimensions of Conflict in Colombia*. New York: Palgrave Macmillan, 2005.

Berry, Albert, and Miguel Urrutia. *Income Distribution in Colombia*. New Haven: Yale University Press, 1976.

Bidegaín de Urán, Ana María. "La pluralidad religiosa en Colombia." In Oscar Collazos, ed., *Arte y cultura democrática*. Bogotá: Instituto para el Desarrollo de la Democracia Luis Carlos Galán, 1994.

Bidegaín de Urán, Ana María. *Iglesia, pueblo y política: Un estudio de conflictos de intereses, Colombia, 1930–1955*. Bogotá: Pontificia Universidad Javeriana, Facultad de Teología, 1985.

Bidegaín, Ana María, ed. *Historia del cristianismo en Colombia: Corrientes y diversidad*. Bogotá: Taurus, 2004.

Bidegaín, Ana María, and Juan Diego Demera Vargas, eds. *Globalización y diversidad religiosa en Colombia*. 1st ed. Bogotá: Universidad Nacional de Colombia, Facultad de Ciencias Humanas, 2005.

Bird, Richard M., James M. Poterba, and Joel Slemrod, eds. *Fiscal Reform in Colombia: Problems and Prospects*. Cambridge: MIT Press, 2005.

Bomann, Rebecca Pierce. *Faith in the Barrios: The Pentecostal Poor in Bogotá*. Boulder, Colorado: Rienner, 1999.

Borjas, George J., and Olga Lucia Acosta. "Educational Reform in Colombia." Pages 245–72 in Alberto Alesina, ed., *Institutional Reforms: The Case of Colombia*. Cambridge: MIT Press, 2005.

Bushnell, David. *The Making of Modern Colombia: A Nation in Spite of Itself.* Berkeley: University of California Press, 1993.

Cepeda Ulloa, Fernando, ed. *Fortalezas de Colombia.* Ariel Ciencia Política. Bogotá: Ariel, 2004.

Cifuentes, María Teresa, and Helwar Figueroa S. "Corrientes del catolicismo frente a la guerra y la paz en el siglo xx." Pages 399–410 in Ana María Bidegaín, ed., *Historia del cristianismo en Colombia: Corrientes y diversidad.* Bogotá: Taurus, 2004.

Cohen, Lucy M. *Colombianas en la vanguardia.* Medellín: Editorial Universidad de Antioquia, 2001.

Colombia. Contraloría General de la República. *Bien-estar—macroeconomía y pobreza: Informe de coyuntura 2003.* Bogotá: Universidad Nacional de Colombia, Facultad de Ciencias Económicas, Centro de Investigaciones para el Desarrollo / Contraloría General de la República, 2004.

Colombia. Departamento Administrativo Nacional de Estadística. *Colombia, una nación multicultural: Su diversidad étnica.* Bogotá, October 2006.

Colombia. Departamento Nacional de Planeación. *Bases del Plan Nacional de Desarrollo 2002–2006.* Bogotá, 2002.

Colombia. Departamento Nacional de Planeación. *La estratificación socioeconómica: El reconocimiento de las diferencias sociales por un país solidario.* Bogotá, 1997.

Colombia. Ministerio de Salud. Programa Universidad de Harvard. *Reforma de salud en Colombia y plan maestro de implementación.* Bogotá, 1995.

"Colombia." Pages 289–321 in Jacqueline West, ed., *South America, Central America and the Caribbean, 2008.* 16th ed. London: Routledge, 2007.

Comisión Económica para América Latina. *Anuario estadístico de América Latina y el Caribe, 2006.* Santiago, Chile: CEPAL, División de Estadística y Proyecciones Económicas, March 2007. http://websie.eclac.cl/anuario_estadistico/anuario_2006.

Corr, Edwin G. *The Political Process in Colombia.* Denver: University of Denver, 1972.

Cruz, Carmen Inés, Francisco Parra Sandoval, and Nelsy Gined Roa. *Armero: Diez años de ausencia.* 1st ed. Ibagué, Colombia: Fondo Resurgir–FES / Corporación Universitaria de Ibagué, 1995.

Cuervo, Luis Mauricio, and Luz Josefina González Montoya. *Industria y ciudades en la era de la mundialización, 1980–1991: Un enfoque socioespacial.* 1st ed. Bogotá: Colciencia / CIDER / Tercer Mundo Editores, 1997.

Currea Lugo, Víctor de, Mario Hernández Alvarez, and Natalia Paredes Hernández. 1st ed. *La salud está grave: Una visión desde los derechos humanos.* Bogotá: Plataforma Colombiana de Derechos Humanos, Democracia y Desarrollo / ILSA / PROVEA, 2000.

Dillehay, Tom D. *The Settlement of the Americas: A New Prehistory.* 1st ed. New York: Basic Books, 2000.

Dion, Michelle L., and Catherine Russler. "Eradication Efforts, the State, Displacement and Poverty: Explaining Coca Cultivation in Colombia during Plan Colombia." *Journal of Latin American Studies* 40, no. 3 (August 2008): 399–429.

Economist Intelligence Unit. *Country Profile 2007: Colombia.* London, 2007.

Espinosa Baquero, Armando, Augusto Antonio Gómez Capera, and Elkin de Jesús Salcedo Hurtado. State of the Art of the Historical Seismology in Colombia. *Annals of Geophysics* 47, nos. 2–3 (April–June 2004): 437–49.

Europa World. "Education (Colombia)." London: Routledge, 2007. http://www.europaworld. com/entry/co.is.80.

Europa World. "Health and Welfare (Colombia)." London: Routledge, 2007. http://www.europa world.com/entry/co.ss.15.

Fals-Borda, Orlando. *Peasant Society in the Colombian Andes: A Sociological Study of Saucio.* Westport, Connecticut: Greenwood Press, 1955. Reprint, 1976.

"La familia colombiana. ¿Crisis o renovación?" *Boletín* (Bogotá: Observatorio de Coyuntura Socioeconómica / Universidad Nacional de Colombia, Facultad de Ciencias Económicas / UNICEF), no. 10 (November 2001). http://www.cid.unal.edu.co/observatorio.

Flórez Nieto, Carmen Elisa, with Regina Méndez. *Las transformaciones sociodemográficas en Colombia durante el siglo XX.* 1st ed. Bogotá: Banco de la República / Tercer Mundo Editores, 2000.

Friedemann, Nina S. de. "Negros, negritudes, afrocolombianos." Pages 80–97 in Alvaro Tirado Mejía, ed., *Nueva Historia de Colombia.* 2d ed. Vol. 9. Bogotá: Planeta, 1998.

Fundación de Atención al Migrante. Consultoría para los Derechos Humanos y el Desplazamiento. *Gota a Gota: Desplazamiento forzado en Bogotá y Soacha.* 1st ed. Bogotá: Consultoría para los Derechos Humanos y el Desplazamiento / Fundación de Atención al Migrante / Arquidiócesis de Bogotá, July 2007.

Fundación para la Educación Superior y el Desarrollo. "¿Al fin qué ha pasado con la distribución del ingreso en Colombia?" *Coyuntura Social* (Bogotá), no. 17 (November 1997). http://www.fedesarrollo.org.co/.

Fundación para la Educación Superior y el Desarrollo. "Incidencia del gasto público en salud." *Coyuntura Social* (Bogotá), no. 7 (November 1992). http://www.fedesarrollo.org.co/.

Gaviria Trujillo, Alejandro. *Los que suben y los que bajan: Educación y movilidad social en Colombia.* Bogotá: Fundación para la Educación Superior y el Desarrollo / Alfaomega Editores, 2002.

Gerardino Rojas, Alberto. *Colombia.* 2d ed. Vol. 2, Geografía. Bogotá: Prolibros, 2001.

Gilhodès, Pierre. "Movimientos sociales en los años ochenta y noventa." Pages 181–86 in Alvaro Tirado Mejía, ed., *Nueva historia de Colombia.* 2d ed. Vol. 8. Bogotá: Planeta, 1998.

Goff, James E. *The Persecution of Protestant Christians in Colombia, 1948–1958, with an Investigation of Its Background and Causes.* Cuernavaca, Mexico: Centro Intercultural de Documentación, 1968.

Gómez Buendía, Hernando. *El lío de Colombia.* 1st ed. Bogotá: Tercer Mundo Editores, 2000.

Gómez Buendía, Hernando. *Para dónde va Colombia? Un coloquio abierto entre Alfonso López Michelsen, Belisario Betancur, Miguel Urrutia, Fernando Chaparro.* Bogotá: Tercer Mundo Editores, 1999.

González, Fernán E., and Ricardo Arias. "Búsqueda de la paz y defensa del 'orden cristiano:' El episcopado ante los grandes debates de Colombia (1998–2005)." Pages 176–79 in Francisco Leal Buitrago, ed., *En la encrucijada: Colombia en el siglo XXI.* Bogotá: Universidad de los Andes, Centro de Estudios Sociales e Internacionales / Grupo Editorial Norma, 2006.

Gutiérrez de Pineda, Virginia. *La familia en Colombia: Trasfondo histórico.* Medellín: Ministerio de Cultura / Editorial Universidad de Antioquia, 1997.

Gutiérrez de Pineda, Virginia. "Familia ayer y hoy." In Patricia Tovar Rojas, ed., *Familia, género y antropología: Desafíos y transformaciones.* Bogotá: Instituto Colombiano de Antropología e Historia, 2003.

Havens, A. Eugene, and William L. Flinn, eds. *Internal Colonialism and Structural Change in Colombia.* New York: Praeger, 1970.

Helg, Aline. "La educación en Colombia, 1958–1980." Pages 111–33 in Jaime Jaramillo Uribe, ed., *Manual de historia de Colombia.* 4th ed. Vol. 3. Bogotá: Procultura / Tercer Mundo Editores, 1992.

Helg, Aline. *La educación en Colombia.* Bogotá: Fondo Editorial CEREC, 1987.

Jackson, Jean. "Colombia's Indigenous Peoples Confront the Armed Conflict." Pages 185–208 in Cristina Rojas and Judy Meltzer, eds., *Elusive Peace: International, National, and Local Dimensions of Conflict in Colombia.* New York: Palgrave Macmillan, 2005.

Jaramillo Uribe, Jaime. *Ensayos de historia social: La sociedad neogranadina.* 2d ed. Vol. 1. Bogotá: Ediciones Uniandes / Tercer Mundo Editores, 1991.

Jaramillo Uribe, Jaime, ed. *Manual de historia de Colombia.* 4th ed. 3 vols. Bogotá: Procultura / Tercer Mundo Editores, 1992.

Jimeno Santoyo, Myriam. "Los indígenas colombianos, hoy: Su situación real, problemas y alternativas." *Revista Credencial Historia* (Bogotá: Biblioteca Virtual del Banco de la República), no. 33 (September 1992). http://www.banrep.gov.co/blaavirtual/revistas/credencial/cred.htm.

Jimeno Santoyo, Myriam, and Adolfo Triana Antorveza. *Estado y minorías étnicas en Colombia.* 1st ed. Bogotá: Cuadernos del Jaguar / Fundación para las Comunidades Colombianas, 1985.

Leal Buitrago, Francisco, ed. *En la encrucijada: Colombia en el siglo XXI.* Bogotá: Universidad de los Andes, Centro de Estudios Sociales e Internacionales / Grupo Editorial Norma, 2006.

Levine, Daniel. *Religion and Politics in Latin America: The Catholic Church in Venezuela and Colombia.* Princeton: Princeton University Press, 1981.

Livingstone, Grace. *Inside Colombia: Drugs, Democracy and War.* London: Latin American Bureau, 2003.

Londoño de la Cuesta, Juan Luis. "Brechas sociales en Colombia." Pages 118–22 in Jaime Jaramillo Uribe, ed., *Nueva historia de Colombia.* 2d ed. Vol. 8. Bogotá: Planeta, 1998.

Mato, Daniel, ed. *Estudios latinoamericanos sobre cultura y transformaciones sociales en tiempos de globalización.* Buenos Aires: Consejo Latinoamericano de Ciencias Sociales, 2002.

Maya, Luz Adriana. "Memorias en conflicto y paz en Colombia: La discriminación hacia lo(s) 'negro(s)'." In Daniel Mato, ed., *Estudios latinoamericanos sobre cultura y transformaciones sociales en tiempos de globalización 2.* Buenos Aires: Consejo Latinoamericano de Ciencias Sociales, 2002.

Montenegro, Armando, and Rafael Rivas. *Las piezas del rompecabezas: Desigualdad, pobreza y crecimiento.* Bogotá: Taurus, 2005.

Moreno, Pablo. "El protestantismo histórico en Colombia: Corrientes y diversidad." Pages 421–49 in Ana María Bidegaín, ed., *Historia del cristianismo en Colombia: Corrientes y diversidad.* Bogotá: Taurus, 2004.

Munévar, Jorge. "La libertad religiosa en Colombia: Orígenes y consecuencias." Pages 252–56 in Ana María Bidegaín and Juan Diego Demera Vargas, eds., *Globalización y diversidad religiosa en Colombia.* 1st ed. Bogotá: Universidad Nacional de Colombia, Facultad de Ciencias Humanas, 2005.

Nagle, Luz E. "Placing Blame Where Blame Is Due: The Culpability of Illegal Armed Gangs and Narcotraffickers in Colombia's Environmental and Human Rights Catastrophes." *Environmental Law & Policy Review* 29, no. 1 (Fall 2004): 1–106.

Ng'weno, Bettina. "Can Ethnicity Replace Race? Afro-Colombians, Indigeneity and the Colombian Multicultural State." *Journal of Latin American and Caribbean Anthropology* 12, no. 2 (2007): 414–40.

Ospina, Guillermo Andres. "Mountains in the Context of War in Colombia: Some Geopolitical Considerations." *Mountain Research and Development* 26, no. 1 (February 2006): 90–93.

Palacios, Marco. *Between Legitimacy and Violence: A History of Colombia, 1875–2002.* Trans., Richard Stoller. Durham, North Carolina: Duke University Press, 2006.

Pécaut, Daniel. "Respecto a los desplazados en Colombia." In Carlo Tassara, Dalia María Jiménez-Castrillíon, Luigi Grando, and Yolanda Zuluaga Torres, eds., *El desplazamiento por la violencia en Colombia: Experiencias, análisis y posibles estrategias de atención en el Departamento de Antioquia.* Proceedings of the international forum Desplazados internos en Antioquia, Medellín, July 27–28, 1998. Medellín: Comitato internazionale per lo sviluppo dei popoli / ACNUR / Arquidiócesis de Medellín Pastoral Social, 1998.

Pereira Souza, Ana Mercedes. "El Pentecostalismo: Nuevas formas de organización religiosa en los sectores populares: Origen, evolución y funciones en la sociedad colombiana, 1960–1995." *Historia Crítica* (Bogotá), no. 12 (January–July 1996): 43–67.

Pereira Souza, Ana Mercedes. "La pluralidad religiosa en Colombia: Iglesias y sectas." Pages 197–206 in Alvaro Tirado Mejía, ed., *Nueva historia de Colombia.* 2d ed. Vol. 9. Bogotá: Planeta, 1998.

Pérez-Olmos, Isabel, Patricia Fernández-Piñeres, and Sonia Rodado-Fuentes. "Prevalencia del Trastorno por Estrés Postraumático por la guerra, en niños de Cundinamarca, Colombia." *Revista de salud pública* (Bogotá) 7, no. 3 (September–December, 2005): 268–80.

Perotti, Roberto. "Public Spending on Social Protection: Analysis and Proposals." Pages 306–21 in Alberto Alesina, ed., *Institutional Reforms: The Case of Colombia.* Cambridge: MIT Press, 2005.

Piñeros-Petersen, Marion, and Magda Ruiz-Salguero. "Aspectos demográficos en comunidades indígenas de tres regiones de Colombia." *Salud Pública de México* (Mexico City) 40, no. 4 (1998): 324–29.

Portes, Alejandro, and Kelly Hoffman. *Las estructuras de clase en América Latina: Composición y cambios durante la época neoliberal.* Santiago, Chile: Economic Commission for Latin America and the Caribbean, Division of Social Development, 2003.

Renner, Richard. *Education for a New Colombia.* Washington, DC: Department of Health, Education, and Welfare, Office of Education, 1971.

Restrepo, Juan Darío, and James P.M. Syvitski. "Assessing the Effect of Natural Controls and Land Use Change on Sediment Yield in a Major Andean River, The Magdalena Drainage Basin, Colombia." *Ambio* (Stockholm) 35, no. 2 (March 2006): 65–75.

Rodríguez, Abel. "La debilidad del Ministerio de Educación y la politización de la educación pública en Colombia: Dos problemas a enfrentar en el Plan Decenal." *Coyuntura Social* (Bogotá), no. 14 (May 1996). http://www.fedesarrollo.org.co/.

Rojas, Cristina. "Elusive Peace, Elusive Violence: Identity and Conflict in Colombia." Pages 210–32 in Cristina Rojas and Judy Meltzer, eds., *Elusive Peace: International, National, and Local Dimensions of Conflict in Colombia.* New York: Palgrave Macmillan, 2005.

Safford, Frank. *The Ideal of the Practical: Colombia's Struggle to Form a Technical Elite.* Austin: University of Texas Press, 1976.

Safford, Frank, and Marco Palacios. *Colombia: Fragmented Land, Divided Society.* New York: Oxford University Press, 2002.

Sánchez T., Fabio, and Jairo Núñez M. "Descentralización, pobreza y acceso a los servicios sociales: ¿Quién se benefició del gasto público en los noventa?" *Coyuntura Social* (Bogotá), no. 20 (May 2000): 165–92. http://www.fedesarrollo.org.co/.

Sánchez-Triana, Ernesto, Kulsum Ahmed, and Yewande Awe, eds. *Environmental Priorities and Poverty Reduction: A Country Environmental Analysis for Colombia.* Washington, DC: World Bank, 2007.

Sarmiento Gómez, Alfredo. "Equity and Education in Colombia." Pages 228–34 in Fernando Reimers, ed., *Unequal Schools, Unequal Chances.* Cambridge: Harvard University Press, 2000.

Sarmiento Gómez, Alfredo, and Blanca Lilia Caro. *Análisis del sector educativo con énfasis en sus aspectos administrativos y financieros.* Bogotá: Ministerio de Educación Nacional, 1987.

Secretariado Permanente de la Conferencia Episcopal. *Proliferación de sectas*. Bogotá, 1989.

Sinclair, John. "Hacia un protestantismo colombiano y venezolano." In Tomás S. Gutiérrez, eds., *El protestantismo y política en América Latina: Entre la sociedad civil y el estado*. Lima, Peru: Comisión de Estudios de Historia de la Iglesia en América Latina y el Caribe, 1996.

Smith, T. Lynn. *Colombia: Social Structure and the Process of Development*. Gainesville: University of Florida Press, 1967.

Tassara, Carlos, Dalia María Jiménez-Castrillón, Luigi Grando, and Yolanda Zuluaga Torres, eds. *El desplazamiento por la violencia en Colombia: Experiencias, análisis y posibles estrategias de atención en el Departamento de Antioquia*. Proceedings of the international forum Desplazados internos en Antioquia, Medellín, July 27–28, 1998. Medellín: Comitato internazionale per lo sviluppo dei popoli / ACNUR / Arquidiócesis de Medellín Pastoral Social, 1999.

Tirado Mejía, Alvaro, ed. *Nueva historia de Colombia*. 11 vols. Bogotá: Planeta, 1989–98.

United Nations Development Programme. *El conflicto: Callejón con salida, informe nacional de desarrollo humano para Colombia–2003*. National Human Development Report for Colombia, 2003. Bogotá, 2003. http://hdr.undp.org/en/reports/nationalreports/latinamericathecaribbean/colombia/name,3213,en.html.

United Nations Development Programme. *Human Development Report 2007/2008: Fighting Climate Change: Human Solidarity in a Divided World*. New York: UNDP / Palgrave Macmillan, November 2007.

United States. Department of State. Bureau of Democracy, Human Rights, and Labor. "Colombia." *2006 Country Reports on Human Rights Practices*. Washington, DC: March 6, 2007.

United States. Department of State. Bureau of Democracy, Human Rights, and Labor. "Colombia." *2008 Country Reports on Human Rights Practices*. Washington, DC: February 25, 2009.

Urrutia, Miguel. "On the Absence of Economic Populism in Colombia." In Rudiger Dornbusch and Sebastián Edwards, eds., *The Macroeconomics of Populism in Latin America*. Chicago: University of Chicago Press, 1991.

Urrutia, Miguel. *Winners and Losers in Colombia's Economic Growth of the 1970s*. New York: Oxford University Press for the World Bank, 1985.

Vélez, Carlos Eduardo, Mauricio Santamaría, Natalia Millán, and Bénédicte de la Brière. "Two Decades of Economic and Social Development in Urban Colombia: A Mixed Outcome." *Archivos de Economía* (Bogotá), no. 192 (June 28, 2002).

Wade, Peter. *Blackness and Race Mixture: The Dynamics of Racial Identity in Colombia.* Baltimore: Johns Hopkins University Press, 1993.

Wade, Peter. *Race and Ethnicity in Latin America.* Chicago: Pluto Press, 1997.

West, Jacqueline, ed. *South America, Central America and the Caribbean, 2008.* 16th ed. Europa Regional Survey of the World. London: Routledge, 2008.

Williams, Raymond Leslie, and Keven G. Guerrieri. *Culture and Customs of Colombia.* Westport, Connecticut: Greenwood Press, 1999.

Wilson, Suzanne. "Inside Colombia: Drugs, Democracy, and War." *Latin American Politics and Society* 47, no. 3 (Fall 2005): 164–70.

World Bank. *Colombia Poverty Report.* Vol. 1. Washington, DC: March 2002.

Yunis Turbay, Emilio. *¿Por qué somos así? ¿Qué pasó en Colombia? Análisis del mestizaje.* Bogotá: Editorial Temis, 2003.

Zambrano Pantoja, Fabio, and Oliver Benard. *Ciudad y territorio: El proceso de poblamiento en Colombia.* Bogotá: Academia de Historia de Bogotá, 1993.

(Various issues of the following publications also were used in preparing this chapter: *Boletines de Divulgación Económica* (Bogotá), Departamento Nacional de Planeación (DNP); *Boletín Cifras de Violencia* (Bogotá), La Dirección de Justicia y Seguridad, DNP, 1966–2005; *Economist* (London), 2006; *El Tiempo* (Bogotá); *Global Information Network*, 2007; *New York Times*, 2007–8; *Semana* (Bogotá); and *World Factbook, 2007.* In addition, the following Web sites were consulted: Acción Social, Presidencia de la República de Colombia, http://www.accionsocial.gov.co; Consultancy for Human Rights and Displacement (La Consultoría para los Derechos Humanos y el Desplazamiento—Codhes), http://www.codhes.org; DNP, Sistema de Indicadores Sociodemográficos (SISD), http://www.dnp.gov.co; Encarta Encyclopedia, http://encarta.msn.com/encyclopedia; Foundation for Higher Education and Development (Fundación para la Educación Superior y el Desarrollo—Fedesarrollo), http://www.fedesarrollo.org.co/; Internal Displacement Monitoring Centre, http://www.internal-displacement.org; National Administrative Department of Statistics (Departamento Administrativo Nacional de Estadística—DANE), http://www.dane.gov.co/files/censo 2005/perfil.pdf; United Nations Development Programme, *Human Development Report*, 2007–2008, for statistics and Human Development Index rankings, http://hdr.undp.org/en/statistics; United Nations Food and Agricul-

ture Organization, http://www.fao.org; and U.S. Geological Survey, http://
earthquake.usgs.gov.)

Chapter 3

Alesina, Alberto, ed. *Institutional Reforms: The Case of Colombia.* Cambridge: MIT Press, 2005.

Angell, Alan, Pamela Lowden, and Rosemary Thorp. *Decentralizing Development: The Political Economy of Institutional Change in Colombia and Chile.* New York: Oxford University Press, 2001.

Arango Londoño, Gilberto. *Estructura económica colombiana.* 9th ed. Bogotá: McGraw Hill, 2000.

Arboleda, Jairo A., Patti L. Petesch, and James Blackburn. *Voices of the Poor in Colombia: Strengthening Livelihoods, Families, and Communities.* Washington, DC: World Bank, 2004.

Asociación Nacional de Instituciones Financieras. *El sector financiero de cara al siglo XXI.* Bogotá, 2002.

Ayala, Ulpiano, Carolina Soto, and Lorena Hernández. "La remuneración y el mercado de trabajo de los maestros públicos en Bogotá." *Coyuntura Social* (Bogotá), no. 20 (May 1999): 83–122.

Banco de la República. Grupo de Estudios del Crecimiento Económico Colombiano. "Comercio exterior y actividad económica en Colombia en el siglo XX: Exportaciones totales y tradicionales." *Borradores de economía* (Bogotá), no. 163 (November 2000).

Banco de la República. "La inversión extranjera directa en Colombia." *Revista del Banco de la República* (Bogotá), no. 12 (December 2003): 5–23.

Barajas, Adolfo, Roberto Steiner, and Natalia Salazar. "Interest Spreads in Banking in Colombia, 1974–96." *IMF Staff Papers* 46, no. 2 (June 1999): 196–224.

British Petroleum. *BP Statistical Review of World Energy 2007.* London, June 2007.

British Petroleum. *Statistical Review of World Energy 2008.* http://www.bp.com/productlanding.do?categoryId=6929&contentID=7044622.

Bushnell, David. *The Making of Modern Colombia: A Nation in Spite of Itself.* Berkeley: University of California Press, 1993.

Cadena Ordóñez, Ximena, and Mauricio Cárdenas Santa-María. *Las remesas en Colombia: Costos de transacción y lavado de dinero.* Documentos de Trabajo, no. 00810. Bogotá: Fedesarrollo, October 30, 2004.

Callahan, Colleen M., and Frank R. Gunter, eds. *Colombia: An Opening Economy?* Stamford, Connecticut: JAI Press, 1999.

Cárdenas Santa-María, Mauricio. *Introducción a la economía colombiana.* 1st ed. Bogotá: Alfaomega Editores / Fedesarrollo, 2007.

Cárdenas Santa-María, Mauricio, and Miguel Urrutia. "Impacto social del ciclo económico en Colombia: 1989–2004." *Coyuntura Económica* (Bogotá), no. 34 (June 2004): 143–62.

Clavijo Vergara, Sergio. *Fallos y fallas de la Corte Constitucional: El caso de Colombia, 1991–2000.* 1st ed. Bogotá: Alfaomega Editores, 2004.

Clavijo Vergara, Sergio. *Impacto económico de algunas sentencias de la Corte: El caso de la "Mesada 14" y de las Regulaciones de Vivienda.* Bogotá: Banco de la República, 2004. http://www.banrep.gov.co/junta/trabajo4-clavijo.htm.

Clavijo Vergara, Sergio. "Política monetaria y cambiaria en Colombia: Progresos y desafíos." *Ensayos sobre política económica* (Bogotá), nos. 41–42 (June–December 2002): 87–142.

Clavijo Vergara, Sergio, Michel Janna, and Santiago Muñoz. *The Housing Market in Colombia: Socioeconomic and Financial Determinants.* Bogotá: Banco de la República, 2004. http://www.banrep.gov.co/junta/trabajo4-clavijo.htm.

Colmenares, Germán, and José Antonio Ocampo, eds. *Historia económica de Colombia.* 1st ed. (revised and updated). Bogotá: Planeta / Fedesarrollo, 2007.

Colmenares, Germán, and José Antonio Ocampo, eds. *Historia económica de Colombia.* 1st ed. Bogotá: Fedesarrollo / Tercer Mundo Editores / Siglo Veintiuno Editores, 1987.

Colombia. Comisión de Regulación de Telecomunicaciones. *El sector de las telecomunicaciones en Colombia, 1998–2001.* Bogotá, 2002. http://www.crt.gov.co.

Colombia. Contraloría General de la República. "El debate sobre el tamaño de la pobreza en Colombia." *Economía Colombiana* (Bogotá) 303 (July–August 2004): 97–106.

Colombia. Departamento Nacional de Planeación. "Cadenas productivas: Estructura, comercio internacional y protección." Bogotá, 2004.

Colombia. Departamento Nacional de Planeación. *Estado Comunitario: Desarrollo para todos, Plan Nacional de Desarrollo 2006–2010.* Bogotá. http://www.dnp.gov.co/PortalWeb/PND/.

Colombia. Departamento Nacional de Planeación. "Hacia un estado comunitario." In *Plan Nacional de Desarrollo 2002–2006.* Bogotá, 2003.

Colombia. Departamento Nacional de Planeación. *Visión Colombia II centenario–2019: Propuesta para discusión.* Bogotá: Planeta, 2005.

Colombia. Departamento Nacional de Planeación. Consejo Nacional de Planificación Económica Social. *Plan de Expansión de la Red Nacional de Carreteras.* Conpes, no. 3085, Bogotá, 2000.

Colombia. Departamento Nacional de Planeación. Consejo Nacional de Política Económica Social. *Balance macroeconómico 2004 y perspectivas para 2005.* Conpes, no. 3341. Bogotá, 2005.

Colombia. Ministerio de Agricultura y Desarrollo Rural. *La cadena del azúcar en Colombia: Una mirada global de su estructura y dinámica, 1991–2005.* Documento de Trabajo, no. 56. Bogotá, 2005. http://www.agrocadenas.gov.co.

Colombia. Ministerio de Agricultura y Desarrollo Rural. *La cadena del banano en Colombia: Una mirada global de su estructura y dinámica, 1991–2005.* Documento de Trabajo, no. 60. Bogotá, 2005. http://www.agrocadenas.gov.co.

Colombia. Ministerio de Agricultura y Desarrollo Rural. *La cadena del oleaginosas en Colombia: Una mirada global de su estructura y dinámica, 1991–2005.* Documento de Trabajo, no. 62. Bogotá, 2005. http://www.agrocadenas.gov.co.

Colombia. Ministerio de Communicaciones. "Políticas para la radiodifusión en Colombia." *Cuadernos de Política Sectorial* (Bogotá), no. 3 (September 2004). http://www. mincomunicaciones.gov.co.

Colombia. Ministerio de Communicaciones. *Telefonía móvil celular: Informe trimestral.* Bogotá, October–December 2004. http://www. mincomunicaciones.gov.co.

Colombia. Ministerio de Transporte. *Anuario Estadístico, 2004.* Bogotá, 2004. http://www.mintransporte.gov.co/Servicios/Estadisticas/ANUARIO_ESTADISTICO_2004.pdf.

Colombia. Ministerio de Transporte. *Diagnóstico Sector Transporte 2007.* Bogotá, 2007.

Colombia. Ministerio de Transporte. *Plan Estratégico de Transporte 2003–2006.* Bogotá, 2003. http://www.mintransporte.gov.co.

Colombia. Ministerio de Transporte. *El Transporte en Cifras.* Bogotá, July 2004. http://www.mintransporte.gov.co/Servicios/Estadisticas/Transporte_en_cifras_2004.pdf.

Comisión de Regulación de Telecomunicaciones. *Informe Semestral Internet* (Bogotá), no. 10 (October 2007). http://www.colombiadigital.net/informacion/docs/Informe_Internet_junio_2007.pdf.

Comisión Económica para América Latina y el Caribe. "Anexo Estadístico." In *Análisis y proyecciones del desarrollo económico: III, el desarrollo económico de Colombia*. Santiago, Chile, 1957.

Consultoría para los Derechos Humanos y el Desplazamiento. "Comportamiento del Desplazamiento, 1985–2004." Bogotá, 2004. http://www.codhes.org.co/cifra/GraficoTendencias1985_2004.jpg.

Crandall, Russell. *Driven by Drugs: U.S. Policy Toward Colombia*. Boulder, Colorado: Rienner, 2002.

de Ferranti, David, William Foster, Daniel Lederman, Guillermo Perry, and Alberto Valdés. *Beyond the City: The Rural Contribution to Development*. Washington, DC: World Bank, 2005.

Dornbusch, Rudiger, and Stanley Fisher. "Moderate Inflation." *World Bank Economic Review* 7, no. 1 (January 1993): 1–44.

Easterly, William Russell. *The Elusive Quest for Growth: Economists' Adventures and Misadventures in the Tropics*. Cambridge: MIT Press, 2001.

Echeverry Garzón, Juan Carlos. "Colombia en la década de los noventa: Neoliberalismo y reformas estructurales en el trópico." *Coyuntura Económica* (Bogotá) 30, no. 3 (September 2000): 121–48.

Echeverry Garzón, Juan Carlos. *Las claves del futuro: Economía y conflicto en Colombia*. Bogotá: Editorial Oveja Negra, 2002.

Echeverry Garzón, Juan Carlos, Ana María Ibáñez, and Luis Carlos Hillón. *The Economics of Transmilenio: A Mass Transit System for Bogotá*. Documento CEDE 2004, no. 28. Bogotá: Universidad de los Andes, 2004.

Echeverry Garzón, Juan Carlos, and Mauricio Cárdenas Santa-María. *The Political Economy of Labor Reform in Colombia*. Documento CEDE 2004, no. 22. Bogotá: Universidad de los Andes, 2004.

Edwards, Sebastian, and Ben Patterson. *The Economics and Politics of Transition to an Open Market Economy: Colombia*. Paris: Organisation for Economic Co-operation and Development, 2001.

Esfahani, Salehi Hadi, and María Teresa Ramírez. "Institutions, Infrastructure, and Economic Growth." *Journal of Development Economics* 70, no. 2 (April 2003): 443–77.

Eslava, Marcela, John Haltiwanger, Adriana Kugler, and Maurice Kugler. "The Effects of Structural Reforms on Productivity and Profitability Enhancing Reallocation: Evidence from Colombia." *Journal of Development Economics* 75, no. 2 (December 2004): 333–71.

España, Rafael. *Estructura y tendencias del comercio en Colombia*. Bogotá: Federación Nacional de Comerciantes, 1994.

Federación Colombiana de Ganaderos. *Fedegan 40 años al servicio de la ganadería colombiana*. Bogotá: Carta Fedegan, 2003.

Florez Nieto, Carmen Elisa. *The Function of the Urban Informal Sector in Employment: Evidence from Colombia, 1984–2000*. Documento CEDE 2002, no. 4. Bogotá: Universidad de los Andes, Facultad de Economía, Centro de Estudios sobre Desarrollo Económico, 2002.

Foster, Vivien. *Colombia: Recent Economic Developments in Infrastructure (REDI): Balancing Social and Productive Needs for Infrastructure*. Vol. 2. Washington, DC: World Bank, 2004.

Fundación para la Educación Superior y el Desarrollo. "El sistema de seguridad social en salud: Logros y retos." *Coyuntura Social* (Bogotá), no. 23 (November 2000): 31–53.

Fundación para la Educación Superior y el Desarrollo. "La reforma a las transferencias y la descentralización." *Coyuntura Económica* (Bogotá) 31, no. 2 (June 2001): 51–72.

Fundación para la Educación Superior y el Desarrollo. "Petróleo y carbón: Situación actual y perspectivas." *Coyuntura Económica* (Bogotá) 34, no. 2 (2004): 11–37.

Galli, Rosemary E. *The Political Economy of Rural Development: Peasants, International Capital, and the State: Case Studies in Colombia, Mexico, Tanzania, and Bangladesh*. Albany: State University of New York Press, 1981.

Garay Salamanca, Luis Jorge. *Colombia: Estructura industrial e internacionalización, 1967–1996*. Bogotá: Departamento Nacional de Planeación, 1998.

García García, Jorge, and Sisir K. Jayasuriya. *Courting Turmoil and Deferring Prosperity: Colombia Between 1960 and 1990*. Washington, DC: World Bank, 1997.

Gaviria Uribe, Alejandro. *Del romanticismo al realismo social y otros ensayos*. 1st ed. Bogotá: Grupo Editorial Norma / Universidad de los Andes, Facultad de Economía, 2005.

Giugale, Marcelo M., Oliver Lafourcade, and Connie Luff. *Colombia: The Economic Foundations of Peace*. Washington, DC: World Bank, 2003.

Junguito, Roberto, and Hernán Rincón. "La política fiscal en el siglo XX en Colombia: Una visión global." *Coyuntura Económica* (Bogotá) 34, no. 2 (2004): 53–75.

Kalmanovitz, Salomón, and Enrique López Enciso. *La agricultura en Colombia en el siglo XX*. 1st ed. Bogotá: Fondo de Cultura Económica / Banco de la República, 2006.

López, Hugo, and Jairo Núñez. *Pobreza y desigualdad en Colombia: Diagnóstico y estrategias*. Bogotá: Colombia, Departamento Nacional de Planeación, 2007.

Lozano, Ignacio. "Colombia's Public Finance in the 1990s: A Decade of Reforms, Fiscal Imbalance, and Debt." Working Paper. Bogotá: Banco de la República, September 2000.

Lozano, Ignacio, Jorge Ramos, and Hernán Rincón. "Implicaciones fiscales y sectoriales de la reforma a las transferencias territoriales en Colombia." *Borradores de Economía* (Bogotá), no. 437 (April 2007).

McFarlane, Anthony. *Colombia Before Independence: Economy, Society, and Politics under Bourbon Rule*. New York: Cambridge University Press, 1993.

McGreevey, William Paul. *An Economic History of Colombia, 1845–1930*. Cambridge: Cambridge University Press, 1971.

McLure, Charles E., John Mutti, Victor Thuronyi, and George R. Zodrow. *The Taxation of Income from Business and Capital in Colombia*. Durham, North Carolina: Duke University Press, 1990.

Montenegro, Armando, and Rafael Rivas. *Las piezas del rompecabezas: Desigualdad, pobreza y crecimiento*. Bogotá: Taurus, 2005.

Moser, Caroline O.N., and Cathy McIlwaine. *Urban Poor Perceptions of Violence and Exclusion in Colombia*. Washington, DC: World Bank, 2000.

Núñez, Jairo, and Silvia Espinosa. *Asistencia social en Colombia: Diagnóstico y propuestas*. Documento CEDE 2005, no. 42. Bogotá: Universidad de los Andes, 2005.

Observatorio del Mercado de Trabajo y la Seguridad Social. "Los sindicatos en Colombia (una aproximación microeconómica)." *Boletín del Observatorio del Mercado de Trabajo y la Seguridad Social* (Bogotá: Universidad Externado de Colombia), no. 7 (September 2004). http://www.uexternado.edu.co/derecho/pdf/observatorio_mercado_trabajo/boletin_7.pdf.

Ocampo, José Antonio. *Colombia y la economía mundial, 1830–1910*. 1st ed. Mexico City: Siglo Veintiuno Editores, 1984.

Pachón, Álvaro, and María Teresa Ramírez. *La infraestructura de transporte en terrestre Colombia durante el siglo XX*. 1st ed. Bogotá: Fondo de Cultura Económica / Banco de la República, 2006.

Palacios, Marco. *Coffee in Colombia, 1850–1970: An Economic, Social, and Political History*. Cambridge: Cambridge University Press, 1980.

Pinzón, Jorge. *Hacia Basilea II: El caso colombiano*. Bogotá: Superintendencia Bancaria, July 2004. https://www.superbancaria.gov.co/comunicadosypublicaciones/discursos/discursos. htm.

Rajapatirana, Sarath. "Colombian Trade Policies and the 1996 WTO Trade Policy Review." Pages 105–18 in Peter Lloyd and Chris Milner, eds., *The World Economy Global Trade Policy, 1998.* Cambridge, Massachusetts: Blackwell, 1998.

Reina Echeverry, Mauricio, and Luis Alberto Zuleta Jaramillo. *El nuevo comercio minorista en Colombia.* Cuadernos de Fedesarrollo, no. 12. Bogotá: Fedesarrollo, 2003.

Richami, Nazih. *Systems of Violence: The Political Economy of War and Peace in Colombia.* Albany: State University of New York Press, 2002.

Rincón, Hernán, Jorge Ramos, and Ignacio Lozano. "Crisis fiscal actual: Diagnóstico y recomendaciones." *Revista del Banco de la República* (Bogotá) 77, no. 923 (2004): 30–135.

Robinson, James, and Miguel Urrutia. *Economía Colombiana del siglo XX: Un análisis cuantitativo.* 1st ed. Bogotá: Fondo de Cultura Económica / Banco de la República, 2007.

Roda, Pablo. "Impacto sectorial de los diez años de la legislación marco de servicios públicos domiciliarios en Colombia." Bogotá: Superintendencia de Servicios Públicos Domiciliarios–Económica Consultores, October 2004. http://www.superservicios.gov.co/ Impacto%20Sectorial.pdf.

Rodríguez, Catherine, Fabio Sánchez T., and Armando Armenta. "Hacia una mejor educación rural: Impacto de un programa de intervención a las escuelas en Colombia." *Documento CEDE* (Bogotá: Universidad de los Andes), no. 2007–13 (July 2007).

Rueda, María Clara. "El mercado mundial de flores y las exportaciones colombianas." *Coyuntura Económica* (Bogotá) 21, no. 2 (July 1991): 113–33.

Safford, Frank, and Marco Palacios. *Colombia: Fragmented Land, Divided Society.* New York: Oxford University Press, 2002.

Salcedo, Fernando. *Historia de la conexión de Uniandes a Internet.* Bogotá: Universidad de los Andes (Uniandes), May 2002. http://www.uque. uniandes.edu.co/~fsalcedo/voc/Historia %20Internet_2002.htm.

Schmidt-Hebbel, Klaus. *Colombia's Pension Reform: Fiscal and Macroeconomic Effects.* Washington, DC: World Bank, 1995.

Solimano, Andrés. *Colombia: Essays on Conflict, Peace, and Development.* Washington, DC: World Bank, 2000.

Steiner, Roberto. "Colombia's Income from the Drug Trade." *World Development* 26, no. 6 (June 1998): 1013–31.

Steiner, Roberto, Adolfo Barajas, and Natalia Salazar. "The Impact of Liberalization and Foreign Investment in Colombia's Financial Sector." *Journal of Development Economics* 63, no. 1 (October 2000): 157–96.

Steiner, Roberto, and Mauricio Cárdenas Santa-María. "Private Capital Flows in Colombia." Pages 192–222 in Felipe Larraín B., ed., *Capital Flows, Capital Controls, and Currency Crises: Latin America in the 1990s.* Ann Arbor: University of Michigan Press, 2000.

Steiner, Roberto, and Natalia Salazar. "Cómo atraer más inversión extranjera a Colombia." Pages 169–213 in Santiago Montenegro and Roberto Steiner, eds., *Propuestas para una Colombia competitiva.* Bogotá: Corporación Andina de Fomento / Universidad de los Andes, Facultad de Economía / Alfaomega, 2002.

Steiner, Roberto, and Patricia Correa. "Decentralization in Colombia: Recent Changes and Main Challenges." Pages 221–57 in Colleen M. Callahan and Frank R. Gunter, eds., *Colombia: An Opening Economy?* Stamford, Connecticut: JAI Press, 1999.

Thoumi, Francisco E. *Drogas ilícitas en Colombia: Su impacto económico, político y social.* Bogotá: United Nations Development Programme / Ariel Editorial / Colombia, Ministerio de Justicia y del Derecho, Dirección Nacional de Estupefacientes, Unidad Administrativa Especial, Entidad de Coordinación Nacional, 1997.

Thoumi, Francisco E. *Illegal Drugs, Economy, and Society in the Andes.* Washington, DC: Woodrow Wilson Center Press; and Baltimore: Johns Hopkins University Press, 2003.

Thoumi, Francisco E. *Political Economy and Illegal Drugs in Colombia.* Studies on the Impact of Illegal Drug Trade, Vol. 2. Boulder, Colorado: Rienner, 1995.

Thoumi, Francisco E. *Some Implications of the Growth of the Underground Economy in Colombia.* Reprint Series, no. 173. Washington, DC: Inter-American Development Bank, 1987.

United Nations. *"Colombia: Censo de cultivos de coca."* Bogotá: Oficina Contra la Droga y el Delito, June 2007.

United Nations Development Programme. *Human Development Report 2007/2008: Fighting Climate Change: Human Solidarity in a Divided World.* New York: UNDP / Palgrave Macmillan, 2007.

United Nations Educational, Scientific and Cultural Organization. *Primer estudio internacional comparativo sobre lenguaje, matemática y factores asociados en tercero y cuarto grado.* Santiago, Chile: Laboratorio Latinoamericano de Evaluación de la Calidad de la Educación, 1998. http://www.unesco.cl/esp/atematica/evalalfabydest/ntrabajo/4.act.

Urrutia, Miguel. *Cincuenta años de desarrollo económico colombiano.* 1st ed. Bogotá: La Carreta Inéditos, 1979.

Urrutia, Miguel. "Políticas para evitar burbujas especulativas en finca raíz." *Revista del Banco de la República* (Bogotá), no. 867 (January 2000): 5–23.

Urrutia, Miguel. "Una visión alternativa: La política monetaria y cambiaria en la última década." *Revista del Banco de la República* (Bogotá), no. 895 (May 2002): 5–27.

Urrutia, Miguel, and Mauricio Cárdenas. "Macroeconomic Instability and Social Progress." Chapter 3 in Rudiger Dornbusch and Sebastian Edwards, eds., *Reform, Recovery, and Growth*. Chicago: University of Chicago Press, 1995.

Urrutia Montoya, Miguel, Adriana Pontón Castro, and Carlos Esteban Posada Posada. *El crecimiento económico colombiano en el siglo XX: Aspectos globales*. Bogotá: Banco de la República, 2002.

Vélez, Carlos Eduardo. "Pobreza en Colombia: Avances, retrocesos y nuevos retos." *Coyuntura Económica* (Bogotá), no. 30 (June 2004): 51–63.

Villar, Leonardo, and Hernán Rincón. "Flujos de capital y regímenes cambiarios en la década de los 90." *Ensayos sobre Política Económica* (Bogotá), no. 39 (June 2001): 5–71.

Williamson, John, ed. *The Political Economy of Policy Reform*. Washington, DC: Institute for International Economics, 1993.

World Bank. *Colombia: Paving the Way for a Results-Oriented Public Sector*. Washington, DC, 1997.

World Bank. *Colombia Poverty Report*. Vol. I. Washington, DC, March 2002.

World Bank. *Colombia Social Safety Net Assessment*. Washington, DC, August 2002.

World Bank. *Review of Colombia's Agriculture and Rural Development Strategy*. Washington, DC, 1996.

World Bank. *Violence in Colombia: Building Sustainable Peace and Social Capital*. Washington, DC, 2000.

World Bank. *World Development Indicators 2007*. Washington, DC, April 2007.

World Tourism Organization. *International Tourism Receipts (US$) by Region, Subregion, and Country of Destination: Americas*. September 2005. http://www.world-tourism.org/ frameset/frame_statistics.html.

World Trade Organization. "Trade Policy Review: Colombia." Documents WT/TPR/S/18 and WT/TPR/S/18. http://www.wto.org/english/ tratop_e/tpr_e/tp39_e.htm.

(Various issues of the following publications were also used in the preparation of this chapter: Central Bank reports to Congress, http://www.banrep. gov.co; Economist Intelligence Unit, *Country Profile: Colombia* (London); *El Espectador* (Bogotá); *El Tiempo* (Bogotá); *La República* (Bogotá); *Portafolio* (Bogotá); and *Revista Dinero* (Bogotá). In addition, the following Web sites were consulted: Aeronáutica Civil de Colombia, http://www. aerocivil.gov.co; Agencia Nacional de Hidrocarburos, http://www.anh. gov.co/; Asociación Colombiana de Exportadores de Flores, http:// www.asocolflores.org/; Asociación Nacional de Empresarios de Colombia, http://www.andi.com.co; Asociación Nacional de Financieras, http:// www.anif.org/; Banco de la República, http://www.banrep.gov.co; British Petroleum (BP), http://www.bp.com; California Public Employees' Retirement System, http://www.calpers.ca.gov; Centro de Estudios sobre Desarrollo Económico, http://economia.uniandes.edu.co/; Comisión Nacional de Televisión, http://www.cntv.org.co; Departamento Administrativo Nacional de Estadísticas, http://www.dane.gov.co; Departamento Nacional de Planeación, http://www.dnp.org.co; Economic Commission for Latin America and the Caribbean, http://www.ECLAC.org; Fundación para la Educación Superior y el Desarrollo, http://www.fedesarrollo.org; Gobierno en línea, http://www.gobiernoenlinea.gov.co; Investorwords.com, http:// www.investorwords.com; Juriscol, http://juriscol.banrep.gov.co:8080; Portafolio, http://www.portafolio.com.co; Proexport, http://www.proexport. com.co; United Nations Development Programme (2007/2008 Human Development Index Rankings), http://www.hdr.undp.org/en/statistics/; and World Bank, *WDI* (World Development Indicators) *Online*, 2007, http:// www.worldbank.org/data/online.)

Chapter 4

Ardila, Martha, Diego Cardona, and Socorro Ramírez, eds. *Colombia y su política exterior en el Siglo XXI.* 1st ed. Bogotá: Friedrich Ebert Stiftung en Colombia / Fondo Editorial CEREC, 2005.

Ardila, Martha, Diego Cardona, and Arlene B. Tickner, eds. *Prioridades y desafíos de la política exterior colombiana.* Bogotá: Friedrich Ebert Stiftung en Colombia / Hanns Seidel Stiftung, 2002.

Arnson, Cynthia, and Robin Kirk. *State of War: Political Violence and Counterinsurgency in Colombia.* New York: Human Rights Watch / Americas, 1998.

Bolívar, Ingrid J., Fernán E. González, and Teófilo Vásquez. *Violencia política en Colombia: De la nación fragmentada a la construcción del estado.* Bogotá: Centro de Investigación y Educación Popular, 2003.

Cepeda Ulloa, Fernando, ed. *Corrupción y gobernabilidad.* 1st ed. Bogotá: Tercer Mundo Editores, 2000.

Cepeda Ulloa, Fernando, ed. *Fortalezas de Colombia.* Ariel Ciencia Política. Bogotá: Ariel, 2004.

"Colombia." *Sentinel Country Risk Assessments.* Coulsdon, United Kingdom: Jane's, December 13, 2006.

Correa Robledo, Ricardo. "Empresarios, conflicto armado y procesos de paz en Colombia." Pages 31–58 in *Síntesis 2002–2003: Anuario social, político y económico de Colombia.* Bogotá: Universidad Nacional de Colombia, Instituto de Estudios Políticos y Relaciones Internacionales / Editorial Gente Nueva, 2004.

Dudley, Steven. *Walking Ghosts: Murder and Guerrilla Politics in Colombia.* New York: Routledge, 2006.

Dugas, John, Angélica Ocampo, Luis Javier Orjuela, and Germán Ruiz. *Los caminos de la descentralización.* Bogotá: Universidad de los Andes, Departamento de Ciencia Política, 1992.

Dugas, John, ed. *La constitución de 1991: ¿Un pacto político viable?* Bogotá: Universidad de los Andes, Departamento de Ciencia Política, 1993.

Echandía Castilla, Camilo. "Territorio y conflicto armado." Pages 335–58 in Ann C. Mason and Luis Javier Orjuela, eds., *La crisis política colombiana: Más que un conflicto armado y un proceso armado de paz.* Bogotá: Ediciones Uniandes / Universidad de los Andes, Facultad de Ciencias Sociales, Departamento de Ciencia Política / Fundación Alejandro Ángel Escobar, 2003.

Estrada Álvarez, Jairo, ed. *Plan Colombia: Ensayos críticos.* Bogotá: Universidad Nacional de Colombia, Facultad de Derecho, Ciencias Políticas y Sociales, 2001.

Gaitán Pavía, Pilar. "Partidos y campañas: Partidos fraccionados en busca de candidatos únicos." Pages 59–65 in *Síntesis '94: Anuario social, político y económico de Colombia.* Bogotá: Universidad Nacional de Colombia, Instituto de Estudios Políticos y Relaciones Internacionales / Editorial Gente Nueva, 1995.

Gaviria Díaz, Carlos. *Sentencias: Herejías constitucionales.* Bogotá: Fondo de Cultura Económica, 2002.

Giraldo, Fernando, with Mauricio Solano, Fredy A. Berrero, and Alberto Cienfuegos. *Sistema de partidos políticos en Colombia: Estado del arte, 1991–2002.* Bogotá: Fundación Konrad Adenauer / Centro Editorial Javeriano, 2003.

Giraldo, Fernando, and Mauricio Solano, eds. *Partidos, reforma política y referendo.* Bogotá: Centro Editorial Javeriano, 2003.

Gómez Buendía, Hernando, ed. *El conflicto, callejón con salida: Informe nacional de desarrollo humano para Colombia.* Bogotá: United Nations Development Programme, 2003.

Helfrich, Linda, and Sabine Kurtenbach, eds. *Colombia: Caminos para salir de la violencia.* Madrid: Iberoamericana / Vervuert, 2006.

Human Rights Watch. "Colombia: Letting Paramilitaries off the Hook." January 2005. http://www.hrw.org/backgrounder/americas/colombia0105/4.htm.

Instituto de Estudios Políticos y Relaciones Internacionales. *Nuestra guerra sin nombre: Transformaciones del conflicto en Colombia.* Bogotá: Universidad Nacional de Colombia, IEPRI / Grupo Editorial Norma, 2006.

Instituto de Estudios Políticos y Relaciones Internacionales. *El Plan Colombia y la internacionalización del conflicto.* Bogotá: Universidad Nacional de Colombia, Instituto de Estudios Políticos y Relaciones Internacionales / Editorial Planeta Colombiana, 2001.

Jaramillo, Juan Fernando, and Arlene B. Tickner. "Colombia: El largo camino hacia la renovación política." Pages 43–64 in Fernando Tuesta Soldevilla, ed., *Sistemas electorales en los países andinos.* Bogotá: Parlamento Andino / Unidad para la Promoción de la Democracia / OEA, 1999.

Kline, Harvey F. *State Building and Conflict Resolution in Colombia, 1986–1994.* Tuscaloosa: University of Alabama Press, 1999.

Leal Buitrago, Francisco. *La seguridad nacional a la deriva: Del frente nacional a la posguerra fría.* Bogotá: Universidad de los Andes, Centro de Estudios Sociales e Internacionales / Alfaomega, Quito: Sede Académico de Ecuador, Facultad Latinoamericana de Ciencias Sociales, 2002.

Leal, Buitrago, Francisco, ed. *En la encrucijada: Colombia en el siglo XXI.* Bogotá: Grupo Editorial Norma / Universidad de los Andes, Centro de Estudios Sociales e Internacionales, 2006.

Mason, Ann C., and Luis Javier Orjuela, eds. *La crisis política colombiana: Más que un conflicto armado y un proceso armado de paz.* Bogotá: Ediciones Uniandes / Universidad de los Andes, Facultad de Ciencias Sociales, Departamento de Ciencia Política / Fundación Alejandro Ángel Escobar, 2003.

Melo, Jorge Orlando. "La libertad de prensa." Pages 76–86 in Fernando Cepeda Ulloa, ed., *Fortalezas de Colombia.* Ariel Ciencia Política. Bogotá: Ariel, 2004.

Mockus, Antanas, ed. *Descentralización y orden público.* Bogotá: Friedrich Ebert Stiftung en Colombia / Milenio, 1997.

Moncayo, Víctor Manuel. *El leviatán derrotado: Reflexiones sobre teoría del estado y el caso colombiano*. Bogotá: Grupo Editorial Norma, 2004.

Orjuela, Luis Javier. *La sociedad colombiana en los años noventa: Fragmentación, legitimidad y eficiencia*. Bogotá: Ediciones Uniandes / CESO, 2005.

Pardo Rueda, Rafael. *Fin del paramilitarismo: ¿Es posible su desmonte?* Bogotá: Ediciones B., Grupo Z, Colombia, 2007.

Peñaranda Supelano, Ricardo. "Los movimientos sociales: ¿Continúa la crisis o se inicia una nueva etapa?" Pages 39–47 in *Síntesis '95: Anuario social, político y económico de Colombia*. Bogotá: Universidad Nacional de Colombia, Instituto de Estudios Políticos y Relaciones Internacionales / Editorial Gente Nueva, 1996.

Peñaranda Supelano, Ricardo. "Movilización y protesta popular en el tiempo de la crisis." Pages 35–45 in *Síntesis '97: Anuario social, político y económico de Colombia*. Bogotá: Universidad Nacional de Colombia, Instituto de Estudios Políticos y Relaciones Internacionales / Editorial Gente Nueva, 1998.

Pizarro Leongómez, Eduardo. *Una democracia asediada: Balance y perspectivas del conflicto armado en Colombia*. Bogotá: Grupo Editorial Norma, 2004.

Pizarro Leongómez, Eduardo. "Hacia un nuevo modelo partidista." Pages 79–89 in *Síntesis 2002–2003*. Bogotá: Universidad Nacional de Colombia, Instituto de Estudios Políticos y Relaciones Internacionales / Editorial Gente Nueva, 2004.

Plataforma Colombiana de Derechos Humanos, Democracia y Desarrollo. *El embrujo autoritario: Primer año de gobierno de Álvaro Uribe Vélez*. Bogotá: Ediciones Antropos, 2003.

Ramírez García, and David Arturo. "Una revisión a las relaciones colombo-japonesas." *Colombia Internacional* (Bogotá), no. 47 (September–December 1999): 5–31.

Ramírez, Socorro, and José María Cárdenas, eds. *Colombia–Venezuela: Agenda común para el siglo XXI*. Bogotá: Universidad Nacional de Colombia, Instituto de Estudios Políticos y Relaciones Internacionales / Tercer Mundo Editores, 1999.

Ramírez, Socorro, and Luis Alberto Restrepo. *Colombia: Entre la inserción y el aislamiento*. Bogotá: Universidad Nacional de Colombia, Instituto de Estudios Políticos y Relaciones Internacionales / Siglo del Hombre Editores, 1997.

Rangel Suárez, Alfredo. *Colombia: Guerra en el fin de siglo*. Bogotá: Tercer Mundo Editores / Universidad de los Andes, Facultad de Ciencias Sociales, 1998.

Rangel Suárez, Alfredo. *La oposición política en Colombia: Debate político*. Bogotá: Universidad Nacional de Colombia, Instituto de Estudios Políticos y Relaciones Internacionales / Friedrich Ebert Stiftung en Colombia, 1996.

Restrepo, Luis Alberto. "Movilización social." Pages 85–102 in *Síntesis '93*. Bogotá: Universidad Nacional de Colombia, Instituto de Estudios Políticos y Relaciones Internacionales / Editorial Gente Nueva, 1994.

Rettberg, Angelika. "Entre el cielo y el suelo: Una mirada crítica a los gremios colombianos." Pages 253–68 in Ann C. Mason and Luis Javier Orjuela, eds., *La crisis política colombiana: Más que un conflicto armado y un proceso armado de paz*. Bogotá: Ediciones Uniandes / Universidad de los Andes, Facultad de Ciencias Sociales, Departamento de Ciencia Política / Fundación Alejandro Ángel Escobar, 2003.

Reyes Posada, Alejandro. "Violencia." Pages 117–28 in *Síntesis '93*. Bogotá: Universidad Nacional de Colombia, Instituto de Estudios Políticos y Relaciones Internacionales / Editorial Gente Nueva, 1994.

Richani, Nazih. *Systems of Violence: The Political Economy of War and Peace in Colombia*. Albany: State University of New York Press, 2002.

Rodríguez, Libardo. *Derecho administrativo general*. Bogotá: Editorial Temis, 1998.

Rojas, Fernando, ed. *Descentralización y corrupción*. Papers from a meeting held in April 1996. Bogotá: Friedrich Ebert Stiftung en Colombia / Milenio, 1996.

Safford, Frank, and Marco Palacios. *Colombia: Fragmented Land, Divided Society*. New York: Oxford University Press, 2002.

Santos, Boaventura de Sousa, and Mauricio García Villegas, eds. *El caleidoscopio de las justicias en Colombia: Análisis socio-jurídico*. Bogotá: Siglo del Hombre Editores, 2001.

Tate, Winifred. *Counting the Dead: The Culture and Politics of Human Rights Activism in Colombia*. Berkeley: University of California Press, 2007.

Tickner, Arlene B. "Colombia: Chronicle of a Crisis Foretold." *Current History* 97, no. 616 (February 1998): 61–65.

Tickner, Arlene B. "Colombia: U.S. Subordinate, Autonomous Actor, or Something in Between?" Pages 165–84 in Frank O. Mora and Jeanne A.K. Hey, eds., *Latin American and Caribbean Foreign Policy*. Lanham, Maryland: Rowman & Littlefield, 2003.

Tickner, Arlene B. "From Counternarcotics to Counterterrorism in Colombia." *Current History* 102, no. 661 (February 2003): 77–85.

Tirado Mejía, Alvaro. *Colombia en la OEA*. Bogotá: Ministerio de Relaciones Exteriores / Banco de la República / El Áncora Editores, 1998.

Tirado Mejía, Alvaro, and Carlos Holguín Holguín. "Colombia." In *The UN, 1945–1995*. Bogotá: National Committee for the Fiftieth Anniversary, 1995.

Tokatlián, Juan Gabriel. *Globalización, narcotráfico y violencia: Siete ensayos sobre Colombia*. Bogotá: Grupo Editorial Norma, 2000.

Ungar Bleier, Elisabeth. "Partidos políticos y trabajo parlamentario en Colombia: Un matrimonio indisoluble." Pages 79–102 in Fernando Giraldo and Mauricio Solano, eds., *Partidos, reforma política y referendo*. Bogotá: Centro Editorial Javeriano, 2003.

Ungar Bleier, Elisabeth. "Repensar el Congreso para enfrentar la crisis." Pages 311–31 in Ann C. Mason and Luis Javier Orjuela, eds., *La crisis política colombiana: Más que un conflicto armado y un proceso armado de paz*. Bogotá: Ediciones Uniandes / Universidad de los Andes, Facultad de Ciencias Sociales, Departamento de Ciencia Política / Fundación Alejandro Ángel Escobar, 2003.

Velásquez, Fabio C., and Esperanza González R. *¿Qué ha pasado con la participación ciudadana en Colombia?* Bogotá: Fundación Corona / Fundación Social, 2003.

Welna, Christopher, and Gustavo Gallón, eds. *Peace, Democracy, and Human Rights in Colombia*. Notre Dame: University of Notre Dame Press, 2007.

(Various issues of the following Bogotá newspapers and periodicals were also used in the preparation of this chapter: *El Espectador, Revista Cambio, Revista Semana*, and *El Tiempo*. In addition, the following Web sites of governmental and nongovernmental organizations were consulted: Amnesty International, Annual Report on Colombia, http://www.web.amnesty.org; Center for International Policy Colombia Program, http://www.ciponline.org/colombia/index.htm; Centro de Investigación y Educación Popular, http://www.cinep.org.co/inicio.htm; Colombian judicial-branch Web sites accessed through http://www.gobiernoenlinea.gov.co/entidad_buscar.aspx?Sitios=4; Colombian Ministry of National Defense, http://www.mindefensa.gov.co/; Comisión Colombiana de Juristas, http://www.coljuristas.org/; Confederación Colombiana de Organizaciones No Gubernamentales, http://www.ccong.org.co/; Congreso Visible, Universidad de los Andes, http://www.cvisible.uniandes.edu.co/; Corporación Nuevo Arco Iris, http://www.nuevoarcoiris.org.co/; Military Penal Justice, http://www.justiciamilitar.gov.co/BancoConocimiento/R/resenaresena.asp; Office of the United Nations High Commissioner for Human Rights, http://www.hchr.org.co/; Presidencia de la República, http://www.presidencia.gov.co/; Programa Presidencial de Derechos Humanos y Derecho Internacional Humanitario, http://www.derechoshumanos.gov.co/; and TransparencyInternational, http://www.transparencyinternational.org.)

Chapter 5

Apter, David E., ed. *The Legitimation of Violence*. London: Macmillan, 1997.

Arnson, Cynthia, ed. *The Peace Process in Colombia with the Autodefensas Unidas de Colombia—AUC*. Woodrow Wilson Center Report on the Americas, no. 13. Washington, DC: Woodrow Wilson International Center for Scholars, Latin American Program, 2005.

Arocha, Jaime, Fernando Cubides, and Miriam Jimeno, eds. *Las violencias: Inclusión creciente*. Bogotá: Universidad Nacional de Colombia, Centro de Estudios Sociales, 1998.

Atehortuá, Adolfo León, and Humberto Vélez. *Estado y fuerzas armadas en Colombia: 1886–1953*. Bogotá: Tercer Mundo Editores / Pontificia Universidad Javeriana, 1994.

Bagley, Bruce. "Narcotráfico, violencia política y política exterior de Estados Unidos hacia Colombia en los noventa." *Revista Colombia Internacional* (Bogotá), nos. 49–50 (May–December 2000): 5–38.

Bailey, John, and Lucía Dammert, eds. *Public Security and Police Reform in the Americas*. Pittsburgh: University of Pittsburgh Press, 2006.

Baud, Michiel, and Donny Meertens, eds. *Colombia from the Inside: Perspectives on Drugs, War, and Peace*. Cuadernos de la CEDLA, no. 18. Amsterdam: CEDLA Inter-University Centre for Latin American Research and Documentation, 2004.

Baum, Dan. *Smoke and Mirrors: The War on Drugs and the Politics of Failure*. London: Back Bay Books, 1997.

Bergquist, Charles W., Ricardo Peñaranda, and Gonzalo Sánchez Gómez, eds. *Violence in Colombia, 1990–2000: Waging War and Negotiating Peace*. Wilmington, Delaware: Scholarly Resources Books, 2001.

Bertram, Eva, and Morris Blachman. *Drug War Politics: The Price of Denial*. Berkeley: University of California Press, 1996.

Bolívar, Ingrid J., Fernán E. Gonzalez, and Teófilo Vázquez. *Violencia política en Colombia: De la nación fragmentada a la construcción del estado*. Bogotá: Centro de Investigación y Educación Popular, 2003.

Bouvier, Virginia. "Evaluating U.S. Policy in Colombia." *Policy Report*. Silver City, New Mexico: International Relations Center, Americas

Program, May 11, 2005. http://americas.irc-online.org/pdf/reports/
0505Colombia.pdf.

Braun, Herbert. *Our Guerrillas, Our Sidewalks: A Journey into the Violence of Colombia.* Niwot: University Press of Colorado, 1994.

Bushnell, David. *The Making of Modern Colombia: A Nation in Spite of Itself.* Berkeley: University of California Press, 1993.

Camacho Guizado, Álvaro, and Francisco Leal Buitrago. *Armar la paz es desarmar la guerra: Herramientas para lograr la paz.* Bogotá: Universidad Nacional de Colombia, Instituto de Estudios Políticos y Relaciones Internacionales, Centro de Estudios de la Realidad Colombiana, 1999.

Camargo, Pedro Pablo. *Justicia de excepción, inquisición en Colombia: El sistema acusatorio.* Bogotá: Editorial CIMA, 1995.

Cárdenas, Martha, and Manuel Rodríguez Becerra, eds. *Guerra, sociedad y medio ambiente.* Bogotá: Foro Nacional Ambiental, 2004.

Carpenter, Ted Galen. *Bad Neighbor Policy: Washington's Futile War on Drugs in Latin America.* New York: Palgrave Macmillan, 2003.

Casale, John, and Robert Klein. "Illicit Production of Cocaine." *Forensic Science Review,* no. 5 (1993): 95–107.

Cepeda Ulloa, Fernando, ed. Minutes of the seminar, Instituciones civiles y militares en la política de seguridad democrática, October 3–5, 2003. Bogotá: United States Embassy in Bogotá, Project Houston, 2003.

Chepesiuk, Ronald. *Hard Target: The United States' War Against International Drug Trafficking, 1982–1997.* Jefferson, North Carolina: McFarland, 1999.

Chernick, Mark W. "Negotiated Settlement to Armed Conflict: Lessons from the Colombian Peace Process." *Journal of Inter-American Studies and World Affairs* 30, no. 4 (Winter 1988–89): 53–88.

Clawson, Patrick L., and Rensselaer W. Lee III. *The Andean Cocaine Industry.* New York: St. Martin's Press, 1996.

Colombia. Departamento Nacional de Planeación. *Hacia un estado comunitario: Plan nacional de desarrollo del gobierno del Presidente Álvaro Uribe, 2002–2004.* Bogotá, 2005.

Colombia. Departamento Nacional de Planeación. *El salto social: Plan nacional de desarrollo del gobierno del Presidente Ernesto Samper, 1994–1998.* Bogotá, 1999.

Colombia. Ministerio de Defensa Nacional. *Los grupos ilegales de autodefensa en Colombia.* Bogotá, 2000.

Colombia. Ministerio del Interior y de Justicia. Dirección Nacional de Estupefacientes. *Colombia's War Against Drugs: Actions and Results,*

2002. Bogotá, 2003. http://www.colombiaemb.org/opencms/opencms/system/galleries/download/id/Libro_ Blanco02ingles.pdf.

Colombia. Presidencia de la República. *Informe Anual de Derechos Humanos y Derecho Internacional Humanitario 2003.* Bogotá, 2004.

Colombia. Presidencia de la República. *Plan de Desarrollo Nacional.* Bogotá, 2003. http://www.presidencia.gov.co/ley812.

Colombia. Presidencia de la República and Ministerio de Defensa Nacional. *Política de Defensa y Seguridad Democrática.* Bogotá, 2003. http://www.mindefensa.gov.co.

Colombia. Vicepresidencia de la República. Observatorio de Derechos Humanos. *Panorama actual del macizo colombiano.* Bogotá, 2002.

Colombia. Vicepresidencia de la República. Observatorio de Derechos Humanos. Programa Presidencial de Derechos y Derecho Internacional Humanitario. *Informe Julio 2003.* Bogotá, 2003. http://www.derechos humanos.gov.co/observatorio.

Colombia. Vicepresidencia de la República. Programa Presidencial de Derechos Humanos y Derecho Internacional Humanitario. "Panorama de la situación de derechos humanos de los docentes colombianos." *Boletín Estadístico* (Bogotá), no. 2 (May 2004): 1–7. http://www.derechoshumanos.gov.co/modules.php?name=informacion&file=article& sid=174.

Colombia. Vicepresidencia de la República. Programa Presidencial de Derechos Humanos y Derecho Internacional Humanitario. "Violaciones cometidas contra los derechos humanos de los periodistas." *Boletín Estadístico* (Bogotá), no. 5 (October 2004): 1–9. http://www.derechoshumanos.gov.co/modules.php?name=informacion&file=article& sid=174.

Consultoría para los Derechos Humanos y el Desplazamiento. *Dimensiones de la crisis humanitaria y de derechos humanos en Colombia.* Bogotá, 2004.

Corporación Excelencia en la Justicia. *Reforma constitucional de la justicia penal.* Bogotá, 2002. http://www.cej.org.co/reforma_constitucional.pdf.

Council on Foreign Relations. *Andes 2020: A New Strategy for the Challenges of Colombia and the Andean Region.* New York, 2004.

Crandall, Russell. *Driven by Drugs: U.S. Policy Toward Colombia.* Boulder, Colorado: Rienner, 2002.

Cubides, Fernando. "Los paramilitares y su estrategia." Pages 151–200 in Malcolm Deas and María Victoria Llorente, eds., *Reconocer la guerra para construir la paz.* Bogotá: Ediciones Uniandes, Centro de Estudios de la Realidad Colombiana / Grupo Editorial Norma, 1999.

Dávila, Andrés. "Ejército regular, conflictos irregulares: La institución militar en los últimos quince años." Pages 283–346 in Malcolm Deas and María Victoria Llorente, eds., *Reconocer la guerra para construir la paz*. Bogotá: Ediciones Uniandes, Centro de Estudios de la Realidad Colombiana / Grupo Editorial Norma, 1999.

Deas, Malcolm. "Violent Exchanges: Reflections on Political Violence in Colombia." In David E. Apter, ed., *The Legitimation of Violence*. London: Macmillan, 1997.

Deas, Malcolm, and María Victoria Llorente, eds. *Reconocer la guerra para construir la paz*. Bogotá: Ediciones Uniandes, Centro de Estudios de la Realidad Colombiana / Grupo Editorial Norma, 1999.

Duncan, Gustavo. *Del campo a la ciudad en Colombia: La infiltración urbana de los señores de la guerra*. Documento CEDE no. 2. Bogotá: Universidad de los Andes, 2005.

Duncan, Gustavo. *Los señores de la guerra: De paramilitares, mafiosos y autodefensas en Colombia*. Bogotá: Planeta, 2006.

Echandía Castilla, Camilo. *El conflicto armado y las manifestaciones de violencia en las regiones de Colombia*. Bogotá: Colombia, Presidencia de la República, Oficina del Alto Comisionado para la Paz, 1999.

Echandía Castilla, Camilo. "Expansión territorial de las guerrillas colombianas: Geografía, economía y violencia." Pages 99–150 in Malcolm Deas and Maria Victoria Llorente, eds., *Reconocer la guerra para construir la paz*. Bogotá: Ediciones Uniandes, Centro de Estudios de la Realidad Colombiana / Grupo Editorial Norma, 1999.

Echandía Castilla, Camilo. "Territorio y conflicto armado." Pages 335–58 in Ann Mason and Luis Javier Orjuela, eds., *La crisis política colombiana: Más que un conflicto armado y un proceso de paz*. Bogotá: Ediciones Uniandes / Universidad de Los Andes, Facultad de Ciencias Sociales, Departamento de Ciencia Politica / Fundación Alejandro Ángel Escobar, 2003.

Escuela Superior de Guerra and Universidad Javeriana. *"El papel de las FFMM en una democracia en desarrollo: Memorias de la conferencia internacional."* Bogotá, April 6–8, 2000.

Estrada, Jairo. *Plan Colombia: Ensayos críticos*. Bogotá: Universidad Nacional de Colombia, 2001.

Fajardo, Luis Eduardo. *From the Alliance for Progress to the Plan Colombia: A Retrospective Look at U.S. Aid to Colombia*. Working Paper no. 28. Crisis States Programme, London School of Economics. London: London School of Economics, 2003.

Haugaard, Lisa, Adam Isaacson, Kimberly Stanton, John Walsh, and Jeff Vogt. *Blueprint for a New Colombia Policy.* Washington, DC: Latin America Working Group Education Fund / Center for International Policy / Washington Office on Latin America / U.S. Office on Colombia, 2005. http://www.lawgorg/docs/Blueprint.pdf.

Instituto de Estudios Políticos y Relaciones Internacionales. Universidad Nacional de Colombia. *El Plan Colombia y la internacionalización del conflicto.* Bogotá: Planeta Colombiana, 2001.

Isaacson, Adam, and Alison Hare. "Colombia's Álvaro Uribe: The First 100 Days." *International Policy Report.* Washington, DC: Center for International Policy, 2002.

Kenney, Michael. "La capacidad de aprendizaje de las organizaciones colombianas de narcotráfico." *Análisis Político* (Bogotá), no. 41 (September–December 2000). http://www.analisispolitico.edu.co/index.asp ?num=41.

Kirk, Robin. *More Terrible than Death: Massacres, Drugs, and America's War.* New York: Public Affairs, 2003.

Kline, Harvey F. *State Building and Conflict Resolution in Colombia, 1986–1994.* Tuscaloosa: University of Alabama Press, 1999.

Lair, Eric. "Colombia: Una guerra contra los civiles." *Colombia Internacional* (Bogotá), 49–50 (2001): 135–47.

Leal Buitrago, Francisco. *El oficio de la guerra: La seguridad nacional en Colombia.* Bogotá: Tercer Mundo Editores / Universidad Nacional de Colombia, Instituto de Estudios Políticos y Relaciones Internacionales, 1994.

Leal Buitrago, Francisco. "La seguridad: Difícil de abordar con democracia." *Análisis Político* (Bogotá) 46 (2002): 58–77.

Leal Buitrago, Francisco. *La seguridad nacional a la deriva: Del frente nacional a la posguerra fría.* Bogotá: Universidad de los Andes, Centro de Estudios Sociales e Internacionales / Alfaomega; Quito: Sede Académico de Ecuador, Facultad Latinoamericana de Ciencias Sociales, 2002.

Leal Buitrago, Francisco, ed. *En la encrucijada: Colombia en el siglo XXI.* Bogotá: Grupo Editorial Norma / Universidad de los Andres, Centro de Estudios Sociales e Internacionales, 2006.

Llorente, María Victoria. "Demilitarization in Times of War: Police Reform in Colombia." Chapter 9 in John Bailey and Lucía Dammert, eds., *Public Security and Police Reform in the Americas.* Pittsburgh: University of Pittsburgh Press, 2005.

Llorente, María Victoria. "Perfil de la política colombiana." Pages 389–474 in Malcolm Deas and María Victoria Llorente, eds., *Reconocer la guerra para construir la paz.* Bogotá: Ediciones Uniandes, Centro de Estudios de la Realidad Colombiana / Grupo Editorial Norma, 1999.

López Restrepo, Andrés. "De la prohibición a la guerra: El narcotráfico colombiano en el siglo XX." Pages 69–112 in Instituto de Estudios Políticos y Relaciones Internacionales, Universidad Nacional de Colombia, *Colombia, cambio de siglo: Balances y perspectivas.* 1st ed. Bogotá: Planeta Colombiana, 2000.

Marks, Thomas. *Colombian Army Adaptation to FARC Insurgency.* Carlisle, Pennsylvania: U.S. Army War College, Strategic Studies Institute, 2002.

Mason, Ann C. "Colombia's Democratic Security Agenda: Public Order in the Security Tripod." *Security Dialogue* (Oslo) 34, no. 4 (2003): 391–409.

Mason, Ann C. "La seguridad democrática de Álvaro Uribe: Retórica, doctrina y práctica." Pages 35–43 in *Anuario Social y Político de América Latina y El Caribe,* no. 6. Caracas, Venezuela: Editorial Nueva Sociedad / Facultad Latinoamericana de Ciencias Sociales, 2003.

Maullin, Richard L. *Soldiers, Guerrillas, and Politics in Colombia.* Lexington, Massachusetts: Lexington Books, 1973.

The Military Balance, 2009. London: International Institute for Strategic Studies, 2009.

Millett, Richard L. "Colombia's Conflicts: The Spillover Effects of a Wider War." *North–South Agenda Papers,* no. 57 (September 2002): 1–21.

Molano, Alfredo. "Coca, Land and Corruption." Pages 63–76 in Michiel Baud and Donny Meertens, eds., *Colombia from the Inside: Perspectives on Drugs, War and Peace.* Cuadernos de la Cedla, no. 18. Amsterdam: Inter-University Centre for Latin American Research and Documentation, 2004.

Montenegro, Armando, and Carlos Esteban Posada P. "Criminalidad en Colombia." *Borradores Semanales de Economía* (Bogotá), no. 4 (1994): 1–26. http://www.banrep.gov.co/docum/ ftp/borra004.pdf.

Oquist, Paul H. *Violence, Conflict, and Politics in Colombia.* New York: Academic Press, 1980.

Ortíz, César. "Agricultura, cultivos ilícitos y medio ambiente en Colombia." Pages 297–352 in Martha Cárdenas and Manuel Rodríguez Becerra, eds., *Guerra, sociedad y medio ambiente.* Bogotá: Foro Nacional Ambiental, 2004.

Ortiz, Román. "De 'país problema' a pilar estratégico: La mutación de la posición de seguridad colombiana en la región andina." In Fernando Cepeda Ulloa, ed., *Fortalezas de Colombia.* Ariel Ciencia Política. Bogotá: Ariel, 2004.

Ortiz, Román. "El estado colombiano frente a las FARC: Buscando respuestas a una nueva amenaza insurgente." Chapter 6 in Reinaldo Botero Bedoya, ed., *Seguridad y Terrorismo*. Bogotá: Editorial Planeta Colombiana, 2003.

Ortiz, Román. "Las nuevas guerras civiles." In Esther Barbé, Carlos de Cueta, and Javier Jordán, eds., *Introducción a los estudios de seguridad y defensa*. Albolote, Spain: Comares, 2001.

Ortiz, Román, and Mauricio Rubio. "Organized Crime in Latin America." In Philip Reichel, ed., *Handbook of International Crime and Justice*. Thousand Oaks, California: Sage, 2004.

Palacios, Marco. *Entre la legitimidad y la violencia: Colombia, 1875–1994*. Bogotá: Grupo Editorial Norma, 1995.

Pardo, Diana, and Arlene B. Tickner. "El problema del narcotráfico en el sistema interamericano." Pages 291–310 in Arlene B. Tickner, ed., *Sistema interamericano y democracia: Antecedentes históricos y tendencias futuras*. Bogotá: Centro de Estudios Internacionales / Ediciones Uniandes / Organization of American States, 2000.

Pardo Rueda, Rafael. "Colombia's Two-Front War." *Foreign Affairs* 79, no. 4 (2000): 64–73.

Pardo Rueda, Rafael. *La historia de las guerras*. Barcelona and Bogotá: J. Vergara, 2004.

Pécaut, Daniel. *Orden y violencia: Colombia 1930–45*. 2 vols. Bogotá: Fondo Editorial CEREC / Siglo Veintiuno Editores, 1987.

Pécaut, Daniel. *Guerra contra la sociedad*. Espasa hoy. Bogotá: Editorial Planeta Colombiana, 2001.

Pizarro Leongómez, Eduardo. *Una democracia asediada: Balance y perspectivas del conflicto armado en Colombia*. Bogotá: Grupo Editorial Norma, 2004.

Pizarro Leongómez, Eduardo. "Revolutionary Guerrilla Groups in Colombia." Pages 169–94 in Charles W. Bergquist, Ricardo Peñaranda, and Gonzalo Sánchez Gómez, eds., *Violence in Colombia: The Contemporary Crisis in Historical Perspective*. Wilmington, Delaware: Scholarly Resources Books, 1992.

Pizarro Leongómez, Eduardo, and Ricardo Peñaranda. *Las FARC (1949–1966): De la autodefensa a la combinación de todas las formas de lucha*. Bogotá: Tercer Mundo Editores / Universidad Nacional de Colombia / Instituto de Estudios Políticos y Relaciones Internacionales, 1991.

Plataforma Colombia de Derechos Humanos, Democracia y Desarrollo. *El embrujo autoritario: Primer año de Álvaro Uribe Vélez*. Bogotá: Ediciones Antropos, 2003.

Rabasa, Angel, and Peter Chalk. *Colombian Labyrinth: The Synergy of Drugs and Insurgency and Its Implications for Regional Stability.* Washington, DC: RAND, 2001. http://www.rand.org/publications/MR/MR1339/.

Ramírez, María Clemencia. "Aerial Spraying and Alternative Development in Plan Colombia." *Harvard Review of Latin America* 4, no. 2 (2005): 54–57.

Ramírez, María Clemencia, Kimberly Stanton, and John Walsh. "Colombia: A Vicious Circle of Drugs and War." In Coletta Youngers and Eileen Rosin, eds., *Drugs and Democracy in Latin America: The Impact of U.S. Policy.* Boulder, Colorado: Rienner, 2005.

Ramírez B., Marta Lucia. *Democratic Security, Transnational Threats and the Rule of Law.* Washington, DC: Center for Strategic and International Studies, 2002.

Ramírez Tobón, William. "Violencia, guerra civil, contrato social." Pages 21–67 in Instituto de Estudios Políticos y Relaciones Internacionales, Universidad Nacional de Colombia, ed., *Colombia, cambio de siglo: Balances y perspectivas.* 1st ed. Bogotá: Planeta Colombiana, 2000.

Ramsey, Russell W. *Guerrilleros y soldados.* Bogotá: Tercer Mundo Editores, 2000.

Rangel Suárez, Alfredo. *Colombia: Guerra en el fin de siglo.* Bogotá: Tercer Mundo Editores / Universidad de Los Andes, Facultad de Ciencias Sociales, 1998.

Rangel Suárez, Alfredo. *El poder paramilitar.* 1st ed. Bogotá: Fundación Seguridad y Democracia: Planeta, 2005.

Rangel Suárez, Alfredo. *Las FARC–EP: Una mirada actual.* Bogotá: Centro de Estudios sobre el Desarrollo Económico, 1997.

Rangel Suárez, Alfredo. "Military and Security Foundations for Peace." In Woodrow Wilson Center, *Peace and Security in Colombia: A Conference Report.* Washington, DC: Woodrow Wilson International Center for Scholars, 2003.

Rangel Suárez, Alfredo. "Parasites and Predators: Guerrillas and the Insurrection Economy of Colombia." *Journal of International Affairs* 53, no. 2 (2000): 577–607.

Richani, Nazih. *Systems of Violence: The Political Economy of War and Peace in Colombia.* Albany: State University of New York Press, 2002.

Rocha, Ricardo. *La economía colombiana tras 25 años de narcotráfico.* Bogotá: United Nations Drug Control Programme / Siglo del Hombre Editores, 2000.

Romero, Mauricio. "Changing Identities and Contested Settings: Regional Elites and the Paramilitaries in Colombia." *International Journal of Politics, Culture, and Society* 14, no. 1 (2000): 51–69.

Romero, Mauricio. *Paramilitares y autodefensas, 1982–2003.* Bogotá: Editorial Planeta Colombiana / Universidad Nacional de Colombia, Instituto de Estudios Políticos y Relaciones Internacionales, 2003.

Rubio, Mauricio. *Crimen e impunidad: Precisiones sobre la violencia.* Bogotá: Tercer Mundo Editores, 1999.

Rubio, Mauricio. "Criminalidad urbana en Colombia." Pages 238–82 in Malcom Deas and María Victoria Llorente, eds., *Reconocer la guerra para construir la paz.* Bogotá: Ediciones Uniandes, Centro de Estudios de la Realidad Colombiana / Grupo Editorial Norma, 1999.

Rubio, Mauricio. "La justicia penal: Juicio sin sumario." In Boaventura de Sousa Santos and Mauricio Garcia Villegas, eds., *El caleidoscopio de justicias en Colombia: Análisis socio-jurídico.* Bogotá: Siglo del Hombre Editores, 2001.

Safford, Frank, and Marco Palacios. *Colombia: Fragmented Land, Divided Society.* New York: Oxford University Press, 2002.

Sánchez David, Rubén, and Federmán Antonio Rodríguez Morales. *Seguridad, democracia y seguridad democrática.* 1st ed. Bogotá: Editorial Universidad del Rosario, 2007.

Sánchez Gómez, Gonzalo. "Guerra prolongada, negociaciones inciertas en Colombia." *Boletín Instituto Francés de Estudios Andinos* (Lima, Peru) 29, no. 3 (2000): 269–305.

Sánchez Gómez, Gonzalo, and Donny Meertens. *Bandits, Peasants, and Politics: The Case of "La Violencia" in Colombia.* Trans., Alan Hynds. 1st ed. Austin: University of Texas Press, 2001.

Sánchez Torres, Fabio. *Las cuentas de la violencia: Ensayos económicos sobre el conflicto y el crimen en Colombia.* Bogotá: Norma / Ediciones Uniandes, 2007.

Schifter, Michael. "Colombia on the Brink." *Foreign Affairs* 78, no. 4 (July–August 1999): 14–20.

Silva García, Germán. "La independencia interna de la justicia: La democracia y la eficiencia como problemas políticos de la justicia." Paper presented at Primer Congreso Latinoamericano de Justicia y Sociedad, October 20–24, 2003. Bogotá, 2003.

Soto Velasco, Andrés, Yaneth Giha Tobar, and Héctor Reyes Riveros. "El gasto militar en Colombia: Aspectos macroeconómicos y microeconómicos." *Revista de la CEPAL* (Santiago, Chile) 69 (December 1999): 163–80.

Sweig, Julia. "What Kind of War for Colombia?" *Foreign Affairs* 18, no. 5 (September–October 2002): 122–29.

Tate, Winifred. *Counting the Dead: The Culture and Politics of Human Rights Activism in Colombia.* Berkeley: University of California Press, 2007.

Thoumi, Francisco E. *Drogas ilícitas en Colombia: Su impacto económico, político y social.* Bogotá: United Nations Development Programme / Colombia, Dirección Nacional de Estupefacientes / Editorial Ariel, 1997.

Thoumi, Francisco E. *El imperio de la droga: Narcotráfico, economía y sociedad en los Andes.* Bogotá: Universidad Nacional de Colombia, Instituto de Estudios Políticos y Relaciones Internacionales / Editorial Planeta Colombiana, 2002.

Tickner, Arlene B., and Rodrigo Pardo. "Estados Unidos, Colombia y sus vecinos: Los desafíos externos de la 'Seguridad Democrática.'" *Foreign Affairs en Español* (Mexico City) 3, no. 4 (October–December 2003): 102–14.

Tokatlián, Juan Gabriel, and Jorge Mario Eastman. *Amapola, coca y....* Proceedings of the international symposium, Drugs: Integral Vision of a World Problem, Bogotá, November 1992. Bogotá: Parlamento Andino / United Nations Drug Control Programme, 1993.

Tokatlián, Juan Gabriel. *Globalización, narcotráfico y violencia: Siete ensayos sobre Colombia.* Bogotá: Grupo Editorial Norma, 2000.

Torres del Río, César. *Fuerzas armadas y seguridad nacional.* Bogotá: Editorial Planeta Colombiana, 2000.

United Nations. "Informe del Alto Comisionado de las Nacionas Unidas para los derechos humanos sobre la situación de derechos humanos y derecho internacional humanitario en Colombia año 2005." Bogotá: United Nations Office of the High Commissioner for Human Rights, 2005.

United Nations Development Programme. *El conflicto: Callejón con salida, informe nacional de desarrollo humano para Colombia—2003.* National Human Development Report for Colombia, 2003. Bogotá, 2003. http://hdr.undp.org/en/reports/nationalreports/latinamericathecaribbean/Colombia/name,3213;en.html.

United States. Department of Justice. *International Criminal Investigative Training Assistance Program Project Overviews: Colombia.* Washington, DC: 2005. http://www.usdoj.gov/criminal/icitap/colombia.html.

United States. Department of State. Bureau of Democracy, Human Rights, and Labor. "Colombia." *2002 Country Reports on Human Rights*

Practices. Washington, DC, March 31, 2003. http://www.state.gov/g/drl/rls/hrrpt/2002/18325.htm.

United States. Department of State. Bureau of Democracy, Human Rights, and Labor. "Colombia." *2003 Country Reports on Human Rights Practices.* Washington, DC, February 25, 2004. http://www.state.gov/g/drl/rls/hrrpt/2003/27891.htm.

United States. Department of State. Bureau of Democracy, Human Rights, and Labor. "Colombia." *2004 Country Reports on Human Rights Practices.* Washington, DC, February 28, 2005. http://www.state.gov/g/drl/rls/hrrpt/2004/41754.htm.

United States. Department of State. Bureau of International Narcotics and Law Enforcement Affairs. "2003 International Narcotics Control Strategy Report." Washington, DC, March 1, 2004. http://www.state.gov/p/inl/rls/nrcrpt/2003/vol1/html/29832htm.

United States. Department of State. Bureau of International Narcotics and Law Enforcement Affairs. "2005 International Narcotics Control Strategy Report." Washington, DC, 2005. http://www.state.gov/g/inl/rls/nrcrpt/2005/vol1/html/42363.htm.

United States. Department of State. Counterterrorism Office. "Colombia." *2004 Country Reports on Terrorism.* Washington, DC, April 27, 2005. http://www.state.gov/s/ct/rls/crt/45392. htm.

United States. Embassy in Bogotá. "El apoyo de Estados Unidos al Plan Colombia." http://www.usembassy.state.gov/bogota/www.spceus.html.

Uribe López, Mauricio. "La droga: Una industria peregrina." *Hechos del Callejón* (Bogotá), no. 3 (May 2005): 12–14. http://www.pnud.org.co/indh.

Urrutia Iriarte, Nicolás. "El gasto en defensa y seguridad: Caracterización del caso colombiano en el contexto internacional." *Archivos de Economía* (Bogotá) 249 (March 15, 2004): 1–74. http://www.dnp.gov.co/paginas_detalle.aspx?idp=688.

Vaicius, Ingrid, and Adam Isaacson. "The War on Drugs Meets the War on Terror." *International Policy Report.* Washington, DC: Center for International Policy, 2003.

Valencia Tovar, Álvaro. *Historia de las fuerzas militares de Colombia.* 6 vols. Bogotá: Planeta, 1993.

Vargas, Ricardo. "Fumigaciones y política de drogas en Colombia: Fin del círculo vicioso o un fracaso estratégico?" Pages 353–95 in Martha Cárdenas and Manuel Rodríguez Becerra, eds., *Guerra, sociedad y medio ambiente.* Bogotá: Foro Nacional Ambiental, 2004.

Villamizar, Andrés. *Fuerza militares para la guerra: La agenda pendiente de la reforma militar.* Bogotá: Fundación de seguridad y democracia, 2003.

Washington Office on Latin America. *Trends in U.S. Military Programs in Latin America.* Washington, DC, 2004.

Welna, Christopher, and Gustavo Gallón, eds. *Peace, Democracy, and Human Rights in Colombia.* Notre Dame, Indiana: University of Notre Dame Press, 2007.

Youngers, Colletta A., and Eileen Rosin, eds. *Drugs and Democracy in Latin America: The Impact of U.S. Policy.* Boulder, Colorado: Rienner, 2005.

Youngers, Colletta A., and Eileen Rosin, eds. "Drugs and Democracy in Latin America: The Impact of U.S. Policy." *Drug War Monitor* (Special Report of the Washington Office on Latin America, Drugs, Democracy, and Human Rights Project) 3, no. 4 (November 2004). http://www.wola.org/publications/ddhr_exec_sum_brief.pdf.

Zabludoff, Sydney. "Colombian Narcotics Organizations as Business Enterprises." In United States, Department of State, Bureau of Research and Intelligence, and United States, Central Intelligence Agency, *Economics of the Narcotics Industry Conference Report.* Washington, DC, 1994.

(Various issues of the following publications, and their Web sites, also were used in the preparation of this chapter: *Boletín Codhes* (Consultoría para los Derechos Humanos y el Desplazamiento), 2003 (Bogotá), http://www.codhes.org.co; Center for International Policy Colombia Program reports, 2004; *Coyuntura de Seguridad* (Bogotá), 2003, 2005; *Economist* (London), 2001, 2005; *Human Development Report* of the United Nations Development Programme, 2003, 2004, http://hdr.undp.org/en; Human Rights Watch reports, 1998, 2000, 2003–5; International Institute for Strategic Studies, *The Military Balance* (London), 2009–10; *Latin American Report* (Bogotá and Brussels), 2003–5; *New York Times* (2003); *New York Times Magazine*, 2001; Programa Presidencial de Derechos Humanos y Derecho Internacional Humanitario, http://www.derechoshumanos.gov.co/; *Revista Cambio* (Bogotá), 2003; *Semana* (Bogotá), 1999; and *El Tiempo* (Bogotá), 2002–3. In addition, relevant information was found at the following Web sites: Colombia, Armada Nacional, http://www.armada.mil.co/; Colombia, Comando General Fuerzas Militares, http://www.cgfm.mil.co/; Colombia, Ejército Nacional, http://www.ejercito.mil.co/; Colombia, Fuerza Aérea Colombiana, http://www.fac.mil.co/; Colombia, Ministerio de Defensa Nacional, http://www.mindefensa.gov.co; Colombia, Policía Nacional de Colombia, http://www.policia.gov.co/; Jurist Legal News and Research, http://jurist.law.pitt.edu/world.colombia.htm; National Drug Intelligence Center, http://www.usdoj.gov/ndic/; Office of National Drug Control Policy

(ONDCP), http://www.whitehousedrugpolicy.gov/index.html; and United Nations Office on Drugs and Crime (UNODC), http://www.unodc. org/unodc/index.html.)

Glossary

alternative development—The officially recognized definition endorsed by the United Nations General Assembly Special Session on the World Drug Problem in 1998 characterizes it as "a process to prevent and eliminate the illicit cultivation of plants containing narcotic drugs and psychotropic substances through specifically designed rural development measures in the context of sustained national economic growth and sustainable development efforts in countries taking action against drugs, recognizing the particular sociocultural characteristics of the target communities and groups, within the framework of a comprehensive and permanent solution to the problem of illicit drugs."

Andean Community of Nations—The Andean Community (Comunidad Andina de Naciones—CAN) is a trade bloc consisting of Bolivia, Colombia, Ecuador, Peru, and Venezuela (it was known as the Andean Pact or Andean Group from 1969 until 1997).

Andean Price-Band System (APBS)—Introduced in 1995, the APBS had the announced goal of reducing domestic price instability by buffering fluctuations in international prices through use of a variable import tariff. The APBS consists of the application of variable levies in addition to a basic ad valorem tariff established through the common external tariff policy of the Andean Community.

barrels per day (bpd)—Production of crude oil and petroleum products frequently is measured in this unit, which often is abbreviated bpd or bd. As a measurement of volume, a barrel is the equivalent of 42 U.S. gallons. Conversion of barrels to tons depends on the density of the specific product in question, which varies by country. In Colombia 7.08 barrels of crude oil weigh one metric ton.

clientelism (*clientelismo*)—Personal relationships that link patrons and clients together in a system in which jobs, favors, and protection are exchanged for labor, financial support, and loyalty.

Common Market of the South (Mercado Común del Sur—Mercosur)—An organization established on March 26, 1991, when the Treaty of Asunción was signed by Argentina, Brazil, Paraguay, and Uruguay for the purpose of promoting regional economic cooperation. Bolivia, Chile, Colombia, Ecuador, Peru, and Venezuela are associate (nonvoting) members.

421

compadrazgo—Literally, copaternity. A system of ritual coparenthood that links parents, children, and godparents in a close social and economic relationship.

crawling-peg system—A system of exchange-rate adjustment in which a currency with a fixed exchange rate is allowed to fluctuate within a band of rates. The par value of the stated currency is also adjusted frequently as a result of market factors such as inflation. This gradual shift of the currency's par value is done as an alternative to a sudden and significant devaluation of the currency.

encomendero—The holder of the administrative authority in a territory, called an *encomienda* (*q.v.*), where indigenous people were settled. The *encomendero* was entitled to some services from Amerindians in exchange for their Roman Catholic instruction.

encomienda—A tribute institution used in Spanish America in the sixteenth century. The Spaniard received Amerindians as an entrustment (*encomienda*) to protect and to Christianize them, but in return he could demand tribute (including labor).

fiscal year (FY)—Calendar year.

Gini coefficient or index—A measure of a country's inequality of income distribution by means of a ratio analysis with values between 0 and 1. A lower Gini coefficient represents better equality and income distribution and vice versa.

gross domestic product (GDP)—A measure of all the production generated by the factors located in a country, regardless of their nationality, GDP is the sum of value added by all resident producers plus any product taxes (less subsidies) not included in the valuation of output.

intermediation—The process carried out by a financial institution, such as a brokerage firm, bank, or insurance company, serving as a link, or intermediary, between borrowers and savers. Savers deposit funds in the institution, which lends those funds to homebuyers and other borrowers. Thus, "intermediation spreads" are the gap between the interest charged by banks for loans they made and the interest paid by the banks for the deposits they received.

liberation theology—An activist movement led by Roman Catholic clergy who trace their inspiration to Vatican Council II (1965), when some church procedures were liberalized, and the Latin American Bishops' Conference in Medellín, Colombia (1968), which endorsed greater direct efforts to improve the lot of the poor. Advocates of liberation theology—sometimes referred to as "liberationists"—work mainly through ecclesiastical base communities, which are grassroots groups consisting of mostly poor Christian lay people.

narco-terrorism—Sometimes defined as terrorism resulting from an alliance between drug traffickers and political terrorists, narco-terrorism may be carried out by either category and may include assassinations, extortion, hijackings, kidnappings, and other violence and intimidation against judges, elected officials, or law-enforcement agents, in an effort to extract concessions from the government.

neoliberalism—A somewhat nonstandard academic term for an economic and social model that is based on the primacy of the individual with only a minimal role for government. Neoliberal policies recommend solutions based on free movement of goods, services, and capital, with reliance on market forces to allocate resources. Neoliberalism is characterized by laissez-faire economic policies and reduction of public spending and social welfare programs.

Organization of American States (OAS)—An inter-American organization that brings together the nations of the Western Hemisphere to strengthen cooperation on democratic values, defend common interests, and debate the major issues facing the region and the world. The OAS is the region's principal multilateral forum for strengthening democracy, promoting human rights, and confronting shared problems such as poverty, terrorism, illegal drugs, and corruption. It plays a leading role in carrying out mandates established by the hemisphere's leaders through the Summits of the Americas.

peso—Colombia's unit of currency. The exchange rate between the Colombian peso and the U.S. dollar as of February 16, 2010, was Colombian pesos (formally abbreviated as COPs and informally as COL$ or Ps) 1,900.8 = US$1.

resguardos—Communal lands held in common by Amerindians during colonial times and formed under an *encomendero* (*q.v.*), that is, the manager of an *encomienda* (*q.v.*), a colonial institution that employed Amerindians as slaves. In present-day Colombia, *resguardos*, or reserves communally owned by indigenous groups, cover about 24 percent of the national territory.

Index

Index

Contributors

David Bushnell is a member of the Emeritus Faculty, Department of History, University of Florida, Gainsville. He has written extensively on Colombian history.

Rex Hudson is a senior analyst for Latin America, Federal Research Division, Library of Congress, Washington, DC.

Ann C. Mason is Executive Director, Fulbright Colombia, Bogotá. Her publications concentrate on Colombian and Andean security affairs.

Roberto Steiner is Director, Foundation for Higher Education and Development (Fedesarrollo), Bogotá. He has written widely on Colombian economic issues, including economic and institutional repercussions of the drug trade in Colombia.

Arlene B. Tickner is Professor of International Relations in the Political Science Department, University of the Andes (Uniandes), Bogotá. She has written extensively on Colombian foreign relations and Andean security.

Hernán Vallejo is Associate Professor, Department of Economics, Uniandes. His research has focused on economic theory and empirical evidence on the Colombian economy.

Published Country Studies

(Area Handbook Series)

Afghanistan
Albania
Algeria
Angola
Argentina

Armenia, Azerbaijan,
  and Georgia
Australia
Austria
Bangladesh

Belarus and Moldova
Belgium
Bolivia
Brazil
Bulgaria

Burma
Cambodia
Cameroon
Chad
Chile

China
Colombia
Commonwealth Caribbean,
  Islands of the
Congo
Costa Rica

Côte d'Ivoire (Ivory
  Coast)
Cuba
Cyprus
Czechoslovakia

Dominican Republic
  and Haiti
Ecuador
Egypt
El Salvador

Estonia, Latvia, and
  Lithuania
Ethiopia
Finland
Germany

Ghana
Greece
Guatemala
Guinea
Guyana and Belize

Honduras
Hungary
India
Indian Ocean
Indonesia
Iran

Iraq
Israel
Italy
Japan
Jordan

Kazakstan, Kyrgyzstan,
  Tajikistan, Turkmenistan,
  and Uzbekistan
Kenya
Korea, North

Korea, South
Laos
Lebanon
Liberia
Libya

Malawi
Malaysia
Mauritania
Mexico
Mongolia

Morocco
Mozambique
Nepal and Bhutan
Nicaragua
Nigeria

Oceania
Pakistan
Panama
Paraguay
Persian Gulf States
Peru

Philippines
Poland
Portugal
Romania
Russia

Rwanda and Burundi
Saudi Arabia
Senegal
Sierra Leone
Singapore

Somalia
South Africa
Soviet Union
Spain
Sri Lanka

Sudan
Syria
Tanzania
Thailand
Tunisia

Turkey
Uganda
Uruguay
Venezuela
Vietnam

Yemens, The
Yugoslavia
Zaire
Zambia
Zimbabwe

$ 35.00

CONNETQUOT PUBLIC LIBRARY
760 Ocean Avenue
Bohemia, NY 11716
631-567-5079

Library Hours:

Monday - Friday	9:00 - 9:00
Saturday	9:00 - 5:00
Sunday (Oct. - May)	1:00 - 5:00

GAYLORD